PREFACE

MIS: Management Dimensions is intended to integrate the basic systems theory with the design, implementation, and application of management information systems. Such an integration should facilitate the understanding of MIS goals and the effect of MIS on organizational structure and corporate management. More importantly, it should provide insight on how organizational structure and management can affect MIS. Thus, by making available a supplemental source of materials about the managerial complexity of MIS in the corporate environment, we hope to help managers and potential managers accomplish needed informational objectives. Hence focus is on informational needs and the design of MIS to meet them rather than on how-to-do-it techniques in computer science.

There is both a technical and a managerial side to MIS. Directed toward managerial dimensions of MIS in a total organization environment, the book is unique in:

1. Time. Management information systems are reaching increased sophistication and use in industry. In addition, colleges and universities are implementing MIS courses and specializations.
2. Approach. Articles included emphasize managerial dimensions of what MIS should accomplish. They point up what managerial information is needed to communicate those needs, how to fit MIS into the organizational structure and management into the design, and what is the appropriate leadership role of top management.

Businessmen cannot continue to be frustrated with rapid technological computer advancement and achievements. To maximize managerial effectiveness and system potential, it is necessary to map the understanding of MIS and to evaluate it by:

1. Pinpointing weaknesses in vulnerable spots that can hinder management systems effort
2. Setting forth the fundamental needs of system design
3. Spelling out the kind of leadership needed for both effective system management and effective total (corporate) management

This volume, a collection of readings that constitutes a single source of recent contributions to the field of MIS, is a convenient anthology of supplementary readings for university undergraduate and graduate courses in MIS as well as a core text for management-development and training programs. The book provides what is fundamental to decision making: the right information at the right time at the right level.

Coverage is given to a wide range of viewpoints expressed in leading professional journals. The book is organized into six parts:

Part I: An overview of the managerial dimensions of MIS, written by the editors. Selected articles on MIS perspectives, written by others, follow.

Part II: Basic concepts in the systems approach to management and total management systems. This section sets the framework for both understanding and optimizing MIS.

Part III: Organizational impact of MIS, approached from a two-dimensional view—the impact of MIS on organization and the impact of organization on MIS. Specifically, these include organizational dimensions, role of top management, and information needs.

Part IV: MIS as a subsystem of the total business system. Purpose, scope, and design in the dimension of MIS environment are stressed.

Part V: MIS pitfalls and problems of the past. Articles are structured to present the crucial role of control and to stress the importance of management training in optimizing MIS design and use.

Part VI: MIS applications (within diversified organizational structures) that reinforce the managerial concepts and implications of MIS as reflected throughout the book. These articles explore the nature of the information needs of managers, as well as point up the vital need for unique design and top management involvement.

For their helpful suggestions and criticisms, we would like to thank Grace Muilenburg, Kansas Agricultural Experiment Station; William R. Cornett, Texas Tech University; Herbert F. Spirer,

University of Connecticut; and Charles H. Smith, University of Texas at Austin. We are also grateful to Floyd W. Smith, Director of the Kansas Agricultural Experiment Station, for his support on related research activities, which contributed to the development of this book.

Raymond J. Coleman
M. J. Riley

CONTENTS

PART I

MIS Perspectives

Information—Decision-making as a System

Decision making, which is essential to implement and to integrate resources so that objectives can be accomplished, is fundamental to man's behavior. Behavior is goal oriented, and man moves toward goals by making decisions from alternative courses of action. Hence, all managerial activity may be considered decision making; according to Simon (1) the two terms are synonymous.

Such an analysis contains the basic elements of a system: a set of interrelated parts with a purpose. It is useful, then, to treat management as a system—an information-decision system—that can be analyzed by the model provided by Miller and Starr (2):

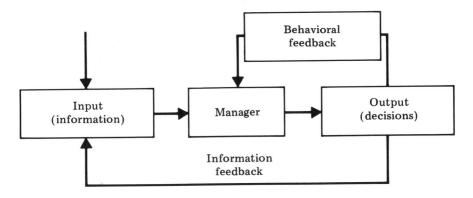

Simply stated, this input-output, feedback model shows that the manager responds to information he receives about his decisions (how they worked, how they failed, how they should be changed, or how and when they might be used again) by modifying his future behavior. A key ingredient is information, which is necessary for making decisions that will integrate activities toward objectives which will maintain a viable, dynamic organization. Therefore, any organizational design must include appropriate information flows to managers.

It is useful then to consider a business firm as a system. The interrelated parts may be analyzed in the following general input-output model:

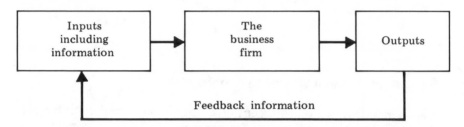

If we define the firm as a total input-output system, such activities as production, purchasing, or data processing may be considered as input-output subsystems that, through interaction, provide information flow for the integrated whole. In such a systems view of management (or a business firm), the interrelationships (the product of combinations that can be identified, studied, manipulated, understood separately and together, and then evaluated) contribute to purpose. As Churchman stated, "The systems approach is simply a way of thinking about total systems and their components" (3).

Can MIS be Defined

"System" and "management information system" (MIS) have been given so many meanings by authorities and have been so overworked that today the terms are used loosely. But, as indicated earlier, the elements of any "system" have some common properties and interacting functions. Thus, a management information system or MIS provides managers with information about a company's activities—presumably information they need to make sound decisions. To maximize our understanding of the components and purposes of MIS, let us look for common threads in available definitions of MIS:

> ... an organized method of providing past, present and projection information related to internal operations and external intelligence. Walter J. Kennevan (4)

. . . produced, for all levels of management, the information required to make decisions in two areas: (1) predicting what will happen by using historical data and simulation to give alternatives and (2) outlining or making changes to a present procedure or decision to make the selected prediction possible. R. L. Martino (5)

. . . provides management with the information it requires to monitor progress, measure performance, detect trends, evaluate alternatives, make decisions, and to take corrective action. R. R. Duersch (6)

. . . facilitates the management functions of planning, organizing, integrating, measuring and controlling. R. E. Breen, H. Chestnut, R. R. Duersch, and R. S. Jones (7)

. . . a computer-based network containing one or more operating systems. . . provides relevant data to management for decision-making purposes and also contains the necessary mechanism for implementing changes or responses made by management in this decision-making activity. Thomas R. Prince (8)

. . . fulfills the requirements of information to plan, direct, evaluate, coordinate, and control business in an economic and efficient manner. Normally it involves a total system linkage concept, whether dealing with one overall system or a main system and subsystems. Nathan Berkowitz and Robertson Munro, Jr. (9)

. . . should include: (1) a standard, integrated data base, (2) a system design that provides for the use of these data in the efficient and timely development of required information, and (3) the facility or plan to utilize these data for projecting future activity and for planning management action. William F. Cooke, Jr., and William J. Rost (10)

. . . a communication process in which information (input) is recorded, stored and retrieved (processed) for decisions (output) on planning, operating, and controlling. Robert G. Murdick and Joel E. Ross (11)

An operational function whose parts corresponding to functional units are information subsystems of other operational functions. Sherman C. Blumenthal (12)

... an evolving organization of people, computers, and other equipment, including associated communication and support systems, and their integrated operation to regulate and control selected environmental events to achieve system objectives. Harold Sackman (13)

... structured to provide the information needed, when needed, and where needed ... represents the internal communications network of the business, providing the necessary intelligence to plan, execute and control. Frederick B. Cornish (14)

... the problems underlying MIS can best be classified in overall systems perspective ... to realize information as fundamentally a three-dimensional concept (pragmatic, semantic, and syntactic) is simple but to incorporate this insight into an information systems definition means to apply the structural and procedural systems notions to the concept of information. Information is then considered as the output of data transmutation processes and is identical to desired knowledge which provides insights into a problem or a particular problem solution. Hartmut J. Will (15)

... a very highly organized combination of personnel, equipment, and facilities performing data storage and retrieval, data processing, transmission and display, all in response to the needs of decision makers at all levels of the business. Hershner Cross (16)

... the combination of human and computer-based resources that results in the collection, storage, retrieval, communication and use of data for the purpose of efficient management of operations and for business planning. Joseph F. Kelly (17)

... a management-oriented system characterized by information elements structured into a data base serving the information requirements of policy and operating management. Norman L. Enger (18)

... the methods by which an organization plans, operates, and controls its activities to meet its goals and objectives by utilizing the resources of money, people, equipment, materials, and information. We extend the use of the term "management system" to include any aspect in the life of an organization to which management personnel devote their attention. Other frequently encountered terms that denote the same concept are: "total system," "unified system," "goal-directed system," "integrated system," and "information system." We use these terms interchangeably. Thomas B. Glans, et al. (19)

There are two ingredients of MIS—management and the information system. Management must define, in order of priority, what it wants, and it must also specify the important characteristics of the information system. Leonard I. Krauss (20)

Implied in all these MIS definitions is the necessity of designing MIS to meet such fundamental questions as: "What is information?" "Are there different kinds?" "Does management need information other than that being received?" "Do different managers have different requirements?" "And what is the nature of the required information outputs from the system?" The definitions reveal, however, a diversity of opinion about what constitutes an MIS and what its purposes are. Difficulties with definition can lead to design and implementation failure. Problems have occurred in conceptualization; e.g., are all MIS computer based? Indeed not; a cardinal rule of any information system is that it must be appropriate to the organization for which it is designed. Not all firms use computers, but all have some type of MIS at some level of sophistication.

The quoted definitions emphasize that an MIS (1) applies to all management levels; (2) has and is linked to an organizational subsystem; (3) functions to measure performance, monitor progress, evaluate alternatives, or provide knowledge for change or corrective action; and (4) is flexible, both internally and externally.

Problems arising from definitions and lack of agreement on a definition's basic components are not unique to writers of MIS. Beckett (21), for example, has pointed out that writers of management texts have defined management differently from viewpoints of principles, functions, processes, systems, and behavior, and from quantitative and nonquantitative aspects. But just as the business world has produced many effective (as well as noneffective) managers, despite lack of a universal definition of management, so should managers be able to optimize MIS.

What, Then, Is the Purpose of an MIS

A sophisticated concept, MIS transcends hardware, software, and management information needs and uses. (22) The principal operating components of a computer-based–data processing system include a central processor (containing arithmetic and control units and internal memory or core-storage facility); file-storage units; input-output processing facilities; and programming software support. (23) The integrated purpose of an MIS, by general consensus, would appear to be to provide a functional whole composed of a standard, integrated data base, a system for using those data to develop required, timely information, and a plan to utilize that information in future management plans and actions. (24) Yet the purpose of an MIS goes beyond getting the right information to the right manager at the right time at the right cost. That analogy fails to consider either the data processing functions necessary in such basic operational activities as billing orders and information storing or the nature of an organization (a dynamic, functional entity). The information-management process encompasses the planning, evaluation, coordination, and control of generating, processing, using, preserving, and disposing of both operational and corporate management information; it also includes records and paperwork management as integral elements.

An MIS, then, is the total complex in which data are generated, processed, and refined to produce the information needed at all levels of organization. To accomplish those goals, objectives must be established; information needed to evaluate performance must be determined; the exception principle must be applied effectively; an effective mechanism must be developed, installed, and maintained; the system's adequacy as a basis of information for management decisions must be reviewed and appraised continually. Thus,

> . . . The purpose of an MIS is to determine and provide, as efficiently, effectively, and economically as possible, what management needs to know. It should facilitate the accomplishment of objectives, prevent failures to reach objectives, and correct conditions which hamper the fulfillment of objectives. (25)

Why MIS Fail

Some companies are using MIS successfully; others are not. Many are using the computer system to record and process data but have not succeeded in using it for planning. Therefore, it is necessary to examine major problems areas of MIS so that designers and business firms can profit from the experience of others.

An effective computer MIS has five elements: (1) a data base with multiple files; (2) various functionally adjacent applications, such as billing and inventory control; (3) an information-retrieval system, which allows for management reports at will; (4) simulation capability; and (5) on-line access to the data base. Firms that have been unable to get these five elements to produce an effective system have failed primarily because (1) their data base was difficult to build on a modular basis, file by file, without interrupting the daily flow of business activities; (2) the adjacent applications were too difficult and costly to design and redesign; or (3) the simulation capability required data factors that were neither built in nor available as needed. Because few MIS designers could foresee all the requirements, there have been more failures than successes with MIS (26).

According to Gale, difficulties in designing and implementing MIS basically result from

1. Orienting, defining, and designing of the system in terms of the computer rather than of the user.
2. Vesting responsibility for the system's development and implementation with computer specialists without involving top management in the design and establishment of priorities.
3. Inadequately explaining to company personnel the nature, purpose, and scope of the system—which results in failure to anticipate resistance to change.
4. Underestimating the complexity in system design and implementation stages. Managers fail to appraise the practicable capabilities of the system, a feasible timetable, and a realistic approach to cost and efforts. (27)

Some systems fail because of inflexibility. To stand the test of time, systems must be changing constantly. Disparity between the potentially achievable and the attained results of computerized MIS was the fundamental concern of more than 1,300 executives interviewed by Case and Company, Management Consultants. The executives' concerns and opinions may be categorized as

1. Inability to use the computer-information system for planning. Executives, action oriented, have thought little about ideal information systems. Operational duties tend to require their full attention.

2. It is unrealistic to expect the computer manufacturer to tell customers in detail how they can use a computer in planning. A salesman cannot be an expert on the information needs for decisions in all firms.
3. There are few recognized computer experts, and the computer executive (like other functional managers) has his daily operating deadlines and personnel problems.
4. To date no one in management information has effectively grasped the responsibility for systems design, development, and evaluation. (28)

To failure factors already noted, Carlson (29) adds inactive supervision by those responsible for the system results, too much attention to computer-room efficiencies, lack of standardization in data elements and in data coding, and inexperienced analysts.

The pivotal issue in a successful MIS program is how well a particular company's interpretation of MIS reflects its information needs. Failure to meet those needs occurs when

1. Crash data are defined and identified and then installed, rather than developed in an orderly, well-thought-out effort.
2. Unreliable data (inaccurate and incomplete) and undependable data sources are used.
3. Hypothetical (instead of actual) information needs are used for design basis and decision making.
4. Information does not distinguish between critical and noncritical organizational factors or does not relate to objectives. (30)

An MIS may fail because control measures and evaluative criteria are inadequate or absent. In 1964, McKinsey and Company (31) studied computer usage in 27 major manufacturing companies (involving more than 300 computer installations); they found that 18 of the companies were not earning sufficient returns on their computers to cover the investments, primarily because of no control or evaluative criteria. If a businessman installs a new piece of machinery, he usually has studied first a proposal and knows the unit's expected performance. But, generally, performance parameters for computers are lacking, and few are competent enough to establish the yardsticks. The essential task thus is to grasp the causes of failure in MIS and then, through design and involvement, prevent such deficiencies.

False Assumptions Lead to System Failure

In establishing an MIS framework, computer specialists and managers make many assumptions. Some assumptions (those based on the relationship between information and management) have implicit, built-in MIS requirements, which some promoters emphasize in pointing out the value of MIS. Unfortunately, the promoters thus point out assumptions, not conclusions, which (if they persist) lead to improperly defined system objectives, failure, or suboptimization. As momentum builds up, it is less likely that design efforts will change or shift to the correct dimension.

Dead-end streets in MIS development are likely to be incredibly expensive, so much so that what at first looks attractive can gradually degenerate into disaster. The project undertaken may be impossible because of what it attempts to do, the money allocated for it, the talent available to work on it, the contemporary state of the art, the timetable for implementation, or any combination of these factors. Also, disaster can result when the MIS simply does not bring about the benefits needed to justify its existence. A number of companies met with failures because they did not work on the right problem or mix of problems; they did not encompass a balance of short- and long-term payoffs. For the right mix, the functional modules of a planned MIS must be identified and ranked according to benefits to management, cost effectiveness, and other values.

At least seven false and commonly made assumptions can blind system designers to the real needs and opportunities (32):

1. *Decision makers can express their information needs. (Management may understand its problems without knowing what information is needed to solve them or even how to state those needs lucidly and unambiguously.)*
2. *Decision making will improve as more information is made available. (More wrong information cannot help; more information of any type will not help unless accompanied by more sophisticated methods of locating and retrieving what is needed. Besides, sheer bulk of information makes it difficult to separate the important from the irrelevant.)*
3. *Managers are starving for information. (Piles of information surround the busy administrator; what is needed is not more information but appropriate information properly presented.)*

4. *Information will improve communication, which in turn will improve executive performance. (Information that is not relevant to the receiver or is not clearly stated cannot be communicated. More communication, even if improved, may be a burden on the manager.)*
5. *Managers need the information they request. (Many managers request available information, which may not meet their needs. Some, being uncertain of their needs, may ask for a lot of information, hoping to discover something by browsing through it.)*
6. *Managers get too much information. (Often true, this assumption may be specious when viewed conversely. Less information is warranted only when it gives the manager the same message.)*
7. *Executives tend to get information faster. (Unless faster is related to something, this assumption falls apart.)*

So MIS fail because of the assumptions made concerning the relationships between information and management. Neither more nor different information necessarily results in better decisions, but an MIS should have better decisions as one of its goals. Few managers can pinpoint their information needs because they tend to center their requests around what they are currently receiving (protection) and what they would like to have (desired) but often fail to request either what is actually needed or to see how different information could meet their needs (projection). To solve the information dilemma, computer specialists and managers must work together to search out the dependent and independent relationships between information and management needs.

Some Important Variables in MIS Design

Designing an MIS that will respond to the user's real need is a critical, complex task. Meeting management's information needs with a poorly conceived system—one either too weak for proper response or too powerful and thus too costly—can spell disaster. Every well-designed MIS is in some respects unique, but all MIS need certain criteria grounded in the nature of management functions. These criteria include

1. Simplicity and brevity of output

2. Concentration on results and goals, rather than on methods and processes
3. Suppression of "noise," or trivial and irrelevant data
4. Integration with the information flow at the operational levels in a particular business so that its managers can be provided detailed information speedily in a familiar form without cumbersome translations (33)

Design to Meet Goals

To guarantee an output designed to serve their real needs, users must help develop MIS specifications. First they must look at the goals: goals of top management (in terms of the firm's future direction and growth rate and of how MIS is expected to contribute to those objectives); goals of middle management (involving timely information, exception reports, and operational data); goals of the MIS management team (who must meet their own time and resource commitments in considering business profit). (34) Though goals originate at various information sources, the most crucial are long-range business plans for the company. From such MIS specifications, designers learn about expected growth rate, product changes, new processes planned, marketing direction of the firm, and space and plant projections.

Integrate MIS into the Managerial Functions

In their 1964 study, McKinsey and Company found that companies having successful computer systems also had (1) quality leadership by top executives, (2) planning and control tools built into the computer system by management, (3) participation by operating management, and (4) competent computer and systems staff. In those systems most successful, management had set clear objectives to ensure that the computer program focused on major problems, adequate resources had been marshaled to get the job done, and human and organizational barriers to progress had been removed. In addition, top management reviewed and challenged the computer plans and programs, monitored progress, and insisted on significant tangible benefits from its investment. This study indicated success of computer systems depended more heavily on executive leadership than on any other factor. (35)

In one survey, which involved 100 top managers of firms using in aggregate more than 120 computers, the managers reported that they made no direct use of the computer for decision making at corporate or division levels and that they rarely received information directly from the computer. Consequently, the decision-making process at the middle-management level was affected by the computer directly; top management was affected, if at all, by middle managers and lower-echelon managers who filtered up computer-generated information. (36)

Zani, in a cost-benefit analysis of selected real-time information systems, found that the system did not automatically generate savings for a company, quicker information flow in and of itself had no value, and real-time systems yielded benefits only if they were meaningfully integrated into management processes. Management perceived the system not as a tool to bring about inventory savings or to gain competitive advantages but as an inexpensive paper processor or simply a convenient replacement for older data processing equipment. (37)

Consider MIS as Part of Total Systems Resources

An MIS that is functionally inadequate, because total resources involved with input and output were not considered, results in suboptimized objectives, with undue emphasis on data maniuplation and insufficient attention to decision making. To be efficient, MIS design must integrate an organization's operational and informational subsystems so as to enhance total organizational effectiveness. To do that, each functional component must be described in terms of its outputs and resources used, documented, and assessed. Separate functional segments, once described, must be pieced together on the basis of output, logic, and/or input relationships to form a mosaic of the total organization as a functional system. (38) Tools used to develop and implement such an MIS consider the organization as one system composed of many subsystems and may range from paper and pencil subparts to highly sophisticated computers. But MIS is not designed around a computer; rather, the proper computer is selected and fitted into the MIS design. (39)

MIS Design Is One of Several Integrated Phases

MIS design cannot be viewed as independent of everything else in the firm. The firm's goals, which add value to materials and ideas and fill a societal need, are accomplished by operating systems consisting of people, machines, energy, and planning efforts. Therefore, MIS cannot be designed in a vacuum; operational systems must be analyzed and MIS designed to complement them. That an MIS is a continuous process, with each phase blending into the following phase and consistent with an overall plan, is a view supported by Murdick (40), O'Black (41), Hodgson (42), Rosner (43), Murdick and Ross (44), Kelly (45), Blumenthal (46), Yaffa and Hines (47), Krauss (48), and others.

According to Krauss (49), the design effort consists of three stages (conceptual, subsystem, and process), each resulting in a progressively more-detailed representation of the system. The conceptual stage, which relates to a diagram (master plan) of the important components and variables in the system, is custom tailored to the company's needs. In the second stage, subsystems and their logical functions first are defined (with details about information flows, sources, appearances, and types of output), and then the exact processing information and program in each subsystem is specified. In the process stage, detailed requirements relevant to input, output, and data processing are set forth as program specifications.

Blumenthal (50) believes that systems development encompasses all activities involved in a systems effort, beginning with a recognition of a systems need and ending with the satisfaction of that need. There are activities carried on directly and specifically in support of a given systems-development effort, and there are those indirect activities carried on in general to support all development activities collectively.

Structuring the Data Base

How the data base is structured is central to the success of any MIS design. This is the view supported by Head (51), Kelly (52), and Enger (53). The design of the data base will dictate (or, conversely, in some situations be constrained by) the type of storage devices to be used, the data-management package chosen to manipulate information in the data base, the degree of security that must be built into the system to protect the data from misuse, and the rapidity of the responses that must be made to management inquiries. To include every possible element of information that could conceivably be relevant at some time to management's information needs would be impractical (with respect both to the amount of data stored and to the impossibility of an effective retrieval). "The key in structuring the data base is to force the designers to be selective in what they include with the understanding that what is included inevitably results in a compromise" (54). Obviously, in making a compromise the hierarchy of objectives should help determine priorities.

Thus those involved in designing and planning ambitious but effective long-range MIS must temper the conceptual system they would like to develop with the reality of what is technically feasible and economically justifiable. Difficult but important tasks include determining what data to collect and how, which medium to use, what retrieval method to adopt, and what analyses to perform. Information cannot be generated if supporting data are absent. Yet the scope of the data base cannot be so broad that the system becomes too costly to implement or too impractical (from standpoints of amount of data stored or the impossibility of an effective retrieval). (55)

The Organizational Impact of MIS

"Information derives its value from the effect it has on the behavior of the organization" (56). But what impact does MIS have, and what are the consequences for management?

The Middle Manager

How computer systems affect middle management are not yet clear. Diverse opinions include eliminating the middle manager or shifting his functional responsibilities. Because most middle managers are involved only in operational-type problems and plans, they have not participated actively in strategic planning. But even if many middle-management decisions can be programmed and implemented directly from computer output (thus bypassing middle managers), the need for motivating and directing employees will remain.

If MIS should eliminate middle managers the span of control at the next higher level would increase significantly. With such a wide span of control, how would such important leadership activities as supervision, motivation, and direction be accomplished? Leadership is a process of interpersonal influence.

So far middle managers seem to have survived the obituaries written for them. Management studies by McKinsey and Company and others show no significant decline in the number of middle managers as firms install computers. Perhaps that, however, is a myth associated with failure to conceptualize the interrelationships in the organizational impact of MIS. But it must be remembered that much decision making is intuitive judgment based on experience and the ability to relate to decision variables, circumstances, and past outcomes. Thus, it would seem implementing an MIS would be more successful if there is greater emphasis on involving and reinforcing middle management. With MIS facilitating and speeding up some decision making and routine activities, middle management could spend more time on leadership activities and humanizing the work environment. MIS with almost unlimited data inquiry and retrieval capabilities can facilitate top-management's job by extending its scope to include more planning and decision-making activities and perhaps by increasing the amount of formerly lower-level operational activities it handles. But there are significant differences in middle- and top-management jobs and in the self-perception of those jobs. Even 15 years ago, Porter and Ghiselli (57) found differentiation in the self-perceptions of top- and middle-management executives. Top executives thought of themselves as active, self-reliant, and generally willing to act on faith in themselves and their abilities; they would take risks when they thought they had good, original ideas, confident their decisions would lead to success. In contrast, middle-management's self-perceptions focused on careful planning, well-thought-out-beforehand actions, and well-controlled behavior; they placed more emphasis on operating by the rules and conditions of the system, had less confidence in their own judgment or ideas, and appeared less willing to take risks or to move ahead when the outcome was uncertain. Those observations of differences between top- and middle-management job levels suggest that MIS may be more compatible with the tasks of middle managers than those of top executives. Top managers make broad, organizational, encompassing plans; middle managers make specific or operational plans. This hierarchial nature of planning appears to support retaining middle managers and shifting more MIS planning to those with expertise in operations research and analysis. Indeed, it tends to be the middle manager who has experience (or seeks it) in computer and management science, which has become so essential in forecasting, simulating, and planning techniques.

Top Management

Most literature on MIS design advocates the need for top management involvement and support (with which we agree), but the extent of involvement and how to accomplish it are uncertain. Because of the nature of the top-management job, the self-perceptions about it, the information requirements necessary to do the job, and the difficulty (if not impossibility) of obtaining many information needs, it appears that for some time yet neither top-management's information needs nor top-management's use of the MIS will be optimized. Not all that can be blamed on inadequate involvement by top management in MIS design; part of the cause is undetermined and unrefined information needs.

Top management can support MIS design, but support is less than involvement. Certainly top management can and should provide the right organizational philosophy and attitude, assign responsibility for design and evaluation high in the organization, help establish the necessary framework, help determine information needs, encourage middle management to be involved, develop a broad calculus of cost, and help apply the test of need (tangible and intangible feasibility) to MIS design. Top management should select, train, and evaluate personnel; participate actively in designing and implementing the MIS program (including equipment acquisition and installation) and in determining the appropriate organizational level, along with responsibilities and accountability; and establish appropriate plans to evaluate and audit.

To become involved and to play the expected and needed leadership role, top management must update itself in computer- and management-science techniques and in so doing develop an appreciation for information exactness and completeness required. Then, top management needs to find avenues to use MIS in planning and decision making (beyond facilitating operational decisions).

Centralization-decentralization Syndrome

Whether or not computers and MIS lead to centralization perhaps need not be resolved, if we are to assume that whichever occurs will lead to optimizing the firm's objectives. Centralization and departmentalization—two related but dissimilar management concepts—have been confused often. Centralization implies that decisions are made at the top of each management level; decentralization implies that decisions are pushed down to subordinate levels. In departmentalization (a concept in organizational structure), an organization's work is divided into tasks that then are assigned and coordinated to facilitate reaching objectives. Hence, consolidating computer facilities is departmentalization, not centralization. Firms that have consolidated computer-based activities at their headquarters move toward decentralization when they communicate processed information to branch locations, where managers use it in decisions. But when MIS output goes directly and only to top management and decisions are made by top management only, MIS leads to centralization. Who uses information, not where it is processed, determines centralization or decentralization.

To be effective, MIS must provide information where it is needed; all managers need information. Thus, effectively designed MIS would seem to be more compatible with decentralization than with centralization. To decentralize requires considering the questions "Who has the capacity to decide?" "Who can obtain the necessary information and act on it?" "Will the decisions have local or broader consequences?" Although decision making is complicated and depends more and more on interrelated variables, middle managers often are closer than top executives to the interrelationships and should, therefore, make the decisions.

If a manager is not making the decisions he wants to make or should make, then he rightfully can charge his organization with being centralized. Behaviorally, the issue is not in numbers of decisions made or in percentages of the total but whether or not subordinates perceive themselves as capable of making the decisions that they are not permitted to make.

The number of variables (other than MIS output) that bear on a decision are indicators of the difficulty in establishing a relationship between MIS and the centralization-decentralization syndrome. Albrook (58) has indicated that business firms shift from decentralized to centralized decision making and control when economic conditions of the firm are tightened. When profits are up, top management is satisfied. When profits are down, top management wants to control and guide their corporations. An opposite view, although related to the economic circumstance of the time, is expressed by Parkinson:

> In times of growth and prosperity, the main-office leaders . . . tend to have increased confidence in their own wisdom and move toward centralization of power. However, with increased competition and declining profits, there may be greater communication with others in the organization who are closer to the action. This, in turn, may lead to decentralization of responsibility (often buck-passing) and eventually to decentralization of authority. (59)

It remains undemonstrated that centralization or decentralization is a function of MIS or computers.

Resistance to Change

The impact of that which is new or different often causes stress between those managing and those managed. Resistance to change is common among managers at all levels; thus it occurs when an MIS is designed and implemented. Often top management assumes that an organizational change automatically changes behavior; it rarely does. As stated by Daniel:

> Where organizational change has successfully influenced behavior, it is a safe bet that considerable thought has been given to the steps involved in implementation—announcing the change, realigning executive personnel, timing the various moves, and securing the participation of those affected as a means of building understanding, acceptance, and commitment. (60)

How to bring about change in such a way as to increase, rather than undermine, the commitment of the people involved could be as important as what is done. The MIS and the MIS-manager group, seen as an integral part of the company's growth, should play an important part in the company's planning and control. But the MIS group often fails to reach the potential expected of it or to fulfill its function adequately. Viewing themselves as system creators or developers, members of the MIS group attempt to develop the best functioning MIS possible; this perspective creates a serious schism in their relationship with other groups of the organization, particularly those expected to use the MIS group output but who feel that the output does not meet their information needs. If this producer-user gap is perpetuated, animosity and hostility between the two groups increase and each perceives the other as incompetent.

Neither acceptance nor use of an MIS can be expected to occur simultaneously with system activation. A positive attitude toward change must be established. This can be done by training managers and exposing them to different job responsibilities so that they will understand what is involved (already there are many sponsored programs*). Failing to do this can plot manager against manager until MIS becomes a victim of the in-fighting.

Despite training programs, trainees may fail to apply the learned

---

*Management and computer seminars have been specifically designed by Control Data Corporation, Washington, D.C., AMR International, Inc., New York, Didactic Systems, Inc., New York, and American Management Association, New York, to cite a few.

concepts when back on the job because of a poor corporate climate in which to apply the newly acquired techniques. Corporate and top managers, through lackadaisical attitudes and minimal support and endorsement, are responsible, according to Butkus (61), Murphy (62), House (63), and others. To be effective, training and applications must be endorsed by management.

The Computer Specialist—Corporate-management Dichotomy

Attitudes between computer specialists and corporate management often become belligerent (perhaps not intentionally) because they tend to defend their different specializations. Computer specialists have technical, mathematical, and systems orientation; corporate managers, unable to appreciate that specialization, are unsympathetic toward its requirements and so tend to be oriented toward their own functional job. Each group regards the other as threatening; such behavior impedes communication and destroys any hope of cooperation. Townsend's *Up the Organization* phrased the schism thus:

> First get it through your head that computers are big, expensive, fast, dumb adding-machine-typewriters. Then realize that most of the computer technicians that you're likely to meet or hire are complicators, not simplifiers. They're trying to make it look tough. Not easy. They're building a mystique, a priesthood, their own mumbo-jumbo ritual to keep you from knowing what they—and you—are doing. (64)

Part of the gap between MIS manager and corporate manager is caused by the difference in responsibilities. The designer (and manager) of the MIS must explain and defend the computer input-output transformation and the logic behind it as well as manage its operation; the corporate manager must plan and carry out the decisions. Devising what we think might be useful is not the same as applying the information in beneficial ways. Thus for MIS (as well as other systems and procedures) to be successful their design and use must be by joint effort rather than defensive behavior.

Determining Information Needs

The success of MIS depends largely upon the ability of designers and managers to determine information needs and to design a unique system to meet them. There are variables that make it difficult, if not impossible, to determine all information needs. Information needed to make decisions is often complex and not easily pinpointed or defined. Also, managers at different levels have different information needs, and each manager has different information needs for different decision problems. New efforts are needed to define such information diversity and to design it into MIS.

There are organizational barriers that tend to prevent securing needed information. Unfortunately, information often has a characteristic of bias. MIS must be uniquely designed and requires a degree of flexibility to meet changing and diverse information needs of managers. In this section we shall search out some of these needs, focusing on problems involved in determining them and behavioral responses to them.

Different Information Needs for Different Objectives

Obtaining information and validating it provide barriers to MIS design and success. MIS designers cannot assume that all needed information is available, all applicable information is needed, or all available information (even if applicable or needed) can be effectively and systematically processed and produced. Neither can a manager's total information needs be determined by the manager or by anyone else—an assumption inconsistent with the decision-making process or the rapidity of corporate and technological change. It is also unrealistic to assume that a manager can always communicate his information needs to MIS designers in such a way that his needs can be correctly and adequately reflected in MIS design.

According to Livingston (65), a manager's decision making centers around (1) problem solving (immediate), in which the manager, for the most part, draws on analyzed data, company policies, and his past decisions; (2) problem finding and then solving, with the manager drawing not only on internal information but also on information that reflects changes in the business environment (including such external variables as changes in raw-material components, products, demand shifts, prices, consumer behavior, distribution patterns, or competitive business practices); and (3) opportunity finding, for which the manager needs information he can use to recognize opportunities and to design strategic plans. Since results in business are obtained generally by discovering and developing opportunities (not by solving problems), the manager needs information (substantively and qualitatively superior to information needed for other decisions) to make strategies and plans for multiple-year horizons. Therefore, the toughest management job in the world is the one which demands that the executive flip ahead to see what is coming and flip back to determine what information and resources are needed to act upon an idea for the future. Anshen, in his McKinsey award-winning article in the *Harvard Business Review*, expressed it this way:

> To prosper in a fast-changing world top business leaders must think more like philosophers than efficiency experts. Improved analytical and administrative tools . . . alone will not be enough for survival in the future, because they are geared primarily to improve the efficiency of present operations. The new business leaders will be those who can stretch their minds beyond the management of physical resources . . . to conceptualize broad new philosophies of business and to translate their vision into operations. To the traditional skills of managing people, material, machines and money, they will add . . . managing ideas. (66)

Can today's managers conceptualize opportunity-finding information needs? Are current MIS flexible enough to meet such needs? MIS designers and top managers in particular must realize that it is just as important to implement new ideas and to reach for new goals as it is to reach a higher level of efficiency in administering yesterday's ideas (which to date they have emphasized).

Organizational Barriers to Information Needs

Because the MIS group and the corporate-management group are far apart in understanding information needs for decision making, communication may fail in the early stages of MIS. After discovering that executives cannot tell them what information is needed, and not comprehending that information needs of corporate decision makers in a competitive environment are infinite and everchanging, the shocked computer specialists retrench and design MIS to meet what seems desirable and feasible. Embarrassed, corporate management recedes, never again becoming involved in design and requests for information, and perhaps never actively using the output data.

When managers ask for new or additional information from MIS, designed without top-management involvement, they may be advised that such data are not available, cannot be determined, or to fulfill such requests would cost a given number of dollars (estimated in terms of convincing cost-benefit analysis). In some cases, managers requesting additional information may be informed by their superior that such data are either not available or too expensive to acquire, which may or may not be so. More likely the MIS had not been designed to provide the data, or managers (not wanting the information made available to that particular management level) apply the "principle of missing information." Managers may use that technique because holding certain information gives prestige only to them; they really do not know how to share information; they fail to realize the importance of the information to subordinate managers; they believe releasing information would violate company security policy; or (in some cases) it is a way to belittle or show belligerence toward subordinates. There is also the practice of protective screening; subordinates use it to ensure that managers at higher levels do not obtain certain information. Unfortunately, such management practices exist; hence, MIS design, regardless of how excellent it is, does not overcome this obstacle but continues to be a victim of it.

Imperfect Information

In many decision situations (certainly in complex ones), the problem is how to reduce risk by obtaining unbiased information. Because some subjective judgment is involved in preparing the basic information, a certain amount of bias in conclusions can be expected. Because human ingenuity is great, hidden assumptions can be introduced into almost any analysis, as witnessed by prejudiced benefit of the doubt, overemphasis of quantitative facts, influential personal opinions, or red-herring techniques. Such bias in information output or objectives can weaken MIS efforts to provide information where needed.

The Need for an MIS Synthesis

To ensure the success of MIS, companies must consider the types of system components, organizational levels to be served, individual manager-information needs, timing required to tie a subsystem to the total system, translation of systems requirements, preparation of standard operating procedures, staffing and training of personnel, the management of MIS, and evaluation to prevent information and facility obsolescence. In addition, it is necessary to establish the data base, set goals, determine priorities, and make financial commitments.

To make an MIS work, managerial support, attitudes, and objectives must be melded with the expertise of computer specialists. To overcome pitfalls of past MIS design requires a constructive course of action, a basic change in philosophy by both artificially dichotomized groups: corporate managers and computer specialists. Thus computer specialists must adopt and apply behavioral-science techniques in their approach to management; corporate management must develop an appreciation for computer technology and the ability to comprehend the detail and exactness required to establish objectives and provide input information.

Considering the success of the subsystem approach (particularly toward achieving inventory control, production, scheduling, and distribution objectives), perhaps some firms should take that approach to their MIS, rather than attempt an unfeasible total MIS. Independent, as well as interdependent, relationships exist in information needs. For some objectives, at some management levels, a subsystem MIS seems highly desirable both in economic feasibility and in objective function.

During the 1960s many organizations were economically effective even though their MIS were ineffective or underutilized; however, during the 1970s we may find greater dependence on MIS and therefore a renewed enthusiasm toward making MIS contribute to management.

It is important that management realize there are both differential and integrative aspects in MIS design. It is unrealistic to attempt to design an MIS to meet every information need (differentiation). It is necessary to integrate information needs with the hierarchy of objectives and with other informational, behavioral, and organizational phenomena. Management needs to look closely at the interrelationships among the MIS, the organization, and the managers; in so doing it can consider what managers with unlimited vision can do if they have access to well-designed MIS of unlimited capacity and flexibility and unrealized objectives and unlimited potential.

Early MIS were suboptimum because of the failure to see the role of human personality in modern systems; hence, behavioral-science dimensions were not integrated with those of computers and associated technologies. What is needed for a new synthesis? The answer is lively and important exchange between management know-how and computer-science expertise to capture the facts and opinions that constitute true information needs. Then systems can be designed to optimize those needs; blending behavioral science with computer-information technology will guarantee a successful design.

Summary

Management is a decision-making process in which information is combined with experience, judgment, and intuition to utilize resources to reach objectives. Management as an input-output system uses information to make decisions to integrate activities toward objectives. In organizational design, then, information flows are fundamental to ensure that managers' information needs are met. The system for meeting those needs is called MIS (management information system).

There are many different definitions of MIS, but their central theme is a system designed to provide managers with information needed to make sound decisions. Such a dynamic system processes and transforms information into required outputs, retains data in storage, simulates information for decision alternatives, implements changes and responses, and integrates itself with total system environment. Although not all firms use computers (yet all have some type of MIS at some level of sophistication), it is popular to conceptualize MIS as being computer based. Such MIS are composed of facilities for information storage, retrieval, and transformation; the data base, unique to the organization's information needs and sources, ideally is integrated with management needs for and uses of information.

The purpose of an MIS—to provide information for management decision making—is accomplished through data processing of operational information; this involves storage, retrieval, simulation capability, functionally adjacent support systems, information refinement and communication, and integration of corporate plans and objectives. Some MIS have succeeded in this objective, but others have failed because of inadequate design in all phases and lack of leadership from top management. MIS designers have failed to foresee information needs and uses, provide needed flexibility, and differentiate assumptions from facts; top management has failed by not becoming involved in design efforts, not using the system, and by not endorsing, supporting, and evaluating it.

Each MIS must be designed to meet goals of the organization. To do this it is necessary to integrate MIS with operational and long-range business plans; if designed independently, the MIS subsequently fails. All managers plan, make decisions, and control; MIS should be designed to facilitate those activities.

Any MIS is part of a larger total system, having as its objective effective use of resources to accomplish desired goals. Designing an MIS so that it can contribute to the total system requires analyzing and describing the organization's functional components in terms of their outputs and their interrelationships and then placing those relationships together to form a mosaic of the total functional organization. MIS design is a continuous process, each phase blending into the next, consistent with an overall plan.

Structuring the data base is essential in MIS design. Keeping the organization's objectives in mind, this structuring requires determining what data to collect, how to collect them and with what medium; what retrieval method to adopt; what analyses to perform; and what supporting data to include. Naturally, this always results in a compromise between what can be developed and what is technically feasible and economically justifiable. (A data base so broad that it prices the system out of feasible implementation is useless.)

Changing variables in an organization make an impact on the organization. In the design and implementation stages of MIS, organizational structure changes may occur in responsibilities assigned, procedures required, the information flows necessary to support the system, or in managerial behavior (particularly with respect to time spent on and emphasis given to planning, controlling, and decision making). When implementing that MIS, changes should occur in the components of the system and in the emphasis required to meet changing objectives of the MIS and the organization. When resistance to change occurs as a natural behavioral response (at either design or implementation stage), management must assume its responsibilities to minimize that resistance. Likewise, the organization can make its impact on MIS through effective design efforts, involvement, support, and use. To date, the MIS-organization impacts have been restricted by lack of involvement, commitment, and use; consequently, MIS has not contributed directly to many planning and decision-making activities. Certain myths would have us believe that computers and MIS lead to centralization, elimination of middle managers, revolutionization of top-management roles, or a system that makes every decision faster and better. Such consequences have not occurred.

Determining information needs (which vary with managers) has been a difficult problem in MIS design. Information needed to solve known problems is different from that required to find problems; that information needed to find problems is different from that required to find opportunities and then to design effective plans to optimize those opportunities. But problem solving and opportunity finding are essential management tasks, and MIS should contribute to them. The success of MIS, therefore, depends largely on the capabilities and attitudes of both designers and users. With any system or corporate structure there are disappointments, inefficiencies, and somewhat opposing managerial forces. MIS is no exception. For effective MIS, designers need to build in avenues that accommodate greater information flexibility, and corporate managers need to improve their skills in information finding and using. Ineffective communication between MIS and corporate-management groups contributes to failure to determine (and to meet) information needs. Managers who apply the principle of missing information or use protective screening to withhold information create organizational barriers that cause MIS suboptimization. The objective in MIS design is to determine dynamic information needs and uses and to build in enough flexibility to meet them.

In addition to bottlenecks in information flows and ineffective communication between MIS and corporate-management groups, information often is biased because of subjective judgment in its selection, processing, interpretation, and use. Consequently, this weakens MIS efforts to provide information where needed.

An MIS synthesis—a melding of managerial support, attitudes, and objectives with computer-science expertise—should lead to constructive action to overcome pitfalls of MIS design. As the gap between behavioral-science concepts and computer-information technology closes, there will be greater understanding of managers and their jobs, responsibilities, and information needs and uses; then there will be effective communication of information needs and uses. The synthesis also must include the possibility of subsystem approaches to MIS, highly desirable both in economic feasibility and in objective function; for many firms the approach has been successful. Integrated with other organizational resources, MIS contributes its part in the managerial process of making decisions, utilizing resources, and accomplishing objectives.

References

1. Herbert A. Simon, *The New Science of Management Decisions* (New York: Harper & Row, Publishers, 1960), p. 1.

2. David W. Miller and Martin K. Starr, *The Structure of Human Decisions* (Englewood Cliffs, N.J.: Prentice-Hall, Inc., 1967), p. 18.

3. C. West Churchman, *The Systems Approach* (New York: Delacorte Press, Dell Publishing Co., 1968), p. 11.

4. Walter J. Kennevan, "Management Information Systems: MIS Universe," *Data Management*, p. 63, September 1970.

5. R. L. Martino, *MIS—Management Information Systems* (Wayne, Pa.: Management Development Institute Publications, 1969), p. 27.

6. R. R. Duersch, *Business Information System Design* (Schenectady, N.Y.: General Electric Company, 1968), p. 2.

7. R. E. Breen, H. Chestnut, R. R. Duersch, and R. S. Jones, *Management Information Systems, A Subcommittee Report on Definitions* (Schenectady, N.Y.: General Electric Company, 1969), p. 1.

8. Thomas R. Prince, *Information Systems for Management Planning and Control*, rev. ed. (Homewood, Ill.: Richard D. Irwin, Inc., 1970), p. 40.

9. Nathan Berkowitz and Robertson Munro, Jr., *Automatic Data Processing and Management* (Belmont, Calif.: Dickenson Publishing Company, Inc., 1969), p. 318.

10. William F. Cooke, Jr., and William J. Rost, "Standard Cost System: A Module of a Management Information System," *Journal of Systems Management*, p. 11, March 1969.

11. Robert G. Murdick and Joel E. Ross, *Information Systems for Modern Management* (Englewood Cliffs, N.J.: Prentice-Hall, Inc., 1971), p. 292.

12. Sherman C. Blumenthal, *Management Information Systems: A Framework for Planning and Development* (Englewood Cliffs, N.J.: Prentice-Hall, Inc., 1969), p. 36.

13. Harold Sackman, *Computers, Systems Science, and Evolving Society* (New York: John Wiley & Sons, Inc., 1967), p. 42.

14. Frederick B. Cornish, "MIS: Cause and Effect," *Managerial Planning,* p. 1, January/February 1971.

15. Hartmut J. Will, "Some Comments of Information Systems," *Management Science*, p. B-171, December 1969.

16. Hershner Cross, "A General Management View of Computers," in *Computers and Management—The Leatherbee Lectures 1967* (Boston: Harvard Graduate School of Business Administration, 1967), p. 15.

17. Joseph F. Kelly, *Computerized Management Information Systems* (New York: The Macmillan Company, 1970), p. 5.

18. Norman L. Enger, *Putting MIS to Work* (New York: American Management Association, 1969), p. 14.

19. Thomas B. Glans et al., *Management Systems* (New York: Holt, Rinehart, and Winston, Inc., 1968), p. 3.

20. Leonard I. Krauss, *Computer Based Management Information Systems* (New York: American Management Association, 1970), p. 3.

21. John A. Beckett, *Management Dynamics: The New Synthesis* (New York: McGraw-Hill Book Company, 1971), pp. 134–144.

22. Robert V. Head, "Management Information Systems: 1970," *Journal of Systems Management*, p. 24, August 1970.

23. Charles H. Kriebel, "Information Processing and Programmed Decision Systems," *Management Science*, p. 159, November 1969.

24. Cooke, Jr., and Rost, loc. cit.

25. Herman Limberg, "How to Meet Management's Information Needs," in *Management Information Systems* (Cleveland: Association for Systems Management, 1970), p. 39.

26. Frederik H. Lutter, "Why MIS Is No Hit," *Administrative Management*, p. 12, December 1970.

27. John R. Gale, "Why MIS Fail," condensed from *Financial Executive, Management Review,* p. 50, November 1968.

28. John H. Barnett, "Information Systems: Breaking the Barrier," *Journal of Systems Management*, pp. 8–10, May 1969.

29. Walter M. Carlson, "A MIS Designed by Managers," *Datamation*, p. 41, May 1967.

30. Krauss, op. cit., p. 25.

31. John T. Garrity, *Getting the Most Out of Your Computer* (New York: McKinsey and Company, 1964), p. 7.

32. Krauss, op. cit., pp. 41–43.

33. Frederick W. Shipman, "Designing MIS for Managers," *Journal of Systems Management*, p. 19, July 1969.

34. Frank P. Congdon, Jr., "Advance Planning for the Systems Function," *Journal of Systems Management*, pp. 13–14, August 1970.

35. Garrity, op. cit., p. 13.

36. Rodney H. Brady, "Computers in Top-Level Decision Making," *Harvard Business Review*, pp. 67–69, July–August 1967.

37. William M. Zani, "Real-Time Information Systems: A Comparative Economic Analysis," *Management Science*, p. B-354, February 1970.

38. Miles H. Hudson, "A Technique for Systems Analysis and Design," *Journal of Systems Management*, pp. 14–15, May 1971.

39. Cornish, loc. cit.

40. Robert G. Murdick, "MIS Development Procedures," *Journal of Systems Management*, p. 22, December 1970.

41. Mary Jane O'Black, "Building a Successful MIS," *Journal of Systems Management*, p. 9, April 1971.

42. R. N. Hodgson, "Design Considerations in Planning and Control Systems," *Managerial Planning*, p. 1, November/December 1970.

43. W. Norton Rosner, "Organizing for Management Information," *Systems & Procedures Journal* (now *Journal of Systems Management*), p. 35, November/December 1968.

44. Robert G. Murdick and Joel E. Ross, *Information Systems for Modern Management* (Englewood Cliffs, N.J.: Prentice-Hall, Inc., 1971), chaps. 12 and 13.

45. Kelly, op. cit., pp. 336–360.

46. Blumenthal, op. cit., pp. 104–105.

47. Earle Yaffa and Paul Hines, "Who Should Control The Computer?", *Management Review*, March 1969.

48. Krauss, op. cit., p. 105.

49. Krauss, op. cit., pp. 105–112.

50. Blumenthal, loc. cit.

51. Robert V. Head, "Structuring the Data Base for MIS," *Journal of Systems Management*, pp. 9–11, January 1969, and "MIS: Structuring the Data Base," *Journal of Systems Management*, pp. 37–38, September 1970.

52. Kelly, op. cit., pp. 336–360.

53. Enger, op. cit., pp. 40–48.

54. Robert V. Head, "MIS: Structuring the Data Base," *Journal of Systems Management*, p. 37, September 1970.

55. Kelly, op. cit., pp. 10, 51, and 60.

56. James C. Emery, *Organizational Planning and Control Systems* (New York: The Macmillan Company, 1969), p. 67.

57. L. W. Porter and E. E. Ghiselli, "The Self Perceptions of Top and Middle Management Personnel," *Personnel Psychology*, pp. 401–402, Winter 1957.

58. Robert C. Albrook, "Participative Management: Time for a Second Look," *Fortune*, p. 197, May 1967.

59. C. Northcote Parkinson, *The Law of Delay: Interviews and Outviews* (Boston: Houghton Mifflin Company, 1971), p. 47.

60. D. Ronald Daniel, "Reorganizing for Results," *Harvard Business Review*, p. 99, November-December 1966.

61. Alvin A. Butkus, "Should Executives Go Back to School?", *Dun's Review*, pp. 37–38, September 1970.

62. Joseph P. Murphy, "Overcoming Supervisory Weaknesses," *Personnel Journal*, pp. 312–314, May 1968.

63. Robert J. House, "Most Manager Training Misses the Mark," *The Iron Age*, p. 43, July 1966.

64. Robert Townsend, *Up the Organization* (New York: Alfred A. Knopf, Inc., 1970), p. 36.

65. J. Sterling Livingston, "Myth of the Well-Educated Manager," *Harvard Business Review*, pp. 82–84, January–February 1971.

66. Melvin Anshen, "The Management of Ideas," *Harvard Business Review*, p. 99, July–August 1969.

Will the Real MIS Stand Up

Robert G. Donkin

Reprinted by permission of
Business Automation, May 1969.

Ten years ago if inventories were turning over too slowly or production were held up by shortages of parts or materials, many company managers turned to the computer as the answer to all their problems. Well, why not? That's the way the computer was being touted in both the business and popular press, and that's the way many equipment manufacturers' representatives and systems designers, who should have known better, were talking it up.

The results, of course, were disastrous. Some managers were burned so badly by oversold EDP systems that they reacted violently. Not only did they get rid of the computers, but to this day they become visibly upset if anyone talks about bringing EDP back into their companies. "Once burned, twice shy" is a vastly understated description of the sentiments of many, perhaps most, of those managers who survived this fiasco of the 1950's.

They're not at all hard to identify: "Don't talk to us," they say, "about designing a computerized system. Just design a manual control system that really works. Then, maybe later, we can talk about automation. . . ." Ask any systems consultant whether those words have a familiar ring.

On the Threshold of a Fiasco

This first major misunderstanding of the true nature of computers probably set the dp industry back five years or more. It is my present concern that we are now on the threshold of a similar fiasco with respect to management information systems which may have even graver consequences. Many managers today—even many of those who survived their first third-degree burns in the 1950's—appear to be in danger of falling into the same old trap, camouflaged with new buzzwords and baited with instant information of any flavor that management might relish.

As a glance at almost any issue of a business journal published within the last 12 months will reveal, the latest rash of "MIS" articles is replete with such phrases as "stratified information matrix," "selective interrogation of a computerized data bank," and the like. If this glib jargon doesn't completely baffle corporate executives, along with the few remaining practical systems designers, I'll be more than a little surprised. There is, unfortunately, a real and present danger that many manufacturers, too brash or too proud to admit their confusion, will turn blindly to the management information system as the ultimate solution to all of their management problems.

If consultants permit these managers to repeat, in connection with management information systems, the same mistake that they and their predecessors made in the 1950's, then they deserve to be banished from the world of business—at least until they can learn to speak in words which the average businessman can comprehend.

When consultants finally agree on a glossary of terms—and if managers still trust them enough to let them "save" management by designing an actual management information system—then consultants will owe management both a debt of gratitude and a practical and workable system to help them manage their business.

In short, I believe that it will be unacceptable to management to "selectively interrogate a computerized data bank" but not be able to determine until three months after the end of an accounting period whether the company is earning a profit or if increasing production backlogs are causing shipments to fall behind schedule.

Having suggested some of the things that a management information system should not be, I suppose it is now incumbent upon me to define what such a system should be.

A management information system should be a totally integrated synergistic analog control system, with digital input and output characteristics, which categorically differentiates the data sets in alternate axes and provides random and sequential access to all planning, operating, financial and other quantifiable nonquantitative transactions in past, present and future data planes in conjunction with selective interrogation of the stratified data matrix contained within the computerized data bank in combination with discriminate differentiation of the magnitude of variance limits of the multiply control variables, providing accurately time-phased exception reports for management decision and executive action.

Any consultant worth his salt should be able to play this buzzword game with perfection if he expects to contribute to the mysticism and confusion associated with management information systems.

The one thing that every consultant should remember in his zeal to develop and sell to management the perfect, ultimate "total system," is that every company now in business already has a management information system of some sort. Normally, it is not the consultant's job to install a system where none exists but rather to improve the ability of an existing system or systems to provide reliable and timely data to support management decisions.

It has been my experience that management usually takes a dim view of revolutionary proposals, and that an evolutionary approach to systems improvements is more likely to gain management's support. It is truly an unusual manager who will wholeheartedly support ringing out the old and bring in the new!

For these reasons, I believe that it is helpful to consider management information systems in terms of the subsystems which they comprise. There are essentially four major subsystems to any management information system:

Management planning/control
Operations planning/control
Financial planning/control
Nonquantitative information

Though it may come as surprise, it is no accident that dp is not included in this list of major subsystems. Data processing systems support all of them, and as such perform a vital service function, but they do not in themselves constitute a major management information system.

Note also that I speak of "data processing" only, not ADP, EDP or even abacus. In my (perhaps simplistic, but indisputably practical) view, data processing is what you and I do when we balance our personal checking accounts each month with a pencil and paper. If we can all begin to regard dp as a service function which manipulates the data generated by our systems according to procedures we have established, then I believe we will have cleared away most of the smoke that camouflages the fundamental subsystems relationships of a management information system.

Conquering a Formidable Foe

Of course data must be gathered, processed, stored, and retrieved many times, even in a simple information system. But I think we must place dp in the role of servant rather than master if we ever hope to achieve a practical management information system. If we can learn to start by designing a competent system and then specify the dp requirements, rather than the other way around, I believe we will have conquered a formidable foe in our fight for systems sanity.

Let's take a closer look now at each of these major subsystems and the part each might play when integrated into an MIS.

The management planning and control function can be divided into three basic types of levels of activity: (1) establishing corporate goals and objectives (long and short range); (2) establishing policies for various functional areas of corporate activity (marketing, finance, R&D, etc.); and (3) establishing and exercising effective management control.

Let's consider the management information system requirements and possibilities of each of these types of activity in turn.

Establishing Goals and Objectives

Corporate goals and objectives, both long and short range, must be established in each of the following areas: financial, products/ services, marketing, facilities, organization, policy and mergers/ acquisitions.

The management level planning represented by this activity will probably never be sufficiently systematized to become an integral part of a practical management information system. It may soon become economically feasible, however, to store huge volumes of data in computers and it is this possibility that gives rise to the speculative talk about "selective interrogation of data banks"—since, to be of any practical value, stored data must be retrieved just as information must be intelligently extracted from a reference book.

In any case, this type of management planning is nonroutine in nature, and small, specialized staffs of analysts and planners are usually involved in securing and manipulating the data required as a basis for management decisions. As a result, this type of management planning will probably not be tied into the management information system except for the possible use of specialized data files.

Monsoons to Meteoric Dust

The specialized data files would be of the type we might expect to find in the "mass information storage data bank." The reference data contained in these files would probably be selected for their relationship to the markets or general sphere of operations in which the company is involved. It seems reasonable to assume that the reference data contained in such files would vary drastically from one company to another. Conceivably such files might contain data ranging from the monsoon season rainfall in Nepal to the daily meteoric dust fallout per square yard on the moon.

I believe it is safe to say that this aspect of management planning should and will remain an essentially manual and non-integrated subsystem of the management information system for a long time to come. Ideally it should some day become an integrated part of the management information system, but in the meantime there are several other areas in which immediate attention and effort would be far more profitable.

Establishing Policies

The management planning function also includes the establishment of policies to govern the various areas of corporate activity, such as: marketing, R&D, finance, personnel and production/service.

It seems to me that, for some time to come, the involvement of this aspect of management planning in the management information system should be limited to changes in systems requirements which result from policy decisions and that interaction in the opposite direction should not now be contemplated. A practical approach for the immediate future would be essentially to ignore the requirements of the policy-making function in the development of management information systems.

There are, as I have already suggested, several other parts of the "total system" in which systems improvements would pay off far more handsomely and more quickly, and we will probably find enough problems in these other areas to keep us all busy for at least one more generation of computers. Then when all of these practical problems have been solved, we can attack the problem of "selective interrogation of a stratified data bank" with vigor.

Management Control

The information requirements in the area of management control can largely be satisfied through the natural information fallout (e.g., exception reports) from competent operating and financial control systems.

Operations Planning and Control

The operations planning and control subsystem embraces, or should embrace, the following activities: advertising, sales forecasting, sales management, collection and credit control, inventory planning, inventory control, production control, production load (scheduling), personnel planning and purchasing control.

Many companies today are tolerating inexcusable conditions of improper organization, poor communications and lack of cooperation between the departments, managers and systems involved in performing these closely related functions. Surely here is an area in which the "total systems concept" can perform a real service in eliminating the empire builders, perforating the communications barrier and leading the way in developing a cooperative company team. Integrated operating and financial control systems are the nucleus of a practical management information system. These are the areas upon which we should focus management's attention and with respect to which we should gain its support for designing and installing competent planning and control systems.

What exactly do we mean by "control" in this context, and what does control have to do with management information systems? Simply defined, control consists in exerting a force equal and opposite to an unbalancing force, thus maintaining a state of equilibrium. I believe that information in and of itself—no matter what its quantity, quality or timeliness—is worthless unless it is properly organized and related to a specific activity or process which is (or should be) subject to management control.

"Control" means to guide, steer or regulate; its synonym is "manage." When we guide, steer or regulate something we are in a sense forcing equilibrium and maintaining a balanced condition between two or more variables. To bring this concept into operating systems design, we must identify and define the variables we are attempting to control and then relate them in a manner which will indicate an "out of balance" condition. When such a condition is indicated, management can take corrective action and restore equilibrium to the system.

Losing Hair and Developing Ulcers

Control must be "designed in" to obtain a balanced operating system. In many business organizations, sales forecasting, order entry, inventory control and production control systems exist within various departments and function independently, with little communication of useful data between the separate systems and departments. What I am suggesting here is that if we want an operating system through which inventory and production can be controlled, it is necessary to include the six prime control variables in a system which establishes and maintains a continuous relationship among them. These six variables are: forecast sales, actual sales, planned inventories, actual inventories, planned production and actual production.

In such a system, the prime control input is forecast sales. The amounts of planned inventories and planned production are derived from or computed on the basis of this prime input. Actual sales, inventory and production data, as the term "actual" implies, are derived from the feedback of results into the system. The difference between planned and actual amounts is called "variance." The larger the variance the more the system is out of balance, and the more drastic corrective action is necessary to restore equilibrium.

Financial Planning and Control

The financial planning and control subsystem includes: variable budgeting, income forecasting, cash flow forecasting, return-on-investment planning, cash float analysis, operating statements, profit and loss statements, balance sheet accounting, job cost analysis, products (marginal contribution), and product mix (contribution analysis).

Accountants have long been "losing their hair and developing ulcers" as they have tried to make sense out of the garbage numbers often fed to them by operating departments. In many companies it is a foregone conclusion that, given accurate and timely data, it wouldn't be at all difficult for accounting to supply management with some really useful reports. Since many accounting systems have already been well enough defined to be programmed and computerized, it isn't hard to imagine how readily truly advanced accounting systems could be developed using good data provided by competent operating systems. I believe that this development can and should proceed apace, just as quickly as we can design and install operating systems of the nature I have described.

Despite the Lack of Empathy

Thus far, accounting and financial control systems have been developed despite the lack of empathy on the part of operating departments. Indeed, in many cases these systems have been developed at management's insistence, because it just couldn't find out what was going on any other way. Surely it is time that the systems designers and managers of these operating departments got together with the accountants to develop some systems that would help everyone know the score. The first company that follows this prescription will probably be the first company to have a practical management information system installed and operating.

Nonquantitative Information

The fourth and last major subsystem of a management information system includes various types of nonquantitative information, such as employe histories, skills inventory, turnover statistics, area skill/wage data, attitude survey data and employe test results.

Such data has no immediate place in an integrated management information system. True, it might be convenient to include it, but as with the nebulous data involved in the management planning function, I believe we should bypass this whole subsystem until more urgent problems have been solved. When we have successfully integrated competent operating systems with financial planning and control systems it will be time enough to tackle these remaining pockets of resistance. And who knows, by then someone may have designed a computer that can program itself to solve the problem.

2

Myths of Automated Management Systems

Edward M. Tolliver

Reprinted by permission of
Journal of Systems Management, March 1971.

Today, many top executives are worried because competitors are reportedly using computers to make major breakthroughs in executive level management techniques and effectiveness. These executives tend to have an uneasy feeling that somehow they have failed to exploit the potentials of modern management science—and that the penalty will soon become painfully visible in the profit and loss statement.*

Relax, Mr. Worried Executive. Computers have not resulted in major breakthroughs in executive level management and none are in prospect. Computers have done little more than perform clerical tasks such as the day to day processing of sales, production and accounting actions. Computers have performed such routine tasks in an efficient manner. But these tasks involve the processing of decisions that have already been made and the principal by-product of value to executives is historical data.

In contrast, the success of a business is largely dependent on decisions concerning future events. Such decisions do benefit from a

---

*The system management concepts in this article are written from the perspective of private business where the success of a system can ultimately be judged by its impact on the profit and loss statement. Such system management concepts are not always applicable in government where criteria of success is not profit.

good and timely analysis of historical happenings which an auto-mated management system can provide. But the basic ingredients of such decisions (and thus of business success) are judgement, initiative, and common sense. An automated management system cannot be endowed with these ingredients. An automated system will no more insure the success of a business than a scalpel will insure the success of a surgical operation. A good automated system is to an executive what a good scalpel is to a surgeon: both increase the chance of success but are certainly no substitute for ability and know-how.

Nevertheless, the purveyors of automated management system miracles continue to promote myths such as the following: (Over-simplification is employed for the sake of brevity.)

Myth: The Successful Executive Will Soon Have a Computer Terminal on His Desk

About as useful as a typewriter on his desk. A computer can provide perhaps 10% of the ingredients of a good executive decision. The executive and his human associates must continue to provide the remaining 90%. (But humor the senior executive who has taken a computer course and wants a computer terminal to play with—he is entitled to some diversion and will likely tire of the gadget before he seriously disrupts the system.)

Myth: Think Big—I: Don't Just Automate the Old Way of Doing Things: Restructure the Company's Operations to Fully Exploit the Potential of Modern Computers

Not if the company's success is dependent on making a profit. It is hard to make really major breakthroughs in management processes while concurrently teaching the computer to do complex new things. Don't venture into unchartered waters too far too fast. Find out how far others have successfully gone, take advantage of their accomplish-ments and mistakes, and go a bit further. If you have a long-range system vision, describe it the best you can and try to channel interim system development in a compatible manner.

Myth: Think Big—II: A Fully Integrated Corporatewide System Will Revolutionize the Company

It sure will. Responsibility is likely to be so defused that almost everyone will have an excuse. An error or failure at one point may jam the gears in several departments. We still can't fully integrate functions without disproportionate risk of operational and economic penalty. Concentrate on automating information near its point of origin and making it available to every concerned department for use by that Department as it sees fit. Promote the multiple use of common items of information.

Don't be too concerned about some duplication in the automated processing of information once it is in computer useable form; computer power is relatively cheap and getting cheaper. Letting each department run its own part of the business will promote initiative and innovation with more effective results in the long run. It is, however, desirable to have a few persuasive but diplomatic system experts around to discover and promote opportunities for integrating across departmental boundaries.

Myth: Think Big—III: Take Advantage of the Growing Capability to Transmit a Tremendous Volume of Data in Microseconds over Long Distances

Business and government is already being buried in an avalanche of data of marginal value. The need is to decrease the flow of data—not increase it. There are valid requirements to transmit electronically over long distances relatively small quantities of data, such as stock transactions and reservations. In contrast, there are very few valid requirements to rapidly transmit large volumes of data hundreds or thousands of miles for business purposes. The next most important goal is to cull out and transmit only what serves a substantially useful purpose.

The next most important goal is to transmit it in the most economical manner—getting business data there in a day or two is usually as satisfactory as getting it there in a microsecond. But, keep in mind that the cost of long distance electronic data transmission is going to decrease very substantially—possibly by 50% or more in the next five years—so don't base a cost-effective evaluation on today's prices.

Myth: Stop the Foot Dragging—Create an Automated System Czar at the Senior Vice-president Level

Another excellent way to defuse responsibility. Just try holding the sales manager responsible for sales when he is convinced (rightly or wrongly) that the Czar isn't giving him the information he needs, is requiring the sales staff to create useless computer input, and is permitting the computer to mistreat customers.

A better way is to create an automated managment service (not Czar) good enough so that the sales manager will go to it for help in implementing his ideas. There is merit in having a senior executive to insure that the service is good, to insure that the service is being fully exploited but not abused, and to impose minimum standardization and other guidelines to the extent clearly justified to achieve corporate-wide objectives.

Myth: Centralize System Design to More Effectively Utilize Systems Experts

Your objective is to operate the company more effectively—not to utilize systems experts more effectively. System design is nothing more nor less than figuring out a better way to get a job done—using rubber stamps, quill pens, computers or anything else that best achieves results. The person who can figure out the best way is usually the department head responsible for the day to day accomplishment of objectives. Make available systems experts to help him.

In contrast, systems experts left to their own devices, will usually end up solving the wrong problem or the right problem the wrong way. Much of what they create may not be used—or may become just an additional (not a replacement) process. After the responsible department head has determined rather specifically how things should be done, it's OK to have the details worked out by a centralized staff of systems experts.

Myth: Our Department Heads Aren't Smart Enough—Get Outsiders to Create a Major New Automated System

If department heads aren't smart and flexible enough to be cruise directors in developing an automated management system they aren't capable of doing their present job and should have been replaced long ago. Probably department heads need only some leadership from you, enough relief from day to day pressures to do some constructive thinking, and the assistance of experts who have know-how in the automated techniques involved.

An essential ingredient in successful development of an automated system is knowledge of the job to be done and understanding of the environment in which it must be accomplished. Another essential ingredient is in-house enthusiasm for a new system. Department heads tend to have a monopoly on both of these essential ingredients. They can very quickly learn enough about computer capabilities to be cruise directors. In contrast, it would take a great many months for a systems expert to acquire a real understanding of your business even if you could find such an expert who has the aptitude and motivation. But, don't overlook the potential value of an outside management firm that has actually solved the specific kind of problem you have.

Myth: Executives Must Determine Their Information Needs

Wait for executives to determine their information needs in the detail meaningful to a computer and you are not likely to develop a good automated management system. Executives get to be executives because they are good at solving broad intangible problems. Computers get to be computers because they are built to handle specific tangible problems. An executive typically doesn't think on a wave length meaningful to a computer. You can and must get executives to meaningfully express their information needs from an overall operational or functional perspective. These needs must then be translated by functional staff people into specific information requirements meaningful to ADP experts.

Myth: Automated Management Systems Are Flexible—Just Put Data in and the Computer Can Use It to Answer Almost Any Management Question You Can Think of

A computer can only answer questions you have anticipated well in advance and taught it to answer. Teaching a computer to answer a question is far more costly and time consuming than teaching an individual to answer a question. So depend primarily on individuals —not automated systems—to answer nonrepetitive questions. This is also another reason why most executives will never have a computer terminal on their desk.

Myth: But a "Data Management System" Can Automatically Re-organize Data Almost Any Way You Want

It sure can re-organize it, like re-stacking bricks in a variety of ways. But that doesn't help much in making management decisions such as how, why, or where you should build a brick house. And, you have to be somewhat of a computer technician to persuade the Data Management System to re-stack the bricks.

Myth: Our Automated Management System Costs Too Much—I

So do groceries, but you don't stop eating. You consider what each item of food contributes to your well being, either nutritionally or emotionally, and you perhaps eliminate filet mignon. You don't cut out vegetables because the penalties and alternatives are not in your best interest. Apply the same common sense to your automated management system. Its segments, like items of food, must be individually evaluated in terms of what they do for you. Such an evaluation should be a continuing process. It makes no more sense to condemn the cost of an automated management system as a whole than to condemn the cost of food as a whole.

Myth: Our Automated Management System Costs Too Much—II

Not the system—but your decisions to do things of marginal value. It's mighty sporty and impressive to know the status of every customer order every hour—but what does it do for you or the customer? Is your decision to have such information costing you $10 for every $1 of benefit? Such illogical decisions/requirements are the principal cause of excessive system costs. (A strictly secondary cause might be the efficiency of the automated system itself.)

Myth: Our Automated Management System Costs Too Much—III

Probably not enough. The really big potential today is in promoting the automation of functions that could be accomplished far more efficiently by automation—even if you have to bribe a major department or facility with a computer of its own.

Myth: Don't Discourage Automation by Prorating Costs among Departments

If you don't prorate costs you'll have the biggest computer system in town and most of what it does won't be cost-effective. First discontinue charging each department with the travel and entertainment costs it incurs: you'll learn the same lesson for less.

Myth: To Have a Successful Automated Management System Depend on an Outside Firm (Computer Utility) for Computer Service like You Do for Electric Service

Follow this logic and you can reduce the size of your organization to a President and a few staff assistants. You could contract out your sales, production, accounting and most other functions to various firms of specialists. But you don't, because such functions are essential to your success and you can't precisely define the requirements or measure the results. It's not like arranging for so many kilowatts and volts of electricity. The same is true of stenographic or computer services. Thus most successful firms (except the smallest) will continue to have in-house computer capability to meet basic requirements and will depend on outside facilities to meet specialized or peak needs.

Myth: Automated Systems Revolutionize Management Processes

To date computers have generally discouraged really major changes in management processes by making it economically feasible to continue doing things the old way. And, once the old way is automated, change becomes more difficult and expensive. In some instances, however, the definitive analysis of management processes essential to automation has revealed significant opportunities for improvement—even if the automated system didn't work as promised.

Myth: Automated Management Systems Are a Myth—There Aren't Any Such Things

Almost true. Mostly, there are automated clerical systems. A very few firms have successfully automated some of the more routine management functions, but to date benefits have usually not justified the expense. A tremendous gap exists between what is theoretically possible and what is operationally and economically feasible.

But don't stick your head in the sand—the potential is there. During the next decade or so the more routine management functions will be gradually automated with substantial payoff. Just avoid the major expense and operational penalties of being a pioneer unless your organization has a great deal to gain.

3

A Manager's Perspective of Management Information Systems

Ward A. Fredericks,
" A Manager's Perspective of Management
Information Systems," pp. 7–13, *MSU Business
Topics*, Spring 1971. Reprinted by permission
of the publisher, Division of Research, Graduate
School of Business Administration, Michigan
State University.

A plethora of seminars, speeches, articles, and scholarly books extolling the virtues of MIS (management information systems) has descended upon the business community. *On-line, real-time, data base*, and *teleprocessing* have become part of the "compleat" manager's vocabulary, albeit with less understanding of meaning than usual. In fact, management has accepted the reality of the concept of MIS with open arms, trusting that the types of key decisions which have to be made daily will somehow become easier when the promised data appear in precisely organized formats.

Major companies have mounted massive efforts aimed at designing MIS with results ranging from disaster to partial success. It is still appropriate to say that well-designed and operating MIS are much easier to find in the pages of technical and management journals than in real life.

In order to look at the concept and the application of MIS, an appropriate starting point is to look at management and its most fundamental actions and processes to see what role systems can play in aiding managers in the attainment of their objectives.

The term *top management* as used in this article will cover those members of management whose perspective must include the operation of the entire company—typically the president and executive vice-president in centralized companies, and division general managers in decentralized companies.

Textbooks list planning, controlling, organizing, and so on, as the major functions of management. In an ongoing business enterprise, however, top management makes key decisions relating to certain aspects of the business which determine the size, character, and long-term viability of the organization. These decisions are made in every company, regardless of size, and represent the most difficult part of the management process. They set the tone for the entire enterprise. To simplify the perspective in these key decisions and actions, a five-way categorization would be: (1) decisions and actions which affect pricing, (2) decisions and actions which affect volume, (3) decisions and actions which affect overhead or structural cost, (4) decisions and actions which affect product (or service) cost, and (5) decisions and actions which affect asset turnover.

In every business enterprise it is the interaction of the decisions made in each of the above categories which determines the viability and profitability of the organization. Any MIS effort, then, should address, both in cause and effect terms, the impact of having systems which can influence the outcome of these various decisions and actions.

Profitability: A Complex Result

In order to put proper emphasis upon the complex interaction of the five main areas for management action just listed, let us investigate the "anatomy of a profit." Profit is certainly one of the major objectives of business enterprise, although not the only objective in today's complex society. Continued existence of the enterprise is dependent upon the generation of acceptable profit, however, and therefore management thrust must be directed toward this result.

Management action aimed at producing profit in an ongoing business enterprise may be looked at in terms of the four parts to the profit equation below:

$$(1) \quad (P \times V) - PC - SC = PROFIT$$
$$(2) \quad \frac{Profit}{Assets} = Return\ on\ Investment$$

Simply stated, price times volume equals gross revenue for the enterprise, from which is subtracted product cost and structural cost (or overhead). Profit-oriented management action must be aimed at impacting one or more of the variables in the equation to have a favorable effect on the result. Return on investment of the enterprise is a function of profit, certainly, but turnover of assets involved in the business plays a major role in determining the resultant rate of return.

It is prudent to begin an analysis with simple truths in order to follow the flow of logic to the desired end. In terms of the actions of management and the impact of various kinds of decisions on profitability and return on assets employed, the "truths" exposed above are certainly simple and both mathematically and judgmentally provable to the most practical manager.

Where does the impact of various elements of the MIS come into the picture? Basically, operating systems in any company form the basis for the information system, and these operating systems impact the profit equation by their very existence.

Systems Impact on the Process of the Business

Perhaps the easiest way to visualize the interrelationships between the business, operating data processing systems, and the overall MIS is to visualize the total enterprise as being made up of intertwined key processes. Then it can be seen that the planning, control, and administration of these key processes constitutes the overall management of the company.

The major interacting processes which together make up the entity called the company include:

The financial analysis and control process

The market research—product definition—product introduction process

The sales planning—forecasting—and monitoring process

The purchasing—provisioning—manufacturing—and finished product distribution process

Each one of the four processes needs to be managed at strategic, tactical, and operational levels. In order to properly manage each process, an information system must exist which provides data to the manager which is a symbolic representation of the process itself. The information system needs to provide the *planning, control,* and *administrative* data necessary to constantly evaluate and take appropriate action upon the process to bring it under control. Therefore, in each area or department of the business, management must go through a disciplined thought process in order to: (1) define the process (or processes) for which the function is responsible; (2) define the information necessary to plan, control, and administer the process; (3) design the operating and/or information systems which will provide operational assistance and reports necessary to plan, control, and administer the process; (4) determine the level of cost which the present and proposed techniques will require to carry out the process; and (5) determine what changes in the method or technique of handling the process are required to minimize costs or allow for greater volume at minimum expenditure.

Let us take the process of acquiring raw materials, transforming them into finished product, and distributing the product, as an example. Let us examine it at operational, tactical, and strategic levels, and then look at the implications. [Table 1] summarizes the aspects of the process.

It is evident that in the development and implementation of information systems in a company, when we view the problem as one supporting the planning, control, and administrative functions of a major process, we must define the operational, tactical, and strategic requirements and considerations which permit management of that process on a continuous basis under constantly changing circumstances.

Conversely, when we are looking at the strategic, tactical, and operational management needs of the corporation, we have to take into consideration and formalize the planning, control, and administrative systems necessary to manage the major processes.

It is obvious that with this approach we are no longer talking about *the* MIS, as if it were some mythical beast like the unicorn; we are talking about an interlocking, coordinated set of management systems designed to optimize the planning, control, and administration of specific processes operationally, tactically, and strategically. Modularity is essential in our approaches to management concepts and to system design.

A Sense of Strategy: MIS

Management information systems don't just happen, they have to be uniquely constructed to fit the enterprise they are to serve.

We have already seen that the management perspective of MIS

Table 1. Aspects of the Business Logistics Process

Functions	Operational Level	Tactical Level	Strategic Level
Planning	(a) Plan the receiving and progress chasing schedule for next day's schedule of material deliveries.	(a) Forecast of sales in detail of each specific product within lead time of material acquisition.	(a) Determine future product line requirements and strategies.
	(b) Plan releases on suppliers to be processed next day.	(b) Translation into future build program.	(b) Estimate long range demand for existing and planned products by demand region.
	(c) Plan machine shop schedule for next day.	(c) Determination of sourcing pattern.	(c) Determine production and warehousing facilities requirements.
	(d) Plan next day's assembly schedule.	(d) Planning of inventory levels of raw material, work in process, and finished goods.	(d) Plan management, administrative, labor, and other resources required for planned growth.
	(e) Plan inspection, packing, and shipping schedule for next day.	(e) Planning of purchasing quantities and orders on suppliers.	(e) Determine capital requirements and financial conditions for successful growth.
	(f) Plan minimum/maximum in-process inventories (short lead items).	(f) Planning and scheduling of utilization of existing facilities and available labor.	
		(g) Planning of requirements for cash to finance any seasonal needs.	

Control	Control all activities (processes) against documented plan prepared yesterday; report and take appropriate action on variances.	Monitoring of accuracy of all forecasts up to cut-off point determined by lead time of materials and components. Continuous feedback in response to market changes and production achievement, modifying tactical plan on a continuous basis.	Control against predicted performance to adjust strategic plans on a continuous basis in response to: economic trend changes, inflationary changes, political situations, industry and competition, technological developments, and current performance accomplishment.
Administration	Prepare and communicate all operational control documentation and capture for future analysis and extrapolation of historical performance. (Receiving documentation, machining orders and instructions, scrap reports, assembly tallies, packing instructions, shipping documentation, production volume data, and so forth.)	Maintenance and communication of all tactical planning and feedback information. Acquisition, maintenance, and extrapolation of historical data.	Maintain continuously updated planning data base containing feedback from the tactical control system and monitoring of external environment.

implies that there are operational elements as well as tactical and strategic planning elements in the hiearchy of systems which together make up an MIS.

From a strategic standpoint, development of an MIS must start with development of operational systems which have immediate benefits to the enterprise in terms of reducing overhead costs or some other major variable in the profit equation.

Information to be used in MIS originates at the operating levels within the company, and in the marketplace. In order to develop an MIS one does not set out to design one, but one should set out to design specific operational and control systems required for the on-going management of individual processes and functions in the company. Further, each operational and control system in a given functional area consisting of a series of specific applications needs to be evaluated and brought into being only after identifying the business goals of the system and performing initial cost/benefit analysis prior to expenditures on design and installation.

In terms of a basic strategy of systems development, one of the key management goals in a manufacturing company is the control of cost of goods sold. In a situation where material is the dominant element of the total cost of finished goods, a key system to be developed would be a manufacturing and logistical control system primarily oriented toward optimizing work in process and raw material inventories, and toward optimization of assets used in the production process, machine tools, toolage, and so forth. Justification of such a system would lie in increased utilization of assets, reduction of inventories in relation to throughput, and, in general, increased throughput through the factories for a given level of investment.

Similarly, in the marketing area as far as control of the flow of finished goods from factory door to retail is concerned, information on order status through the distribution system leads to better information on product mix and volume. Relating production mix to demand mix makes lower inventories in the distribution pipeline possible for any given level of sales activity. This again leads to conservation of assets employed in realizing a given level of revenue.

We find that if we define and implement an information system designed to control the process which has to be carried out (such as purchasing, production control, machining, assembly line scheduling, wholegoods warehousing, wholegoods distribution, and so forth), the data which have to be maintained to do so almost automatically include information needed to control costs—to account for the operation, and to develop historical data for statistical and forecasting purposes. It is really right at the basic level of operational control data that a computer-aided MIS is anchored, because it is at that level that facts for planning, extrapolation, and monitoring of progress have to be captured.

These examples are given in an attempt to illustrate the point that the foundation of an MIS is in the information and operating systems designed to control and support operations in the manufacturing, distribution, marketing, financial, and logistics areas.

Back to the Basics

We began this analysis with a discussion of the basic tools open to the manager and of the arena in which he could take actions to increase profits. Where then, does the construction of an MIS aid him in the manipulation of the variables which determine the result of his efforts? Let's look again at the variables and indicate where the elements of an MIS impact each and what abilities the manager has with operating management systems which he would otherwise forego:

(1) Structural Costs (Overheads)

Perhaps the most difficult group of decisions made by top management revolve around the ongoing costs of administering the company. Early EDP (electronic data processing) applications typically address segments of this expense in terms of mechanizing payroll, accounting, and billing. The key decision factors in mechanizing these areas are those which relate to the relative simplicity of accomplishing the EDP application and the high level of predictability that savings in overhead will, in fact, occur as a result of the mechanization effort. Order processing, warranty claim processing, purchase order preparation, and work in process inventory status are all applications which form the most basic parts of an overall MIS, and which, if properly conceived and executed, should provide for a reduction in overhead cost at expected levels of volume.

Many technical writers bemoan the fact that companies tackle the administrative and accounting applications first rather than some abstruse decision-making types of functions. Business logic and the realities of commercial life strongly suggest that these applications are, in fact, the most appropriate bases upon which to build a MIS effort.

(2) Price and Volume

It is in the marketing and sales area of price and volume that creativity in systems design can pay off for the knowledgeable businessman. The customer of any company is looking for a supplier and a product which minimizes his total cost of doing business. Development of systems which make it easier to do business with your company than with competitors can provide opportunity to maximize price without attendant loss of volume. Providing the customer with an inventory control system and maintaining his inventory records allows for reductions in his costs while giving sales management useful information on product movement.

Price and product cost analyses with the kind of detail possible by use of EDP systems may suggest different pricing approaches where basic models of the product are sold at low margin while typical add-ons carry higher profit. In addition, the relatively fixed nature of the cost of mechanically handling administration activities may make it possible to go after incremental volume at less than fully absorbed price when circumstances are appropriate.

(3) Product Cost

While product cost may be reduced by better scheduling of manpower and assets utilized in the company, many other opportunities also exist to employ EDP-generated intelligence to minimize costs. Product-by-product cost/price analysis will invariably show up specific products where inflation or other factors have seriously deteriorated margins. Decisions can then be made on pricing action or product phase out. Purchasing systems which analyze bought-out materials by commodity type, vendor, frequency of usage, commonality of usage, or multiple vendors in various geographic locations are relatively straightforward systems applications which typically yield profitable results. These applications will often provide summarized data which establish different make/buy situations than had been previously recognized.

(4) Asset Turnover

The critical elements which lead to improved asset turnover are summarized in the ability to tightly and precisely schedule usage of assets, and in the ability to react to changes in need for assets quickly enough to avoid acquisition of unnecessary dollars of inventory. Sales analysis and forecasting systems can provide intelligence on shifts in needs for inventory and production. Combined with appropriate production control and material provisioning systems, lead times to react to market changes may be reduced by months. The ability to react to change should, in fact, be the overriding objective in design of material and production control systems, since an overly precise result which cannot be changed quickly in the face of market shifts will straitjacket management instead of providing the flexibility necessary to maximize results.

The Management Questions

We have seen that an MIS is not one system but a series of interrelated operating elements which support different ongoing processes of the business. How then does operating top management select and determine priorities of effort in the systems area, and how does the management know when the efforts it is sponsoring are paying off?

Basically, there is a set of questions to which management needs to know the answers in order to effectively run the business. The questions are simple, their answers straightforward, and their interrelationships obvious. They are:

What are we selling?—Product and dollars.

Where are we selling it?—Geography and product mix.

What will we be selling and where?—Forecast—units and dollars.

What do we own?—Company inventories—product and dollars and age.

Where is it?—Locations of inventory.

What are we producing for sale?—Production schedules.

When will it be ready for sale?—Future product availability.

What will it cost us?—Product cost.

What should we be producing and selling tomorrow?

Any MIS which is truly responsive to the needs of top management should provide the answers to these questions—accurately and quickly. The system will be composed of a number of sub-systems which address certain aspects of one or more questions—and which are used by operating personnel as an inherent part of their activities. The answers to the questions will provide management with data indicating whether action needs to be taken in the arena of price, volume, structural cost, product cost, or asset turnover—and should indicate the basic area for action. And it should be paying for itself, in reduction of structural costs or product costs; the MIS benefit should be a product of the "gestalt" equation where $2+2=5$.

If the EDP systems in a company can answer the questions posed above then they represent truly an MIS.

It is managements' responsibility to ask "why not?" if the systems efforts in their company do not appear to produce the desired end results. If systems in a company do not provide answers to the key questions, then management hasn't been providing enough input to the systems development process and the technicians have been practicing their own brand of footwork. One can consider the projects currently underway in any systems group and determine if they meet *all* the tests of relevance contained below:

Will existence of the system being designed help to answer one or more of the nine key top management questions about the business?

Has the system been cost justified by the operating area which is to use it?

Are the systems people working with (and for) the staff of the operating area of the business which is the sponsor of the effort?

Are there explicit time targets for the systems people to meet in order to finish the project?

Does overall systems management know and recognize where this systems effort will fit into the total information system needs of the company?

If systems efforts in a company can meet the tests of relevance, chances are good that an overall MIS is coming into being. If not, management is not being served, and whatever is to be produced by the systems effort will not aid in making the kinds of decisions necessary to produce profits.

It remains up to management to produce an MIS which will produce profits instead of costs for the company. The final product of management is, after all, profits.

Reassessing Marketing Information Systems

Malcolm McNiven
and Bob D. Hilton

Reprinted by permission of *Journal of Advertising Research*, February 1970.

Until very recently, it would have been sheer heresy for a management scientist or "up-to-date" businessman to refute or doubt the many claims being made for computerized information systems.

There is mounting evidence that this is no longer true. An article in a recent issue of *Fortune* described the progress that has been made in setting up management information systems in business. It states that "Many corporations are waking up to the fact that they were oversold (on MIS). Now they recognize that the most important business decisions cannot be reduced to neat mathematical terms."

A recent survey by the Research Institute of America of some 2,500 companies disclosed that only half the companies with in-house computers could give an unqualified "yes" to the question of whether they were paying off, and only 28 per cent believed that the machines were doing a good job. According to the survey, the majority of computer users felt they were too precipitous in acquiring their machines.

Roy Ash, president of Litton Industries, contends, "Business has gone through a stage in which it was popular to consider it as a science. Now it is increasingly regarded as an art. For there are no absolute answers, and if there are no answers, how can it be a science?"

In another article entitled "Management Misinformation Systems," Professor Russell Ackoff, one of the leading proponents of management information systems, speaks frankly of the weaknesses of existing systems. He says: "Contrary to the impression produced by the growing literature, few computerized management information systems have been put into operation. Of those that I have seen which have been implemented, most have not matched expectations and some have been outright failures."

Other leading figures in the field of management science have expressed disappointment and dismay and, in some cases, indignation at the lack of progress made in implementing computerized decision systems in American business. A distributor of automotive parts recently won a court suit against a division of IBM for failure to fulfill contract obligations in setting up a computerized control system. He was promised an exception-reporting system but he got only stacks of computer printouts and even they were late.

There has been a surprising growth in the use of case study methods in business schools around the world. Those teaching methods, which present judgmental situations with which a businessman may be faced, may be returning to their previous position of strength in the curriculum of some business schools in place of more quantitative techniques.

What does all of this mean? Have we had our fling with computers, with decision theory, and with mathematical models? Have we finally found the type of problems that computers cannot solve? Does the future of executive decision-making lie in well-trained intuition gained from years of experience in the business?

Certainly not! There is no turning back in the rapid development of information systems. It does mean, however, that management is beginning to recover from the dazed shock of having the computer age thrust into its midst. It also means there is a definite need for reassessment of the promise and the reality of management information systems in today's business world.

There is little doubt that decision-making problems in business are much more difficult than originally perceived. In addition, decision-making procedures developed by businesses over the years are not necessarily the best or most efficient procedures. And to try describing these procedures in mathematical terms for the computer is not the answer.

It has become necessary to revise the entire manner in which decisions are made and, in some cases, to change the way a company does business in order to realize the full power of modern management science techniques. To restructure a business in this sense is truly a monumental problem.

A more specific problem is that hardware progress has outpaced that of software, personnel, or concepts. A high percentage of third generation 360's are still operating using 1401 or comparable second generation concepts. Although computers are expensive, only 20 percent of present computer systems' cost is in hardware. The other 80 per cent is for keypunchers, operators, programmers, and other personnel.

Human problems are the key stumbling block in resourceful use of the computer. Programming is still an art. No two programmers would solve a problem the same way; therefore, there are few standards of performance. Good programmers do not necessarily make good systems analysts. Good systems analysts may not make good managers. Management people often tend to regard analysts as either mere technicians or threats to their position. They are unwilling to spend adequate time with the analyst to devise a good system. Equipment manufacturers provide numerous courses for programmers, and it takes only months to train them; however, few courses exist for systems designers, and it may take several years before they are fully competent. This shortage will limit the development of MIS more than any other single factor.

One of the greatest areas of disillusionment has been in marketing. Marketing information systems have not developed as expected. This failure is due to several causes. Marketing decisions as a class are more difficult to model than other business decisions. Many of the methods that have been developed for modeling these decisions don't seem to work when checked with real world results, and it is very hard to measure them. All of these factors together have brought about a series of unproductive attempts to develop marketing information systems, and failure to produce has led to skepticism on the part of marketing management. They (perhaps more so than any other area of business) have continued to rely on traditional, though inefficient, means of decision making.

Presently, marketing systems are made up of six distinct areas of effort, all of which are necessary to some degree.

These are: (1) classification, (2) measurement, (3) analysis, (4) reporting systems, (5) information retrieval systems, and (6) decision models. The last three identify major areas or kinds of systems; the first three are more traditional marketing research areas,

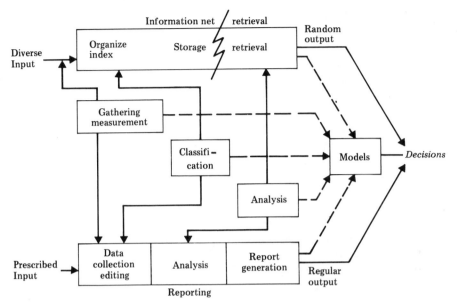

Figure 1

and they affect the quality of the overall system's effort (see Figure 1).

The first requirement in a marketing information system is a *Classification* scheme, or a taxonomy of marketing elements. These are carefully selected structural building blocks, or standard units, that make the creation of integrated systems possible. They provide important guidelines for operations and reduce the need for programming change and data modification.

One should clearly distinguish between the problem of identification and classification. People, in general, can be "classified" by blood type, whereas they are "identified" by a unique social security number.

Identification coding schemes, such as customer numbering, are tending toward being unique "non-significant" numbers. These are grouped and linked together where needed by separate modifiable linking systems. Furthermore, classification should not be integrated within the identification code. For example, all too often the first or last digit of a customer number has some meaning, such as big or little customer, chain or non-chain.

The approach to both these problems is essentially the same, and certainly there is some overlap. A recommended approach is:

1. *Identify the important areas of classification and identification (A, B, C, D, etc.). For example, outlet identification, product identification, outlet description, or package description.*
2. *Within each identification area*
   (a) determine the maximum size code required.
   (b) determine the needs for this code (e.g., billing, sales reporting) and support these needs with a good linking system.
3. *Within each classification area delineate the mutually exclusive dimensions, if any (B_1, B_2, B_3, etc.). For example:*

   B_{1-n} = *Outlet description (classification area)*
     B_1 = *Primary business function (dimension)*
     B_2 = *Proprietorship/ownership and control (dimension)*
     B_3 = *Product class handled (dimension)*
     B_4 = *Primary type of consumer service (dimension), etc.*
4. *Within each classification area dimension, specify a list of terms and associated codes. In dimensions where a single or primary term is required of each classification unit, care must be taken to avoid overlap. For example:*

   B_1 *Primary business function (dimension)*
     21 Full-line grocery
     22 Specialty food store
     31 Movie theater (indoor)
     32 Movie theater (outdoor), etc.

   In those dimensions where combinations are possible, provide for them. For example:

   B_3 *Product class handled (dimension)*
     1 Soft drinks
     2 Coffee/tea
     3 Soft drinks/coffee/tea

The outcome of this approach is that, within each classification area, any unit to be classified *fully* must be categorized in each of the mutually exclusive dimensions of that classification area. Of course, it will not always be feasible or even desirable to classify a unit (e.g., an outlet) by a given area of classification (e.g., outlet description). Furthermore, even if it is desirable to describe an outlet by certain dimensions (e.g., primary business function), data on other dimensions (e.g., product class handled) may be excluded or ignored.

The point is that a standard taxonomy should exist for use where applicable.

The second area is called *Measurement*, or data gathering systems. This area figures heavily in the traditional idea of marketing research. It includes all kinds of sales data, outlet data, consumer surveys, store auditing data, and various testing procedures which are used to measure changes in the marketing environment.

Most market researchers and analysts are aware of the current level of knowledge on measurement factors. A great deal has been written and taught about the pros and cons, what to measure, and how best to measure it. Generally, though, these measures can be divided into two categories: (1) monitoring and (2) problem solving. The monitoring activity refers to measurements regularly taken of basic elements in the marketing systems (for example, sales or advertising awareness) in hopes that they will alert management to problems that exist. The most common marketing reports are merely regular summaries of monitoring measurements. In some companies, marketing information systems are limited to this type of information.

Problem solving procedures are an attempt to develop specific information or measures related to a specific problem that is facing a marketing manager at that time. These measurements are obtained for that specific purpose.

The third area is *Analysis*, and a great deal of progress is being made here. The capabilities of the computer now allow us to use many statistical techniques which have been around for some time but which have not really been feasible due to the large amount of computation required. These include multivariate techniques such as multiregression, factor analysis, and a variety of other techniques which are described in modern textbooks. Most of these statistical and operations research analysis methods are available in the form of several software packages, and they allow detailed inferences from marketing data. The techniques also permit a reduction of massive data down to a few important conclusions. These data reduction techniques must be built into any marketing information system since they reduce the information to a manageable set with which the manager can cope.

So far we've been talking about merely systematizing our information, and being systematic is not being scientific. Science is an attempt to find causal relationships between variables. Once these relationships are established, so that one can make very accurate predictions, it usually can be considered a law or a theory. Many laws of marketing are yet to be discovered, and the best way to set about finding these laws is to undertake a series of controlled measurement studies (CMS).

In order to conduct CMS, certain marketing variables like advertising, promotions, and price can be manipulated, and the effects of dependent variables, such as sales, profits, or perhaps attitudinal responses, can be observed.

It is surprising that the CMS still has not been widely accepted in the field of marketing. Generally, it is felt that the marketing environment is much too changeable to study these relationships. However, these studies have been done quite successfully by many companies over the last ten years (duPont, Ford, Anheuser-Busch, USDA). It is important to embody a CMS program in any marketing information system.

The most widely used CMS method uses the retail outlet as the measurement unit where certain variables are manipulated within the store. The movement of the product through the store is measured and related to changes in the experimental variable.

For example, a CMS of different package designs was conducted to determine which sold more products. A rational design was used with all test packages appearing at the same time in each outlet. In addition to the three test packages, a control package was included. Therefore, four groups of outlets and four time periods were used. The sales and cost indices are shown in Table 1.

Table 1

Package	Sales Index	Cost Index
1	151	114
2	149	116
3	135	112
Control	100	100

In this case, the higher sales index for package 1, coupled with the slightly higher cost, made package 1 generally the most profitable.

Another CMS technique, with an entire market as a measurement unit, is used when the variables being tested cannot be studied in a retail outlet (e.g., advertising distribution). The variable of interest is changed from market-to-market in a planned way using one of the variety of experimental designs available for this purpose.

The response measure is usually some form of sales measurement (e.g., market share change, actual unit sales), and this is compared across markets to estimate the effect of the experimental variable.

The relationships between marketing variables and sales must be measured or estimated if efficient allocation of resources is to be accomplished by a marketing manager. For example, he must know which media are providing the most in sales response to his advertising if he is to allocate funds rationally to these media. This is also true when allocating funds among marketing variables such as advertising, promotion, sales effort, distribution, etc. A CMS program produces information about these relationships which are used as input for marketing models.

Reporting Systems

The first of three major areas of Marketing Information Systems is *Reporting Systems*. These are the systems which can easily be thought of as having a beginning, middle, and end. In the beginning, prescribed data are gathered from one or many sources. In the middle, it is processed in a prescribed way. Finally, some prescribed output is emitted. This output may be produced periodically or upon request.

Three points can be made about reporting systems.

First, they should be designed with the user in mind. That is, each management person has a particular form in which he likes to receive information. It may be in charts; it may be in tables of numbers; it may be in written narrative. But whatever the form, output of a reporting system should be designed to help the user interpret it quickly and readily.

Second, it should be as brief as possible. Computers can produce enormous quantities of information very rapidly. This has scared many management people away from making requests because they only receive a huge stack of computer printouts. Exception reporting systems are, of course, a solution to this problem, but they also leave something to be desired since business people want to be able to see everything that is happening, not just those things that the computer selects out for them to see. In this case, an exception reporting system should be backed up by a good on-request program. Then if management wants something other than exceptions, it is available upon request.

Third, the type of reporting system is unlikely to be real-time or on-line reporting. There has been a great deal said about real-time output, instant reporting, and conversational mode. This can only be accomplished by utilizing huge storage capabilities in computers and with a great deal of complex programming. In most cases, it turns out to be unfeasible at the present stage of development. It also has become apparent that most top management people prefer to have someone else talk with the computer. In spite of this, real-time reporting systems will still be the most useful marketing information system for middle management in the near future.

The second of the three major areas is *Information Retrieval Systems*. The distinction for this type of system is neither in the media format, such as documents or microfilm, nor even in the type of information input or output. The distinction is in the type of function it is expected to perform.

The function of an information retrieval system is to accept isolated and significant items of information from many sources and organize, index, and store these data, and to disseminate logical sets of information later upon inquiry from requestors.

Natural Cleavage

The marketing information void existing because of the lack of efficient information retrieval systems is astonishing. For example, what per cent of the documents normally passing over an executive's desk are prescribed output from reporting systems compared to the vast amount of other documents, reports, etc.? The latter are potential input to an information retrieval data base, but because there has been no really efficient information retrieval system, this segment of the decision-making process has been effectively programmed out of the pattern. So a typical "rational" decision might be made without even considering related past data or experience.

There is a natural *cleavage* in all information retrieval systems that is not found in other types of systems. This cleavage is between the storage and the output. The human mind acts as an information retrieval system. It gathers information from whatever the source, stores it, and later uses part or all of this knowledge to fulfill some random, unanticipated demand.

It is true that most information retrieval systems to date are non-computer systems. However, this is changing. Many existing computer systems are at least quasi-information retrieval systems.

Incidentally, the multidimensional nature of the marketing activity makes this type of system highly desirable.

Within the last few years, information retrieval systems have undergone a revolution with the rise of microfilm, computers, telecommunications, the Uniterm principle, etc. The old versions of files based on subject classification schemes are, or should be, a thing of the past.

For example, the systems currently being built within The Coca-Cola Company utilize the Uniterm or concept-coordination principle. This idea is applicable to any size file from that of an individual to that of a major marketing or technical information center, such as are being built within The Coca-Cola Company.

The basic principle is very simple. The units of information used in the system are called Uniterms. These terms, usually individual words selected directly from the document being indexed, are key words that are descriptive of ideas or concepts embodied in the documents. Although Uniterms are usually single words, they may also be simple combinations of words; and they may even be proper names, dates, or numbers.

Each Uniterm is typed on a separate card, which is then placed in alphabetical order in the card file. A document number (serial) is assigned to each report or document as it is added to the collection. The document number is recorded on all Uniterm cards that pertain to that document.

Typical Uniterms are "plastic," "sleep," "budgeting," and "oxidation." The Uniterm card, "oxidation," for example, contains the document numbers of all documents that pertain to oxidation.

The terms chosen are considered "concepts," and the system operates on the principle of "concept-coordination."

The operation of the system may be illustrated by the following example. Suppose we wish to retrieve all reports that apply to the subject, "U. S. Government Forecasting of Weather." The words, or Uniterms, are "U. S. Government," "Forecasting," and "Weather."

The principle of the search, concept-coordination, is illustrated in Figure 2.

In actual operation, there would be three cards headed "U. S. Government," "Forecasting," and "Weather," respectively. The numerals at the top of each card represent the last digit in the document number. Listing in this manner facilitates comparison of the numbers in the columns on the cards as they are examined for common document numbers. The document number of each report

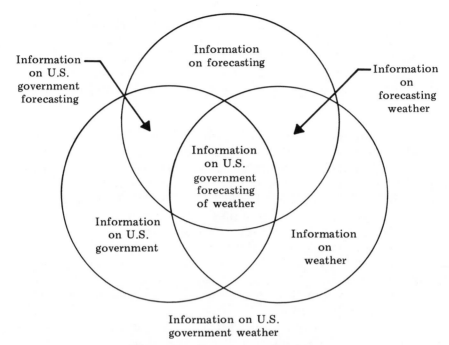

Figure 2.   Concept coordination.

pertaining to these three Uniterms would be posted on each card as the report is received. The three cards might then appear as illustrated in Figure 3.

A mechanical version of this system using punched holes in plastic cards is being used within The Coca-Cola Company and is operational and inexpensive to install.

In addition, within Coca-Cola USA's Marketing Intelligence Center, the push is heavily in the direction of microfilm. Over one-half million frames can be stored in a single drawer. Any document can be located on film in a minute or two, and if desired, a hard copy can be made. In addition, with the use of microfiche, one can obtain a postcard-sized duplicate containing as many as 72 pages of data which never has to be returned. Simple, cheap readers are utilized for reading documents.

The most promising and least developed of the six major areas of marketing information systems is *Decision Models*. A model is a mathematical description of the marketing decision-making process which serves as a structure within which marketing information is used. This is an area which has provided the most disillusionment in

U.S. Government

0	1	2	3	4	5	6	7	8	9
90	41	22	33	104	75	46	57	98	109
370	101	592	103	1194	115	716	157	478	219
	291	1022	493	1574	875	986	307	888	839
	1101	2502	2003		1025	1136	1317	1208	1009
			3203			1446			

Forecasting

0	1	2	3	4	5	6	7	8	9
370	21	52	73	104	115	56	57	148	109
890	131	1002	953	794	225	286	497	328	789
1300	291	1852	1193	1194	525	816	1197	888	1179
	301	2502	2113	2564	1015	1126	2317	918	1909
	3221		2213	2964	2205		2447		2349
				3004					

Weather

0	1	2	3	4	5	6	7	8	9
120	21	702	113	104	15	76	17	88	219
890	131	1492	813	504	125	186	147	178	309
	291	1852	1123	784	305	326	237	528	809
	401	2502	2213	1004	1055	786	1027	888	1019
				2014	2035			1128	

Document numbers 291, 2502, 104, and 888 are found on all three cards. These four documents, therefore, all pertain to U.S. Government, forecasting or weather.

Figure 3

marketing since much has been promised and little delivered. Nevertheless, models must be built, however crude, to serve as guides to the marketing information required for marketing decisions.

Following is one example of a marketing model that has recently been developed. The purpose of the model is to allocate funds to advertising. It was developed by Management Division Systems of Lincoln, Mass., and it is available on time-sharing terminals. It uses a conversational mode, and a representative problem is shown in Figures 4 and 5. The output is shown in Figure 6. In between, the computer asks a number of questions of the user, and he must provide certain input.

This model, although general, can be made directly applicable to a company's marketing problems, and, over time, it evolves into a far more specific model relating directly to those factors that are important to a company's business. As these models become part of a brand manager's operating procedure, they allow him to start developing a control procedure. As he develops more and more

ADBUDG II — A multiperiod advertising budgeting model

1 Computer asks questions in standard form
2 Computer asks questions in short form

Answer = 1

1 Enter new data
2 Use saved data

Answer = 1

Brand name: Groovy
No. of time periods (Max. = 8) :4
Length of period: quarter
Name of first period: 1st 69
Geographic area: U.S.

> Brand data for reference case. Two consecutive periods, called A & B, with seasonality, trend, or other nonadvertising effect removed

Market share in period A (% of units): 1.86
Advertising rate in period A (dollars/period): 486000
Market share in period B if advertising reduced to zero in period B:1.77
Market share in period B if advertising increased to saturation in period B:2.25
Market share in period B if advertising in period B increased 50% over period A: 1.95
Market share in long run if advertising reduced to zero: 0
Index of media efficiency (e.g. average efficiency = 1.0): 1.0
Index of copy effectiveness (e.g. average copy = 1.0): 1.0
Units in which sales are to be measured (to be used for both brand and product class, e.g., pounds, gallons, cases, thousands of dollars, etc.): hogsheads
Contribution profit (exclusive of advertising expense) expressed in dollars/sales unit: .68

Average brand price (dollars/sales unit): 1.812
Other brand data
Market share at start of period 1: 1.86

> Product class data for reference case. Two consecutive time periods, A & B with seasonality, trend, and other nonadvertising effects removed.

Name of product class: Treacle
Product class sales rate in period A
  (units/period): 290000000
Consider response to product class advertising ? No
Average price for product class (dollars/sales unit): 1.88

> Time varying data. If time variation not specified, reference data will be copied into all periods.

Product class sales rate has seasonal or other nonadvertising time effect ? Yes
Index of product class sales (reference case = 1.00) for period:
  1: 943
  2: 1.012
  3: 1.065
  4: .959

Brand share has a nonadvertising time effect? Yes

Figure 4.   Trace of a user putting input data for Groovy into the computer.

Media efficiency varies ? No

Copy efficiency varies ? No

Contribution varies ? No

Average brand price varies ? No

Average price for product varies ? No

Brand advertising rate varies ? Yes

Brand advertising (dollars/unit) in period:
  1: 486000
  2: 606000
  3: 876000
  4: 414000

1 Save data

2 Print data

3 Change data

4 Output

5 Restart

Answer = 1

Data file name: Groovy 69

Figure 5.   Index of nonadvertising effects (reference case—1.00) for period
            (1) 1.0; (2) 1.03; (3) 1.0; (4) 1.0.

experience with the model, he will be refining the estimates of the effects of different marketing variables. This, in turn, will allow the model to predict the effects of his actions much more accurately.

This brings up a concept called "Adaptive Control Systems," developed by J. D. C. Little, whereby a marketing model is used as a guiding structure, and the relationships among the marketing variables in the model are continuously modified by the results of controlled-measurement studies. The model is always moving closer and closer to a representation of reality as the CMS provide improved input. In this way, the marketing research functions and the computer systems are wedded to produce better estimates of the effects of marketing strategies. These models are crucial and must

No	Item		1	2	3	4
1	Output for		Groovy			
2	Period length:		Quarter			
3	Starting period:		1st 69			
4	Area:		U.S.			
5	Sales unit:		Hogsheads			
6	Data from file:		/Groovy—69/			
8	Period		1	2	3	4
9	Market share: (% of units)		1.860	1.961	2.043	2.009
10	Prod. class sales (units/per)		273M	293M	309M	278M
11	Prod. class sales (dollar)		514M	552M	581M	523M
12	Brand sales (units/per)		5.09M	5.76M	6.31M	5.59M
13	Brand sales (dol/per)		9.22M	10.4M	11.4M	10.1M
14	Contribution (dol/per)	3.46	3.91M		4.29M	3.80M
15	Brand adv. (dol/per)	0.486M	0.606M		0.876M	0.414M
16	Cont. after adv. (dol/per)	2.97M	3.31M		3.41M	3.39M
17	Cumulative cont. after adv.	2.97M	6.28M		9.70M	13.1M
23	Slope	1.634	1.169		0.241	0.379
24	Brand decay constant	0.048				
26	Brand adv. exponent	2.357				
27	Brand den. constant	4.333				

Figure 6.   Output for Groovy brand for the input.

exist in some form at the early stages of the development of a sophisticated marketing information system.

In building decision models of marketing decisions, it is of utmost importance to realize the existence of directive informational needs, as well as rational informational needs. This means that certain components of a decision-making model must be variable, depending upon the individual who is currently the decision-maker. Since the manager is the key element in the decision-making system, the system should be modeled for him and consider his style of decision-making.

In order to build and use marketing models, a better understanding is needed of the decision-making process. Quantitative decision theory, as it exists today, has very little to do with methods used by managers in making decisions, and it may be worthwhile to consider some of the points made in psychological studies of decision-making.

When a manager is in a decision-making situation, he is trying to obtain information for two purposes: First, information is sought which will help him identify and select the alternative that best meets his decision criteria; second, after having made the decision, he will seek out information to support the decision he has made. His motivation to obtain information is a function of the degree of uncertainty he has in a situation, as well as the importance of the decision that is being made. Of course, individuals differ widely in their levels of uncertainty in a given decision situation and in their ability to select an alternative, given the appropriate information. Once the decision-maker is motivated to acquire information, then his preference for a source of information is directly related to the uncertainty-reducing properties of that source.

Sources of information generally reduce uncertainty with two kinds of information—either directive information or rational information. Directive information is that type of information which will directly reduce the uncertainty in the situation due to past experience with the source. This may be called irrational or unconscious evaluation of the information source. For instance, women continue to seek the advice of their mothers when making purchases; a government official seeks the opinion of high status university figures; or a businessman uses a consultant as an information source.

Rational information represents that which ought to be considered in making a rational decision—that is, the type of information that we usually include or should include in our decision-making models. There is a great deal of difference between the decisions which might be made based on the information provided by a directive source or a rational source. Generally, directive information incurs less cost and effort than rational information. Because of this and emotional reasons, there is generally a bias in favor of directive information.

Managers' perceived informational needs are evolving rapidly, and as they change, the types of information systems to support them must change. This has resulted in an revolutionary process in the resulting information systems area which has caused some controversy.

There is a logical explanation of why business is in an unsatisfactory position with regard to marketing information systems. The explanation has to do with the inter-relationship between managers' perceived information needs and actual fulfillment of those needs. It also concerns the unusually large amount of skilled manpower required to develop new information systems. Perhaps the following will clarify the situation.

Reporting systems have been around for some time. They are also the easiest to develop. Figure 7 shows that, although most reporting systems take less time to develop than either information retrieval systems or models, the average time for development is still increasing and perhaps will for awhile longer. The reason is the increasing complexity and degree of integration required as a company's systems expand. As a general rule, all types of systems are becoming more complex and time-consuming to develop. However, for any one class of systems, the software support, etc., finally reach a point of efficiency and use to enable the developmental time-curve to actually turn down. For example, much of the sorting, selecting, ranking, cross-taping, etc., normally required in reporting systems can be routinely handled by built-in utility features.

Figure 8 is a pictorial representation of how the specific outputs will change and vary in the relative contribution to management needs over time.

Gradually, the switch will be away from periodic reports into the area of special or exception reporting. This switch is attributable primarily to more sophisticated reporting systems. However, as information retrieval systems begin to come into their own, a new type of random open-end inquiry will be possible, and this is represented by "variable output." Finally, with the utilization of better models, the output will become more intelligent or decision-oriented.

The overstatements on one hand and the problems that have

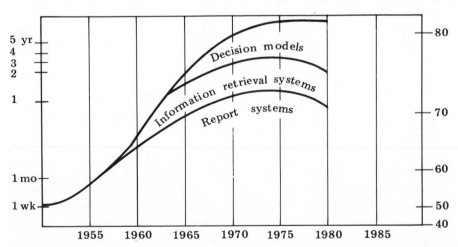

Figure 7.   Information system development. Maximum project span in man years.

been pointed out on the other hand have widened the gap between perceived needs and fulfilled needs. This is demonstrated by the "fulfilled needs" line in Figure 8, which represents the sum of the

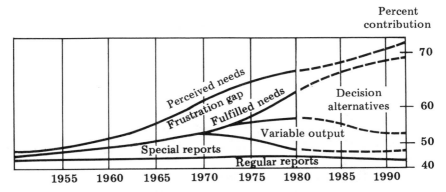

Figure 8.   Type of systems output and needs.

output currently available to the manager. The "perceived needs" line represents the manager's desire for information based on the promises and dreams of computer manufacturers and management scientists. As it can be seen, the frustration gap is at its widest point in 1970-1975, but narrows after that as systems design and programming begin to be implemented. As management reassesses the situation and as software and personnel begin to catch up with hardware, this gap should narrow.

The evolution of types of systems in Figure 7 and the evolution of types of output to management in Figure 8 are, of course, directly related as shown in Figure 9. Growing information needs have not been satisfied due to the extensive effort being placed on the development of new reporting systems and a beginning of information retrieval systems. These new systems are not yet operational, except in a few isolated instances (e.g., airline and hotel reservation systems). Of course, the frustration gap will continue to be large as management's perceived needs continue to grow faster than the systems' development and increased output.

Marketing information systems have been seriously oversold to marketing management, and most attempts at setting up sophisticated systems have not performed as expected.

Still, a great deal of progress has been made in understanding the problems of marketing and how they should be supported by marketing information. It is possible at this time to set up an interim

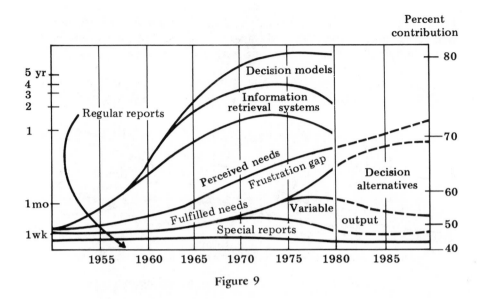

Figure 9

marketing information system which will be helpful and compatible with future systems when operational.

In summary, a marketing information system which can be implemented at the present time should include the following:

(1) Standard classification of elements, (2) marketing measurement, (3) analytical packages, (4) information retrieval systems, (5) reporting systems, and (6) simple marketing models.

In each of the above areas, there have been significant changes in technology in the last year which make a marketing information system more feasible and efficient.

However, interaction of management information requirements and system planning capability has produced a frustration gap which is not likely to be reduced in the near future.

A general conclusion one can reach is that there is a good deal to be done by most companies to improve their marketing information systems quickly, with a minimum of expenditure. This will not put them into the wonderland of futuristic systems, but it will give them a good, solid base on which to build for the future. In order to achieve this, professional people, either outside or inside the company, must be used extensively to make some of those critical decisions regarding equipment and systems, which can either send the company on the right path for future development or send them down the wrong path to frustration and loss of faith on the part of management.

It is time to stop living in the world of delusion regarding marketing information systems and come back to reality. But then, reality isn't all that bad.

PART II

The Systems Approach to Management

Introduction

The fastest-growing field in the business administration curriculum during the 1950s and 1960s was management. Quite naturally, significant changes in approaches to the study of management paralleled that expansion. Before 1950, students had been exposed to management as a somewhat comparatively neat set of principles of traditional, classical, and administrative theory with little concern for relationships or interrelationships. Emphasized in conjunction with those "good principles of management" were such finitely defined managerial functions as planning, organizing, directing, coordinating, acquiring, staffing, and controlling. In classroom and textbook the theoretical dimension of those functions was emphasized, and a student quickly learned to go along with the managerial-function breakdown as seen by his professor. Although universality of management was a commonly adopted principle, universality in managerial functions was indeed not a characteristic of the times. A few writers gradually shifted from the functional approach to what they called managerial processes, to which they neatly fitted the same old managerial functions. Today, almost all popular management texts are subdivided according to some variation of this theme, but interrelationships among the management functions (processes) are being stressed.

With the realization that managing includes more than memorizing and applying certain distinguished principles or that certain principles constitute only part of what management involves, management has expanded to include what is called the systems approach. Through that approach, an effort is being made to build an inclusive picture of the manager's job and his world. The idea of a system, a set of interrelated parts with a purpose, seems to fit the concept of the manager's job and the complexity of the internal and external environment in which he operates.

Articles selected for this section conceptualize the idea of a system and system concepts of a manager's job and his managerial environment. Through them, our specific purpose is to help the reader grasp system concepts in the context of the business organization so that he may gain a broad perspective of the organizational-managerial interrelationships and impacts. Viewed as a system, management entails coordinating all its separate but inter-related parts to accomplish organizational objectives and sub-objectives. Obviously, conflict and stress occur between those making the budget and those budgeted, between the leader and those led, and between salesmen and producers of products for sale. And delivery times and production times don't always meet customer satisfactions and needs. Different goals, work flows, managerial styles, and organizational dimensions (both formal and informal) impose restrictions on behavior and performance. The idea (which becomes the manager's problem) is to conceptualize first the patterned organizational and behavioral relationships into a meaning-ful whole with a purpose and then to conceptualize the problems in designing the systems and subsystems, along with strategies, that are necessary to accomplish objectives of the whole system.

Neither the fact that a manager's job is an information–decision-making system nor the fact that the business organization is a total system composed of interrelated subsystems (such as personnel, production, finance, and distribution) is new. What is new is our conceptualization of the using of those facts. Management writers and philosophers have tended to stay with what they believed were the fundamentals, when actually integrating those fundamentals into a meaningful and purposeful system was the key, rather than independence or the differentiation in functions.

This section of the book is designed to give the reader a synthesis of the systems approach to both management and the business organization by focusing attention on systems definitions, concepts, and components. We propose it as a framework for integrating the contributions of several writers of systems and system analysis toward the end of helping the reader to: understand the interrelationships in any system; gain a concept of the interdisciplin-ary nature of the systems approach; become familiar with the various types of systems, including the design and purpose of subsystems and of a total system; and to encourage him to develop a synthesis of his own about what is a system and what are its purposes.

To ease the reader's task of conceptualizing a system, it is necessary to cite several definitions of systems. The definitions can be a focal point for grasping system concepts and their interdisciplinary nature as reflected in the background, experiences, and interests of the authors of the included articles. We offer this prelude to these definitions: experience indicates that systems are conceived, designed, built, and operated even in the absence of common language, definitions, diagrams, or a firmly established theoretical base. In the most general sense, a system can be thought of as being synonymous with order; it is a set or arrangement, a relationship or connection, unity or wholeness.

> A system is a set of objects together with relationship between the objects and between their attributes. A. D. Hall and R. E. Fagen (1)

> A system is an organized or complex whole; an assemblage or combination of things or parts forming a complex or unitary whole. Richard A. Johnson, Fremont Kast, and James E. Rosenzweig (2)

> A system is, roughly speaking, a bundle of relationships. Anatol Rapoport (3)

> A system is a purposeful, organized interrelationship of components in which the performance of the whole exceeds the individual outputs of all the parts. Dan Voich, Jr., and Daniel A. Wren (4)

> A system is a collection of entities or things (animate or inanimate) which receives certain inputs and is constrained to act concertedly upon them to produce certain outputs, with the objective of maximizing some function of inputs and outputs. Richard B. Kershner (5)

> A system is defined as some on-going process of a set of elements, each of which are functionally and operationally united in the achievement of an objective. Stanford L. Optner (6)

> A system is a complex of elements or components directly or indirectly related in a causal network, such that at least some of the components are related to some others in a more or less stable way at some time. Walter Buckley (7)

> The essential characteristic of a system is that it is composed of interacting parts, each of which has interest in its own right. R. L. Ackoff (8)

A system is a complex unity formed of many diverse parts subject to a common plan for serving a common purpose. James H. Greene (9)

The purpose of a business system is to produce a profit. This includes preparing the way for profitable operations; therefore, one of the larger management responsibilities is to see that systems purposes are achieved. Paul T. Smith (10)

An organization is a cooperative system . . . a complex of physical, biological, personal, and social components which are in a specific systematic relationship by reason of the cooperation of two or more persons. Chester I. Barnard (11)

A system can be defined as a complex of elements standing in interaction. There are general principles holding for systems, irrespective of the nature of the component elements and of the relations or forces between them. Ludwig von Bertalanffy (12)

Organization is a system of structural interpersonal relations. Robert V. Presthus (13)

A system is the organization of all the procedures and operations needed to produce information about one major activity of the business. Gilbert Kahn (14)

A system is any related set of events and objects; the collective organization of information these possess, and the means for acquiring, storing, transforming, transmitting, controlling or otherwise processing such information, all in relation to, but distinct from the external environment in which the behaviors and history of the object system are embedded. Harold Sackman (15)

Personality represents the totality of a person's characteristics, and emphasizes that each of an individual's characteristics are interrelated with all of the others. That is, personality represents an organization of forces within the individual—it may be viewed as a dynamic system. Max D. Richards and Paul S. Greenlaw (16)

The integrative conceptual framework utilized in this book is one which views the business organization as an information-decision system, in which decision making represents the focus of activity performed by managers. Max D. Richards and Paul S. Greenlaw (17)

Systems are all around us, but the problem is to see them, understand them, use them, and learn from them so that we can conceptualize and design better ones. In our daily conversations we talk about the economic, social, two-party political, educational and other systems. We even use popular phrases such as "You can't beat the system" or "We are a victim of the system" or "Employee X has no system."

In a general systems model, the parts take the form of inputs, outputs, something that transforms input into output, and feedback. The transformation function to be performed may be simple, as in the transformation of cold air into warm air or a customer's order into an invoice, or it may be complex, as the transformation of multiple sources of data into meaningful reports. It is important to remember that boundaries of a system usually are determined arbitrarily, consistent with the objectives sought. When systems are combined as a total system, they become subsystems of that system.

It is essential also to conceptualize a system as being dynamic, that is, being subject to changes in input and in output of objectives sought. Because of changing technology, transformation functions change, both in process and in speed of that process. Basically, a system must be going through a process of learning and adapting continuously, with perhaps changes being less frequent in structure than in process. Obviously, a system can fail. A system's suitability depends critically on the thoroughness of the designed structure and its capacity to meet the requirements imposed, subject to the built-in constraints. A structure's failure to meet changing requirements is one form of confirmation that the system also has failed. Some business firms, following the keep-up-with-competition syndrome, have installed poorly designed and poorly oriented systems that have been given an importance not justified by their performance. Yet such systems are expected to work automatically and instantaneously.

One of the most positive contributions of the systems approach to management has been the means for organizing elements into an integrated network designed to achieve predetermined organizational goals. Systems, which are of many kinds, are here to stay. Many, through management's determination to make them workable and profitable, have been designed to accomplish the goals sought. The real task now is to improve the way systems are planned and used, to close the gap between what is feasible and what is useful. To make a system work, whatever that system is, management must be committed to it and must understand it.

References

1. A. D. Hall and R. E. Fagen, "Definition of System," in L. von Bertalanffy and A. Rapoport (eds.), *General Systems* (Ann Arbor, Mich.: the Society for the Advancement of General Systems Theory, now Society for General Systems Research, 1956), p. 18.

2. Richard A. Johnson, Fremont Kast, and James E. Rosenzweig, *The Theory and Management of Systems*, 2d ed. (New York: McGraw-Hill Book Company, 1967), p. 4.

3. Anatol Rapoport, "General Systems Theory," *International Encyclopedia of the Social Sciences,* (New York, 1968), vol. 15, p. 452.

4. Dan Voich, Jr., and Daniel A. Wren, *Principles of Management: Resources and Systems* (New York: The Ronald Press Company, 1968), p. 21.

5. Richard B. Kershner, "A Survey of Systems Engineering Tools and Techniques," in Charles D. Flagle, William H. Huggins, and Robert H. Roy (eds.), *Operations Research and Systems Engineering* (Baltimore: The Johns Hopkins Press, 1960), p. 41.

6. Stanford L. Optner, *Systems Analysis for Business Management*, 2d ed. (Englewood Cliffs, N.J.: Prentice-Hall, Inc., 1968), p. 3.

7. Walter Buckley, "Society as a Complex Adaptive System," in Walter Buckley (ed.), *Modern Systems Research for the Behavioral Scientist* (Chicago: Aldine Publishing Company, 1968), p. 493.

8. R. L. Ackoff, "Systems, Organizations, and Interdisciplinary Research," in Donald P. Eckman (ed.), *Systems: Research and Design*, Proceedings of the First Systems Symposium at Case Institute of Technology (New York: John Wiley & Sons, Inc., 1961), p. 26.

9. James H. Greene, *Operations Planning and Control* (Homewood, Ill.: Richard D. Irwin, Inc., 1967), p. 1.

10. Paul T. Smith, *Computers, Systems, and Profits* (New York: American Management Association, 1969), p. 98.

11. Chester I. Barnard, *The Functions of an Executive*, 2d ed. (Cambridge, Mass.: Harvard University Press, 1968), p. 65.

12. Ludwig von Bertalanffy, *Problems of Life* (New York: Harper & Row, Publishers, Incorporated, 1960), p. 176.

13. Robert V. Presthus, "Toward a Theory of Organizational Behavior," *Administrative Science Quarterly,* p. 50, June 1958.

14. Gilbert Kahn, "The Study of Systems and Procedures," *Business Education World*, p. 16, April 1969.

15. Harold Sackman, *Computers, Systems Science, and Evolving Society* (New York: John Wiley & Sons, Inc., 1967), p. 5.

16. Max D. Richards and Paul S. Greenlaw, *Management Decision Making* (Homewood, Ill.: Richard D. Irwin, Inc., 1966), p. 113.

17. Ibid., p. vii.

Section **1**

Systems Parameters

5

Toward a Systems Theory of the Firm

August William Smith

Reprinted by permission of *Journal of Systems Management*, February 1971.

Systems defy concise and precise definition because of the wide diversity of systems interpretations and applications. The problem is further compounded by the fact that there may be an almost endless array or hierarchy of systems within still other larger systems. In addition, there may be numerous subsystems within larger, more complete systems. Thus, the concept of systems represents a "theory of relativity," where the scope and completeness of a given system may only be defined in relative terms to larger systems or to component subsystems.

Johnson, Kast and Rosenzweig recognize that the "only meaningful way to study organization is as a system."[1] This premise is based on the need for a conceptual analytical base which synthesizes and integrates the firm as a total entity worthy of independent empirical study. This concept of systems is more in line with a systems theory of the firm, as contrasted to the original concept of "general systems theory" coined by Von Bertalanffy (1947) who based his approach upon biological processes.[2] While Von Bertalanffy developed the conception that biological processes

[1] Richard A. Johnson, Fremont E. Kast, and James E. Rosenzweig, *The Theory and Management of Systems* (New York: McGraw-Hill, 1967), p. 8.
[2] Kenneth Boulding, "General Systems Theory—The Skeleton of Science," *General Systems Yearbook*, vol. 1, 1956, p. 11.

can be related to other processes related to engineering, science, management, and organization, he did not undertake investigations to experimentally test or verify these relationships. While he expounded a number of systems concepts which he deduced into systems theories, he failed to substantiate his systems theories with experimental designs, or with applications to large enterprises.

Perhaps the best working definition of "systems" is provided by Hall who defined a system as a "set of objects with relationships between the objects and their attributes."[3] Each system is described as consisting of component parts or objects which have certain properties. The ties between the components, defined in terms of these properties, identifies the structure of the system.

Closed-systems Approach

Traditionally, problems were viewed in the context of a closed-systems approach. This idea originated from the traditional scientific viewpoint that systems are self-contained entities. This "inward" approach involved an analysis of the components which make up a system. This mechanistic approach to systems completely ignored environment. This led to the establishment of a term, "entropy", taken from thermodynamics as being applicable to physical systems. This term described the condition that systems move toward equilibrium (order or balance) or toward a random state where there is no further potential for transformation or change. The fact that closed systems were self-limiting in terms of entropy, rather than subject to the dynamic properties of environment noted with change over time rendered this concept invalid as a systems theory of the firm.

Von Bertalanffy's research on biological systems recognized the impact of the environment on the functioning of living systems, and the fact that in biological systems there is a tendency toward order. This led to the conception of open systems which are subject to continual interaction with the environment, to inflows and outflows to interact with the environment and to the design (building up and breaking down) of components which are never in equilibrium or finalized. Yet the paradox is that these conditions of open systems eventually lead to a more steady state condition, or negative entropy, based on orderly change and revised organization structures, than in

[3] Arthur D. Hall, *A Methodology for Systems Engineering* (Princeton, N.J.: D. Van Nostrand Company, Inc., 1962), p. 60.

the case of closed systems.[4] Closed systems may die on the vine because they are not adaptive and subject to orderly change over time. The open system concept is visualized in the following input-output model [Figure 1]:

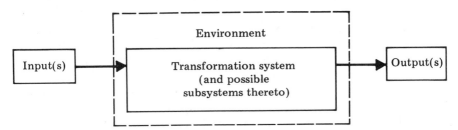

Figure 1.   General conceptual model of an organization as an open system.

The open-systems approach consists of elements of input from the environment which enter the system and through some transformation process internal to the system are converted to output which is then returned to the environment. An industrial example would include a production process as the transformation process, and an environment based on consumer desires and demands for particular types of outputs from the production process. Thus, the internal subsystem of the firm, the transformation process, is only one major part of a larger system, the firm, and its organization, which in turn, is but a part of an even larger system called the environment.

The environment not only consists of customers, but also of competitive industries and in situations which react to induced changes in customer desires and demands with technological innovations and economical efficiencies. In fact, survival and perpetuation of the firm is directly linked to environment. Before a firm can adjust to environment or the "larger-than-the-firm" system, managers must first adjust the organizational system of the firm. This requires a systems theory of the firm.

Identifying Boundaries

In order to develop a systems theory of the firm, it is necessary that managers identify boundaries and constraints imposed on the firm in

[4] Ludwig Von Bertalanffy, "General Systems Theory," *General Systems Yearbook*, vol. 1, 1956, p. 5.

terms of objectives, goals, and resources (i.e., plant goals and capacity limits, and so forth). These constraints should either facilitate the transformation process (or similar process by which the firm's resources are allocated) and set the domain of the activities or else facilitate the environment (i.e., distribution of end products). More important is the concern to maintain equilibrium in the various systems. This equilibrium is maintained by means of information feedback and communication channels which exist between the various processes and systems within the system hierarchy.

All open systems have a characteristic called "equifinality" which will allow orderly change. This concept indicates that there is no one best way to arrive at an end product. Rather, systems operations are dependent upon initial conditions and constraints as well as upon human and mechanistic interaction. Yet different initial conditions applied with different interactions may result in the same end result or output based on equifinality. Thus, systems changes are hard, if not impossible to reconcile in particular instances. This flexibility in interpreting systems results should be incorporated into the systems theory of the firm.

Changes made in the components of a system may have varying degrees of effect on the complete (whole) system. The property of wholeness or independence determines the effect on the total system. When changes to a component result in orderly changes in other components of the system, the system is said to act coherently, and to indicate system completeness or a "total system." Just as the term "synergy" can be applied to an organization to indicate that the total is greater than the sum of the parts, so can this term be applied to the systems concept that system wholeness is greater than the sum of the various integral systems.

At the opposite end of the spectrum, when changes in a component do not affect other components, then system independence results. The concepts of wholeness and independence should be incorporated into the systems theory of the firm.

The problem confronting many managers today is one of understanding open socio-technical systems. Such socio-technical systems include at least five major subsystems: goals and values; technology; structure; psychosocial; and, managerial.[5] Each subsystem is indeed complex. The subsystems coexist but are divergent, and hence, are subject to continual conflict.[6] An organization as a socio-technical system can be visualized [as shown in Figure 2] thus:

[5, 6] Fremont E. Kast, and James E. Rosenzweig, *Organization and Management: A Systems Approach* (New York: McGraw-Hill, 1970), p. 2.

Figure 2.   Conceptual model of an organization as a set of socio-technical subsystems.

The primary task of management is to coordinate the total system of the organization or firm relative to its environment in terms of the interactions of internal activities of the socio-technical subsystems. In this case, the transformation system is composed of a set of structured socio-technical subsystems. Within the transformation system, there exists an interdependent relationship between the social and technological components. For example, the technology base involves all tasks to be performed including the input and output subsystems. The goals and values of the individuals and the psychosocial interactions of individuals within groups and between groups make up the social system of the organization. The social system considers these relationships between the human elements of the system and strives for effectiveness and efficiency in the utilization of technology.

The managerial components must relate the goals and values of the organization to the human elements. This involves the interaction of people, ambitions, expectations, and values which are intangible subsystems, and which may not be reconcilable with the values and goals of the organization. Hence, a manager is a systems artist in terms of relating human intangible subsystems, and a systems scientist in terms of relating the human subsystems to larger technical systems. This constitutes a dual responsibility of the manager of an organizational system, which approximates a systems theory of the firm as viewed by the industrial manager.

In fact, it is possible to relate the systems process to the management process based on this dual responsibility as shown in Figure [3].

In step one, both processes are concerned with problem identification. A complete analysis of needs is required. Without a complete analysis of needs it is impossible to design the right approach or system for meeting these needs. The environment affects anticipated future needs, and hence these needs must be identified.

Systems process[1]	*Management process*[2]
1. Analysis of the problem situation	1. Perception of need
2. Synthesis of solutions	2. Design
3. Evaluation and decision	3. Production
4. Optimization	4. Delivery
5. Revision	5. Utilization
6. Implementation	

[1] Morris Asimow, *Introduction to Design* (Englewood Cliffs, New Jersey: Prentice-Hall, Inc., 1962), p. 39.
[2] Richard A. Johnson, Fremont E. Kast, and James E. Rosenzweig, *The Theory and Management of Systems* (New York: McGraw-Hill Book Company, 1967), p. 142.

Figure 3.   The systems process compared to the management process.

Second, the design of a particular system is undertaken in terms of selected design parameters which relate to the conditions and constraints imposed on that system. This leads to the actual design of the system (i.e., production system), the outputs of the system (delivery of products), and the utilization of the system (feedback) from customers concerning these products. All of these steps are essential to the concept of a systems theory of the firm. Yet, each step is in need of further clarification and extension based on empirical evidence.

Conclusion

The empirical testing of a systems theory of the firm can only occur through the efforts of managers in organizations (industrial, military, governmental, and institutional) who will attempt to reconcile systems theories and concepts in terms of systems applications and case studies. This is a real challenge for managers in the 1970's to develop an integrative model of systems theory relative to particular organizations, including industrial firms, which can be readily understood and used by managers. This challenge will prove to be the reality or fantasy of a systems theory of the firm.

6

Management Systems Engineering

Reprinted by permission of the publisher from *Management Review.* © October 1969 by the American Management Association, Inc.

Faced with increasingly complex problems in achieving his business objectives, today's manager is turning more and more to the discipline of management systems and to their orderly development and maintenance.

Management systems themselves consist of the arrangement and integration of personnel, equipment, services, and data for the effective planning, direction, and control of an organization. The basic elements of a management system, therefore, are people (and their relationships), equipment, information, integration, and objectives.

Thus, the financial management system consists of the controller, his staff, cost accountants, and clerks; accounting machinery, calculators, and computer equipment; and the chart of accounts, financial policy, accounting procedures, and the flow of information. But superimposed over this is the organization of people, equipment, and information by which management can be provided with financial and accounting information for purposes of control. Other operating systems may be described in the same way.

Need for a New Discipline

The process of logically sequencing activities and decisions leading to the definition, development, and operational implementation of business management systems is the concern of the relatively new discipline called management science, management technology, or management systems engineering. The development of this discipline has been hastened by a number of factors:

Complexity. As business operations become more complex, connections between operations tend to multiply geometrically. Control at the intersection or even the design of the intersection itself is an increasingly technical job to which mathematical and engineering techniques alone seem to provide an answer.

Dynamics. People, equipment, and information channels are undergoing constant change. To ensure a fairly normal or predictable output of operations, the system itself must be designed with precision and be kept up to date.

Communication networks. In many American companies, this requires graphic, reproduction, and telecommunication equipment of all kinds—closed-circuit television, computers, consoles, and displays; reports, charts, and graphs; operations centers and war rooms. This massive flow of data cannot be left to chance. The very term "network" is used to describe an orderly arrangement of information senders and receivers. To reduce randomness in information—and therefore in decision making—the information flow itself and the equipment involved must be carefully designed.

Interfunctional systems. Functional procedures that have a tendency to multiply by themselves must be interlocked. In its normal growth, a firm gradually develops from a small, highly integrated, and centralized organization to a decentralized and functional organization. Eventually a point is reached where a strictly vertical and functional structure will be unable to solve—perhaps even to detect—problems that relate to the horizontal flow of goods and services through the operation. It's at this point that the need for the systematic engineering of operating procedures into a set of integrated management systems becomes apparent.

The computer. Perhaps the major reason why management systems must be engineered is the permeating influence of the computer. The economics of large-scale computer applications are realized best when functionally oriented, proceduralized operations are knit together in a manner that eliminates redundant or overlapping reports and operations but does not degrade performance and production. This trend toward integration by the computer is a forcing factor. It means that nothing less than careful design and engineering of systems will be equal to the task of effective computer utilization.

Management systems engineering also applies to business operations the tools and techniques of systems analysis, math modeling, trade-off studies, functional analysis, process flow charting, and associated documentation. The objective is to arrive at an optimum, integrated, and operational management system.

This approach is now being used with apparent success under a number of different names. One authority in the field cites the case of a large company that created a management systems department, one section of which employs 54 systems analysts and technicians, 17 of whom are Ph.D.'s.

Management systems engineering works primarily through the phased application of a systems approach to conceptualization, definition, design, development, test, evaluation, and operational implementation of the business system.

The Systems Approach

Before considering the phases of management systems engineering, it might be well to review some of the more significant characteristics of the systems approach as it applies to business operations:

All parts of the business operation (or at least a well-bounded portion of the total operation) must be considered from a systems aspect from the very beginning.

System needs, requirements, and objectives must be defined initially.

The systems concept must be expanded in terms of operations and functions that will satisfy those requirements.

Alternative solutions to operational problems must be defined in terms of hardware that will satisfy the functional requirements, considering such limiting factors as schedule, cost, performance, and risk.

Interfacing systems, subsystems, operations, and hardware must be carefully evaluated and accommodated.

Hardware must be specified in terms of performance characteristics, output, and operating modes.

Supporting operations, personnel, facilities, equipment, training, and data must also be specified.

The manner in which the hardware will be maintained for its anticipated life span must be detailed.

The system and its subsystems must be designed, developed, documented, tested, and installed in accordance with specifications.

The engineering of a management system, like that of a military, space, commercial or socioeconomic system, is best accomplished in phases, as shown in [Figure 1]. The chart is essentially a logic flow diagram indicating orderly progression from concept to final operational use. Each of the phases implies a potential recycling until the output of the phase is optimized. Outputs of each phase constitute a definitive and documented baseline for entry into the next phase.

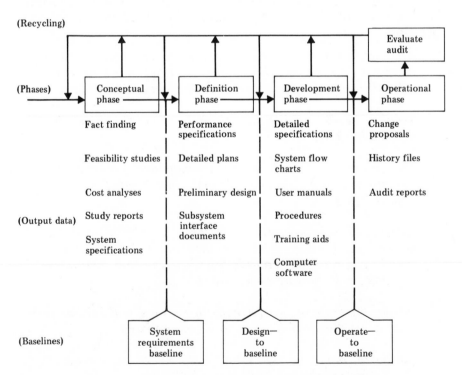

Figure 1.   Phases of management systems engineering.

Conceptual Phase

During the conceptual phase, the preliminary idea of the system is formulated. This means identifying the requirements that would seem to make the management system necessary. Frequently, the requirement may be to overcome an operating deficiency, such as the inability of the production process to keep up with orders or frequent customer complaints.

In many respects, this identification of the true problem, peeling away layers of symptomatic deficiencies, may be the most difficult part of the entire process. Certainly, it may well be the most important, because unless the fundamental problem or system requirement is clearly identified, there may be a great deal of wheel-spinning in trying to arrive at a solution.

A considerable amount of discipline is necessary in concept formulation to avoid the inclination to "solve" the problem prematurely by bypassing the step of specifying in plain English what it is the solution is supposed to accomplish. To do so may result in the anomaly of having a solution in search of a problem.

In those instances in which the use of automatic data processing is possible, the concept formulation phase is particularly important. To assume a requirement for computerization unnecessarily may provide an ample backlog of work for system designers and programmers, but it may also result in drastically reduced profits.

Preliminary Report

The primary output of the conceptual phase will be a report that summarizes the origin and nature of the problem or requirement and a concept of the management system solution. The component parts or modules of the system may also be defined. In effect, the system specification provides sufficient detail on which management can base a decision to proceed with further definition. An example will make this clear.

Suppose there has been a breakdown between a company's ordering process and production. The company wants a new system engineered to overcome the problem. The conceptual phase of the work may cover a study of the flow of paperwork from the sales operation through to the finished product. Fact finding will describe the current process and isolate specific instances where the process is defective, inefficient, or too costly.

An analysis of the facts may result in a general concept, based on current experience in the same or a similar industry. Study may also show the need for a single system, using a minimum number of standard forms, with proceduralized routing, carefully chosen approval checkpoints, and use of a computerized management information system for production control if production volume warrants it.

The conceptual phase results in a preliminary report and general system specification; it does not define the solution in detail, nor does it plunge into system design. It merely provides management (at an appropriate authorizing level) with sufficient facts (including cost data) and a concept to make possible the decision whether to proceed as suggested.

Definition Phase

Assuming that the conceptual phase has resulted in a confirmed system requirement and that management has given its go-ahead, a distinct phase called definition now begins. The objective here is to detail the general system concept and to provide plans and specifications for design and development.

Generally, this involves the development of alternative functional and hardware solutions to the problem, their evaluation and comparison, and the preparation of back-up material supporting one selection. Trade-off studies are prepared that weigh the relative merits of each solution in terms of total costs, system effectiveness, schedule for implementation, and constraints or limitations placed on them.

During the definition phase, the management systems engineering process will follow a well-specified routine. [Figure 2] illustrates the flow of this process.

Optimum Solution

The iterative nature of the process is particularly important. In going from preliminary requirements to final specifications, it may be necessary to recycle several times. This will continue until the solution (the proposed management system) has been optimized in relation to original requirements, constraints, and the capabilities of the organization to support the solution. In a few instances, this recycling may show that the original requirements were unrealistic and should be modified.

In this phase of management systems engineering, many of the techniques associated with operations research and systems analysis

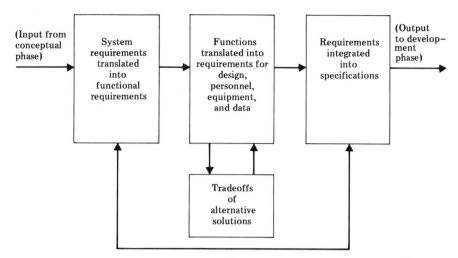

Figure 2.   Management systems engineering during definition.

can be used. Mathematical modeling, linear programming, sensitivity analysis, life-cycle costing, and cost-effectiveness studies may be used to advantage.

The output of the definition phase is a set of specifications and plans sufficiently well documented to provide a baseline for a management decision on whether to proceed with design and development.

This is the baseline that tells the authorizing manager:

What the scope of the intended system will be

How long it will take to become operational

What resources will be required to complete design and development, go operational, and maintain the system thereafter

Who will be responsible for developing and implementing each part of the system

Given this planning information, system and subsystem specifications, and cost figures, management is ready to decide to proceed with development of the system, to redefine requirements, or perhaps even to stop all further effort on the system. In many instances, the last may well be the wisest decision, particularly if the proposed system represents an overkill of the problem—like swatting an operating gnat with a system sledgehammer.

Development Phase

Plans and specifications prepared during the definition phase are prerequisites for the development phase. They also provide a documented baseline that can be referred to (1) to determine whether management's intent is being carried out, (2) to assess progress, and (3) to provide a measurable point for evaluating changes to the system and its specifications.

At this stage, the dynamics of systems development is most evident. Conditions change. The problem may look different now from what it appeared to be some months before. Budgets have a way of expanding and contracting. During this phase, which will probably last many months, there is no guarantee that the original requirements will sit still.

It is both unrealistic and hazardous to assume a static condition. Fortunate is the project manager who has a well-documented set of plans and specifications to which he can refer and from which he can document changes to the system concept. Without them, he will be in the position of Mr. Blandings, building a dream house that grows in physical size and—more disastrously—in cost as the work proceeds.

In systems involving computerized information subsystems or modules—and what systems today do not?—the development phase is most critical. It is here that the developing system succeeds or fails in meeting the objectives originally planned, in solving the problem, and in complying with specifications.

Documentation

The documentation of the steps through which the design is proceeding is especially important. The designer's notebook, the formalized flow diagrams for individual subsystems and modules, the truth tables comprising the logic of the computerized systems, the interface analyses, and the tabulated programming operations are essential to the documentation of the total system. These are usually the property of the firm.

What it means to develop a computerized system without proper documentation may be illustrated by the legendary case of the system developer who had access to a computer and managed to develop a computerized system for forecasting market information.

Unfortunately, after the system had been operating for some time and the developer had left the company, someone discovered that there was no extant documentation. It was also revealed that reprogramming and documentation would cost a quarter of a million dollars. The lesson was expensive.

It is of the essence of scientific method that performance be repeatable. The recurring performance of certain methods and the ability to duplicate a programming routine or to change it if need be makes the detailed documentation of the system absolutely essential to system effectiveness.

Integration

A second aspect of management systems engineering that is vital during the development phase is the integration of parts of the system and the establishment of compatible external interfaces with related systems and subsystems.

An illustration of the potential complexity of a major management system can be cited from the experience of the Autonetics Division of North American Rockwell Corporation. In this division, a management system called Integrated Quality Information System is now in the development phase. This involves integrating a variety of existing procedures and operations with the addition of special computerized modules to provide management information.

In the development of this system, as many as 22 major interfaces with other functional systems must be considered. When intrasystem and subsystem relationships are considered, the number of interfaces may be many times as great. The urgency of a systems engineering approach to a problem of this magnitude is apparent.

The final output of the development phase will include the following: a completely documented system design, including flow charts; all necessary computer programs; detailed procedures for the operation of the system; input document formats; output report formats; training manuals; qualitative personnel requirements lists; equipment requisitions and purchase orders or lease agreements.

Operational Phase

The final phase of management systems engineering takes the output of the development phase as baseline documentation for the operational phase. Again, an explicit management decision must be made on whether to proceed with implementation. The alternatives, of course, are to recycle part or all of the preceding phases or even to stop further effort.

The explicit nature of this commitment or noncommitment sharpens the effort of system designers and others to focus on a set of system documents that will justify operating status. In the absence of such a decision point, there may be an inclination to slip into an operating mode with inadequate preparation, deficiencies in equipment, personnel, or training, or partially documented software.

In practice, there may be an overlap of the development and operational phases because of some urgency. Final debugging of the system in the latter stages of the development phase, completion of training courses, and final documentation may continue even after the system has become operational. It is important, however, that the distinction between phases be apparent and that there has been a decisive pause at the baseline before proceeding further.

While management systems engineering effort falls off during the operational phase, it does not cease altogether. Maintenance of the system itself, correction of deficiencies, evaluation of recommendations for system changes and improvements all require a level of effort from the management systems engineering unit.

Audit

Of particular importance during the operational phase is the necessity for periodic audit. This may and probably should be conducted by people other than those responsible for system development and maintenance.

Audit encompasses the discipline with which the system is operated. It will invariably review compliance with written procedures and policy. It may even extend to system effectiveness. Thus, if an inventory control system is operating smoothly but with top-heavy overhead costs, the audit should indicate this as a system deficiency.

It should be the responsibility of the management systems engineering unit to review the system to determine whether new system requirements should be established. Audit reports, however, might conceivably result in recycling any phase. If the audit shows deficiencies in output reports, training manuals, or procedures, this may simply indicate that additional development effort is required.

The operational phase concludes with final system close-out. Here again it is desirable that the system should not be allowed to linger on, ultimately dying a slow death. Formal recognition should be given to the demise of the system or its possible rebirth in another system. The reason is obvious: It is extremely expensive to maintain obsolete systems. And too often there are large numbers of people within the organization who are busily engaged in preparing forms and performing operations, but who may be totally unaware that the system itself is really obsolete.

A fairly simple solution to this problem is for the designated management systems engineering group to maintain an up-to-date list of operating systems and to conduct a periodic check of their status. A more sophisticated approach would include identification of intersystem and intrasystem interfaces, possibly in a matrix format. This permits rapid recognition of impacted areas when a system changes or new systems are introduced. The Management Systems Framework used by the Autonetics Division of North American Rockwell is a formal approach to this problem. It consists of a complete listing of the division's systems and subsystems, together with flow charts and inventory sheets identifying system names, codes, references, abstracts, status, equipment, interfacing systems, and responsible organizations.

Appraisal

What contribution can management systems engineering make to improve operating systems, and what are its limitations?

Discipline

The key contribution of management systems engineering is the discipline it introduces into the development and installation of business systems. It is easy enough to become enamored of management systems and the computer programs with which they are associated. Unfortunately, these systems do not come cheap. For the sake of economy, therefore, it is essential that strict controls be exercised over the initiation and implementation of these systems. In some form or other, business systems themselves must be system-managed.

The disciplinary aspect of management systems engineering is evident in a number of ways:

1. *The total management systems development process is subdivided into phases that can be readily controlled.*
2. *Clear baselines are established for making management decisions on whether to proceed.*

3. *The baselines also provide for a definite point for determining whether changes should be made to requirements, specifications, and design.*
4. *Budgets for each phase can be established that relate to very specific outputs and milestones for that phase.*
5. *Resources need be committed only after considering current progress on the system. (This is particularly important in relation to EDP equipment.)*
6. *Planning (detailed who, what, when, where, and how) is related to specifications, with improved chances of control.*
7. *An improved structure is provided for the use of modern management tools and techniques, with consequent sharpening of capabilities in problem solving, solution synthesis, and decision making.*

In effect, the discipline inherent in the management systems engineering process is ultimately related to economics—the preparation and installation of the most effective and efficient business systems with the least expenditure of time, effort, and money. This is what constitutes the ultimate justification for applying it.

The Human Factor

On the other hand, management systems engineering is not a magic wand for the solution of operating ills. In point of fact, it does not, in itself, solve problems. People solve problems. Used without constant monitoring, it may result in the overemphasis of computerized solutions. Used by the wrong people, it may lead to an overly mechanized approach in which the importance of the human element for system success or failure may be neglected.

It is well to remind ourselves occasionally that a business system is a social system. It is made up of human beings as well as equipment and communication devices. It is totally unrealistic to imagine that the antiseptic routines that work so well in the laboratory (or computer) can be transferred without adjustment to an operating environment.

Arnold E. Keller, editor and publisher of *Business Automation*, recently warned that "the machine is not a system." An understanding of people and the human aspects of change may determine whether a sound management system can be implemented effectively.

A final caution in regard to the application of management systems engineering may be in order. This concerns the optimum level of operating scope and complexity at which management systems engineering would appear to be justified. In a small to medium-size plant, whoever is responsible for business systems development and documentation might profitably use the general concepts of management systems engineering. In larger, more complex organizations with many interfunctional operations requiring integration, the use of specialized management systems engineers, analysts, and information systems experts should be considered carefully. As in any similar decision, their potential contribution to total operating effectiveness and profit should be the primary yardstick.

Organization, Perception, and Control in Living Systems

Avery R. Johnson

Reprinted by permission of *Industrial Management Review*, Winter 1969.

Introduction

Ever since I came barging into the ranks of industrial management, there to pay attention to the structure and behavior of "intelligent" systems, I have relied, for the purposes of my own understanding of the issues involved, upon what I know of physiological organisms and of how they deal with their world. I have, at the same time, been somewhat appalled on occasion by the essayed anthropomorphic descriptions so often applied to the observed or intended behaviors of information-handling systems: those "aids" toward which we find ourselves turning in the endeavor to stem the tide of meaningless paper and to simplify our grasp of business process. We are being inundated by the flow of data and statistics and carefully charted relationships to the point where what we seem to know *about* a situation threatens to exceed by far in complication the workings of the situation itself. Let us take another and quite different look at what we are doing and why.

Animals deal with a highly complex, ambiguous world while performing the simplest of behaviors. Let us consider how they collect and use their information, and then take a similar view toward improving the health and functioning of those larger systems of which we form but part. In what follows I am not going to suggest that we hook up our computers to animal brains in order somehow to put to use some abstract ability that we have as yet not learned to imitate in hardware. I will, however, suggest that we must seek far better ways to connect computers to people: to make their services much more congenial to obtain, more "conversational," of the nature of a shared dialogue.[1] The alienation we are coming to feel in our confrontations with those superfast, infallible, compulsive, unforgiving electronic beasts is one that may stem largely from our own failure to demand that they not make such demands for sophistication from us in their use. Let us see what we ourselves are doing "on-line" in the world and note whether we would like our computing or management systems to be of the same ilk.

As we approach the eighth decade of the twentieth century, we find ourselves moving into a world in which we must learn to take account of "triadic" relationships.[2] The diadic attitude of "if this, then that," irrespective of context, is no longer adequate. It served us fairly well in setting up an industrialized society of interlocking, working parts whose roles could be expected not to have to change much in the course of a human lifetime, and even less over the span of a year or of a professional commitment. We were once a *monadic* race, as are the other species: setting our sights on making satisfactory the objects and events of our immediate surroundings. We later became *diadic*, requiring the emergence of symbolisms and metaphoric embodiments of our identity: names, money, property, and clothing styles, to name but a few. We are now fast approaching the *triadic*, which will have its own forms and will serve to relate and give meaning to the other two. The "three-valued" world is one which demands the participation of the individual in a dialogue with his environment in order that he be able to generate for himself a meaningful existence. Psychologists are discovering that grasp is a more fundamental perceptual mode than mere touch, and that looking is more essentially descriptive of vision than is seeing. It is the active involvement of the organism which is paramount.[3]

I find the use of physiological analogy in teaching to be significant, partly because it allows me to elicit from the student a description of how he thinks he perceives his world, thereby providing the raw material for discussion in his terms, but more because it allows the student to develop in himself his own

[1] See Pask [14].
[2] See McCulloch [13].
[3] See Held [6].

laboratory for experiment and for a start along the path to an active participation in the processes he is studying. Rigorous arguments employing equations and tables are akin to bricks and mortar; I am more interested in the thrust of architecture.

The Role of the Perceiver

We seek to ask, then, as living examples of the organisms about which we theorize, what are we and how do we go about our business. What is our highly developed central nervous system *for* anyway? How does it serve itself and the rest of the corporal system in which it resides? And ultimately, what can we learn from such considerations that will lead us to better formulations of the larger organizations of management?

If called upon to state the overriding purpose of the central nervous system as an evolutionary phenomenon, I would characterize its role as the organizing of the total behavior of the organism in the task of discovering the meanings of the objects and events surrounding it. The senses measure data flowing in from the environment, but of themselves those measurements are meaningless. Sensory input is metaphoric: there is an implied comparison between it and the event which produced it. The sensory input is not the event. I repeat. THE SENSORY INPUT IS NOT THE EVENT. It is a metaphoric statement about the event or object. It remains for the organism to discern the meaning of the metaphor through some further behavior which is more than simply a passive, sensory observation.

What is meaning? For the most part, it is an identification, but it is far more than a simple naming. The identification of an object or event by name is the result of a *common sense*, an agreed upon correspondence between metaphors of an event-like kind, as experienced, and metaphors of a symbolic kind, as stated. The apprehension implies that some meaning has been assigned to the object and therefore that some appropriate response is available within the organism's repetoire. In fact, that is the crux of it. MEANING IS TO BE FOUND IN THE RESPONSE WHICH THE ORGANISM FINDS APPROPRIATE. Note, however, that the response is not necessarily carried out; it may be latent or potential. Note also that we have as yet failed to consider how the response and its appropriateness came to reside within the available repetoire, and how these are elicited. There is, of course, the element of past experience to be considered, but of much more immediate importance are the elements of present experience, of participation in the event. No object or event can exist totally without relation to the observer and still have meaning. It is the manipulation of the relation of event to observer that allows him to discern meaning. This is a roundabout way of saying that the context of the event acts as an operator to assign meaning to the sensory metaphor, and that the discernment of context is an active process on the part of the observer.[4]

Let us try another tack.

Here is a man, I show him a photograph of an object: a piece of mechanical apparatus. He has never seen such a thing and so it has no meaning for him whatever. Since the photograph shows the object only, devoid of any context of use, he cannot even estimate its size, material, color, orientation, or where he might expect to see one. I tell him the object's name. It is a dibble.[5] A what? A dibble. Sorry, still no enlightenment; the name means nothing to him yet.

Here, my friend, are a few hundred plant seedlings I would like you to put in the ground for me. Just make a little hole for each and stick it in. It's easy, you can do them all in about. . . . Aha, he says, now if I had a gadget like the one in that picture and it was the right size on the blunt end to fit my hand, then the sharp end would make holes just the size I need for the plants.

Here you are, how does it feel?

Fine! Very comfortable to grasp.

How does it work? Try it a bit.

Works fine. Just what I wanted. What do you call it?

A dibble.

And he will never forget what a dibble is because now his *mind* knows. The feel of it in his hand, the sensation of the earth parting as it makes the hole, the satisfying moment of insight as he "reinvented" the dibble for himself are all his forever. His *participation* in dibbling and the changes wrought in him by that participation *are* his knowledge of it. Any metaphor implying the dibble—picture, name, hand-feel, seedling—can now evoke the context of the dibble through his experience and consequently that metaphor can take on meaning for him.

Ask a friend who can type where, on the typewriter, the Y is to be found relative to the H. Almost without exception you will observe his or her hand to rise to near chest height, there to make the motion in space of moving from the H to the Y. Where lies the most convenient route to the "memory" of that relationship? Somewhere in functioning of the circuits that mediate the appropriate *responsive*

[4] See Hermann [7].

[5] Webster's New World Dictionary, College Edition, 1966, p. 406.

behavior. The illustration gives us a clue to what we mean by "knowing."

Spend some time in a supermarket and contemplate what the meaning of a food package is to each person who must relate to it. As the housewife reaches for it, she is already anticipating its use in cooking, its aspect in serving, and its flavor in the tasting of it. The meaning for the checkout girl is simple price; she probably goes home at night, looks at the shelf, and automatically thinks numbers rather than aromas—and her hand may start to tap out the keyboard pattern. The kid who puts the groceries in bags sees packages solely in terms of size, weight, and relative fragility. His reach and grasp must reflect the spaces remaining within the bag. Price and flavor are irrelevant to whether the bundle will maintain its integrity from there to your kitchen.

Everyone sees objects or events within a context that serves to provide meaning for him. Earlier I suggested that context be thought of as an operator which assigns meaning to metaphor. Now you will want to know what context is. You will want me to point to it as if "background" were a sufficient description. It isn't. The context which you discern involves your participation in it, not mine. However, I think I can be of help to you here if you will let me make the argument sound circular.

Let us consider context to be everything which serves in some way to assign meaning to an object or event. Since we have already seen that meaning is embodied by the appropriate response to the object or event, context must then be that which allows us or helps us to organize our responses appropriately. The usefulness of this obverse way of defining context will become more apparent later.

Structures and Their Changes

We talk a lot about information and its entropic nature. We talk about redundancy and channel capacity and all the gamut of description of data flow, yet seldom take account of how a part of the system may be changed by the information which it processes. A simulation model of a municipal government is formulated.[6] In one branch of the flow chart we find the mayor with information pouring in from many places and going out to others. For all the simulation runs, that mayor is imagined to have ears and eyes with

[6] Paper presented by a member of New York City Mayor's office at the October 1968 meeting of American Society for Cybernetics.

which to take in data, and a mouth with which to give out orders, but he is never allowed hands with which to pick up and dial a telephone, thereupon to access information for himself. Most of the information flow into the mayor's office is of high speed and of fairly low resolution: not erroneous, but lacking in detail, and so it should be. It is his job to sense a situation of growing novelty somewhere and to make the active effort to increase the resolution of his view in that specific area until he feels he knows what is happening and what the appropriate municipal response should be. His very participation in the process of refining the grain of the picture he sees—doing so in a limited area and to as high a resolution as he feels is necessary—is what assigns the meaning to the events therein. He is not a simple transformer of information. He is more than tactile flesh; he has a reach and grasp which can serve him to identify what he touches.

There is no doubting that data come at us in many forms, some of which will hit us even if we sat still and some of which we must go after for ourselves. To an extent we have predictive models of what our participation must be in order to sort out meaning from the mess. At the outset all is ambiguity. Redundancy is all of that which has been anticipated by the predictive model and for the aperception of which no active participation was required. Information is ambiguity resolved by transaction with the environment. It is not just that the active transaction delivers us the information. OUR PARTICIPATION IN THE PROCESS IS THE PERCEPTION OF THE INFORMATION. The leftovers are generally called noise, but we should not lose sight of the possibility that through further transactions we may be able to diagnose their context and thus rescue them from meaninglessness. It is up to the organism to change itself for the purpose of acquiring elucidation. Discovery of an appropriate response takes trial and error, trial and success. Trial? Not as such, for no trial is carried to completion in the form with which it commenced. The organism changes itself and evolves continuously. No unitary error or success may be identified. The handy phrase, "cut and try," is too simplistic and even misleading, because to cut the system in time, to take a stop-frame view of it, is tantamount to murder.

What, after all, do our piles of data and statistics and charts on hard copy in endless fan-fold stacks tell us of living, changing, growing organisms? Our computer technology has provided us the opportunity to have at every hand a responsive model of the systems we envision, one which is up-to-date, anticipating, predicting, resolving, and available at all times. No office should require a file or shelf wherein to store away a lot of paper. Any particular aspect of the system about which we want to know should be available at a terminal and should perhaps be printed out on a scope or in ink that has a half-life measurable in minutes or seconds, thus to underscore the relevance of the data only to the temporal context in which they were requested.

Our manners of taking data, of organizing them into "meaningful" statements, and then of applying the inferences of those statements in the processes of management are far from reflecting a real world of things, events, and people, and are also largely unsuited to use by the complex information-handling systems that are available. For the most part, the espoused theories and techniques are only slightly modified versions of those prevalent prior to the invention of the computer. In those days, the purpose of a statistical measure or test was to minimize the manual labor for the investigator while maximizing the probability of success of his interpretations. Who needs that first requirement any more? Let us stop lumping data which have been husked of their context of time and of the marks left by the hand that grasped them.

We are so accustomed to being asked to distort our vision so that a model will look like the original that we forget to ask for the model to be placed in our own hands that we may examine it ourselves. We are likewise prone to crow loudly when in visual aspect a real situation is found which appears to fit one of our models with ease. I am sorely reminded of expressions of aesthetic enthusiasm when a scene looks "pretty as a picture postcard." I would rather we asked why postcards usually fail to convey more than a negligible aspect of the experience of being there.

Decision, Control, and Self-organization

We hear a lot about decision theory, but I wonder if we really have a clear notion about what a decision is and how it differs from "doing what comes naturally." My principal interest is in the latter, the informal ways in which we generally go about getting things to work without ever thinking very explicitly about how and why we are taking each step along the way. There is a clear class of situations, however, in which it is appropriate to make a decision and then to act upon it. Let me illustrate with a somewhat extreme case from the psychophysiological realm.

There are moments in the life of any organism when a state of emergency arises. What is a state of emergency? Whence its urgency? How do we learn to recognize it? What do we do about it?

An emergency may be said to exist when it appears that there is not enough time available for an adequate exploration of the meaning of incoming data. Something must be done *now*; a decision has to be made. A commitment to responsive action must be commenced immediately and its selection must be based upon what we already know or can guess. Exploration takes time because it is an interactive dialogue and involves changes in both the perceiver and his environment. Emergencies are of a stop-frame character. Here is a snapshot of the world. Act upon it. Time has run out. The clock is stopped.

Animals do not enter an emergency mode of behavior for the sole reason that a threat to survival is present. If the threat is explicit, and its meaning in terms of an appropriate response is clear, then no decisionary procedures are necessary because, in a very real sense, the correct response is already under way. Emergencies are produced by an overload of ambiguity (some would say an "information overload," but this in incorrect), and the danger is that hidden among the ambiguous data may be something which is of a threatening nature. One cannot take chances with survival. Action must be initiated which has the highest probability of moving one out of the ambiguity overload and back to a condition of dialogue. That action should be unitary in the sense that it is a single, well-formed pattern of behavior already available in the repertoire of such patterns, and commitment must be made at any one time to only one of them. Dialogue is a many-eyed, many-armed transaction. The response to emergency should be cyclopian, immediate, and uni-directional.

Such is the nature of decision. It is not a gesture which tells you more about the world. Quite the contrary, a decision is made as the shutter closes and no more metaphors will acquire meaning until the action to which you are now committed is either carried to completion or is otherwise terminated. Decisions freeze structure and proceed to turn the behavioral crank. They put the blinders on us, rendering us unaware of meaningful twists in the path. Decisions are for those moments when you cannot do otherwise.[7]

The next time that you find yourself in the act of "making a decision," ask yourself: (a) whether you would not instead prefer the opportunity to explore the data more fully and then deal with them

[7] See Kilmer [10].

in smaller pieces, (b) whether the decision you are making has more the character of "timeless relevance" than of specific applicability to a one-of-a-kind situation, and (c) how soon the behavior you are commencing as a result of the decision will give way in its inflexibility to a more informal, congenial groping.

Cybernetics in Perspective

Lest you think I am inveighing totally against structure or policy, let me change my tune to a more positive one. I am concerned with the nature of self-organizing systems. To be sure, they have a structure or mechanism which is put together in a fairly immutable way and which cannot disobey the laws of physics in the use of its parts while engaged in a dialogue with its environment. However, there may and should be a highly flexible set of relationships possible between the sensors that detect changes and the effectors that produce them. The system itself must never be content to remain as a passive observer of incoming data; it must participate in exploration. In fact, it is becoming increasingly evident that any self-organizing system must, in effect, play with itself in a manner which includes part of the environment in the loop. Furthermore, the most meaningful information to be found anywhere in that loop is not the raw data with which the system is dealing but the behavior in which the system must engage in order to deal with the data.

Let us take a look at cybernetics from a somewhat historical perspective in order to see where this trend of thinking is taking us.

Initially, as the principles of feedback control gained in popularity and interest, purposive, "goal-seeking" systems were envisioned as altering their outputs in order to reduce the "error" discrepancies between their inputs and some desired state of the inputs. The sensory metaphors were to be analyzed by a central processor and appropriate action was to be taken by the effectors to make corrections (Figure 1a). There was little serious concern as to how "appropriateness" was to be determined, since it was presumed that such considerations would be provided for by the designer. Performance assessment was to be prearranged; the systems had no need to learn for themselves what the meanings of the sensory metaphors were because someone had already performed the task of translation. Where a symbolic manipulation was necessary, the symbols were delivered as symbols; where the error to be minimized was physically measurable, the notion of "good" or minimum was explicitly defined. These systems did not have to be born and

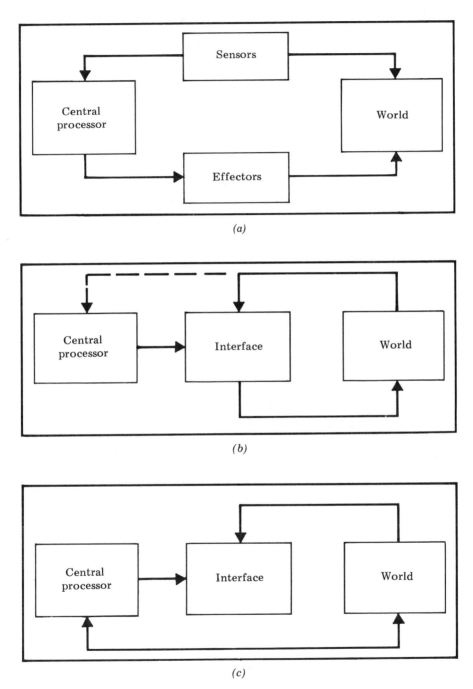

Figure 1.   (*a*) 1930; (*b*) 1950; (*c*) 1970.

nurtured; they were made of whole cloth and turned on. And if the gadget did not work as intended, the fault was laid at the designer's feet because he had not forseen all of the consequences of his design. The system was not supposed to *be*, or to seek a favorable identity; it was simply supposed to *do*.

Even now, as we look at diagrams of management systems and at organizational charts and read the descriptions of the information channels depicted, we know implicitly (and then promptly forget) that at the nodes, where information enters and is relayed onward, there are men, self-organizing human beings whose task it is to understand that information in its context, to know the policies of the company in relation to that context, and to transform the data into new symbols relevant to the next stage of processing. Fine. People are good at this task and have been doing it for a long time. But every day I see claims that there are systems that are doing it. I claim they are doing no such thing.

About 20 years later (Figure 1*b*), around the time when cybernetics acquired its name and formulations, it became apparent that a new attitude was gaining popularity. Partly as a result of physiological studies and partly arising from the development of servomechanical controls, an advantage was recognized in the use of "interfacing" systems which would deal with the environment in a goal-seeking, "homeostatic" way and not belabor the central processor with the problems of calculating the necessary adjustments. The higher centers could then concern themselves with higher things and would in turn produce their effects upon the environment by altering the goals or null settings of the interfacing systems. In the use of such a mechanism, the designer no longer needed to know precisely what kind of environment the system would be called upon to face but had only to assure himself that the effector apparatus would be capable of finding a route toward satisfaction of the goal structure assigned to the interface.

There was, however, still a reluctance to accept as meaningful descriptors of the environment anything but the sensory metaphors received as inputs. *Looking* appeared to be merely a useful adjunct to *seeing*; *feeling* seemed to come before *touching*; and *shape* was considered somehow to have a message of its own even before *grasp* came along to define it. In short, the organism was still being viewed as a passive observer of information and its active role in accessing that information for itself was no more than an additional feature. The interpretation of meaning by the system was still the a priori responsibility of the designer or programmer. One still needed people at the nodal points to make the transformations called for by the context of the data. The system had no way to explore such operations for itself.

A new trend is in the making.[8] It is becoming apparent that the necessity for the participation of the perceiver in the act of perception is more than fortuitous. IN FACT, THE PROCESS OF PARTICIPATION IS ITSELF THE MEANINGFUL STATEMENT OF OBJECTS AND EVENTS IN THE ENVIRONMENT. The interface required is not much different from what it was, but the useful information we derive from it has taken a profound shift. Any system which has the responsibility for organizing itself and for discovering the meanings of things must trust, at least at first, to what it can learn from the behavior of its interface with the world (Figure 1c). After some experience with a sensory metaphor and the rediscovery of responses appropriate to it, the system can learn to apprehend meaning as a passive observer. At the outset, however, no such sophisticated interpretation is possible: the system must trust its interface to deal with a new aspect of the environment according to the goal structure (policies) which it has set for that interface. The meaningful data are to be found in the statement of resulting behavior, not in the raw environmental measurements. The topology of initial exploration and later of interpretation is that of an "effector map," which in its turn has no meaning if removed from the context of the interfacing mechanism which produced it. If you turn off the system and disassemble it in order to describe the parts, you will not be able to discern that quality which makes it work. If you document its behavior out of the context of the situation which produced it or of the structure which responded as described, you will likewise tell me nothing. Self-organizing systems are of a devious ilk and hide their colors when you try to isolate them. Instead, present the system in some active, responsive embodiment and let the observer explore its responsiveness. Allow him the opportunity to tweak it with his interface—his reach, grasp, poke, stratagem, and perturbation—so that he in his turn may "know" the system as only an active participant can ever know it.

This shift of attention from a reliance upon the input as the source of environmental fact to a confidence in the behavior of an exploratory interface which is adept at dealing with the environment is not a trivial change in point of view. It says, for example, that a representative or ambassador to be selected should be a man who is

---

[8] See Johnson [9].

familiar with the culture into which he is to go and trustworthy in his understanding of and belief in the policies that are to guide his actions. Thereafter he should not be asked for reports of the details of his negotiations but only of what he did about them. He is the one who knows the meaning of the details because he is immersed in the context of their happening. No authority further up the pyramid can be expected to grasp their significance (the ambassador himself is the grasper for us), nor should responsive actions be dictated from above, but only shifts of policy. Gradually he may educate us by his actions into the meanings of the events with which he must deal; but at the outset those events are meaningless in our context and only his actions may convey to us their import.

A mountaineer returns from a climb exhausted. Do we ask him metric questions about the mountain if what we wish to know is the effect the climb will have upon us? No, for his very exhaustion is message enough. The metric details would be meaningless by themselves.

Refer for a moment to our earlier considerations of the activities of the perceiver and his search for meaning. If, as was suggested there, we define context to be all of that which allows us to organize our responses appropriately, then it would appear immediately that the interfacing system described above is especially well suited to the exploration of context. The responsive behavior of the interface *is* the message to which the central processor attends. Since the interfacing system is going to manipulate its effectors so as to explore the ways in which to fulfill the role assigned to it by the next higher level, it will by that very process refrain from isolating a metaphor away from the context of its occurrence.

There lies within this notion of an autonomous interfacing system the seed of the direction which I think our considerations must take when we speak of decentralization of industrial management. A hierarchical structure may be imagined in which each higher level accepts as meaningful statements of reality the behavior of the next rank below and receives as instruction from above a slowly varying goal structure (role assignment). Each rank is trusted to be diligent in the pursuit of the role assigned to it, to be responsive to variation of goals, and to be capable of reporting the actions taken (goals set) upon the next rank below.

I am not suggesting that it is out of bounds for an upper level to observe the raw data serving a lower one. I only submit the warning that that raw input may well be meaningless to one who is not in the habit of immediate and extensive participation in it. The lower ranks—"down where the rubber meets the road"—are more sophisticated in the meanings of events at their levels because they are more colloquial with the appropriate responses to them. The higher levels may learn those meanings, but only by observing the events in the context of the behavioral responses dealing with them. Direct command for specific action should rarely flow downward except under the conditions discussed above, when a decisionary procedure is mandatory. Even then, the decision reached should give evidence of the redundancy of potential command throughout the system. I will not elaborate here; Kilmer, McCulloch, and Blum have done so at length elsewhere.[9]

Intelligent Behavior of Systems

Another concept we hear and talk and write about, without ever being very specific about what we mean by the term, is "intelligent behavior." Let us consider for a moment how we might arrive at a useful, operative definition.

An intelligent act certainly is one which takes account of the context in which it is performed. But there is more to it than that. One can imagine ritual acts carried out in conditions where the context never changes and which are therefore appropriate for all time. So we say, aha, there must be something of adaptability in the process of intelligence, something which takes account of changes in context. All right, but how would we as observers know that this had been the case? We cannot expect our aperception of the conditions surrounding an event to be the same as that of some other complex organism. How would we know whether the change in system response were or were not appropriate to the change of conditions?

Consider an artificial situation and a human parallel. Someone brings a black box into your office and claims that it is a machine capable of intelligent behavior. He demonstrates the means of communicating with the device and then departs, leaving you to convince yourself of the truth or falsehood of his assertion. Note that we are not trying to decide whether there is a man or a computer inside the box, but rather to exercise our concept of what constitutes intelligent behavior. Any good definition should be capable of statement, independent of the object to which it is to be applied. Note also that if we wait for a demonstration to take place which does not include us as an active participant, we will be disappointed, for if the definition allowed us to be passive observers,

[9] See [10].

then the box might as well contain nothing more than a magnetic tape playback unit loaded with suitable prerecorded tapes. No, there is more to intelligence than utterances. There must occur a transaction between us and the system.

Consider a human parellel about which you may have fantasized at some time in the past. You have been unwillingly incarcerated in a mental institution and have been brought before a board of psychiatrists for examination. It is your task to demonstrate your sanity. How would you go about it?

Again we come to the immediate conclusion that there is no statement you could make which would be convincing. You may not even have a clear notion as to what sanity is, inasmuch as the rest of your world appears to be insane at this very moment. You do know, however, that you want the board to ask you questions and that the onus will be upon you to provide responses which the board will consider appropriate. In the case of an investigation of sanity, the board will most likely be seeking affective (emotional) responses while our accustomed thoughts about intelligent behavior center around rational responses. Let us not quibble. The test is essentially the same. For the sake of brevity, let us consider one familiar form it might take.

A partial, though certainly insufficient, test for sanity is to tell the patient stories, some of which are funny and some of which are not. We will be watching for the appropriateness of his amusement and laughter or lack of it. We must, of course, take into account the cultural context from which the patient comes, for otherwise we would have no estimate of appropriateness to him. Let us accept that as a "given" in the problem.

But what, after all, makes a story funny or straight? Wherein lies the humor of a joke? It is really quite simple when you think about it. A joke, prior to the punchline, is a story told in some context with which you are familiar and which appears to assign meaning to all of the metaphors involved. What the puuchline does is to shift the context in such a way that some or all of the metaphors suddenly take on new meaning. Your amusement is the natural response evidencing your enjoyment at participating in the construction of the new meanings which have been assigned by the new context. Think up any adequate test for sanity or for the ability to perform intelligent behavior and you will find that the same fundamental structure underlies the test.

The test involves a transaction in which metaphoric (but not necessarily verbal or symbolic) statements are to be made by one party and the meanings are to be discerned by the other. You will remember that meaning, to an organism, is implied by its response. Assuming that the appropriateness of the response can be estimated, we may say that INTELLIGENT BEHAVIOR IS THE DETECTION OF THE CHANGE OF MEANING BROUGHT ABOUT BY A SHIFT OF CONTEXT. Great elaborations of this basic definition are possible. I will not indulge in them here, but will leave the definition in its simplest form for now.

Consider if you will, however, the fact that most of the more serious problems faced by management systems arise in the form of an apparent irrelevance of an older, previously successful system for dealing with new problems. It often appears that the problems are, in almost every sense, identical with the old ones, but they are now appearing in a different context. The system has failed to react intelligently. It has failed to detect the change of meaning brought about by a shift of context.

Some Attitudes and Predictions

One idea which is becoming inescapably clear in many areas of human experience is that the sources of motivation for mankind are not limited to actions that promote physical survival or satisfy physiological appetites. Man has an undeniable need to maintain his "information level" and will go to great lengths to do so. Extreme examples are Saturday night fights at home, car theft, narcotics experiments, vandalism, exhibitionism, or even alcoholism, a reverse attempt to suppress the need to where it is relatively tolerable. It should be clear by now that "information" for the individual is not simply what is beamed at him for his consumption, but is rather that which invites his involvement: i.e., something that will respond to him, that will tell him *he is there*. In the years to come we are going to see many instances of people rebelling against a world which lacks courtesy, lacks a responsiveness to them. They will kick cigarette machines that swallow their money without giving anything back, and will kick government just as hard when it gives back irrelevance. We will see more students wondering why the university experience prepares them for nothing that they care to be and therefore demanding at least some role in the determination of that preparation. We will see people more prone to ignore traffic lights when the irrevocable rhythm is irrelevant to the present traffic conditions: unmindful, that is, of the original context and purpose of those lights.

We are also going to see arising the use of involvement itself as a motivator at all levels of industry and of society at large. I predict a higher demand for involvement than for financial compensation as an inducement to productive creativity. There is nothing mysterious about this trend except perhaps its late appearance. Its latency is most plausibly assignable to the lessons of the industrial revolution which pronounced the edict that each could afford the products that all enjoyed provided that he was willing to accept their sameness. We learned not to expect individual difference, but to be content with a ubiquitous value system. However, such conformity need no longer be the case.[10]

We now have the information handling systems that can keep track of routine matters, and if we can get away from the industrial notion that computers are there for the purpose of cranking out mountains of hard copy on call and demand instead that they interface with us in a conversational way, then we can get on with the business of making this world a far more congenial one. Who needs a system that can spit back absolutely detailed and accurate statistics and correlations of data in predigested form about a past that is by now virtually irrelevant, when what we want are systems that allow us to play on-line and in real time with relationships that exist *now*? We don't need ten-place precision! What we want is self-organizing models that update their structures continually and offer us a 4-bit dialogue in real or fast time so that we come to "feel" what the system is like. Our on-line involvement is crucial to our growth and to our knowledge of the current state of affairs and of the meanings of the events to follow.

I will also predict that there will be a gradual de-emphasis of the qualities of inclusion and precision in the writing of proposals or reports. Rather, a company will consider as its major salable asset the ability to adapt its services in a relevant way as conditions change. Artists' conceptions of the "city of the future" will show some cranes and torn-up streets and the urban designers will be asked to provide the means for making future changes more comfortable to effect. That is, the graphical presentation itself will show that the process of change has been taken into consideration. The areas of the social sciences should be the first to show a useful grasp of the principles of self-organization. Projects will be undertaken which start at high speed in many areas at once. They will have a clear, over-all purpose, but will be initially defocused as to the means for effecting that purpose. As a project progresses, there will be internal

[10] See Brodey [3].

shifts and refocusing of attention and effort onto those specific active parts that are showing the best promise for achievement of the original intent. In this manner, the resolution or clarity of the picture of social change will arise in the form of effective action taken rather than "statements of the problem."

Later the technique should become more pervasive in scope and will reach maximum fruition with the maturity of a generation of students who have been educated by a system that attends at all times to the relevance of the education to the individual. It could start now, and some attempts have been made, but their approaches are not sufficiently general and do not reach enough students on a continuing basis. Eventually they will, but it will be expensive, initially clumsy, and widely resisted except by the students themselves and their teachers. The principal focus should be upon ways to interface the systems with the student for the maximum of multi-sensory, multi-effector dialogue so that the system can learn enough about the student to model him and to teach him concepts in the contexts with which he is the most facile.[11]

A far brighter, more fascinating future lies in store for us in a "turned on" world if we can get around to developing it. Its major product will be our own participation in the events around us and it will require that our informational technologies provide us with a maximum of on-line facility.

[11] See Wiener [16].

References

1. Barron, R. L. "Self-Organizing and Learning Control Systems." In: H. L. Oestreicher and D. R. Moore (eds.), *Cybernetic Problems in Bionics*. New York, Gordon and Breach, 1968.

2. Bentley, A. F. *Inquiry into Inquiries: Essays in Social Theory*. Boston, Beacon Press, 1954.

3. Brodey, W. M. "Soft Architecture: The Design of Intelligent Environments," *Landscape*, vol. 7, no. 1 (Autumn 1967).

4. Gibson, J. J. *The Senses Considered as Perceptual Systems*. Boston, Houghton Mifflin, 1966.

5. Gurwitsch, A. *The Field of Consciousness*. Pittsburgh, Duquesne University Press, 1964.

6. Held, R. "Plasticity in Sensorimotor Systems," *Scientific American* (November 1965).

7. Hermann, H., and Kotelly, J. C. "An Approach to Formal Psychiatry," *Perspec. in Biol. and Med.* (Winter 1967).

8. Ittleson, W. H., and Cantril, H. "Perception: A Transactional Approach." In: S. W. Matson and A. Montagu (eds.), *The Human Dialogue.* Toronto, Free Press, 1967.

9. Johnson, A. R. "A Structural, Preconscious Piaget: Heed Without Habit," *Proc. Nat'l Electronics Conf.,* vol. 23 (1967).

10. Kilmer, W. L., McCulloch, W. S., and Blum, J. "Some Mechanisms for a Theory of the Reticular Formation." In: M. D. Mesarovic (ed.), *Systems Theory and Biology.* New York, Springer-Verlag, 1968.

11. Kotelly, J. C. "Survey of Concepts of Content." *NASA Report,* 1968.

12. MacKay, D. M. "On Comparing the Brain with Machines," *American Scientist,* vol. 42 (1954).

13. McCulloch, W. S. "Lekton." In: L. Thayer (ed.), *Communication: Theory and Research.* New York, Charles C. Thomas, 1967.

14. Pask, G. "My Prediction for 1984." *Prospect,* London, Hutchinson, 1962.

15. Storm, H. O. "Eolithism and Design," *Colorado Quarterly,* vol. 1, no. 3 (Winter 1953).

16. Wiener, N. *The Human Use of Human Beings: Cybernetics and Society.* Boston, Houghton Mifflin, 1950.

Section **2**

Management as a System

8

Management Information-decision Systems

G. W. Dickson

Business Horizons. Copyright, December 1968
by the Foundation for the School of Business, at
Indiana University. Reprinted by permission.

Management is on the verge of entering a new era. A new technology is being developed in order to cope with the problems of administering the monolithic and complex organizations that have emerged over the past decade. The vast business conglomerates—such as Litton Industries, Texas Instruments, or the giant diversified and decentralized firms found in the aerospace and electronic industries—are examples of organizations in which sheer size and complexity demand new managerial techniques. The Department of Defense (DoD), the National Aeronautics and Space Administration (NASA), state governmental offices, and large "multiversities" represent organizations in the public sector with similar management problems caused by some of the same organizational characteristics.

As the interfaces between the public and private sector increase in number, scope, and complexity, and organizations grow in size and diversity of goals and functions, the need for improved management techniques becomes acutely critical. "Operations research," "systems analysis," and "integrated data processing" have been developed in response to many of these needs. A new academic discipline, "management information-decision systems," is emerging to integrate these techniques and to provide the analytical frames of reference and the methodologies necessary to meet the new management requisites.

The purpose of this article is to attempt to define some of the characteristics of this new field, to raise some of the unsolved problems and issues, to explore briefly the current state of the art, and to identify some of the kinds of research being conducted and the kind of educational programs becoming available.

The System Defined

The emerging discipline of management information-decision systems views information as a resource parallel to land, labor, and capital. This resource, too, must be subject to managerial planning and control. The potential for progress from the management of information has only recently been recognized. McDonough, for example, notes: ". . . some 50 per cent of the costs of running our economy are information costs. No other field offers such concentrated room for improvement as does informational analysis, and yet it is only now that formal approaches are starting to appear."[1]

Perhaps the identification of the new discipline as a separate area can be traced to Leavitt and Whisler. These authors first described what they called "information technology" as composed of several parts:

> One includes techniques for processing large amounts of information rapidly, and it is epitomized by the high-speed computer. A second part centers around the application of statistical and mathematical methods to decision making problems; it is represented by techniques like mathematical programming, and by methodologies like operations research. A third part is in the offing, though its applications have not yet emerged very clearly; it consists of the simulation of higher-order thinking through computer programs.[2]

It is now possible to be somewhat more specific than Leavitt and Whisler were in 1958 and to add another level to the hierarchy because of recent technical developments and a change in the way of thinking about management information systems. This additional part emphasizes the interaction of man and machine in cooperative problem solving. Table 1 represents a restructuring of the Leavitt and

[1] A. M. McDonough, *Information Economics and Management Systems* (New York: McGraw-Hill Book Company, 1963), p.11.
[2] H. J. Leavitt and T. L. Whisler, "Management in the 1980's," *Harvard Business Review* p. 41, November-December 1958.

Table 1. The Hierarchy of Management Information-Decision Systems

Level	Area
1	Clerical systems
2	Information systems: Manual Mechanized
3	Decision systems: Independent Integrated
4	Interactive systems: Man-machine Man-man
5	Programmed systems

Whisler framework and is intended to depict a hierarchy within management information-decision systems. The levels within the hierarchy indicate the relative sophistication of the concepts that are employed.

Speaking functionally, management information-decision systems is a blend of organizational theory, accounting, statistics, mathematical modeling, and econometrics, together with exposure in depth to advanced computer hardware and software systems. This field is centered on expanding the horizons and integrating the decisions of organizations, both public and private, which must operate within the dynamics and functional demands imposed by their organizational size and degree of complexity. In order to more fully understand the content of this field and its implications, it is instructive to consider each level of the hierarchy shown in Table 1 in detail and to examine the current state of affairs in each subarea.

Clerical Systems

"Clerical systems" refers to the substitution of computer processing for manual record-keeping procedures. This level is totally analogous to Leavitt and Whisler's Part I. It is safe to say that most of the advances in the entire area of management information-decision systems have been on this level, and these advances are indeed impressive. Everyone is familiar with computerized payroll systems, dividend calculation systems, accounts payable systems, customer billing systems, and so forth. The important feature of these systems is that they are to a great extent routine and repetitive and readily lend themselves to computerization.

Almost any up-to-date progressive organization is employing computerized clerical systems and reaping the benefits of faster processing and the ability to deal with vast amounts of input data. One recent trend on this level has been toward on-line data input by the way of typewriter and teletype consoles. On-line teller systems and on-line insurance agent systems such as that of the Travelers Insurance Company are examples. The distinguishing characteristic of the clerical level is that the systems are oriented toward the processing of data rather than toward providing managers with decision-oriented information. When the orientation is toward providing information to be used in managerial decisions, the transition has been made from a clerical to an information system.

Information Systems

When a system provides information to be used in the managerial decision process, then it is a true information system. Few, if any, of this sort operate today, but a substantial effort is being made to develop systems that meet the definition. Perhaps the best way to identify these requisites is to say what the characteristics of an information system are not.

A true information system is not aimed at the processing of data as is a clerical system. Thus, payroll systems, accounts payable and receivable systems, and even many inventory systems, although computerized, are not information systems. Furthermore, an information system contains information, not data; the content of the system output is not a vast sea of numbers, but conveys a message to the decision maker.

A true information system contains only the information that is pertinent for making decisions and, in addition, presents it in a meaningful form and has it available at the correct time. Information from such systems obviously warns when managerial action is necessary and assists in deciding what action to take. The level of information systems thus refers to providing the correct input for the managerial decision process. Stated simply, it is providing accurate, timely, reliable, and valid information on which to base an effective management decision.

Note in Table 1 that two levels of information systems exist. The first is manual. Many firms or subunits of large firms have information which is produced manually rather than by computer. Too often the term "information system" automatically brings to mind extensive computer systems, but there is nothing in the philosophy of an information system that requires computer processing. There are those who advocate the point of view that many organizations would be better off with a few good manual information systems instead of misusing what is essentially a computerized clerical system by attempting to obtain information that the system does not provide. Of course, in many instances, because of problems of size and the necessity for rapid presentation, a computer system is required; such a case is indicated in Table 1 as a mechanized information system.

When one concentrates on assisting the decision process itself instead of simply providing the information, the next level of the hierarchy is reached—the decision system level.

Decision Systems

This part is characterized by the fact that it concentrates on the decision process rather than upon the inputs to the process. That is, procedures are presented to the decision maker that assist him in the way he makes his decision. At the previous level, no emphasis is placed upon how the decision is reached, but only upon the provision of the right information no matter what the process.

In recent years, considerable attention has been given to the subject of applying operations research or management science to organizational problems. Since these techniques and methodologies are focused upon expanding the decision horizons of the manager, operations research and similar approaches are an integral part of what has been identified as management information-decision systems. Typically, one hears only about management information systems, and one of the major points of this article is to point out that management information cannot be disassociated from management decisions. It is for this reason that, like information technology, the critical importance of treating management and information as being linked by the decision process is recognized.

Table 2 identifies some of the techniques that are available to assist in making certain management decisions; many have been highly developed within the last decade. In the table these tools are roughly divided into levels of sophistication and also into areas of application. There is considerable room for argument with regard to what is basic and what is advanced and also with respect to

Table 2. Techniques Available to Assist the Managerial Decision Process

Basic	Advanced
Economic and financial analysis:	Mathematical modeling:
Break-even analysis	*Deterministic*
Capital budgeting analysis	*Inventory theory*
Ratio analysis	*Stochastic*
Marginal analysis	*Queueing theory*
Incremental analysis	
Analysis for planning and control:	Resource allocation:
Time study, motion study, work sampling	*Transportation methods*
Learning curve analysis	*Assignment methods*
Forecasting techniques	*Mathematical programming*
Regression analysis	
Exponential smoothing	Cost-benefit analysis:
Statistical techniques	*Systems simulation*
Network analysis	

application areas. The reader should recognize that the classifications are imprecise and that obviously many of the tools have application in areas other than the one in which they are classified. The object of the table is simply to identify and illustrate the techniques.

Finally, it should be noted that decision systems is divided in Table 1 into two parts, independent and integrated. An integrated decision system would be one in which the decision technique is directly coupled to the information system. A simulation model, for example, would manipulate information provided by a "data" (information) base in investigating decision alternatives without the discoupling that is characteristic of independent systems. In the latter case, the inputs required by the simulation analysis are unavailable in the correct form, and considerable massaging of existing data must be performed before the simulation can take place.

Interactive Systems

One level of the field of management information-decision systems is seldom identified, and yet it is the area which is the most exciting and where recent technical developments have occurred that will have far-reaching consequences. This area concentrates on the development of cybernated (man-machine) interactive information-decision systems in which the manager and the information system are coupled together into a problem-solving network. Two thrusts of activity are identifiable on this level. The first is shown in Table 1 as the man-machine type of interactive system.

A man-machine interactive system is one in which the decision maker is coupled to the information system by means of a remote console such as a typewriter, teletypewriter (TTY), or cathode ray tube (CRT) terminal. Through such a system, the decision maker may ask for information upon which to base a management decision or, if the system is integrated, he may even simulate the consequences of alternative courses of action.

A second type of interactive system is increasingly used, but is seldom recognized as a type of management information-decision system—perhaps because it is more a philosophy than an entity. In such a system, a man (the decision maker) interacts with other men (the staff information specialists) in a problem-solving network. The decision maker states the problem as he sees it. Then the information system specialists assist in additional problem definition and finally present the decision maker with alternatives and options, together with quantitative measures of the consequences of each. The best example of such a system is the one that existed between 1961 and mid-1968 at the Pentagon. Here the decision maker, Secretary of Defense McNamara, posed the problems, and the group known as systems analysis acted to provide decision alternatives and an analysis of each. The systems analysts, of course, are highly trained (over fifty have Ph. D.'s), broad-gauged technical persons each having an academic specialty such as econometrics, mathematics, or management science.

Although the DoD experience is best known, a definite trend toward the use of similar high level information-decision specialists in all types of organizations is becoming evident. Even many medium-sized firms are beginning to hire employees to worry about designing the systems to provide managerial information and to assist managers in making decisions where the quantitative techniques have application.

In many instances, of course, the staff specialist will employ a machine-based information-decision system in his analysis of the problem given him. In such cases, a man-man-machine system can be said to exist. The important thing is to recognize the interactive philosophy. In other words, the man uses the system to investigate many aspects of a complex problem. He may get a response from the system that changes the nature of his question. He then restates the question and again queries the system. Thus, he iterates toward a solution, and a true interactive system exists.

Note that on this level, as well as the previous ones, the decision still rests with the person referred to as the decision maker. On the highest level, this is no longer true.

Programmed Systems

When the decision discretion is removed from the human decision maker and turned over to the information-decision system, the system is of the programmed type. Leavitt and Whisler identify this area of activity as their Part 3. Most activity on this level is research. Two doctoral dissertations, for example, have dealt with the construction of computer models in which the system was actually capable of "making" a decision. Clarkson's model replicated the decision of a bank's trust officer selecting stock portfolios for customers with varied objectives.[3] My model simulates the decision of industrial purchasing agents selecting a supplier from among a number of potential vendors.[4]

Few programmed decisions actually exist in ongoing organizations. Inventory control systems, which have automatic order quantity determination and computer order placement, are primitive programmed systems utilizing built-in decision rules. Since so much of the activity at the programmed level is research oriented, this subtopic will not be discussed further in this article.

Problems and Issues

Because management information-decision systems is in its early stages of development, many problems exist and issues remain on which the managerial implications are by no means clear. Perhaps the most basic problem is noticeable in the previous discussion: a clear definition of management information-decision systems is still under development, and the content of the field is still subject to question. As work goes on and our sophistication and understanding increase, this problem undoubtedly will be solved. However, a number of other

[3] G. P. E. Clarkson, *Portfolio Selection: a Simulation of Trust Investment* (Englewood Cliffs, N. J.: Prentice-Hall Inc., 1962).
[4] G. W. Dickson, "A Simulation Model of Vendor Selection Decision," in E. Weber and G. Peters (eds.), *Management Behavior: Models of Administrative Decisions* (New York: International Textbook Co., forthcoming).

problems can be identified, many of them resulting from the fact that the field is still in its infancy. Before management information-decision systems as an approach or philosophy can truly contribute to universal organizational effectiveness, these problems must be solved and several issues must be faced.

Some Problems Identified

Many of the existing management information-decision systems problems are suggested by the following statements with regard to the use of computers and associated techniques as aids to the management process.

> Many companies today are faced with serious problems in utilizing the capabilities of computers. Computers are not being used effectively in providing management with the best information available for decision making; they are not being used efficiently in terms of properly integrating the various information systems. Moreover, the situation appears to be getting worse rather than better.[5]

> Substantial investments have been made at many companies in the hope of securing better procedures for handling operating information. This has been true particularly in the past ten years during which electronic data-processing equipment has been available. But the progress toward better information systems has been disappointing at a number of companies.[6]

> Automatic data processing (ADP) has certainly arrived. But somehow it has not produced changes of the order of magnitude that we who have pioneered in the field expected.[7]

The Management Information Crisis This problem is one of the more specific ones. As was pointed out in the previous section, managers are deluged with numbers (data), but little managerial information is provided with existing systems. Little is really known about the relationship between the effectiveness of management

[5] J. Dearden, "How to Organize Information Systems," *Harvard Business Review* p. 65, March-April 1965.
[6] P. H. Thurston, "Who Should Control Information Systems," *Harvard Business Review* p. 135, November-December 1962.
[7] J. Diebold, "ADP—the Still Sleeping Giant," *Harvard Business Review* p. 60, September-October 1964.

decisions and the information used to make them. Precisely, no one knows what the content of the information system should be, the form in which information should be presented to the decision maker, the media through which information should be presented, or what the time availability of information should be.

Thus, an opportunity for research exists in the area of determining how to use the computer to assist management decision making and how to integrate quantitative decision systems with organizational information systems.

The Management of Information Systems   One of the bases of managerial decentralization is that an information system exists to provide coordination among the decentralized units and to control the performance of these units according to standards. To see what can happen in a decentralized organization when a system of this sort is not working properly, one has but to consider the disaster that befell the General Dynamics Corporation in their Convair 880 and 990 jet transport program.[8]

Other than through such empirical evidence, however, no one understands exactly how a firm's information system optimally fits into the organization structure. Should the information system be centralized? Decentralized? Or perhaps a combination of these approaches should be employed?

Another great problem of a similar sort involves the economic evaluation of an information system. Other than a few vague, nonoperational approaches, there is no way to evaluate the information provided by the system in relation to the cost of system development and operation.

People and Systems   Another gap in the knowledge relative to management information-decision systems concerns the way people react when they are part of such a system. In order to realize the technical advantages of management information systems, the dysfunctional behavior of people associated with the system should be minimized. Such behavior may run the gamut from ignoring the informational output to outright sabotage of physical components such as data recorders. The manner in which management information systems are introduced to an organization is obviously of critical importance to its acceptance, but again guidelines are absent to a large extent. Since all three levels of management information-decision systems under discussion here

[8] For an account of this interesting tale, see R. A. Smith, *Corporations in Crisis* (Garden City, N. Y.: Doubleday & Company, Inc., 1963).

involve people as a component, knowledge of their behavior as a part of the system is important to the success of the entire field.

Automation, Cybernation, and Society   Automation is the substitution of machine control for human control in a system. Cybernation is a term that has been applied to "office automation," but can also be used to apply to the combination of human beings and machines (computers) as a part of a decision-making network. The effects of automation on society, such as unemployment and increased leisure time, have been the subject of considerable discussion. Similar problems associated with cybernation must also be studied. Additional problems involving the increased educational requirements of a cybernated society and the dangers of an "information elite" should also be considered. Here is an entire area that must be given thought and subjected to research if we are to achieve the maximum societal benefit of organizational management information-decision systems.

Other Issues

In addition to actual problem areas like those identified above (and obviously many more), a great number of what might be called issues must be faced and resolved by those wishing to see management information-decision systems recognized as a tool for increased organizational efficiency. Some of these issues are suggested by the following questions:

How will (and should) computer-assisted management, integrated with the use of quantitative decision aids, affect the structure of organizations?

Using these systems, what will be the content of the manager's job, and what training and experience will (and should) he have?

What will (and should) the relationship be between the general manager and the so-called "whiz kids" (the information systems specialists)?

In general, it can be concluded that the area offers a vast range of opportunity for research on how computers and decision aids ought to be used to assist the management process. On this point there is support for the contention that an academic field exists, but something must be done to make order out of chaos and to provide normative guides for action to replace the current practice of "keeping up with the Joneses."

Despite the rather unsettled situation, much progress has been made and more is on the immediate horizon. To demonstrate these conclusions, one has but to examine the existing state of the management information-decision systems art.

The State of the Art

During the past ten years or so, much routine clerical work has been turned over to computers by large, medium, and even small organizations. Today clerical functions are synonymous with computer processing. Because of their widespread use and wide acceptance, clerical systems as a part of the field of management information-decision systems do not require additional discussion. At the other end of the continuum, programmed systems have likewise been excluded from further discussion for the opposite reason; developments in this area are research oriented and almost totally lacking in practice. The middle parts—information systems, decision systems, and interactive systems—do merit treatment because "this is where the action is."

Much of the action is on the information system level, where technological developments are making it easier to provide management-oriented systems. Here are two examples:

A large milling company has developed an information system to analyze cost-volume relationships as well as to provide other financial information in a decision-making form as opposed to a traditional accounting report form.

A totally integrated wood-products producer has an information system that will provide managers with order information of any stage—from order receipt to payment for the finished product.

Many recent occurrences, such as the development of third generation computer equipment and advanced problem-oriented computer languages such as COBOL and GIS, are making it easier to build management information systems. More of the burden is being placed on the computer and less on the programmer so that more attention is being paid to the problem—getting *information to* the decision maker.

On the decision systems level, an increasing use of operations research, systems analysis, and the like is continuing. Most exciting on this level, however, is the development of integrated decision systems. For example:

A computer manufacturer has developed a system for managing the inventory of fashion goods. The system is integrated because it uses a quantitative technique, statistical decision theory, coupled with a computerized data base for assisting inventory decisions. The system will, for example, tell a department manager early in the life of a style whether reordering is necessary because it is a hot seller, or whether to mark down the price and sell out because the item will not sell.

Another computer manufacturer has also integrated quantitative techniques with a data base for use in estimating its computer market by type and buyer.

It is on the interactive level that developments are being made that have the most far-reaching implications for the management process. Hardware developments, such as random access storage and remote CRT and TTY terminals, coupled with software improvements (like time sharing and multiprocessing) and communications breakthroughs (like microwave, microfilm, and optical scanning) may revolutionize management by making possible man-machine management systems.

Even today many managers are coupled to information systems or even information-decisions systems by means of remote terminals:

A major food producer has a "war room" in which corporate officers meet regularly to model their decisions by means of a time-sharing terminal.

In the same company a product manager can get inventory decision information by means of a remote console.

A major computer manufacturer has developed a system whereby sales personnel can get national marketing information on a CRT display.

In a large hospital, a doctor can check in, check a patient status, and order patient tests or medications simply by touching *the face of a CRT display.*

It is safe to say that we are just beginning to understand the ways the computer can be used to assist in the managerial decision process, either by providing better information or by expanding the decision horizons by using quantitative techniques—or both. Thus, though it is clear that progress has been made, it is also clear that much remains to be done, especially in terms of integrating existing knowledge and techniques and in doing research to develop new understanding and methods. It is legitimate, therefore, to ask what lies ahead.

A Look to the Future

With new developments in computer hardware and software and with new quantitative decision models, together with increased experience in applying these tools to the management process, a new sophistication on the part of managers of the future can be expected. Much of this development will, of course, come through trial and error. Just as important is the fact that academicians are becoming aware that a new discipline exists, and this group is beginning to assume its role in doing research and in training persons to operate in the field of management information-decision systems.

One major university, for example, has created a Management Information Systems Research Center to tackle many of the problems and issues.

New M.S. and Ph.D. majors are in the offing in the area of management information systems (MIS). Thus MIS will be taking a place alongside management, accounting, marketing, production, and so on as a recognized field of study. Undoubtedly, many schools associated with the organizational process will soon be offering work in MIS.

In view of the research and training activity of the universities, coupled with increased application of and experience in management information-decision systems by organizations, it is logical to assume that notable developments in this field will be forthcoming. With such experience, research, and training reinforcing each other, one can expect that the associated techniques and concepts will cope with the current and future demands of organizations.

9

Behavioral Science, Systems Analysis, and the Failure of Top Management *

William H. Gruber

Reprinted by permission of *The Industrial Management Review,* Fall 1967.

Introduction

During the last decade there has been a significant increase in the resources available to high-level managers. New techniques and better trained professional personnel have become available to assist executives in achieving the objectives of their companies. Studies of the utilization of the new managerial resources have begun to appear,

*This paper is based upon a seminar given by the author at the Fourth IBM Personnel Research Conference, January 11, 1967. The discussion at the Conference was of great assistance in the writing of this paper. The concepts developed in this paper represent a merger of the contributions received from two sets of colleagues. The organization facet of work was assisted by my work with three psychologists: Donald Marquis, George Farris and David Sirota. The systems input owes much to the work of Arnold Amstutz, James Emery and Edward Roberts. All errors in the integration of these two disciplines are the sole responsibility of the author. Leo Moore's work on the management of change in corporations was a third source of ideas for this paper. A grant from the M.I.T. Center for Space Research (funded by NASA grant NsG 496) provided time for research. This financial support and the assistance of my colleagues are warmly acknowledged.

such as *The Impact of Computers on Management*,[1] and there are now available textbooks such as *Systems Analysis: A Diagnostic Approach.*[2] The increase in the supply of econometricians, operations researchers and psychologists and the improved quality of graduates from schools of business have provided top managers with a new kind of assistance that is of very recent origin.

Competitive pressure has increased, however, as a result of (1) these new tools available to managers, (2) the increase in foreign competition[3] and (3) the greater competition between materials as reported recently by the President's 1965 Council of Economic Advisors. The pressure for managerial effectiveness has been increased further by the actions of the United States government to hold down prices[4] as well as to direct the attention of executives to a "public interest" that may, at least in the short run, have an adverse effect upon a company's performance (as when the government sets safety standards that are not in popular demand). Thus, we have a set of forces that make it necessary for top managers to improve their performance, and we have a set of new tools to help them to manage more effectively.

One might expect that the availability of these new tools would have altered significantly the manner in which top executives make decisions and manage their operations. There appears to have been a negligible change to date. Charnes and Cooper[5] compared Thucydides' *History of the Peloponnesian War* and Eisenhower's *Crusade in Europe* and were able to find that there was little difference between observations on organizational practice and problems, despite the fact that nearly 2500 years separated the authors.

Klahr and Leavitt concluded after reviewing the uses of computer that ". . . it seems clear that top managers' jobs have not been much affected by computers, although many lower-level routine jobs have."[6]

Mason Haire, in a review of the work of behavioral scientists, sadly noted: "When I say the contribution of the behavioral sciences to management has been disappointingly small, I mean this: in the past 15 years there have been perhaps 150 books and 1,500 articles

---

[1] See [21].
[2] See [12].
[3] See [23].
[4] See [6].
[5] See [7].
[6] See [15], p. 108.

written on the subject. And yet the practice of management remains almost the same. To be sure, managerial vocabulary has changed. The well-rounded manager now speaks of T-groups, cognitive dissonance and role conflicts, but he does just about the same things he's always done."[7]

The reasons for the small contribution to top management from the staffs of psychologists, economists, and operations researchers that have been added to the overhead expenses of corporations will now be analyzed.

The Training and Work of Professional Staffs in Corporations

The work of management scientists (psychologists, sociologists, economists, operations researchers) in corporations is a relatively new phenomenon. In the area of organization research, social scientists have been engaged in attempts to improve performance of the personnel (white-collar and blue-collar; high-level and low-level) working in corporation. Some examples of this kind of work are attitude surveys, managerial appraisal and development, research on the relationship between worker satisfaction and productivity, and organizational development work. By definition, the focus of the organization research staff involves the company employees.

Economists and operations researchers, through the use of systems analysis, attempt to provide the information needed for corporate decisions. "Systems analysis" is a staff activity of even more recent origin than "organization research"; it is so recent that this functional staff group does not exist in many corporations. Ford is one corporation that does have an effective systems analysis capability. The work of this group has been described as the "continuous evaluation of Ford's costs, prices and profits, long-term planning for major capital investments and the far-out world of mathematical simulation."[8] It is interesting to note that the systems analysis group at Ford is part of the financial staff, while the organization research staff is usually associated with the personnel or labor relations staff functions.

The lack of interaction between the organization research and the systems analysis staff may be a major reason why the contribution to top management of these two staff groups has been retarded. We have one set of scientists who work with people in such

[7] See [10], p. 110.
[8] See [14], p. f–13.

activities as attitude perception surveys, and another set of scientists who work with economic data such as sales, profits and rates of return. Though the ultimate purpose of trying to understand the data on people is to improve the economic functioning of the corporation, those who work with the human factor have almost completely neglected the economic and financial consequences of their findings.[9] The scientists who measure the economic output of the system have an inadequate understanding of the human input that generates the output. This situation shows a grave lack of communication between two groups, both of which should perform functions vital to the welfare of a corporation but neither of which can see more than half of the picture. This has reduced the contribution that these two staff groups make. This disparity between the actual and potential contribution of the new professional staffs within corporations is too serious to continue indefinitely.[10]

It is important to note that this disparity continues because of the failure of top management to recognize the contribution available from these two staff groups. If part of a system is not functioning properly, it is the responsibility of a higher level manager to step in and correct the problem.

Cooperation and Coordination

Mason Haire has tried to answer the question, "Why have the social sciences contributed so little to the practice of management?" He has suggested that too little *developmental research*, based upon the recognized needs of corporate management, is performed.[11] The work of the new behavioral science–systems analysis (BSSA) staffs is

[9] The reader who doubts this observation is invited to attempt a frequency count of articles written by organization researchers who present empirical evidence relating attitudes, laboratory training and the other interests of their trade with measures of economic performance such as change in profits or rate of return on investment. David McClelland (see [17]) has analyzed acutely the propensity of professionals trained with one focus to contribute in terms of that focus, and to neglect a problem that requires another perspective that is not in harmony with their professional training or values.

[10] In addition to the powerful forces leading to change that have been enumerated, there is evidence from within the community of professionally trained social and managerial scientists that an awareness of the problem is developing. For examples of ferment within the ranks, see [2] and [10].

[11] See [11], p. 3.

too much science, not enough technology. The work has not been integrated in a meaningful way and remains dormant in bits and pieces. "Development" research has the connotation of work that leads to a product to be used. Random findings will not solve the needs of top management. The BSSA staffs should have precise responsibilities with performance expectations well defined by top management. And only top management can create the internal mechanisms for the self-analysis that will lead to improvement of management. Resources are now lacking for: (1) the collection and evaluation of critical systems information; and (2) the development of procedures for the testing and diffusion of managerial innovations.

Given the need for better performance and the new tools that are available, top management has the responsibility for creating a system internal to the firm for the self-analysis and improvement of managerial practices. To achieve this capability, it will be necessary for top management to:

1. *Facilitate the shift of interest of traditionally trained social scientists away from their professional disciplines and toward the problems of management.*
2. *Provide a means of identifying the problems that require the attention of social and management scientists, and permit a more rational allocation of BSSA resources.*
3. *Integrate the research findings of the various BSSA specializations by using models that link the research findings, thus better enabling the BSSA efforts to be applied to management practice.*
4. *Increase the communication between men who understand the human resources in an operation (the organization research people) and the men who know how to keep score with the financial information of operations (the systems analysts).*
5. *Provide a staff capability that has enough potential contribution to managerial performance to warrant the attention of top management.*

The Behavioral Science–Systems Analyses (BSSA) Relationship: A Definition

Whenever anyone uses the word "systems" today, he must be prepared to define terms, because a wide range of meanings has been used in connection with the word. The definition we use is not a generally accepted one because there is probably no definition available that is inclusive enough to contain all the meanings that are used. Ours is a functional definition of the systems perspective, which we propose to be the natural center for the work of organizational research.

Assume that there are people in a box. They produce output, and they are motivated by rewards, punishments, instructions and standards. This idea is presented in Figure 1 and is a first approximation to what we call the systems approach to organization research. This is a simple system with one output, information inputs from top management, some unseen factors, and a feedback loop to top management. This is a first approximation to the model that will be expanded later, and it is used here to develop an awareness of what we mean by a system. It is useful to integrate the BSSA components of the model. The link between the behavioral facets and systems information is critical. Failure to establish this integration between the behavioral and systems components of the total BSSA function has been a major weakness in the traditional efforts in corporations.

Note that there is information going into the box in the form of rewards and instructions. Each bit of input information has a behavioral and a systems component. This information is processed somehow within the box, and the output that appears also has behavioral and systems content. By definition, a system has, as we show here, interrelationships and a feedback mechanism.[12]

Systems are hierarchical in nature. It is possible to conceive of the flow of information and the organizational effects of actions by top managers as taking place along a series of action nodes, as in Figure 2. One of the major contributions of BSSA in a corporation is to break the pattern shown in Figure 2 in order to give top management contact with lower levels of activity. Thus some of the

---

[12] "Systems watching" is a game with marvelous entertainment potential and those of us who play this game are often surprised at the blindness of those in power who seem not to understand the system. An interesting example of a situation that may fool the untrained observer is the fact that a poorly functioning system may appear not to have a feedback mechanism. This does not mean that a feedback system is not present. The people who take advantage of the fact that there is no feedback system to top management are receiving feedback. Feedback to top management may come in a discontinuous manner that is sometimes called a crisis. The quality of the feedback system is perhaps one of the most useful tests of the efficiency of an operational system.

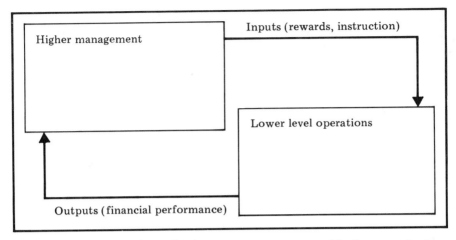

Figure 1.   A simple information input-output systems model of an organization.

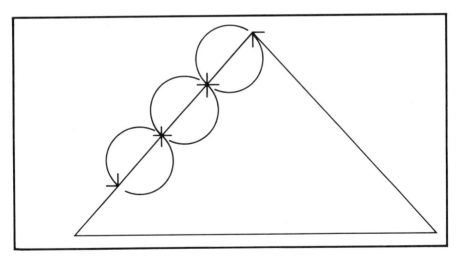

Figure 2.   A simple information flow systems model with hierarchial relationships.

distortions inherent in this kind of filtering process may be
eliminated.

From this background information we may outline the stages of
a systems approach:

1. *Identify the organization to be studied (establish
boundary conditions).*

2. *Determine the goals of this organization.*
3. *Seek key activities that occur in the effort to fulfill the organizational goals.*
4. *Examine the activity for sets of relationships and patterns of behavior or action.*
5. *Begin simulation or other forms of modeling at this stage.*
6. *Test first results and adapt the BSSA effort.*

A major advantage of a systems perspective is that it leads to analysis of the total organization; a view of the total system permits an evaluation that can provide for the best allocation of resources for the BSSA effort. The work should be adaptive and each step will require an adjustment of the prior conceptions of the total system.

The Involvement of Top Management

Managerial style and the organizational tone are set by the top management of a corporation. Since it is this group that sets goals, evaluates progress and applies pressure or gives rewards in a corporation, it is vital that the higher levels of management be involved closely with the BSSA effort. The participation of top management in BSSA will increase the effectiveness of the BSSA effort because:

1. *Progress toward better corporate management begins at the top.*
2. *The performance of top management contributes the most to the fulfillment of corporation goals. The BSSA will result in improved corporate performance to the extent that top managerial decisions utilize the BSSA efforts.*
3. *Many of the findings or procedures developed for top management will be applicable to lower level management.*
4. *Findings first developed with the participation of top management are more readily diffused throughout the corporation.*

Some schools of organization research have developed the idea that when *lower level* people participate together with their superiors in decision making that involves their work, they become involved and their contribution to corporate goals is increased (for example, the "theory Y" approach of Douglas McGregor[13]). In our case, participation of *top* management is necessary in order to improve the performance of top management. And the work of lower level people also will be improved as a direct result of the improved performance of top management; our concern is to increase the effectiveness of the personnel in the whole corporation, including those who control it.

The proposition that top management should recognize the value of the BSSA function and participate actively in its activities is based on the hypothesis that such involvement is necessary for the realization of the potential contribution that this effort can make to the management of a corporation. The basis for this proposition should become evident when we examine (1) the functions of top management and (2) the need for better veridical perception by top management, a need that the organization research–systems analysis effort can help to meet.

The Functions of Top Management

If a systems focus must begin at the level of top management, it is necessary to specify the inputs from this source. Although the nature of the contribution that top management makes to a corporation is very complex and subject to investigation, we will use the following list as a first approximation:

1. *Selection of corporate goals such as rate of growth in profits and sales.*
2. *Implementation of some of the corporate goals through personal actions such as negotiation of acquisitions.*
3. *Action on critical decisions such as corporate debt policy, consideration of major innovations in marketing or product development.*
4. *Attempts to attain good performance from lower levels in the corporation.*

One way of viewing the function of top management is shown in Figure 3. At any given point in time top management faces an environment that offers opportunities such as markets and constraints such as competition. Top management has a set of resources at its command which, based upon environment and resources, sets

[13] See [18].

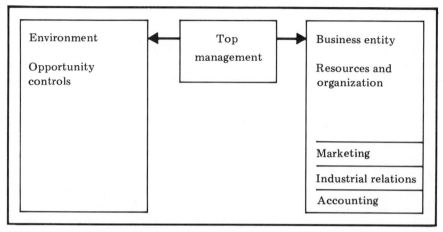

Figure 3.   The position of top management linking the resources of a firm to the external environment.

high level corporate goals and strategies.[14]   It is impossible for the BSSA group to work on a model for the fulfillment of the corporate goals unless these goals have been defined. Tradeoffs between goals, and the willingness to accept risk or to increase pressure on subordinates are examples of the inputs that must be specified through the participation of top management

The work of the BSSA group will only begin at the top management level; much effort (in terms of units of research input) will also take place at lower levels in the organization. A corporation of any size is not one system, but a set of subsystems that are often only remotely related. The whole process of decentralization and the development of profit centers is an attempt to factor down a total system into relatively independent subsystems.[15]   Then the subsystem—an operating division, for instance—is again factored down into a set of more related subsystems. Each major subsystem has an interface relationship with top management, and with the rest of the corporation. A subsystem has its own top management—thus it and the total corporation may be examined in like manner. This situation is presented in Figure 4.

[14] This is somewhat too rational and does not consider the values of top management, which vary between the managements of companies and even within the top management groups in a given company. It is therefore necessary to take the personal values of top management as an input.
[15] The trend toward decentralization has resulted in operating divisions that are large enough in size to justify calling the presidents or operating managers of such divisions "top management."

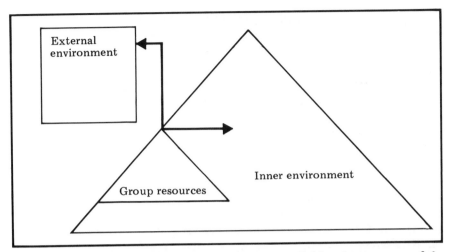

Figure 4.   The position of group top management, linking the resources of the group to the external environment and to the inner environment provided by the larger organization.

The position of a division top management may be represented by an input-output model like the one that was presented in Figure 1. Much of the work of the BSSA effort at the corporate level would be devoted to the evaluation of the division subsystems—total system relationship. The work of the BSSA effort at the division level would be to evaluate the functioning of the division subsystems. Note, however, that considerable attention would also be devoted to the interface between the subsystem and the total system. The input of a set of rewards, punishments, standards, and instructions from corporate top management is of critical importance to the operations of a subsystem.

The Importance of Veridical Perception

Veridical perception in this case is the accuracy with which top management seeks and obtains information about its environment, its resources, and the functioning of its organization.[16] Information, as we can easily see, is the central element of systems analysis. A major reason for the establishment of a BSSA capability is to improve the veridical perception of top management. Since this is a major reason for the existence of the effort, it is difficult to conceive of success here without the active participation of top management.

[16] See [24].

The exercise of working in a BSSA of a corporation is itself a valuable activity and is helpful in improving veridical perception. This idea was expressed by a top executive involved in a marketing simulation: "Even if there are significant errors in prediction, it is worth the expense because of the way it makes people think."[17] The effect it has on the thinking of top management, the usefulness of a systems model for improved veridical perception, and the criticial importance of information in this whole sphere of activity cannot be overestimated.

Development Work in BSSA

We are now ready to examine the BSSA group whose function will be to do the developmental work for improved corporate performance. A first observation is that once a set of relationships, filters, perceptual barriers to understanding and communication, and the sources of inputs and outputs has been specified, it becomes possible to develop an integrated research program to study the functioning of the system. This kind of systems approach is adaptive, and the system will be altered as better managerial understanding is developed because of the research effort.

When top management sits down with the manager of the BSSA function and studies the boundary conditions of a preliminary model, a list will be made to specify the relationships that are to be studied and the information that is to be gathered. Top management will be forced to think about the expectations from operations and the quality and usefulness of the feedback that top management has been receiving. What is the level of agreement between performance and the rewards, punishments, standards, and instructions given by management? How accurately do lower level people in the box seem to understand the information inputs from higher level management? Is there harmony between the understanding of the performance/ standards ratio as seen by various levels in the organization? How do any differences in this understanding affect the response of the operating personnel to the rewards/performance ratio?

The findings described by Lawrence Ferguson[18] may help to illustrate the nature of this development work. In a study of

---

[17] See [4], p. 45.
[18] See [8].

managerial career patterns, he found that out of a population of managers ranked by performance after five years of service, 83 per cent of the managers who ranked in the top ten per cent had left the company by the end of 20 years of service while only 43 per cent of the managers ranked in the bottom 50 per cent had left the company. This is the kind of information that should be generated in order to develop the veridical perception needed by top management.

If Ferguson had been working with the close participation of top management on a long-range development program to complete a detailed model of a firm, his finding could have been related to such other systems information as (1) the relationship between salary level and managerial performance; (2) the speed with which managers with high potential are recognized; (3) the reward structure for management development (in other words, does it pay managers to hide good men in order to keep them for their own operations[19]) and (4) the communication channel upward for new ideas and the degree of facility with which the organization is able to accept innovation. One would expect that Ferguson's finding would be relevant to all these other questions.

Just as there are now procedures for checking out physical systems, in time, the art of improving the veridical perception of managers will become a science, and there will be a set of BSSA programs for checking on the health of an organization. Some of these will be in real time or continuous; others will be in the form of an annual physical; and still others will be ad hoc problem solving procedures designed to cope with specific situations. The program we have just described is one that can be seen to improve over time. The improvement occurs because of the learning curve produced when feedback from the work of the BSSA effort is utilized. Each stage of work in the development of a systems understanding of an organization leads to the next stage of analysis.

Just as a total system is factored into subsystems for analysis, the development work done by the BSSA group will be factored into stages of effort and fields of specialization. The systems perspective first permits this factoring of activity to be divided into manageable units, and then allows for the accumulation and integration of the research findings that result from this development work. The activity of the BSSA group will take place more at the development level, once our suggested proposals have been implemented.

[19] See [3].

Diffusion of Findings

In production, product development and marketing, firms are often aware of what other firms are doing, and there have been any number of imitation studies.[20] If an improved technique is introduced in one company, it is possible to calculate the loss of competitive position that would result if it were not introduced by other companies, and the acceptance of the new technique usually follows. The recent studies of the lag by U.S. steel firms in introducing the basic oxygen furnace are examples of this kind of analysis.[21] Diffusion of more efficient techniques, and the calculation of the financial returns that occur as a result of such innovations, are activities vital to any organization—but there has been a surprising absence of this kind of study in the field of organization research.

In the literature of organization research and systems analysis, there now exist many research findings that have been very poorly diffused. How many firms have applied the methodology suggested by Ferguson to determine their success in keeping good managers? What organizational procedure exists in most firms to integrate the findings of social scientists over time and to apply these findings in managerial practice? A review of the literature uncovers numerous research findings. Vroom,[22] for example, gives a report of Bingham's work in 1932 in which it was discovered that there was a marked increase in performance when a measuring device was made available to keep visible score of the work of physical laborers. How many firms have tested such a finding and, if validated, how many have applied it in locations where similar work was involved? How many firms have used the findings of Meyer, Kay, and French[23] and altered their performance appraisal procedures to achieve the increases in improvement reported in that study? How many of the firms that did alter their appraisal procedures as a result of the Meyer, Kay, and French findings also utilized control groups and other methods of verifying through their own experience that these findings were generally applicable and not merely a set of findings resulting from errors not caught in the research methodology that was utilized?

[20] See [19] and [20].
[21] See [1].
[22] See [26].
[23] See [21].

David Sirota[24] has reported the experience of an IBM plant where blue-collar productivity was raised through the utilization of a reward system based upon improvement over a worker's past performance instead of the more traditional use of engineering standards. His discussion of the contribution of blue-collar employees in methods improvement is very much in harmony with other findings.[25] How many firms have developed a formal prodecure for intracompany diffusion after a managerial innovation in one part of the firm has been made and found to be effective? How quickly will Sirota's findings on the success of one IBM plant be utilized in, say, the majority of IBM's operations? How many firms that do apply Sirota's findings also have a system of evaluation to assess the improvement resulting from the adoption of his recommendation?

Researchers in the field of technology[26] report that innovation (the adoption of inventions) is more costly and involves greater risk than invention, and this is probably also true in the field of organization research. If this is the case, what procedures have been developed to protect a corporation from introducing an imperfect invention from the field of organization research or systems analysis? Some of these questions have been raised by Ferguson[27] and Haire,[28] but because (1) a systems perspective capability has not been part of the organization research function, (2) organization research people do not attempt to develop measures of their contribution to the financial performance of corporations, (3) top managers have not participated in this work[29] and (4) the whole focus of organization research has been at a low level within the corporation, the suggestions of Ferguson, Haire and others have gone largely unheeded. The set of forces and facilitating factors discussed in this paper will help bring about the practical implementation of this new BSSA capacity, whose purpose, as we have seen, is to improve this situation by concentrating on the creation of an improvement process within the corporation.

[24] See [25].
[25] See [16] and [18].
[26] See, for example, [20].
[27] See [9].
[28] See [11].
[29] If this assertion were not accurate, more affirmative answers could have been given to the previous set of questions about procedures for the implementation of organization research findings within corporations.

Information, Understanding and the Education of Managers

Collecting and analyzing information and developing an understanding of a system will be only the first stages of the work of the BSSA function. Successful systems development *requires* the cooperation of the managers involved in the operations that are being studied. BSSA effort is not one short, quick look at a problem.[30] It is a continuing program that provides adaptive models that reflect the actual operations better as the models are tested and altered by experience in their utilization.

The BSSA function should be as involved with the education of management as it is with its work on the analysis of operations. The resulting improvement of operations will be the product of a *cooperative effort;* success, measured by progress toward specified organizational goals, will be a result of the ability of line management to work with the new BSSA professional staff function. As new managerial techniques are developed with increasing rapidity, the *educational* facet of the work of the BSSA staff will be of great importance in the diffusion of new knowledge. The combination of an analysis function with an education responsibility should result in better communication between the managers and the BSSA staff. The success of this new staff will depend as much on the ability to educate as it will on the ability to analyze and develop a systems understanding of an operation.

A commitment to understanding and improving the operations of a corporation or of an operating division is necessary to utilize the BSSA function successfuly. Corporate self-analysis on a continuing basis requires that managers at all levels be willing to continue their education, to improve their managerial capabilities, and to increase their understanding of the operations for which they are responsible. The development of a BSSA capability also creates the ability and commitment to measure and evaluate the progress of the operating divisions.

The present economy, with its rapid change and intense competition, requires precisely this commitment to improvement and attainment of rapid rates of progress. The development within corporations of a BSSA function requires more than the needs and facilitating conditions; the commitment of top management is also necessary. A crisis is one way to gain an understanding of what is

---

[30] See [5] and [13] for examples of the problems resulting from the traditional training and relationships that professional management science people tend to have.

needed. One would expect, however, that top management will prefer to build an evaluation function into the corporate system through the use of BSSA activities as described in this paper.

References

1. Adams, W. and Dirlam, J. "Big Steel, Invention and Innovation," *The Quarterly Journal of Economics,* LXXX, *2* (May, 1966), 167–189.

2. Albrook, R. C. "Participative Management: Time for a Second Look," *Fortune,* May, 1967, pp. 166–167 ff.

3. Alfred, T. M. "Checkers or Choice in Manpower Management," *Harvard Business Review,* January-February, 1967, pp. 157–169.

4. Amstutz, A. E. and Claycamp, H. "Simulation Techniques in the Analysis of Marketing Strategy," Alfred P. Sloan School of Management Working Paper No. 208-66, July, 1966.

5. Beged-Dov, A. G. "Why Only Few Researchers Manage," *Management Science,* XII, *12* (August, 1966), B-580-593.

6. Burns, A. F. "Wages and Prices by Formula?" *Harvard Business Review,* March-April, 1965, pp. 55–64.

7. Charnes, A. and Cooper, W. W. "Management Science and Managing," *The Quarterly Review of Economics and Business,* May, 1962, pp. 7–19.

8. Ferguson, L. L. "Better Management of Managers' Careers," *Harvard Business Review,* March-April, 1966, pp. 139–152.

9. ____. "Social Scientists in the Plant," *Harvard Business Review,* May-June, 1964, pp. 133–143.
10. Haire, M. "Coming of Age in the Social Sciences," *Industrial Management Review,* VIII, *2* (Spring, 1967), pp. 109–118.

11. ____. "The Social Sciences and Management Practices," *California Management Review,* Summer, 1964, pp. 3–10.

12. Hare, V. C. Jr. *Systems Analysis: A Diagnostic Approach.* New York: Harcourt Brace and World, 1967.

13. Heany, O. F. "TIMS Talking to Itself?" *Management Science,* XII, *4* (December, 1965), B146-B155.

14. Heinemann, H. E. "Ford's Lundy: A New Model," *The New York Times,* February 5, 1967, pp. f-1, f-13.

15. Klahr, D. and Leavitt, H. J. "Tasks, Organization Structures, and Computer Programs," in C. A. Myers (ed.). *The Impact of Computers on Management.* Cambridge, Massachusetts: M.I.T. Press, 1967.

16. Lesieur, F. G. *The Scanlon Plan.* Cambridge, Massachusetts: The M.I.T. Press, 1958.

17. McClelland, D. C. "The Role of an Achievement Orientation in the Transfer of Technology," paper presented at the M.I.T. Conference on Human Factors in the Transfer of Technology, May 18, 1966.

18. McGregor, D. *The Human Side of Enterprise.* New York: McGraw-Hill Inc., 1960.

19. Mansfield, E. "Size of Firm, Market Structure, and Innovation," *Journal of Political Economy,* LXXXI (1963), 556–576.

20. ———. "The Speed of Response of Firms to New Techniques," *The Quarterly Journal of Economics,* LXVII, *2,* 290–311.

21. Meyer, H. H., Kay, E. and French, J. R. P., Jr. "Split Roles in Performance Appraisal," *Harvard Business Review,* July-August, 1965, pp. 123–129.

22. Myers, C. A. *The Impact of Computers on Management.* Cambridge, Massachusetts: M.I.T. Press, 1967.

23. Quinn, J. B. "Technological Competition: Europe *vs.* U.S.," *Harvard Business Review,* July-August 1966, pp. 113–130.

24. Schrage, H. "The R&D Entrepreneur: Profile of Success," *Harvard Business Review,* November-December, 1965, pp. 56–69.

25. Sirota, D. "Productivity Management," *Harvard Business Review,* September-October, 1966, pp. 111–116.

26. Vroom, V. H. *Work and Motivation.* New York: John Wiley & Sons, Inc., 1964.

Section **3**

Total System

10

Organization as a Total System

Stanley Young

©1968 by The Regents of the University of
California. Reprinted from *California Management Review*,
Spring 1968, pp. 1–32, by permission of The Regents.

Increasingly, organizations are being considered from a systems point of view in both descriptive and normative context.[1] Ashby's work would exemplify some of the descriptive work. Systems Development Corporation, Strategic Air Command, and Lockheed are effectively using the systems concept to redesign major phases of organizations in an operational and normative sense.[2] Many companies have expanded similar efforts to certain subsystems, such as steel-rolling mills, oil refineries, and so on.[3]

Our conception of the organization is changing from one of structure to one of process. Rather than visualizing the organization in its traditional structural, bureaucratic, and hierarchical motif, with a fixed set of authority relationships, much like the scaffolding of a building, we are beginning to view organization as a set of flows,

[1] For example, see Joseph Litterer, *Analysis of Organizations* (New York: John Wiley & Sons, Inc., 1965); Claude MacMillian and Richard Gonzales, *Systems Analysis* (Homewood, Ill.: Richard D. Irwin, Inc., 1965), Chaps. 11–14; Ross Ashby, *An Introduction to Cybernetics* (New York: John Wiley & Sons, Inc., 1958, Chaps. 10–14.

[2] For example, see Donald G. Malcolm et al., *Management Control Systems* (New York: John Wiley & Sons, Inc., 1960).

[3] See Cornelius Leondes, *Computer Control Systems Technology* (New York: McGraw-Hill Book Company, 1961), Chaps. 15–20.

information, men, material, and behavior. Time and change are the critical aspects. When we consider the organization from a normative point of view, we find another reason for this trend which is of more immediate concern. This is the working hypothesis of my article. Only when the organization is designed (organization planning) from a systems engineering orientation will it be able to take full advantage of the new and emerging managerial technologies, such as quantitative methods, the computer, information sciences, and the behavioral sciences. The engineering sciences have illustrated unusual success in the rapid creation and application of new technology and will, therefore, represent the guiding model of this analysis.

However, before taking up my thesis, let us note the current problems concerning the effective utilization of managerial technology. One problem relates to the absence of a construct as to how this new technology is to be used in an integrated and systematic manner; or consider it as the absence of a meaningful gestalt, or whole, into which such a technology would logically fit. What does exist might be categorized as a tool chest or "bits and pieces" state.

For example, let us suppose that a personnel manager has a problem of excessive absenteeism. Given the external and internal environment of the firm, the organizational constraints he has as a manager, and a set of behavioral information and managerial tools that he has acquired, how does he reduce the absenteeism rate? He knows something about psychology—perception, cognition, learning, and motivation theory. From social psychology, he should be aware of theories of attitude formation and resistance to change. From sociology, he recalls the implication of group theory. He can calculate the median, mean, and mode, run a correlation, and find a derivative. He is a qualified MBA student. Yet, what specifically should he do to reduce the absenteeism rate? Students and practitioners are given a tool chest filled with some mathematics, some psychology, and so on, and the manager is then admonished to build a better house.

Although one can appreciate the value of these various approaches, one is still confronted with the problem of their integrated application in order to be relatively assured of achieving a desired result. What is missing is the bridge or discipline between tools and organizational results. The engineering sciences represent such a discipline.[4]

---

[4] See Arthur D. Hall, *A Methodology for Systems Engineering* (Princeton: D. Van Nostrand Company, Inc., 1962); and Harry E. Goode and Robert E. Machol, *System Engineering* (New York: McGraw-Hill Book Company, 1957).

Although one can raise many serious questions as to the reality, validity, predictability, and effectiveness of the classical principles approach, nevertheless it can be said that it roughly holds together as a whole or single unit, and its parts are related in logical fashion. Starting with the concept of private property and the delegation of authority, the organizational chart is drawn; authority is allocated; a division of labor is specified; and the functions of management, planning, organizing, and staffing are outlined. A certain internal logic is present, not unlike the economist's model of perfect competition. The parts are related to each other in a particular manner. Viewed as a single construct, the traditional model is understandable and operational to students and practitioners alike.

A Systems Approach

The same cannot be said for the newer managerial technology. The general management or organization theorist's domain is the whole. One is concerned with the problem of organization space or the distance between subfunctions, subprocesses, tools, and techniques—the interface problems. To those who are concerned with the whole, the partial approach of the new technology is disconcerting. Where and how do all these parts fit together, and what is the relationship between one and another? Sprinkling behavioral and quantitative courses about a business curriculum is of questionable effectiveness. Therefore, as far as the newer technologies are concerned, a gestalt, or general, model has been missing which will integrate all the parts meaningfully. What is being suggested is that the systems approach will provide this model.

Another problem which has emerged, which requires that the organization be designed as a total system, is that all too frequently the organizational context into which the newer technologies are inserted tend to be inappropriate. We are attaching sophisticated techniques to a primitive vehicle—the bureaucratic structure. Organizations should be designed around the technology; technology should not be forced to fit an existing structure. Thus, some corporations, to be fashionable, have created operations research departments which in fact have been given little or nothing to do. One case was reported in which the primary duty of the O.R. official was to solve the school mathematics problems of the corporate president's daughter!

In the history of innovation, one frequently finds that when a new device is invented it is attached to the existing model. For example, when the gasoline motor was first invented, it was connected to a buggy. However, as additional innovations occurred, the vehicle itself eventually had to be modified. If advantage was to be taken of additional improvements, obviously one could not unite a 300-horsepower motor to a light wooden shay. If innovation follows its usual course, we can expect the new managerial techniques to force a modification in the traditional organizational arrangements. This, indeed, has been taking place. The exploitation of the computer has led to a weakening or abolishment of the traditional divisional or departmental lines of authority. Improvements in the control and measurement of operations have the same consequences.

The differences between administrative and engineering analyses that will be taken up are:

The engineering sciences view of the operation to be analyzed as a system or subsystem.

The design and implementation of such systems as a sequential analysis of a team effort composed of appropriate specialized personnel.

Research, development, hardware specifications, and pilot and field studies are conducted with at least one purpose: to create and apply an improved technology to the functional operations being considered. Further, historically, the engineering sciences have incorporated the basic sciences of physics, chemistry, and quantitative methods into their analyses.

To demonstrate how the organization may be treated from an engineering point of view, it will first be analyzed as a system, and then the design process will be briefly outlined. In the presentation of the organization as a system, the approach will be analytical—a successive breakdown of the whole into increasingly smaller parts.

Organization as a Total System

In Figure 1, the business organization is presented in its most simplified form. The basic input is economic resources, the organization is the process, and the output is economic welfare. Other organizations can be represented by changing the inputs and outputs. For example, the hospital has a human input (sick patient) and a healthy patient as the output.

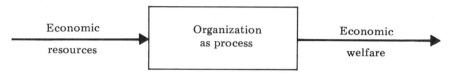

Figure 1.   Organization as a system.

In Figure 2, the control or feedback mechanism is added to the organization, which is represented by management. Or, in terms of control theory, the management segment constitutes the basic control element of the organization. Thus, given a certain welfare objective or expected welfare output (a profit increment), actual welfare is measured against expected welfare. If a difference exists, then a problem is indicated. This information is sent to the management segment which formulates a solution that is then input into the organization process. This feedback device will operate until the actual and expected welfares are approximately equal.

In Figure 3, the control unit is further broken down into a series of parts, in order to provide an adaptive capability for the organization.[5] Given a change in certain environmental inputs, one

[5] For a review of adaptive systems, see El. Mishkin and Ludwig Braun, Jr., *Adaptive Control Systems* (New York: McGraw-Hill Book Company, 1961), and J. H. Westcott, *An Exposition of Adaptive Control* (New York: The Macmillan Company, 1962).

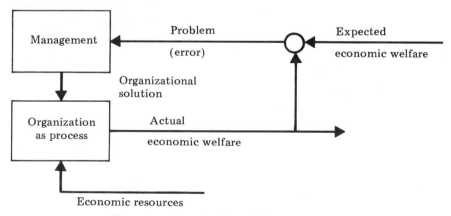

Figure 2.   Organization with control unit.

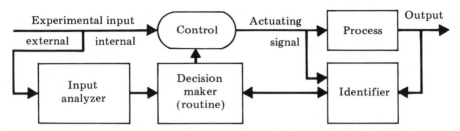

Figure 3.   Organization as an adaptive system.

initially has an input analyzer, which indicates the nature of such changes. This is an information-gathering or sensory device; somewhat analogously, market research might be so categorized in terms of sensitizing the organization to some of the external variables, as accounting functions for the internal changes. One has also a display device, the identifier, which indicates the state of the organization or any of its subprocesses at any given time.

Hence, if the subprocess were a production plant, the identifier at a given time could indicate the productive capacity, current running capacity, order backlog, inventory conditions, orders in process, production lines in operation, and machine breakdown. Such information is fed to a decision-making unit along with the information from the environment. We assume that a set of rules has been programmed, one of which will be selected for a particular environmental input and a given process point to achieve a certain output.

For example, if the initial input is a large order with a required completion date, the rule may be to go to overtime. This information is called a control signal and is sent to the control unit. The control unit is that element which actually changes the input before it enters the system, or the process itself. The order could have been put into a queue. Such information is simultaneously sent to the identifier. Therefore, at any given time, the identifier tells us what inputs have entered the process, the state of the process, and its outputs.

Because the control signal and the control unit are frequently confused, the difference between the two should be explained. The example that is usually given is the driving of an automobile. If one wants to stop an automobile by depressing the brake pedal, information is relayed to the brakes of the car. It is not the brake pedal that stops the car, but the brakes, which constitute the control unit. Similarly, in a man-to-man system, the control signal and the control unit would appear as shown in Figure 4.

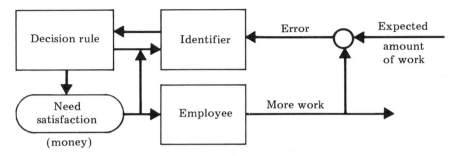

Figure 4.   The control signal and the control unit.

Let us suppose that the total employee population is the basic system, and we want a higher work output. Further, assume that we know exactly what the relationship is between need satisfaction input and expected work output. Given the figure for expected work output, the decision maker will increase or decrease the amount of need satisfaction (for example, money) via a control signal to the financial department, where need satisfaction is stored in the form of money. This department would release funds until the expected work output was achieved. It is not the decision to increase work output or its relay to the employee that constitutes the control element or even the decision to augment wages and salaries, but the reservoir and release of funds that is the control element. In other words, a salary may be to the employee what brakes are to an automobile. For our particular purposes, those subparts of the organization control mechanism—input analyzer, and so on—give the process an adaptive capability or the ability to adapt to changing inputs so as to maintain a desired or expected output.

In Figure 5, the organization is further broken down into a series of major subprocesses: marketing, production, and so on, with its own adaptor. The adaptor consists of an input analyzer, decision rules, identifier, and control for each subprocess. Moreover, it is assumed that each of these subprocesses can be identified and separated from other subprocesses. A super-adaptor applies a series of decision rules for subdecision makers, to assure appropriate adjustment between processes. It is further assumed that each subsystem's adaptor has this same capability concerning subprocesses. Consequently, the production system may have subsystems of purchasing, inventory control maintenance, and so forth. The inputs and outputs of these subsystems would have to be controlled appropriately with the proper decision rules.

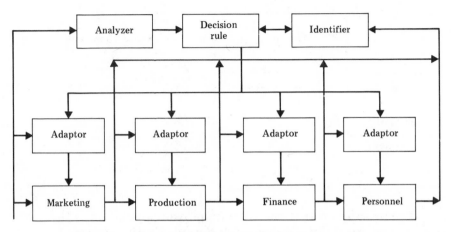

Figure 5. Major subprocesses, each with its own adaptor.

In Figure 6, a learning capability in the form of a designer is added to the adaptive system. A learning capability can be thought of as the ability of the system to redesign itself or learn from past mistakes so as to improve system performance. Given the environmental state of the system and the application of what is thought to be the correct rule, the expected output may still not be produced. This indicates design problems.

The designer would receive information as to system performance. Then, to increase welfare output, he would attempt to improve the adaptive mechanism: by formulating more effective decision rules for the decision-making routine, by improving the

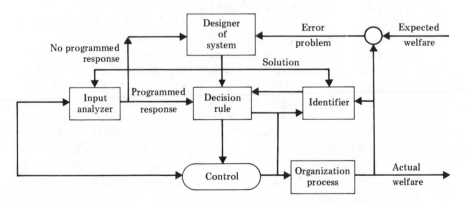

Figure 6. Adaptive system with learning capability.

identifier in terms of more and better information, by achieving a more rapid response in information from the input analyzer, by improving the sensory devices, and by improving the control mechanism.

In Figure 7, we now see the total system in some detail. We have our environmental inputs on the left, both external and internal (psychological, sociological, etc.). Two basic subsystems are shown: marketing and production, in which the marketing output becomes a production input. Each of these subsystems has its own adaptor, and although not shown, a coordinating adaptor to integrate the two. Further, each subsystem has its own design capability.

The only new feature of the schematic is the box at the top: Design of system design. This particular function would integrate the work of subdesigners. For example, if the organization is viewed as an aircraft, the design of which is generally broken down into such areas as weight and structures, air frame, power, information system, and so on, design coordination is required. Moreover, this function would also advise as to design technique and strategy, and, ideally, one should be able to reach a stage in which the design itself of subsystems could be programmed.

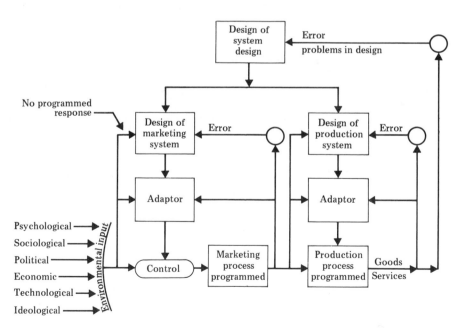

Figure 7.   Organization as a total adaptive system.

Thus, in looking at Figure 7, we see in some detail the organization as a total system which is self-regulating and self-learning, at least partially closed, in which the environment can be detailed and in which subsystems are integrated. Further, the adaptor provides for appropriate internal adjustments between subsystems. In other words, the organization without too much difficulty can be considered as a total system. All of its essential elements can be incorporated into a design. Also, with an appropriate index, one can detail the subsystems. Each subsystem can be broken down into its subsystems, and so forth. The indexing of the system's subparts is a complex but not an insurmountable problem. For example, it is estimated that the blueprints for a new aircraft may finally weigh two or three tons—more than the aircraft itself!

System Design

In Figure 8, we can briefly go through the design process, which further analyzes the function of the designer. Given a statement of the problem or the type of system with which one is concerned, the next, and key, step is the construction of a model of the system. Such a model would be essentially stochastic in nature and would stipulate the output or mission of the system and the inputs, of which there are three:

The input upon which the process is to operate or that input which enters the system.

Environmental inputs which affect the process.

Instrumental or control inputs which modify the operation of the process or the process itself—and here we are concerned with the technology of processing the load inputs. For example, in a marketing subsystem, if the initial input is a potential customer, he has to be processed through the subsystem so that a sale will result.

The system's logic relates to the set of decision rules or, given certain inputs, the state of the system and a certain control capability, such as more or less advertising—what particular decision rule should be utilized to achieve some expected output? Information requirements relate to the classification, amount, and timing of information, so that the system will operate as expected. Hence, concerning the environmental variables, what information about which variables should be gathered? How often? How much? And how soon would this information have to reach the decision role?

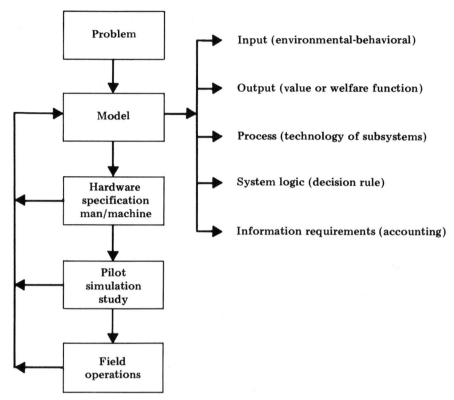

Figure 8.   System design. [see Harry Goode and Robert Machol, *System Engineering* (New York: McGraw-Hill Book Company, 1957)].

At the outset, it would be a highly worthwhile investment to construct a complete stochastic model of the system with which one is concerned, in which output is the dependent variable, and inputs, environmental and instrumental, are the independent variables. For example, one might be concerned with a personnel selection subsystem in which the output is a certain number of qualified employees. The environmental inputs might be the labor demand for certain occupations, amount of unemployment, the number of graduates, and so on; the instrumental variables might be the recruiting budget, the number of recruiters, the training program, etc.

It is more efficient to construct one model to which various decision rules can be applied than to construct a new model every time a new decision rule is formulated. With the latter approach, one would always be reconstructing the model, given a change in tools.

Once the model is constructed, the research and development begins. One can experiment—try different decision rules and different hardware specifications—in terms of devising appropriate controls and measuring devices.

Experimentation requires a certain ingenuity. A grocery chain may have to set aside one of its representative stores for research purposes. It would not only be important to establish the consequences of various pricing strategies, but if possible, the causes for such consequences or, at least, the ability to predict their outcome. Given a new rule on a pilot basis, one can apply it to actual hardware. Naturally, one has to be sure that the data from pilot studies are meaningful in terms of the total system with which one is concerned. Research and development represent the essence of the engineering effort. Experimentation is costly and uncertain, but there is little doubt that the payoff is greater than using an intuitive approach.

If it is successful, the new rule can be applied, and data can be fed back regularly to the designer, so that he can continually improve and refine his initial model. Although one may begin with a relatively unrefined model, with successive experimentation and field experience, hard data will constantly flow back to the designer. This will enable him to improve his model in terms of the nature of the variables, the preciseness of the parameters, and the model's predictability.

Over time, an improvement in the state of the art should occur, if research development is effectively executed. Our grocery chain should have an everimproving pricing strategy. As for hardware specifications, apart from the consideration of costs, one is concerned with providing components that will execute the operations as specified.

In terms of Figure 8, of particular concern is the problem of how to convert what is essentially a paper model into something that approaches operating reality. We can construct reasonably good stochastic or econometric models which can be used to simulate different decision rules, but the conversion of these into operating reality with appropriate hardware is a different matter. In an operating context, the stochastic model or identifier becomes an information panel for a decision or rulemaker. In terms of hardware, information collection or sensory devices are needed which survey the environment and send such data to a central location, so that the values of the variables of the model can be displayed. An example is the control room in a public utility, in which the operator watches continually the changing values of significant variables. Only with such a display can appropriate action be taken. However, wiring such a system is a particularly difficult task.

For example, as a member of a team that has been given the responsibility of designing a metropolitan poverty program as a total system, the primary inputs are poverty families, and the outputs are supposed to be self-sufficient economic units. Although there exists some technical assurance that a stochastic model can be constructed, we have not yet been able to reach this design step, because we are at the initial stage of inventing a sensory machine that will give us some running idea of the nature of our changing inputs which, in this instance, is the changing mix of the characteristics of our poverty families. This program appears in Figure 9.

Another area that requires additional work is the control element, which actually modifies the operation of the system. In a man-to-man system, we do not have sufficient information about which variables to vary and by how much, in order to achieve the desired human behavior. The crude reward and punishment system that we have all too often gives us dysfunctional results. Presumably, in the design process, when serious deficiencies arise, research and development should be directed to those areas.

Managerial Technology as Utilized in System Design

Although this view of the organization as a total adaptive system and the design process has been brief, it has been sufficient to indicate how one can take advantage of the newer managerial techniques in the use of system analysis.[6] In terms of the system presented, where and how do these techniques fit? As for the behavioral sciences, our environmental inputs or variables are behavioral in nature. To build a model and eventually a display panel, such knowledge is essential. In the decision box, we would utilize our various decision rules, such as Linear Programming, Game Theory, Dynamic Programming, PERT, and so forth. Because system design requires one to deal eventually with a total subsystem such as marketing, in all likelihood we will become increasingly concerned with the problem of combining various decision rules. For example, Gerald Thompson has indicated that we must combine appropriate decision rules to achieve the most satisfactory system output. Under what conditions is it advisable to move from Linear Programming to rule of thumb, and then back to Linear Programming? As Professor Thompson has noted,

[6] For a more complete review, see Goode and Machol, *System Engineering*.

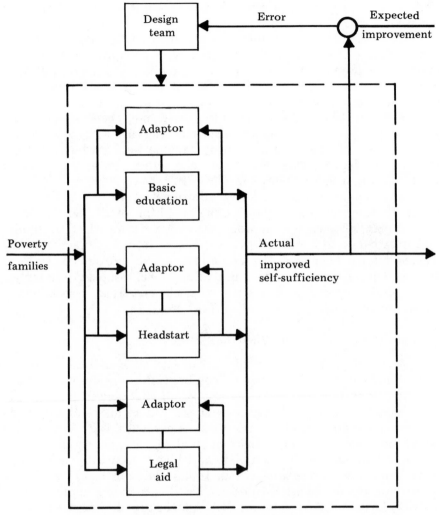

Figure 9.   Poverty program as a system.

We need to develop heuristics about using heuristics. That is, an executive program that would accept a problem and then decide which of a list of heuristics (decision rules) should be employed to give its solution.[7]

[7] Gerald L. Thompson, "Some Approaches to the Solution of Large Scale Combinatorial Problems," Carnegie-Mellon University, Pittsburgh, working paper, p. 25.

The information sciences relate to the input analyzer and the collection, manipulation, and relay of information. Here we have all our data collection and processing problems. The control element relates to the area of control theory, specifically, the direction of human effort. Finally, in designing a specific subsystem, such as personnel or marketing, one should have some knowledge with regard to the technology of these systems; for example, one should be able to use employment tests correctly in the selection process.

In designing the organization as a total system, it would appear rather apparent that one would not only have to be familiar with but also be able to use a wide array of sophisticated managerial techniques and knowledge. The understanding and use of managerial techniques is an integral part of the design process. This is distinctly counter to the bureaucratic structure, which merely attaches such techniques to it with little purpose or place.

Design Criteria

Design criteria are rules which are utilized to evaluate designs as to their acceptability. Given a number of designs, which one is the best? Although there are numerous rules, the most widely used are: *measurability, feasibility, optimality, reliability,* and *stability.* We will consider only the first three.

Measurability is the system's ability to evaluate its performance. If its performance cannot be measured, a system's desirability or undesirability cannot be established. Its particular excellences or deficiencies cannot be known. When models are measurable, the superior system can be inferred from the specific measuring devices used in each. In the model that has been suggested, the identifier as a display panel is the primary measuring mechanism, in that we would know the actual inputs, process, outputs, and decision rules. If the model is not working as expected, the errors would be fed to the designer on a more or less continual basis, so that the system could be redesigned for more effective results.

One of the most serious weaknesses of the bureaucratic design as a management system is that it lacks measurability. When the bureaucratic system is redesigned, for example, from a product to a functional arrangement or when the line of command is lengthened by the introduction of additional levels of managers, no measuring devices exist either in the previous or subsequent design that will indicate what improvements, if any, have occurred.

Feasibility relates to the question of whether or not the model will operate as planned. As the model must be realistic, it must be capable of being installed, of achieving expected payoff, and of performing its task requirements within the environment of the system. If a particular quantitative decision-making tool is suggested, can we be reasonably certain that it can be employed in an operational context? The use of pilot studies or experimental models relates to the question of feasibility.

Given any managerial device, we of course want to know if it will increase organizational payoff when it is utilized; will stockholders, employees, and consumers be better off than before? Organizations are normative systems. All too often, the student and practitioner are exposed to quantitative manipulations and behavioral research that are interesting, but either no directions are provided as to how these findings are to be incorporated into the operations of the firm or no measuring devices are suggested that will establish the quantity of welfare that the research results will actually produce.

The end purpose of the manager, as it is viewed in this analysis, is to design subsystems which will actually increase human well-being. The manager is not, per se, a mathematician, statistician, sociologist, or psychologist. However, he must rely on these disciplines in much the same way that the engineer has to rely on physics. This does not mean that continuous research is not required in these disciplines, if designs are to improve. However, such research will not automatically lead to improvements. It is only when the designer is able to incorporate findings into an operating reality that he can achieve the full value of the research.

A corollary to the feasibility criterion relates to the question of balance between the parts of the system. All parts of the system must not only be integrated, but they must also be mutually consistent. One would not put into practice a primitive input analyzer and follow this with a complex regression analysis in the identifier. The final system output will be no more productive than the least productive part of the system. Each part acts as a constraint on all other parts. Consequently, the identifier can never be any better than the input analyzer, and so on. The absence of integration and/or balance is self-defeating.

For example, we frequently find information systems personnel providing voluminous data; that is, the input analyzer is well developed. However, the rest of the system may be missing; there is no identifier or set of decision rules. In other instances, we may have analyses of the use of a single decision rule, linear programming, but nothing else.

As long as we find this type of analysis, managers will always revert, out of necessity, to the most primitive part of the total system, because this part represents the primary constraint. In such a context, increasing sophistication will not meet the criterion of feasibility. Even if it is used, no increment in organizational payoff will result.

For example, in the design of the poverty program system that was mentioned earlier, the staff's initial impulse was to design an econometric model of the program including exogenous variables. We immediately ran into the constraints of the rest of the system and realized that, until we had a relatively effective input analyzer, a set of decision rules, and a control element, we could not move to the sophisticated model we wanted. In other words, when one designs a total system, he is generally forced to start with a fairly elementary model. Then, when all the parts are developed, he can progress to a more complex system.

The management sciences may be overly concerned with the *optimality* criterion and ignore such other criteria as measurability and feasibility, on the assumption that if one has an optimal solution there is little else that has to be done. But unless all criteria are considered, we will not get the hoped-for results. To have a solution that is optimum but nonfeasible is meaningless. Obviously, a solution has to be measurable, feasible, and reliable, before we can consider its optimality.

For the most part, operating managers stress the feasibility criterion. At the outset, they want something that will work and actually function and are not overly concerned with optimality. In dealing with a complex system, I am not sure what constitutes an optimal solution. Russell Ackoff has said:

> One of the things Operations Research has learned about putting results to work is having considerable effect on its methods. This means the team must either translate elegant solutions into approximations that are easy to use or side step the elegance and move directly to a quick and dirty decision rule. Operations Research is learning that an approximation that is used may be a great deal better than an exact solution that is not.[8]

[8] Russell L. Ackoff, "The Development of Operations Research," *Scientific Decision Making in Business*, Abe Shuchman (ed.) (New York: Holt, Rinehart and Winston, Inc., 1963), pp. 59–60.

Because design methodology imposes a specific discipline on the designer, we can be assured that new techniques will be effectively utilized.

Conclusions

Some Implications

Although this has been a rather broad treatment of the organization as a total system, certain implications can be inferred.

1. *On a normative basis, organizations should be viewed as a total system if we are to increase organizational output. Different organizations, corporations, universities, poverty programs, and so on can be categorized. Further, although this is by and large an article of faith, nevertheless some empirical evidence does exist (certainly in the area of complex weapons systems) that, if organizations are viewed as a total system, better results will be obtained. We are in the initial stages of this development, and, at this time, we can only block out the basic characteristics of total systems.*

2. *There has been an attempt to demonstrate that the systems approach is a highly conducive vehicle for the incorporation of current managerial technologies, unlike the bureaucratic structure. Irrespective of the developing managerial concepts, the bureaucratic structure itself represents such a serious constraint that only minimal advantages would accrue.*

3. *When viewed in this context, the essential role of the manager is that of designer of organizational or behavioral systems, just as the engineer is the designer of machine systems. The design of a large complex system, however, will necessitate a team effort: mathematicians, psychologists, and information specialists. But, as in large machine systems, system specialists will be required to integrate the team effort. There is little reason why efforts cannot be organized to design a marketing system in the same fashion as the F-111 aircraft was designed.*

In conclusion, the engineering and management sciences face the same fundamental problem—the creation of improved systems. Both suggest that quantitative modeling be performed, based on their respective underlying sciences, physical and social. However, in the engineering sciences the design and implementation of machine-to-machine systems tends to be organizationally highly systematic, whereas such a development is yet to occur with respect to the management sciences in their design of man-to-man systems.

11

Are Total Systems Practical

Reprinted by permission of
Business Automation, June 1969.

Much of what is being said and written these days about information systems is devoted to persuading corporate executives that the "total information system" which they heard described and discussed so enthusiastically a few years ago has proved to be a will-o'-the-wisp, not to be pursued by profit-minded businessmen. Both in the academic research oriented literature, and in the harder-nosed business press, there seems to be a concerted effort to dissuade high level decision makers from investing their hard earned dollars in broadly conceived information systems that are "total" either in concept or in their intended contribution to managing the enterprise.

John Dearden, author of a series of much discussed articles in the *Harvard Business Review*, is popularly identified with the professorial position that such systems are dreamy-eyed and premature. "Some Dreams Have Turned to Nightmares" is the similarly ominous caveat carried as the subtitle of an article on management information systems by a consultant writing in the prestigious *Business Horizons*. *Dun's Review* has, from its own penny-wise practical point of view, led its readers to a similar conclusion.

Step Forward

Our purpose is to bring this record into balance, based on experience in designing information systems that have achieved practical and profitable objectives, both short-term and long-range. The systems we are talking about are, in fact, total management information systems, if one avoids falling into one of several semantic traps. Nothing in the world of business is ever "total," if the word is defined as connoting all-inclusiveness to the point of impracticality. Nor should "total" be used in any absolute sense, since clearly what is total for one company is certainly not total for another with different problems and policies, with different management style and different markets. More important, total is relative to time. What is total today will probably be partial tomorrow. On the other hand, what is partial today may, if properly conceived, be a necessary step toward tomorrow's total information system.

What we are talking about, then, is the feasibility of total management information systems that can be designed and installed now to serve today's critical top management needs and, in turn, enable top management to see that each responsible executive has the detail and depth of information he needs at the moment that critical decisions can most productively be made. But the systems we are talking about are future oriented in the sense that they do not preempt the step-by-step development of more inclusive systems that will bring more and better information to bear on more of the decisions that are important to the well-being of the enterprise.

To illustrate our point, we propose to track in some detail the history of the design of such a system in one company. We have chosen this company because it is, in our experience, typical of most major middle-size businesses with broadening and increasingly variegated product lines and widening—though increasingly frag-mented—markets. The experience of this company provides a basis for some general comments in defense of the total information system concept.

What makes this case additionally relevant to the problems facing most companies today is that this is a well-managed company in which islands of information had grown up at different points in the organization, each developed for different purposes by people with different responsibilities. It was recognition of this that led management to invite us to explore the practicality of a total system that would integrate isolated accumulations of information. Manage-ment wanted a system that could increase corporate effectiveness in the near term and at the same time establish guidelines for the continuing development of improved information flow.

Of special interest to those concerned with the design of information systems is that this was a pure systems problem involving no significantly new hardware or software.

Semantics aside, two characteristics make a management information system a total system. First, on a priority basis, it has to provide both top management and operating management with the information required for their most important decisions. It has to be valid information—timely, precise and complete. And it has to be integrated information—not bits and pieces of data. How many decisions are included in the roster of important decisions is a matter of practicality and time-phasing. In the near term, one goes as far down the list as is possible and practical. In this sense, possible means that the inputs are available and the skills and disciplines present in the company. Practical means just what it says—that the cost of the information can be justified by its contribution to growth and profitability.

Bearing on the Mode

The second operational characteristic of a total system is that it provides all of the information that has an important impact on these decisions. What information describes the factors that will significantly affect the design of alternative solutions? What information describes the meaningful interrelationships among these factors, relationships that will have a critical bearing on the mode of operation and on decisions? What information is necessary for the selection and implementation of the alternative that promises to contribute most to corporate objectives? It is these dimensions, and not dictionary definitions, that explain what we mean by a total management information system [see Figure 1].

In the company we are discussing, the following critical decisions are among those which top management must make to maintain profitable growth in the immediate future.

How much will the company's inventory needs affect its financial requirements for the year ahead?

To keep up with competition, this company faces substantial financial requirements to make necessary changes in its product line which require new facilities and new equipment. At the same time, the company's investment in inventory is equal to about one-fourth of its dollar sales, and the value of its inventory has been increasing rapidly. The rising cost of inventory is accordingly a major factor in the diminishing return on investment.

To make its critical financial decisions, top management needs more precise information on how much inventory will be needed to maintain acceptable levels of customer service. In what form should

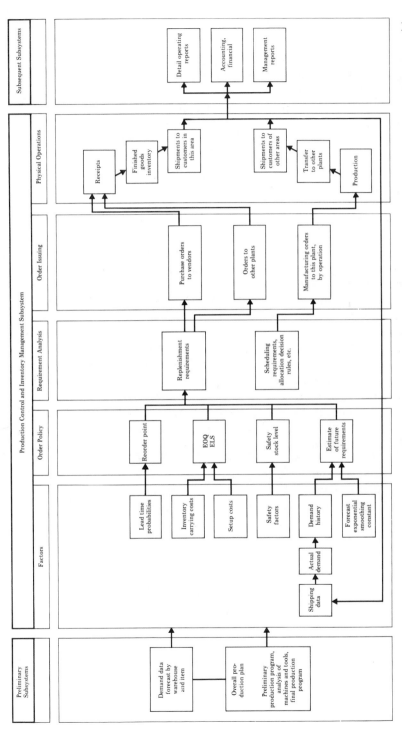

Figure 1. Demand (warehouse and product) and production schedules (plant, machines, and tools) are forecast in computer memory. An exponential smoothing constant corrects forecasts for longer term trends. Actual demand (warehouse shipping data) is fed into the system to bring demand up to date and to correct estimates. Then, the system applies accumulated data on lead time, reorder points, inventory carrying, and set-up costs; EOQ's, ELS's, and reorder points are then calculated. These feed into a requirement analysis subsystem, providing the basis for purchase orders and manufacturing requirements, plant by plant. Inventory is recalculated and allocation decisions are made. The ultimate outputs are operating, financial, and management reports.

the inventory be raw material, in-process or finished goods? Where should it be? This same information provides management with an objective way of measuring alternative approaches to inventory management that would optimize the use of inventory at any level of investment. At the same time, this information should give management all the advantages of committing the company to inventory investment as late as possible in the production-selling cycle.

Top management needs to plan allocation of products to plant and allocation of equipment and tools to those plants.

Facilities planning that will cut both production and distribution costs is a once-a-year decision that involves conflicts of interest among different operating executives which can be resolved only at the top management level. To negotiate these decisions in a manner acceptable to the operating executives, the information system has to provide cost data by plant and by processes and relate that data to product plans and market forecasts. Only this kind of information can lead to decisions that are in the best interests of the company as a whole.

In addition to providing information for annual allocation decisions, this same information system should provide feedback on variance from projected costs that will continually enable the company to improve its facilities decision making.

Top management needs information that will enable it to set customer service standards objectively and to monitor the performance of each operating unit and each responsible manager.

Once customer service objectives are defined, top management can select from a range of alternative levels of service as they impact profitability and growth. Furthermore, feedback on service performance will make it possible to identify responsibility for that performance and appraise the contribution of line personnel.

In addition to these specific needs for making priority decisions, top management also had the responsibility for structuring a system to provide operating management with the information it needs for day-to-day decisions that determine the effectiveness of the company's operations in the field. This company has four major plants and several minor production facilities. Its markets are divided among a number of executives and customer accounts and assigned to representatives responsible for the relationship between the company and its major customers across the country. With this kind of decentralized responsibility, it was particularly important that the information system provide all operating executives throughout the company with a common information base to guide their day-to-day decisions.

The problem of total systems design is, therefore, two-fold: A total system must satisfy the present needs and do this in a way that will make it possible to meet future needs.

To provide management with its requirements for high priority decisions, a system had to be developed that would generate certain continually updated data not hitherto available in the form in which it was needed. In fact, one advantage of the total information system approach is that it defines as early as possible the kind of data that will be required for the kind of information system that management is likely to require at predictable points in the future. Without this kind of prescience, the company inevitably will be involved in constant and costly revisions of its corporate data base as additional informational needs are defined and appropriate systems developed to meet these needs.

At this point, we identified the need for the following data:

1. *Information that would make it possible to maintain up-to-date cost schedules on alternative levels of customer services, in terms of which management could select, on a cost-effectiveness basis, a customer service policy that the company could live with.*

Prior to the development of this kind of precisely defined policy, customer service levels had been loosely described. Customer service policy decisions were actually made largely on the basis of the number of complaints sales representatives received from customers. Since each had his own subjective evaluation of how many complaints is too many complaints, and each had his own concern for a complaint-free record, safety stocks varied widely from product to product and from warehouse to warehouse.

Significantly, until precise data on service standards and performance was made available, management was deprived of an important control tool.

2. *Data on inventory carrying costs, including the cost of money.*

Prior to this, consideration had been given to certain costs of carrying inventory, but not to all of these costs. For example, those making inventory decisions did not have current information on the costs of money to the company.

3. *Continually updated data on set-up costs.*

Obviously, this would be important for defining optimum production runs.

4. Continually updated transportation cost information.

Three kinds of transportation costs entered into management decisions. Paper had to be shipped from the mill to the plant where a particular product was to be produced. The product then went from that plant to customers. A third element of transportation costs was the transfer of in-process or finished products from one plant to another, depending on availability of production capacity.

5. Historical demand data, product by product, continually updated.

From this historical data it was possible to develop an exponential smoothing constant to bring forecasted demand into line with past experience.

With this data in hand, and with the growth forecast available, it was possible to develop the information needed for this cluster of both top level and operating decisions. Furthermore, by relating estimates of future requirements to actual shipments, it was possible to keep these decisions corrected for actual movement of merchandise to customers.

At the top management level, this system provided management with foreknowledge of the investment and inventory it would have to maintain for the year ahead and the cost of maintaining that inventory. It provided them with this figure for a level of inventory adequate to meet the customer service policy deemed appropriate for effective market growth at costs the company could live with. Furthermore, it provided top management with data on the responsibility of production efficiency.

This latter consideration is related to the fact that each operating executive now had available information on how much of each product should be held in inventory at any particular time; at what point a product should be reordered and how much of a particular product should be produced in a production run.

Pointing at Profits

Whatever else this system accomplishes, it has the merit of pointing directly at profits. It puts the management of this company in a near-term position to increase its margin on sales and thus upgrade its return on investment. Aside from this obvious and short-range benefit, the hardnosed approach to information system design means that each phase of the information system can pay for the next phase. The immediate benefits from the current system fall into three categories:

1. Tangible and measureable benefits. *This system will enable the company to meet its presently defined objectives with an increase in profits of between $800,000 to $1.35 million per year at the projected level of sales.*

These benefits will come from reduced inventory carrying costs of between $200,000 and $300,000; improved customer service which should, at current profit margins, earn added profits of from $400,000 to $800,000 a year; and reduced back orders which should add another $200,000 to $250,000 in profits.

Significantly, only about $250,000 of this amount represents cuts in direct costs. Most of the benefits of this information system will come from improved management decision making.

2. Tangible but difficult-to-measure benefits. *This information system will generate additional savings from better purchasing practices and from a reduction in per unit production costs that will follow from more efficient utilization of existing equipment. In addition, there will be savings from a reduction in seasonal inventory buildup.*

One very tangible benefit is that the sales people now know what products each sales area should concentrate on to make best use of available production capacity. Similarly, industrial relations and production planning can now, for the first time, consider together the impact of union contract vacation provisions.

3. Intangible benefits. *The most significant benefits to management from this information will most certainly not be these tangible benefits, measureable or nonmeasurable. This management will now have information on the basis of which organizational responsibility can be clarified and managerial performance motivated, measured and rewarded. For example, it will now be possible to identify the responsibility for each element of marketing costs. It will be possible to assign to each marketing manager the responsibility for the inventory carrying costs which he generates, and this will, in turn, motivate him to sharpen his decision-making. The most intangible benefit this information system provides is the fact that it is compatible with the longer range needs of management.*

Reporting on Management

What is significant, in the context of the current controversy about total management information systems, is that this approach to systems is open-ended. While the information generated by the proposed system serves current needs and generates near-term profit improvement, it makes it possible for management to contemplate moving steadily and soundly toward a more all-embracing information system.

For example, this present system integrates marketing and production management needs. The outputs of the system should then enable the company to improve its financial decision making and integrate financial decisions with production and marketing forecasting and scheduling.

Also, this information system will improve personnel planning at all levels of the company from the plant to the front office. In a period of dynamic growth, within the framework of rapidly changing technology and markets, this will enable the company to know what kinds of people it is going to need and how many of each kind it will require to achieve its objectives at each point in time.

Further in the future, this information system can be linked to long and short term corporate planning. This would make it possible to integrate all of the company's operating activities into a single corporate plan, oriented to its growth in the marketplace at improved levels of profitability. At the same time, this developing information system will provide top and middle management with better information about the performance of each member of management. This will result in the kind of achievement oriented environment in which the optimum development of managerial capability can be expected.

The current polemics about management information systems does a disservice to the effort to put the present state-of-the-art to work on behalf of corporate growth and profitability, both near-term and long range.

It is true that those who try to design and install total systems in companies that are not ready for them are heading for trouble. By the same token, however, to use this argument to discourage management from reaching as far as it can as fast as it can is to deprive executives of information which can improve performance.

People-ware

The controversy about total information systems is largely a matter of words. Systems can be designed and put to work in a short period of time that will meet management's critical information needs and in doing so earn handsome returns on the investment in designing and implementing them. In these terms, the phrase "total information system" means *practical* total, rather than theoretical and ideal total.

What is important about practical total systems is that they should be designed with at least the broad outlines of a larger term total system in hand. The purpose of the longer range total system is to provide guidance to management for its shorter term efforts to make certain that nothing is done now to preempt what management wants to do and is able to do in the future.

In all of this thinking about total systems, the decisive ingredient of management decision making has to be the competence of its people. What is wrong about the total systems concept is not that they cannot be designed or that the necessary hardware and software are not available. They are. The missing ingredient in most cases is "people-ware." Well-conceived time phasing takes this into account by moving the company ahead as fast as its people can perform productively and profitably, using the kind of information the system provides at each point in its development.

PART III

Organizational Impact of MIS

The organizational impact of MIS seemingly focuses on the future role of the middle manager, the centralization-decentralization syndrome, responsibility for MIS and location of the electronic data processing department, needed organizational structure changes to accommodate necessary information flows, the dilemma of information needs and uses, and the crucial role of top management. Obviously these problems are not mutually exclusive.

The future role of middle management, discussed in Part I, may be summarized in the following statements. Middle-management responsibility can be expected to move toward more direct involvement in corporate planning. A change will occur also in the interrelated nature of operational management functions. However, middle management will retain the important leadership functions of directing and motivating employees. Because the middle-management job is characterized by close association with employees and what is often referred to as "operations management" it seems unlikely that the middle manager will be replaced by an intricate, interpersonal system for influencing relationships among employee behavior, attitudes, beliefs, or values toward specific goals in given situations. One might also observe that eliminating the middle manager would be inconsistent with Parkinson's law, which states that work expands to fill the time available without regard for the volume or usefulness of the tasks to be carried out. (1)

Centralization and departmentation—two related but dissimilar concepts in management—often have been confused. Centralization implies that decisions are made by top management; decentralization implies that they are made at appropriate lower levels. Departmentation, a concept in organizational structure design, deals with dividing an organization's work into tasks and then assigning and coordinating the tasks in such a way as to facilitate organizational objectives.

Hence, locating computer facilities or consolidating them is departmentation, not centralization. A direct relationship between MIS and centralization has yet to be demonstrated.

Diverse patterns exist in industry for locating the electronic data processing (EDP) department and assigning responsibility for MIS. Some firms departmentalize the MIS function, for example, placing it with accounting and finance; others make it a division; some rely on a computer committee composed of operating staff and top-level managers; and some use liaison men. (2) These patterns can be expected to be shifted somewhat as the MIS management discipline gains greater organizational prestige. Simultaneously, there undoubtedly will be increased development of MIS subsystems, structural changes in the MIS currently in operation, or addition of appropriate MIS requirements directed toward total MIS. Accountability to top management probably will receive new emphasis.

The dilemma has been created by the tendency of computer specialists to overromanticize the equipment capability and management to underutilize the equipment. As in any other system, the value of an MIS is a function of the data selected for input and of the persons who use the information output. Certainly additional information is not the only need. The danger of reasoning that more information implies better decisions is placed in perspective by Hertz, Director of McKinsey and Company, management consultants:

> Too often, information available to management is plentiful without being relevant, extensive without being adequate, and detailed without being precise. Its seeming comprehensiveness is illusory and, although it flows in without respite, it is not timely. In short, it is less a help than a hinderance to effective decision making and control. (3)

To put it another way, the design antennae of the computer specialist are well tuned to facilities expectation; those of management are tuned to daily operational problems. Fundamentally, some MIS designs have had more symbol than substance because management has failed to concentrate on how well they will meet needs and to keep a cost surveillance during the early development stages.

MIS literature has focused on the call for top-management involvement. Smith expresses it this way:

> When the curtain goes up on new developments in computer technology, management applauds the opening

up of new horizons in management methods. After the curtain goes down, management too often leaves the show to the stage hands. (4)

Some responsibilities of management include selecting, training, and evaluating personnel; actively participating in the design and implementation, including equipment acquisition and installation; determining the appropriate organizational level for the department, its responsibilities, and its accountability; and establishing appropriate plans for evaluation and audit.

Organizational structures change—they cannot remain a constant. Therefore, to appreciate the complexities involved in organizational structure, including MIS and its management, it is essential to grasp the significance of change, the variables causing change, and the relation of changed structures to planning for such changes. It is important to make changes that are a function of planning, not of chance. Planning, similar to decision making, occurs at all organizational levels and varies with scope and type of plans made. A general principle is that top managers make general but encompassing organizational plans; lower-level managers make specific, or operational, plans. Planning, a difficult management task, requires considerable time and effort; evidence supports the view that in the past insufficient planning has characterized both large and small business enterprises. Most have failed to develop the philosophy that plans are actually resources to be used in guiding and developing the firm. Much planning, short range and inadequate, has contributed to failure to integrate the relationships between planning for an MIS and corporate planning, particularly with respect to planning for change in corporate organizational structure. In the McKinsey and Company management survey on computer and systems experience, the most successful companies had built planning and control tools into their computer-system programs and had set clear objectives to ensure that the computer program focused on the major problems of the business. (5)

McFarlan, who recently made a study of a diverse group of heavy users of computer equipment, pointed out that "In general, computer-based management information system planning today is at roughly the same stage of development as corporate planning was in 1960." He further observed that

1. The volatile environment of today requires building a flexible framework to manage change in an orderly and consistent fashion.

2. Failure to recognize and plan for interdependency and coordination can lead to future revision of a system that cannot accommodate new requirements.
3. Quality and detail of written plans are the most significant factors differentiating the companies that have effective computer-based information systems from those that do not.
4. Companies that formally plan their computer-based information systems have more effective systems than companies that do not.
5. A strong correlation exists between a company's ability to develop an effective information system plan and the maturity and scope of its total corporate planning process. (6)

With reference to large corporations, McFarlan concluded, "We found overwhelming evidence that companies are tending toward consolidation. This trend increases the need for, and the payoffs from, central computer-based information system planning." (8)

In another study of the *Fortune* top industrials, Glueck observed that

Although there are few fullfledged organization planning and development departments in the United States today, this author believes that the number will grow . . . because of expansion, consolidation of planning activities resulting in a new type of organization function, and because of the establishment by top management of these new departments (9).

Daniel of McKinsey and Company found in a study of the country's 100 largest corporations that 66 percent of the firms had realigned their organizational structures. Furthermore, in several additional studies of organizational characteristics, Daniel observed that the largest firms had experienced a major organization change every 2 years; thus, Daniel concluded that the larger the firm, the more likely it is to change organizational structure. (10)

In a study of small farm-equipment manufacturing firms, we found that organizational structure tended to change with growth of the firm but that planning in the specific areas of budgeting and forecasting and planning for organizational change was inadequate. (11)

Thus it would seem that corporations are dynamic entities when changes are made to cope with technology, growth, and the residual factors and when management actively plans for these changes so that their nature and direction may be controlled. Planning and change have organizational impacts; obviously, then, planning for an MIS has an organizational impact.

In this section of the book the reader should look for the organizational interrelationships at work in an MIS and examine their causes and effects. Not all of a manager's time can be spent reacting to operational crises and fires and other outside stimuli; some must be devoted to effective, sound planning. As complexities and technology continue to increase in the business world, still more of the manager's time must be given to developing action plans, which constitute the road map for guiding a company toward its goals. Business transactions are becoming complex and the systems so integrated that a company cannot drift along and then react only to circumstances and chance. Corporate planning is a must, and along with continued top-management direction there must be greater involvement of middle and lower levels of management. Our primary purpose, then, is to show that, through the readings and these introductory remarks, management can—by planning, assigning responsibilities, and becoming involved—make an impact on a company's organizational structure, it is crucial that management develop this viewpoint, and an MIS is a significant part of the organizational structure which management must consider.

References

1. C. Northcote Parkinson, *Parkinson's Law and Other Studies in Administration* (Boston: Houghton Mifflin Company, 1957), p. 2.

2. Joseph Poindexter, "The Information Specialist: From Data to Dollars," *Dun's Review*, pp. 36–37, June 1969.

3. David B. Hertz, *New Power for Management* (New York: McGraw-Hill Book Company, 1969), p. 30.

4. Paul T. Smith, *Computers, Systems, and Profits* (New York: American Management Association, 1969), p. 13.

5. John T. Garrity, *Getting the Most Out of Your Computer* (New York: McKinsey and Company, 1964), p. 13.

6. F. Warren McFarlan, "Problems in Planning the Information System," *Harvard Business Review,* p. 76, March–April 1971.

7. Ibid., pp. 77–85.

8. Ibid., p. 85.

9. William F. Glueck, *Organization Planning and Development*, AMA Research Study 106 (New York: American Management Association, 1971), p. 4.

10. D. Ronald Daniel, "Reorganizing for Results," *Harvard Business Review*, pp. 96–104, November–December 1966.

11. Raymond J. Coleman and M. J. Riley, *Chief Executive Behavior and Corporate Growth Rate in an Agribusiness Industry* (Manhattan, Kans.: Agricultural Experiment Station, Kansas State University, 1971), pp. 8–9.

Section **1**

Impact of MIS on Organization and Management

12

Emerging EDP Pattern

Charles W. Hofer

Reprinted from the March–April 1970 issue of *Harvard
Business Review*. © 1970 by the President and Fellows
of Harvard College; all rights reserved.

It is commonplace that there has been a great increase in management's understanding of how to apply the computer to a wide variety of tasks, ranging in complexity from simple, routine accounting applications to large simulations of entire industries.

But there has been little knowledge about the overall impact the computer has had on the organizational structures and processes of the companies—both large and small—using EDP.

The purpose of this Special Report is to present the findings of a recent study I conducted in this area, which I feel make some needed additions to our knowledge. But first let me comment that there have been many speculations, opinions, and previous research studies devoted to the effects of the computer on organizations. Each has differed to such a degree, however, that no clear-cut pattern of the total impact of this technology on the organizational structures and processes of businesses has heretofore emerged.

For example, the *predictions* of such observers of the business scene as Harold J. Leavitt, Thomas L. Whisler, Melvin Anshen, John F. Burlingame, and John Dearden differ substantially, as indicated in the ruled insert on pages 215 to 218.

Likewise, the accompanying *findings* of researchers such as Ida Russakoff Hoos, Donald Shaul, Hak Chong Lee, and Rodney H. Brady differ, although each of their independent studies supports one of the sets of predictions.

Research Focus

In search of a clearer understanding of how the use of the computer and related technology has made an impact on industrial companies, I conducted a study of two manufacturing organizations. One was an independent division of a large multiproduct corporation whose total divisional sales exceeded $200 million. The other was a small company with sales of about $8 million. Both organizations were considered to be leaders in their respective industries in the application of computer techniques to management problems.

For example, both utilized nonconversational systems in a batch-processing operation in which the major files were updated daily. Both also had electronic data-collection devices which gathered and transmitted input data from remote locations. In addition, the larger organization utilized a corporate time-shared computer for some engineering and managerial applications.

Unlike previous researchers who had focused their efforts on one or two components of the companies they studied (usually the accounting and/or production scheduling and inventory control activities), I examined the effects of the computer in every type of organizational *component*—such as marketing, finance, engineering, manufacturing, employee relations, general management, and so on—and at every *level* in the hierarchy (from the president's office to the production floor).

Over a period of two years in the two organizations, I interviewed nearly 80 managers, with each set of interviews covering from one to six hours although no single interview took longer than two hours. To supplement and confirm the data obtained from my interviews, I also (a) studied organizational charts, statistics, and job descriptions; (b) analyzed budgeting, operational planning, and measurement and evaluation procedures; (c) constructed detailed decision matrices; and (d) examined computer and noncomputer company reports, all covering a period of 12 years in each organization.

Obviously, however, I could not possibly examine the effects of the computer on all organizational characteristics and processes. Consequently, I focused my attention first on the more important characteristics of formal structure, such as—

the method of task specialization;
the method of coordination;
the span of control;
the size of organizational components.

Then I examined such important organizational procedures as—

the various operational planning processes;
the budgeting process;
the measurement and evaluation process.

Synopsis of Findings

With but a few exceptions, my research—which is summarized in [Tables 1 and 2]—shows that the effects of the computer were the same in both companies even though the one organization was nearly 25 times larger than the other, both in dollar sales and in total employees, and even though the larger one had a rate of growth of less than 2% in dollar sales for the period covered by the study while the other had a compounded growth rate of over 10%. In both companies, the effects of the computer varied according to the organizational characteristic or process examined, the hierarchy level involved, and the nature of the principal tasks of the organizational component involved.

For example, on the one hand, the computer had no effect on the methods of coordination at the general management level or in components whose principal tasks did not involve the processing of large amounts of quantitative data. On the other hand, it did affect both the measurement and evaluation process at the general management level, and the methods of coordination in components whose principal tasks did involve the processing of large amounts of quantitative data.

In general, the research findings showed that the effects of the computer were:

Greater on organizational processes and delegation of authority than on the characteristics of formal structure.

Greater at the operations level than at the top functional level, and greater at both of these levels than at the general management level.

Greater on the organizational components whose principal tasks involved the processing of large amounts of quantitative data than on components whose tasks did not.

Table 1. Summary of Computer Impact in a Large, Multidivision Manufacturing Corporation

Level in hierarchy	Methods of specialization	Methods of coordination	Span of control	Size of components	Decision making and delegation of authority	Operational planning	Budgeting	Measurement and evaluation
General management	No change	No change	No change	No change	No change	No change	No change	Managers able to ask for more detailed back-up statistics on problems
Top functional: Components that do not process large amounts of quantitative data	No change	No change	No change	No change	De facto delegation of some decisions or some aspects of the decision making process to subordinates	Managers devoted more time to examining ways to improve systems and procedures at the operations level	Managers able to change budgets quickly as projects changed in nature or scope	Quantitative measures of the performance of operations level personnel and components improved in both content and accuracy
Top functional: Components that process large amounts of quantitative data	Creation of position of information systems manager	Some components transferred in hierarchy to improve implementation of computer technology	No change	Some role positions reduced in number because of decrease in size of components at operations level	Additional time allocated to other activities, such as operational planning			

Operations: Components that do not process large amounts of quantitative data	No change	No change	No change	Size of components per dollar sales decreased slightly (about 10%) because of increased efficiency of remaining personnel	Better decisions because of more accurate information	Managers better able to direct attention to areas where efforts would be most productive	Accuracy of manager's budgets increased because of more accurate information on indirect costs and greater detail on direct costs	Quantitative measures of the performance of employees, distributors, suppliers, etc. improved in both content and accuracy
Operations: Components that process large amounts of quantitative data	Creation of roles related to data processing, such as programmers and systems analysts; Elimination of some clerical role positions; Some roles upgraded	Coordination activities increased in frequency, become more formalized; Some components transferred as a result of systems changes	No change	Size of components per dollar sales decreased substantially (30% to 50%) because of elimination of clerical personnel	Some decisions programmed into computer	No change		

Table 2. Summary of Computer Impact in a Small Manufacturing Company

Level in hierarchy	Methods of specialization	Methods of coordination	Span of control	Size of components	Decision making and delegation of authority	Operational planning	Budgeting	Measurement and evaluation
General management	No change	No change	No change	No change	No change	No change	No change	Managers able to ask for more detailed back-up statistics on problems
Top functional: Components that do not process large amounts of quantitative data	No change	No change	No change	No change	De facto delegation of some decisions or some aspects of the decision making process to subordinates	Managers devoted more time to examining ways to improve systems and procedures at the operations level	No change	Quantitative measures of the performance of operations level personnel and components improved in both content and accuracy
Top functional: Components that process large amounts of quantitative data	Creation of position of data processing manager	Some components transferred in hierarchy to improve implementation of computer technology	No change	No change	Additional time allocated to other activities, such as operational planning		No change	

Operations: Components that do not process large amounts of quantitative data	No change	No change	No change	Size of components per dollar sales decreased moderately (about 20%) because of improved methods	Better decisions because of more accurate information	Managers better able to direct attention to areas where efforts would be most productive	No change	Quantitative measures of the performance of employees, distributors, suppliers, etc. improved in both content and accuracy
Operations: Components that process large amounts of quantitative data	Creation of roles related to data processing, such as programmers and systems analysts / Some roles upgraded	Coordination activities increased in frequency, become more formalized	No change	Size of components per dollar sales decreased substantially (about 40%) because new activities performed with existing personnel	Some decisions programmed into computer	No change	No change	

Effects on Formal Structure

Although I examined all of the changes (over 200) in formal structure which had occurred in both organizations during the 12-year period covered by the study, I found no instances in which the computer had caused changes in structure at either the general management level or at the top functional level in those components whose principal tasks did not involve the processing of substantial amounts of quantitative data.

(In one instance, a computer report served as a catalyst for a change from a functional grouping to a product grouping at the top functional level, but the computer did not influence the nature of the change.)

There were limited changes at the top functional level in components whose principal tasks involved the processing of quantitative data and at the operations level in components whose principal tasks did not. In the former case, the majority of the changes were related to changes in structure which occurred at the operations level. For example:

In the larger company, a 30% reduction in the number of personnel in the general accounting and cost accounting sections permitted the consolidation of these two components, with the consequent elimination of a managerial position.

In the smaller company, the responsibility for the purchasing component was transferred to the manager of finance, who was also in charge of data processing, when the system and procedures in that area were automated.

The major changes in formal structure brought about by the computer occurred at the operations level in components whose principal tasks involved processing large amounts of quantitative data. Here, new roles were created, while old roles were modified or eliminated. In addition, the coordination mechanisms became more frequent and formal, and organizational components were transferred or combined as a result of new systems and new procedures.

Effects of Computers on Organizational Structures and Processes

Here are some of the predictions and research findings concerning EDP's impact on manufacturing companies.

A. The observers' predictions

Harold J. Leavitt and Thomas L. Whisler[1]
Jobs at today's middle management levels will become highly structured.

Top managers will take on an even larger portion of the innovating, planning, and other "creative" functions.

The programmers and R&D personnel will move upward into the top management group.

Large industrial organizations will recentralize.

Melvin Anshen[2]
The new technology will not erode or destroy middle management jobs. Instead it will present opportunities for expanding management capacity and performance in areas that have suffered from scant attention.

The tasks of middle managers will more closely resemble those of top management.

Computer personnel will not assume top management responsibilities or become the fundamental source for top management personnel.

The trend toward decentralization of decision making will be slowed down.

John F. Burlingame[3]
If the company's philosophy is one of centralization, then the likely evolution will be along the lines predicted by Leavitt, Whisler, and others.

---

[1] "Management in the 1980's," HBR November–December 1958, p. 41.
[2] "The Manager and the Black Box," HBR November–December 1960, p. 85.
[3] "Information Technology and Decentralization," HBR November–December 1961, p. 121.

If a company's activities are centralized because of difficulties involved in achieving a harmonious unifying of individual creativity and initiative, then the computer will provide a basis for the adoption of a decentralized approach as a more desirable and more effective way.

If the company's philosophy is one of decentralization, then the technology should strengthen the existing decentralization of operations. Middle management should grow and flourish rather than wither and die.

John Dearden[4]

The computer will have no impact on the organization of top and divisional management, relatively little impact on the ability of the top manager to control profit centers, and limited impact on management levels below the divisional manager even though there may be some centralization of data processing and logistics systems.

With the exception of certain routine operating control problems in such areas as logistics, production scheduling, and inventory control, it will not be practicable to operate a real-time information system; and, even if it were, such a system would not solve any of top management's real problems.

B. The researchers' findings

Ida Russakoff Hoos[5]

Computer applications have led to drastic changes at the middle management level (supervisory to executive junior grade). Many jobs have been either combined or eliminated.

EDP has systematized and standardized formal information flow and also has seemed to dam up the upward and downward flow of information through both formal and informal channels.

---

[4] "Can Management Information Be Automated?" HBR March–April 1964, p. 128; "Myth of Real-Time Management Information," HBR May–June 1966, p. 123; and "Computers: No Impact on Divisonal Control," HBR January–February 1967, p. 99.

[5] "When the Computer Takes Over the Office," HBR November–December 1960, p. 102.

As more and more operations are programmed, the power and status of new computer personnel have been expanded, while the functions of other departments have been undercut, and the authority of their managers truncated.

EDP stimulates two distinct kinds of recentralization—one type referring to the integration of specific functions, the other involving regrouping of entire units of the operation and causing sweeping changes of the external structure as well.

Donald Shaul[6]
While EDP has undoubtedly eliminated a vast amount of monotonous, detailed administrative work, there has been no accompanying reduction in the need for middle managers. Actually, EDP has made the middle manager's job more complex.

The centralization of activities has not been accompanied by an elimination of managerial positions. On the contrary, EDP and the new activities have resulted in the addition of over 50 middle management positions in the companies studied.

Hak Chong Lee[7]
The nature and magnitude of the EDP impact is basically governed by the computer technology and the management attitude toward the use of the technology.

Drastic changes (centralization of the decision-making process and reduction in the number of middle management jobs) have not occurred to date in the companies studied during the early period of industrial experience with EDP.

Rodney H. Brady[8]
Top management does not seem to use the computer directly for decision making.

[6] "What's Really Ahead for Middle Management?" *Personnel*, November–December 1964, p. 8.

[7] *The Impact of Electronic Data Processing Upon Patterns of Business Organization and Administration* (Albany, New York, State University of New York at Albany, 1965).

[8] "Computers in Top-Management Decision Making," HBR July–August 1967, p. 67.

The use of the computer by middle management permits top management to:
Make some decisions at an earlier date.

Gain time in which to consider some decisions.

Consider more thorough analysis of some situations.

Review several courses of action on many problems.

Examine analyses of the impact that recommended courses of action will have on the problem or opportunity identified.

Obtain additional information from middle managers concerning problems, opportunities, and promising alternatives before making decisions.

Finally, there were substantial decreases in the total number of personnel per total dollar sales at this level, even after taking into consideration the additions of computer-related personnel. For example:

In the larger company, as the result of the development of a computerized production scheduling system, there was a threefold increase in the number of formal meetings between market forecasting personnel and production scheduling personnel to discuss major changes in production schedules.

In both companies, after data-manipulation activities had been programmed into the computer, the tasks performed by cost accountants were upgraded.

In the larger company, because of increased efficiency resulting from the use of computer models in design work, the number of product design engineers decreased about 10%.

In the smaller company, the automation of accounting records resulted in a 40% decrease in the number of accounting personnel per $1 million of sales.

Why Not More Changes   Since the effects of the computer on formal structure which I found were far less than many business observers had predicted, I attempted to ascertain why this was the case and also to learn whether further changes in structure were anticipated in the future. In general, the interview responses were to the effect that the computer had not affected formal structure at the general management level or in those components which did not process large amounts of quantitative data because it did not basically alter either the tasks performed by these components or the way in which those tasks were performed. The interviews also predicted that this would continue to be true in the future.

Typical of these kinds of interview responses was this observation by a corporate staff specialist on organizational design and development:

> I do not expect the computer to have much effect on our approach to managing and organizing at the general management level in the near future.

> Most of the information in a business is recorded inside people's heads. All the computer contains is a series of abstractions, and usually financial ones at that, which may serve to alert the general manager to a situation in which he should become involved. When he actually does get involved, it is necessary for the manager to go far beyond these abstractions by talking with the people involved to get at the underlying factors affecting results.

A sales manager offered this explanation as to why there are not more changes in his area:

> There is not much potential for changes in structure in the sales section due to the computer. The way we organize depends on our sales volume, the size and location of our customers, the number and nature of our channels of distribution, the number and diversity of our product lines, and so on, and these factors are not affected by the computer.

An engineering manager viewed the computer's impact in this way:

> I do not expect major changes in the organizational structure of the engineering section in the near future due to the increased use of the computer, although I do feel that the computer will increase the productivity of our present personnel.

> The reason for this is the fact that in the engineering section organizational structure is based on the physical characteristics of the products we produce, the nature of the production process, and the level of new product development and cost reduction activities rather than on the ways we process data.

Finally, this comment was given by a manufacturing manager:

> First, let me say that I could supervise more people than I do now. However, the computer really could not increase the number of men I could supervise. I must evaluate the man as well as the job he does, and the computer could not help there.
>
> In addition, the real limitation I have is understanding the nature of the tasks performed by each man well enough to evaluate him. The computer does not help too much there, either.
>
> In the case of my subordinates, the computer has given them better measures, so they could probably supervise a few extra employees. But I prefer them to spend their time improving their supervision of the employees who currently report to them.
>
> Moreover, the computer has not given them that much more time, because they spend only a small portion of their time in evaluating employees. Most of their time is spent in trying to improve operations by training personnel or by improving methods, and the computer does not help there.

Effects on Decision Making

My study revealed no direct effects of the computer on decision making or delegation of authority at the general management level. At the top functional level, however, there was considerable de facto delegation to subordinates of the analysis and evaluation phases of certain classes of decisions.

The major reason for this appeared to be the fact that the executives involved felt that the improved systems and procedures enabled their subordinates to handle these tasks on their own. One financial manager put it this way:

The computer has enabled me to become less involved in day-to-day activities because the system design is such that many tasks that used to occupy my time are now handled routinely by my subordinates. This is possible because the parameters are spelled out in such a way that I know my subordinates can do the job.

For example, I used to have to worry about our overdue accounts receivable. Now we have a report which indicates accounts receivable for each customer by billing date. We send a copy of this report to each of our customers every month. This eliminates a lot of calls we used to have to make.

In addition, my subordinates can now follow up on the routine cases so that I only have to handle the exceptional ones.

At the operations level, managers in components that did not process large amounts of quantitative data felt they were able to make better decisions as a result of more accurate data. In the components that did process large amounts of quantitative data, a substantial number of decisions were programmed into the computer. These were usually associated with activities such as production scheduling, machine loading, determination of inventory levels, and so on.

Effects on Operational Planning

The majority of the general managers I interviewed did not become heavily involved with operational planning. Their participation was usually limited to keeping tabs on the activities of their subordinates. The use of the computer did not change this. Thus one general manager commented:

I do not get deeply involved in the day-to-day operations of the departments reporting to me. In the first place, I do not have the time, and, besides, that is not my job; it's the job of the department general manager. Rather, I just monitor the departments' activities to make sure the managers are doing their jobs.

In a sense, I'm really not evaluating plans, I'm evaluating people and the way they think, and to do this I must talk with them. A set of statistics cannot tell me how a man thinks.

At the top functional level, however, the computer enabled managers to devote more time to examining ways to improve existing systems and procedures, and it had given them better information to do this. For example, one manufacturing manager described this incident:

> We have three or four peak demands for our punch presses each year. In the past, after each peak period, trained personnel were either laid off or moved to other jobs. Last year, I noted that we were using a lot of overtime and part-time labor to produce these parts during one of the periods of peak demand, so I asked our information systems people to explore our requirements for these parts for the past several years.
>
> Their figures showed that the total demand was large enough to keep all regular employees busy all year. It did not take me much longer to calculate that it would cost us substantially less to keep those men on full time and build up inventories than to lay them off and then have to work overtime and part-time.
>
> Without the computer, however, it would not have been possible for me to do this because we would not have had the information stored anywhere. Even it if had been, it would probably have been prohibitively expensive to try to pull it out and process it.

At the operations level, the increased accuracy of computer-prepared reports enabled managers to improve their planning and to direct their attention to areas where their efforts would be most profitable. For example, in the large company, computer reports on tool usage, dollars of expense on tooling, and dollars of maintenance by machine have enabled the engineers to plan replacement, repair, and maintenance work more accurately and profitably than ever before.

Effects on Budgeting

Inasmuch as my study only tangentially examined the effects of the computer on the budgeting process, I observed only two types of changes. At the top *functional* level, managers were able to change their budgets far more rapidly when the circumstances on which they were based were also changed.

Thus one engineering manager developed a program for use on a time-shared computer which contained his yearly expense budget broken down by project. Whenever a project had to be changed, he used the program to generate several "alternative" budgets for discussion purposes. When agreement was reached on the changes to be made, he then revised the original program to incorporate the new inputs.

At the *operations* level, utilization of the computer resulted in an increase in the accuracy of the manager's budgets. This occurred because the computer permitted direct costs to be broken down in greater detail than was previously economically feasible. The computer also permitted the development of detailed reports on indirect costs at this level for the first time. The result was better decision making by the managers involved. Typical was the comment of one supervisor who remarked that he was now able to do his job on the basis of facts rather than on intuition or guesswork.

Effects on Measurement

One of the few areas in which the computer directly affected the activities of the general manager was that of measurement and evaluation. The major result was that these men were able to request more detailed backup statistics on many problems than previously. In addition, one general manager said that he used the additional information in running his business:

> The availability of almost any sort of information I want makes it possible for me to know where to apply pressure, and/or how I ought to organize activities. For example, before the computer, I had little idea of our costs or profits for our smallest business in the XYZ market on a current basis because these data were buried in other statistics on our major markets. The development of such information has permitted me to examine the problems in a given area more closely and to evaluate the managers involved on the basis of facts.

At both the top functional level and the operations level, the computer changed the measures managers use to evaluate the performance of their subordinates. Here is a typical comment:

> In some cases the computer has affected the way I, and other managers like me, evaluate our subordinates. The ideal measure has not changed, of course, but the actual measure has. For example, we have always felt that the best way to measure the performance of our manufac-

turers' representatives was by the share of market our distributors got.

However, since we had no way to estimate total sales for their territories, we used other, less desirable measures. Thus, in the past, if a distributor sent in a large order or if his personal contact with us was good, we felt he was doing well.

After we got the computer, we started generating reports of quarterly and annual sales by distributor. This revealed that for several distributors the big order did not repeat or that the good contact was a substitute for good sales. These reports have enabled us to upgrade the performance of both our manufacturers' representatives and our distributors, even though we still are not able to measure market share.

A manufacturing manager offered this comment on performance evaluation:

Previously, I used to have to judge performance on the basis of output. Now I have reports which indicate both machine and labor efficiency for the section as a whole, as well as for each machine and each employee. They have helped me to identify areas where efficiency could be improved. I suspect, however, that these reports are of even greater value to my subordinates than they are to me.

For example, the other day one of them told me about a situation in which our labor efficiency report helped him to increase productivity. We had started making parts using a nonstandard material, and he was worried about productivity. But, when he went through the shop, everyone looked busy enough, so he felt pleased.

The next day, however, the labor efficiency report indicated that one employee's productivity had been extremely low. A quick check revealed that the worker did not know how to machine the new material. A little on-the-spot training solved that problem.

The point is that without the report the situation would probably have gone unnoticed, since it was a short run. As a consequence, we would have suffered decreased productivity.

Generality of Study Results

The fact that my research covers only two somewhat similar companies is not as limiting as it might initially seem to be. The results are applicable to many companies in many industries.

I say this because the independent studies described previously (and others like them) tend to support my own research findings. As I mentioned earlier, all of these studies appear to be contradictory when taken individually. However, when one views each as a piece of a larger pattern, rather than as the entire pattern, and then compares each piece with the corresponding portion of my findings, the fit is good indeed.

For example, Hoos's observations of the impact of the computer on the structure and processes of government agencies, banks and insurance companies, and manufacturers of industrial and consumer products dealt primarily with organizational components at the operations level whose principal tasks involved the processing of large amounts of quantitative data.

When her findings (see the ruled insert on page 216) are compared with mine [see Table 1 and Table 2] at the same level for the same types of components, the similarity is unmistakable even though the characteristics of the organizations involved are different.

Similar comparisons of my findings with those of Shaul, Lee, Brady, and others yield the same results. In fact, I found *no* study whose findings are in disagreement with mine when compared in this manner.

Since these studies covered a wide variety of businesses and industries, it would seem that my findings possess substantial generality. Because of limitations in the data available, however, it is not possible to develop a detailed classification system of the types of companies to which the figures would apply.

Future Changes

As we have seen, the computer's impact on organizational structure and processes has varied according to the characteristics of the process, the level of the organization, and the nature of the task of the component involved. Will the pattern and magnitude of the effects observed so far remain the same in the future?

It depends. In my opinion, companies which are just starting to use the computer will experience changes such as those described in this Special Report. However, I feel this pattern will change in the future for the two manufacturing companies I studied, as well as for others like them. More specifically, I predict that in such companies this pattern will emerge by 1975:

The computer will not have any significant effects on any of the major characteristics of formal structure—methods of specialization, coordination, span of control, and so forth—at either the general management or the top functional level.

The effects on formal structure at the operations level will be similar to those observed here, but the magnitude of these changes will be substantially less than those that have occurred to date.

For certain important operating decisions, general management will delegate the analysis and evaluation phases of the decision-making process to top functional management. As better information becomes available, and as top management becomes convinced that functional managers can do the job, top management may also delegate the responsibility for the final choice.

Top functional managers will become even less involved in routine, day-to-day decision making. Instead, they will concentrate their time on the important operating decisions delegated to them (for which they will probably begin to use simulation models), and on improvement of system design.

At the operations level, managers will increasingly be able to focus their attention on those areas with the greatest payback. Fewer decisions will be programmed into the computer than in the past, but the caliber of decision making will increase as information is processed and summarized in more pertinent ways.

At the general management level, the introduction of financial and other complex simulation models will permit the development of variable budgets. The latter will in turn permit better evaluation of the performance of the general manager involved. Such models should also be useful to general management in the investment planning process.

There will be continued improvement in the quantitative measures available to evaluate performance at both the functional and operations levels. In a real sense, the computer will make the concepts of both management-by-exception and management-by-objectives operational at these levels.

In general, the computer is going to affect management decision making and processes—such as operational planning, and measurement and evaluation—substantially more than it will affect the various characteristics of formal structure. This will hold for all levels in the hierarchy and for all types of organizational components.

Conclusion

The computer has brought a number of changes in the structure and processes of businesses. These changes have been less than some would have liked and more than others have wanted. If the same effort and original thinking had been applied to existing operations as was applied to the development of computer systems, some of the changes probably could have been made without the computer. In other cases, the speed and accuracy of the computer were absolutely essential in bringing about the changes.

Further changes will occur in the future. These will primarily involve increases in management efficiency and effectiveness, especially at the top functional level. They will be more subtle and more complex than those changes which have occurred to date and will be more difficult to justify economically, since they will not be accompanied by such substantial decreases in the total number of clerical personnel at the operations level as in the past.

To accomplish these changes will require advances in our knowledge of organizational relationships and business processes, as well as advances in computer hardware and software. Such advances can be aided by management support and training, but they cannot be halted. Kenneth Boulding described the reasons in another context:

> There is probably no way back. The growth of knowledge [computer systems] is one of the most irreversible forces known to mankind. It takes a catastrophe of very large dimensions to diminish the total stock of knowledge in the possession of man. Even in the rise and fall of great civilizations surprisingly little has been permanently lost,

and much that was lost for a short time was easily regained. Hence there is no hope for ignorance or for morality [management] based on it. Once we have tasted the fruit of the tree of knowledge, as the Biblical story illustrates so well, Eden is closed to us.[1]

The computer is a tool. Tomorrow's manager will use it in the same manner that today's manager uses a slide rule, or an adding machine, or a telephone.

[1] *The Meaning of the 20th Century: The Great Transition* (New York, Harper and Row, 1964), p. 23.

13

Computers and Middle Management

Robert S. Jackson

Reprinted by permission of *Journal
of Systems Management*, April 1970.

Since 1958 there has been considerable controversy among students
of management as to the impact the computer had upon organizational structure. Most controversy has centered around middle
management positions. Professors Leavitt and Whisler predicted a
dichotomous structure with the middle manager gravitating either
toward top executive positions, or downward to toilsome positions.
Professor Drucker doubts that the computer will eliminate middle
management jobs, but will force the middle manager to make
important decisions. Thus his job would become more challenging
and rewarding. Others have contended that, although the computer
will serve to enhance the job of the future middle manager, the
number of such managers will be reduced.[1]

What, then, has actually taken place in the past decade? Have
middle managers experienced the predicted demise; have their jobs
become challenging and rewarding; or has the effect of the computer
been neutral, allowing for a maintenance of *status quo*? The
following study attempts to answer these questions by measuring the
current experience of today's manager. Five top executives and 20
middle managers in the banking, chemical, oil and steel industries

---

[1] Reference to selected readings relevant to existing controversy are cited in the
Appendix.

were surveyed.[2] The sample was selected from five companies, all of which had owned or leased a computer for three or more years. All respondents have been users of computer software for two years or more. The responses, compiled from written questionnaires, were used to relate the present consequences of the computer upon the environment in which the managers work. More specifically, the study asked what effects the computer had upon: (1) the nature and scope of the job, (2) the extent of job specialization, (3) the overall skill level required, and (4) the basic managerial functions performed.

Broadening Perspectives

Despite earlier predictions, it is doubtful that middle management positions will be downgraded, nor is it likely that the need for this level of management will be lessened. The findings offer substantial evidence of certain trends that depict job content with expanded scope and broader perspective.

Eighty per cent of the middle managers interviewed said that their responsibilities had increased as a result of the computer. The increased amount of accurate and timely information enabled these managers to cope with more activities than had been possible prior to the computer. Eighty per cent claimed that their decision-making capabilities had been expanded because: (1) the number of important decisions required had been increased, (2) authority had expanded proportionally, and (3) the needed information was available.

Four of the five top executives indicated that they were able to delegate most of the authority relative to the organizations' short-term objectives where the middle managers could be trusted to react dependably. The middle manager who met those criteria said that many of their repetitive tasks could be further delegated, thus allowing more time for creative endeavors requiring intuition, judgement, and experience.

Increasing Specialization

Early speculation contended that the only middle management positions to survive the impact of the computer would be those

---

[2] Middle management is defined as those positions below the top executives of a self contained unit, and above the lowest level of supervision.

directly associated with the hardware and the information systems. This survey showed little evidence to support this hypothesis.

Three-fourths of the middle managers responded that the performance of their jobs required increased specialization. This was attributed to the increased responsibilities, authority, and activities of the job content. Some typical comments were:

> The computer has broadened the requirements for the job functions. It has also gone a long way towards the establishment of various specialized functions within the department.

> The mere fact that information technology has expanded the work content of the job forces the manager to become a specialist. A mistake can be very costly and possibly fatal to his career.

According to four of the top executives interviewed, the introduction of the computer allowed for a reduction of specialization in terms of their own positions. They could now depend upon the middle manager to interpret, analyze, and then relate necessary details to the appropriate executive. For example, evaluation of detailed financial statements in order to determine the organization's cash flow was no longer the responsibility of higher echelons.

Rising Skill Levels

When asked how the computer has affected the overall skill level of their jobs, top management responses were divided. Two executives indicated an increase, and three saw no noticeable effect. According to this latter group, the only new skills associated with the new information system were those that required a working knowledge of the system. It was, however, discovered that 100 per cent of the middle management interviewees noted a substantial increase in the skill level required to perform their jobs. This, they said, was due mainly to: (1) the increased number of reports pertaining to external as well as internal data, (2) the necessity of coordinating several operations with the computer, and (3) the necessary capability of communicating with the computer. One middle manager told of an interesting effect the computer had had upon his job:

> One of my tasks has always been to maintain the level of inventory. Bi-weekly reports reached my desk and seasonal guidelines for minimum levels were established by my

boss. The reports received since the employment of the computer no longer singularly relate to the inventory level but are now integrated with marketing, production, and purchasing data. Previous guidelines are no longer used. I must interpret overall needs from a much larger picture.

Weighing these responses with the earlier predictions, there is little evidence that the need for middle management positions will decrease, nor will they become highly structured and ladened with characteristics of Theory X. Accordingly, the top executives interviewed declared that the need for these positions are both dependent upon and relative to many factors, both internal and external to the computer and the information technology that evolves. They went on to say:

However, we are always looking for opportunities to expand, and the computer has given tremendous impetus to this desire as well as some favorable results.

Similarly, these same top executives said that they would continue to delegate marginal activities to a point of diminishing returns, with the cut-off point determined by the middle manager's degree of ability to perform and make accurate decisions. Findings that further support this thesis can be seen with a brief discussion of each managerial function.

Managerial Functions

The interviewees were asked to comment on the effect the computer has had upon the performance of their job functions.

Seventy-five per cent of the middle managers claimed that they spent more time with the planning function. This was mainly because the complexity of the associated problems had been increased. Some of the reasons were: (1) the work content of their jobs entailed more long-term objectives, (2) planning decisions are required at more frequent intervals, (3) the decisions relative to the function are more important, and (4) most decisions can no longer be made on an *ad hoc* basis but require greater foresight and ingenuity.

Direction

The computer has had no noticeable effect upon the function of directing. Eighty-five per cent of the middle managers interviewed said that they spent more time on this function, but could not say whether or not this was a consequence of the computer. A few of these managers did pin-point major portions of the time increase as time allotted to directing departmental personnel on the use of the computer systems. Computerization of work usually requires thorough understanding of the information system's demands, abilities, and limitations; thus, it is necessary to revamp and upgrade the skill levels of the entire department.

Staffing

Middle management interviewees saw little evidence that the staffing function had been affected by the computer. Several did, however, comment that the allocation of the time spent with the related function of training had increased considerably.

Top executives noted that finding the right personnel became more difficult as many jobs became more specialized. Furthermore, existing jobs became more technical, and re-training of personnel became a necessity.

Control

Middle managers agreed that the time spent on control had decreased, but the responsibilities connected with the function had increased substantially. The reasons given placed emphasis upon the timeliness and accuracy of computerized reports. These reports (monitoring, triggered, and demand) make possible earlier recognition of and response to problems.

Innovation

The only limitations connected with innovation are determined by the manager's knowledge of and ability to discern the present and long-term needs of the organization, as well as his knowledge of the computer systems. The middle managers who indicated that the computer's impact upon this function is negligible also indicated that they had not fully examined its capabilities and opportunities in this light.

It appears that the important variable is the skill level of the middle manager. It is evident that in considering each function within the organization, as long as this skill level is adequate, the computer enhanced the efficiency of operations as well as helped the manager to be a responsible and necessary director.

Each middle manager found that the peculiar characteristics of his job were affected in a different way. However, all recognized the opportunity to concentrate more on the functions of planning and innovation with less time being allotted to the function of control. With more time available for creative tasks and less required for routine matters, middle management positions tend to become more challenging and the rewards offered are greater and more numerous.

Conclusions

Organizational structure has been affected at all levels by the computer, and the implications of these effects will continue to become evident. Elimination of middle management positions is not one of the implications; instead quite different developments will evolve. Top executives depend upon the specialization and skills of their middle managers to a great extent. Now that the computer has allowed for an increase of this specialization and these skills, the attributes of the middle managers will be in greater demand and their number will increase with computer use. Middle management positions will be upgraded due to increased need and the greater amount of responsibility inherent in the new aspects of these positions.

These changes in the nature of middle management presage a lessened need for top managers. It is these echelons that will be decreased. Further changes in organizational structure will also take the form of decentralization of authority structure. Not only will there be fewer top managers, but their decision-making authority will be further delegated to the middle management ranks.

This predicted development is dependent upon the philosophies and preferences of the top managers presently in control. These philosophies and preferences are contingent, to a great degree, upon the capabilities of the middle manager to perform well in his newly achieved status. Therefore, it is recommended that every manager become sensitive to the computer and its systems, and that he evaluate his position in the light of these important implications. He must examine how the computer has affected each task associated with his job, and ask: (1) Is he required to spend more or less time with the task? (2) Are problems inherent to this task increased or decreased? (3) Is he able to delegate more or less of the tasks? (4) How can the computer enhance the possibilities of his job content? The key to effective utilization of information systems is people. These people are the middle managers who are cognizant of the dimensions and capabilities of the computer.

Appendix

Peter Drucker, "What the Computers Will Be Telling You," *Nations Business*, August, 1966, pp. 84–90.

Glenn Gilman, "The Computer Revisited," *Business Horizons*, Winter, 1966, pp. 77–89.

"How the Computer is Changing Management Organization," *Business Management*, July, 1967, pp. 26–30.

H. T. Leavitt and T. L. Whisler, "Management in the 1980's," *Harvard Business Review*, November–December, 1958, pp. 41–48.

Hak Chong Lee, "The Organizational Impact of the Computer," *Management Services*, May–June, 1967, pp. 39–43.

Donald H. Sanders, *Computers in Business*, New York: McGraw-Hill Book Company, 1968, pp. 324–332.

Donald R. Shaul, "What's Really Ahead for Middle Management?", *Personnel*, November–December, 1964, pp. 8–16.

T. L. Whisler, "The Manager and the Computer," *Journal of Accounting*, January, 1965, pp. 27–32.

14

Modular Method of Structuring MIS

James V. Milano
Reprinted by permission of
Data Management, February 1970.

The concept of a management information system has been highly promoted and taken seriously by a large number of enterprises. Large amounts of money, talent and time are being expanded by both government and industry in this general area with very little success. There is little question that the promised goals of management information systems are not as readily achieved as would be apparent from the budget outlay and computer systems in existence today.

Generally, there is a great deal of disenchantment with what is being received from such systems. A critical examination indicates that most systems provide, at best, only dated and voluminous reports. This situation raises the question of why it is important to create a disciplined management information system. The premise is made that the advent of the computer and its allied management science techniques for all major enterprises to progress in this area for efficiency and competitive purposes.

The subject under discussion involves many facets in the management information spectrum. These include such items as planning an MIS, determining information requirements, structuring a data base [see Table 1], systems development, systems implementation, etc. These are the traditional components of systems development and design. Other components discussed here may assist in solving the dilemma of making the concept of a computer-based MIS a practical reality.

Table 1. Structuring the Management Information System

MIS must be developed on an evolutionary basis.

The MIS must be structured along functional lines with the understanding that the functional managers must comprehend what happens to "their" data in the system.

The MIS must be developed as an extension of what is being done today.

Hardware won't solve the MIS dilemma; hard systems work will.

MIS must be developed and controlled in manageable segments, i.e., into pieces of a size that can be honestly estimated, forecasted and monitored effectively.

Don't ask executives what are their MIS requirements. Lay out for them what you think they should be so the executive will have something to vote on.

Integrate your MIS modules on a related basis. An example would be to integrate budget and accounting before taking on any other module.

For the purpose of this paper, an MIS is defined as a concept of managing an enterprise as an integrated whole with the assistance of a systematic application of information and computer technology—in short, automating and integrating data from the various functional management areas.

Since the professionals associated with data processing, hardware manufacturers and many functional managers have been hard at work resolving the MIS dilemma for over a decade, why has progress been so limited? As one reviews history to find the answer to this question, we find that much of it lies in our constant seeking to find a quick solution based on the notion of breakthrough.

In the early years, we all went through the hardware romance. The hardware manufacturers could solve any problem, just so long as you placed orders. From this we progressed to the applications approach, then to the total systems approach, and now to the MIS approach.

We have learned a few things from this migration from one approach to another approach to solve our information problems. One of the key lessons learned is that hardware is not the answer. Secondly, arriving at a solution is tough, slow, hard work; there are no easy packaged solutions available. Thirdly, perhaps we haven't been looking deeply enough at the factors which have definite influence on structuring an MIS. For discussion purposes these may be categorized as environmental, systems, and administrative factors.

Environmental Factors

Historical Significance of Functional Management

Historically, the grouping of like activities and skills into departmentalized units of the total organization was the accepted and most efficient method for the management, direction, and control of integrated human effort. This functional approach as an organizational philosophy was initially developed by the military and used with success and efficiency. Commercial enterprises, therefore, as they grew and developed, adopted the functional approach as a natural and logical managerial method of known success.

The growth of electronic data processing activities has its origins in functionalized entities such as accounting, payroll, personnel and finance. This association was based primarily on the need for utilizing data processing machines to reduce the large clerical workload in these fuinctions. The functional applications are still a large segment of any MIS application.

There is no question that the integration of data through the MIS concept strikes a blow at functional management. Managers feel at home in their functional environments and it remains to be determined whether the functional approach should be altered as would be indicated by the integration of data in an MIS.

Staff Interpretation of Data

Another very important constraint mitigating against the integrating concept of an MIS is the insistence of the functional managers on their right to interpret data which emanate from their area of responsibility. The executive in charge of production normally wants to pass on all production-generated data going to top management. He wants to make certain they aren't misinterpreted from his department's point of view. He feels at home with these, has a definite proprietary sense about the data, and he knows his advice is desired and sought.

By the same token, it must also be assumed that decisions coordinated with functional area managers have a functionalized bias or a functionalized flavor at very best. MIS designers must recognize this factor of staff interpretation of data, and provide for a workable solution to managers for preserving this deeply embedded prerogative.

Centralization vs. Decentralization

There appears to be a great deal of misunderstanding over what centralization and decentralization of information systems really mean. To most management people, a decentralized organization is interpreted as one having great autonomy and decision-making authority below the corporate level. Centralization, on the other hand, is viewed as retaining more autonomy and decision-making authority within the corporate group.

Almost invariably, company executives view the centralization-decentralization issue with respect to computers and information systems in the same manner as they view the degree of centralization or decentralization established in the corporate organizational structure and its style of management. Such thinking certainly serves as a deterrent to centralized MIS activities, even when they may be considered desirable.

Centralization of the control of information systems on a planned basis need not diminish the autonomy and decision-making capability among the lower echelons of the organization. In fact, it can and probably will enhance the effectiveness of these activities. I think it is incorrect to assume that a company is increasing centralization simply because it makes extensive use of computers and controls input. Information processed by computers can improve all aspects of management and can strengthen either centralization of decentralization efforts.

Role of the Systems Analyst as a Catalyst

In an effort to adjust to the ever-changing conditions of the business world, many executives are now using computer-produced information in managing their companies. This gives the MIS director (and his senior systems personnel) the opportunity to act at a catalyst. In this role, he can assist the executive so that the latter can spend his time examining operations in a more judicious manner, with more time for future planning. The analyst can do this by showing how data can be arrayed to depict trends, how it can be used for long-range planning and how it can be used for business analysis of special areas of the company. The analyst can concern himself more with the kinds of data to be processed, rather than being overly concerned about how the data are processed.

The analyst must constantly demonstrate that management

information systems are a means to an end, not an end in themselves. The old adage of the analyst—if the executive will describe his requirements, I will design his system—is no longer acceptable. Executives have not and possibly should not, diagnose their detailed information needs. It is up to the analyst to give him something to vote upon. In other words, the analyst must visualize outputs and present them to executives as the basis for discussion in determining requirements.

Decision Making

The literature is replete with statements that a new MIS is needed in order that top executives can make better decisions in a shorter reaction time. This is a fine generalized position to take, but it is an oversimplification of the issue at hand.

Top executives make relatively few decisions based on reports emanating from information systems, but they ask many questions based on these reports. The nature of the questions sets a pattern which triggers action at many levels. Secondly, top level decisions are made from data in reports after this data has been thoroughly analyzed by business analysts, operational analyst and long-range planners. Thirdly, the decision-making process is in many instances the accumulative effect of many small decisions at lower levels based on very general policy guidance from top policy makers.

All of these decision-making methodologies have a profound effect on the MIS structure and must be recognized and accounted for in making the system operable.

Man-machine Relationship

In our zeal to structure systems which will take advantage of hardware and software developments, we have a tendency to minimize the impact of such systems upon people. As decision rules are placed in computers, the element of job security looms very high in the minds of the individuals affected by these rules. The impact of this factor must be constantly reviewed because no system will work without the understanding assistance, and desire of employees to make the system work.

Responsibility for the Integrity of the Data Base

A significant organizational problem that an MIS brings to the forefront is one regarding the data base. The fundamental question to be resolved is determining who should be held responsible for the integrity of the information itself. By way of example, data are entered into the system, they are manipulated and combined with other data, then reformatted and summarized and finally flashed on a visual display output device in the president's office. Who should be held accountable for the reliability of the information? In the final analysis, whoever is held responsible for data that have been integrated from various functional areas must have some form of control over all aspects of the system.

In the early years of electronic data processing, the accepted rule was that the proponent for whom the data were prepared was responsible for the data that went into the report. This often resulted in a great deal of manual checking of reports. Such a concept is not practicable in an MIS environment.

One answer to the problem is simply to say that the MIS director is responsible for the integrity of all of the data in the system. This gets a bit complex when one considers that much of the contents of the data bank originates and often resides in plants, distribution branches, field sales offices and subsidiary firms, all of which have their own line management structure. There are many other possible solutions to the problem. The important fact is that it must be recognized and solved if the automated MIS is to be effective.

Day-to-day Business

The day-to-day data processing requirements are a reflection of the dynamics of the business environment. The entire structure is usually in some form of change at all times. This makes the business of systems and programming maintenance a critical issue. It also means that the designers of the MIS must understand and, to a degree, live with these changes. Also, they must dispel the notion that they will come up with a new masterful system which will replace the on-going system. The on-going system of today will not be the on-going system tomorrow. One answer is to make the MIS implementation an extension, on a modular basis, of today's systems.

Systems Factors

Data Flow Analysis

Most systems analysts follow the basic premise that the entire spectrum of data flow is analyzed in detail in structuring an MIS. This has gotten to be such a tremendous, time consuming job, we should revise our thinking in this area. We would do better to concentrate on decision analysis and data station analysis.

Decision analysis is locating and trying to determine the impact of the decision-makers in any chain of events. One of the keys to finding the decision-makers is by physically tracing the system, discussing what each individual's function is and the basis for any decisions he may make. Once the decision points are determined, their interrelationships will also undoubtedly begin to emerge. It is important to determine the impact of the total process of the previously unnoticed or unknown decision-makers. Secondly, it is well to determine what might be termed the cumulative effect of a series of little decisions. An example is the rounding off of figures to the next highest number by a group of clerks in a process run in a plant. The cumulative effect can certainly be significant. It will probably be necessary to return several times to discuss a given situation with certain decision-makers. This technique is termed data station analysis.

The primary objective of data station analysis is to structure the data flow to the decision-making point, determine the use of that information at the decision point in arriving at the decisions made, and the flow and type of information that leaves the point of decision. This process will allow for the structuring of the information network. Data station analysis involves the study of the functions of various decision-makers, the information used to make decisions and the results that are generated by the decisions.

Data Discipline

Regardless of the organizational placement of the MIS, there are certain factors concerning these systems which have an impact throughout the organization of the enterprise. Among them, that an MIS requires a strong element of discipline which must be adhered to if the MIS is to be successful. Term this data discipline.

The common concept of data discipline implies a concern for clean and accurate input. This has been a problem with automated information systems since their inception. The problem extends beyond the simple control of input. The significance of discipline in the field of processing data stems from the binary basis upon which computers operate. As a consequence, all of the thought processes that bear upon what a computer can be expected to do must be structured in a "go"–"no go" mode.

The development of the logic which goes into the designing of the system to be automated, the writing of the machine programs, the format of inputs and outputs, must conform to this philosophy. Thus not only must the systems specialists think in highly structured, disciplined terms, but the users of MIS must also think in these terms. They must exercise discipline in formulating their requirements.

Information Discipline

Beyond the data discipline stage, there is another equally important aspect of discipline related to MIS development, that is "information discipline." It involves the problem of continuity of data summarization and presentation to management. The need becomes obvious when you appreciate the fact that part of the corporate communications problem stems from using the same label to tag different segments of information.

Example: companies of any size these days prepare formal budget documents. Within these budget documents, one generally finds a section on profit leaders by product line or group. Subsequently, during the monitoring cycle for the budget, we find such reports being prepared as weekly and monthly sales reports, inventory reports, production reports and actual statements of operating profit by product line. The reports are frequently used to serve several purposes and the assumption is made that the product line groupments in the various reports contain the same products. All too often, this is not the case. Often, there are a few significant differences among the various product lines used in these reports. The users are generally unaware that this could happen. Thus, even though there are different reports for different purposes, information discipline is essential in reports that are supposed to be comparing plans with actual results. This involves the successful institution of information discipline within the firm, if the MIS is to be effective.

Levels of Systems

There are three levels of systems. This fact must be kept in mind by the designers of an MIS, if the MIS is to serve all levels of management. Level I deals with transactions, files and reports. The specifications are clear and the system generally supports or replaces clerical functions. Level II deals with decision rules, requires item data such as prices, and weight. Such systems are concerned with alternatives and the people involved with such systems are there to exercise judgments (exceptions to the decision rules). Level III is concerned with how we run the business. The people involved are negotiators. Management sets policies and considers the alternatives and consequences of such policies. Such systems imply top management's knowledge and participation in such systems.

Administrative Factors

Systems Planning and Project Control

There is little unanimity regarding the best method to follow in developing, documenting and controlling systems efforts. Systems planning can be defined briefly as the continuous process of isolating and defining systems projects, allocating resources to these projects and controlling the progress of their development.

A systems project is defined as the activity and the resource investment required to change an existing system. This definition is based on the assumption that all projects involve instruments that transform what is used today into systems to be used in the future.

Once systems have been sorted, the next major step is one of setting systems targets. These are reference points which can be used as a basis for resource allocation and control of individual projects. The job of structuring systems into projects and targets have been poor. We have not applied ourselves to this area in an effective manner and we must concentrate on this to properly inform management and gain their confidence.

Standards

The area of standards for the development of an MIS fall into two broad categories. The first is methods standards which serve as a guide in establishing uniform practices and common techniques. These include specific yardsticks such as checks against the details of systems analysis programming and computer operations. The second category of standards is performance standards. These standards are used to evaluate capital assets that are allocated to an MIS project, as well as personnel and equipment.

In order to provide a third and necessary means of controlling an MIS, it is proposed that there be established another group of guidelines in addition to the two previously described. These can be termed management standards. They have applicability to any segment of the enterprise concerned with information flow, systems design and data processing. The need for such standards stems from the fact that an MIS is involved with integrating data and systems from all aspects of the corporation.

Management standards for MIS can be derived from two general areas. One is the benchmark variety, which is based on criteria within the firm's industrial environment; an example would be the ratio of sales dollars to MIS costs. The other type of standard is the one developed for internal control purposes based on data within the firm. An example would be some form of a time/phase chart to display interdependencies of the various parts of sub-systems within an application.

We all have to work at evolving new standards by which we can be judged as well as judge others. We have been negligent in developing this phase of EDP management.

Assessments

In precise terms, assessments may be defined as customer charges. More realistically, however, assessment includes all of the activities necessary to develop and substantiate charges for information and forms the basis for billing the user. The question is often asked: "Why go through the effort of assessing information services?"

The answer lies in a combination of three factors. First, user demands against the system increase rapidly when the service is without charge. Secondly, a charge-out system can be used to evaluate the effective use of MIS resources. The third reason is the budgetary purposes.

It is very difficult for the MIS activity to formulate and defend a budget which has to respond to the demand of users. Ideally, the MIS activity should ultimately be budgeted at zero by charging out all services and overhead and receiving payments from the user's budgets. This is very difficult to achieve from a practical point of view but still remains a worthwhile planning objective. Some form of assessment is vital to assist in controlling the development of a Management Information System.

15

Management in the Computer Age

William Karp

Reprinted by permission of
Data Management, December 1970.

The computer revolution is here, and it is proceeding at high speed. More, perhaps, than any other group, management is feeling the impact of the computer. Traditional management concepts are being obsoleted rapidly.

Where previously management was the initiator of changes in industry, today the tables are being turned. In the age of the computer, it is clear that managers will be subject to change—with little notice and less choice.

The efficiency of the typical "practical manager" today may be impaired by the rational behavior of the computer. Computer competition may become too much for him, leading to frustrations. Unless, of course, he is able to divert his energies into more creative channels such as art, poetry, theatre and creative human relationships, on and off the job. Otherwise, we may suffer a rise in ulcer victims. An ulcer is often recognized by psychologists as symbolic of an unfulfilled human personality. John Ciardi defines an ulcer as "an unkissed imagination taking its revenge" of the dehumanized personality of, in this case, the "practical manager."[1]

In the future, industry may exchange the "practical manager" for a new model, one with a creative imagination and a broad outlook. The specialist with narrow-gauged skills will be less in demand since the computer will take over all such specialized functions.

[1] Charles A. Myers (ed.), The M.I.T. Press, Cambridge, Mass., February, 1967.

The computer is transforming the "nature and practice of management."[2] Even management's basic philosophy is being put to the test. Management values, attitudes and life styles are undergoing change as computer technology permeates organizations. Organizations themselves are being restructured in the process. It is evident already that traditional organizational structures, management philosophy and practices require radical adaptations to meet the new conditions. The longer the delay in making changes, the greater the expected disturbance of the equilibrium of the organization and disruption of the management social system.

Role of Data Management Personnel

Data management personnel are the professional experts in automated data processing. They hold positions of growing importance since their expertise will influence the direction in which information technology and decision making goes in organizations. What are their chances of entering the elite corps of top management tomorrow?

Undoubtedly, some will reach the highest management positions in time, but the majority will remain in highly structured jobs. Certainly, at present, continuing shortages of programmers, systems designers, information technologists and EDP managers prevent transfers to operating departments. Without the broadening experiences to be obtained in operating departments, however, data specialists will not be able to advance their careers, and, therefore, are not likely to be selected right now for top-management posts.

Perhaps of greater significance is the factor of specialization itself. A highly-developed technical competence in any field does not qualify a man for top management responsibilities. There is more to a policy or executive position than expertise in information processing or programmed decision-making. A good example of this point is the late President Eisenhower's "forceful criticism of attempts by professional soldiers to determine the size of the nation's military budget."[3] Their special know-how was valuable in the military field but too narrow and limited to encompass a broader range of federal budget decision-making.

---

[2] Ibid.
[3] Melvin Anshen, "Technology and Managerial Decision," in John T. Dunlop (ed.), *Automation and Technological Change*, (American Assembly), (Englewood Cliffs, N.J.: Prentice-Hall, Inc., 1962), p. 75.

In time, as data processing specialists move creatively from structured, programmed decision-making to total management information systems, their contribution to problem-solving and decision-making in broad areas of the enterprise will come to be recognized. When that day arrives, those who operate the information systems that integrate various functions of an enterprise, will become candidates for a step up the ladder to top management posts, especially those who become versed in the management sciences so that they can view the business organization as a system.

At the present, and for some time to come, data processing management will face a challenge from the operating management. There is need for better understanding between them. On the one hand, data processing managers complain about the fuzzy and misleading inputs of operating managers. On the other hand, operating managers accept the expertise of data processing managers but charge them with a lack of understanding and failure to address themselves to the needs of the business, and they cite examples. They complain about computers that continue to spit out reports that supposedly were stopped months ago; meanwhile, they cannot get data they really need.

The gap will be closed between data processing and operating managements when operating management is involved in the development of information systems. Where companies regularly use operating managers on information development projects, there is usually a successful outcome. The interface between computer and operating people in such projects serves to link them together, resulting in improved understanding and better communication.

In presenting new projects, the key test should "not be computer feasibility, but relevance to the business."[4] The question uppermost in the mind of data processing management should be the potential impact of a project upon profits. Perhaps, most importantly, data processing specialists must become involved in the total processes and goals of a business or an agency.

Changing Characteristics of Managerial Work

The "shopkeeper" type of executive is on the way out. A new breed of top management has become essential in the age of computers. There must be receptivity to change. Innovation must become a way of life, the "trademark" of leadership. Creativity must be encouraged

[4] J. Sanford Smith, *The Growing Maturity of the Computer Age.*

and rewarded in an environment where risk is accepted as a calculated policy of corporation action.

Top management in the computer age no longer can depend upon large files of information organized along functional lines into bureaus and departments for inputs to decision-making. The specialized attitudes, jargons, forms and perceptions of personnel in the various bureaus and departments tend to obstruct communication flow, diffuses authority and dislocates responsibility. Under the worst conditions, a department head becomes what Friedrich Juenger calls a "white-collar scribe:"

> . . . such a man . . . gets the notion that all is well with the world because his files are in order. He tends to confuse the world with a bureau, since the card file is his world, the center of his life. To conceive of the universe as a huge bureau would be an excellent idea if only nature had intended us to live on red tape.[5]

One of the positive benefits which accrues to top management from computer based information-processing systems is the withering away of bureaus and departments with their large files. At the same time, behavior patterns which are derivatives of the bureau mentality are wiped out. Channels of information are shorter, less distorted and more effective. Authority is exercised directly. And responsibility is easily fixed. Perhaps, the greatest benefit of all for top management is the impact of information processing systems upon their thinking. For the first time, they begin to see the business enterprise as an integrated system. Along the way, the computer opens up a view to the mysteries of human red tape which were heretofore locked up in a maize of the bureaucratic organization.

Computers have already relieved executives from a considerable amount of work. They have benefited from computer applications in accounting, inventory control, production scheduling and control, purchasing, customer ordering, marketing and shipping, among others. There will be further extensions in the 70's to cover many more repetitive tasks either in the factory or the office.

By 1980–85, computer techniques will have advanced to the point where they will take over a large number of programmed decisions made by managers across the board. The focus of information technology will be upon problems which are structured and subject to programmed solutions.

Freed from routine activities, managers will address themselves

---

[5] Friedrich G. Juenger, *The Failure of Technology.*

to a range of problems which cannot easily be defined—problems that are unstructured and do not yield easily to programming—such as the problems encountered in determining organization objectives; selecting, developing and motivating employees; improving collective-bargaining relations; humanizing the work environment; facilitating company relations with federal, state and local governments; and learning to interact with the community which buys its wares and from which it draws both employees and public support. These aspects of the managerial job will rise in importance and will require broadly trained personnel who are sensitive to social, economic, political as well as technical changes.

One of the most painful phenomena brought about by the "knowledge explosion" in general and the computer revolution in particular is management obsolescence. That is, those who have fallen behind in knowledge, technique, or skill required by decision-making or job performance standards. A recent study by Stanford Research Institute showed that technical know-how and versatility of 50% of engineers and 25% of physical scientists have become obsolete. The rate among top management and other executives is not known, but may indeed run higher. The introduction of automation and computer technology into manufacturing, engineering and service industries, such as banking and insurance, has taken its toll in managerial obsolescence. Thousands of executives are caught up in the chilling realization that they are no longer capable of coping with the increasing complexity of their jobs.

The application of management sciences, including operations research, to a whole range of problems in management has widened the obsolescence gap among top and middle management groups. Since the management sciences are based upon mathematical know-how developed after World War II, the built-in obsolescence factor in many older company managers may be beyond redemption. Even today, top management and other executives in many industries who lack the mathematical "tools" of problem-solving such as linear programming, dynamic programming, game theory, statistical decision theory, heuristic programming, among others, are at a competitive disadvantage.

In the future, managers must be equipped with a comprehensive understanding of the new technology. Top level executives must know both its capabilities and limitations. Above all, they must become familiar with the thinking of professionals in the field, and their approach to problem-solving, otherwise, they run the risk of becoming incapable of effectively managing experts in the new technology. More importantly, they will not understand how to use the new tools to help them adapt the structure and administer the organization. Too many company managements have failed thus far to take full advantage of the potentials of computer technology. In fact, one study by Baum and Burack shows that the "general lack of technically qualified administrative and functional personnel in . . . insurance and banking has acted as a restraining factor in incorporating information technology."[6]

Despite the emphasis attributed to the in-roads made by computers and the management sciences upon the functions of management, much of the area of managerial activities remains ill-defined, unstructured and heuristic. Relations within the firm and with external social and economic forces remain largely unpredictable. This will require the continuing applications by managers of such irreplaceable human qualities as experience, judgement, imagination, initiative, perception, sensitivity and courage in decision-making. And even if eventually these cognitive processes are taken over by man-machine intelligence systems, managerial functions will push out yet to other activities which are not now being done because there is not enough time to do them. Thus, computers will not so much replace management capacities as extend their problem-solving and decision-making capabilities. As Jay W. Forrester has asserted, "about 90% of what matters to the success of a business enterprise lies outside the EDP system. . . ."[7]

Group Decision-making

The complexity of decision-making has already grown beyond the expertise of the top executive in many companies. Decisions often call for inputs of many people, each with unique knowledge and experience.

Before arriving at a decision, the top executive must bring together all of those who have a special input. He must consider all the alternatives presented. Only then can he arrive at a judicious decision in which risk has been minimized.

This process may be designated as group or participative decision-making. The effects of such a process is to distribute

---

[6] Bernard B. Baum and Elmer Burack, "Information Technology, Manpower Development and Organization Performance," *Academy of Management Journal*, (September, 1969).

[7] Charles A. Myers, "Some Implications of Computers For Management," paper prepared for Annual Meeting, I.R.R.A., December, 1966.

influence and power in the organization. Although one man may ultimately finalize a decision, he cannot wisely make it alone. A sharing of decision-making responsibilities established interdependence among the parties. Thus, a new kind of decision-making model replaces the old authoritarian one. Psychologically speaking, the decision-making environment in the organization will never be the same. The need for cooperation becomes a categorical imperative; success depends on it. Those who fail to cooperate increase the risk of failure and eventually must lose their position on the team. Cooperation replaces competition as a dynamic for organizational progress.

Man-machine systems have facilitated centralization of information needed for decision-making of a routine and programmed type. For the most part these affect more or less lower level decisions. What concerns us at this point are top management decisions which depend upon unstructured and unprogrammed information. There is every reason to believe participative group decision-making will grow over time. Many executives may come to respect the power and effectiveness of democratic processes and seek to apply group decision-making elsewhere in society.

On the other hand, as we get closer to the "total management information system," top management can become a self-sufficient "big brother." By means of tight control over a computerized total management information system, "big brother" can restrict access to the system. Thus, as Professor Jay W. Forrester has said, "It appears that we can use computers and information technology to create more confinement or more freedom."

Future of Middle Management

As far as supervision goes, computer operated man-machine systems ease the supervisory burden of middle management which is largely concerned with supervision and handling well-structured tasks in accounting, inventory control, purchasing, shipments, production scheduling, marketing, among others. When the work pace is pre-determined, "work-pushing" plays a much smaller role in meeting production quotas or goals. Middle management responsibility for getting the work out, under such conditions, is assured. For machine-paced operations do not depend upon workers maintaining a standardized rate of work.

The consequences of computer operated man-machine systems

upon middle management are not altogether clear. Diverse opinions prevail. Among them are the following:

Fewer middle management people will be needed to perform supervisory routine tasks. Many of those now in such positions are in danger of skill obsolescence.

Middle management organizational structure is being changed, sometimes radically, with down-grading in the status of some jobs and up-grading of others.

Computer skilled professional types are taking over middle management slots; however, their relationship to top management is more in the nature of staff rather than line operations. Under man-machine systems, the old relationship between staff and line has been blurred.

The demarcation line between top and middle management has become sharper and harder to penetrate.

Top management is absorbing former middle management functions in the areas of planning, budgeting and forecasting.

Overall, the work environment for middle management will become more satisfactory. It will be less frustrating and more wholesome than those we often encounter today. The reason is that the need for middle managers to exercise authority over others will diminish. Conditions for reducing conflict with subordinates will improve human relationships.

Supervision

Lower level management, namely, supervisors and foremen, is in the process of being divorced from the typical work roles. The function of controlling work procedures and maintaining employee productivity rates is being taken out of their hands by machine paced programming. Under those conditions, men are removed from their hallowed historical position in the production system.

In a recent comparative field study between two high-volume production facilities in the baking industry, it was found that "supervisors in the more advanced technological system devoted significantly less time to direction and control activities."[8] It was evident that "normal" supervisory functions were diminished.

As technology advances, the erosion of supervisory direction and control will continue. Supervisory relations and time commitments will be disengaged from production processes. The supervisory contribution to production is being relegated to a secondary role.

Employee Relations

Employee relations are undergoing change. Perhaps no other area of business requires it more, certainly, no other area is loaded with greater emotional overtones.

The conditions upon which companies based employee relations policies and practices are rapidly disappearing:

The work force is changing from blue to white collar. Except for maintenance crews and skilled technicians, blue collar employees are becoming an ever smaller component of the work force. On the other hand, the white collar group is growing, with no end in sight.

The white collar group has an educational level of high school, college and beyond. Of the professionals among white collar employees, you have an elite corps with the highest intellectual attainments, equal to or greater than that of top management.

The character of work itself places ever greater emphasis upon innovation and creativity.

The balance of power between companies and unions is shifting. With declining numbers of blue collar workers, unions are losing their constituency, unless they learn to organize white collar people.

The authority employers commanded over employees by virtue of their dominant position in hiring has dissipated under present labor market conditions. Moreover, white collar employees demand treatment as equals. They shun

[8] Elmer H. Burack, "Technology and Supervisory Functions: A Preliminary View," *Human Organization*, (Winter, 1967).

*superior-subordinate   relationships.   Unless   treated   as
equals, they won't stay.*

The use of authoritarian methods in employee relations is
counter productive for white collar employees, particularly professions. Motivation, innovation and creativity do not flourish in an
authoritarian work environment. A new type, sophisticated executive
is needed who can lead and inspire smart, young and energetic
people. One who is flexible and places creative accomplishment
above discipline or rules. If he finds an employee works better at
home, or at the seashore, or a cabin in the mountains, he will not
hesitate to go along.

Loyalty to the company can no longer be demanded. It must be
earned.

The unique qualities of each employee must be recognized and
treated with due regard to individuality. Company failure to treat
professionals according to individual standards causes them to seek
employment elsewhere. Although these people are not yet demonstrating in protests against the company, they can and do resign.

The work environment must be humanized. People must count
in the organization. The company must demonstrate that it puts
human resources first.

Unions and companies will seek to resolve differences before
they erupt. Computer techniques have already come into play in
developing wage and fringe benefit packages. More fact-finding and
conflict resolution methods will be employed to avoid disruption of
delicate human relations. On the other hand, unless companies vastly
improve their human relations, you can expect some form of
organization of white collar personnel to develop for collective
bargaining with employers including professionals.

A New Management Philosophy

Computers and the management sciences have done much more than
place new "tools" in the hands of managers. They have also created a
new way of thinking. No single concept has emerged in recent times
which has had a more powerful impact upon management than the
systems approach. No longer can we view "things" piecemeal. To
understand how "things" work, we must understand how various
sub-systems link together to form a total system. All are interdependent. A breakdown in a subsystem immediately affects the whole
system.

Thoughtful business leaders have come to realize the implications of the systems approach for their companies, internally and externally. To function at optimum levels, company management must link together towards a common goal.

Viewed from the outside, each enterprise is a subsystem within a local business community, within an industry, within a social, economic and political structure. There are wheels within wheels within wheels—all interrelated. No business leader worth his salt today can fail to recognize that his company is a link in a long chain. A pressure upon the chain at any point can affect his interests.

Yet, there are business leaders—all too many of them—who still think bad schools, bad housing, unemployment, poverty or crime is no concern of theirs. These are problems in their view that should be left to politicians and to governments. "The corporations," according to them, "do the most good for society when they just stick to business and maximize their profits."[9]

In the last few years, there has been a major breakthrough in the attitude of management towards their social and community responsibilities. Perhaps Roger M. Blough, chairman of the board of U. S. Steel, best epitomized it in a speech before the Iron and Steel Institute, when he said:

> Today, there is another great social change now aflame in which business has an unperformed social responsibility— one as inescapable, I believe, as the responsibility for operating at a profit. . . .

Another business leader, David Rockefeller, summarizes a philosophy of social action for the 1970's. He says:

> It is my firm conviction that in the years ahead business corporations will find it increasingly necessary to fulfill a social as well as an economic function. If private enterprise is to retain any real degree of autonomy—and, in my judgement, it must do so if it is to continue to play a creative role in society—it will have to accept heavy social responsibilities.

> To put it more specifically, the men who manage private corporations will be obliged, as part of the daily course of business, to confront a wide range of social problems.

[9] R. C. Albrook, "Business Wrestles With Its Social Conscience," *Fortune*, (August, 1968), 89–91.

They will have to recognize that although business men can justly claim having played an important role in creating the affluent society which has spread its benefits to millions of people all over the world, they should also share in the blame for creating other problems of a social and environmental nature which as yet have not been solved.

As matters stand, a gross imbalance exists between technological and sociological progress. It is widening. Transition to the technological society has been too rapid for human beings, social and political institutions to absorb. As a result, the behavior of our social and political institutions is becoming more and more obsolete. Social patterns are disintegrating. Value systems are in sharp conflict. Social distance between generations is reaching a point of noncommunication. The fabric of common interests which underpins community life is under severe strain. Society itself is in a process of disruption.

It is being recognized, but all too slowly, that a major effort must be mounted to build a viable body of authentic information about the dynamics of human behavior. Social innovation must be integrated into our way of life. In the past, changes in human institutions have taken hundreds of years. Usually, war and revolution accompanied such social transformations. Bloody battles are no longer an acceptable model for instituting change. A more orderly and rational route must be found to social change.

Perhaps, with the help of computer technology, we will unravel the most elusive phenomena of all—man himself.

16

The Computer Comes of Age

Neil J. Dean

Reprinted from the January–February 1968
issue of *Harvard Business Review*. © 1968 by
the President and Fellows of Harvard College;
all rights reserved.

The survey to be reported on in this article is the second such study made by Booz, Allen & Hamilton Inc.[1] The 108 manufacturing companies covered were selected on the basis of their superior records of sales growth and return on equity compared to the averages for their industries. Every significant manufacturing industry group was included. The companies' experience with the computer ranged from one to eighteen years. Annual sales volumes ranged from under $50 million to more than $10 billion. Both centralized and decentralized companies participated. The manufacturing processes of the companies included "continuous process" companies which convert raw materials into finished products by a flow-through process, "fabrication and assembly" companies which build discrete finished items from component parts, "industrial products" companies which make products that are used largely by other businesses and by the federal government, and "consumer products" companies which make items used by the general public.

Author's note: The research for this study was conducted by Leroy S. Brenna and James M. Beck.

[1] The first was reported by Neal J. Dean and James W. Taylor in "Managing to Manage the Computer," HBR September–October 1966, p. 98.

Emergence of the 'TCE'

A significant finding of the study is the emergence of the top computer executive (TCE). In one way or another, this man is responsible for the company's computer effort. He typically coordinates the activities of other computer managers and is responsible for overall quality, performance, and forward planning in the company's computer effort. In almost all instances, the TCE is found at the corporate level, and most managements seem to feel that it is absolutely necessary that he have considerable power. As one TCE said:

> You must have centralized direction as well as centralized coordination if you expect to manage information systems successfully. Centralized coordination alone without corporate direction wouldn't give us the compatibility of systems that we must have to compete effectively in today's market.

Of the 108 companies covered in this survey, 97 have established such an executive position. As shown in [Figure 1], a TCE is found in different reporting relationships in these companies. This relationship tends to be determined by the general pattern of organization in each firm. In about one third of the companies, the TCE reports to corporate controllers; in the remaining two thirds, he reports directly to a president or vice president who, in turn, reports directly to the president.

The TCE performs his role in ways similar to those of other top corporate executives. As shown in [Figure 2], he may direct all computer activities on a centralized basis, or provide overall direction to decentralized computer groups—or do a little of both, if the company organization pattern contains elements of both centralization and decentralization. Whether his management is direct or through other managers, he is expected to be on top of all computer activities in the company program. An oil company executive made this comment:

> Centralized control and decentralized operations of data processing is our present practice. We had a lot of duplication of effort, so we decided to centralize the control of our computer effort. This move runs counter to the basic organizational philosophy of the company. But we are attempting to seek equilibrium by decentralizing control over expenditures and by adding to the autonomy of operations.

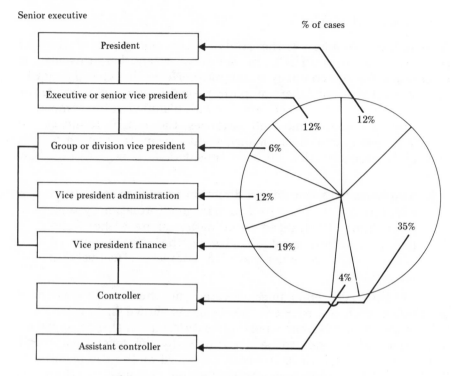

Figure 1.   To whom does the TCE report?

A key part of the TCE's job is working with noncomputer executives, who are becoming more and more involved in specifying what the computer is to do for them. This is particularly true because of the increasing trend toward participation of functional, divisional, branch, and plant operating executives in creating short-term systems-development plans. The TCE also works increasingly with the chief executive officer—president or chairman—on the company's overall use of the computer both in current operations and longer-term programs.

Activities Managed

The TCE, more often than not, is responsible for activities other than the computer activity. In fact, in only 32 companies out of the 108 surveyed are his responsibilities limited to computer activities. His

Responsibilities   % of companies having a TCE

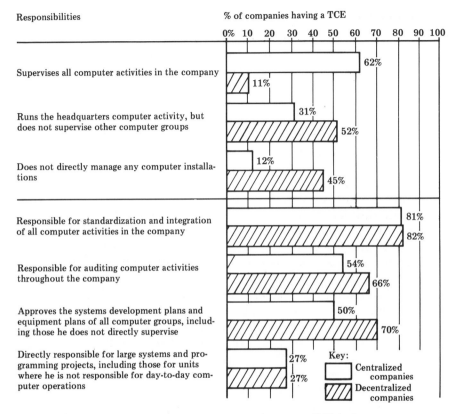

Figure 2.   What are the TCE's responsibilities?

other activities often include operations research, clerical systems and procedures, and even, in a few instances, broad corporate planning activities.

The study shows that 48% of the TCEs supervise operations research (OR) groups. Clerical systems and procedures are the next most commonly found noncomputer activity of TCEs, with 46% of them having responsibility for this function.

It used to be the practice to assign responsibility for computer activities to a financial executive (or an executive whose responsibilities were largely financial in character). Today, however, only about one tenth of the companies with specifically established TCE positions make financial planning and financial auditing a part of the TCE's responsibility.

Location Patterns

Decentralized companies tend to have most or some of their computer operations and systems analysts at division, branch, or plant locations. But in a large number of the centralized companies, too, the responsibility for some computer activities is decentralized (see Part A of [Table 1]). There is clear recognition in these companies that their interests are best served by having the computer where it can directly support company operations.

The dichotomy of having companywide central control and decentralized computer operations has been reconciled in a pattern commonly found in certain other company functions. In both centralized and decentralized companies, there are computer systems planning and development people at the corporate headquarters level. These are the computer systems developers—planning personnel, systems analysts, and programmers. This group assures coordinated development of systems and consistency of hardware and software throughout the organization (see Part B of [Table 1]).

The computer systems operating personnel—computer operators, keypunchers, and electronic accounting machine (EAM) operators—working under the direction of this headquarters group, are more commonly found in the divisions, branches, and plants than are the planners and analysts (as shown in Part C of [Table 1]). An interesting indication of the importance of on-site computer operations activities is the fact that clerical systems and procedures specialists are less commonly found at branches, divisions, and other decentralized operating locations than are their opposite numbers, the computer systems analysts.

A little more than one third of the companies in this study have computers in foreign countries. The mix of computer people at various locations in these foreign countries generally is similar to that in domestic operations. Those capabilities involved in operating the computer are more commonly found in the operating divisions and plants, while the planners and systems developers are typically located at the foreign headquarters level or at corporate headquarters in the United States.

Specialized Functions

Many companies use computers for specialized purposes—that is, for activities other than processing business information. Often these

Table 1. Location of Computers and Personnel

A. Where is the equipment located?

Location	Percent of companies having computers at indicated location	
	Centralized	Decentralized
Headquarters	93%	70%
Domestic divisions or plants	57	91
Foreign subsidiaries or branches	16	42

B. Where do the systems analysts work?

Location	Percent of companies having systems analysts at indicated location	
	Centralized	Decentralized
Headquarters	93%	89%
Domestic divisions or plants	43	81
Foreign subsidiaries or branches	16	42

C. Where do other specialists work?

Specialists	Percent of centralized companies employing the indicated specialists at:		Percent of decentralized companies employing the indicated specialists at:	
	Headquarters	Domestic branches/plants	Headquarters	Domestic branches/plants
Planners	100%	36%	95%	68%
Analysts	93	43	89	81
Programmers	93	46	79	94
Computer operators	93	57	70	91
Keypunchers	93	64	70	95
EAM operators	86	57	57	89
Clerical S&P	79	39	68	76

groups have their own systems and programming staffs, and may operate their own computers as well, depending on the nature of the type of data and hardware requirements involved. For instance, separate systems and programming staffs for research, development, and engineering (RD&E) are found in 65% of the surveyed companies, and 39% have separate RD&E computers. The larger the company, the greater the likelihood that the RD&E organization will have its own computer, as shown in Part A of [Table 2].

In those companies that have separate OR groups, the group often includes systems analysts or programmers. However, only three companies have separate computers specifically for OR purposes. Most OR computer work is done on business data processing equipment or on RD&E computers; little work is done on analog computers.

As might be expected, the percentage of companies which have a separate process-control computer capability is much higher for process-oriented industries than for fabrication and assembly industries (see Part B of [Table 2]).

At present, process-control computers are usually the responsibility of that operation of the firm in which they are used, such as a production unit or a research laboratory. However, there is a growing recognition that process-control computers can be a source of data for regular business computers. As systems integration progresses, process-control computers undoubtedly will come under increasing control, if not within the direct responsibility, of the TCE.

Part C of [Table 2] shows that machine tool numerical-control programming is being done on computers in 17% of all the companies—in most cases, on normal business data processing computers.

Varying Cost Patterns

The amount of money spent in using the computer, and the way the money is being spent among the different activities in computer operations, varies by length of computer experience and sales volume of the individual company. As for the future, only four companies in the survey expect computer costs either to hold at the present level or to decline.

The longer a company has been using its computer, the more money it spends on this operation; the median for all companies in the survey now stands at $5,600 per $1,000,000 of sales volume. Around this median, individual company computer costs ranged

Table 2. Computer Use for Special Purposes

A. How widespread is RD&E specialization?

	Percent of companies having RD&E systems and programming groups	Percent of companies having RD&E computers
All companies in survey	65%	39%
By sales volume*		
Up to $99 million (9)	33	0
$100 million to $199 million (16)	50	21
$200 million to $499 million (23)	75	35
$500 million to $999 million (21)	55	40
$1 billion and over (39)	85	65

B. How widespread is specialization in process control?

	Percent of companies having process-control systems and programming groups	Percent of companies having process-control computers
All companies in survey	28%	25%
By type of industry*		
Continuous process (65)		
Industrial products (33)	38	38
Consumer products (32)	41	41
Fabrication and assembly (43)		
Industrial products (27)	9	0
Consumer products (16)	20	13

C. What is the extent of specialization for numerical-control programming?

	Percent of companies having numerical-control systems and programming groups	Percent of companies having numerical-control computers
All companies in survey	17%	5%
By type of industry*		
Continuous process (65)		
Industrial products (33)	17	7
Consumer products (32)	0	0
Fabrication and assembly (43)		
Industrial products (27)	30	9
Consumer products (16)	20	0

*Numbers in parentheses refer to number of companies in category.

from $200 per $1,000,000 of sales for a crude-oil refiner which was just launching a computer operation, to $34,000 per $1,000,000 of sales for a large aerospace company (see [Figure 3]). Smaller firms and firms with relatively short computer experience spend less on systems planning and programming than do the companies that are larger and have longer experience.

Another common factor among all companies surveyed is that they spend more money on equipment rental and other operating costs than they do on systems planning and programming. The average expenditure for all companies for systems planning and programming is 29% of computer costs; equipment rental accounts for 38% of costs, and other computer operating expenses come to 33% of the total.

Increasing costs for systems planning and programming are consistent with the historical patterns established by companies that have made successful use of data processing capabilities.

When a company initially acquires a computer, its primary need is for programming personnel to convert existing systems to the computer. Later, it obtains systems analysts to improve the already converted systems and to develop new computer-based systems to improve the efficiency and profitability of company operations. However, it is not uncommon for a company to establish a

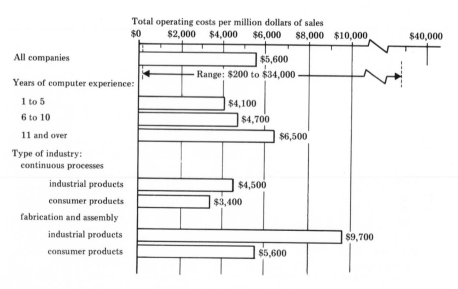

Figure 3.   Computer costs.

considerable number of systems analysts in separate groups *without coordinating their efforts.*

So, when companies recognize the high cost of duplicate systems, they frequently acquire planning personnel to coordinate the efforts of systems analysts and to ensure standardization of practices and procedures in data processing systems. Professional systems analysts and planning personnel then recognize and move into the more sophisticated systems that need to be developed. For example, operations research personnel may be employed to put mathematical techniques to use as an essential ingredient for capitalizing fully on the benefits of the computer. This sequence accounts for the trends of the figures in [Table 3].

Table 3. Use of Functional Specialists at Domestic Divisions

	Percent of companies employing specialists in:			
	Programming	Systems analysis	Planning	Operations research
All companies in survey	78%	69%	57%	48%
By years of computer experience:				
1–5 years	57	52	43	33
6–10 years	78	66	47	48
11 or more years	90	82	74	54

Increasing Use

The study clearly indicates a trend away from restricting the computer to finance and administration. It is used more and more often in major operating areas—marketing, production, and distribution. In the next three to five years companies in the survey expect to direct over half of the total computer effort to serving operating areas, and company executives expect to double the proportion of effort given to planning and control (see [Figure 4]). This trend toward more emphasis on applications in operating functions is more pronounced as a company's years of computer experience increase.

The study reveals some interesting differences in emphasis among various types of applications within industry groups. These variations directly reflect the characteristics of different types of business and the recognition that different functional areas are critical to a company's success. For example:

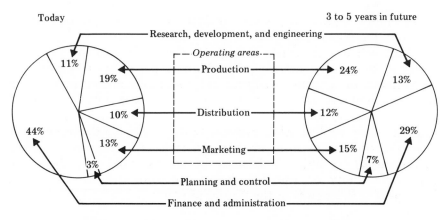

Figure 4.   How is computer use expected to change?

In fabricated and assembled products companies, RD&E computer applications represent 18% of the computer effort, and manufacturing or factory applications account for 24% of the computer effort; by contrast, the comparable percentages are 7% and 14% respectively in continuous-process companies. This difference reflects the contrasting requirements of product engineering, production, scheduling, and control in the two types of businesses.

In consumer goods industries, computer applications in marketing account for 16% of total computer effort, as compared to 11% for companies producing industrial products.

Systems Integration

The median company in the survey now has some computer systems which are integrated within functional areas; that is, major data processing systems within a function (such as marketing or production) are linked together, coordinated, and run as a unit. In three to five years, the median company expects to have integrated systems which tie together two or more functional areas. And, in the future, all companies in the sample expect their computer systems to be integrated to some significant degree, as shown in [Figure 5].

Predictably, computer systems in decentralized companies are less integrated now than in centralized companies primarily because of the complexities of multiplant and multiproduct activities. But,

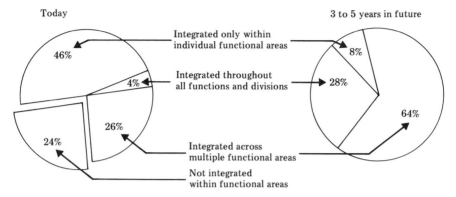

Figure 5.   What changes are expected in the degree of integration of computer systems?

the survey shows, in three to five years both centralized and decentralized companies expect to be at about the *same* level of integration of computer systems. In other words, the decentralized companies expect to overcome most of the difficulties of standardizing and integrating diverse and independent product groups.

Most of the companies (82%) also regularly prepare long-range plans to guide their computer activities. The most common time span for long-range plans is three to four years. About a quarter of the long-range plans reported in the survey cover five years or more.

As part of their long-term planning, many companies are investigating the pros and cons of eventual integration of computer activities into total "management information systems." However, most of the companies, including many of those with the longest computer experience, do not intend to go that far in the next three to five years.

Planning and Control

Executives of 90% of the companies say they maintain planning and control of their computer operations by the use of a formal short-range plan. Of these companies, over half include in the plan costs and schedules for all projects, while the remaining companies include costs and schedules for major projects only.

Short-range computer plans are an important control mechanism in all of the companies in the survey. In more than two thirds of the companies, in fact, short-range plans are the most significant control device for management. In the remaining third, short-range plans are used primarily as guidelines.

Nearly all of the companies in the survey use some measure of relative profit improvement as a means for choosing among different systems projects proposed for consideration. Formal return-on-investment analysis is the major criterion in 24% of the companies, less formal analyses of operating improvement are used in 61% of the cases, and direct cost reduction or other measures of selection are used in the remaining companies.

Auditing Activities

The managements of two thirds of the surveyed companies use regular audits to improve their control of computer activities and performance. The larger the company, the greater the likelihood that management regularly audits computer work. Of increasing significance is the degree to which operating managers are involved in making these audits. The managers typically serve as members of a committee that reviews the findings of the audit and reports to top divisional and corporate executives.

Of the companies that perform regular audits, most (62%) confine the audits to critical computer applications, while the others (38%) cover all areas of computer activity. In the companies performing audits of either type, there is major emphasis on the following activities (numbers in parentheses refer to the portion of the sample engaged in the activity):

Appraisal of budgets for new computer systems developments and new equipment (78%).

Determination of appropriateness of present systems as management and control tools (75%).

Review of the usefulness of present systems to operating people (70%).

Checking on adherence to operating budgets and output deadlines (67%).

Analysis of systems and operations for potential susceptibility to fraud or other financial irregularity (63%).

Evaluation of personnel and management practices affecting computer systems (62%).

Review of adherence to development project budgets and schedules (60%).

Conclusion

The computer systems function, not only technologically but also managerially, has come of age. As a result, it has become an extraordinarily important quantitative tool at the disposal of management at all levels in the intense competitive market which manufacturing companies in the United States face today.

The survey clearly shows that the computer increasingly is penetrating and permeating all areas of major manufacturing corporations. Indeed, the computer is becoming an integral part of operations in those companies. Several findings give solid evidence of this. Most of the companies in the survey are expecting to increase their financial commitments for computer services at a rate which is more rapid than their anticipated annual sales growth. In addition, and because of these increasing financial commitments, the chief executive officers are taking a more active role in the computer function of their companies. Increasingly, other levels of management—operating group as well as staff groups—also are participating in planning for computer usage.

Along with this increasing involvement in money and manpower, the computer activity is becoming a more integrated and established part of company operations. Computers are being used more and more for management planning and control as well as for record keeping. More companies are using OR and advanced mathematical techniques in computer operations.

Accepted management techniques typically used in other parts of company operations are being applied to the computer function. Companies are planning, budgeting, and auditing the computer function. More and more often, computer project selection is being made on the basis of overall benefits to the company. Also, the growing number of TCEs at high levels of responsibility in the corporate structure attests to growing recognition of the importance of computer management.

In reporting Booz, Allen & Hamilton's first study of computer management, an executive was quoted as saying: "Our real goal is to make sure that we achieve more benefits from computers than our competitors do."[2] This kind of aggressive, competitive thinking has doubtless played a large part in speeding the development of computer systems. It also spells a real threat for laggards in such development, for it means that the gap between effective users, on the one hand, and ineffective users and nonusers, on the other, will widen ever more swiftly. The day may not be far distant when those who analyze annual business failures can add another category to their list of causes—failure to exploit the computer.

[2] Ibid., p. 99.

Section **2**

The Work Environment

Information Technology, Manpower Development, and Organizational Performance

Bernard Baum
and Elmer Burack
Reprinted by permission of *Academy of Management Journal*, September 1969.

Introduction

This study provides increased insight into variations in the organizational implementation of manpower programs for education and training in information technology. Dislocation of clerical personnel, rapidly burgeoning computer usage, greater involvement of manpower resources with computer systems and the increased threat of manpower obsolescence provide ample rationale for undertaking these analyses. This paper first clarifies some of the organizational considerations in launching education and training (E&T) programs focusing on computer based (information) systems. Then the structuring of a field research study is described which provided data on education and training efforts of a diverse group of firms. Next, the results of the field study are reported and analyzed in terms of factors influencing individual company approaches in education and training. Finally, the initial approaches to analysis set forth in this study are reexamined and an approach proposed for improving organization performance in E&T programs focusing on computer based systems.

Background

Rapid expansion of information technology in a wide variety of manufacturing and service type organizations suggests a growing involvement of manpower resources of the firm within or in relation to computer based systems.[1] Personnel at all levels of the organization are called upon to exercise varying levels of conceptual ability, understanding and technical competency regarding introduction or emergence of information systems within their organizations.[2] These necessities highlight the potential needs or problems of preparing manpower resources in the functional requirements of their jobs as well as for newer, innovative approaches in management technique emerging in this area.[3] Issues include: What role has education and training played in the advanced position of companies utilizing information technology? What new education and training needs are emerging at varying organizational levels? Are education and training needs more pressing in particular departments, types of companies or industries? What role has top management played in overall company usage of computers and how does the recognition of this additionally bear on education and training needs?[4] This study seeks to provide insights into some of these important questions.[5] It is instructive to consider several notions which suggest approaches to dealing with the questions raised in this section.

Underlying Assumptions

Based on past studies in this area it is possible to anticipate that sophistication regarding the incorporation and use of information technology will be greater in:

[1] Martin Greenberger (ed.), *Management and the Computers of the Future* (Cambridge: M.I.T. Press, 1962); also, see Herbert A. Simon, *The Shape of Automation for Man and Management* (New York: Harper & Row, 1965).

[2] For an instructive discussion, see Charles A. Myers, *The Impact of Computers on Management* (Cambridge: M.I.T. Press, 1967).

[3] Broader dimensions of the problem are presented in Paul Armer, "Computer Aspects of Technological Change, Automation and Economic Progress", *The Outlook for Technological Change and Employment*, Appendix, vol. 1. Report of the National Commission on Technology, Automation and Economic Progress, Government Printing Office (Washington, D.C.) (February, 1966).

[4] Organizational considerations are suggested in Elmer H. Burack, "Impact of Computers on Business Management", *The Business Quarterly*, vol. 30, no. 2 (Spring, 1966).

[5] For some dimensions of this problem including the influence of centralization/discentralization of the firms' activities, and history of usage, see Neal Dean, "The Computer Comes of Age", *Harvard Business Review*, vol. 46, no. 1 (Jan/Feb, 1968).

1. Service enterprises *as distinguished from manufacturing industries. The service enterprise frequently being based on information processes exhibits computer potential not present where the constraints of production ("state of the art") exist.*[6]
2. Large companies. *Size,* per se, *involves the number and combination of variables, as well as volume of business activity, that encourages the implementation of a computer based system.*
3. Companies with longer histories *of using information technology; because such companies have developed an information and data discipline which should encourage a positive attitude toward new areas of application.*[7]
4. Companies where information processing is more crucial to effective performance. *Where speed and manipulation of data are crucial factors in the decision making process (e.g., logistics management) information technology will tend to be more highly developed.*[8]
5. Companies where personnel with a background of formal, technical education (engineering sciences and mathematics) are central to success. *Chemical and petroleum units would be examples of these operations. Note that some of these characteristics may tend to*

---

[6] Publications of various U.S. Agencies, including Labor (insurance industry, electric light and power, telephone, and Internal Revenue Service), Commerce and special commissions such as those on automation. Also, see U.S. Department of Labor, "Technology and Manpower in the Telephone Industry, 1965–75", *Manpower Research Bulletin*, no. 13, Manpower Administration (Washington: U.S. Government Printing Office, Nov., 1966); "Four Routes to Small Bank Computerization", *Bankers Monthly Magazine*, July 15, 1968, pp. 30–32 and other issues; Richard A. Hansen, "Planning, Installing and Controlling the United States Army Material Command Management Information System," *Annual Proceedings Academy of Management* (Boston, 1963), pp. 84–95; and Alfred L. Kahl, "Computer Usage by Financial Institutions", *Commercial and Financial Chronicle* (September, 1968), p. 10.

[7] Some feel for the impact of history of computer usage may be gleaned from Floyd C. Mann and L. K. Williams, "Observations on the Dynamics of a Change to Electronic Data Processing Equipment," *Administrative Science Quarterly*, vol. 5 (September, 1960), no. 1. Floyd C. Mann and Laurence K. Williams, "Organizational Impact of White Collar Automation", *Annual Proceedings, Industrial Relations Research Association*, 1958.

[8] Herbert Simon, "Programs as Factors of Production", *Proceedings of the Nineteenth Annual Winter Meeting, Industrial Relations Research Association*, San Francisco (December 28–29, 1966), pp. 177–188.

work in opposite directions so that the net resultant is indeterminate. For example, in 1 and 4 a given service company may be built largely on information processes (encouraging computer usage) while a particular manufacturing system is heavily dependent on logistics management for successful operation.[9] Thus, both types (service and manufacturing) of firms could have substantial stakes in E&T for information systems.[10]

As a final point in this preliminary analysis, we would assume that the greater the sophistication regarding information technology, the more highly developed and extensive the accompanying information technology education and training program and effort will be. Such a program would include (a) a wider range of employees, (b) more responsibility levels and (c) greater utilization of in-house and outside resources and education beyond functional job requirements.

Selection of Companies Incorporated in the Study

Our study is based on survey responses from 78 companies, supplemented by extensive interviews in 26 of these companies. Our sample constitutes a 50 per cent response from the total 1967 membership of a Midwestern (industrial) association; it included 35 service-type companies (insurance, banks, merchandising organizations, etc.), 23 manufacturing concerns (metal products, equipment, etc.) and 20 utilities, transportation and process (chemical) type companies. Of these, 40 per cent exceeded an annual sales volume of $250 million. No firms included in the study were less than 10 years old and some 70 per cent of the firms exceeded 50 years of corporate activity. Finally, some 60 per cent of the firms had decentralized (nine or more) production, distribution or administrative units to a considerable extent. In short, the sample can be

---

[9]The technical features of production processes, both in encouraging or complicating the introduction of information technology are suggested in Charles R. Walker, *Technology, Industry, and Man: The Age of Acceleration* (New York: McGraw-Hill, 1968), especially pp. 85—146; 158—172; 217—226; for effects in a traditional area of usage, see W. J. Bruns, Jr., "Accounting Information and Decision Making; Some Behavioral Hypotheses", *Accounting Review* (July, 1968), pp. 469—480; finally, changes in particular industries and institutions are to some extent suggested by J. A. O'Brien, "How Computers Have Changed the Organizational Structure", *Banking* (July, 1968).

[10] For some of the managerial effects, see Robert H. Guest, "Today's Trends for Tomorrow's Management", *The Business Quarterly*, vol. 31, no. 4 (Winter, 1966).

characterized as comprising older, larger and more complex firms. Research data were secured primarily from top level personnel-manpower officials, supplemented by managerial personnel in computer systems, administrative or supporting departments.

Findings

The results of the research are summarized under the following topical points: (a) History of information usage; (b) Bases for endorsing information technology; (c) Restraints in incorporating computer systems; (d) Influence of product versus information orientation; (e) System planning; and (f) Management's computer literacy.

Background and Past Usage of Information Technology

The companies in our sample largely follow the characteristic mode of computer introduction, that is, an outgrowth of business machines usage and centered in the accounting function. Almost 40 per cent of these companies had installed computer equipment before 1961. The obvious applications of computer based equipment to routine work are high where there is a desire to effect cost economies. Updating of mechanical (Chullarath) business machine functions provides a common point of departure characterizing (early) computer introduction. However, other important reasons are also found including recommendations by consultants, exercise of top management leadership, competitive response, need for operational control and the pressure exerted by parent companies, sophisticated in computer system usage. A few of the "pioneers" in early computer usage displayed extraordinary insights into future computer possibilities in the period of the early and middle 1950's as exemplified by the following response:

> In the mid 50's it was apparent that volume would rise, forcing computer usage at some point. But, more importantly, computers would be able to provide much more planning and control information. Subsequently, we established a six man task force to study the adaptation of a computer based system to our operations.

Here, education and training approaches to computers were essentially confined to those departmental personnel directly affected by the new applications.[11]   It seems clear that historical development of computer usage follows no single pattern and thus E&T programs as a response to emergent need varied considerably.

Management's Willingness to Innovate

Here, an attempt was made to both determine and distinguish between top management philosophy on endorsing *functional* (approven application) computer usage as distinguished from willingness to *innovate in management techniques* (still an unknown) such as information technology. Our respondents were asked to rank their companies in terms of the following: "Top management's willingness to experiment or innovate in management techniques such as information technology" and "Top management's endorsement of the use of the computer". In general, personnel in the service activities view their top managements as somewhat more willing to innovate than companies in the manufacturing sector (Table 1). Furthermore, this distinction (service-manufacturing) carried through to top management's endorsement of computer usage (Table 2). It probably comes as little surprise that virtually no companies were willing to claim "low" willingness to innovate or endorse computer usage.

Table 1. Top Management's Willingness to Innovate in Management Techniques

	Service		Manufacturing		Other	
	No.	%	No.	%	No.	%
Low	...	...	...	...	1	7
Moderately high	11	32	11	50	8	50
High	23	68	11	50	7	43
	34	100	22	100	16	100

Although one might assume that both the willingness to innovate in management techniques such as information technology and top management endorsement of computer usage are necessary concomitants of effective computer implementation, a joint view of Tables 1 and 2 suggests greater support for the functional application

[11] For application problems, an example is provided by "Hire Fast, Train Slowly to Solve EDP Personnel Puzzle", *Bank Equipment News* (October, 1968), p. 26.

Table 2. Top Management's Endorsement of Computer Usage

	Service		Manufacturing		Other	
	No.	%	No.	%	No.	%
Low	...	...	1	4	...	...
Moderately high	4	12	5	23	2	13
High	28	88	16	73	14	87
	32	100	22	100	16	100

("proven") usage than ("untried" and "expensive") innovative management approaches involving the computers.

The distribution pattern in Table 2 provides a summary view of top management perspective on computers but their underlying strategies are not discernible.

Underlying Rationale for Information Technology Endorsement

Six major problem areas of business organization and operation were identified, encouraging the use and extension of information technology. In the realm of corporate policy, (1) the rapid gains made by competition may require a defensive posture by some companies whereas for others (2) incorporating information technology (and/or other novel information approaches) reflects a persistent pattern of company leadership in marketing or production. Information technology is viewed as (3) bolstering decision making processes and the quality of decisions made and (4) providing new promise for future planning strategies. Also, (5) cost reduction continues to persist as a compelling reason for endorsing information technology usage. Finally, (6) information technology may well constitute an indispensable part of modern company operation and for the service (information) oriented unit (company, functional or department activity), be a basic necessity for effective operation. It is clear that such considerations as policy outlook or improved decision making do not exhaust the areas of philosophical rationale for promoting information technology usage. In some cases, internal organizational processes further encourage information technology extension. For example, active top management involvement and an internal job of supporting and "selling" applications—aptly described by one respondent as "enlightened self interest" help to support computer usage. Although many factors present compelling reasons for extending information technology usage, respondents also set forth significant considerations in *curtailing* system extension.

Factors in Restricting Computer Usage

For companies which have curtailed or cut back on the utilization or extension of the information technology system, underlying considerations span a range from the rather obvious to those quite discreet. Low volume of activities relative to computer costs is an obvious point in limited information technology activity and E&T programs. Yet, even where data possess a high volume attribute, important institutional factors such as "being hamstrung by old procedures" or a "new concept as yet unappreciated by the board" reflect the realities of company life even in a period of the "information revolution." Some companies have taken tentative steps towards enlarging their scope of information technology usage and development but highly mixed results have instilled a "note of caution in making radical procedural changes." In addition, preoccupation with other company programs or attempting to grapple with the dynamic problems of rapid growth provide sufficient rationale to limit top management's interest (and time) in expanding information technology.

Manufacturing versus Service Type Institutions

Top management's position on use of information technology reflects business strategies and in some cases, basically different institutional problems. Some of these are peculiar to manufacturing (product oriented) or service (information oriented) companies. Other areas of difference may also be ascribed to differences in supporting departments. It will come as no surprise that one-fifth of service oriented companies (e.g., insurance companies and banks) view information technology as an *indispensable* part of current and contemplated operations, in many cases necessitated by an almost overwhelming volume of information needs. For the manufacturers, although viewing information technology as a *major factor* in such areas as "improved decision making" and "cost reduction," none identified an "indispensable need" for incorporating information technology systems.

Contrasting Patterns in Information Systems, Planning and Manpower Development

Both manufacturing and service oriented units indicated similar (and considerable) interests in widening or extending existing computer applications (Table 3) given comparable historical usage (importance of information technology—Table 4).

Table 3. Top Management's Planning for Extending Information Systems

A. Widening applications:

	Yes		No		Uncertain	
	n	%	n	%	n	%
Service (n = 31)	28	90	1	3	2	6
Manufacturing (n = 21)	16	76	1	5	4	19
Other (n = 15)	14	93	. . .	. . .	1	7

B. Deepening applications:

	Yes		No		Uncertain	
Service (n = 31)	27	87	1	3	3	10
Manufacturing (n = 21)	18	86	. . .	. . .	3	14
Other (n = 15)	13	86	. . .	. . .	2	14

The most striking inference to be drawn from the responses (Table 3) regarding computer usage or plans for widening or extending information systems is that an overwhelming number of companies, across the board, have plans. Thus, the implications of such system planning, if the plans are to be implemented, heavily involve managerial and professional groups and importantly underscore the need for education and training programs. Does the man-power programming match the hardware programming? No!

Table 5 indicates that some 40 per cent of companies do not conduct nor have any general plans for educational efforts, irrespective of industry affiliation or size. It is this type of confused, almost paradoxical thinking that seems to fairly characterize the realities of upper management thinking.

Corporate thinking in launching education and training programs in information technology encompasses a narrow range of management strategies. Firstly, the larger, frequently more profitable firms were early entrants into computer applications. They had already achieved a high level of maturity in attempting to capitalize on information technology and enhance management performance in conjunction with information technology systems. These firms view general management education and the potentialities of future applications as sufficient reason for developing a serious education and training effort. This approach holds promise for both updating current managers not conversant with information technology as well as insuring a nucleus of young, knowledgeable managers in the future.

Table 4. Maturity in Use of Information Technology

A. Date of computer installations:

	Before 1961		After 1961	
	n	%	n	%
Service (n = 30)	12	40	18	60
Manufacturing (n = 22)	8	36	14	64
Other (n = 16)	8	50	8	50

B. In transaction (e.g., accounting) use:

	Level of Usage			
	Low		High	
	n	%	n	%
Service (n = 33)	4	12	29	88
Manufacturing (n = 23)	1	4	22	96
Other (n = 11)	2	13	14	87

C. In computation or analysis (statistical studies, research, control):

	Level of Usage			
	Low		High	
	n	%	n	%
Service (n = 31)	13	42	18	58
Manufacturing (n = 23)	8	35	15	65
Other (n = 15)	6	40	9	60

A second corporate strategy of considerable importance visualized the establishment of a nucleus of key managers at all levels who can spawn new information technology applications and ease the introduction of current computer based programs. Information technology applications were not conceived of as being so broad as to dictate a *generalized* management training effort.

Finally, the single most important reason for launching education and training programs (almost one half of those actively engaged in planning educational programs) pertained to preparing managers, supervisors or workers who would be affected by new system applications. Necessarily, these were specific and application oriented. Impending applications such as production control (scheduling, inventory and forecasting), accounting extensions, and operations research and market studies triggered specific educational programs. Realistically, company planning for launching education

Table 5. Forward Planning in Education Training Programs
Encompassing Information Technology

A. General planning-institutional lines:*

Orientation	Definite Plans		Continue Current Programs		No Plans		No Response	
	n	%	n	%	n	%	n	%
Service (n = 33)	14	42	5	15	14	42		
Manufacturing (n = 23)	10	43	4	17	9	39		
Other (n = 6)	8	50	3	20	5	30		

B. Specific programs to begin within next twelve months—by size: †

	Definite Plans		Continue Current Programs		No Plans		No Response	
	n	%	n	%	n	%	n	%
Large	12	40	9	30	7	23	7	6
Small	18	43	15	36	6	14	3	17

*72 firms responding
†Sales volume used as a crude measure: large = over $250 million; medium and small firms = 250 million and under.
Note: Totals vary slightly from 100 per cent because of rounding.

and training programs may fairly reflect top management's *judgment* of managerial understanding and insight in this area.

Management's Computer Literacy

In general, the findings reported in Table 6 suggest that the diversity of manufacturing, process and service type firms incorporated in this study view their upper managerial ranks ("middle" and "top" management) as relatively computer literate in terms of terminology, hardware and general information concepts. This view encompasses three-fifths of these upper-level managers. Yet, some three-fifths of the *supervisory groups* are judged to be relatively "low" in comprehension of information concepts. These wide differences between managerial levels most frequently reflect different corporate attitudes towards managerial and supervisory personnel. Computer training for supervisory levels often turns on specific information—computer applications touching a particular functional area. Consequently, for the supervisory group, computer training is typically more limited, functionally rather than conceptually oriented, and leans on individual initiative (self-development) to go

Table 6. Judgments Regarding Management's Computer Literacy*

A. All industrial groupings:

Level of Management	Estimate of Computer Literacy					
	High		Low		Uncertain	
	n	%	*n*	%	*n*	%
Top management	46	69	19	28	2	3
Middle management	42	63	24	36	1	1
Supervision	25	37	41	61	1	1
Employee-clerical	8	12	56	86	1	1
Plant employee	7	12	44	77	6	10

B. Selected industrial groupings (service vs. manufacturing):

Level of Management	Estimate of Computer Literacy											
	High				Low				Uncertain			
	Serv.†		Mfg.‡		Serv.		Mfg.		Serv.		Mfg.	
	n	%	*n*	%	*n*	%	*n*	%	*n*	%	*n*	%
Top management	25	78	12	57	5	16	9	43	2	6	...	...
Middle mgmt.	21	66	14	67	10	31	7	33	1	3	...	...
Supervision	17	53	5	24	14	44	16	76	1	3	...	...
Employee-clerical	7	22	...	...	23	74	20	100	1	3	...	...
Plant employee	4	17	1	5	18	45	16	84	2	8	2	10

*n ranges from 57 to 67 respondent firms because of no response.
†n = 32
‡n = 21

beyond the company's education-training effort. Thus, the lack of innovative suggestions for computer applications at the supervisory levels, a frequent complaint, should come as little surprise. Here, a heavy dependency exists on the expertise of computer specialists. On the other hand, computer orientation for middle level and senior managers is viewed as important since a conversational level of comprehension is frequently a must for communication with associates or in day-to-day activities. However, the adjudged view of upper level management familiarity with the world of the computer does not hold equally for various industrial sectors.

Table 6 indicates that both the top management and supervisory groups of *service* oriented units are seen as possessing a stronger background ("Computer Literacy") in computer based processes (78 per cent and 53 per cent respectively) than their counterparts in manufacturing (57 per cent and 24 per cent respectively). At first blush, these results would seem to follow from the assertions which we made initially when we proposed that the service oriented institution with its heavy information orientation and dependency *should* be considerably ahead of the manufacturing units (constrained by the complexity of the production technology) in the incorporation of the computer. Yet, the historical pattern of computer installations and usage suggests manufacturing leadership in computer numbers and breadth of applications. It is likely that service institutions started to realize their potentialities (as evidenced by the judgments of computer literacy), well into the 1960's. Another factor which appears difficult to reconcile is the discrepancy between judgments of computer literacy and the lack of involvement of personnel in education and training programs.

A Paradox

In attempting to distinguish between service and manufacturing oriented concerns in terms of information system (computer) training and knowledge of computer utilization, a paradox emerged. Service oriented institutions included less top management personnel in computer training than their counterparts in the manufacturing sector. Only 29 per cent (nine) of the service firms indicated over one-half of top management involvement whereas 77 per cent of the top managements in manufacturing concerns indicated more than one-half their groups were involved in computer training. Middle management, supervisory and clerical-worker groups showed little significant differences.

Conclusions and Implications

The computer potentialities of information based *service* units are as yet to be realized in some companies or departmental functions as compared with developments in the manufacturing sector. Among other factors, the general lack of technically qualified administrative and functional personnel in service firms such as insurance and banking has acted as a restraining factor in incorporating information technology. In manufacturing, the natural, number-symbol facility typical of the technically trained individual (for instance in petroleum and chemicals) has permitted information development, aside from process restraints. However, the accounting areas and numbers oriented departments ("actuarial") of these service firms have provided more of a natural point of entry for computer applications. Here, there is a typical number-symbol orientation. In the case of accounting, past machine accounting applications may simply be extended. Departmentally oriented applications permitted limited organizational involvement, and disruption. One might speculate that these early, "obvious" applications of the computer may have constituted a trap constraining broader information thinking and permitting system thinking to be "swept under the rug." However, the difficulty of re-orienting the nontechnical supervisor or manager in the service enterprise may well be matched by the restraints imposed on additional information extensions into the production function of manufacturing units beyond current computational and transaction applications. In this regard, service based units should be able to increasingly capitalize on the large base of computer potential emerging from the basic information character of their operations. Thus, education and training considerations bulk up as more crucial ones.

As expected, the focus of education and training programs involves a scale from general familiarization and conceptionalizing at the top level to problem applications ("nuts and bolts") at the lower levels of the organization hierarchy. However, this tends to lead to parochial thinking by supervision which is the antithesis of systems orientation essential for optimizing information technology usage. Some contemporary top managements, particularly in larger companies, see limited possibilities in developing any depth in information technology knowledge for higher echelon managers. Consequently the thrust of the effort is in grooming *tomorrow's* top management. (In some cases, self-diagnosis capabilities of top managers have been realistically applied to their own situations). The relative priority of information technology and related education and training programs is the realistic recognition of the issues or problems facing (a) a particular industry and (b) a particular management. It appears that the successful (in terms of morale, working relationships, efficiency) extension in depth and breadth of computer based information systems, has been paralleled by

(a) The concomitant extension of education and training efforts at all management levels
(b) A more highly placed information technology officer

Conversely, the relative lack of formal programs and relative dependence on informal efforts for education and training lead to obsolescence potential, limit expansion and blunt usage. All of which is to say that unless top management does more than heretofore, company organizations are falling far short of their potential.

The decentralized, corporate units reflect wide differences in computer undertakings and educational approaches. The evidence suggests a lack of unified approach to information technology, on a corporate basis. These multi-segmented organizations (where units are largely autonomous) display degrees of information technology sophistication largely dependent on the characteristics of the division head. One would of course expect diversity; but the degree of diversity and lack of sophistication go beyond the potential inherent in the original unit, to questions of management background, sensitivity to changes such as information technology, etc. In cases of acquisitions and mergers where the acquiring company has computer sophistication, one technique for rapid extension of information technology is the "seeding" of the acquired organization with corporate personnel who have the appropriate background or by directing the acquired company to secure such personnel.

Top management endorsement and willingness to innovate with the computer are clearly important, but care should be taken to establish a solid organizational base of working relationships, applications, involvement and avoid premature establishment of an EDP unit. Such hasty action typically represents the "buying" of a technique or "package" rather than a management philosophy or functional system.

Even in companies where in-house potential exists for information technology staffing, some companies have nevertheless chosen to recruit EDP personnel from outside to provide new and broader perspective for innovative management undertakings, particularly with mathematical and/or technical background.

18

Management Information Systems: The Challenge to Rationality and Emotionality*

Chris Argyris†

Reprinted by permission of
Management Science, February 1971.

Management science theorists and practitioners would tend to agree that some day management information systems (MIS) will probably be designed that perform many critical managerial functions. Many also would agree that the realization of this potential is a long way off.

What would happen if an MIS system were developed that could achieve this potential? How would individuals react to increased rationality in their lives? Will they think as many humanists believe, namely that information science rationality can lead to a mechanistic and rigid world which, because of its narrow concept of efficiency, will dominate man and eclipse his humanness (Argyris [9])? Will individuals believe, as many futurists argue, that the scope of our society has become so great and the interdependence so pervasive, that without the rationality possible from sophisticated information

*Received December 1969; revised July 1970, September 1970.
†The author would like to express his deepest appreciation to the members of the management services division who participated in this study. Their excellent support helped him immensely. He is also indebted to Professor Robert Fetter for his advice during the research and his helpful comments on the manuscript.

systems we run the risk of losing control over our everyday life and our destiny?

These critical questions require much research from many different perspectives. We have chosen to focus on these issues by conducting empirical research in actual settings where they are being played-out (or, more accurately, fought out). The setting is the study of a management services division in a multibillion dollar corporation. One objective of the division is to introduce new management information systems into certain management processes, that are now possible with the advent of more sophisticated management information systems, within the firm. The professionals in the management services division see themselves as consultants to the entire corporation with the mission of unfreezing "This colossus and pushing it into the twenty first century". They genuinely believe, like the futurists noted above, that organizations have become so complex and cumbersome that the only (best?) answer for effectiveness is management through the expanded and deepened rationality possible from sophisticated information systems.

What has caused organizations to develop internal processes that lead to increased ineffectiveness? In order to shed light on this question, we need to focus on the pyramidal structure which is the most dominant organizational design in use. It assumes that within respectable tolerances man will behave rationally, that is, as the design requires him to behave (Argyris [4]).

The Formal Organization and Its Impact on the Participants

There are three aspects of the formal organizational design that are important in generating work requirements for the participants at all levels. They are (1) work specialization, (2) chain of command, and (3) unity of direction. These properties of formal organization have been shown to place (especially the lower level employees) in situations where they tend to be dependent upon and submissive to their superiors; where they experience a very short time perspective and low feelings of responsibility about their work.

Those employees who prefer to experience some degree of challenge, to have some control, to make some decisions will tend to feel frustration and a sense of psychological failure. They may adapt to the frustration and failure by such activities as apathy, indifference, work slow downs, goldbricking, the creation of unions, absenteeism and turnover. Those employees who do not prefer challenging work or control over their work activities will not tend to feel frustrated. They will tend to report satisfaction and involvement, but the latter will not be deep or enduring.

The impact of task specialization, chain of command, and unity of direction is different at the upper levels. At the upper levels the formal design tends to require executives who need to manage an intended rational world, to direct, control, reward and penalize others, and to suppress their own and others' emotionality (Argyris [5]). Executives with these needs and skills tend to be ineffective in creating and maintaining effective interpersonal relationships; they fear emotionality and are almost completely unaware of ways to obtain employee commitment that is internal and genuine. This results in upper level systems that have more conformity, mistrust, antagonism, defensiveness, and closedness than individuality, trust, concern and openness.

As these dysfunctional activities become embedded in the system and as the defenses that hide their original causes are rigidified and locked into place, there is a tendency in the system to reduce the probability that accurate information will flow through the system. Top management reacts by establishing further controls which feed back to reinforce the original condition that began this causal sequence.

These reactions again tend to reinforce the initial conditions, and so there is a closed loop creating a system with increasing ineffectiveness in problem solving, decision making, and implementation. *In the social universe, where presumably there is no mandatory state of entropy, man can claim the dubious distinction of creating organizations that generate entropy, that is, slow but certain processes toward system deterioration.*

To some readers this analysis may seem overly pessimistic; to others overly optimistic. John Gardner [20], for example, has gone so far as to suggest that the "dry rot" in organizations will become so bad that they eventually will collapse (a view shared by the writer). Admittedly empirical research is needed if the analysis is to become convincing.

The relevant point for the operations researcher-management scientist however is that his field has been born at the very time our institutions are becoming increasingly ineffective. This will place his professional wares in high demand. It will also have the (temporary) advantage of increasing the probabilities that even his early and primitive modelling attempts will be useful. To put it somewhat coarsely, things are so bad that the only way is up. The success however may come as much as a result of the hard thinking and the facing of reality that is required if one attempts to model the world as it does from the use of the models developed. This advantage is not to be disparaged. All of us working in these new fields need all the honeymoon period that we can get.

The difficulty in being born at this time stems from the very advantage just described. As organizations become increasingly ineffective, they tend to produce *valid* information for the *unimportant* and programmed problems and *invalid* information for the important and nonprogrammed problems (Argyris [11]). The development and successful introduction of a sophisticated MIS is an example of an important and nonprogrammed problem. Thus the climate of rationality needed for the effective construction of an MIS may be very difficult to create.

The Properties of Management Information Systems, (MIS), and Their Impact on Management[1]

We are concerned with MIS whose usage can alter significantly the way top managers make important decisions (not those that deal with trivial data that are easily programmable). These are the MIS that help the executive to order and understand the complexity of the present. They are the systems that provide the executive with an opportunity to experiment with different possible future states of his environment and to learn what might be the possible consequences for each state. These are the systems therefore that a top executive may use to simulate the future so that he can increase the probability that his decision processes will produce outcomes which are in some sense fulfilling prophecies.

It is agreed that such systems may be a long way off. However, it seems useful to study these systems as if they existed in order to identify some of the problems that may accompany their introduction and use. Thus the MIS studied in this project, as is the case for many such models, is far from constituting complete systems of this kind. The state of the art is too primitive for such claims. However, in studying the human problems associated with the introduction and acceptance of MIS to management, it is acceptable to focus on the potential of the MIS and the extent of its realization in an application such as this because executives react to the potential as much as (if not more than) to our present delivery capabilities.

[1] Because the research focussed primarily on management, the data to be reported will be related to management.

MIS, like formal pyramidal organizations, are based upon the assumption that organizations are, and should continue to be, intendedly rational. Whereas the traditional scientific management designer of organization attempts to construct organizational structures as they ought to be (forgetting provisionally, at least, the personality interpersonal and group factors) the designer of MIS is more interested in modelling the system in accordance with how individuals actually behave. He focuses on aspects of the functional *and* dysfunctional activities described above. In doing this he acknowledges the relevant formal *and* informal activities. The important criterion for inclusion is that the factors are relevant to solving the problem at hand.

> *(1)* Reduction of space of free movement. *Whereas the traditional management expert limits his plans to the formal system, the MIS expert enlarges his domain of interest to all relevant factors. Consequently, the MIS expert may ask that behavior, policies, practices and norms that have been operating covertly be surfaced so that their contributions to the problem be made explicit. This requirement can be threatening because what has been hidden may be incriminating to some participants.*

Equally important however is that, as the informal is made explicit, it comes under the control of the management. The result may be that the participants will feel increasingly hemmed-in. In psychological language the participants will experience a great restriction of their space of free movement. Research suggests that a restriction of the (psychological) space of free movement tends to create feelings of lack of choice, pressure and psychological failure. These feelings, in turn, can lead to increasing feelings of helplessness and decreasing feelings of self-responsibility resulting in the increasing tendency to withdraw or to become dependent upon those who created or approved the restriction of space of free movement.

> *(2)* Psychological failure and double bind. *The second impact of MIS upon management is related to the eventual thrust of the MIS on what Carroll has called "global real time" or "on-line, real-time" (Carroll [17]). The salient characteristics of this structure are formal and continuous flows of global information throughout the system and machine involve-*

ment in all decision making. The system makes all the important decisions. If the local decision maker sees an opportunity to alter the plan, he asks the console to evaluate his idea and give him a yes or no response. The real-time decisions are made centrally. Ultimately, the real-time decisions will be automated completely (Carroll [17, p. 402]). Moreover future planning will be a continual activity primarily carried out by MIS as it is fed information about possible changes.

The impact of such a system can be eventually to create a world for the local decision maker where his daily goals are defined for him, the actions to achieve these goals will be specified, and the level of aspiration will be determined, and the performance evaluated, by a system that is external to him. These conditions may lead individual managers to perform as expected. However, they will also lead to a sense of psychological failure (Lewin, Dembo, Festinger, and Sears [21]). Psychological failure occurs whenever someone else defines the individual's goals, path to his goals, his level of aspiration, and criteria for success. Psychological failure, in turn, leads those managers who aspire toward challenging work that requires self-responsibility to be frustrated while those who prefer less challenge and less responsibility are satisfied. The former may leave, fight, or psychologically withdraw; the latter usually stay and withdraw. The manager, in short, because of the MIS, will now tend to experience the frustrations that the employees have experienced in the past as a result of the industrial and quality control engineers who have designed their work and monitored their performance.

The sense of psychological failure is distasteful to human beings such as successful managers who have been accustomed to psychological success. The manager is now in a double bind. If he follows the new rationality he will succeed as a manager and fail as a human being. He is damned if he refuses to obey, and he damns himself if he does obey.

(3) Leadership based more on competence than on power. *A third impact that the MIS can have upon management is its emphasis upon the use of valid information and technical competence, rather than formal power, to manage organizations. It is not accidental that in models of the actual flow of work events, there is*

> *rarely a hierarchy of power positions independent of the work flow. If a decision maker exists, he is in the diagram along the work flow and not above it, as is the case in the traditional models. McDonough and Garrett have described this characteristic of MIS as emphasizing what and how things are done (McDonough and Garrett [22, p. 18]), whereas in traditional models there was an equal, if not greater, emphasis upon who did it.*

The MIS is not, however, completely devoid of emphasis on power. In defining a "good criterion" Hitch has been quoted as saying, "The criterion for good criteria is consistency with a good criterion at a higher level" (McDonough and Garrett [22, p. 19]). With this definition the MIS expert places himself under the control of the upper levels of management; an action that probably helps to account for his "acceptance" by the upper levels given the problems that we have discussed above and will discuss below.

The difficulties with making valid information and technical competence the new currency for power are several. First, one greatly reduces the probability that managers can order others simply because they have power. This may be threatening to executives who have, up till now, been free to make the organization "move" even if they had incomplete or invalid information.

Second, as we have seen above, is the tendency for organizations to produce invalid information about important issues. An effective MIS will ask the executives to produce precisely that information that they may have learned to withhold (until the appropriate moment) in order to survive.

Thirdly, organizations with properties described above require those executives who enjoy ambiguity, the manipulation of others, and the making of self-fulfilling prophecies. The latter skill is a particularly important one. One of the marks of a successful executive has been that he was able to marshal human and financial resources to make his decisions come true even if others felt that the decision could not be accomplished. These executives enjoyed, indeed needed, to feel that they were fighting and confronting and overcoming a system (Argyris [6], Bennis [14], Dalton [19]).

> *(4)* Decreasing feelings of essentiality. *As MIS becomes more sophisticated there will be less need for ambiguity and self-fulfilling prophecies; there will be less need for "taking hold of the goddam place and turning it*

*around and tightening it up". These activities will now
be carried out in a planned and rational way by the
MIS.*

In other words success, in the past, may have come from
selecting an admittedly ambiguous course of action but, with
resources and power, making it come to reality. The manager,
therefore, had good reason to feel essential and powerful. If a
decision was successful, he could point to where his influence was
important. With optimal ambiguity and fluidity he could also reduce
the probability of being convicted of incompetence if the decision
was not successful. The ambiguity and fluidity could have helped
him to protect himself from his competitors *and*, when successful,
made it possible to assign the feelings of success to himself. The use
of sophisticated quantitative models therefore could tend to reduce
this protection and the feelings of essentiality on the part of the line
manager. One might argue that a line manager could take more risks
with an MIS because he could blame the model or those who develop
it. Our research suggests such an action is not a psychological risk to
the individual. Moreover a line executive would not enhance his
position with those above him if his strategy is to blame others.

(5) Reduction of intra and inter group politics. [*Fifthly*],
*a mature MIS reduces the need for organizational
politics within but especially among departments. The
basic assumption of traditional organizational theory
is that the subordinate should focus on fulfilling his
departmental responsibilities. It is the superior's task
to integrate the several departments into a meaningful
whole. Because of such factors as competition, lack of
trust, and win-lose dynamics, the subordinate tends to
build walls around his department to protect it from
competing peers or arbitrary superiors. Given the
interdepartmental rivalries and barriers, interdependence becomes only partially effective, and success
may come primarily from constant monitoring by the
superior.*

Researchers have documented the existence of interdepartmental rivalries where one side must lose and the other win (Blake,
Shepard, Mouton [15]). Competition for scarce resources is high.
Indeed many managers believe that interdepartmental competition is
healthy. They see it as the best way to assure that departments will

make the best possible demands upon the management. This "rabble hypothesis" of management can be shown to have many dysfunctional effects upon interdepartmental cooperation. It is probably the major cause of subordinates developing and maintaining a departmental view whereas their superiors wish that they had a concern for the whole.

The reduction of organizational politics for managing the whole system requires that the relevant departments provide valid information and abide by decisions made by the MIS. The sophisticated MIS no longer views the organization as an aggregate of "hungry, competitive, and angry" units but as a set of interrelated activities that have to be meshed into a whole. In order to do this, the MIS follows a principle that most managers agree with in theory but seldom follow in practice. "The idea is that the activity of any part of an organization has some effect on the activity of every other part. . . . Therefore, in order to evaluate any decision of action . . . it is necessary to identify all the significant interactions and to evaluate their *combined* impact on the performance of the organization as a whole, not merely on the part originally involved" (Ackoff [1]). In order to capture the wholeness of the problem, the technology must deal not only with the behavior of each department, but also with the interrelationships among the departments. This leads the information scientist to seek information from the parts about their relationship with each other and the whole. He hopes to build a model that will show how the departments can be integrated into a fully functioning whole. To succeed means that the departments which have been locked into win-lose conflicts will have to learn to cooperate with each other. Departments with a long history of survival through combat will understandably be skeptical and cautious about being "required" to cooperate.

> *(6)* New requirements for conceptual thinking. *Finally the sophisticated MIS will require of managers a different level of intellectual and conceptual competence. However, the historical emphasis upon power over competence and fuzziness over explicitness has naturally attracted executives with qualities and competence that are different than those needed if one is to manage with a sophisticated management information technology.*

One major difference is the level of conceptualization they are able to employ. In the past, when data was very incomplete much of the intuition used by a manager was to fill in the many blanks with possible valid data. This meant that managers focussed on immersing themselves "in the facts" especially as revealed by past practice.

A sophisticated management information system is able to develop a much richer set of data or facts. Past and present experience can be efficiently summarized and presented. The new skill that may be required is for the manager to deal with the interdependence among the facts. But since he has many facts and these produce complex interdependences and since the human mind is a finite information processing system, the demand will be for more effective conceptualization of the data in higher order concepts (Miller [23]). This skill typically has been lacking with many managers (Anshem [3]).

Management science specialists might wish to point out, at this time, that the ultimate goal of a valid information science system is to free the manager from the routine data and permit him to focus on being creative and innovative. Indeed, as Ackoff states, the objective of a valid management information system is to reduce the overabundance of irrelevant information because many managers suffer from information overload. The writer agrees.

Unfortunately, our studies so far indicate that the majority of managers still do not know how to use models as the basis for creative experiments. This is partly due to the fact that experimentation, risk taking and trust, as we say above, have been largely drummed out of managerial systems. This, in turn, tends to assure that men who do not enjoy experimenting will become managers. And for those few brave souls who prefer to experiment, they will probably be faced with an array of control systems to keep their innovations "within bounds."

To summarize: Line management and MIS experts probably agree upon the necessity for organizations being essentially rational phenomena. However, the MIS experts' view of rationally designing systems could lead to some basic changes in the present world of management. The managers may find themselves (1) experiencing increasing amounts of psychological failure yet system success and therefore more double binds; (2) being required to reduce interdepartmental warfare and intradepartmental politics; and (3) finding that the concept of managerial success changes its base from one of power, ambiguity, and self-fulfilling prophecy to valid information, explicitness, and technical competence.

Therefore, sophisticated MIS that introduce in organizations a quantum jump in rationality represent a stressful and emotional problem to the participants.

The "New" Degree of Rationality Creates a "Deeper" Degree of Emotionality

How would MIS professionals tend to react to stress and emotions?

Before an attempt is made to answer this question a caveat seems in order. The analysis, to date, has attempted to predict the world if and when MIS were fully mature. No claim is made that we have reached such a state or indeed ever will. The position is that as MIS become more sophisticated they will tend to create the conditions described above. However, as we shall point out below, man need not be reactive and submissive to a system. Indeed, it will be our argument that if the MIS were used effectively, they could actually free the manager rather than restrict him. Our pessimistic prediction is that man will not tend to use MIS effectively because of the norms of the existing world and the way he has programmed himself to be more incompetent than competent in dealing with people.

The Behavior of the MIS Professionals

Recently I conducted a study that hopefully will shed some light on parts of the analysis above as well as the assertion that man may have programmed himself to tend toward interpersonal incompetence rather than competence. I studied a management science-operations research team (MSOR team) operating as a management information group in a multibillion dollar corporation. The number of professionally trained core members on the MSOR Team was about twenty. They were housed in modern facilities and were located as part of a management services department which reported in a staff relationship (and through five layers of management) to the top corporate management. The team was headed by a professionally trained mathematical statistician who, for years, had been championing the relevance of quantitative analytical methods to management.

Although the group had been given a generous budget and excellent facilities, top management's receptivity to quantitative analytical thinking had left much to be desired. Several reasons may be offered. First, as mentioned above, the executives had succeeded because they had the capacity to make choices, based upon intuitive heuristic understanding. Once a decision had been made they were experts at marshalling human and financial resources to implement the decisions. They were skilled at making their decisions "come true"; they were skilled at turning a decision into a self-fulfilling prophecy.

Second, the organization had developed quantitative financial analyses which were used to manage the corporation. These financial systems which seemed, to the MSOR Team, to be inadequate, antiquated, and tied to reporting history were buttressed by a powerful organization that had influence with the top management.

Finally, the state of the art in management science information systems is still primitive compared to the demands of the management. Thus the MSOR Team could not, in all honesty, make promises of major innovations with spectacular results (which would be required to unfreeze the financial department from its position).

The head of the MSOR Team plus his superiors used the admittedly primitive state of the field to "sell" the MSOR Team as developing modest experiments which would not rock the boat while hopefully providing new insights and methods for management. The opportunity to develop an MSOR Team in terms of experimentation and research attracted the team members because it would reduce the probabilities of creating unrealistically high expectations on the part of the clients while giving the team members more time to develop valid models.

The Research Methods Used

The writer interviewed (in individual and group sessions) all of the MSOR Team members plus the superiors two layers above the head of the group. The interviews were semistructured and tape recorded. They lasted about an hour with a few being as short as thirty minutes and some (primarily the group sessions) about four hours. The interviews served to provide the background information and the perceptions of the team members of their problems.

The major research method however was observation of actual work meetings plus analysis of tape recordings of meetings. Tape recordings of twenty five meetings were obtained and analyzed. Fifteen of these meetings were analyzed in great detail. It is these fifteen meetings that provide the core of our data for this paper.

The meetings were tape recorded and analyzed by using a set of categories whose reliability and predictive validity are described in detail elswhere and presented briefly in Table 1 (Argyris [7]). Those above the middle or zero line are hypothesized to facilitate, and those below to inhibit, interpersonal relationships and problem solving. The further away from the zero line, the more difficult is the behavior to perform. Thus, openness to ideas (i) or feelings (f) is hypothesized to be more difficult than owning ideas or feelings (i.e.,

Table 1. Categories of Behavior

Level I		Level II
Individual	Interpersonal	Norms
Experimenting i f	Help others to experiment i f	Trust i f
Openness i f	Help others to be open i f	Concern i f
Owning i f Zero	Help others to own i f	Individuality i f
Not owning i f	Not help others to own i f	Conformity i f
Not open i f	Not help others to be open i f	Antagonism i f
Rejecting experimenting i f	Not help others to experiment i f	Mistrust

stating one's ideas or feelings), and experimenting is more difficult than openness. Each unit of behavior is scored on two levels. Level I represents the individual and interpersonnal. Level II represents norms of the group. For example:

Sample Statement	Would be Scored as		
(1) "I believe that we should reject the idea even though we are told not to."	own i	individuality i	
(2) "I feel tense."	own f	individuality f	
(3) "Would you please tell me more about your theory?"	open i	concern i	
(4) "This is not easy for me to talk about. I feel like my whole life has been a shambles. I feel frightened and bewildered."	experimenting f	trust f	

When both scores represent categories above the zero line or below, the behavior may be said to be *consistent*. For example, in the four cases above, the categories representing the personal and norms levels are all positive. If behavior was positive and negative, it would be viewed as *inconsistent* (e.g., owning *i*—conformity *i* or open *i*—antagonism *i*). Inconsistent behavior presents a special class of problems which is very important in understanding individual or group attempts to be effective.

The Results of Observations

The results of six meetings are presented. (Table 2) The first three compose a pattern to be identified as A (which represents 7 of the 15 meetings). The second three compose pattern B (and are representative of the remaining 8 meetings).

Pattern A was characterized by a high degree of stating or *owning* up to ideas. Ideas were stated in such a way as to contribute most frequently to the norm of *concern* for ideas. The second most frequently scored norm was *conformity* to ideas (but that was significantly lower). These results may be interpreted to mean that the discussion was straightforward where the facts spoke for themselves.

Openness to ideas occurred significantly lower than owning up to ideas. An analysis of these scores indicated that openness was found mostly (1) when a member wanted to learn something from a superior or a client and (2) when presentations were being made of quantitative models and the people listening asked questions to understand them.

There was little behavior of the members helping or not helping each other to own up to, be open, and experiment with ideas. The members seemed to be on their own, concerned with their contribution and less with helping others. Inconsistent behavior tended to be somewhat more frequent than the openness, but the scores were not very high.

Behavior that was *rarely* observed was (a) expressing feelings; (b) openness to feelings; (c) experimenting with ideas or feelings; (d) helping others to own up to feelings; (e) helping others to experiment with their ideas and feelings; (f) the positive norms of trust or individuality and the negative norm of antagonism and mistrust; and (g) overtly refusing to express, to be open, to experiment with ideas or feelings and overtly and directly trying to prevent or inhibit others.

These results suggest several characteristics of the dynamics of the groups.

Table 2. Group Scores for Six Meetings

		1 n = 90		2 n = 80		3 n = 100		4 n = 200		5 n = 200		6 n = 15	
		n	%	n	%	n	%	n	%	n	%	n	%
Personal													
own	i	67	74	56	70	74	74	116	58	132	66	112	74
own	f												
open	i	22	24	16	20	21	21	50	25	29	14	16	10
open	f												
exper	i												
exper	f												
Interpersonal													
ho* own	i												
not ho own	i			8	10	4	04	50	25	39	20	21	14
Group norms													
conc	i	75	83	47	53	66	66	108	54	75	39	51	34
conc	f												
indiv	i	7	08	3	05	6	06	8	04	3	02	2	01
indiv	f												
trust	i												
trust	f												
conf	i	8	08	30	70	30	30	83	41	104	53	73	48
conf	f												
antag	i							1	01	18	07	22	14
antag	f												
mistrust	i												
mistrust	f												
Inconsistent behavior													
own i conf	i	7	08	22	27	23	23	50	25	59	30	53	36
own i antag	i					3	03			13	06	23	16
open i conf	i											6	04
open i antag	i									4	02	8	06
Total imbalance		7	08	22	27	26	26	50	25	86	43	90	60

*Helping others.

1. *Behavior that facilitates or directly inhibits others'
behavior and feelings was rarely expressed. The norms
for openness to new ideas, for expressing feelings and
for taking risks were very weak. These groups, therefore, should not be settings where creative and innova-*

tive work is done. Also, any risk taking or conformation should tend to be inhibited (Argyris [12]).

Such a conclusion may seem to be at variance with the findings reported by several recent studies (Churchman and Schainblatt [18], Mumford and Ward [24], Pettigrew [25]) to the effect that MIS people perceive themselves as wanting to be, and as being, creative or innovative. These data are based upon individual reports. Indeed, most of our population reported similar needs and self-perceptions. The conclusions above are focussed on group behavior. We are, in short, predicting that if these individuals are creative they will tend to have their creativity cancelled out or reduced when they are operating in these groups.

2. *Individuals rarely express positive or negative feelings in the group setting while striving to achieve their tasks. This may be due to several possibilities:*
   (a) *The individuals rarely generate positive or negative feelings;*
   (b) *The individuals do generate positive and negative feelings but are inhibited in expressing these feelings (e.g., their view of effective problem solving may include the suppressing of feelings or their personality inhibits them from expressing their feelings);*
   (c) *The individuals develop positive and negative feelings but feel group and cultural norms exist about expressing them.*

These findings are very similar to the ones found to exist for top and middle management groups (Argyris [8]). Thus the MSOR team members tend to behave in ways that are similar to line executives. Although the similarity of behavior may lead one to infer that feelings of commonality and effective communication should exist, our observations suggest a different outcome. The reason may be found by observing what actually happens when the MSOR Team meets managers. These conditions tended to be stressful and tension producing because here were the times when the MSOR Team was trying to convince line executives to accept an MIS. Here is where the new rationality produced the deeper emotionality.

The behavior of the MSOR Team under stress changed significantly. The results are identified as pattern B. We note that pattern B is again characterized by a high degree of *owning up* to ideas. However, *conformity* to ideas becomes the predominant norm.

People are doing much more persuading and "selling". *Openness* to ideas is reduced but not altered significantly. *Helping others* is sharply reduced to zero. *Not helping* others increases dramatically. People may be observed cutting each other off. *Antagonism* increases significantly in two of the three meetings. Inconsistent behavior also increases dramatically.

Again, feelings are hardly ever expressed; experimenting, trust or mistrust are rarely observed.

Under stress, the MSOR Team loses some of its composure; it produces more behavior scored as conformity and antagonism; it suppresses its feelings of tension by intellectualizing them; it does little to help its own members or others to become more open, to explore new issues, and to take risks.

The research of top management behavior cited previously concludes that they too react in similar ways when under stress. *We have two groups who react to stress and tension in ways that will tend to inhibit effective problem solving.*

Thus MIS professional and line managers have a comparable degree of interpersonal competence. Under stress, people with this degree of interpersonal competence tend to react in ways that inhibit effective problem solving. These conclusions are supported by Pettigrew's results. Operations researchers report that they run into interpersonal and interdepartmental problems when they are trying to do the job the way they think it should be done (68%). "The biggest single difficulty lay in communicating with and convincing 'user' departments that a change or a series of changes was in fact in their and their company's interests" (Pettigrew [25, p. 211]).

To summarize:

Under Minimal Stress Both Groups Will Tend To:	Under Stress Both Groups Will Tend To:
1. encourage the expression of nonrisk taking ideas	1. encourage the expression of non-risk ideas
2. encourage concern for nonrisk taking	2. discourage concern for ideas and encourage conformity, encourage inconsistent behavior (as much as it encourages concern under minimal stress), and antagonism more than helping others.

3. encourage mild expressing of selling and persuasion	3. encourage strong expression of selling, persuasion. Listening to others is primarily in terms of winning arguments, supporting colleagues, or agreeing with what is being said
4. encourage mild competitive behavior of not helping others	4. encourage strong competitive or withdrawal behavior and increase not helping others
5. encourage individuals not to be concerned about group effectiveness	5. encourage individual members not to be concerned about group effectiveness
6. discourage the expression of risk taking, deviant news, issues loaded with conflict, trust or mistrust, feelings of any kind	6. discourage the expression of risk taking, issues loaded with conflict, trust, or mistrust, feelings of any kind

The overemphasis on persuasion and selling, the increase in competition or withdrawal, the discouragement of openness and risk taking, the discouragement of helping others and of showing concern for group effectiveness *are basically emotional responses, even though the feelings may be intellectualized.* Thus two groups whose members prefer to be intendedly rational, who prefer to manage rationally, who seek new intendedly rational designs of managing human behavior develop a design for dealing with confrontation of the introduction of a new MIS that is basically emotional and threatening to them.

Adaptation by the Clients to Threat

The clients' reactions to threat can be predicted from the analysis to date. First, the feelings of mistrust, suspicion, and fears of inadequacy will rarely be discussed openly. If information science groups are destroyed or slowly permitted to atrophy, the announced reasons will be consistent with present managerial practice. For example, not enough clients can be persuaded to pay for the services. Or management still does not understand the value of the new systems and therefore does not know how to use an operations research group effectively (Burack [16]).

If the specialists are kept, management may react by assigning them projects that are of low level importance or of critical urgency. In both cases, the attending conditions help to assure the poor use of management information concepts and models. In the former case, since the status of the project in the client's eyes will be low, the specialists may find it difficult to get the cooperation from all levels of the organization in supplying the necessary data or in permitting observations of the activities to be modelled. In the case of the latter, the pressures are so great and tensions so high that deadlines are usually defined that make it difficult for the specialist to study the problem thoroughly and to develop a systematic model. The clients, who typically do not understand the time required to collect the data and, more importantly, to develop abstract models that are relevant to their particular requirements, become impatient, frustrated, and disappointed. The specialists develop the same feelings for having their ultimate value assessed on the basis of the sophistication of these admittedly incomplete models.

Adaptation of the Team

Team members developed several ways to cope with their dilemmas. First they convinced themselves that it was their mission, "To force people to become more explicit in their thinking in order to be more effective". Another put it this way, "It is my job to make people think through what the hell their objectives are". Given that their task is now conceived as *coercing* others to become more explicit and rational, then any coercion on their part becomes consistent with their mission.

Another mode of adaptation was to be as diplomatic as possible. This came in the form of translating their ideas into "simple" (but "sloppy") managerial language, by suppressing (they thought) their disrespect for the low calibre of intellectual capacity among managers, and by not confronting any issue that might be threatening to the line.

To be sure, there came moments when the team members could no longer be diplomatic. At that moment, they either withdrew (behavior that tended to upset aggressive line managers because an important reason for their aggressiveness was a fear of being rejected) or, they too became aggressive and competitive. To make matters worse, once the latter occurred, whatever success the team members had in hiding their feelings of intellectual superiority was greatly reduced, and they came across (in the eyes of line management) as arrogant. For example, one computer expert responded to a line manager (who had just asked him to explain his proposals), "Do you understand the concept of the half life in physics" (Mumford and Ward [24, p. 247]).

Another way to adapt was to meet in their private rooms and complain loudly to each other and to their superiors about the inhibiting behavior of their clients. This not only provided an opportunity for catharsis, but it created pressures on the supervisors to calm the group down, to assure them that the project was going well, and to promise to do their best to meet with some senior line representatives to ask for better cooperation. The team members tended to feel cheered and left the meeting thanking the superior and asking him to make their requests to the higher levels without upsetting them. If the top line people became upset, they could upset the lower level line people who, in turn, could make it very difficult for the lower level management scientists. One can imagine the tension felt by superiors. They were asked to complain "carefully" to already defensive line managers, but to do so with enough "force" to assure some action on their part "against" their subordinates.

These contradictory demands made of their superiors were compounded by the contradictory games they tended to play with their clients. For example, the clients experienced the information science technologists to want:

(1) All relevant information made explicit and subject to correction	yet	(1) they kept many of their change strategies about the clients secret.
(2) Organizations should be based more on competence than power	yet	(2) they used power and manipulation to get their work accepted.
(3) Management to reduce their intuitive and seat-of-the-pants thinking	yet	(3) they used primarily intuitive thinking in developing their strategies to introduce their technology to the clients.

These basic inconsistencies between stated philosophy and actual behavior helped the clients who were defensive to rationalize their myopia and resistance as necessary protective activity. Under these conditions the distance between the clients and the technologists became greater.

Attempts could be made to reduce the distance by having as head of the specialists someone who "understands, gets along with, and speaks the language of the line". This may mean that the head of a management science-operations research group would be selected primarily for his abilities to succeed with line executives rather than for his technical competence.

Unfortunately, this frequently used strategy tends to fail in several ways. Since the head of the technical group also will not tend to deal with the emotional dimensions openly, he will find himself becoming increasingly diplomatic and cautious with line management. This, in turn, may create increased anxiety in the team members who could interpret this as a potential sellout to the line.

To make matters more difficult, the head may also feel that in order to obtain paying customers for his group, he may have (1) to accept, for the group, assignments that are not challenging; (2) to oversell the capabilities of information science technology and thereby create unreal expectations; (3) to agree with the line that information technology specialists are somewhat odd and difficult; (4) to agree to reductions in the quality of effort and in the time available; or (5) to remain indefinitely vague about what can be accomplished, thereby preventing the clients from having realistic expectations.

The more the subordinates find themselves caught up in the consequences of such behavior, the more hopeless and frustrated they may become. The first-rate men may leave while the others may stay but come to condemn their superior for the problems of ineffectiveness.

One can predict that if the MSOR Team members attempted to resolve the issues among themselves, there would be a high probability that the meeting would be a highly stressful one. Consequently, the behavior described at the outset would tend to predominate. For example, those who valued the competitive, win-lose dynamics would tend to make their contributions as articulately and persuasively as possible. They would generate a pervasive mode of "selling". Selling would tend to make the speaker feel that he was being articulate and intellectually powerful. However, this very power may act to reduce the probabilities that the "customer" would buy because the customer would sense (a) that the emotional component was stronger than the rational, yet (b) the speaker was insisting that he was being rational and asking others to be the same. (Let's look at the facts.) The listener would tend to mistrust the "sales pitch". He would see it more as the speaker trying to win him over, to protect his own interests, rather than to help create a climate where the best solutions or a new idea could be created.

Under these conditions the participants would also tend to immunize themselves from being infected by the enthusiasm of the seller by (a) turning him off, (b) not listening but preparing their own sales pitch, or (c) if they did listen, it would lead the original seller to feel less effective. He may react by increasing his selling and by evaluating the others as somewhat stubborn for defending their "narrow departmental or personal view".

Thus, there would be a recycling which would tend to increase the selling and competitiveness. This, in turn, would make them be very careful and articulate in verbalizing their thoughts. Thus, they may focus more on preparing their contributions than on listening to others. Moreover, once they spoke, they would continue until all of their accumulated ideas had been heard. The time available to be "on the air" would become scarce. This would result in ineffective group meetings and problem solving.

Some Thoughts on Coping with the Problems Identified

The reader may ask what can the MSOR team members and the line executives do to reduce the problems identified above and to increase the probabilities of effective introduction of MIS? The first step is that both groups become aware that the MIS per se is *not* the basic problem. The basic problem is that modern organizations, as we indicated at the outset, are designed with power centralized at the top, with specialization of tasks which results in many concealed dysfunctional components that are revealed by a MIS and that MIS implies a different design for organizations, one where competence is more important than power and collaboration and interdependence are more important than competition. This tends to create many fears and resistances on the part of individuals, groups, and intergroups.

In order for valid advice to become available, much empirical research is needed on the differential impact of the different degrees of these consequences. Rubenstein, *et al* [26] has identified ten variables that could be used in such studies. They are

(1) Level of management support
(2) Client receptivity
(3) Organizational and technical capability of the OR/MS person or group
(4) Organizational location
(5) Influence upon organization
(6) Reputation

(7) Adequacy of the resources
(8) Relevance of projects
(9) Level of opposition
(10) General perception of the level of success

Many researchers have suggested that one way to reduce these problems is to teach managers the basic knowledge about management information science technology. Others suggest that both managers and MIS professionals need to be taught to hold a position of "mutual understanding". Under such conditions both react to each other in order to enhance their personal gains (Churchman and Schainblatt [18]). The difficulty with these suggestions is that no one, to the writer's knowledge, has ever shown that if such learning is achieved it transfers to real situations when the individuals are fighting a win-lose game and are under high stress. Indeed, our data show that the MIS people, who are well educated in information sciences, have similar emotional problems with each other. They frequently challenge each other's work which leads to the same kinds of strains that exist between themselves and the line managers.

Suggestions to bridge the two cultures by placing line managers in MIS groups and vice versa may help. However, in the writer's experience, when these "fully" educated men enter the arena of conflict and win-lose they may use their knowledge about the other side to decrease the probability that they will win.

In the organization studied, the strategy used was to place a member of the line management on the MIS team to act as a liaison. He was in constant touch with both groups. He made significant inputs into the development of the model. However, these men reported great role strain. They described themselves as men-in-the-middle trying to please and help both sides only to wind up as a hero or a traitor (depending upon which way the decision went).

Others have suggested that MIS may be helped if the team is housed in a management services division, if it has easy access to influential top management, and if it has adequate funds to support some of its activities on a research basis. This group was housed in a management services division and was encouraged by top management to take on a few jobs, primarily on a research basis. The access to the top management however was not easy. But it is not clear what such an access could have achieved. Perhaps both sides would hesitate to go to the top because the nature of their win-lose intergroup dynamics and lack of communication would become evident to the highest officers.

The primary difficulty with all these strategies is that they assume the problem can be solved rationally. Education and structural rearrangements assume that people will respond rationally to the new stimuli these learnings and changes create. This assumption is valid up to the point where people begin to threaten each other and are in conflict. Then both sides regress and respond ineffectively. Rational solutions may delay the moment of conflict, but they do not get at the underlying problem, namely, no one has been able to program human activity significantly to eliminate or reduce conflict and threat. Moreover, in the cases where it has been attempted the "success" has been due to the fact that the protagonists got the message and suppressed the expression of conflict in front of top management.

This does *not* mean that rational solutions such as education and structural changes will never work. The strategy being suggested is that the competence of *both* managers and MIS professionals in dealing with emotionality and strain in interpersonal and intergroup problems must be raised. As their interpersonal competence in these areas increases they will naturally turn to education and structural changes. We would predict, on the basis of other research, that their commitment to education and the changes will then be internal, not merely external (imposed) (Argyris [7], [8]). Under these conditions the participants would also tend to develop a responsibility of continually monitoring their solutions to correct the failures. In short, the team members may need to be helped to modify their behavior.

Behavioral science research suggests that in order to increase one's interpersonal competence the individual needs to be aware of his self and his defenses. Next, it is helpful if the individual strives to attain a minimum of psychological conflict and an acceptance of his self so that he can create conditions that lead to trust, openness, risk taking, and effective confrontation of conflict (Argyris [13]).

The focus on interpersonal relations and the expression of feelings should *not* be interpreted to mean that rationality should be substituted for emotionality and interpersonal competence for technical competence. As Rubenstein et al. [26] pointed out, a reputation for professional excellence is central to the success of an MIS unit. Openness requires a particular combination of rational *and* emotional communication. Openness does *not* mean that each individual should express whatever is on his mind regardless of any concern for the feelings of others. The aim is to create a situation in which the MSOR Team members can express how they feel in such a manner as to help the line executives express themselves in a similar open manner. The theory is that emotional problems within organizations do not simply disappear when they are not faced; rather they tend to obstruct the carrying out of rational plans.

Also, the utilization of behavioral science technology requires an awareness of, and competence in, the use of a different set of concepts and conceptual schemes. These schemes, primitive as they may be, are presently either unknown or incompletely known to the MSOR Team members. Moreover, to learn these concepts in such a way that the individual can use them he would be required to undergo learning experiences that may be somewhat painful to him. Concepts about human behavior are most effectively learned by first experiencing them and later relating the concepts to the experience (Schein and Bennis [27]). This means that the learning situations can be designed to help individuals experience and openly talk about their feelings regarding many different complex emotions. But, as we have seen, the expression and exploration of feelings was not one of the strengths of the MSOR Team members.

Developing and increasing interpersonal competence includes becoming aware that high competence is maintained by constant feedback of valid information from others about one's own impact on the others. In order to get relatively valid feedback from others, one must help to create conditions for minimal defensiveness for one's self and the others. These conditions include (1) reducing the formal power of the superior, (2) focussing more on interpersonal competence as a basis for influence, and (3) creating conditions where others can feel free to confront one's self and others on the difficult interpersonal and substantive issues. Such a relationship is significantly different from the way the various team members dealt with authority and influence. They were consistent with their line executives who tend to be controlling and directive.

Finally, there is a necessity to recognize and deal openly with interpersonal interdependence. Individuals are incomplete without others. Again this tends to be at variance with the feeling and beliefs of most of the MSOR Team members. They felt "completed" by relating themselves to a world of symbols, models, and concepts. They tended to resist getting into interpersonal interdependence.

The point being made is that the introduction of a sophisticated information technology is as much an emotional human problem that requires interpersonal competence (as well as technical competence) and that requires knowledge about the human aspects of organizations such as personality, small groups, intergroups, and living systems or organizations norms. Those of us working in these fields are painfully aware of the inadequacy and primitive state of our knowledge. We need help from the management scientist-operations research professional if the relationships between thought and action, as played out in this world, are to be understood and made more effective.

References

1. Ackoff, R. L. (Ed.), *Progress in Operations Research,* vol. 1, John Wiley and Sons, 1961, p. 26.

2. _____ , "Management Misinformation Systems," Management Science Center, Wharton School of Finance and Commerce, University of Pennsylvania, 1968, Mimeograph.

3. Anshem, M., "The Management of Ideas," *Harvard Business Review,* (July–August, 1969), pp. 99–107.

4. Argyris, C., *Personality and Organization*, Harper and Row, 1957.

5. _____ , *Interpersonal Competence and Organizational Effectiveness,* R. D. Irwin and Co., 1962.

6. _____ , *Integrating the Individual and the Organization*, John Wiley, 1964.

7. _____ , *Organization and Innovation*, R. D. Irwin, Inc., 1965.

8. _____ , "Interpersonal Barriers to Decision-Making," *Harvard Business Review*, 44(2) (1966), pp. 84–97.

9. _____ , "How Tomorrow's Executives Will Make Decisions," *Think*, 33(6), (1967a), pp. 18–26.

10. _____ , "Today's Problems With Tomorrow's Organizations," *Journal of Management Studies*, 4(1), (February 1967b), pp. 31–55.

11. _____ , "On the Effectiveness of Research and Development Organizations," *American Scientist*, 56(4), (1968), pp. 344–355.

12. _____ , "The Incompleteness of Social Psychological Theory," *American Psychologist*, 24(1), (October 1969), pp. 893–908.

13. _____ , *Intervention Theory and Method: A Behavioral Science View*, (in press).

14. Bennis, W. G., *Changing Organizations*, McGraw Hill, 1966.

15. Blake, R. R., Shepard, H. A. and Mouton, J. S., *Managing Intergroup Conflict in Industry*, Gulf Publishing Co., Houston, 1964.

16. Burack, E. H., "Operations Research: Its Future Place in Business Organization," *Michigan State University, Business Topics*, 17(4), (Spring 1969), pp. 9–16.

17. Carroll, D. C., "On the Structure of Operational Control Systems," *Operations Research and the Design of Management Information Systems*, John F. Pierce, Jr. (Ed.), Special Tech. Association Publication Stap. no. 4, Chapter 23, (1965), pp. 398–402.

18. Churchman, G. W. and Schainblatt, A. H., "The Researcher and the Manager: A Dialectic of Implementation," *Management Science*, vol. 11, (February 1965), pp. B-69–B-87.

19. Dalton, M., *Men Who Manage*, John Wiley, New York, 1958.

20. Gardner, J., "America in the Twenty-Third Century," *New York Times*, July 27, 1968.

21. Lewin, K., Dembo, T., Festinger, L., and Sears, P. S., "Level of Aspiration," in J. M. V. Hunt (Ed.), *Personality and the Behavior Disorders*, Ronald Press, New York, 1944, pp. 333–378.

22. McDonough, A. M. and Garrett, L. J., *Management Systems*, R. D. Irwin and Co., 1965, pp. 18–19.

23. Miller, G. A., "The Magical Number Seven Plus or Minus Two," *Psychological Review*, vol. 63, (1956), pp. 81–97.

24. Mumford, E. and Ward, T., "Computer Technologists," *Journal of Management Studies,* 3(3), (October 1966), pp. 244–255.

25. Pettigrew, A., "Inter-Group Conflict and Role Strain," *Journal of Management Studies*, 5(2), (May 1968), pp. 205–218.

26. Rubenstein, A. H., Radnor, M., Baker, N. R., Heiman, D. R. and McColly, J. B., "Some Organizational Factors Related to the Effectiveness of Management Science Groups in Industry," *Management Science*, vol. 13, no. 8, (April 1967), pp. B508–B518.

27. Schein, E. H. and Bennis, W. G., *Personal and Organizational Change Through Group Methods: The Laboratory Approach*, Wiley, New York, 1965.

Section **3**

Management Information Needs

19

Management Misinformation Systems*

Russell L. Ackoff

Reprinted by permission of
Management Science, December 1967.

The growing preoccupation of operations researchers and management scientists with Management Information Systems (MIS's) is apparent. In fact, for some the design of such systems has almost become synonymous with operations research or management science. Enthusiasm for such systems is understandable: it involves the researcher in a romantic relationship with the most glamorous instrument of our time, the computer. Such enthusiasm is understandable but, nevertheless, some of the excesses to which it has led are not excusable.

Contrary to the impression produced by the growing literature, few computerized management information systems have been put into operation. Of those I've seen that have been implemented, most have not matched expectations and some have been outright failures. I believe that these near- and far-misses could have been avoided if certain false (and usually implicit) assumptions on which many such systems have been erected had not been made.

There seem to be five common and erroneous assumptions underlying the design of most MIS's, each of which I will consider. After doing so I will outline an MIS design procedure which avoids these assumptions.

*Received June 1967.

Give Them More

Most MIS's are designed on the assumption that the critical deficiency under which most managers operate is the *lack of relevant information*. I do not deny that most managers lack a good deal of information that they should have, but I do deny that this is the most important informational deficiency from which they suffer. It seems to me that they suffer more from an *over abundance of irrelevant information*.

This is not a play on words. The consequences of changing the emphasis of an MIS from supplying relevant information to eliminating irrelevant information is considerable. If one is preoccupied with supplying relevant information, attention is almost exclusively given to the generation, storage, and retrieval of information: hence emphasis is placed on constructing data banks, coding, indexing, updating files, access languages, and so on. The ideal which has emerged from this orientation is an infinite pool of data into which a manager can reach to pull out any information he wants. If, on the other hand, one sees the manager's information problem primarily, but not exclusively, as one that arises out of an overabundance of irrelevant information, most of which was not asked for, then the two most important functions of an information system become *filtration* (or evaluation) and *condensation*. The literature on MIS's seldom refers to these functions let alone considers how to carry them out.

My experience indicates that most managers receive much more data (if not information) than they can possibly absorb even if they spend all of their time trying to do so. Hence they already suffer from an information overload. They must spend a great deal of time separating the relevant from the irrelevant and searching for the kernels in the relevant documents. For example, I have found that I receive an average of forty-three hours of unsolicited reading material each week. The solicited material is usually half again this amount.

I have seen a daily stock status report that consists of approximately six hundred pages of computer print-out. The report is circulated daily across managers' desks. I've also seen requests for major capital expenditures that come in book size, several of which are distributed to managers each week. It is not uncommon for many managers to receive an average of one journal a day or more. One could go on and on.

Unless the information overload to which managers are subjected is reduced, any additional information made available by an MIS cannot be expected to be used effectively.

Even relevant documents have too much redundancy. Most documents can be considerably condensed without loss of content. My point here is best made, perhaps, by describing briefly an experiment that a few of my colleagues and I conducted on the OR literature several years ago. By using a panel of well-known experts we identified four OR articles that all members of the panel considered to be "above average," and four articles that were considered to be "below average." The authors of the eight articles were asked to prepare "objective" examinations (duration thirty minutes) plus answers for graduate students who were to be assigned the articles for reading. (The authors were not informed about the experiment.) Then several experienced writers were asked to reduce each article to 2/3 and 1/3 of its original length only by eliminating words. They also prepared a brief abstract of each article. Those who did the condensing did not see the examinations to be given to the students.

A group of graduate students who had not previously read the articles were then selected. Each one was given four articles randomly selected, each of which was in one of its four versions: 100%, 67%, 33%, or abstract. Each version of each article was read by two students. All were given the same examinations. The average scores on the examinations were then compared.

For the above-average articles there was no significant difference between average test scores for the 100%, 67%, and 33% versions, but there was a significant decrease in average test scores for those who had read only the abstract. For the below-average articles there was no difference in average test scores among those who had read the 100%, 67%, and 33% versions, but there was a significant *increase* in average test scores of those who had read only the abstract.

The sample used was obviously too small for general conclusions but the results strongly indicate the extent to which even good writing can be condensed without loss of information. I refrain from drawing the obvious conclusion about bad writing.

It seems clear that condensation as well as filtration, performed mechanically or otherwise, should be an essential part of an MIS, and that such a system should be capable of handling much, if not all, of the unsolicted as well as solicited information that a manager receives.

The Manager Needs the Information That He Wants

Most MIS designers "determine" what information is needed by asking managers what information they would like to have. This is based on the assumption that managers know what information they need and want it.

For a manager to know what information he needs he must be aware of each type of decision he should make (as well as does) and he must have an adequate model of each. These conditions are seldom satisfied. Most managers have some conception of at least some of the types of decisions they must make. Their conceptions, however, are likely to be deficient in a very critical way, a way that follows from an important principle of scientific economy: the less we understand a phenomenon, the more variables we require to explain it. Hence, the manager who does not understand the phenomenon he controls plays it "safe" and, with respect to information, wants "everything." The MIS designer, who has even less understanding of the relevant phenomenon than the manager, tries to provide even more than everything. He thereby increases what is already an overload of irrelevant information.

For example, market researchers in a major oil company once asked their marketing managers what variables they thought were relevant in estimating the sales volume of future service stations. Almost seventy variables were identified. The market researchers then added about half again this many variables and performed a large multiple linear regression analysis of sales of existing stations against these variables and found about thirty-five to be statistically significant. A forecasting equation was based on this analysis. An OR team subsequently constructed a model based on only one of these variables, traffic flow, which predicted sales better than the thirty-five variable regression equation. The team went on to *explain* sales at service stations in terms of the customers' perception of the amount of time lost by stopping for service. The relevance of all but a few of the variables used by the market researchers could be explained by their effect on such perception.

The moral is simple: one cannot specify what information is required for decision making until an explanatory model of the decision process and the system involved has been constructed and tested. Information systems are subsystems of control systems. They cannot be designed adequately without taking control in account. Furthermore, whatever else regression analyses can yield, they cannot yield understanding and explanation of phenomena. They describe and, at best, predict.

Give a Manager the Information He Needs and His Decision Making Will Improve

It is frequently assumed that if a manager is provided with the information he needs, he will then have no problem in using it effectively. The history of OR stands to the contrary. For example, give most managers an initial tableau of a typical "real" mathematical programming, sequencing, or network problem and see how close they come to an optimal solution. If their experience and judgment have any value they may not do badly, but they will seldom do very well. In most management problems there are too many possibilities to expect experience, judgement, or intuition to provide good guesses, even with perfect information.

Furthermore, when several probabilities are involved in a problem the unguided mind of even a manager has difficulty in aggregating them in a valid way. We all know many simple problems in probability in which untutored intuition usually does very badly (e.g., What are the correct odds that 2 of 25 people selected at random will have their birthdays on the same day of the year?). For example, very few of the results obtained by queuing theory, when arrivals and service are probabilistic, are obvious to managers; nor are the results of risk analysis where the managers' own subjective estimates of probabilities are used.

The moral: it is necessary to determine how well managers can use needed information. When, because of the complexity of the decision process, they can't use it well, they should be provided with either decision rules or performance feed-back so that they can identify and learn from their mistakes. More on this point later.

More Communication Means Better Performance

One characteristic of most MIS's which I have seen is that they provide managers with better current information about what other managers and their departments and divisions are doing. Underlying this provision is the belief that better interdepartmental communication enables managers to coordinate their decisions more effectively and hence improves the organization's overall performance. Not only is this not necessarily so, but it seldom is so. One would hardly expect two competing companies to become more cooperative because the information each acquires about the other is improved. This analogy is not as far fetched as one might first suppose. For example, consider the following very much simplified version of a situation I once ran into. The simplification of the case does not affect any of its essential characteristics.

A department store has two "line" operations: buying and selling. Each function is performed by a separate department. The Purchasing Department primarily controls one variable: how much of each item is bought. The Merchandising Department controls the price at which it is sold. Typically, the measure of performance applied to the Purchasing Department was the turnover rate of inventory. The measure applied to the Merchandising Department was gross sales; this department sought to maximize the number of items sold times their price.

Now by examining a single item let us consider what happens in this system. The merchandising manager, using his knowledge of competition and consumption, set a price which he judged would maximize gross sales. In doing so he utilized price-demand curves for each type of item. For each price the curves show the expected sales and values on an upper and lower confidence band as well. (See Figure 1.) When instructing the Purchasing Department how many items to make available, the merchandising manager quite naturally used the value on the upper confidence curve. This minimized the chances of his running short which, if it occurred, would hurt his performance. It also maximized the chances of being over-stocked

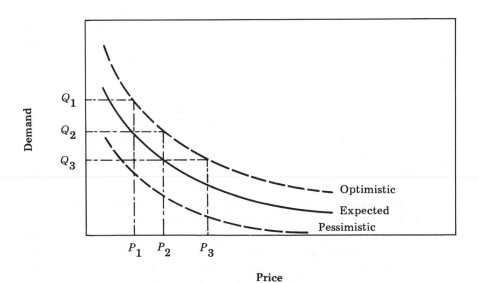

Figure 1.   Price-demand curve.

but this was not his concern, only the purchasing manager's. Say, therefore, that the merchandising manager initially selected price P_1 and requested that amount Q_1 be made available by the Purchasing Department.

In this company the purchasing manager also had access to the price-demand curves. He knew the merchandising manager always ordered optimistically. Therefore, using the same curve he read over from Q_1 to the upper limit and down to the expected value from which he obtained Q_2, the quantity he actually intended to make available. He did not intend to pay for the merchandising manager's optimism. If merchandising ran out of stock, it was not his worry. Now the merchandising manager was informed about what the purchasing manager had done so he adjusted his price to P_2. The purchasing manager in turn was told that the merchandising manager had made this readjustment so he planned to make only Q_3 available. If this process—made possible only by perfect communication between departments—had been allowed to continue, nothing would have been bought and nothing would have been sold. This outcome was avoided by prohibiting communication between the two departments and forcing each to guess what the other was doing.

I have obviously caricatured the situation in order to make the point clear: when organizational units have inappropriate measures of performance which put them in conflict with each other, as is often the case, communication between them may hurt organizational performance, not help it. Organizational structure and performance measurement must be taken into account before opening the flood gates and permitting the free flow of information between parts of the organization. (A more rigorous discussion of organizational structure and the relationship of communication to it can be found in [1]).

A Manager Does Not Have to Understand How an Information System Works, Only How to Use It

Most MIS designers seek to make their systems as innocuous and unobtrusive as possible to managers lest they become frightened. The designers try to provide managers with very easy access to the system and assure them that they need to know nothing more about it. The designers usually succeed in keeping managers ignorant in this regard. This leaves managers unable to evaluate the MIS as a whole. It often makes them afraid to even try to do so lest they display their ignorance publicly. In failing to evaluate their MIS, managers delegate much of the control of the organization to the system's designers and operators who may have many virtues, but managerial competence is seldom among them.

Let me cite a case in point. A Chairman of a Board of a medium-size company asked for help on the following problem. One of his larger (decentralized) divisions had installed a computerized production-inventory control and manufacturing-manager information system about a year earlier. It had acquired about $2,000,000 worth of equipment to do so. The Board Chairman had just received a request from the Division for permission to replace the original equipment with newly announced equipment which would cost several times the original amount. An extensive "justification" for so doing was provided with the request. The Chairman wanted to know whether the request was really justified. He admitted to complete incompetence in this connection.

A meeting was arranged at the Division at which I was subjected to an extended and detailed briefing. The system was large but relatively simple. At the heart of it was a reorder point for each item and a maximum allowable stock level. Reorder quantities took lead-time as well as the allowable maximum into account. The computer kept track of stock, ordered items when required and generated numerous reports on both the state of the system it controlled and its own "actions."

When the briefing was over I was asked if I had any questions. I did. First I asked if, when the system had been installed, there had been many parts whose stock level exceeded the maximum amount possible under the new system. I was told there were many. I asked for a list of about thirty and for some graph paper. Both were provided. With the help of the system designer and volumes of old daily reports I began to plot the stock level of the first listed item over time. When this item reached the maximum "allowable" stock level it had been reordered. The system designer was surprised and said that by sheer "luck" I had found one of the few errors made by the system. Continued plotting showed that because of repeated premature reordering the item had never gone much below the maximum stock level. Clearly the program was confusing the maximum allowable stock level and the reorder point. This turned out to be the case in more than half of the items on the list.

Next I asked if they had many paired parts, ones that were only used with each other; for example, matched nuts and bolts. They had many. A list was produced and we began checking the previous day's withdrawals. For more than half of the pairs the differences in the numbers recorded as withdrawn were very large. No explanation was provided.

Before the day was out it was possible to show by some quick and dirty calculations that the new computerized system was costing the company almost $150,000 per month more than the hand system which it had replaced, most of this in excess inventories.

The recommendation was that the system be redesigned as quickly as possible and that the new equipment not be authorized for the time being.

The questions asked of the system had been obvious and simple ones. Managers should have been able to ask them but—and this is the point—they felt themselves incompetent to do so. They would not have allowed a handoperated system to get so far out of their control.

No MIS should ever be installed unless the managers for whom it is intended are trained to evaluate and hence control it rather than be controlled by it.

A Suggested Procedure for Designing an MIS

The erroneous assumptions I have tried to reveal in the preceding discussion can, I believe, be avoided by an appropriate design procedure. One is briefly outlined here.

1. Analysis of the Decision System

Each (or at least each important) type of managerial decision required by the organization under study should be identified and the relationships between them should be determined and flow-charted. Note that this is *not* necessarily the same thing as determining what decisions *are* made. For example, in one company I found that make-or-buy decisions concerning parts were made only at the time when a part was introduced into stock and was never subsequently reviewed. For some items this decision had gone unreviewed for as many as twenty years. Obviously, such decisions should be made more often; in some cases, every time an order is placed in order to take account of current shop loading, underused shifts, delivery times from suppliers, and so on.

Decision-flow analyses are usually self-justifying. They often reveal important decisions that are being made by default (e.g., the make-buy decision referred to above), and they disclose interdependent decisions that are being made independently. Decision-flow charts frequently suggest changes in managerial responsibility, organizational structure, and measure of performance which can correct the types of deficiencies cited.

Decision analyses can be conducted with varying degrees of detail, that is, they may be anywhere from coarse to fine grained. How much detail one should become involved with depends on the amount of time and resources that are available for the analysis. Although practical considerations frequently restrict initial analyses to a particular organizational function, it is preferable to perform a coarse analysis of all of an organization's managerial functions rather than a fine analysis of one or a subset of functions. It is easier to introduce finer information into an integrated information system than it is to combine fine subsystems into one integrated system.

2. An Analysis of Information Requirements

Managerial decisions can be classified into three types:

(a) *Decisions for which adequate models are available or can be constructed and from which optimal (or near optimal) solutions can be derived. In such cases the decision process itself should be incorporated into the information system thereby converting it (at least partially) to a control system. A decision model identifies what information is required and hence what information is relevant.*

(b) *Decisions for which adequate models can be constructed but from which optimal solutions cannot be extracted. Here some kind of heuristic or search procedure should be provided even if it consists of no more than computerized trial and error. A simulation of the model will, as a minimum, permit comparison of proposed alternative solutions. Here too the model specifies what information is required.*

(c) *Decisions for which adequate models cannot be constructed. Research is required here to determine what information is relevant. If decision making cannot be delayed for the completion of such research or the decision's effect is not large enough to justify the cost of research, then judgment must be used to "guess" what information is relevant. It may be possible to make explicit the implicit model used by the decision maker and treat it as a model of type (b).*

In each of these three types of situation it is necessary to provide feedback by comparing actual decision outcomes with those predicted by the model or decision maker. Each decision that is made, along with its predicted outcome, should be an essential input to a management control system. I shall return to this point below.

3. Aggregation of Decisions

Decisions with the same or largely overlapping informational requirements should be grouped together as a single manager's task. This will reduce the information a manager requires to do his job and is likely to increase his understanding of it. This may require a reorganization of the system. Even if such a reorganization cannot be implemented completely what can be done is likely to improve performance significantly and reduce the information loaded on managers.

4. Design of Information Processing

Now the procedure for collecting, storing, retrieving, and treating information can be designed. Since there is a voluminous literature on this subject I shall leave it at this except for one point. Such a system must not only be able to answer questions addressed to it; it should also be able to answer questions that have not been asked by reporting any deviations from expectations. An extensive exception-reporting system is required.

5. Design of Control of the Control System

It must be assumed that the system that is being designed will be deficient in many and significant ways. Therefore it is necessary to identify the ways in which it may be deficient, to design procedures for detecting its deficiencies, and for correcting the system so as to remove or reduce them. Hence the system should be designed to be flexible and adaptive. This is little more than a platitude, but it has a not-so-obvious implication. No completely computerized system can be as flexible and adaptive as can a man-machine system. This is illustrated by a concluding example of a system that is being developed and is partially in operation. (See Figure 2.)

The company involved has its market divided into approximately two hundred marketing areas. A model for each has been constructed as is "in" the computer. On the basis of competivive intelligence supplied to the service marketing manager by marketing

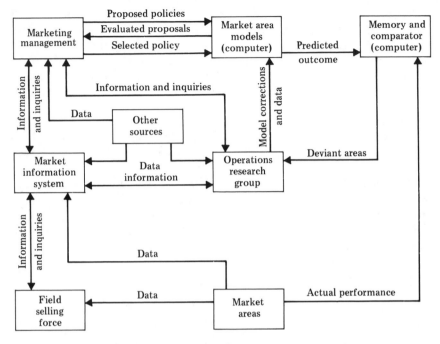

Figure 2.   **Simplified diagram of a market-area control system.**

researchers and information specialists he and his staff make policy decisions for each area each month. Their tentative decisions are fed into the computer which yields a forecast of expected performance. Changes are made until the expectations match what is desired. In this way they arrive at "final" decisions. At the end of the month the computer compares the actual performance of each area with what was predicted. If a deviation exceeds what could be expected by chance, the company's OR Group then seeks the reason for the deviation, performing as much research as is required to find it. If the cause is found to be permanent the computerized model is adjusted appropriately. The result is an adaptive man-machine system whose precision and generality is continuously increasing with use.

Finally it should be noted that in carrying out the design steps enumerated above, three groups should collaborate: information systems specialists, operations researchers, *and managers*. The participation of managers in the design of a system that is to serve them, assures their ability to evaluate its performance by comparing its output with what was predicted. Managers who are not willing to invest some of their time in this process are not likely to use a management control system well, and their system, in turn, is likely to abuse them.

Reference

1. Sengupta, S. S., and Ackoff, R. L., "Systems Theory from an Operations Research Point of View," *IEEE Transactions on Systems Science and Cybernetics*, vol. 1 (Nov. 1965), pp. 9–13.

20

How Intelligent Is Your "MIS"

Robert L. Johnson
and Irwin H. Derman

Reprinted by permission of *Business Horizons*.
Copyright, February 1970 by the Foundation for
the School of Business, at Indiana University.

Business organizations provide for the accomplishment of corporate objectives through the delegation of accountability and authority. The organizational hierarchy represents a network for the flow of communications without which such delegation and reporting activities would be impossible. Except for such institutions as the press and schools, few organizations have been formed with the objective of producing and utilizing information. Few businesses, in fact, consider themselves in the information business, yet none could long exist without information and effective distribution channels.

"Totality of Information" Concept

Since most organizational activity is centered around the acquisition, production, or transfer of information in various forms, employees are the targets of a conglomeration of data, information, and intelligence. Decisions are communicated by passing information to those with the delegated authority and responsibility for performance. Standards are established against which product quality, cost, and completion time are measured; evaluation procedures are developed for checking performance against the standards. The entire operation is continually monitored by a reporting system that communicates performance information to the manager, who uses a control system to feed back instructions to correct or prevent deviations from planned performance.

Within the operational framework, the words, "data," "information," and "intelligence" do not represent the same entity. The distinction lies more in usage than in format. Data represent facts catalogued according to a retrieval scheme, maintained either by computer or manually, and, as elements of knowledge at the statistical level, are passive. Information, on the other hand, represents data to which the need to satisfy a requirement has been added. In other words, information consists of data combined with direction. In contrast to data, information pertinent to the understanding of a situation or to forming the basis for action is active and has a limited useful life expectancy. Finally, in the business communications hierarchy there is intelligence resulting from the analysis of organized information that provides the decision maker with a preferred course of action after having evaluated available alternatives.

Businessmen are subjected to a barrage of data—organized and random—that impinge on their conscious as well as their subconscious minds. These data may be meaningless or pertinent at either level, and only a small amount relates generally to work interests or specifically to work projects. That which is relevant comes from a variety of sources, not exclusively through a formalized information transfer structure. From the entire universe of data, a finite amount is applicable to a specific decision. Because a decision maker never has all the data needed to guarantee the correctness of an action, decisions ultimately must be based on imperfect intelligence made up of a combination of data, experience, opinions, and intuition.

Information as a Resource

A resource is an entity that has present or potential utility. Until recently, information was neither recognized nor appreciated as a corporate resource valuable to management when used to effect the operation of an organization. Without information, day-to-day or long-range organizational functions cannot be carried out. The executive commands a higher salary than the janitor because he has learned to use information more profitably for the organization; the more scarce the possessors of knowledge on a given subject, the more valuable is the master of that information.

Information has many of the characteristics of material resources. It can be produced, stored, and distributed; it is perishable to the extent that it has no utility beyond the time it is needed; yet it is not consumable in the sense that it can be used up. As for its worth, the less a decision maker knows about a problem and its possible solutions, the higher the cost he must pay for potentially useful information. The greater the potential value of information, the larger the investment management must be willing to make for its acquisition.

Information Resource Management

Since information has value as a resource, it must be treated like other valuable resources. Because of the costs associated with procurement, transfer, storage, and conversion, information should receive consideration similar to that given such corporate resources as materials and facilities. To estimate the worth of a piece of information, its cost-value factors must be carefully examined, including the cost of acquisition and conservation, and the cost of not having it available when needed. In the latter case, the cost of raw data depends on the cost consequences of making a decision without that data.

The cost of the procurement of information on an *ad hoc* basis is high and sometimes intolerable. Nevertheless, most information needed for top management decision making is procured in this manner, since the formal management information system rarely is responsive to the special needs of the corporate executive. When gathering data, he must either search for, find, and exploit an external source or assign the task to a staff information specialist. Consequently, the search for, and isolation of, required data from the available universe and the conversion to information and intelligence results in the consumption of another valuable resource—time.

In short, an information system designed for the orderly and systematic procurement, transfer, storage, and conversion of data will reduce time, effort, and cost, and increase the utility of information. The cost of developing and implementing such a system must be weighed against the cost of searching for, finding, and handling data on an *ad hoc* basis or, worse, the consequences of making a decision without pertinent information.

Impact on Top Management

Executive Awareness

The executive often feels he is deluged with data, but rarely feels he is receiving enough information. To replace intuition and opinion, he sifts a mass of data to satisy his information needs; nevertheless, he must often intuitively evaluate the risks of a poor decision in the absence of perfect information about the probable consequences of his actions.

All modern corporations have some form of information system that is supposed to reduce the cost of decision making and lower the probability of making poor decisions because relevant information is lacking. These systems have been designed to provide information to support corporate studies. Typically, however, they lack the essential elements of an intelligence system required to support top management marketing and investment decision making and so imperil the very survival of the corporation. Even detailed information about company resources and activities is of limited value to top management for planning corporate response to major technological, political, or economic shifts. A class of facts relating to the environment in which the corporation operates is what is really required by top management.

Today's top executives are aware of this knowledge gap in decision making. Information systems have proved their worth in supporting operating level activities by assuring a steady flow of tools, materials, and information essential for production and distribution of goods. Existing data processing systems also do a reasonable job of helping top managers get a general indication of corporate efficiency from accounting summary reports, from which financial and market reports can be extrapolated. The top executive must know that these information systems, efficient and useful as they may be to the functional managers, are not much help in making those decisions on which corporate prosperity or even survival depend.

The Problem

Too much of the executive's time is spent searching for the technical, economic, and political intelligence needed to make policy and strategy decisions. Existing information systems, generally, cannot tell him the potential impact of industry, government, and corporate threats and opportunities; he lacks, therefore, the essential elements of intelligence required for evaluating the risks and rewards associated with various options. An executive cannot obtain, remember, or retrieve all available facts pertinent to a strategic situation.

Because of the differences in the needs for facts at various levels, the corporate information system has rarely been designed to satisfy upper management requirements. Appeals by top management for more pertinent information usually bring the same data—a summary of what has happened or what is happening—not what is likely to happen "if," or how the firm can exploit an opportunity or cope with a threat, or what cost or profit may result from a future action.

To perform their tasks, top management planners need intelligence on threats, opportunities, risks, and information about future resource requirements and sources (both economic and technological), investment-payoff criteria, and techniques for evaluation of alternatives. A complete system designed to collect data, process them into information, and convert them to intelligence suitable for goal setting and strategy determination would indeed be costly. Weighed against the value of such intelligence in terms of competitive advantage, however, the investment may well be warranted. If the cost of getting and processing the information top management now uses is considered, the investment may be even more justified.

Unfortunately, few executives are aware of how much it is costing them to get strategic intelligence. They do not consider the cost of consultants, corporate staff planners, and economic analysts; business periodical and service subscriptions; and the expenditure of their own time in searching for and processing information in the same way they might calculate the costs and benefits from the operational support of management information systems.

Information Economics

The value of information to a business is a function of timeliness and the hierarchial position of the user in the organizational structure. With regard to production work, the value of an instruction, job order, or job sheet is the profit obtained from the sale of a product. If the sale is forfeited because of mistiming or incomplete information, the cost to the firm is more than just the worker's wages; it is also the lost profit from the potential sale. It is obvious that the potential loss will exceed the cost of having provided the worker with necessary information. Therefore, management willingly commits the required funds to establish a system to provide job-related data to the operating level personnel.

People in resource management, on the other hand, have different requirements for data than do production workers. It is more difficult, for example, to justify economically such long lead time activities as an information system where the purpose is to facilitate resource management data acquisition, processing, and reporting. These systems generally begin with the limited objective of developing an operational management data base and a reporting system to account for the expenditure of time and materials. Where time is especially valuable, as in managing high cost, potentially automatic processes, the extension of the system to real time monitoring, might even be justified.

Sharing of repetitive resource and program management information can justify a high investment in a computer-based information processing system, relieving the manager of *ad hoc* data collection and processing. A computer system has an obvious advantage—its ability to "remember" facts useful to a number of management problem solvers. Inventory management, for example, may be systematized to monitor stock levels to optimize the time and effort of production control, purchasing, and stock control personnel. With a computer monitoring out-of-control conditions, the inventory manager is free to devote more time to research, creative planning, managing, and communication, the work he is best qualified to perform. Having the computer provide the manager with exception reports removes him from the normal crisis management loop to which he now devotes much of his day-to-day activity.

The computer, then, can make planners out of managers instead of forcing them to "plan on the fly." The computer, with its ability to remember rules and recall stored transaction data, introduces elements of predictability, reliability, and capability that go far towards establishing a true management environment. Since the computer is not under pressure to do "more important things," there is little danger that priorities could develop that would result in the postponement of decisions vital to production efficiency.

Limited Utility of Operating Activity Data

A look at the business oriented activities performed by computers shows that day-to-day applications predominate. Payroll, accounts receivable, accounts payable, inventory control, and tax processing—all activities that involve simple manipulations of data— comprise the major portion of business data processing. This is because of the ease in identifying potential cost savings that result from automating such operating activities. Since computers can handle simple, repetitive tasks, the overwhelming majority of past design activity has been directed toward installing operating level information systems.

Although the survival of the firm is rarely threatened by operating level decisions, the financial consequences of a poor decision can easily exceed the cost of reducing the probability of making such a decision. With the development of computer programs to systematize operating procedures, it was expected that the data base would provide information pertinent to long-range business activities. Planning was to be facilitated by the use of modeling techniques and simulation routines that operate on the data to identify preferable courses of action. The computer capability to recall, manipulate, and integrate large masses of data was supposed to ease the problem of handling data required for top management activity.

What has happened, though, is that top management has found operating data no more than vaguely useful for executive decision making. Therefore, those companies that went the computer/data base route have discovered information systems have little effect on middle and upper management activities.

If the information system is not providing sufficient data to allow management to carry out planning activities, what kinds of information are lacking? It is difficult, at best, to make a definitive list of information required to run a company. First, industry considerations are important in determining the kinds of information needed to carry out all kinds of activity. Next, such factors as the size of the company, its market share, objectives, interest in acquisitions, and growth pace strongly influence the establishment of a comprehensive information base. In general, certain classes of information can be identified as potentially useful to a manager during a study or planning activity.

Fact-opinion Dichotomy

Executives are paid for their knowledge, the relative use made of that knowledge, and their decision-making guts. Knowledge, in this case, consists of some combination of factual information, insight, and opinion. Even though some decisions must be made on the basis of insight and intuition in the face of data contradicting such judgments, the executive should have the integrity to examine pertinent facts when they are available. In other words, he must be aware of the dichotomy of fact and opinion. The information system should provide for this dichotomy by separating fact from opinion, and making the collected mass available to the manager in the form of information or intelligence.

An intelligence system for top management then can provide both data and opportunities to use those data in testing probable consequences by use of simulation prior to actual decision making. Such simulations can provide a feedback of more information to improve the odds of making a good decision.

Types and Sources of Information

Some kinds of information are not now included in corporate information system data bases. Although such information is available in some form, it is the ability to retrieve a fact within a specified time frame that is crucial. A key piece of information needed to make the optimum decision, but not available at the right time or not known to be in existence, may make the difference between success and failure. Certain information classes, if included in the corporate data base, will upgrade operational capabilities of computer systems into true corporate-wide information systems.

Middle Management Information Sources

Although it is the function of a company library to maintain a complete file of *general business publications* like the *Wall Street Journal, Forbes, Business Week,* and *Fortune,* imagine a situation in which the index of these publications is stored in the corporate data base. When a manager needs information relevant to a particular topic, he would use a computer terminal to communicate his request for citations to a retrieval program that would scan all indexes to produce a list of pertinent articles. A simple approach to the scanning problem would be the use of a KWIC (Key Word in Context) program to scan the indexes. Information retrieval would then be reduced to a document retrieval problem. The importance of this step lies more in focusing the power of the computer on the speed-of-retrieval problem than in the replacement of the manual search of a card file.

Trade association publications constitute a source of information relevant to particular industries. Besides maintaining an index of available material in the computer, it would be well to monitor selected association publications and data releases for industry wide information that could be included in the company data base as support material.

Because of the difficulty of obtaining proprietary information about competitors, a structured data format for *competitive information* would be hard to specify and maintain. Certainly there are sources of information on such matters as competitor sales, long-range plans, research activities, and plant location announcements that have a direct effect upon company plans. Although most information would be of a qualitative nature, some form of structure, including retrieval codes, could be imposed, and the data base could be designed to accommodate such qualitative information.

The *federal government* publishes a wealth of statistics on a wide range of subjects. Although most of this is unrelated to the interests of a particular company, general categories of material, besides specific industry-oriented publications, can be invaluable in supporting planning activities. For example, reports of pending legislation can be used to determine the effect of laws on the conduct of business on a nationwide basis. The same would be true, of course, for state and local communities passing legislation directly affecting manufacturing, distribution, or sale of company products. For example, federal legislation on truth-in-packaging is of immediate interest to product planning and manufacturing activities.

A general class of information published by the Bureau of Labor Statistics is also useful. Information such as salary surveys in selected areas would be of interest to personnel managers for salary comparisons or to planning managers for new facility location determinations.

Consumer purchasing behavior is, after all, the final determinant of company success. Even companies not selling consumer products are affected by the percentage of the consumer dollar remaining after purchases of necessities and conveniences, leisure services, and savings. It is in the long-range interest of a company to monitor closely shifts in consumer preferences, not only to protect future profitability in existing product lines, but also to guide potential development of related or diverse products and services. In addition to reports of trends that can be found in magazines and newspapers, the federal government is a potential source of long-range information; a government staff, headed by the Special Assistant for Consumer Affairs, could be a valuable source of consumer related facts.

Closely related to consumer expenditure statistics is the

information on the *gross national product* published by the government. Many companies look to this information to help establish trends for consumer and industrial purchases. Research has attempted to relate the trends of certain key indicators to company sales. By isolating leading and lagging indicators in the components of GNP, a firm would be able to predict sales based on the over-all activity of the economy. GNP information could supplement the data normally contained in the company data base to assist management in the conduct of predictive studies and economic simulations.

With the federal government sponsoring so much *research*, it is reasonable to assume that discoveries will be made outside a company's R&D activity that will affect the future course of the firm. In the medical field, for example, research is conducted not only at the National Institute of Health but also in universities and private laboratories. The results of these projects will shape the activities of companies directly and indirectly allied to the health field. Although such results may be "far out," some kind of project directory with supporting descriptive information should be available to planning managers who must predict future health developments. The same is true in other fields of commercial interest in which there is government supported R&D.

Predictions are being made constantly, with varying degrees of supporting material, that can be used to plot the course of future company activities. Even qualitative information gleaned from these reports and included in a supportive section of the data base would be of assistance to company planners. What effect will a coming election have on the business and consumer climate for the following period? What are the weather predictions by the U.S. Weather Bureau for the coming year? What is the extent and duration being forecast for a flu epidemic that may hit the United States? (How many employees will probably miss work and how long will they be out?) These are examples of questions that have a direct bearing on every business.

Top Management Information Sources

What has been examined is a class of information, not normally formalized for inclusion in a company data base, that should be useful to management—especially middle managers—in planning beyond day-to-day company activities. Were such information to be included in a company information base with ready access provided to middle managers, there would be a marked improvement in the coverage and completeness of studies performed at the middle management level.

Yet this is not the whole story. An existing data base stands in relation to operating personnel as the preceding information stands to middle management in fulfilling its missions. That does not complete the evaluation of information for the firm as a whole. There is a class of activities, performed primarily by top management, that must also be considered. Here, the act of management must be viewed more nearly as an art. Consequently, it is significantly more difficult to isolate the data needed by top managers to carry out their roles successfully. Whereas middle managers have a more clearly defined set of information requirements, top management needs are seen as a series of dimensions to the art of management. Several kinds of activities are representative of top management interests.

Threats to the firm encompass such areas as the political climate of the firm in relation to governmental agencies and consumers. There are also the internal problems such as organizational structure, labor constraints, and individual executive power plays, as well as external threats—competitive action, substitute product development, and natural disasters, for instance. Where possible, the data base should contain information pertinent to all forms of threat to organizational integrity.

Risks include such areas as resource allocation, setting priorities for undertaking new projects, research and development decisions, new product development and integration, and investment decision making.

Top management must be aware of *future resource cost*. This calls for knowledge of developments in the money market; keeping a satisfactory debt-to-equity ratio, given the varying conditions of the investment community and awareness of general stock market trends as well as the effects of particular actions on the company stock in order to protect stockholders' interests.

Future resource technology is a top management interest. Product development of competitive firms must be monitored, and the effects of developing technology must be projected to ensure that current products and production processes are not made obsolete by competitive action. This includes a continuing need to evaluate the cycle time from development to implementation of a process, product, or service.

Top management must take the lead in *concept developments*—

determining the nature of the firm and its policy. Where is the expertise of the firm and how can it be best exploited?

What are the *goals* of the business? Is the effort of the firm to be directed toward maintaining the highest return on investment, the highest return on sales, the highest earnings per share? What are the short-term goals and the long-term goals, assuming they differ?

Strategy determination is required. Given the goals of the firm, what steps must be taken to implement them? In the short run? In the long run? In the growth area alone, a range of strategies might be followed. Growth could come from existing product lines; diversification into complementary lines or unrelated services; product and facilities acquisition in either complementary or competing industries; acquisition of an entire subsidiary; the sale of the firm to another company; or liquidation, if the assets are deemed more valuable than the going concern.

Company Posture

A company is more than a production and distribution entity. In the complex society of today, a company must have a posture on public issues. It must be able to react to consumer pressures, be aware of pending legislation as it may affect the firm, be prepared to handle the problems of minority employment, and know the dimensions of the government interface.

The preceding list is neither exhaustive nor set out in any order of priority. Items were selected to point out the areas of concern for top management decision making. In each of these areas, some combination of experience and available information must be used to arrive at the optimum answer for the firm. Although operating daily activities can be carried out by operating personnel using a maximum of data and a minimum of "creative art," the opposite is true of the kinds of decisions made by top management. Even though it is more difficult to isolate those items of information that top management must have, the requirement that they be available when needed is critical. *A lack of information at the operating level may cost the firm some money or time. A lack of information at the top management level may cost the firm its entire existence.*

Information technology, associating the power of the computer and advanced techniques for management planning and control, has significantly improved the practice of management in the past fifteen years. The phrase "management information system" is widely understood in business and government organizations. Many corporations are installing computer-based systems to support operating managers with the information needed for effective planning and control of resources and programs; some provide varying levels of opportunity for the manager to interact with the computer.

Current operating systems provide for status and performance accounting, with a variety of detail from a high level of summarization and consolidation to a mass of operational level data. Because such data have been recognized as a corporate resource, management generally is aware of its value and the wisdom of investing in systems for its economical production and distribution.

Top management, and middle management to a lesser degree, has not yet reaped similar benefits from the information revolution. The bulk of knowledge relevant to major corporate decisions is still a personal resource; decisions with life-or-death impact on the corporation are often made more on the basis of intuition and guts than on valid information. The cost of collecting and processing the information currently used is high, especially in the use of executive time. The "typical" management information system with its operation-oriented data base is of low utility in major decision-making situations, since the character of data needed for internal operations differs significantly from that used in policy making and strategic planning.

Top management is aware of its need for strategic information and is frustrated by the failure of existing systems to satisfy that need. It is apt to be unaware of the low investment required, relative to the cost of maintaining present intelligence gathering methods, to develop a strategic intelligence capability as a logical extension of an existing or planned system. Corporate management must first recognize the utility of a strategic intelligence system, then consider the options for development of such a system appropriate to the corporate and industry environments. It must consider the investment and payoff implications of the viable options; then, with that imperfect information plus its intuition and guts, the investment decision can be made. Implementation of a strategic intelligence system should prove of significantly greater value to top management than current management information systems to middle management.

PART IV

The Management Information System

> An MIS is an organized method of providing past, present, and projection information relating to internal operations and external intelligence. (1)

MIS supports the functions of an organization by providing uniform information in the proper time frame to assist the decision-making process. An MIS should not be viewed as a high-speed computer that, when installed, will meet total organization needs, but neither should it be considered as something to purchase ready made, to plug in and to use if it works or, if it doesn't, to install a larger one. A system borrowed from another company cannot be used without being changed significantly. An MIS must be designed to meet specific information needs. Ignoring the hierarchical nature of planning, differences in information needs, the necessity of both operational and companywide plans can lead to suboptimization or failure. In spite of the large number of systems that have been designed and are in use today, there is no clear-cut optimum approach to MIS design. Rather, it seems, we are just beginning to explore the really basic, possible variations of designing and using MIS.

The key variable in the scope of an MIS is the diversity and range of the information needs of the users. Not every firm needs a complex MIS or a complex computer-based MIS. However, every organization definitely needs some type of MIS at some level of sophistication. Perspective for levels of sophistication and independent needs is given by Gilmore:

> While many sophisticated concepts of formulating corporate strategy are being studied with interest by large corporations, they hold little promise for medium-sized and smaller companies—at least, in the foreseeable future.

What is needed is a conference-table approach to strategy, based on executive judgment and intuition, not computers and operations research. Actually, systems analysis may offer more promise . . . and for the foreseeable future, managements in medium-sized and small companies will have to use the generalizing, inductive, empirical method which has evolved out of the size-up approach. (2)

In defining the scope, Sollenberger noted that

unwillingness or inability to accurately state the scope of data handling problems leads to confusion in information management. Improvements need to be made in specifying the job to be done and in communicating all facts of the project to those involved. (3)

The first important step in developing and managing any system is to define the scope so that factors involved can be identified and related. This approach leads to a common understanding of the job to be done; aids in selecting economically the proper facilities and resources; defines the necessary boundaries of the project; and makes it possible to coordinate efforts of designers and managers, to refine the necessary managerial controls, and to integrate the system into organizational subsystems.

In designing and implementing MIS it is difficult to bring its components (management and information) into proper perspective. Design problems are inherent in the assumption that if information needs could be determined a system could be designed to meet those needs. The other variable that must be integrated to make the system work is management. The basic problem has been to secure the necessary management support and involvement so that a system is not designed independent of management's needs and capacity to meet them. Information derives its value from the effect it has on the behavior of the organization. (4) Thus, new information has value if it is used to improve the nature and direction of the organization or its goals; that could happen if decisions are sensitive to the new information or result from its directional impact or if tangible and intangible benefits result from changes in decisions.

The logical structure of an MIS consists of three basic parts: the information input, the processing mechanism, and the information output. The input device is a means of communicating to the system the data (in many forms and from many sources) to be used or processed. The processing mechanism, designed to transform the input into the desired output, consists of three subparts: arithmetic-logic, storage, and control. Output flows, subject to the constraints established in the processing section, to areas of the organization needing the information. An additional part, feedback, is required to make the system dynamic with respect to change and operational efficiency. A system flow of the data (from origin to use) through the business organization obviously is fundamental to design as well as for uniformity and understanding. It is also essential that the system be economically feasible. The rationalization seems to be that the MIS should stand this test: The value of the system is the difference between the benefits derived and the associated costs. In designing an MIS, it is good business philosophy to use where possible system parts already in existence and to shape them with appropriate add-on dimensions. Thus, MIS design can be viewed as a continuous process of phase blending toward the optimum.

Cohen lists five basic criteria for designing successful systems:

1. Relevance. *The first, and paramount, point is that the system, to serve the stated business need, must be relevant. It is necessary to articulate clearly the objective, to specify who will use it and how they will relate to it, and to describe how the system will satisfy the stated objective.*
2. Timeliness. *It is critical to define the response-time criteria in advance of implementation. If the lapse between a useful time frame and the actual time frame is excessive, it may be better not to proceed with the system.*
3. Cost effectiveness. *In such determination, tangible and intangible values should be blended to cost effectiveness before developing the system.*
4. Accuracy. *Basic controls, checks or balances, must be merged with data sources and components plus assumptions to insure users that information is correct and usable, not just efficient.*
5. Flexibility. *A system should be flexible enough to handle (1) normal growth for a period into the future and (2) inevitable changes in the planning process or the operations of the company.* (5)

On perspective and orientation of MIS design Smith commented: "Let us cease finding new ways to do old things and instead find ways, with or without the computer, to do old and new things in a profitable way" (6). Smith also exemplifies the need for planning in this way: "No one would plan a motor trip without a map; yet most business systems are never planned, they just happen" (7).

The importance of management judgment and responsibility in designing an MIS is given perspective by Romnes, Chairman of the Board, American Telephone and Telegraph Company:

> Which results we get will depend, not so much on our technical competence in linking computers and communications, but on the range and depth of the management judgement we bring to the job. This means to me that the responsibility for managing the information revolution cannot be delegated. Designing a business information system isn't the exclusive province of a specialized department. In the final analysis it is a general management responsibility. And it needs to be a concerted understanding, reflecting a balanced consideration of the needs of the entire organization. (8)

Pertinent information should make an impact on the behavior of the firm; thus it is crucial to "zero in" information needs. The behavioral relationship between information and management is pointed out by Meltzer:

> But good technical and management information is no cure-all for bad management. Bad information always leads to bad management, but good information does not of itself insure good management. Information is only one of the tools of management. The ability to put the information to work is what determines the successful manager. (9)

Articles for this section were selected to help the reader visualize the multiple dimensions of information needs and what an MIS can do to sort out and provide needed information. We also hope they will help the reader crystalize in his mind the importance of the individual aspects of an MIS design. An MIS is unique with respect to both the organization and its functions, size, and structure and to the manager's needs. In this section and throughout the book the reader should develop a repertory of expertise on management dimensions in MIS and realize that those dimensions are a function of both systems design specialization and behavioral-science disciplines. In MIS planning and design, it is essential to understand that it is *people* who will use the system, however sophisticated it may be or become.

References

1. Walter J. Kennevan, "Management Information Systems," *Data Management*, p. 64, September 1970.

2. Frank F. Gilmore, "Formulating Strategy in Smaller Companies," *Harvard Business Review*, p. 71, May–June 1971.

3. Harold M. Sollenberger, "Defining Project Scope," *Journal of Systems Management*, p. 39, September 1970.

4. James C. Emery, *Organizational Planning and Control Systems* (New York: The Macmillan Company, 1969), p. 67.

5. Burton J. Cohen, *Cost-Effective Information Systems* (New York: American Management Association, 1971), pp. 13–16.

6. Paul T. Smith, *Computers, Systems, and Profits* (New York: American Management Association, 1969), p. 176.

7. Ibid., p. 105.

8. H. I. Romnes, "Managing the Information Revolution," *Signal*, p. 23, October 1966.

9. Morton F. Meltzer, *The Information Center: Management's Hidden Asset* (New York: American Management Association, 1967), pp. 136–137.

Section **1**

Purpose

21

Advance Planning for the Systems Function

Frank P. Congdon, Jr.
Reprinted by permission of *Journal of Systems Management*, August 1970.

Hopes and promises to process data faster and provide greater service are continually thwarted by complications and overly optimistic planning. These methods can only lead to embarrassment and questions directed towards the competence of the activity. Add to this the runaway costs associated with slipped schedules and management will believe that: *"MIS is the orderly process of losing money."* If such an impression exists in a company it is probably due to weak communications. Plans and estimates were not realistic in the beginning. Management was not told the facts when asked to make its commitment.

To improve one's approach to advance planning of systems efforts the systems analyst should consider the lessons already learned. Now is an ideal time to practice some self examination and improve one's skills in this vital area of planning. Now is the time to re-examine our systems design to focus more on the information content and the impact of the system upon management rather than exploiting techniques. It is also becoming more important that the system be designed for the *user* and scheduled with appropriate priority to result in realistic delivery to generate greatest return on investment to a business.

Management and Systems

The inseparable interdependency of management and systems has been an accepted fact in today's dynamic business environment. No longer can managers carry everything in their head—no longer can customers be serviced competitively without the speed and accuracy inherent to good information systems and their high speed data processors.

A user must become deeply involved in the systems specifications to assure that the output is to serve his real needs. As each user's requirements are integrated into the framework of an overall MIS, careful analysis is essential to guarantee that the final structure of the total MIS will be right for the company. Force fitting packaged systems for expediency can be dangerous and create unending problems.

Plans, once established, must form the input to an effective Project Control System chosen to provide a means for both MIS management and user upper management to keep abreast of both progress and problems. The depth of detail and the overhead cost of maintaining a Project Control System must be carefully examined. It does not need to be too elaborate but must collect and report significant data by major milestones. Planning and control methods should be reviewed with management to establish the proper rapport and through this level of communication and commitment to minimize the concern management has when investing heavily over a long period of time in a program whose results are not immediately visible.

Goals for Planning

Increasing costs and failures to achieve promised results highlight the need for goals. The goals must be developed from many sources and be compatible to one another. Examining the various sources one will find at the following levels that:

> *At the corporate level one must learn what direction the corporation expects to move in during the planning period and also what it expects the MIS activity to contribute to its objectives.*

> *Top management will undoubtedly want better information, want to provide its middle management with effec-*

tive tools to perform, and also exploit the advantages inherent to modern MIS concepts.

Middle management will ask for more specific help to meet their goals such as: more timely information, exception reports, greater visibility, and means to cope with load problems.

MIS management also has its own set of goals such as: meeting their commitment to higher levels of management, promoting MIS concepts throughout the organization, contributing to the profitability of the business, and the ability to keep pace with the dynamics of their field.

Systems analysts individually and as a group also have a vested interest in the development and achievement of the goals. They are highly motivated as contributors because they want to: support overall MIS achievement, promote MIS concepts, learn new techniques and skills, achieve growth within their career, and qualify for promotion to management.

The origin of goals must lead to various sources. The most crucial is the Long-Range Business Plan for the company. From it we can learn such things as: expected rate of growth, product changes, employment level changes, new processes planned, and space and plant projections.

The need to automate versus hiring may be very evident as well as the need to contribute to the reduction of product costs. Increased sales, more diversified plants and warehouses, etc., will certainly demand enhanced customer service. Looking at the plan from a "people" point of view, shows the intertwining of the need to provide for human satisfaction and growth.

Management Today

The exposure of top management to MIS concepts has pretty well convinced management that it should implement such a system. The advantages are self evident, but the associated costs can cause considerable apprehension because of their magnitude and the fact that the area is somewhat strange. Current experiences by companies who have had difficulties can cause management to be concerned about the end results and generate an impatience waiting a long time for results from a major investment. Not to be discounted is the fear that many levels of management experience when MIS and related computer systems imply that human decision-making prerogatives will be usurped.

MIS Approach

To capitalize on an eagerness to support MIS and to eliminate management's concerns, it is important to establish a strong and effective communication with top management. From the beginning, one must establish guidelines defining the scope of the MIS effort; determine objectives and priorities; develop factual and realistic plans and criteria to govern significant rescheduling. Implicit is the assurance of adequate progress reporting to maintain proper control of the effort.

One approach to establishing a plan is to relate expenditures to available funds. In other words, determine the available resources and break down how they can be used for maintenance, day-to-day requirements and new projects. This analysis will display the amount of resources available for new work. List in proper priority those suggested tasks and show how this load will fit into your budget. Let us call this Increment no. 1 [Table 1]. Develop other groups of

Table 1. Priority 1 (Man/Month)

Projects	Supervision	Programmers	Analysts	Computer Operators	Keypunch
Present staffing	22.0	58.0	46.0	154.0	238.0
Increment no. 1					
Project A	2.7	19.5	16.0		
B	1.4	4.0	4.0		
C	2.5	3.9	4.0		
D	3.0	6.5	8.0		
E	1.6	2.6	4.0		10.0
Maintenance	8.2	16.5	8.0		
Training	1.6	5.0	2.0		
Total requirements	22.0	58.0	46.0	-0-	248.0
Present resources	22.0	58.0	46.0	154.0	238.0
Resources needed	0.0	0.0	-0-	-0-	10.0

Note: Must add 10 keypunch operators.

appropriate systems into a series of increments with their extended man/months of effort and dollars. The cost impact of each can then be shown cumulatively and agreement reached with management as to the scope of work to be implemented. All of the projects must be backed up by cost justification studies and assurance given to maintaining schedules.

This sample clearly indicates how resources will be used and immediately highlights the fact that one of the projects will impact significantly on another activity—namely, keypunching, and require additional personnel. Don't be surprised if the project should be rescheduled or the approach reviewed before being committed to 10 additional salaries.

The number of projects that can be afforded is graphically outlined on this cumulative analysis and lets management submit a budget figure that is compatible with the total expense budget for the year. Agreement at this level automatically generates the first year's input to a five-year plan. Projects deferred are now defined for inclusion in a succeeding time frame together with requests for future projects solicited from various users.

How many projects can we afford?		
Priority	Cost ($000)	Cum. Costs ($000)
I	950.0	950.0
II	65.0	1015.0
III	36.0	1051.0
IV	70.0	1121.0
V	14.0	1135.0
VI	8.0	1143.0
VII	16.5	1159.5
VIII	32.5	1192.0

MIS Long-range Planning

Considerable effort should be spent laying the ground work leading up to this most important phase of advance planning. It is essential because this document will become the major factor in measuring performance. If separate locations are concerned the planning techniques should be followed by each and a consolidation developed.

Long-range Plan Structure

As a guide in formatting a plan, establish a structure similar to that shown below:

Section	Title
I	MIS program description: A. Current plan highlights B. Narrative C. Business system diagram
II	Priority projects: A. Project name B. Project scope C. Project description D. Project plan
III	Other projects: A. Project name B. Project scope C. Project description
IV	Manpower—position analysis
V	Communications
VI	Cost analysis
VII	Utilization summary

In Section I, the significant highlights of the MIS long-range program within your operating unit should be developed. This should emphasize the major systems elements in your plan and illustrate the relationship between them and the business operations of your unit.

A. Current Plan Highlights—Stress the major areas of concentration and pinpoint significant goals in the MIS program for the next 18 to 24 months. This section, together with Section II, priority projects, are the most important sections of the entire report. The evaluation of the total program is based principally on the content of these two areas.

B. Narrative—The narrative should provide a general understanding of the MIS program, and place the current highlights and all supplementary sections in perspective. Describe the major systems of the MIS program in terms of the operating areas served. Indicate briefly the objectives to be attained from the cumulative impact of these systems on the business operations of your unit, and the benefits which will accrue to management. The techniques that will be required for implementation of the program are not germane. It is expected that technical back-up will be available if required during the review of this plan. Historical information should only be included when it is required to bridge the gap between the previous long-range plan and this one.

C. Business System Diagram—Develop a business system diagram to illustrate the interrelationships of the systems described in Section B. The purpose of the diagram, and the corresponding level of detail is to show the *major* system or application areas. If desired, a more detailed chart or list of other projects may be attached as an appendix. It is not as important as the objective of capturing the basic nature and direction of the MIS program. However, it should highlight the areas of concentration.

Priority Projects

This section will provide specific details on the priority projects in your operating unit. A priority project is one which is of major significance because of its proved or expected contribution to the business operation of your division. Their significance is normally reflected in the manpower allocated to them. The number of projects described is optional but should include those which have the greatest potential for contributing to operating benefits. Select the critical or high priority projects to which the major portion of systems effort should be devoted in the next one to two years. For each of these priority projects, complete Section II in full, Sections A through D.

A. Project Name

B. Project Scope—Briefly describe the scope of the project in terms of the business areas served and its functions. Be as specific as possible.

C. Project Description—Describe the basic flow or function of the system, indicating users, interface between functional areas, and timing of significant events in the work-flow. Where a project involves several phases, describe each phase clearly.

C1. Major Input Sources—Indicate in gross terms the type of input required and the source or activity providing it.

C2. Major Outputs—Indicate the type of information or classes of reports provided by the system.

C3. Master Files Used—Describe briefly major files used. Keep names consistent across all projects.

C4. Special Technology Applied—Where applicable, indicate specific management science or information systems methodology used or planned; e.g., linear programming, simulation, game theory, on-line input-output, use of data display, etc.

D. Project Plan—This section serves to show in summary form the implementation schedule, manpower, costs and operational evaluation of each project. Cost figures should be those required to bring the project to operational status. No systems operation costs are to be included.

D1. Schedule—Show the planned dates in this section for each project. If the system is to be implemented in several phases, the definition of each phase should be shown in the Project Description.
(a) Initial project approval date.
(b) Performance Specifications—The date on which operating management in the involved departments or functions approves the performance objectives of the planned system.
(c) Design and Analysis Completion—The date at which the major program specifications will have been completed and actual programming can begin.
(d) Systems Test—The Date when parallel and/or pilot systems tests will begin.
(e) First Operational Use—Where there is a significant period between the first operational use of a phase indicate also a completion date for that phase.

D2. Project Manning and Costs—Show the manpower and costs that will be necessary to support the schedule planned for each project, by year, including all manpower and costs from project inception to date through 12-31-71. Only project development costs are to be shown. Do not include costs of operation for the project. (See [Figure 1].)
(a) Systems Personnel—Show the total number of man-months and annual expense (in thousands) of all MIS systems personnel that will be required for each project by year as shown.

D. Project plan

1. Schedule

Benchmark dates			Phase 1	Phase 2	Phase 3
(a) Initial project approval date					
(b) Performance specifications approval					
(c) Design and analysis completion					
(d) Begin systems test					
(e) First operational use (Start date Completed date)			/	/	/

2. Manning and costs to become operational

Total costs to date →	Thru 12-31-70		1971		1972		1973		1974		1975	
Through 12-31-70 in first column	Man mon.	$	Man mon.	$	Man mon.	$	Man mon.	$	Man mon.	$	Man mon.	$
(a) Systems personnel												
(b) User personnel		x		x		x		x		x		x
(c) Outside personnel												
(d) Total personnel												
(e) Equipment cost												
(f) Other costs												
(g) Total cost												

3. Operational evaluation

Criteria	Measurement of performance

Project name	Original date	Revision date

Figure 1

(b) User Personnel—Estimate the total number of man-months and annual expense (in thousands) of User Personnel that will be required for each project by year as shown. This should include "user" department personnel assigned to support each project.

(c) Outside Personnel—Show the total number of man-months and annual expense (in thousands) of Outside Personnel who will be required for each project by year as shown. This category would include outside consultants, contract programming, systems design, etc.

(d) Total Personnel Costs = a + b + c.

(e) Equipment Costs—Show the total equipment cost to be allocated to each project by year prior to operational use of the system. Such costs would include program

compilation and testing, pilot installation and check-out of data communications equipment, etc.
(f) Other Costs—Show the total other costs attributable to the accomplishment of each project such as travel expenses, significant supply purchases expressly required for this project, remote site preparation, etc.
(g) Total Cost = d + e + f.

D3. Operational Evaluation—Show the criteria by which the value of the proposed projects can be judged; in time, costs, equipment benefits, results, or whatever seems most appropriate to evaluate the new system. Measurements of performance are the quantitative results by which the degree of attainment of the criteria can be determined. Where relevant, show the comparative operational improvement over the present system as one of the criteria for system evaluation.

Section III—Other Projects is intended to include other significant projects shown on the MIS business system diagram, which cannot be classified as priority projects because they have not been finally approved, staffed or definitely scheduled.

Section IV—Manpower and Position Analysis—Use this section to show the number of present and planned personnel by job category as of January 1 for each of the years listed. This schedule should show actual work assignments. Only those actively and currently performing the work listed should be shown in each category regardless of their educational background or work experience. Use Category E to indicate any full-time personnel performing systems or data processing work not included in the information systems department. Use the space provided at the bottom of this form to identify the location, functional area and activity to which these personnel are assigned. Use the following definitions for primary classification of personnel. (See [Figure 2].)

A. MIS Managers—Management and administrative personnel directly concerned with Management Information Systems and Services. Include all personnel above leaders.

B. Management Systems Personnel—Personnel (up to and including leaders) primarily engaged in systems, operations research, data processing, systems and/or programming work. Do not include persons who are not in an information systems department. See E., below.

Number of personnel during plan periods

	1970	1971	1972	1973	1974	1975
A. MIS managers						
B. Management systems personnel						
Operations research						
Systems specialist						
Programmer analyst						
EAM systems						
Manual systems						
Total						
C. Operations						
EAM						
EDP						
Data preparation						
Data communications						
Total						
D. Administrative/clerical						
E. Other systems personnel*						
Total personnel						
Other systems personnel*						

Location	Functional area	No. in 1971

*Other systems personnel — people who do systems work but are not in the MIS department.

Figure 2.   Position analysis.

Operations Research—Personnel currently engaged in the application of business models, quantitative analysis, and EDP to business requirements.

Systems Specialist—Senior systems personnel who have considerable experience in the design, development and implementation of business sytems, including but not limited to the use of EDP. These people should be capable of assuming a project leader level of responsibility.

Programmer/Analyst—Personnel engaged in computer programming and/or systems investigation and development.

EAM Systems—Personnel who work on the development of EAM systems including panel wiring, operating instructions and procedures.

Manual Systems—Personnel primarily involved in the research, development and implementation of manual systems and procedures.

C. Operations—Personnel, including leaders, involved in data processing operations, both EAM and EDP, including data preparation and data communications. Do not include employees not in the data processing department. See E., below.

D. Administrative/Clerical—Miscellaneous data processing clerical personnel, such as control clerks, librarians, etc.

E. Other Systems Personnel—Complete if there is a significant number of people performing systems work who are not included in the information systems department and identify in the block below.

In section V, Communications, indicate plans in time sharing, data collection and data communications. Terms appearing on the form which are self-explanatory are not covered below.

A. Number of Terminals—Indicate the number of time sharing terminals, either teletype or video data terminal.

B. Number of Users—Indicate the total number of users of the system.

C. Applications—Specify the percentage of your time sharing operations spent on engineering, business or other applications.

D. Under costs project the total computer costs, i.e., bulk storage, core memory, and computer time, indicate the combined costs of all terminals and data sets, and project the total line charges to be incurred.

When obtaining in-plant data collection information, indicate the number of stations, specifying the manufacturer and model number. Data communications information should include all on-line data transmission exclusive of manufacturing data collection. Then add total costs from all categories as shown.

Section VI—Cost Analysis

Location: A separate report must be prepared for the *total operating* unit and *for each site*. Where there is a small quantity of equipment at a remote site, it may be combined, for reporting purposes, with a larger site.

Submit all dollar figures in thousands. If equipment is purchased enter "PUR" on this line and show costs as annual depreciation amount before tax adjustments, plus maintenance. Otherwise, show rental cost. Include all extra shift charges and taxes. Show cost of all computers (including process control) installed or planned. This cost figure would include all equipment within the computer room. List rental cost of punched card equipment installed or planned.

Show rental cost of data preparation equipment installed or planned. This includes all data origination equipment, such as keypunches, key verifiers, tape punches, add punches, etc. Show rental cost of remote data communications or data collection equipment, such as Digitronics, Transceivers, 1001s, RCA, DGS, Video terminals, Teletypes, etc. Include the rental cost of digital sub-sets, plus all line charges. Total Equipment Cost—Total of all Classes.

The categories of personnel have previously been defined. The only additional item is employee service expense for all personnel included in this report, if reported separately from salary expense. Use total payroll dollars (in thousands) including overtime. One now has total personnel costs.

Other Data Processing Expense

A. For fixed charges and assessments include items for site preparation, air conditioning, rearrangement, etc. B. Supplies and miscellaneous should include general costs attributable to data processing installations, including forms and supplies. C. Costs paid other company sites should include charges for both equipment use and programming service paid to all other company data processing locations. D. Data processing service charges should include all outside service costs, such as consulting fees and contract programming, incurred both by data processing installations and by other division activities. Attach separate schedules breaking out items C and D above, indicating the type of service performed, the location, the rate and the cost.

Sales

A. DP service sold to other companies should include all data processing transfer charges to other company locations for equipment use and programming services. B. DP service sold to outside customers is the sales of data processing time or service sold outside the company. C. To get net total data processing expense, subtract total sales for total data processing expense. Attach separate schedules breaking out items A and B above, showing customer, type of service, the rate and total charges.

Complete Section VII both for presently installed EDP systems and for any EDP systems projected to be installed through 1975 (including process control). A separate page is to be used for each location. (See [Figure 3].)

For each computer system, show the projected or actual installation date, and date to be released, where appropriate. In the case of replacement systems, identify the systems being replaced by Manufacturer and Model Number.

For each system, show the time in hours required for the stated purpose during January 1972. Only Scheduled Time and Total Production Time are to be completed for January 1973 and January 1974. Do not complete this section for equipment to be installed after January 1974.

Total Production Time—The sum of A. Operating Applications— How much of Total Production Time was used for the performance of production programs; B. Program Compilation, Test and Maintenance—How much of Total Production Time was required for these

	System no.	System no.	System no.	System no.
Manufacturer				
Model number				
Date installed				
Date to be installed				
Date to be released				
Replaces system no.				

Utilization summary—complete for present and future systems installed through June 30, 1971

Scheduled time (avg. scheduled hrs. per mo.)				
Total production time, %				
MIS applications, %				
Program test, etc., %				
Multi prog. made with, %				
Business operations, %				
Process control, %				
Remote terminals connected				

Figure 3.   Project requirements through 1975.

purposes; C. Customer Rerun—What time was required for rerun due to program or operator error.

For set-up and idle time show the time in hours that the equipment was idle, or required for operational set-up. For manufacturer's rerun and downtime show the time in hours used for these purposes. Show the time in hours for each system required for non-scheduled maintenance during scheduled hours of operation, and for each system show the percent of total production time in which the system was run in multi-programming mode.

22

Marketing Information Systems

Conrad Berenson

Reprinted from *Journal of Marketing*, vol. 33 (October 1969), pp. 16–23, published by the American Marketing Association.

During the past several years the words "marketing information systems" have appeared with increasing frequency in the marketing literature. Unlike some other words which are in vogue and then disappear from sight, this phrase has prevailed and, indeed, provided a great deal of substance and meaning for the entire marketing community.

This paper focuses on marketing information systems, examines them vis-à-vis the traditional market research function, studies the background of the needs which initiated the development of such systems, and reviews the benefits, pitfalls, myths, and structure of marketing information systems. Obviously, with so many critical facets to cover in such a brief period of time, one can do little more than indicate the major considerations that fall within the purview of any of these categories. A comprehensive analysis of marketing information systems requires far more attention than just a brief paper.

Let us turn first to a definition of "marketing information systems." This is defined as an interacting structure of people, equipment, methods, and controls, which is designed to create an information flow that is capable of providing an acceptable base for management decisions in marketing.

The question that logically arises when definitions of marketing information systems are presented is "How does it differ from the traditional function of marketing research?" Market research ordinarily follows an eclectic path—one time examining the prices of one product line, and at another time reviewing competitors' packaging innovations, and the like. Usually, the marketing research department provides only a fraction of the data needed to make marketing decisions which have great and far-reaching impact upon the company. This is not to be construed as a criticism of marketing research; all too often marketing research in both consumer and industrial areas fails to receive either adequate budgets, or adequate organizational support.[1]

Furthermore, its mission is different from that of a marketing information system. The latter differs from marketing research in that it provides, for example, *continuous* study of the marketing factors which are important to an enterprise—not just intermittent examination. It utilizes far more data sources—both internal and external—than does marketing research; and it accepts the responsibility for receiving, analyzing and distilling a far greater volume of information inputs than market research is structured to do.[2]

The market research department should be considered to be one part of the marketing information system. The latter would also include or work very closely with such organizational units as: economic research, operations research, long-range planning, the controller, the computer center, marketing planning, and sales management.

Marketing research's traditional role as the primary supplier of information to management for marketing decisions is, consequently, somewhat different in firms with a marketing information system. In the latter, market research concentrates more upon spot projects, fire-fighting, new areas in which the inputs to the system have not yet been established, on data other than that likely to be found in the controller's office or the billing department, and on utilizing a variety of techniques in order to study a particular area which is of momentary interest to the firm. In firms without a marketing information system, market research concentrates more upon such routine information as sales analysis by product line and customer, determination of end-use patterns, and the projection of price and demand trends. It does this on a somewhat eclectic basis.

[1] Philip Kotler, "A Design for the Firm's Marketing Nerve Center," *Business Horizons*, vol. 9 (Fall, 1966), pp. 63–74.
[2] Lee Adler, "Systems Approach to Marketing," *Harvard Business Review*, Vol. 45 (May–June, 1967), pp. 105–118.

The Need for Marketing Information Systems

It is not at all surprising that at this time there is a good deal of discussion and development of marketing information systems. Long-term trends, both in marketing and in business in general, are intersecting in the present time to crystallize the systems activity which is presently taking place. Some of these trends are outlined below:

> *The increased complexity of business calls for more data and for better performance. Markets are no longer local but are national in scope. The organization that previously may have had firm control of its business in a limited area such as New England, now finds itself on uncertain grounds when competing with similar enterprises in the Midwest, on the West coast, and in the South.*
>
> *Product life cycles have become far shorter—thus requiring more skillful management in order to extract a profit during the reduced time available.*
>
> *The marketing concept, in which the various marketing functions of the enterprise are organized under one individual—the marketing manager—has taken root in American industry. Since one manager now more than ever before has the responsibility for integrating a far-ranging variety of marketing activities, he needs a good deal more information so that this can be done effectively.[3]*
>
> *More companies have grown so large that unless they make an intensive effort, such as the development of marketing information systems, their existing marketing information will be dispersed in so many places that its effective use will be virtually impossible.*
>
> *The speed with which today's business decisions have to be made has increased, and therefore marketing systems must be developed to provide information for such rapid decision making.[4]*

---

[3] D. Maynard Phelps and J. Howard Westing, *Marketing Management* (Homewood, Illinois: Richard D. Irwin, Inc., 1968), pp. 9–11.
[4] Same reference as footnote 1, p. 63.

*The advent of techniques which can provide information
for effective decision making has gone hand-in-hand with
the development of marketing decision tools. Thus,
Bayesian analysis, PERT, decision trees, and factor analysis, all require more information than could previously be
made available by normal market research approaches.*

*Although the marketing information system is not entirely
dependent upon the use of computers, nonetheless the
evolution of these machines to the role of a relatively
commonplace article in many enterprises, and the concomitant development of qualified personnel to work with
these computers, means a good deal of information which
previously could not be handled by more archaic methods,
now can be effectively organized and retrieved.*

Benefits of a Marketing Information System

An effective marketing information system may provide the following benefits:

1. *It may provide more information within the time
   constraints required by the firm. Concomitantly, better
   performance could be achieved by the entire enterprise.*
2. *It may permit large and decentralized firms to use the
   information which is scattered in many places, and
   integrate it into a meaningful perspective.*
3. *It may permit fuller exploitation of the marketing
   concept.*
4. *It may provide selective retrieval of information—users
   can be given only what they want and need.*
5. *It may provide quicker recognition of developing
   trends.*
6. *It may permit far better use of material which is
   ordinarily collected by many firms in the course of
   their business activities; for example, sales by product,
   by customer, and by region.*
7. *It may permit better control over the firm's marketing
   plan; for example, it may raise warning signals when
   something is amiss in the plan.*
8. *It may prevent important information from being
   readily suppressed; for example, indications that a
   product should be withdrawn.*

The Environment Needed for a Successful System

In a speech presented to the American Marketing Association, Arnold Amstutz of M.I.T. has suggested that successful marketing information systems need four environmental characteristics.[5] First, the system must be designed to provide information in a form which can be used in the present management decision processes. The information given to management, furthermore, must be refined to the point where management is capable of acting upon it. In other words, management must not be deluged with mountains of paper.

Second, management must participate in creating the parameters of the system's capability. After all, it is management that will be using the information derived from this system. Therefore, it is this same management that must undertake the specification of what is needed and how it will be used.

Third, the information which is gathered by the system must be filed in what is known as a disaggregated data file. In such a file new information input is maintained together with previously received input. The net effect of such procedure is that all previous transactions can be recreated by the system at any time. This is particularly important with new systems, since such information systems are bound to change, and an aggregated file, that is, one in which all information is combined, may have to be completely discarded as being unsuitable for the changes made in the system. A disaggregated file, however, contains the inputs in such a way that they are adaptable to any form of system change.

Finally, the system must be designed so that it can evolve to fit the continually changing needs of the enterprise. Obviously, when the system is first introduced it will only use a few of the many techniques that are available. As the system users become more familiar with its capabilities, their needs will evolve. Thus, the system must be designed so that it too can cope with these new needs.

Elements of the Marketing Information System

Figure 1 shows a graphical representation of the marketing information system.[6] The input and output shown in that Figure are

[5] Arnold E. Amstutz, "The Marketing Executive and Management Information Systems," *Science, Technology and Marketing*, Raymond M. Haas (ed.) (Chicago: American Marketing Association, Fall, 1966), pp. 69–86.
[6] Walter Buckley (ed.), *Modern Systems Research for the Behavioral Scientist* (Chicago: Aldine Publishing Company, 1968), passim.

illustrative only. Obviously, they will change, depending upon the need of the enterprise. Not only will they change within any one firm over a period of time, but they will differ from one enterprise to the next.

The inputs to the system are those items of information which can be used to generate the required output. The output consists of that information which is needed by marketing management for

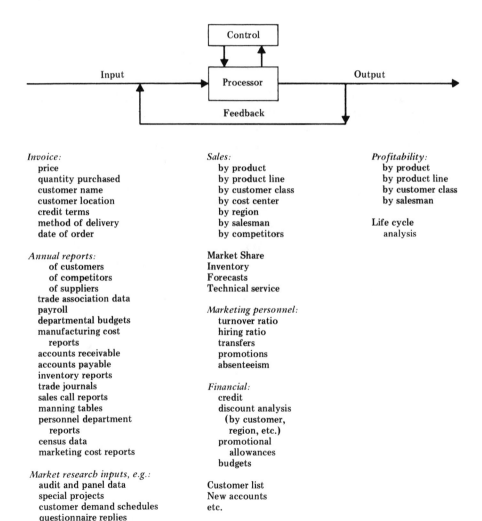

Invoice:
    price
    quantity purchased
    customer name
    customer location
    credit terms
    method of delivery
    date of order

Annual reports:
    of customers
    of competitors
    of suppliers
    trade association data
    payroll
    departmental budgets
    manufacturing cost
        reports
    accounts receivable
    accounts payable
    inventory reports
    trade journals
    sales call reports
    manning tables
    personnel department
        reports
    census data
    marketing cost reports

Market research inputs, e.g.:
    audit and panel data
    special projects
    customer demand schedules
    questionnaire replies

Sales:
    by product
    by product line
    by customer class
    by cost center
    by region
    by salesman
    by competitors

Market Share
Inventory
Forecasts
Technical service

Marketing personnel:
    turnover ratio
    hiring ratio
    transfers
    promotions
    absenteeism

Financial:
    credit
    discount analysis
        (by customer,
        region, etc.)
    promotional
        allowances
    budgets

Customer list
New accounts
etc.

Profitability:
    by product
    by product line
    by customer class
    by salesman

Life cycle
    analysis

Figure 1.   The marketing information system.

decision-making purposes. The illustrative outputs shown in Figure 1 can be considerably augmented by an effective system. For example, the sales category shows that the sales volume will be indicated by product, by product line, by customer class, and by region. For each of these categories we can also design the system so that it will print out the budgeted or forecasted sales figure, the cumulative sales to date, and a graphical representation of curves of cumulative sales, both actual and forecast. Similar expansion of output can be obtained for the profitability data.

The section of the chart market "Processor" is the system itself. This system consists not only of hardware and software, but of the human machinery which is necessary to carry out the mission of the system, and to accomplish the required marketing objectives. The "Processor" sector contains a number of sub-systems, each devoted to a different facet of the input and output sectors. Thus, there could be a sub-system dealing with price, one with marketing personnel, another with life cycle analyses, and others with sales, profitability, market share, and advertising effectiveness.

There are several types of *controls* which can be imposed upon a system.

1. *The MIS can be managed by some group within the firm.*
2. *The MIS can be at a higher stage on the information-decision hierarchy than merely the "information system" stage—the stage at which the system provides timely, reliable, and sufficient information for managerial decisions. It may have advanced to the stage at which* control *capabilities are coupled to the system in the form of remote consoles, cathode ray tube terminals, and other devices by which the manager and the information system are joined into an* interactive man-machine problem-solving network.[7]
3. Control *or "limits" exist which are set by the market and the environment in which the firm operates; examples are social, legal, political, economic, financial, technological, and temporal.*
4. *The "feedback" loop also serves as a control. It monitors the output so that the nature of the input can be varied in order to provide subsequent output in*

[7] G. W. Dickson, "Management Information-Decision Systems," *Business Horizons*, vol. 11 (December, 1968), pp. 17–26.

accordance with the current decision-making needs of the marketing executive.

It should be noted that the third type of control mentioned above is utilized in the *processor* of the system shown in Figure 1. For example, if we are concerned with an information system for an enterprise manufacturing women's bathing suits, we know we need a system which has an extremely fast capability for gathering and processing information. Markets such as those for bathing suits change with extreme rapidity, and last week's information is of relatively little value. On the other hand, if we were dealing with the manufacture of office furniture, the system would be quite different; although there are style changes and technological advances in such a business, these changes are, relatively speaking, far slower. The information system's controls, accordingly, must be changed to correspond with this different sort of market.

Who Is Responsible for the System

One of the basic decisions which has to be made early in the program of any company that wants to develop a marketing information system is that of fixing the responsibility for the daily operation of the system. There are several aspects to this that must be considered.

The primary support for the system must come from top management. Unless the principal executives of the organization, both in marketing and in other areas, are firmly convinced and will support fully the operation and the implementation of a marketing information system, it is bound to fail.[8] Beyond this concept of top management support is the problem of whether or not the system should be run on a daily basis by either a specialist in data processing, or an operating manager who is more of a generalist and is consequently more knowledgeable within the area of marketing itself.

Both the specialist and the generalist have their supporters and critics. The advantages of specialist managers are obvious. They have the technical skills for running a system. On the other hand, their deficiencies are equally obvious. Too often the specialist simply has not had a sufficient background in marketing so that he can properly handle the principal flows of information that are relevant to the

[8] Donald F. Cox and Robert E. Good, "How To Build A Marketing Information System," *Harvard Business Review*, vol. 45 (May–June, 1967), pp. 145–154.

important marketing decisions. As a result, costly mistakes are inevitable. Also some specialists overemphasize the system at the expense of the job which the system is designed to accomplish.

The generalist, or operating manager, has the advantage of a detailed knowledge of the areas about which decisions are being made. This can be extremely valuable in designing the system output. The manager, however, is handicapped by his lack of knowledge relative to information-handling techniques. Such generalists tend to concentrate upon information which will provide immediate profit to the marketing sector at the expense of the long-run profitability.

Responsibility for the system should rest with the top marketing executive who, after all, is accountable for the performance of the entire marketing sector of the enterprise. This is not intended to infer that the specialist-technician should not have a good deal of responsibility; nonetheless, the task which is being performed is a *marketing* task and it is the marketing manager's responsibility to supervise all marketing activities. In consequence of the duality of roles, the last several years have seen the development of a new position title in many business firms, that of director of marketing information services. This title is ordinarily held by an individual who is primarily a technical specialist who, hopefully, has some marketing knowledge as well, and who is capable of utilizing expert staff assistance in marketing. This individual usually reports to the marketing manager who, as stated above, really bears the ultimate responsibility for all facets of the marketing task.

Organizational Problems of Marketing Information Systems

In the few years in which marketing information systems have been used, it has become obvious that there are some typical organizational problems which occur unless extensive foresight, as well as care in execution of the system, is exercised. These are briefly discussed below.

1. Faulty Integration between Sub-systems

It must be recognized that the marketing information system is just *one part* of a total management information system; the other part embraces such areas as finance, production, and personnel. Too great an emphasis upon the objectives of any one of these parts without constant realization that it is the entire enterprise's efficiency which must be optimized can result in a failure of the system to achieve its objectives economically. The problem some-times becomes particularly acute when the output from one organization is needed as part of the input for the other.

2. Changes in Jobs and Skill Requirements

The implementation of a marketing information system will require the marketing department to bring new skills into its organization and to create new job functions to utilize these skills. In addition to these totally new jobs and skills, there will certainly be changes in existing work patterns. After all, many new documents and new information will be generated, and the traditional ways of handling information will probably no longer be adequate. Conse-quently, we are going to have problems of personal conflict, of adjustment to new types of work, of dissatisfaction with new work environments, of human inertia, of obstruction, and the like.

3. Relationships between the System's Designers and the System's Users

Those who are using the system's outputs must get involved with the system's design—otherwise there will be excessive friction at the interface between designers and users. Some marketing decision makers with authoritative positions in the enterprise must be assigned to work with the system's designers. It must be borne in mind that the users must develop plans for utilizing system output. They should not simply expect a mass of data to be deposited with them several times each day, and then sit around and wonder what to do with it.[9]

The System's Relation to Other Corporate Functions

One question that must be raised is "What is the relationship of the marketing information system to the other functions of the organization?" The easiest way to present this relationship is in the form of a chart, and this is shown in Figure 2. Here, it can be seen that the marketing information system is a part of the marketing area. The latter area is led by a single marketing executive who,

[9] Emanuel Kay, "Some Organizational Problems Which Arise As The Result of Large-Scale Information Systems," in Samuel V. Smith, et al (eds.), *Readings in Marketing Information Systems* (Boston: Houghton Mifflin Company, 1968), pp. 323–329.

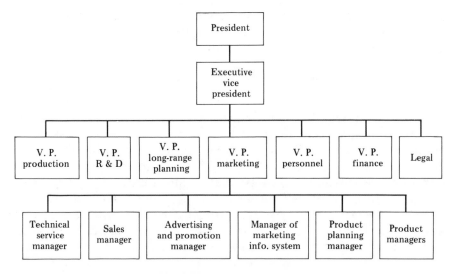

Figure 2.   Organizing for marketing information systems.

ordinarily, would have a title such as vice president of marketing, or marketing manager. The organization shown is one for a company which is organized along what has come to be known as the marketing management concept. This concept requires all of the marketing operations of the enterprise to be so organized that one individual only has responsibility for all such operations and that he be equal in rank with other top corporate executives. The latter relationship is also shown on the chart and indicates that the vice presidents of production, research and development, finance, and so forth are in the same echelon as the top marketing executive.

Relation to the Marketing Plan

The marketing plan is the basic working document by which the marketing department conducts its activities. Obviously, every facet of this plan requires information so that appropriate decisions can be made. The output of the marketing information system hence provides the input to the marketing plan for these marketing decisions. Therefore, the relationship of the information system to the marketing plan is two-fold: (1) the marketing plan uses the output of the information system, and (2) provides control criteria for the marketing information system.

A Brief Look at Some Operating Systems

Chemstrand

The Chemstrand Company has an advanced marketing information system. For example, the Chemstrand system will provide detailed sales analyses by product, by category of product, by sales district, type of process, type of end-use, the type of mill, and so on. Reports are sent to the company's salesmen concerning their transactions with their customers; different marketing groups get specific reports which are relevant to their particular sphere of interest. For example, product managers receive analyses of the marketing operations of their particular area of responsibility. Records are kept of consumer behavior in 7500 households which represent a sample of the national market, so that these socio-economic backgrounds and attitudes can be analyzed to determine buying trends and other related information.[10]

The system also keeps close tabs on Chemstrand's competitors and, in addition, also turns out a number of short-, medium-, and long-range forecasts. These forecasts are made by industry, by company, and by end users. Projections are made for approximately 400 different products on a short-term basis.

Lever Brothers

Lever Brothers has a system that produces 2500 different pages of daily reports, 3000 pages of weekly reports, and 40,000 pages of monthly reports. Thus, managers have daily tabulations for the sales of their brands by geographic districts. Data are also provided as to whether the sales quota is being achieved, and how close to this the salesman is coming. It is possible to compare brands by zones, by districts, and by regions.[11]

Every month there are reports on more than 3000 important customers and, best of all, they are available during the first week of the new month. These reports show a variety of information such as how well a particular account is doing vis-à-vis its performance in a prior year.

[10] Phyllis Daignault, "Marketing Management and the Computer," *Sales Management*, vol. 95 (August 20, 1965), pp. 49–60.
[11] Same reference as footnote 10, pp. 58–59.

RCA

Another example can be found with RCA, whose system can provide sales analyses by product, by territory, comparisons with quota, and so forth. They have a program to determine the amount of each model of the product line which is to be sold to each distributor. It is based on the distributor's sales history, and the knowledge of his territory's market potential, as well as RCA's market share within that area.

Another program combines 100 variables to determine the gross margin for individual models or families of products. In addition, there are monthly reports which show sales by product, by dealer county area, and by distributor. These outputs represent, of course, only a fraction of the output of the RCA system.[12]

Myths and Pitfalls of Marketing Information Systems

Because there has been so much talk about marketing information systems and very little hard fact concerning how well they have operated under a variety of industry types and conditions, a number of myths have evolved concerning the nature and capabilities of marketing information systems. Of course, there are some pitfalls that are well recognized, since they are generally the same as those associated with other information systems, such as management information systems.

Several of these myths and pitfalls are briefly discussed below:

Not every firm should have a computer-oriented marketing information system. While it is true that it is fashionable to talk about one, there are some companies that are equipped neither to run one nor to utilize the output. For these firms the expenditure on the development of this system would be a waste.

The marketing information system should not be based solely on the computer. While this is a vital tool, there are still many "old-fashioned" forms and procedures which are quite good.

Be careful of a revolutionary effect upon the enterprise. The firm simply may not be able to handle both the personnel problems and the output of the system.

[12] Same reference as footnote 10, pp. 59–60.

The marketing information system is not a substitute for basic market research of the traditional type. Such market research is still required for specific studies of particular marketing problems and for handling information needs which are outside the sphere of interest of the system.

It is too easy to accept a computer print-out with 100% confidence, simply because it is neat and voluminous. However, this does not make it right and the marketing manager must remember that outputs are only as good as the inputs used to generate them.

Marketing information systems are not new. Obviously, they have existed for some time, since managers have for a long period had reliable and comprehensive and timely sources of information. What we do have at the present time is a capability for making the system far more comprehensive and for equipping it to handle vastly increased quantities of input with effectiveness and promptness.

The same marketing information system cannot serve all levels of management, nor can all levels benefit equally from such systems. The top managers, for example, require information which is of such a nature that it permits them to make strategic choices. Middle managers and lower level supervisors require different types of information. [13] *Within any one level, the sophistication of the system must be selected carefully so that it is compatible with the managers who will use it.*

Because computers have such an enormous capacity, there is a tendency to make the information too detailed and wide-ranging. This is a mistake. The marketing manager should be provided with an amount of information sufficient for decision making and no more. If there is too much information, that which is relevant and useful will be hidden in the mass of excess input and output.

Insofar as the marketing manager is concerned, the proper design of the marketing information system is one which emphasizes not the outpouring of great masses of

[13] Ridley Rhind, "Management Information Systems," *Business Horizons,* vol. 11 (June, 1968), pp. 37–46.

*data, but rather the filtration, condensation, and evalua-
tion of masses of information into more manageable
form.* [14]

*You cannot expect to develop at one time a total system
that will handle all of the marketing information needs of
your enterprise. Instead, the system must be developed
and implemented in small, manageable stages. How much
time is required for the development of the system to its
fullest capacity is very difficult to state. One company
may be able to implement a fairly comprehensive system
in one year, while other companies may require five or ten
years before their systems are fully operational.*

*There is a danger in the fact that many marketing
managers do not know what information they really need,
yet one of the precepts of designing a good marketing
information system is that the marketing manager must be
consulted. Unfortunately, the great tendency is for people
to demand more information about areas of which they
are uncertain. The result, of course, is that in those
decision-making areas about which the marketing managers
are not too confident, they require the system designers to
provide far more information than they really need.*

*Do not take it for granted that simply because your
marketing personnel will be given more information than
they had previously they will know what to do with it.
Therefore, during design of the marketing information
system, firm steps must be taken to insure that the
managers are prepared to use the output of that system
effectively.*

*The final pitfall is that too often managers feel that they
do not have to understand how the system works, but
merely to take advantage of its capability. While this is
true to a certain degree, nonetheless it requires them to
place too much faith in a system which simply may not be
functioning properly insofar as their decision needs and
marketing objectives are concerned. While the managers
who use the system need not be specialists in its design and*

---

[14] Same reference as footnote 8, p. 152.

implementation, they must be sufficiently aware of the mechanics of the system so that they can evaluate its output and provide suggestions for improvement of the system.

Summary

Marketing information systems are part of the marketing wave of the future. They are important, and they are beginning to function very well. However, like any radical change imposed upon an organization, they can be very expensive and have great potential for damage. Hence, they must be used carefully and with a recognition of their potential for damage. The rewards of struggling with the many problems of developing a successful system are, however, well worthwhile.

Section **2**

Scope

23

MIS in Perspective

Charles H. Nicholson
Reprinted by permission of *Chemical
Engineering Progress*, January 1970.

While there have been many articles carried in business periodicals on the subject of Management Information System, there exists an inadequacy of existing interpretations of MIS. While evermore information becomes available about the component parts of MIS (including such "hot" items as concordant files, data banks and the like), very little progress has been made in clarifying an understanding of MIS as a whole.

The problems involved in attempting to describe MIS are compounded by the plethora of what one might refer to as "dictionary" definitions of MIS. Such explanations add little to an improved understanding and, in my judgment, all too often they vary only insofar as they play on words to convey similar impressions concerning information systems and management's relationship to this area. As a case in point, articles have been published which describe the advantages or disadvantages of management information systems versus information management systems—in other words, MIS versus IMS. It requires no great effort to ascertain that the real difference between the two is a semantic one. (One author apparently reached such a state of confusion that he wrote an article entitled, "The Myth of Real-Time Management Information." (1) Perhaps a timely question is simply "What are we talking about?" Is it possible to picture the essence of MIS in a manner which will clarify an understanding of the subject?

Not long ago I had the pleasure of a visit from a young

Australian graduate student majoring in management sciences at a well-known business school. The young man became convinced through his studies that before long MIS would bring about a major displacement of middle management personnel because the decision-making functions of middle management would be fully computerized. I am sure most will agree that the student's perspective was not in proper focus, and that such an occurrence is not likely to take place, at least for quite a long time. However, in one sense the student posed a valid and timely question: what is a useful perspective within which to consider the relationship of MIS to the business environment?

This presentation will not attempt to establish a single, all-encompassing definition of MIS which might be used to answer this question. There are many "dictionary definitions" available in business periodicals for those interested in abbreviated, concise explanations. The purpose of the presentation will be to consider some fundamental problems involved in making effective decisions in terms of the factors which result in both good and bad management decisions; within this framework specific computer-based systems applications will be reviewed in order to assess the nature of MIS in what might be broadly viewed as the decision-making environment.

Key Factors in Making Decisions

Everyone makes decisions which involve choices and, in most situations, a degree of risk. In arriving at business decisions, we must be able to identify the alternatives, evaluate them and then decide among them. It is a basic truism that *people, not machines, make decisions*. The essential human dimension of business is sometimes overlooked in the market place, in factories and offices and also in designing automated information systems. People buy, people produce, people sell, people decide. Decision-making in business is a valuable human skill and not a science (2).

Business decisions have an important time aspect. Delays can be costly. In general, the longer it takes to make the decision, the more time and money is expended in fact finding and gathering background data. There is also the risk of a competitive countermeasure which could have an undesired effect. For instance, company A might be delaying a decision on marketing a new product only to learn that company B has seized the initiative by announcing a competitive product. On the other hand, proceeding too rapidly can also be risky because of the uncertainty of acting without adequate supporting facts.

In theory, there is a "best time" to decide and that is when considerations of timing and information gathering are in approximate balance. Paul Green of DuPont suggests that "time and money should be spent on the information gathering activity until the sum of the expected costs of information collection and delay, plus the expected costs of acting under uncertainty, are minimal." (4) This concept is illustrated by the diagram in Figure 1.

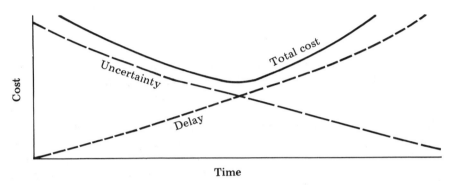

Figure 1.   Schematic depicting theoretical best time to decide.

Introducing New Products

It is clear that good decisions require good data and, of course, different kinds of decisions require various amounts and types of information. One of the challenging decisions management must make involves the introduction of new products in the market place. A wide range of data are usually studied before decisions of this magnitude are undertaken; (3) for example:

Financial
  Return on investment
  Estimated annual sales
  Investment required
  Fixed costs
  Operating costs
  Selling price
Technical
  Research and Development time and costs

> *Availability of knowhow*
> *Patentability*

Production
> *Availability of raw materials*
> *Production knowledge and personnel required*
> *Equipment necessary*

Marketing
> *Effect on present products*
> *Marketability*
> *Number of potential customers*
> *Suitability of present sales force*
> *Market development factors*
> *Anticipated competitive situation*

It takes time and money to obtain data such as these. On the other hand, poor timing can nullify a basically sound decision which is supported with good data. Hesitant decision makers are often criticized because of their desire to clarify exactly every little detail before reaching a final judgment. It is sometimes alleged that they would rather be precisely wrong than vaguely right or, to put it another way, have a well-documented loss rather than an unexpected profit! But it can also be costly to act too quickly without sufficient facts. Most good decision-makers seem to possess an intuitive sense of timing which can amplify the benefits of sound decisions.

In summary, a decision can be described as consisting of two major parts: the analysis and a willingness to act in the face of uncertainty. Important ingredients are facts, people and timing. New analytical methods can help clarify the issues, but they are not a substitute for the final decisive judgment of one person. In the introduction of the Mustang automobile, Donald Frey, Vice President of Ford, remarked that he "knew of no way of running a styling problem through a computer." (5) Thus, a spectrum of human qualities is required to make effective business decisions.

The Impact of MIS

In reviewing the factors involved in making business decisions, it was pointed out previously that good decisions require good data. The decision-maker must evaluate these data in order to make a judgment. A variety of analytical techniques are available which can be used to facilitate the evaluation process: for example, value analysis, decision trees, mathematical models and computer simulation. One of the most provocative and complete procedures, Bayesian Decision Theory, is described by Paul Green of DuPont in an article entitled, "Decision Making in Chemical Marketing." (4) Management science and operations research specialists can identify many other techniques which would also be useful.

There are those who consider MIS as a kind of magnificent octopus which embraces all the techniques from value analysis through Bayesian Decision Theory with the computer included for good measure. This "umbrella concept" of MIS argues that indeed MIS is all-encompassing in terms of techniques and furthermore, that it will provide top management with nearly instantaneous information on what is happening throughout the company. Citing an opposing argument, John Deardon, writing in the Harvard Business Review, questioned the validity of this approach. "One of the most common mistakes in management information systems has been that of providing one level of management with information designed for use by another level. Not only is this information frequently meaningless to those at one level, but it obscures the fact that certain decisions must be made there and the necessary information for making these decisions is absent." (6)

It seems reasonable to believe that the main question is not particularly whether one prefers a broad or a narrow viewpoint concerning MIS, but what the likely impact will be on the vital problems of managerial decision making. To the extent that MIS can result in improving the business decisions which management at all levels of the organization must make, then the so-called MIS approach, regardless of the manner in which it is defined, will have paid its way in terms of the final determinant—improved profit per share.

An MIS Case History

It is axiomatic that MIS and vital business activities are intimately related. The sensitivity of this relationship is illustrated by the following case history of a computer-based information system.

A midwest plant sold products in a regional market in which it faced aggressive competition for orders; its products were of a non-proprietary nature.

Two years ago the sales manager of the plant met with a computer specialist to discuss the difficult problems involved in quoting prices to customers using outdated information on basic costs. He explained that although he could not present concrete evidence to back up his opinions, he was convinced that the inadequate information was largely responsible for his plant's mediocre sales performance. Inadvertently, prices were being set below the breakeven point of profitability which, were the true facts known, would either be adjusted upward to a profitable level or the business would be rejected. Turning the coin on the reverse side, the sales manager felt that opportunities for selective price reductions were being overlooked which would not compromise profitability and would boost sales volumes. But without better support on the underlying cost realities the sales manager was powerless to make improvements in decisions on selling prices. What such improvements might accomplish in practical dollar and cents terms was also uncertain.

It was agreed that the development of a computer-based cost system would be undertaken to supplant the inadequate existing system which was basically a manual procedure. Certain ground rules were decided upon: under no circumstances would the computer be programmed to calculate the selling price of any item, even on a "suggested" basis. The decision on selling price would in all cases be made by the sales manager and his staff in terms of their relationship with customers, markets, product characteristics and pertinent subjective factors. The role of the computer system would be limited to determining the accurate cost facts and making these data available in time for decision by the sales manager; in turn, he would respond to the customer with a price quotation.

It was also established that the system would not result in any out-of-pocket cost savings; in fact, the new system represented such a major change in procedures that additional sales personnel were required to supplement the efforts of the computer programmers. Certainly, the project had little or nothing to recommend it in terms of conventional measurements of anticipated savings, tangible benefits and similar criteria. The proponents of the system were in the lonely position of believing a change would be beneficial but, like voices in the wilderness, they were in no position to back up this judgment with conclusive evidence.

After several months of breaking in the new computer-based cost estimating system, it began to take hold. During this time the sales manager and his staff were learning how to utilize the output of the computer in order to make better pricing decisions. It is true of change in any human endeavor that a departure from a familiar method requires a period of adjustment. At times the computer-produced statistics differed from the established figures by such a wide margin that there was a strong feeling the computer system was wrong!

Certainly, the new system was not without inaccuracies, due primarily to poor input data; however, on balance the accuracy was far superior to the former manual procedure which was subject to human error. Gradually, the sales manager began to detect some clues which bolstered his initial opinions concerning the inadequacy of previous pricing decisions. Where it was evident that prices were being set below the breakeven level, decisions were made to increase prices on a selective basis. Many times this involved negotiation with the customer to explain the reasons for the increase and to persuade the customer to accept the change. In a few instances unprofitable orders were refused outright! In other cases decisions were made to effect selective price reductions where it was believed such reductions would bring in additional sales without prejudicing profitability. In other words, many new decisions on pricing were put into effect in the market place as a result of the cost portfolio which was prepared by the computer in a timely manner and which became, in effect, a sort of "Bible" for the sales manager and his staff.

As to the results of these changes, the plant experienced an increase in sales of over $300,000, within a period of a relatively few months and the profit picture, after lackluster performance during the previous two to three years, turned upward as well. Several months thereafter it became clear that the plant would set new records for sales and profitability which would exceed by a wide margin any previous performance. In addition, when these results were compared with the performance records of 20 of the company's plants serving other regional markets, the plant utilizing the new computer system ranked number one. It is hardly surprising that management decided to install the system in all comparable plants on a "crash" basis. Three regional computer complexes will be tied to a network of data transmission and terminal equipment blanketing the country; these facilities will provide this computer service to 20 plants whose combined annual sales exceed $100 million.

A Substantial Impact

No one can be certain what the ultimate contribution of the system is likely to be in terms of the company's future sales and profitability but its impact will obviously be substantial. What is certain is that the computer-based information system is the instrument by which alert marketing personnel are able to make effective decisions and implement these decisions in highly competitive market places. The sensitive interaction between the information system and skilled marketing specialists yields dramatic results which have meaning in a practical, tangible way. Within this context, the costs incurred for developing the computer system and supporting it with a panoply of computer and communications hardware represent an investment in the increased effectiveness of the company's marketing capability.

To summarize, in the preceding illustration we observed the contribution which an effectively conceived information system can make in facilitating problems in decision making in a dynamic business environment. The computer system prepared the data in a timely fashion but the decision-maker was fully responsible for evaluating these data and making the final decision. It was pointed out also that the computer system was not programmed to provide a "suggested" selling price. Technically, this feature could be easily programmed but there are no plans to provide it in the future. Thus, the decision-maker has full flexibility to make and implement effective decisions in the market place.

However, many decisions management makes are more complex than decisions on selling price, important as these may be to profitability. The information required to make the decision may be available, but sometimes it is simply not enough to know the facts. How to interpret them in a meaningful way can present difficult problems in reaching effective decisions. The effect of such decisions may be far-reaching in their implications; the subject may be very involved from a technical standpoint; or perhaps no method is at hand for testing the impact of the decision on a limited basis before making the choice. In such circumstances, decision-makers often utilize various analytical procedures to facilitate the problems of evaluating information before rendering a final judgment. The following illustration will describe briefly the analytical procedures used by St. Regis Paper Co. in the management of its forestry resources.

A Natural Resource Management

St. Regis holds stewardship on more than 8,000,000 acres of forestry land, an area roughly equivalent to that of Massachusetts and Connecticut combined. (7) Altogether, these timber lands are growing every year wood worth more than $20 million on the stump. The management of such a forestry enterprise presents many unique challenges. For instance, of the 8,000,000 acres managed by St. Regis, a portion of this land is controlled under long term contracts held by the company. Ownership of these lands is in private hands. Nevertheless, it is a contractual obligation of the company to return these lands to the private owner in a specified condition at the completion of the contract period. Considering that it takes more than twenty-five years to grow a single tree to maturity, these obligations present formidable challenges indeed!

Under the leadership of the U.S. Forest Service, techniques for measuring the growth and yield from a forest have been developed to an advanced degree. A continuous forest inventory procedure was developed to record basic forest data on a sampling basis. I emphasize *sampling basis* because, given the enormity of the forest areas with millions of acres of trees, no practical alternative to sampling exists. St. Regis and other paper companies developed important refinements of the sampling technique; the company refers to this new technique as the cutting units appraisal method. The important consideration is that these techniques offer statistically valid inventory data which measure forest growth, projected yield, wood volumes and related vital information.

A few years ago St. Regis along with several forest products companies entered into a cooperative project with the University of Georgia to experiment with the use of mathematical modeling and computer simulation of forestry management problems. Each of the companies agreed to furnish facts and funds which the University staff would use for development purposes. Initially, a simulated forest of 300,000 acres was used to develop a mathematical model from random numbers that would help to predict the results and measure the effectiveness of a given set of management decisions. (8) These predictions were developed on a large-scale computer at the University of Georgia and the results were made available to all the companies participating in the program.

When this program yielded interesting results in an academic sense, it spurred interest in the possibility of utilizing techniques of modeling and simulation for real life problems. One area in particular was of interest: namely, what is the optimum cutting cycle for a given forest area. For instance, should the cut be made every five years for trees of a certain caliber and size or should the cut be made sooner or later than five years? This question oversimplifies the complexity of the cutting problem; in reality, 54 alternative cutting cycles exist in most cases for a given forest area; this area may contain 300 discreet stands of timber. Thus, the analysis involves consideration of possibilities which can be stated statistically as $54.^{300}$ The selection of an optimum method is further complicated by reforestation requirements, constraints arising from good forestry management practices involving conservation considerations, extensive internal revenue requirements and other complex factors. It is clear that evaluation of this magnitude can be greatly simplified by the use of computer simulation procedures and St. Regis developed computer programs for these purposes.

An interesting dimension of the problem is that once a decision is made and implemented, it may take 20, 30 or more years to find out that the decision is a bad one, if this should prove to be the case. In other words, reforestation and growth cycles are measured in decades in a forestry enterprise. Good management procedures make it essential that forestry decisions which will be reflected many years hence are based not only on valid data but also utilize sophisticated analytical techniques for evaluation purposes. In the last analysis, however, it is the decision-maker, the forestry manager steeped in the traditions and experiences of the forest, who alone renders judgment. Effective decision-making in a forestry enterprise is doubtless of critical importance to the companies in the forest products industry whose concern is the efficient and profitable management of vast forestry resources. But in a real sense the decisions which wisely husband these resources are serving the interests of all Americans for whom the forest is a grand national heritage.

The characteristics of the decision process are such as to lead one to the conclusion that decision making is not a science but a valuable human skill. This skill is practiced by men who alone act in the fact of uncertainty when making decisions. To the extent that MIS techniques can present timely and valid facts and also facilitate evaluation of pertinent information, then MIS, irrespective of a broad or narrow scope of interpretation, pays its way by contributing to the increased effectiveness of business decisions. In this sense, the basic impact of MIS is reflected in the common denominator of a business enterprise—improved profit per share.

References

1. Deardon, John, "Myth of Real-Time Management Information," *Harvard Bus. Rev.*, May–June, 1966, p. 123.

2. Hewson, T. A., "Making Effective Decisions," a presentation before the American Management Assn., Mar. 4 and Aug. 18, 1965.

3. Hertz, David B., "Risk Analysis in Capital Investment," *Harvard Bus. Rev.*, Jan.–Feb., 1964, p. 95 ff.

4. Green, Paul, "Decision Making in Chemical Marketing," *Ind. & Eng.*

5. Wright, Robert A., *New York Times*, Feb. 21, 1965. *Chem.*, vol. 54, no. 9, Sept. 1962, p. 30 ff.

6. Deardon, John, "Can Management Information Systems Be Automated," *Harvard Bus. Rev.*, Mar.–Apr., 1964 p. 134.

7. Adams, William R., President's Remarks at the St. Regis Co. Ann. Mtg., New York City, April 24, 1969.

8. Barker, G. Robinson, "Data Processing and the Forest," a presentation before Forest Products Res. Soc., Dec. 1, 1966.

24.

Blueprint for MIS

William M. Zani

Reprinted from the November–December 1970 issue of
Harvard Business Review. ©1970 by the President
and Fellows of Harvard College; all rights reserved.

Traditionally, management information systems have not really been designed at all. They have been spun off as by-products of the process of automating or improving existing systems within a company.

When a company's information system comes into existence in this second-hand manner, it is largely fortuitous whether the information the system provides is exactly the sort of information the managers in the company need to help them make their decisions. If it does turn out to be exactly what they need, then, well and good. If it does *not*—and this is much more likely to be the case—then clearly the so-called "management information system" is merely a mechanism for cluttering managers' desks with costly, voluminous, and probably irrelevant printouts.

No tool has ever aroused so much hope at its creation as MIS, and no tool has proved so disappointing in use. I trace this disappointment to the fact that most MISs have been developed in the "bottom up" fashion that I have just described. An effective system, under normal conditions, can only be born of a carefully planned, rational design that looks down from the top, the natural vantage point of the managers who will use it.

Rather than mirroring existing procedures, in other words, an information system should be designed to focus on the critical tasks and decisions made within an organization and to provide the kind of information that the manager needs to perform those tasks and make those decisions.

This obvious truth has largely escaped the attention of businessmen, information specialists, and computer specialists alike. In this article I should like to present an approach to MIS design that is oriented squarely to decision making. I have presented this approach in the framework shown in [Figure 1], which diagrams out the major determinants of MIS design and their relationships to one another. These determinants are:

Opportunities and risks
Company strategy
Company structure
Management and decision-making processes
Available technology
Available information sources

These are the factors that should structure the characteristics of information provided to management, and therefore the design of the system itself.

From the Top Down

By exhibiting the relationships between these factors, the framework helps establish goals and priorities for MIS development, and hence focuses information technology where it will do the most good. If management sees to it that this framework is used when an information system is being designed, then the resulting system will be smartly tailored to the company from the top down, and not merely patched together from the bottom up in a crazy quilt of residues from automated clerical procedures.

The system, in other words, is likely to support the critical areas of decision making in the company effectively, as it should.

To ensure that the framework will actually be used, however, top management must take a more prominent role in the design process than it has hitherto. Most experts agree that top-management support and participation are necessary for effective system design, but they generally state that this support is necessary only for budget control and control of the data-processing group.

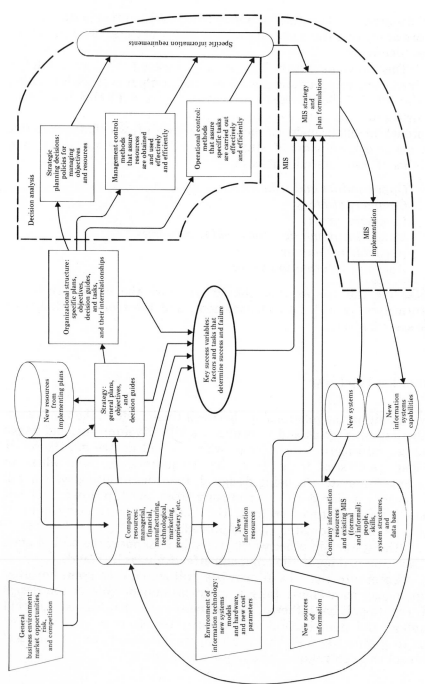

Figure 1.   Blueprint for MIS design.

The framework I am presenting, however, implies a much more extensive participation than this. It assumes that top management itself must start the design process—i.e., must first delineate the organization's strategy, structure, and decision-making processes for the specialists in the design group, and then make sure that the specialist designers integrate these elements fully into the basic system design.

An Ideal, Not a Recipe

I do not offer this framework as a panacea that will solve all of a company's information problems, nor as a step-by-step procedure for the whole design process. I offer it as a concept—an ideal, if you will—of how top management should think about the whole question of the management information system.

Its application does not guarantee that managers at all levels will be fully informed at all times about all matters important to the organization. This is obviously impossible. Further, there is nothing about the framework that implies that management can create a finished system by a single masterstroke of planning and development. Quite the contrary—the framework is only a guide to be used in the ongoing process of creating useful systems large or small, simple or complex, for immediate purposes or purposes farther away in the future. But, as such, it has enormous value.

Framework of MIS Design

The upper left quadrant of [Figure 1] indicates that a company strategy is a blend of internal company resources with external forces—market opportunities, risks, and competitive activities. The general strategy then determines organizational structure and also the practical strategy for augmenting the company's resources with new ones via short- and long-range planning.

The study of corporate strategy has occupied many books and journals, but the implication of corporate strategy for MIS design has largely escaped attention. Strategy should exercise a critical influence on information system design, to ensure that the resulting system is on the same "wave length" as the company as a whole. If, for example, a company changes its strategy so that its MIS focuses on factors no longer relevant—if it now urgently needs cash-flow data, say, where it formerly needed sales data—then the system is no longer valuable. Strategy dictates firm, explicit objectives for system design.

Key Success Variables

Opportunities, risks, competences, and resources, plus the strategy derived from them, yield the company's organizational structure. This structure subdivides the essential tasks to be performed, assigns them to individuals, and spells out the interrelationships of these tasks. These tasks, and the organizational structure they compose, determine the various information needs of the company.

Internal resources, external forces, strategy, and organizational structure define the key success variables of a company. These variables are activities on which the company must score high if it is to succeed. For example:

> For a consumer goods company manufacturing nondifferentiated products, the key success areas might be product promotion and understanding customer responses to product, marketing, and competitive changes.

> For a manufacturer of commodity products, manufacturing and distribution cost control and efficiency might be the major determinants of success.

The key success variables name the key tasks of the company and thus help identify the priorities for information system development. The system must provide information that makes the individual managers' performance of these tasks easier and better.

Decision Analysis

The only way to isolate the specific information requirements of individual managers is to isolate the nature, frequency, and interrelationships of the major decisions made in the company.

One can ask a series of questions which will help isolate the specific information requirements for these decisions:

> What decisions are made?

> What decisions need to be made?

> What factors are important in making these decisions?

How and when should these decisions be made?

What information is useful in making these decisions?

It is obviously not possible to answer all these questions for every decision made, in even the smallest organizations. But the key success variables help identify the *major decision areas* for detailed analysis.

The decision-analysis section of the framework is divided into three segments—*Strategic planning decisions, Management control,* and *Operational control.* Examples of activities falling under these headings are given in [Table 1].

It is particularly important and useful to recognize these three distinct subprocesses of management in information system design because each requires different types of information and analysis. Within the operational control area, for example, many decisions can be programmed—that is, one can build a program that identifies the time at which a decision is needed, the alternatives available, and the criteria for selecting the best alternative under different circumstances.

Within strategic planning, on the other hand, it is frequently extremely difficult to determine when a decision is needed; and developing alternative solutions to a problem of strategic planning is a creative process that cannot be predefined or prescribed. Hence, the kinds of information and analyses needed for strategic planning are quite different from the kinds needed for operational control. [Table 2] displays the informational characteristics required by each of these subprocesses.

Systems designers who fail to understand the differences between these subprocesses and fail to take them into account may make the mistake of applying to all of them a system that is applicable to only one subprocess and not to the others. Decision analysis should filter information requirements for the appropriate management subprocess. Thus far, then, the framework makes explicit:

Objectives dictated by strategy

Specific tasks and their interrelationships, displayed via organizational structure

Key success variables

Using these elements as a base, an analysis of a company's decision-

Table 1. The Characteristics of Input into the Three Decision-analysis Processes

Strategic planning process
  "External" data
    Market analyses
    Technological developments
    Government actions
    Economic data
  Trends
  Predictions

Management control process
  Control
    Internal formation
    Historical summaries
    Goal/performance comparisons
    Monetary reports
    Rhythmic reports
  Decision making
    Future trends & past trends
    Monetary & nonmonetary reports
    Special studies
    Rhythmic reports
    Product & market data
      Market share/potential market share
      Customer & product profiles
      Production-process efficiencies, etc.

Operational control process
  Precise logistic and product data
    Inventory reports
    Production schedules
    Product costs
  Nonmonetary reports

making patterns in strategy, managerial control, and operational control draws out the specific information requirements for the critical areas of company operations. It is by identifying these factors and guiding their analyses that managers make their contribution to MIS development.

To fulfill their roles properly, managers must be aware of the major sources of information, of alternative methods of supplying data, and of the impact of the major changes of information

Table 2. Examples of Activities in the Three Decision-analysis Processes

Strategic Planning	Management Control	Operational Control
Choosing company objectives	Formulating budgets	
Planning the organization	Planning staff levels	Controlling hiring
Setting personnel policies	Planning working capital	Controlling credit extension
Setting marketing policies	Formulating advertising programs	Controlling placement of advertisements
Setting research policies	Selecting research projects	
Choosing new product lines	Choosing product improvements	
Acquiring new divisions	Deciding on plant rearrangement	Scheduling production
Deciding on nonroutine capital expenditures	Deciding on routine capital expenditures	
	Formulating decision rules for operational control	Controlling inventory
	Measuring, appraising, and improving management performance	Measuring, appraising, and improving workers' efficiency

Source: Adapted from Robert N. Anthony, *Planning and Control Systems: A Framework for Analysis* (Boston, Division of Research, Harvard Business School, 1965), p. 19.

technology. The major contribution to information systems in these areas, of course, must come from the information and data-processing specialists.

Information Technology

The field of information technology has undergone and will continue to undergo rapid change. One funnel in [Figure 1] symbolizes the influence of change in information technology, and also of information sources, on the development of information systems. Through this funnel are added new methods of processing and storing data, new models, changes in computer and peripheral equipment, and changes in the costs of hardware and software development to the design process. These generate new system ideas and make them feasible.

The barrel labled "Company information resources. . . ." is a reminder that new systems cannot and should not be developed in the abstract. Existing systems and practices cannot be changed overnight, and many times it is too costly and risky to change the existing systems radically. Proposals for system changes must also consider the level, quality, and kinds of skills present in the data-processing group. And finally, of course, the computer configuration is fixed in the short term and may be difficult and expensive to alter. New systems must therefore be designed and developed with the limitations and constraints of the old systems clearly in mind.

Using the framework, then, encourages understanding of the critical areas of operations, identification of specific information requirements, and recognition of the technological, economic, and personnel constraints within which an MIS develops. As important as anything else, perhaps, is the fact that systems are of necessity dynamic, changing with the environment and the organization.

In essence, the difference between my viewpoint on MIS design and what I call the bottom-up viewpoint is analogous to the difference between the new, customer-oriented concept of marketing and the old marketing concept. Philip Kotler has spelled out the latter difference as follows:

> The new marketing concept replaces and to some extent reverses the logic of the old one. . . . The old concept starts with the firm's existing products and considers marketing to be the use of selling and promotion to attain sales at a profit. The new concept starts with the firm's existing and potential customers; it seeks profits through the creation of customer satisfaction; and it seeks to achieve this through an integrated, corporate wide marketing program.[1]

The old MIS design approach begins with existing systems, and produces benefits by chance. The approach I advocate focuses on key tasks and decisions leading to more effective decisions, and then attacks the problem of designing information systems to support those tasks.

[1] *Marketing Management* (Englewood Cliffs, New Jersey, Prentice-Hall, Inc., 1967), p. 6.

The framework I have proposed helps management structure MIS so that it can and will influence the decision-making processes in the critical areas of the company, and thus focuses information technology and resources where they do the most good. It also demonstrates that general and operating management must be directly involved in the design of systems. Only management's understanding can delineate the organization's critical success factors for the information specialist or systems designer.

If the design of management information systems begins on a high conceptual level and on a high managerial level as well, a company can avoid the unfortunate "bottom up" design phenomenon of recent history and begin to develop the real, and very great, potential of MIS as a tool for modern management.

Section **3**

Design

25

How to Approach a Quality Information System

Lester Ravitz

Reprinted by permission of *Quality Progress*, June 1969,
pp. 22–23. Copyright 1969, Quality Progress magazine.

Management Information Systems (MIS) are many things to many people: cost data collections and reporting to the accountant; trend analyses to the salesman; profit and loss statements to the board chairman; production status reports to plant managers; vendor rating reports to quality managers.

Should quality control involve itself with a management information system? Quality control, or quality assurance, whatever the name of the department, must operate within the same management framework as any other element of the company. It must realize a profit from its operation, which necessitates management controls of cost and effectiveness. Costs are easy to measure. Effectiveness, on the other hand, is not that easy to measure, although many familiar ways to do so have been developed. MIS can provide measurement tools, but management must continue as the controlling element.

It has been shown over the years that a more economical means of control may be effected through strong before the fact quality assurance. This assurance takes many forms: design and specifications reviews, drawing and change control, vendor surveillance and many other product-oriented activities. Also, it is control of shop floor variables such as processes, machines, materials, tools and personnel skills. It is from these shop floor variables that a shop quality data base may be realized.

Approval and Backing

No one should embark on a management information system without securing the solid approval and backing of top management. When management backing is secured, general concepts should be defined. Do you want to begin with a top-down or a bottom-up approach? Should you begin by doing what you can to collect data more effectively or do you want to develop a higher order system first and worry later about how to clean up the detail?

Information systems come in three categories: strategic, tactical and clerical. The manner in which system planning, design and implementation is affected is dependent upon the information category in question.

A clerical system generally is concerned with such matters as labor collection for payroll and contract fund utilization. A tactical system will use labor collection to update operation or flow time standards, or perhaps to effect changes in personnel and skill mix on a given operation. A strategic system will utilize labor data to estimate, plan and forecast.

Regardless of the natural categorical split, data bases must exist that have been developed naturally by the lower echelon systems. Strategic systems, for instance, could not be implemented properly without the flow time standards derived by the tactical system, which itself would be in difficulty without the clerical system collecting basic labor data. The systems are mutually dependent, just as the organizational elements of a business must dovetail and complement each other in their everyday activity.

Requirement Determinations

During the concept definition phase, a determination of whether to use manual or computer based systems is in order. Sometimes, combinations are most practical. One generally finds that a given quality system will contain some effective manual systems that complement a planned system. Regardless of direction chosen, basic criteria must be considered before the choice is made:

1. *Can the planned system be handled practically without help from a computer?*
2. *Can manual systems update the data base rapidly enough to be useful?*
3. *Will a manual system provide the required information*

in every fashion in which the information may likely be required?

4. *Will a manual system respond rapidly enough to be useful?*

5. *Is a manual system more economical to operate?*

One of the most difficult phases of information system development will occur now: determination of system input and output requirements needed to satisfy users of the system when they often do not know, in the kind of detail an analyst needs, what they want. The analyst must attempt to second-guess the needs of users. By judging their needs and working backwards, they can derive their data requirements. Then he must determine the practicality of recording each data element, accepting only the practical.

So armed, the analyst can set user limits by presenting possible output information. This generally will stimulate enough interest in the user to get him to discuss his needs in specific terms.

Too Much Too Quickly

A danger in information system design is too much system too quickly. Many operations have failed dismally due to an attempt to create the ultimate system at the intial cut. Many companies take four or five years to develop a system. This, incidentally, is to achieve minimum results and does not include refinements.

The most practical way that the required effort at any one time can be decreased appreciably, and at the same time provide for manageable segments of a total system design, is to break the effort into unrelated segments.

If one were to segment a quality control system, a natural tendency might be to consider vendor operations, detail part quality, assembly, test and final quality as natural subdivisions. Another might use MIL-Q-9858A or MIL-I-45208A as a guide to define areas of desirable control. No one is better than any other.

For example, take MIL-Q-9858A and four major headings in the body of the specification: Quality Program Management, Facilities and Standards, Control of Purchases and Manufacturing Control. These sections can be taken individually or in combination as system segments.

Quality Program Management includes organizational require-ments necessary to an effective quality program, a review of requirements and detailed planning for satisfaction of those requirements, provision of necessary work instructions, maintenance of records, provision for effecting positive corrective action and maintenance of quality cost data. Facilities and Standards includes drawing and documentation control requirements, measuring and test equipment, tooling control and metrology requirements. Control of Purchases deals solely with vendor controls. Manufacturing Control deals with in-house controls of materials, processing and fabrication, inspection and test, handling, storage and delivery, control of nonconforming material, use of statistical control methods and inspection status indicators.

For the sake of discussion, consider the several requirements in three subdivisions: general controls, vendor controls and in-house controls. We'll start with general controls. Quality planning, provision of work instructions, and some portion of provisions for records and corrective action are part of a general control system, and they apply both in-house and vendor controls.

Some portions of manufacturing control and facilities and standards requirements such as drawings, documentation, change controls, nonconforming material control, measuring, test equipment and tooling controls also are general control elements. Control of purchases and in-house manufacturing are quite specific and often are dissimilar in nature. We now define the three subdivisions of control as follows:

General control (in-house and vendor)
1. *Quality planning*
2. *Quality records, statistical analysis*
3. *Corrective action*
4. *Drawing, documentation and change control*
5. *Measuring, test equipment and tool control*
6. *Control of non-conforming material*
7. *Inspection status identification*

Vendor control
1. *Quality requirements—requisition or purchase order review*
2. *Vendor rating*

In-house control
1. *Work instructions*
2. *Material control*
3. *Processing and fabrication control*
4. *Inspection and test*

The general control area contains elements that are by nature general work systems applying to both in-house and vendor sub-systems or divisions. If any one facet were to be automated first, it should be quality records since most interaction takes place around this element. It is totally dependent upon input from the quality system and provides, in turn, feedback to the other system that provides information necessary for work system adjustments— through quality planning—and for reporting of general health conditions. The automation of input to the records system and the automation of the other satellite elements can then be effected as resources allow.

Examination of the data flow to and from quality records reveals that this element receives both "what's happening" and "what was supposed to happen" data. It receives performance-to-plan information that provides a necessary measure against a baseline, information of vendor quality requirements and in-house work instructions, vendor inspection performance, processes and fabrication control data, and inspection and test information. It provides corrective action feedback to quality planning and quality reports for in-house and vendor ratings.

A Proper Mix

This interplay of elements mixes automated and manual systems. Where practical, systems that can be operated manually should be handled that way.

Measuring equipment, test equipment and tool control systems lend themselves to automation. Non-conforming material control can be automated if the input to the quality record element is automated. The idea is to get a data element on a computer file once and then use it wherever necessary.

The next undertaking is the system design. The only new factor that may be involved is the use of somewhat unfamiliar computing or teleprocessing equipment. I suggest that maximum use be made of EDP professionals. The quality analyst's job is quality control; the EDP man's area is data processing.

A conversational knowledge of EDP equipment and processing by the quality analyst is certainly a plus in his favor, but a little knowledge can be a great danger. This axiom, however, is reversible in that a little knowledge of quality control can be dangerous in the hands of the data processing specialist.

Data processing problems, while naturally a constraint on system design, should not be the sole guiding factor in that design. A computer is a tool, one of many available, that can be used to serve management; it must never be permitted to dictate system requirements. It must be used to handle detail dictated by the system.

Let us recapitulate here:

1 *In order to effectively manage today's complex business in its dynamic market environment, timely information with requisite accuracy must be developed for management at various levels so that it may be employed efficiently in the decision-making process.*

2. *Quality control, as a functional department and as a function, requires an information system to provide it with: production management information dealing with its operation; quality reports dealing with its operation; and quality reports dealing with its own and other departments' effectiveness.*

3. *Development of an MIS requires a thorough understanding of departmental objectives.*

4. *Development of an MIS requires management backing.*

5. *Development of an MIS requires thorough and accurate planning.*

6. *An MIS must be made a part of quality control, not just added to it.*

7. *An MIS must be made to serve its users.*

8. *A computer is a tool that may be used to handle the detail required by the system. It must be kept in its proper perspective.*

I would like to end with a quote used by our late President John F. Kennedy, who told of French Marshal Lyautey's request to his gardener to plant a tree. The gardener objected that the tree was slow growing and would not reach maturity for a hundred years. The Marshal replied, "In that case, there is no time to lose, plant it this afternoon."

26

14 Rules for Building an MIS

Joel N. Axelrod

Reprinted by permission of
Journal of Advertising Research, June 1970.

The Peter Principle holds that a manager rises to the level of his own incompetence. A corollary, Axelrod's Axiom, is that a writer writes to the level of his own ignorance. While I have helped to design one specific type of marketing information system, here I reveal my ignorance on information systems in general. Two issues ago, Malcolm McNiven covered aspects of this topic, notably those dealing with current technological hardware that marketing managers can use.

My plan of exposition is to answer the following questions: What is a marketing information system? What are the different types of MIS? What makes marketing information systems feasible? Why do we need them? How should we design and operate an MIS? How do today's marketers use MIS? What major problems must one overcome to get them used?

My favorite definition of a marketing information system comes from a 1968 *Journal of Marketing* article by Brian and Stafford:

> A structured interacting complex of persons, machines, and procedures designed to generate an orderly flow of pertinent information collected from both intra and extra firm sources for use as the basis for decision making in specified responsibility areas of marketing management.

Note that their definition begins with *people.* Too often we fail to consider the user, the decision maker, or the manager as part of the system. But they are a vital part of any information system—with all their anxieties, concerns, willingness (or lack of willingness) to take risks, delegate authority, etc.

William Massy of Stanford University has classified MIS into three types: The first type, *The Librarian*, is simply a massive data bank. When the manager needs a certain type of information, he asks the computer to retrieve items with specified descriptor characteristics—e.g., how many gross orders were received by Branch X during the recent sales push? How many of these orders subsequently resulted in machine installations?

This class of MIS consists of procedures for collecting, checking, and filing information in a computer; procedures for organizing information for retrieval, procedures for processing retrieval requests, and procedures for calculating summary statistics from the raw data and preparing report formats and displays. Although very crude, this type of information system per se can be extremely valuable to the marketing manager. It provides basic feedback on what is happening in the real world.

The second type, *The Predictor*, enables the manager to ask "what if" type questions—e.g., what would happen if I raised the minimum price on machine X? What would happen if I increased the compensation for a machine Y installation? This type of MIS is based on mathematical relationships and correlations.

The third class, *The Searcher*, helps a manager identify the optimum solution. It is a normative system; it tells him what he *should* do. Some of the advertising media selection models fall under this heading. In my opinion, such optimization models are blind alleys. It may be possible to optimize distribution routes and warehousing, but optimization of marketing allocations requires a lot more information and understanding of the relationship than we are likely to be able to provide in the near future.

Among the *Predictor* type of MIS, there are three important sub-categories: deterministic, stochastic, and behavioral. A *deterministic* model, for example, tells with a given price change, how many customers would trade to the machine that gave them the lowest cost per copy for their volume, if all who were eligible did trade.

A *stochastic* model tells how many would trade to the machine with the lowest cost per copy based on their volume if the same historical relationship between those eligible to switch and those actually switching was maintained.

A *behavioral* simulation model tells the same thing more precisely—in theory, that is.

The behavioral simulation model represents in the computer several thousand decision makers in a cross-section of companies, taking into account their values, exposure to advertising, visits by salesmen, machine breakdowns, etc. In other words, it deals with a disaggregate data base. Other things being equal, we should get the most accurate prediction from this kind of model. But as with optimization models, the problems of getting valid data are such that I personally am not very sanguine about the possibilities for MIS's based on behavioral simulation.

Underlying Technology

Implicit in these descriptions has been the availability of certain technologies: high-speed electronic computers which process huge volumes of data, time-sharing capability of third generation computers, and cost effective large random access files. Without them, management could not get information on a timely basis or they had to make use of massive printed files which were expensive and cumbersome to handle.

Other relevant technologies speed communications. Satellites and telephone lines permit the transmission of data from point to point over thousands of miles. Information terminals permit us to get information into and out of machines fast enough to use it. Input terminals include point-of-sale recorders, factory shop records, optical readers, and many other devices. Output devices include television display tubes, audio answer-back, remote printers, microfilm, and others.

Why We Need MIS

The preceding technologies make marketing information systems feasible, but they do not explain why we need them. We need them because the marketing manager is in danger of being drowned in data.

Business Week reports that the executives of a Washington, D.C., retailing chain will be soon getting a daily 81-page breakdown of the previous day's sales. At Xerox Corporation, at least 40 levels of data can be brought to bear on a decision regarding a single product. This forest of undigested data is hardly the answer to a manager's prayers.

What we need are marketing information systems which reduce data to the point where it can be used by the marketing manager in reaching a decision. Yet we must not just deal in averages; the true significance may lie in the variations around the mean. Therefore it is more meaningful to say that we need MIS to reduce and compact data while keeping us sensitive to variations in the marketplace.

Moreover, we need marketing information systems to help the marketing manager plan and control the activities of his organization. We must distinguish between information systems for planning and information systems for control. The need for control systems has been much more widely recognized, primarily because it is easier to gather information on what has happened than information that tells you what is going to happen.

Most real planning has been carried on without any marketing information systems; instead, we talk about intuition and judgment. However, in my judgment MIS for planning will become increasingly important. Some feel that their use is limited to tactical planning— e.g., should we shift more media dollars into a particular geographic area to take advantage of the potential? They feel MIS are of little value for strategic planning—for example, finding out what would happen as a result of change in a brand's copy strategy. I disagree, mainly because MIS can readily tell you that the greatest leverage on revenue would come from a change in copy strategy and to what markets the copy platform should be addressed. The MIS by itself cannot identify the specific copy platform, but identifying the point of greatest leverage is a big step forward.

Following are some do's and don'ts of building and operating a marketing information system, drawn, in part, from my experience at Xerox Corporation with a project called MARS. Each marks a roadblock on which someone has tripped. By being forewarned, perhaps you can avoid the same experience.

Rule 1—Get Top Management Involved

If there is any point on which all information experts agree, it's that top management's support is vital throughout the process of setting up a marketing information system. Otherwise, top managerial needs are neglected by middle management as the system is set up. Most problems in setting up an MIS can be traced to insufficient top management involvement.

Rule 2—Set Objectives Carefully

Don't get lost in the details of implementation. There are many technical tricks, and there are many kinds of information you can meaningfully provide. Unless you have a clearly defined picture, you may wind up doing some of the trivial things before doing the essentials.

Set up a marketing information system policy group consisting of all key people who will use the MIS. These people then make the decisions about which direction the MIS work should move. For example, should an information system be developed that will enable you to allocate sales force according to potential, or should you focus on building a modeling system that will enable you to consider alternate feature trade-offs for new products?

Rule 3—Figure Out What Decisions Your MIS Will Influence

This rule is intrinsically related to Rule 2. To define objectives, know what decisions you are trying to influence.

When building an MIS, there are perhaps three different approaches to figuring out what should go in it. One is simply to ask the marketing people what information they need. Another approach is to find out what questions they had asked but for which they were unable to get answers. A third is to find out what decisions they were trying to make, and then work backwards to figure out what would be relevant to those decisions.

The first two alternatives are fraught with disaster because not many marketing men can tell what information they need. They are as likely to ask for interesting but irrelevant information as they are to request what is really critical to their decision-making process. But they can define the decisions they have to make—and that's the key to solving the problem.

Rule 4—Communicate!

We use the acronym KISS regarding presentations and reports. This stands for "Keep It Short and Simple," although, it frequently gets translated to "Keep It Simple, Stupid."

Jerome Weisner, science advisor to President Kennedy, eloquently said, "If you can't explain it in simple English, you don't understand it." There is nothing more important than creating and maintaining an understanding among top management and marketing and planning people regarding how an information system is going to help them. Don't try to explain programming or systems work, but do try to communicate what the MIS means in terms of making their performance better.

Another facet of "communicate" relates to the format of reports. Frequently when marketing reports arrive at their destination hot off the computer, the users then begin to manipulate them. They abstract, rearrange, plot, adjust, truncate, percentage, subtotal, and direct. If you find this happening, it means you are not doing your job properly. The computer should have produced it in a usable form to begin with.

Rule 5—Hire and Motivate the Right People

Among the most desirable of characteristics is an undefinable creative spark. Look for people who are not inhibited by knowing that something cannot be done or believing that it has to be done a certain way because that is the way it's always been done before. Implicit in this philosophy is bringing in people who have had little experience with programming or systems work, if they are bright and have a good knowledge of the marketplace, the manufacturing operation, development activities and/or financial analysis. Also bring in other personnel who have considerable experience with systems work but who, on the other hand, know nothing about the market. Cross-fertilization of these two groups produces some very innovative results.

Keeping a staff motivated is just as important as hiring them. With the strong demand for systems and programming people, there is constant pressure to leave for more lucrative jobs or for jobs that appear to be more challenging. One solution is to provide them with a sense of challenge by giving them an overview of the entire effort. Another is to give them meaningful projects rather than little, unrelated bits of work to do. Still another is to give them the opportunity to deal with the users. If people can see that they are having some impact rather than only working in a corner, they will be less likely to pack their bags.

Rule 6—Free MIS from Accounting Domination

Historically, business computers have been controlled by accountants, since they were initially acquired for handling accounts receivable, billing, inventory control, etc. As a result, MIS are used to fill the crevices between accounting crises each month. This can lead to a marketeer getting a report two weeks after it will do him any good or getting data which may be great for accounting purposes but totally nonsensical for marketing purposes. It's not that the accountants bear any malice toward marketing—though this may occasionally be the case. Rather, their orientation is so different that they cannot effectively serve the needs of marketing.

There seems to be only one viable solution. That is for marketing to have control of the MIS and, of necessity, of a computer. I do not necessarily suggest starting off with a computer; there may not be the workload to justify that step at first, but plan on having a computer for taking tapes from the billing and accounting systems and reorganizing them into a form usable for a marketing information system.

Rule 7—Move the Mountain One Teaspoonful at a Time

There are several reasons for not recommending a bulldozer approach to building an MIS. One is that, if you develop a big system which is not productive until it is totally finished, you could be in big trouble. You may be asked to produce results after you have spent much money but before you can make any contribution. Management may not be very understanding about this. It requires much faith on their part, and they may not be prepared to have such faith based on past history.

Still another reason relates to the gambling odds. In any MIS, the chances are fairly good that there are mistakes—in programming and/or the basic data. Perhaps in a small MIS the odds are 100 to one that there is a mistake. The larger the system, the higher the probability that there are mistakes. In fact, with a big system, there may be so many mistakes that you'll be snarled for months, meanwhile antagonizing potential customers.

The approach Xerox has taken to its simulation effort is to build a series of small MIS, each of which can be operated independently. We have designed systems so that they can be operated with estimates plugged in by the planners or with real data if they are available. Depending upon the nature of the problem, we can then select any particular modeling system, or combination of modeling systems, and run them together. For example, for some pricing analyses, we have as many as six different modeling systems involved. Other problems, however, require only a single modeling system.

Xerox has found a host of other benefits from this modular approach. For example, it avoids the all-too-common problem of running a long, complex problem for several hours only to finally discover that there was an error in the input or in one of the routines. Frequently it is possible in attacking new problems to use some existing models, thereby permitting a focus on the innovative aspects of the problem. As more is learned—and there is a constant learning process—one model can be pulled out of a system and replaced with a better one, without rewriting the entire system.

Rule 8—Run a New MIS in Parallel with Existing Procedures

This is one of the most important rules. It is critical to hedge when becoming operational. Don't shut down the existing system because there is a new MIS ready to go. Regardless of how good debugging procedures are, when a system is working with live data, there are frequently unanticipated flaws. If there is no parallel system, you're in deep trouble. In the short run, this may be somewhat more expensive than a complete switchover; but in the long run, it will save a considerable amount of money as well as embarrassment.

Rule 9—Earn Your Way Instantly If Not Sooner

Provide results very quickly after you are funded. Start with a very simple information system, then get more complex. Perhaps this is another way of stating a previous rule—Move the Mountain One Teaspoonful at a Time—but the focus is somewhat different.

As it relates to work in which I have been involved, we started by building deterministic models because we could do so quickly. Subsequently, we developed probabilistic or stochastic models to do a better job of solving the same problems while operating the simple models. Ultimately, while operating the stochastic models, we may even build true behavioral simulations, though I am skeptical about the fruitfulness of investing much time and effort in this direction.

The main point is that we were able to provide some results very quickly, thereby showing management that they were getting something for the money they had invested. If we had asked them to wait for a considerable length of time, while money was being spent in large quantities, I think the project would have been cut off.

Rule 10—Provide Fast Turn-Around Time

In any good MIS, fast turn-around time is critical to success. For example, in simulation efforts, most models are designed to operate from a remote terminal in no longer than three-minute bursts. To do this, start by placing large data bases in the computer. Then design the system so that only the key data is printed out in the proper format. Thus, it can be sent to customers immediately without any typing, drawing, or other work.

Another dimension of fast turn-around is that only a few inputs are required from users. This relates to people being part of a marketing information system; this is particularly true of "what if" type models. Preliminary new product analyses, for example, required that the planner tell us the estimated manufacturing cost, the pricing plan he would like to use, the time at which the machine will be introduced, the estimated number of units, and a few other assumptions; the model is able to give a preliminary estimate of all ROI and ROS within minutes. This is possible because of the large data base and because of willingness to trade precision for the ability to test numerous alternatives within a brief time-span.

Rule 11—Tie Your MIS to Existing Procedures

One of the shortest roads to disaster is to try to change the data collection procedure so it will fit your MIS. Changing the way to enter data in an organization is a massive endeavor, and often it can take many years and affect customers and salesmen alike. As a result, you will not be able to be productive before management patience wears out. This is not to say one should not have a long-range plan for producing changes. But build on what already exists. The main concern should be to clean up the quality of the data that is gathered via existing procedures. We have found that feedback from the field can be enormously helpful in this regard. For example, when we print out lists of customers and send them to salesmen, they correct names, addresses, SIC categories, etc.

Company records provide an invaluable source of data for models, although considerable effort is required to synthesize and organize the data. We have tapped the billing system for data on how customers use our machines, the type of SIC in which our units are placed, order rates, installation rates, cancellation rates, service statistics, etc. These are enormously useful in forecasting and analyzing the behavior of present equipment and markets in the planning process.

Rule 12—Watch the Balance between Development and Operational Work

The MIS needs of tomorrow are going to be different from the needs of today. This means that you have to provide a group to operate an MIS system that serves current needs while, concurrently, you have another group that is busy designing the MIS for the future.

One great danger is the great temptation to focus on the current operational system and to neglect the development work. In the short run, of course, this strategy pays off handsomely, but in the long run you will be doing your company a disservice.

One critical problem is manpower. The kind of people who are good at development work often get bored with the operational aspects. They want to move on to new and more challenging problems. Therefore, if you try to force them into an operational mode, they may well go elsewhere.

Rule 13—Avoid GIGO

GIGO stands for Garbage In—Garbage Out. It is a basic fact of computer life that, regardless of how much one processes garbage, it is still garbage. Be sure to feed valid, meaningful data into your system. Build checks in, both manual and computer, to reject ludicrous data. Don't collect data just because it looks like it might be interesting. Maintaining and updating large data bases are expensive and, if there is much nonsense for which you have no use, this merely adds to the cost. Keep the data in a highly disaggregated form. Once you start to condense data before you put it into the system, there can be trouble; the flexibility in output is highly limited. But if you have highly disaggregated data in your system, it can be combined into almost any form on the output side.

Rule 14–Design a Security System

Many MIS ... work with a series of remote terminals. In order to be of maximum value, they contain some highly confidential information. Therefore, be careful that the wrong people do not get their hands on the data. You can do this via the use of security codes. This involves putting in a code number on the beginning of a tape. Unless one knows what that code is when he puts it on the tape drive, it will not operate. Only people who need to know the information on a particular tape should have the code number.

Not only does a security code prevent the wrong people from having access to the data, it also prevents people from accidentally or otherwise putting in changes. Some rather unfortunate experiences can happen when people add bits of data without telling.

This summarizes some basic rules to keep in mind if you attempt to build a marketing information system, regardless of type.

George Santayana once said, "Those who cannot remember the past are condemned to repeat it." If you could review these guidelines every few days as you went about the process of building an MIS, perhaps you might avoid some major catastrophes.

When talking about building and maintaining a marketing information system, one should also look at the ways marketing men will use an MIS, what some of the problems will be, and the implications for management structure.

Massy pointed out that there are two ways in which a marketing information system can be used. The first involves the marketing man delegating some authority to the computer for making decisions with the expectation that the system's output will be acceptable. In doing so, the marketing manager does not abdicate his managerial responsibility; he is simply assigning certain decision-making functions to the computer just as he might to a subordinate. He monitors decisions to the same degree he monitors the decisions of a trusted employee.

The second kind of implementation can occur in situations where the manager is unwilling to delegate any real authority. In this case, the computer might be viewed as a foil for the manager's thought process. He asks the model for opinions—just as he might do with members of his staff.

The difference between the two viewpoints lies in the manager's expectations and his focus of attention. In the first case, he expects to believe and act on the information predictions or recommendations provided by the computer without focusing much attention on the matter. In the second, he expects to question the computer's results as a part of the process by which he will arrive at his own subjective conclusions.

How Much Risk

What determines whether an MIS will be granted authority or used as a thought-provoking device? Here Massy pointed out that an analogy to delegation of authority to subordinates is helpful for exploring the relationship between managers and models. The manager has the responsibility. When given a choice, he will delegate authority if and when he believes that the delegates can perform the function better, faster, or more economically—and with the risk of error that is within reasonable bounds.

The decision as to how much risk is involved in using a computer is, of course, a highly subjective one. In a sense, it depends upon the marketing man's past experience with the model builders and with the computers. If his past experience has been favorable, he probably would be willing to delegate more authority to the computer. If he has had bad experience or little experience with the computer, he is probably more likely to use it, if at all, as a foil for his judgment.

This subject of risk is a major topic unto itself. It should be briefly mentioned, however, that it is very important in building modeling systems to take into account any experiences marketing men have had with MIS in the past. Even though it may be very logical to place great reliance on super-systems, keep in mind the fact that the marketing manager wants to minimize his risks. Therefore, he is not going to eagerly grasp the great tools at his disposal.

There is one final point concerning risk. Assuming that information sources are good and that appropriate skills have been well applied, the largest potential return will be from information systems whose results are "surprising" in the sense of being different from current decision-making practices. But surprise is the equivalent of risk as managers compare demonstrated results with their own conceptions of the process in question. Thus, this leads to the conclusion that an MIS should be surprising, but not too surprising. There will always be conflict between what we call "quality" and what managers call "believability." Surprises may be right, but they may have very low credibility. As Artemis Ward commented, "It ain't what you don't know that hurts you, it's what you know that ain't so."

Getting MIS used involves some mechanical considerations, too, as well as balancing risk versus credibility. There are some people who say that top executives in business are used to communicating verbally: They talk to people in person or by telephone or ask their secretaries to look up things. But will they use a key-driven device? Will they use something like a Touch-Tone telephone for inputting to the computer?

Some say that it will be necessary for an executive to talk to an expert who will then deal with the computer. Perhaps when the information is out of the computer, the expert will direct it into the executive's office on some sort of cathode ray tube.

Others—myself included—believe that the marketing manager will be willing to use a typewriter-like device or a Touch-Tone telephone to talk to the computer. This seems feasible if the executive can use a fairly normal English vocabulary as a means of addressing the computer. Systems are now in operation where the user simply types a question in English and the computer spews forth the right answer.

I believe that, in the near future, we will see the growth of "war rooms" or strategy rooms in businesses. Key managers will sit around a large display screen, and "what if" type questions will be put to the computer in conversational English. The answer will be displayed on the screen prior to deciding on the next question. After discussion and iterations, the team will arrive at a decision. Of course, it need not be a team, it can simply be an individual.

I think this development will have fundamental implications for management structure, including far more centralization of management planning and control. There will be no need to delegate decisions to less experienced, lower-level personnel because of time pressures and lack of relevant data. The key facts will be in the computer ready to be brought to bear on a decision in an organized fashion.

As a result, the organization will consist of three distinct groups. The first will be the key decision-makers who use the MIS. The second will be the technicians who design and operate the MIS and are responsible for the data inputs. The third group will be those who implement the decisions made by management.

A dilemma is the question of how subsequent generations of decision-makers are to be trained. There will be fewer opportunities for making the small decisions and mistakes that lower- and middle-management now make in preparation for becoming top decision-makers. Staff personnel involved in developing and operating the models will understand the process, but more than understanding is required; to be an effective top-management decision-maker requires courage, audacity, and leadership.

Perhaps there will be something analogous to the amphitheater in which the students watch the master surgeon. The middle- and lower-level managers will watch the top decision-makers go through the process of reaching a decision. Or perhaps they will have sub-unit strategy rooms in which they can experiment with the system and make recommendations to management. Management can then verify these in their own war room. I'm not sure which, if any, of these approaches will become dominant. But I am sure that, as a result of the advance of marketing information systems, the structure of American business is going to undergo some profound changes.

References

Atwater, H. B., Jr. Integrating Marketing and Other Information Systems. Speech to 15th Annual Marketing Conference, National Industrial Conference Board, October, 1967.

Brien, Richard and James Stafford. Marketing Information Systems: A New Dimension for Marketing Research. *Journal of Marketing*, vol. 32, no. 3, July 1968, pp. 19–23.

Clark, William. What Marketing Information Systems Are Made Of. Speech to Cleveland Chapter, American Marketing Association, February, 1969.

Kearns, David T. The State of the Art in Systems Development. Speech to 15th Annual Marketing Conference, National Industrial Conference Board, October, 1967.

Massy, William. Information and the Marketing Manager: A Systems Analysis. Speech to 9th Annual Paul D. Converse Awards Symposium, University of Illinois, April, 1967.

Peter, Laurance and Raymond Hull. *The Peter Principle*. New York: William Morrow and Company, 1969.

Reinhart, Andrew J. Marketing Information: The Systems Approach. Speech to 15th Annual Marketing Conference, National Industrial Conference Board, October, 1967.

Smith, Robert E. Practical Pointers in Building an Information System. Speech to 15th Annual Marketing Conference, National Industrial Conference Board, October, 1967.

Zannetos, Zenon. Toward Intelligent Management Information Systems. *Industrial Management Review*, vol. 9, no. 3, Spring 1968, pp. 21–38.

27

Capturing the Development Costs of an Integrated MIS

Dr. Noble S. Deckard
Reprinted by permission of *Journal of
Systems Management*, January 1970.

The concept of an integrated management information system is that of developing an information system that is usable by all management of the organization. To accomplish this, the system must do two things. First, the system must be such that all data related to organizational operations are gathered. This has been referred to as a common *data base or data banks.* A data base is where elements or data bits are introduced to a common storage medium to form the foundation for all information provided to management. Second, the system must provide for data to become information through combining, constructing, and organizing in such a way that a message, which is relevant to the situation or problem, is communicated. A management information system then provides management with information that is useful to them in performing their activities.[1]

The accomplishment of these two factors is the goal of an integrated management information system.[2] Crucial to its develop-

[1] In general management information systems (MIS) have been thought of as only providing control information but certainly planning information can and should be a part. See "Management Information Systems: A Critical Appraisal", R. V. Head, *Datamation*, May, 1967, pp. 22–27.

[2] An excellent detailed discussion of these two goals may be found in *Information Economics and Management Systems*, by Adrian M. McDonough, McGraw-Hill, 1963, Chapter 5.

ment is the building of the data base, but this means that instead of limited data being gathered for a particular departmental system such as inventory control, the data are something the system analysts must analyze in light of the total organization. This analysis may be costly and time-consuming, yet when the data base is developed the combining, structuring and organizing of data into information are much easier. Also, use of the data in several areas and hierarchial levels means that the benefits increase. However, the project manager must begin to gather and control the cost information needed to evaluate the integrated management information system. How will he do this? Here is an analysis of the classes of costs he will have.

Cost Classification

The integrated management information system project will encompass the total management information needs. The project is a long-term undertaking and therefore the accumulation of costs during the actual development is important.

The primary consideration for classifying the project costs is the major systems area in which the costs are being incurred. The systems identification is the type that Dearden calls "vertical systems".[3] Dearden distinguishes the major systems of an integrated management information system into three major classifications. These are "financial information", "personnel data" and "logistic information."

In addition to the systems classification, there are steps or phases of activities that must be performed to develop fully the particular system. These steps become a convenient and meaningful method for cost classification within the major systems. This is especially true when the project is a long-term effort and, hopefully, the developments will be transferred to all levels of management.

There are four major steps of effort that can be distinguished in accomplishing each system:

Step I: Organization Functional Review and System Identification

This involves interviewing organizational members, reviewing their functional responsibilities, and identifying information needs and the timing requirements of those needs. Identification of how

[3] J. Dearden, "How to Organize Information Systems", *Harvard Business Review*, March–April, 1965, pp. 65–73.

the information needs are presently being provided and how the information flows into and out of the particular organization is also accomplished. Another activity is reviewing the standardization or uniqueness of the information formats. Broadly, the activities in this step are performed to build an organizational synopsis including functions and information needs.

The main category of costs in this step is that of manpower. This includes both the manpower in the task group and the organization people being interviewed.

Step II: Systems Analysis and Synthesis

Activities in this step are those of identifying the systems structure and organization. Analysis of the findings in Step I is made to determine how to best fill the using organization's information needs. Synthesis of the individual organization's information needs is made to provide the basis for designing and developing the system that will furnish from the one data base source the several organizational information needs. These activities form the major foundation of building an integrated management information system. Generally, these activities utilize the expertise of the systems analysts and the organizational specialists to develop the systems network.

Again, the principal category of costs in this step is manpower. As in Step I, there would be manpower expenditures by both the task group and the organization people. There is also a possibility of some expenditures for computer time which may be used to do some preliminary testing of tentative systems programs.

Step III: Systems Development

Activities in this step relate to the detailed analysis and development of systems' files, report formats, programming, and training of the user management. Here there will be a more explicit identification of the various systems that make up the integrated management system. The breakdown into subsystems may also be under development at the same time, and therefore many activities may be occurring concurrently, so the need to identify which subsystem is being worked on is most important.

The cost data in this step will fall into several categories. There will be analyst and programmer time, also computer time for testing and developing the system programs. An additional area of cost data is the training of using organization personnel. This category includes both the project personnel's time and the time of the using organization's personnel. This is an important activity if the full and efficient use of the systems potential is to be achieved.

Step IV: Systems Implementation

This step keeps the system operating and growing. Again in this step the identification of activities may be by various subsystems or several major systems making up the integrated management information system. The using organization's personnel and the data input organization's personnel will do the most. In addition there will be the data processing organization's personnel and the computer time to process the data.

The major cost category in this step will be the computer time and related processing activities. There will be some effort by the personnel supplying input data and those analyzing and reviewing the output reports.

These major Steps are similar to Dearden's "stages of development" in his "horizontal classification".[4] But even more generally, the steps identified are similar to those that are used in the scientific method, problem solving, or decision-making process.[5]

One other process that has been described is the "creative process". The identified phases in this process are as follow:

1. Orientation: Stating the problem
2. Preparation: Gathering pertinent data
3. Analysis: Breaking down the relevant material
4. Hypothesis: Finding alternatives by way of ideas
5. Incubation: Letting up, to invite illumination
6. Synthesis: Assembling the pieces
7. Verification: Judging the resultant ideas[6]

---

[4] Op. cit. Dearden identifies three phases which he calls "stages" and considers these to be "horizontal classifications", i.e., activities that are performed on any system. They are, "System Specification," "Data-Processing Implementation," and "Programming."

[5] A discussion of the problem-solving process may be found in: H. A. Johnson, F. E. Kast, and J. E. Rosensweig, *The Theory and Management of Systems* (New York: McGraw-Hill, 1963), pp. 121–215. The authors also reference several others who have written on problem-solving and decision-making such as: John Dewey, Herbert Simon, and Stuart Chase.

[6] Ibid. These authors cite Alex F. Osborn, *Applied Imagination* (New York: Charles Scribner's Sons, 1953), p. 115.

These seven phases can be compared to the four major steps that are identified in our management information system development as follows:

1. Orientation

          Step I: *"Organization functional*

2. Preparation   *reviews and system*

                      identification"

3. Analysis

          Step II: *"Systems analysis and*

4. Hypothesis   *synthesis"*

5. Incubation

          Step III: *"Systems development"*

6. Synthesis

7. Verification   *Step IV:*   *"Systems implementation"*

The objective in trying to establish the various classifications is to have a basis for comparing costs with benefits.[7]

Cost Reporting

Two major objectives of the cost reporting procedures are the identification of the various costs by the Steps of Effort for historical purposes, and the identification of the types of costs within each of the systems, i.e., the costs for analysts, programmers, computer time, keypunching, and data preparation. The gathering of information on the types of costs provides data for the administration of the project.

The method used to identify the costs relating to the project is that of establishing reporting categories. A major consideration in establishing these categories is that they be relatively easy to use and not highly detailed. With this consideration, a generalized list of categories is established as follows:

1. Organizational requirements analysis
2. System development and design
3. Equipment specifications

---

[7] An article by V. La Bolle, "Development of Aids for Managers of Computer Programming," *The Journal of Industrial Engineering,* Nov., 1966, pp. 564–571, gives an excellent summary of some research being done in trying to forecast computer programming costs.

4. *Systems programming and testing*
5. *Systems documentation*
6. *Training of organization personnel*
7. *Input data preparation*
8. *System maintenance*

This list is general enough that it could be used for any subsystem or system that is identified, and the categories can be classified into the identified steps. For example, the first category fits the activities of Step I, categories two and three fit Step II, categories four, five, and six fit Step III, and categories seven and eight fit into Step IV.

Initially, the coding procedure is primarily used for administrative purposes; however, the data provide a part of the historical information which is one of the objectives of cost data collection. The difficulties of determining costs in management information systems are (1) the time from start of the project to functional operation is long (several years) and (2) the total impact on the organization and thus the magnitude requires that it be accomplished by a subsystem, time phased, approach to the total MIS.

The cost classification categories and cost reporting categories, given above, provide the basis for two project management reports which serve as administrative tools for reviewing current project cost and gathering cost information for future cost-benefits comparisons. The first report, entitled Monthly Expenditure Report, shows the dollar amount expended for a month, detailed by the two cost categories (see [Figure 1]). This report is a straightforward presentation of the total dollar amount expended on the overall project

Date _____			Total $ _____	
Cost Categories	System Analysts	Programmers	Computer Time	Admin. Services
Organizational requirements analysis				
System development and design				
Equipment specifications				
Systems programming and testing				
Systems documentation				
Training or organization personnel				
Input data preparation				
System maintenance				
Monthly total				
Total to date				

Figure 1. Monthly expenditure report.

defined by the classes. Totals for the MIS project can be shown by using this matrix presentation. The second report is one that consolidates the dollar expenditures by the various major subsystems. This report, Subsystem Expenditure Report (see [Figure 2]), would be compiled for each major subsystem to provide cost information as the subsystem develops through the major phases.

These two general reports can provide management the administrative tools for both project management and top management to evaluate current accomplishments and costs. The cost information and detailed data from which it is generated are the beginning of historical cost information that may be used in comparing costs with benefits from the MIS installation.

Date _____

Expenditure Areas	STEPS				
	I Organization Review	II Systems Analysis	III Systems Development	IV Systems Implementation	Total
System analysts					
Programmers					
Computer time					
Administrative services					
Monthly total					
Total to date					

Figure 2.   Subsystem expenditure report (major subsystem).

Conclusion

Before attempting any change in management techniques or tools, serious consideration must be given by management in relating the costs of the change to the benefits from that change. This comparison usually becomes exceedingly difficult even for the simplest of changes. Questions of how to allocate the costs of those activities and material elements affected by the change require skillful analysis to arrive at even the minimum of accuracy. The picture is usually further clouded by the difficulty to collect even a portion of the extra costs to develop the change.

Management information systems development and implementation are one of the more difficult and complex areas to evaluate real costs. Without a good program of cost data collection and reporting, it is easy to become disenchanted and highly criticized as initial costs mount and the system appears to be more costly than it warrants. With the many cost areas that go into developing an integrated management information system, to collect even the obvious costs requires a well defined system; just as establishing the management information system requires systematic planning, coordinating, and implementation.

28

Twelve Areas to Investigate for Better MIS

Robert W. Holmes

Reprinted by permission of
Financial Executive, July 1970.

Computer systems directed to management planning and assistance in making decisions for most companies are still a myth. Executives failing to exploit the computer are facing a grim future, and they are well-advised to investigate in depth the reasons for their failure with the computer and to profit from the successes of others.

Impressive MIS achievements of many large companies have received wide exposure and publicity, and they should serve as models of what can be accomplished through the computer. For each instance of noteworthy achievement, however, there has been a multitude of unsatisfactory results, ranging from minor dissatisfaction to serious lack of progress and, finally, to complete failure.

Management generally has not come to associate high profit return directly with strong information capability. (By "information," I refer to all computer output after its conversion from raw data input by computer processing.) The definition of MIS put forth by the Management Information Systems Committee of the Financial Executives Institute makes clear the relationship between the two. The definition is, in part, as follows:

> MIS is a system designed to provide selected decision-oriented information needed by management to plan, control, and evaluate the activities of the corporation. It is designed within a framework that emphasizes profit plan-

ning, performance planning, and control at all levels. It contemplates the ultimate integration of required business information subsystems, both financial and non-financial, within the company.

A successful management information system must consider the current and future management information needs of the administrative, financial, marketing, production, operating, and research functions. It will have the capacity to provide environmental (competitive, regulatory) information required for evaluating corporate objectives, long-range planning (strategy), and short-range planning (tactics).

The development of MIS within a company is a continuous process, phase by phase, all blending together, with additions made as required to meet the needs of management.

By and large, senior management has been unable to come to grips with the organization and operation of its information processing function. Well-defined objectives of the function are almost nonexistent. Major applications have been hurriedly computerized, piecemeal, without over-all plans, without concern for management's needs, and without updating basic systems.

Current writings reveal the strong trend toward turning over data processing activities completely to outside service organizations for facilities management. Large and small companies alike are using this escape hatch. The complexities of the computer itself, high costs with poor return on investment, shortage of qualified technicians, and problems which seem to defy solution are exhausting a disproportionate amount of top management's time and patience.

Passing off the facilities management or operational problems, however, attacks only the portion of the iceberg above water. Management is still faced with a very basic problem which extends beyond systems development and operations: the organization and management of information technology for maximum competitive leverage.

The real advantages that can be gained from computers come from the operating intelligence it provides to assist management. A sensitive and quick-acting intelligence/information system can arm a company with a most formidable competitive weapon. Such a system can figure in a company's present and future strength as forcibly as the more exotic influences, like acquisitions, product research and development, new product lines, market development, and manufacturing process breakthroughs. In the present period of extraordinary high costs, management leverage through information becomes the most significant factor in insuring a maximum return on invested capital. Timely, relevant information enables management to make key decisions and to take action promptly with minimal risk. The outcome of decisions can be predicted with reasonable accuracy before they are implemented, and knowledgeable choices can be made between many alternatives.

To use outside facilities management could have the regrettable impact of allowing management to continue in its failure to exploit the computer. Management is better advised to investigate thoroughly and to deploy constructively the factors contributing to the success of a management information system. These factors, largely nontechnical, will vary with the viewpoint of the person assessing them.

Investigation of these factors will illuminate the causes of any unsatisfactory condition and, more importantly, will ascertain the proper responses leading to desired improvements. [A table ranking these factors in order of their importance follows]:

Twelve Areas to Investigate for Better MIS

1. Top management's involvement with the system
2. Management's ability to organize the MIS function
3. The use of a master-plan
4. The attention given to human relations between functions involved
5. Management's ability to identify its information needs
6. Management's ability to apply judgment to information
7. The condition of basic accounting, cost, and control systems
8. The degree of confidence generated by accuracy at the input level
9. The frequency of irrelevant or outdated data provided
10. The competence of systems technicians and their grasp of management problems
11. The justification for projects undertaken
12. Reliance on equipment vendors

Top Management's Involvement with the System

Computer failures have caused disillusionment and management withdrawal at times when greater management involvement is needed. Some managers even consider the computer an encroachment on and a threat to their traditional decision-making rights. Perhaps they feel this way because the presence of decision-oriented information—specific facts and figures—can force management to take action in distasteful situations which they are otherwise able to ignore. General knowledge does not trigger action, but facts and figures cannot continually be ignored.

Management's abdication has been interpreted by technicians as a complete delegation to them of the active direction of computer systems concepts, applications, and, more importantly, of implementation. This unfortunate delegation of great responsibility to technicians usually does not correspond with their skills in human relations. In fact, the technicians have tended to hammer their systems creations through, sometimes against all odds. As a result, almost all implementation problems or failures are traceable to the human element.

It is interesting to note some of the impressions of top management held by persons down the line involved with systems creation, design, and implementation.

Management has not made itself aware of the computer's capacity for developing relevant information directed toward problem solving.

Management normally cannot define problem areas clearly, yet it quaintly regards the computer as a challenge to its decision-making prerogative.

Management does not understand the absolute necessity of securing accurate input data to insure the success of a system, and the difficulties in accomplishing this.

Management does not understand or appreciate the time span required to implement a system properly.

It is clear that management must come to realize much more fully the competitive significance of information systems and that, with the proper approaches, eminently successful systems can be developed. Further, management must gain a much broader knowledge of computer systems, possible applications, and implementation problems than it now possesses. With this knowledge, it can confidently demand specific information that is relevant, fresh, accurate, and obtainable.

Management should not feel incapable of understanding computers nor should it fear that computer technology challenges its decision-making rights. The computer is a valuable aid and can remove much of the guesswork and risk. The over-all decision-making function, however, remains the province of management.

Finally, it is absolutely certain that any softening in interest, involvement, or support demonstrated by top management will flow freely down through all segments of the organization and present a major handicap to the success of any information system.

Members of senior management have felt that they should not try to grapple with the technical mysteries and complexities of computer systems. Computer technicians, to a large extent, have added to the confusion by failing to assist those outside technical circles in understanding the capabilities and limitations of the computer, thereby making what is a relatively simple problem unnecessarily complex.

Management's Ability to Organize the MIS Function

Limited understanding of information systems coupled with the dynamic nature of systems have made it difficult for management to deal with policy formulation, organization, and control of this critical resource. The sum presents a continuing, nagging, and major problem for senior management.

Management is groping for answers to such questions as what skills, qualifications, and background should the head of information systems possess? Where should information systems report in the top organization? How much in the way of resources should be devoted to the function? Who should participate heavily in the planning and development of objectives? How should the function be staffed?

Another element often contributing to the problem is the incumbent head of the established information system who continually strives to convince his management that his policies, objectives, and qualifications are the best obtainable and should not be challenged. Management, in not resisting this kind of persuasion, allows the old and largely ineffectual methods to linger on.

The cornerstone of effective MIS organization and performance is the link between senior management and the personnel which form the technical staff. The individual serving as this link must have special qualifications. He must have a heavy background in upper management practices and good knowledge of computer systems and operations, and he must enjoy the confidence and cooperation of both the senior management group and the technical staff. Such qualifications are exceedingly rare, a fact which may help to explain why this position has undergone more failures in recent years than any other key management position. A common mistake has been to assign a person with only a systems background to a managerial position. In other instances, the position has been filled at a time of crisis by someone in the company not remotely qualified.

There are no hard and fast rules for guidance in setting organizational relationships. The function can report to the chief financial officer, to an "independent" executive, such as the head of administration, or directly to the president. Experience has shown that all can work successfully. The key, again, is the ability of the MIS head to gain the confidence and cooperation of senior management as a group. Likewise, the matter of centralization is dependent upon company organization, concepts of profit responsibility, and degree of commonality of the segments of the business.

The Use of a Master Plan

Setting over-all company objectives and planning to meet those objectives still leaves much to be desired in most companies. The real orphan within such imperfect planning is the information gathering system. Management's abdication of MIS leadership has required the system's technical staff to proceed with applications of its own selection. The more simple, low-risk applications have, therefore, tended to be selected on a piecemeal basis. Management information needs have been largely ignored. The result has been the failure to tap MIS' full potential.

Planning for information systems by involving management, other users of the service, technicians, and related clerical staff can save an enormous amount of backtracking, opposition, time, and expense. The full economic impact of charging ahead without planning can never be completely quantified. The costs of applications never completed, of other lost opportunities and poor decisions, however, are often painfully real. The more subtle effects of poor planning, on the other hand, usually lie hidden and manifest themselves only in general dissatisfaction and lack of steady progress.

Planning must start by setting long-term company objectives followed with a detailed profit plan. Information needs within the plan must then be determined and provided for in the creation of the data bank. All separate subsystems should be coordinated into one integrated system. Planning should cover the gathering, transmission, and dissemination of data as well as its processing. Never should individual major applications be started without a complete integrated plan. Above all, the matters of systems concepts, goals, and long-range planning must not be left to the discretion of the technical staff, but assumed entirely by top management.

Individual project planning should assign responsibilities, time schedules, and a means for project progress reviews and project monitoring.

The Attention Given to Human Relations between Functions Involved

People problems in information systems cause disappointments and failures to a much greater extent than do technical problems. The lack of participation by users of the service or by related clerical staffs can result in a deficiency of interest which alone can cause the system to fail. Forcing service upon users that they neither ordered nor helped to conceive may cause the system to die. Clerical personnel, who must make the system work, will not be predisposed toward cooperation if they are brought aboard only in the final implementation stage. Sloppy input, arising out of clerical indifference, leads to erroneous information that can destroy all confidence in the system.

The success of any information system is dependent largely upon the effective use of behavorial sciences *well in advance* of the application of systems techniques. It must be realized that an effective system is composed of a preponderance of nontechnical factors—concepts, attitudes, acceptance, and enthusiasm.

How can human relations techniques be better applied to modern information systems with success? What are the approaches which should be taken to assure success? These requisites can be categorized as follows:

All functional management as well as information systems management serve on the planning and review committee

Active participation by all users of the service

Clear support of technical staff by management

Involvement of related clerical persons in all planning and implementation as it affects them

The following are comments applicable to each of these requisites.

Planning and Review Committee

In order to achieve its maximum benefit, an information system must fulfill the needs of all company functions. In fact, to ignore certain functions is to risk aborting the effort of the entire system. A good human relations approach must be premised on a clear delineation of the technicians' role: that they should serve operating management; they are the specialists to whom management looks for technical tools. But their technical expertise must be tempered with consideration, humbleness, and patience. A group of systems managers and functional managers working together in harmony can accomplish amazing results. Comprehensive forward planning and a united implementation effort will insure a high rate of success.

The committee preferably should consist of the head of each function which reports to the chief executive or another high-level executive with decision-making authority. Information systems representation should consist of the MIS head and project managers. The committee should meet regularly, reshaping ultimate goals, assigning new major applications, and reviewing progress on existing applications. Priorities should be changed where beneficial.

Participation by Users of Service

After objectives and priorities for major applications are set by the planning and review committee, individual projects are set up within the context of an over-all plan. It is at this juncture—establishing individual projects—that the systems technicians and the specific users of the information must be joined in the effort. Again, if projected goals are set or a new system is originated without complete user participation, failure is practically guaranteed. In many instances, the users do not make any outstanding contribution to the formulation process. If, however, their participation has been invited, they will view the system somewhat as a creation of their own and will be more likely to support it enthusiastically.

The degree of user satisfaction is probably the most useful index of measuring the success or effectiveness of an information system. A mediocre system can be eminently successful when supported by user participation, while a model technical system, without such support, can be a dismal failure. Human relations has much greater impact here than is generally realized; it at least equals technical expertise in importance.

Support of Technical Staff

The enthusiasm and interest with which technicians approach their assignments appears almost in direct relationship to the support openly demonstrated by higher management. Management interest cannot lie on the surface; to be influential, it must be deep-rooted.

Support means involvement—active participation in both application assignments and application reviews. It means honest discussions, knowledgeable commentary, and substantial ideas. Support, above all, means commendation where appropriate.

It is virtually impossible in today's competitive market to retain the loyalty of capable computer technicians where they feel a lack of direction or interest from upper management. The choice, therefore, is to give full support or to settle for an inferior technical staff.

Involve Related Clerical Persons

This is the area in which information system delays and ultimate failures are very prevalent. In the development of a system, extensive data must be gathered and considered. Omission of any relevant, although seemingly unimportant, particulars can create the need for extensive redesign and costly delays. Complete involvement of clerical personnel gives them the opportunity to make important contributions and encourages their support of the system, thus helping to assure its successful operation. All approaches should emphasize the objective of work simplification for them.

The time of change is time for crucial added attention to human relations. Change means resistance (usually hidden) and often creates much deeper people problems than it does technical problems. Change upsets stable routines and threatens security. The benefits of change must be shared with those affected wherever practicable. When understanding, pride of accomplishment, and job satisfaction are added to the particular skills of an individual, his efforts can be astounding.

Management's Ability to Identify Its Information Needs

Management chronically deplores that it "does not have enough information to go on." This criticism, more often than not, is entirely correct. Yet management often has not identified its needs, nor has it demanded that these needs be identified by subordinate staff members. Human judgment alone must decide what questions to ask.

A logical approach to defining management's information needs is to review the adequacy of the present information received. Much of this will be excellent. Management certainly will not want any major overhaul that might jeopardize what it presently finds useful.

To determine its information needs, management must review the types of decisions it is called upon to make, the frequency of these decisions, and the specific information that might assist in securing the ultimate success of the decisions. Companies well advanced in MIS can logically use their present cost of capital as a focal point for information requirements, initially comparing this to the present return on investment rate. Relative return on assets employed can be used to evaluate segments of the business. In any case, the information flow can be directed to identify problem areas and to propose solutions. Information should give deep insight into all operating areas so that necessary action is clear and timely.

Management's Ability to Apply Judgment to Information

The span of answers that modeling techniques can develop under differing situations is infinite, but human judgment must make the final selections. Present-day practices of making such selections can be dramatized by the example of the senior executive faced with a major decision who, surrounded by stacks of computer runoffs, closes his door and flips a coin.

To a great extent, seasoned management believes that decisions, even the critical ones, must be made on pure judgment and intuition alone. Many very successful businesses have been built with this type of management. And budget-minded management members are leary of the cost to produce management-oriented information. Applications using the management sciences tend to appear exotic and are not considered to be economically sound.

Thus, the practicality of using scientific techniques, management sciences, and operations research is always a problem. Companies with basic data processing problems, including organizational problems, usually are not remotely interested in the more abstruse facilities of the computer. Management's attitudes toward the utility of simulation, risk analysis, and the relative weighting of alternatives have a strong bearing on the final successes of the scientific techniques applied. Finally, the nature of the particular business, such as the need to make frequent decisions under a multiplicity of uncertain conditions, also has a large role in determining company needs.

On the whole, company management is beginning to realize that scientific management approaches, including financial models of the company or parts of the company, are important to future success. The next few years should witness rapid growth in the use of these techniques. To exploit fully the computer and the leverage derived from information obtained by the computer, management must learn more about the computer, its power, and what it can do to serve management's information needs.

The Condition of Basic Accounting, Cost, and Control Systems

Computer-based information systems are not a solution to outmoded and deficient accounting, cost, and budgetary control systems. There is some tendency to concentrate attention on MIS and to neglect these basic systems. An alarmingly large number of companies today are using antiquated basic systems that have not changed to meet the needs of a dynamic business—systems that produce inaccurate and irrelevant data. Job costing on repetitive production is expensive to administer; often the cost fluctuations reported are not meaningful. To make matters worse, the causes for excess costs cannot be determined because the excesses simply flow in as unidentified cost and are neither isolated nor reported in accounts under a standard cost approach.

Overhead expense accounts are commonly not sufficiently particularized to be meaningful. Account codes are not clear, and considerable cost is reported erroneously. The principles of responsibility reporting are neglected many times. Losses in the work-in-process production flow are not currently reported and cannot be detected until inventory. For many companies, special price quotations are vital to obtaining business; yet their quotation cost data is deplorable.

Budgetary controls using historical data as the principal basis for evaluating new budgets can be most detrimental when grounded on inaccurate data.

Such deficiencies can make the most carefully developed MIS fail. Until basic foundation systems are effective, bad decisions continue to be made based on bad data fed through the computer at a faster rate. A major problem in correcting outmoded basic systems is, again, people. Changes here disrupt their ingrained working patterns and are most subtly resisted.

Continual review by qualified individuals is necessary to assure that the basic systems are meeting the changing needs of the business. Encouraging participation by the users of the systems and the systems specialists is again the most fruitful approach. Fresh and independent viewpoints by outside specialists are usually very helpful.

The Degree of Confidence Generated by Accuracy at the Input Level

Well-conceived and well-designed technical systems can fail miserably with poorly directed implementation. During implementation, inaccurate careless input can produce data so erroneous that the users lose all confidence in the entire system. Moreover, the memory of failure becomes so fixed that successful operations and enthusiastic support can be set back for years. The presence of the computer has created new disciplines for obtaining accurate data. Clerical errors traditionally have prevailed in abundance. The contemporary use of formal systems for handling data on a mass basis and the recent sophistication acquired by the information user have required that much greater attention be given to input.

Important involvement of the clerical personnel and a thorough testing of the system followed by adequate training—all contribute to successful implementation. Most important, going on-stream cannot be rushed, and all inaccurate output must be traced back to its source. Data isolation and correction devices are helpful in preventing bad data from causing damage or delay.

The successful operation of major applications involves substantial time, sometimes years. The high cost of development and implementation over such long periods wears management's patience thin. They demand "something from the system." If such demands are unreasonable, compliance will assure failure or set-back.

The Frequency of Irrelevant or Stale Data Provided

It is unbelievable under present-day concepts of exception reporting to find stacks of machine runoffs being delivered to senior executives. Sometimes the user finds the appropriate pages to keep, but more often all is discarded. It is not uncommon to find deliveries of the data lagging three to four weeks behind the period being reported.

In these instances, it it obvious that the system technicians are completely insensitive to the process of management, and management simply goes along for the ride. Often the unfortunate consequence of this indifference is the effort by members of management, unable to deal with the situation, to set up their own informal information systems. Such independent efforts on the part of management are not isolated cases; they are appearing with alarming frequency.

For a system to be effective, MIS managers must observe the principles of exception reporting and reporting by appropriate levels. Top management cannot accept less than this.

The Competence of Systems Technicians and Their Grasp of Management Problems

In the section covering problems of organization, the importance of the qualifications of the head of MIS was discussed. The casualty rate in MIS reaches into all levels of the technical staff. In particular, the MIS managers, including the systems project leaders and data processing supervisors, have a high turnover.

Although the most serious failings by technical personnel have been related to human relations aspects, there have also been serious technical deficiencies in much of the systems work. Such deficiencies stem largely from the absence of a clear understanding of management's desires and objectives. Systems men do not know what they are expected to accomplish, and they usually do not have a keen sensitivity to management's needs and problems.

To a lesser extent, technical deficiencies are traceable to outright incompetency. Technical qualifications are often overlooked due to the tremendous demand for skilled senior systems designers and programmers resulting from the explosive growth of computer sciences. In spite of the shortage, however, it is usually prudent to defer systems project work until fully qualified personnel can be assigned. Continuous upgrading of the staff has been necessary in most companies to pursue a solid constructive effort. Close coordination with company management has broadened the skills of technicians and has assisted them in better understanding of management. A very successful policy has been to select highly qualified accounting supervisors and train them for systems work.

The Justification for Projects Undertaken

A policy of economic justification for all major projects provides for the allocation of resources and for maximum payoff, and prevents time and cost from being expended beyond the reach of practical application. As an example, the basic data required might not be in the data base, or even worse, it might not be obtainable by any reasonable means. A clear disclosure of what a project will accomplish prevents subsequent controversies.

In charging ahead without a master plan, many companies undertake major projects without sufficient formalized justification. All major projects should be analyzed under the following criteria:

Strategy for profit return maximization and investment considerations

Planning and decision-making information for management

Improved service to customers and other company units

Improved short- and long-term processing of data and

Direct cost reduction

All assignments should be approved by the head of MIS. Major projects should be approved by an operating committee.

Projects undertaken without a sophisticated evaluation of benefits versus cost can very likely cause negative payback and abandonment soon after implementation.

Reliance on Equipment Vendors

Until recently, systems and programming support service was supplied on a limited basis by all equipment vendors. This service, being "free" under the equipment rental arrangements, has been used extensively to save on in-house staffing. Equipment companies have tended to oversell their limited services and have dampened interest in developing ambitious MIS programs. As a result of the intense competition between equipment vendors, some sales representatives have put a gloss on the capabilities of their hardware. Smaller companies are frequently the victims of such a sales pitch. Many times the false confidence inspired by sales representatives has resulted in serious delays and temporary failures. Fortunately, the hardware capability problem has become less critical now that more companies have the skills necessary to review hardware proposals with a realistic approach. Reviews excluding equipment vendors' representatives are most necessary, and full reliance for equipment selection must be placed on in-house staff.

Opportunity to Exploit the Computer is Enormous

Many of the larger, well-managed, forward-looking companies have taken advantage of modern techniques and the computer's power enabling management to plan, control, and enhance the company's future return on investment. All these companies have dealt with the factors discussed here, but they have been able to profit from past errors. Problem identification must precede problem solving.

As a business continues to grow and more blind spots appear, management tends to reach out for assistance. Positive action toward acceptance of facts, figures, and probabilities using computer systems is still a critical point and a difficult step. Realization that members of management will make the final decisions with or without MIS—but with greater chance of success with MIS—should facilitate acceptance of the new concepts.

There is enormous opportunity to profit through the exploitation of the computer's capabilities, and the degree of opportunity will intensify in the future. Although past problems and failures have generally manifested themselves as being technical in nature, very often they are not. The key to computer opportunities, optimum costs, and maximum profit leverage through information will be realized only by management involvement, solid planning, and over-all company coordination.

29

Get the Computer System You Want

Roy N. Freed

Reprinted from the November–December 1969
issue of *Harvard Business Review.* © 1969 by the President
and Fellows of Harvard College; all rights reserved.

In April 1969, a data-processing service company was ordered to pay three automotive and electrical parts-distributing customers $480,811 in damages for losses suffered from misrepresentations concerning the capabilities of an inventory system which had been used to serve the company's customers; the misrepresentations were considered tantamount to fraud.[1] That incident is fast becoming merely another example of the large lawsuits brought by unhappy customers against suppliers of computers and computer service. It shows how unwise it can be for top management to leave the purchasing and leasing of computers or data-processing services in the wrong hands. Too often these decisions are turned over to subordinate financial, procurement, and engineering personnel, who then proceed on their own without guidance.

Senior managers must exercise control over the acquisition of computer services for their companies. Bitter experience now is proving what ordinary business judgment should have indicated long ago: guidance and oversight from the very top is essential in most cases if mistakes in contracting are to be avoided and if full

[1] *Clements Auto Co. et al.* v. *Service Bureau Corp.*, 298 F. Supp. 115 (D. Minn. 1969). Decision reported in *The Wall Street Journal*, April 19, 1969.

advantage is to be taken of new approaches to securing the use of the computer.

The accelerating pace at which lawsuits are being brought by users against practically all types of suppliers of computers and computer services is fair warning that customary contracting practices have been grossly deficient and need prompt change; usually, recourse to litigation indicates inadequate contracting. The proper procurement method is relatively easy to adopt. Essentially all that is required is a genuine policy determination by top management to procure computer services in the same business-like way used to buy less complicated (and less critical) goods and services. Strange as it seems, failure to do just that is largely the root of current difficulties.

High Price of Failure

It is not necessary to recount all of the computer contracts that have gone sour and ended up in court in order to demonstrate the advisability of using proper procurement practices. Let me note only a few cases which, in addition to the introductory example, point up elements in the acqusition process that need particular attention from management:

> *A food wholesaler recovered damages of $53,200 (and a remission of rent) in 1968 from a computer manufacturer because of a breach of warranty involving faulty software supplied in connection with a leased computer system.* [2]

> *In 1964, a hardgoods distributor overturned a sales agreement in court because of a breach of warranty by a data-processing equipment manufacturer. The distributor received a refund of the purchase price for equipment delivered in 1957.* [3]

> *In 1967, a computer manufacturer was sued by a textile manufacturer for $4 million in damages for breach of contract and fraudulent representations in connection with the lease of a large computer system in 1964. An injunction was granted against the removal of the equip-*

[2] *Food Center Wholesale Grocers, Inc.* v. *International Business Machines Corp.*, U.S. District Court for District of Massachusetts (Docket No. C.A. 64-45-C). Jury verdict reported in *The Wall Street Journal*, March 27, 1968.

[3] *Sperry Rand Corp.* v. *Industrial Supply Corp.*, 337 F. 2d 363 (5th Cir. 1964).

ment until alternative arrangements could be made by the lessee. [4]

A computer manufacturer was held liable to a cement manufacturer in 1968 for failure to deliver a computer system under a contract entered into in 1961. [5] *Damage claims of about $138,700 were settled.*

Corporate buyers may get some solace from the realization that their difficulties are shared by others. Even the federal government (probably the world's largest customer for computers) and computer system manufacturers themselves have not been immune from contractual blunders such as those described. For instance:

In 1965, a computer manufacturer that failed to deliver a computer in 1957 was required to pay the federal government $235,806 (consisting of $46,300 for liqui- dated damages, $179,450 for excess reprocurement expense, and $10,056 for unnecessary preparation costs), plus interest. [6]

A manufacturer of peripheral equipment was sued by a producer of computer systems in 1967 for breach of warranty between 1965 and that year. The $145,000 damage claim was settled out of court. [7]

Undoubtedly, countless situations of the same nature either have been resolved short of litigation or could not be taken to court for some reason. Certainly my own experience has been that court cases reflect only a part of the controversies created by poor contracting.

Steps to Better Contracting

Improvements in contracting are required at this time not merely to "tighten up" procurement and avoid costly errors, but also, more

[4] *Springs Mills, Inc.* v. *General Electric Co.*, U.S. District Court for District of South Carolina (Docket No. C.A. 67-544). Suit reported in *Electronic News*, September 11 and 25, 1967, and October 3, 1967.

[5] *Lone Star Cement Corp.* v. *Royal McBee Corp.*, Supreme Court of New York, New York County, Index No. 7250, 1967.

[6] *U.S.* v. *Wegematic Corp.*, 360 F. 2d 674 (2nd Cir. 1966).

[7] *Astrodata, Inc.* v. *Bolt, Beranek & Newman*, U.S. District Court for District of California (Docket No. 67-1486 CC). Suit reported in *Electronic News*, December 25, 1967.

importantly, to enable computer users to benefit from the variety of new offerings in the marketplace today. Before most of us have learned how to lease or buy a computer system properly from a single source, we are tempted by the apparent advantages of securing central processing units, peripheral equipment, and software from different sources and making up the systems ourselves. We are also invited to leap into time-sharing systems. Instant sophistication seems to be required of computer users.

The effort to assess the economic advantages of acquiring software separately is dramatizing for some executives the serious deficiencies in their contracting practices. As they examine the hardware and software offered by their suppliers, many of them are amazed to discover that their contracts for entire systems have not stated the type or quality of the software to be furnished. For example, the lease of one major manufacturer simply assures "the use of the below listed machines" and its sale agreement refers only to the "machines . . . listed below."

Sound procurement of computer services, regardless of the nature of the transaction, involves three primary steps:

1. *Establishing basic company objectives for computer utilization.*
2. *Conducting negotiations so that the objectives will be achieved.*
3. *Writing a usable contract that really describes the transaction negotiated.*

Senior management probably can make its greatest contribution simply by steering procurement back on the right route. Management should help to choose the objectives and evaluate the procurement team's performance during and after each acquisition. To perform such evaluations effectively, executives must be thoroughly acquainted with the proper subject matter and techniques of negotiations and with the related contract drafting. The discussion that follows is intended to remind senior management of those items, not to qualify them to do the negotiating.

Objectives and Implementation

Early establishment of objectives for computer utilization is indispensable if management is to make the best possible arrangements. Computer users have a wider choice of approaches than many people realize. Bear in mind that, regardless of the form of the transaction, all that is being acquired in essence is the *use* of a computer system. The system comprises both hardware and software, rather than simply the machines making up the central processing unit and related peripheral equipment. So long as this basic fact is recognized, computer users are free to survey the entire market for the best approach to satisfy their particular needs. They should regard the different types of transactions as merely means to that end.

The present market basket includes, in addition to the traditional lease or purchase of entire computer systems, the lease or purchase of separate system components (such as central processing units; peripheral equipment; compilers, sort routines, and similar programs; application software; and maintenance) and the purchase of time sharing, batch data processing, or merely time on someone else's computer. Entire systems may be bought from special system houses as well as from the manufacturers, and some systems may be leased from third-party lessors. Moreover, with the growth of the used system market, it is possible to buy used equipment (as well as to sell it).

Each of the possible arrangements mentioned has qualities that might either promote or frustrate efforts to obtain specific company objectives such as (to mention only a few):

Smallest possible capital investment

Minimization of effects of technological obsolescence

Lowest possible net cost of computer system use

Greatest possible privacy of company records

Maximum ability to enlarge or improve the system

Maximum assurance of continued operation of the system

Protection against losses from data-processing errors

Choosing the Right Approach

In view of the multiplicity of factors that are pertinent in selecting the right approach, it is impractical to try to designate which procurement arrangements will best achieve particular objectives. However, some examples can be provided:

A company's initial capital investment can be kept down by using almost any approach other than outright purchase.

It is easier to assure privacy of company records if they remain under the company's control rather than being sent outside (as in, say, a time-sharing system).

The impact of technological obsolescence can be lessened either by using a short-term lease or by buying with a readiness to resell in the used system market.

Losses resulting from errors and omissions of employees can be avoided by buying data-processing services under a contract that imposes liability on the supplier. (Data-processing service companies can buy errors and omissions insurance that is not available to companies using computer systems for their own work.)

In view of the increasing rate of change in the marketplace, continuing thought must be given to the question of ways and means. A particular acquisition method should not be routinely repeated by a user from one transaction to the next; rather, the selection process should be performed afresh each time in the light of prevailing market offerings as well as current company objectives. For example:

Short-term leasing was the logical hedge against early obsolescence—until a market for used computers developed. In years past, leasing could be prohibitively expensive for some users. But then third-party leasing evolved. Also, manufacturers started to offer long-term leases. Likewise, third-party leasing is satisfactory only if the bundle of "support services," consisting of system design, programming, and maintenance, can be secured on economical and satisfactory terms and conditions from some source.

Despite the insistence of a supplier on its "standard" lease or sale contract form, each customer must make a strenuous effort to secure contractual provisions that protect its interests. More than ever before, it is possible to shop around if the suppliers first approached turn out to be inflexible or unreasonable.

Effective Negotiations

Computer contract negotiations (and inevitably the resulting agreements themselves) have tended to be seriously deficient in many critical respects. To illustrate:

> *Although customers almost invariably procure computer systems, not just individual machines, few if any agreements with nongovernment users have specified the software to be provided. In fact, many customers actually accept computer systems that are "blanketed in" under leases of tabulating equipment which involve no internally stored programs. (The failure to describe the software involved probably results from habits developed in using punched-card system lease forms for computers.)*

> *Contracts with nongovernment users usually do not contain specifications describing either the design or the performance of the items to be delivered or the precise nature of the services to be furnished. Software and engineering service contracts should at least specify the items they cover.*

> *Very few agreements state objective acceptance tests for determining whether delivered items are exactly what the customer was to receive.*

> *Agreements practically never include meaningful milestones for the production of systems or software, or for the commencement of sub-contracted services, so that the customer cannot spot delivery failures early enough to arrange for their correction or, as a last resort, to go to another supplier.*

But, some may ask, do not all corporate users receive basically the same treatment from supplier companies? Actually, despite apparent insistence on standard supplier forms which tend to leave little room for negotiation, suppliers do *not* treat all customers alike. Up to now, at least, many customers have secured special treatment in practice. Such treatment usually is camouflaged in a number of ways, such as by supplying greater amounts of system designing and programming without extra charge and without specifying any of it in the contract, or by giving lower prices under the guise of buying back the right of the supplier to use the system for demonstrations or information-processing work.

Of course, achieving uniform treatment for all customers in itself would be no major improvement as long as the forms used and the resulting contracts are deficient. It merely would perpetuate the basic difficulties resulting from the lack of understanding concerning what is to be delivered and what may be done in case of nonperformance.

As past cases of substantial damage awards to disgruntled customers show, deficient contracts can be harmful to suppliers as well as to computer users. Frequently, suppliers suffer in court largely because, in the absence of positive, well-considered contractual statements of what goods or services are to be delivered, customers are able to introduce into evidence the substantially less precise and occasionally somewhat exaggerated statements of salesmen attempting to make a sale. When unhappy customers seek redress from contracts that limit the supplier's warranty liability, they are charging fraudulent misrepresentation and are permitted to use salesmen's statements as proof. Clearly, *both* parties to a contract should prefer to live with specific, comprehensive provisions based upon careful negotiations and written formulation.

Makeup of the Team

Negotiations can be effective only if conducted by a properly qualified and supported team. The team should include the different types of specialists necessary to handle the complex aspects of the transaction, and all team members should be sophisticated in computer-communications technology.

More specifically, a team should include, as a minimum, a financial man, a purchasing agent, a computer system specialist, and a contracting or legal expert (just as in any other major procurement). And each specialist should be qualified to deal with the unique subject of computers. For example, the legal specialist should appreciate, at the very least, the significance of these facts:

1. *Systems, not merely machines, are involved.*
2. *Thorough program debugging is extremely difficult.*
3. *Acceptance tests should include objective criteria that readily and adequately reveal acceptability.*
4. *Computer use usually makes management substantially more dependent on the continued operation of the system than does practically any other form of mechanization.*

Lack of sophistication about computers is far more significant than many people have been willing to acknowledge. It is, in my opinion, the major cause of inadequate computer contracts. It shows up in other ways, too, as the following case illustrates:

> *In a suit involving the failure of a computer system to provide proper inventory control and correctly calculated invoices, it was alleged that the computer was not as ordered. Actually, the testimony indicated that the machine itself was entirely satisfactory. It was the programming that was deficient. Hence, the complaint properly should have charged that the delivered system, rather than the machine, failed to satisfy contractual requirements.*

Obviously, it is the negotiating team that must think of all the technical and business requirements of the user and see that they are provided for.

Key Points to Cover

What matters should be taken up in the negotiations? The talks should deal completely with the usual variety of provisions appropriate for leasing, purchasing, or other types of transactions—and agreements on these points should, of course, be recorded in the contract. As indicated earlier, computer-use contracts are plagued by omission or inadequate treatment of a number of provisions that normally are found in well-drawn documents for the acquisition of complex machinery. I shall discuss these provisions briefly, not in the expectation that senior management will do the negotiating but rather to help it make certain that the negotiating team does its work properly.

When all of the appropriate kinds of provisions are included, it is essential that the scope and content of each be developed in as much detail as the state of the art requires. In short, individual attention is extremely important. A number of characteristics of computer system use justify such attention. The technology is still very novel and has numerous qualities that differ substantially from the more traditional items of machinery acquired by companies. For example:

> *It can be extremely difficult to achieve complete accuracy in many software packages. Despite the frequent assur-*

ances of salesmen to the contrary, people simply do not have the ability to anticipate the wide range of possible circumstances that must be provided for in designing and programming many varieties of systems.

Computer systems frequently constitute a more integral part of a company's operations than do other types of machines, and the user quickly becomes completely dependent on their scheduled availability, continued functioning, and easy expandability.

The creation and adoption of computer systems can require very substantial periods of time and major financial investments. Yet, at the same time, computer technology is extremely dynamic, and its most significant qualities can change from time to time.

Accordingly, experience proves the advisability of paying close attention to the following items even though they may appear elementary:

Descriptions of all goods and services to be furnished

Specifications of those goods and services

Acceptance tests

Time of delivery

Penalties for unexcused delays and other defaults

Place of delivery

Price, including discounts

Terms of payment

Warranties

Protection against patent and copyright infringement

Limitation of the supplier's liability

Action to be performed by the customer

Options

Duration of agreement

Full lists of all potential provisions for each of the above would, of course, be too extensive to include here. I shall limit myself to making general suggestions concerning the listed provisions and to provide some general observations on the acquisition of computer use.

Adequate Specifications

All goods and services to be furnished to the customer should be stated, so that complete strangers to the transaction (including court judges) can find in the agreement exactly what is included. The deliverable items should be described well enough so that receiving clerks can prepare adequate receiving reports for all items, and accounts payable clerks can authorize proper payment for them solely on the basis of routine paperwork. This means that contract negotiators should, in addition to identifying and listing all such items, establish acceptance procedures. In the case of software, for example, it is frequently advisable to specify not only the names of the items but also such components as flow diagrams, print-outs, punched-card decks or reels of punched-paper tape, and sample inputs and outputs.

In a great many cases there should be adequate descriptions of goods and services to be furnished so that delivery of them can be determined by proper inspection procedures at a specific time and place. Such descriptions are familiar ones in procurement. They might show either how the deliverable items are composed, in which case they are called design specifications, or how the items will function, in which case they are called performance specifications. Often, either type of description is feasible, and the parties simply choose which one they want. On occasion, however, performance specifications really are preferable from the customer's standpoint, as he does not care how the item is made up so long as it produces the required results. A case in point is certain types of time-sharing services. (Suppliers, in contrast, usually prefer to work to design specifications.)

Incidentally, it should be noted that the sale of software to a customer usually constitutes the delivery of goods rather than the performance of services. Software packages are tangible items that are delivered physically. Consequently, they satisfy the definition of "goods" in the Sales Article of the Uniform Commercial Code, and contracts for their production and delivery are subject to that law. This is important because it automatically incorporates warranties into transactions and requires that certain warranty exclusions be stated prominently. Moreover, characterization as "goods" may affect the application of sales taxes and have other legal consequences, such as expanding the scope of legal liability of the software producer.

Conformance with Standards

In addition to describing the things to be delivered, negotiators should establish the means for determining whether each delivered item meets its standards before payment is due. Invariably, an inspection procedure of some sort is utilized in major business purchases of equipment. The criteria for computer system or component acceptance should be selected not only so that they will assure that the specifications are met but also so that their fulfillment can be determined objectively and unequivocally, even by an outsider. Except in very unusual cases, the exercise of judgment or discretion should not be necessary to determine acceptability.

In its Federal Supply Schedule contracts covering computers, the federal government insists on actual performance of installed systems in accordance with the manufacturer's technical specifications at effectiveness levels of at least 90% for 30 consecutive days and involving at least 100 hours of productive time. The model lease of the Council of State Governments has a similar requirement and provides for the listing in the lease of the supplier's documents containing specifications.

Preparation of specifications and acceptance test routines for special computer systems or software can be laborious, expensive, and time-consuming (even for the most highly skilled specialists). Nevertheless, these matters are critical elements and well worth considerable effort. In many proposals, their preparation is postponed until after the contract is entered into. This is done in order to avoid incurring expenses for designing a test until a contract for the system is assured. However, the eventual contracts should require that preparation of specifications be completed early enough so that the customer can escape from his obligation if acceptable test criteria cannot be agreed on promptly. When a supplier has had sufficient experience with similar systems to permit economical formulation of a test at the proposal stage, the test should be included in the offer.

Delivery and Damages

Delivery is another important contract factor to be negotiated. It triggers the customer's obligation to pay; frequently it is also the time when the customer starts running the risk of loss and should insure the property involved.

As for the place of delivery, in some cases sellers prefer this to be at their own plants. However, buyers sometimes find that unacceptable, especially when performance standards are to be met by the new system. As for the time of delivery, agreement should be reached on precisely what the supplier must do with respect to the system or other items on or before the delivery date. Bear in mind that, since use of the system is the important thing to the buyer, delivery of such individual components as line printers or other terminals is, by itself, of no value to him; nor is he interested in delivery of a full complement of components that do not perform as specified.

When a computer system becomes a key part of the customer's operations and he must make lengthy and elaborate preparations for its introduction (particularly programming and coding of records), normal legal remedies for delivery default are not likely to provide adequate protection. Once contract performance has been under way for a significant period of time, the customer usually cannot attempt reprocurement elsewhere because of the long production lead times he would have to face anew. This is especially true when default is not discovered until the delivery date has arrived. The receipt of money damages rarely compensates for the expense and inconvenience suffered, many aspects of which are not measurable in dollars.

Consequently, a wise customer will try to establish meaningful concrete performance milestones throughout the period of production of the computer system. This enables him to spot many delivery failures (or potential failures) early, before his bargaining power is weakened; also, he can take advantage of actual or anticipatory contract breaches, depending on how the contract is written. Designing those milestones is a very important item for negotiations. They might include the receipt of confirmations of delivery dates for major items procured outside, the successful passing of in-process tests of critical elements, or the completion of design steps.

The establishment of such milestones can be essential even when buying time-sharing service under a short-term contract. I know of one situation in which the customer had to accept grossly deficient service because it could not abandon the supplier and get prompt help from another company. Moreover, it could not prove monetary damages for the clear breach of contract because of the difficulty of valuing in money its great inconvenience and the burdens of providing makeshift complementary arrangements.

Since, as suggested, the normal judicial type of damages measured by provable loss frequently is not adequate, consideration should be given to using liquidated damages in amounts large enough to serve as "prods" for on-time delivery. The federal government customarily uses that remedy, especially in its contracts under which computer systems are placed on federal supply schedules for easy ordering by agencies. Currently, the penalty is set at the greater of $100 per machine or 1/30th of the basic monthly rental, with a ceiling of 180 days. Admittedly, the government enjoys substantial bargaining power by virtue of its large volume of acquisitions. Commercial customers might encounter supplier resistance to that approach.

Payments and Warranties

When very large systems are bought, it is important to consider how payment will have to be made. The supplier might be entitled to some payments as his work progresses and before final performance. However, any such payments should be made as advances (the so-called progress payments under government contracts) conditional upon acceptance of the entire system. Individual components of a system bought as such should not be paid for finally unless the customer is willing to keep them in any event, whether or not the whole system is accepted.

Meaningful operational warranties are probably even more important for computer systems than for many other items of equipment. Failure of electronic components of computers during the initial "burn in" period probably is more common than for parts of mechanical items. More significantly, many software packages require considerable tinkering because of the great difficulty of designing and debugging complicated programs. Hence, it is essential to secure a proper scope for warranties on a system as well as to specify that they remain in effect for a suitable length of time. In current contracts that do not identify the software furnished, the express warranty provisions probably do not cover the programs. However, implied warranties might apply.

When system elements are obtained from different sources, it may not be easy to take advantage of operational warranties; many times it is difficult to identify the source of a system failure. In such cases the negotiation of warranties obviously calls for special care.

Traditionally, computer system suppliers have given adequate protection to users against patent infringement claims affecting the hardware furnished. But until recently the software supplied was neither specified nor protected by patents or copyrights. The situation has now changed radically, largely because many software houses are undertaking to get patent or copyright coverage on their proprietary products. Hence, system users should seek such indemnification commitments covering software and, in the process, should identify the software so protected.

Limiting Liability

A very important point to cover is the limitation of the supplier's liability. Although in years past suppliers secured merely waivers of claims for consequential and special damages, they now seek to exclude also the broader liabilities introduced in the fraud suits of customers. For example:

> A major manufacturer states that its warranty obligation to keep leased machines in good working order is "in lieu of . . . all obligations or liabilities . . . for damages, including but not limited to consequential damages, arising out of or in connection with the use or performance of the machines." Interestingly, the failure to mention liability in connection with software might have the effect of not achieving any limitation for the manufacturer in that area.
>
> The same manufacturer imposes the following obligation (or one like it) on purchasers of equipment:
> "The purchaser will be responsible for assuring the proper use, management, and supervision of the machines and programs, audit controls, operating methods, and office procedures, and for establishing all proper check points necessary for the intended use of the machines."

This relatively unobtrusive approach probably is taken in an effort to escape from claims for losses that could be avoided by programming techniques and other measures for verifying the accuracy of system operations at relatively frequent intervals. It thus is another attempt at limiting liability.

Putting Agreements in Print

Skillful negotiations can be futile if not summarized well in written agreements. These agreements not only must cover all of the points agreed on, but also must do so in simple language that can (a) guide the people on both sides who carry out the transactions and (b) communicate adequately to nontechnologically oriented tribunals that might be called in to resolve any disputes.

Obvious as the need for completeness in contracts may be, it is difficult to achieve in practice. Points hammered out orally in negotiations often are not reduced to writing for these reasons:

1. *It usually is much more difficult to formulate under-standings in writing than to arrive at them orally, because absence of precision becomes more apparent in writing. Prompt feedback and superficial analysis in oral discussions tend to create an illusion of full coverage.*
2. *Statements on highly technical subjects such as specifications and acceptance tests are difficult to write; relatively few people have the patience and the skill to work them out.*
3. *Some aspects of oral agreement may seem so clear to the participants who have "lived with" the negotiations that their restatement in writing is considered to be unnecessary. Even lawyers can be lulled into such a false sense of security.*

The written agreement must tell the entire story to an outsider, preferably one who is nontechnically oriented. It is remarkable how quickly negotiators' memories of details fade and how rapidly they cease to be available for interpretations of agreements. The ultimate test of the adequacy of documentation, of course, is how well the interests of a party to the contract would fare before a judge.

Incidentally, applicable written sources of information, such as specification sheets, test routines, and the like, should be identified precisely if they are not included in the agreement physically. For example, the model computer lease of the Council of State Governments requires, in the case of equipment specifications, the "manufacturer's document name, number, and date which defines the physical performance characteristics of the machine." Titles of documents alone are not enough; dates of revising the material also are essential.

Simplicity of statement in agreements has many virtues. If written in the language of laymen, agreements will not repel or defy understanding by the persons who are intended to use them. They then can serve the purposes for which they are created, namely, day-to-day guidance on action to be taken. This requires that the words should be nonlegalistic and that the statements should be more complete than "tight" legal writing, even at the risk of redundancy. Laymen are not as adept as lawyers with implied conditions or exclusions; they function better when points are made expressly. Technical jargon and buzz-words must be avoided as much as legalistic words. Most of the former have no clear definitions and merely create a dangerous illusion of expertness or precision. If the use of technical terms is unavoidable, they should be defined clearly and precisely.

Supplementary Files

In many situations it is not possible to achieve the ideal of completeness in a formal written agreement. If so, all is not lost. Many legal as well as business purposes can be served by contracts made up of numerous components, some formal and others informal, oral as well as written.

To provide for this possibility, the parties to a contract should start building a central contract file just as soon as possible. That file should contain relevant items such as those listed in [Table 1]. This

Table 1. Examples of Information to Keep in a Central File

Items generated by the customer:
  Requests to supplier for proposals
  Letters to supplier
  Document drafts submitted to supplier
  Memoranda of conversations with personnel of supplier
  Memoranda of other actions of supplier
Items received from the supplier:
  Advertisements
  Brochures
  Letters
  Proposals
  Document drafts
  Manuals
  Specifications
Formal agreements signed by the parties

---

data will be useful while the transaction is being carried out—and invaluable if litigation is necessary. Responsibility for its maintenance should be assigned carefully.

Evaluating Progress

How can top management best evaluate the work of the acquisition team while the negotiations and contract drafting are in process and after completion? Mere general attention to the activities of the team is not enough. Attention must be focused on specific goals and steps toward those goals.

As a minimum step, management should have an acquisition timetable and budget drawn up. This timetable will provide a means for determining whether adequate progress is being made. Moreover, since one of the chronic and serious problems of buying the use of computers has been unexpected delays in delivery, the timetable should be tied in to any milestones established for contract performance. It should include such steps as those listed in [Table 2].

Table 2. Topics for a Timetable

Preparation of specifications of the system to be used
Selection of type of procurement transaction to be used
Receipt of proposals from potential suppliers
Choice of supplier for negotiation
Commencement of negotiations
Completion of negotiations
Drafting of agreement
Approval of draft
Signing of agreement
Adoption of acceptance test procedures
Activities in connection with delivery:
    Availability of hardware for advance programming
    Training in programming, operation, and maintenance
    Delivery of hardware and software
    Start of acceptance tests
    End of acceptance tests
Start of operation of computer system
End of parallel operation of system being replaced
Evaluation of cost of the procurement effort

Since the financial aspects of the acquisition process also should be reviewed periodically, a budget should be established at the outset (and revised periodically as new data become available) to reflect both the cost of the acquisition activity and the cost of utilizing the system. By this device, effectiveness of the effort can be measured and efficiency in its performance can be promoted by discouraging recourse to costly spur-of-the-moment decisions when delays or other difficulties crop up.

Conclusion

As the record indicates, there has been a serious, inexcusable failure to use normal contracting practices in acquiring the use of computer systems. This failure has been harmful to computer suppliers (the possibly unwitting perpetrators of the errors) as well as to customers, at least where litigation has occurred.

Fortunately, the remedy is relatively easy to adopt. Top management must take the reins and require the use of recommended procurement practices, much as it does in the case of other major purchases of equipment. The apparent complexity of computer technology is not a valid objection to such a policy. In fact, that complexity makes care in contracting even *more* important than in other areas of procurement.

Management's involvement in buying computer services will be rewarding in itself by making executives more familiar with the devices that are already reshaping the structure of many businesses. It will pay substantial dividends by reducing the unnecessary expenses that have resulted from poorly chosen systems, delivery delays, and disputes. And it will help computer users to take full advantage of the rapidly enlarging variety of procurement approaches becoming available in the marketplace.

PART V

Implementing the MIS

Once the MIS has been designed, and all the groundwork has been done to ensure its acceptance and use, implementing the MIS can be considered. If we arbitrarily divide an MIS project into phases of proposal, design, implementation, and evaluation, it is immediately apparent that those phases are interdependent and need to be interfaced. Thus, successful implementation greatly depends on how well management has succeeded in reducing resistance to change and in creating a proper organizational environment that cannot be expected to occur simultaneously with the activation of the system. Resistance to and frustration with change can be anticipated; hence it is imperative that ways to ease tensions be included in the planning in the early stages of the proposal.

Resistance to change takes many forms, including fear of the potentially unknown, threat to economic security, threat of measurable responsibility, fear of increased responsibility, threat to organizational status, and disruption of interpersonal relationships. To reduce such resistance, management must, from the start, endorse the MIS and its objectives, make use of participative management, communicate, take part in training and development programs, support necessary formal and informal organizational changes, and sometimes make economic or psychological guarantees.

Some of the problems and pitfalls that have gripped MIS design because of management's failure to do the necessary homework are cited in several readings in this section. A basic theme is the failure of an MIS because it was not put together to meet the information needs of the users, information needs weren't identified, or top management did not provide the necessary executive leadership to ensure success. To understand part of this failure, as reported in the articles, one should keep in mind that many of the top managers felt inadequate to assume the leadership role of a technical activity alien to their expertise.

Diebold expressed it this way:

> A particularly significant problem exists with regard to top management itself. From all indications, computer activity in most companies does not receive the serious top management attention which one would expect in view of the magnitude of the investment and its potential benefits. Nor are the strategic importance and sensitive nature of the investment generally reflected in top management reporting, control and operations planning. (1)

Haslett, in reinforcing this viewpoint, called on management to assume its responsibility:

> Concern from the top management vantage point in the development and continuing appraisal of computer objectives is a vital part of the responsibilities of the highest level. For it must be presumed that the broadest of corporate insights is required in matters of such consequence. . . . (2)

Research evidence indicates that the results from existing computer-based MIS have been less than expected and that lack of adequate support by management remains the number one cause of failure. Thurston (3) found that when control of information systems was shifted to computer specialists, generally MIS results were not as satisfactory as results from management-supported systems. One study, concerned specifically with marketing-information systems in fifty selected firms, revealed that the most striking characteristic of the successful company was its commitment to an information system as a responsibility of both top management and operating management. (4) In a study of computer effectiveness in twenty-seven companies, Garrity (5) concluded that the companies utilizing computers effectively were those that involved operating management in selecting and managing computer projects and in being responsible for those projects.

But of course the problem goes beyond inadequate involvement of top and middle management; actually, no one has taken command—neither computer specialists, middle management, top management, nor sales representatives of computer manufacturers. As noted by Barnett, "The problem to date is a know-how and responsibility gap" (6). In a research study designed to determine how important and necessary it is to educate noncomputer oriented executives about the computer and its capabilities, Barnett listed these consequences in support of management training in implementing a computer system:

1. The development of a systems relation to a function must come from the managers of that function. Executives of companies using this functional-level involvement in their approach to computer MIS are significantly more interested in the subject of computer usage.
2. All executives of all companies and of all functional responsibilities are interested in computer usage.
3. Executives who have had computer training have more positive attitudes toward their company's computer efforts.
4. The management of information systems relating to a function should not be separated from the management of that function. (7)

Laying the groundwork and establishing a positive attitude toward resistance to change was accomplished at B. F. Goodrich Company in a four-stage program, as described by Becker, training director:

1. Several manufacturer and association training programs were implemented. They included a wide range of computer-concept programs for executives and the American Management Association's programs pertaining to computer use in managerial functions, such as marketing and personnel.
2. Next, we developed our own computer-concept program for internal management. It included sessions on technology, programming, implemented systems, and future applications.
3. Third, several sessions on math-for-management were presented as an in-house seminar.
4. Last, Goodrich followed up this basic core of programs with a series on computer applications, directed toward informing both middle and top management. Included also were sessions devoted to rotation through the information systems departments, construction of models, and exposure to MIS. (8)

In designing and implementing MIS there has been too little emphasis on what management is (resulting in confusion about what constitutes information) and too much attention to the system's computer. The missing efforts have resulted from a failure to develop a clear and precise understanding of the manner in which the information-system output will benefit the manager. This has occurred because of three human weaknesses, as seen by Pelham:

1. Too much zeal by the users to see something installed and operating. Once a project is approved, the fastest path to having something to show is to order the computer, install it, and start logging data.
2. Overselling by vendors of computers and the ease in defining a computer as an information system plus the rationalization that the ill-defined computer is the buyer's problem.
3. The human trait of avoiding those things we do not understand, and working instead with those we do understand. The part we do not understand is the interaction between management and information. (9)

In this section we are concerned with implementing the MIS; our emphasis is on avoiding some of the problems and pitfalls of the past, understanding the contribution of training to successful implementation, and realizing the importance of managerial control and the necessity of assigning a responsibility for it. In any project it helps first to identify the tasks that must be assigned as specific responsibilities and completed. For implementing an MIS, Murdick and Ross provide such a list:

1. Organizing the personnel for implementation
2. Acquiring and laying out facilities and offices
3. Developing procedures for installation and testing
4. Developing the training program for operating personnel
5. Completing the system's software
6. Acquiring required hardware
7. Designing forms
8. Generating files
9. Completing cutover to a new system
10. Obtaining acceptance
11. Testing the entire system
12. Providing system maintenance (debugging and improving) (10)

References

1. John Diebold, "Bad Decisions on Computer Use," *Harvard Business Review*, p. 16, January–February 1969.

2. J. W. Haslett, "Management by Abdication," *Journal of Systems Management*, p. 42, April 1969.

3. Philip H. Thurston, "Who Should Control Information Systems?", *Harvard Business Review*, p. 135, November–December 1962.

4. Donald F. Cox and Robert E. Good, "How to Build a Marketing Information System," *Harvard Business Review*, p. 154, May–June 1967.

5. John T. Garrity, "Top Management and Computer Profits," *Harvard Business Review*, p. 6, July–August 1963.

6. John H. Barnett, "Information Systems: Breaking the Barrier," *Journal of Systems Management*, pp. 8–9, May 1969.

7. ___, "Non-Computer Executives and the Computer," *Journal of Systems Management*, p. 21, December 1969.

8. Richard T. Becker, "Executives Use Computer to Develop EDP Skills," *Administrative Management*, pp. 28–29, February 1971.

9. Roger O. Pelham, "Putting Information Systems into the Company Control Structure," *Data Processing Magazine*, p. 24, July 1970.

10. Robert G. Murdick and Joel E. Ross, *Information Systems for Modern Management* (Englewood Cliffs, N.J.: Prentice-Hall, Inc., 1971), p. 508.

Section 1

Problems and Pitfalls

30

Computerized Information Systems

James R. Ziegler

Permission from *Automation*, April 1970.

There is very little solid achievement behind all the talk about management information systems (MIS). Despite the emergence of specially designed MIS "packages" and a few reports of purported successes in implementing computerized information systems, MIS must still be regarded as more of an art than a science. Yet, the time is rapidly approaching when designing and implementing some sort of MIS will be a management necessity.

What Are the Major Problems

Although there are countless problems that can and usually do emerge during an MIS project, the greatest number of them lie in three general areas:

1. Organizational level of implementation. *Because management information systems generally involve computers, there has been a tendency to try to implement MIS programs through the same techniques commonly used for conventional data processing systems. MIS projects have too frequently been left chiefly to operating and line management personnel for conception, design, development, and implementation. When this happens, the system which goes into operation will probably not deliver the results which top management wants. Top management learns, too late, that they have bought a system designed to solve somebody else's idea of what their problems are.*

Top management jobs are unique—in the problems they involve and in the kind of decision making tools they require. No one knows what information is needed to run a company except the people living with the everyday pressures and responsibilities. Therefore, if management is not ready to make a commitment about the information it wants and to establish value criteria for such information, an organization is better off not trying to implement a true MIS.

2. Scope of MIS projects. *Those who initiate MIS projects tend to aim for a scope which is beyond the pocketbooks of their sponsoring organizations. The MIS bug seems to spread a special sort of contagion. Once people get started, MIS appetites tend to get out of hand. Companies try to do too much, too soon, with MIS programs. It is well to remember that all of the rules of caution which apply to any routine computer system hold true to a far more critical degree for management information systems.*

3. Cost overruns. *In many cases, this problem area is directly related to the first two: lack of management commitment and failure to delineate the exact scope of a system to be developed lead to a looseness of control which lets costs get out of hand. Cost problems are usually related to ignorance or insecurity on the part of making final commitments and exercising ultimate control.*

What Is MIS

It is time that top executives face up to their responsibility of managing computer operations as an integrated, budgeted part of their business. It doesn't take extensive technical education to do this. Rather, the prerequisites are that a manager know what he wants in the way of analytical information and be able to put a realistic value on the acquisition of this information. Such values should be firm. Information availability must be evaluated in terms of its impact on the running of the company. The manager unwilling to establish values for acquired information should probably not authorize an MIS program for his company.

A management information system integrates equipment, people, and procedures in such a way as to deliver analysis-supporting and analytical information pertinent to management decisions. While a computer is not a prerequisite for an MIS, many organizations are large and/or complicated enough to require a computer-aided MIS.

To an increasing degree, modern management is an information science. The top executive, in turn, is a processor and analyzer of information. Conventionally, our concept of information has tended to be historic. In a business sense, information delivered to management has generally been thought of as a distillation and evaluation of facts generated by past experience. Also, the future has tended to be relegated to the realm of intuition.

Today, however, management must find the tools and the methods for factual appraisal and intelligent decisions involving the future. These skills are generally referred to by such names as planning or forecasting. Management information systems are tools for their implementation.

Many potential users of MIS assume the necessity for on-line, real-time, or closed-loop operating capabilities. In the world of business decisions, this can be a costly hang-up. The main questions to be answered are: What information is necessary for management to execute its responsibilities? When should that information be delivered? According to what requirements and stipulations?

Management people must be aware of the relationship between costs and degrees of service. The more flexibility and speed a system delivers, the more it will cost. Therefore, one of the big determinations which management must make is in scheduling access to, and availability of, information. Specifically, an MIS does not require an on-line computer system. Depending on the criteria stipulated by management, printed reports delivered by messenger or mail may prove adequate.

In many instances, a natural relationship emerges between automation and MIS. To illustrate:

Automated systems tend to involve relatively high costs of installation and operation. These factors alone tend to attract management attention and generate a need for information.

Automated systems tend to generate data in formats suitable for processing within an MIS.

The types of people involved in automation are more likely to understand and appreciate the implications and values of an MIS.

Tracing Information Flow

Much of the published material and promotional literature on MIS currently in circulation offers schematic diagrams supposedly showing standard flow patterns for management information, Figure 1. Such diagramming can be helpful for those who have problems in grasping the intrinsic importance of compiling and developing management information. But such an approach might result in a dangerous oversimplification. Management skills do not come in "packages." Information flow in a given company will be uniquely shaped by its management people who will, by nature, apply different standards in the execution of their responsibilities and the meeting of their objectives.

Rather than assuming that the flow-of-information needed to meet management support requirements will be the same for all companies, it is recommended that sources and availabilities be studied and identified for each organization. Unless an MIS implementation program begins with exact information rather than general diagrams or patterns, projections of costs, and equipment and personnel requirements can only be approximate.

The first step in any determination of MIS feasibility is to establish what top management wants and what this information is worth in the running of the company, Figure 2. Generally, it will be advisable to begin the information analysis for an MIS by conducting whatever studies are necessary to develop flow diagrams tracing the handling, documentation, and filing of information pertinent to delivering MIS end products which meet management specifications. Standard flow diagramming techniques can be used. This approach, it should be stressed, applies to manual as well as computerized systems.

In performing an information flow study for an MIS, quantitative elements become critical. That is, it is not enough merely to show the flow of documents and the existence of files. Rather, it is

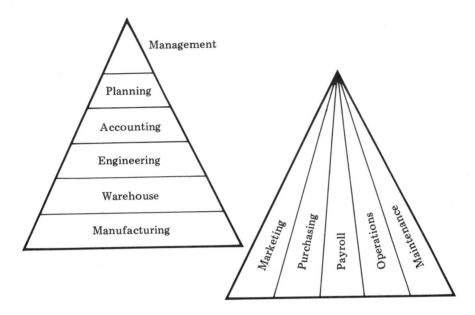

Figure 1.   Standard information flow diagrams picture management reporting as a cross-hatching of vertical and horizontal data areas. Horizontal reporting patterns (left) tend to follow departmental lines: manufacturing, engineering, accounting, etc. Vertical divisions (right) are pictured to represent general information such as marketing, payroll, etc. By superimposing the vertical patterns over the horizontal, these diagrams are purported to show how management information flows through all levels of a company's operations. While convenient, such diagrams can unjustifiably stereotype organizational structure. A better approach is to trace the information flow as it actually occurs in a specific company.

essential that volumes of documents and sizes of files—in terms of numbers of records and record sizes—be pinpointed as closely as feasible.

Remember that every task connected with MIS development should be responsibility-oriented. Thus, in making studies of information flow and file content, data gathered on volumes of documents, file sizes, etc., should be certified in writing by responsible department heads.

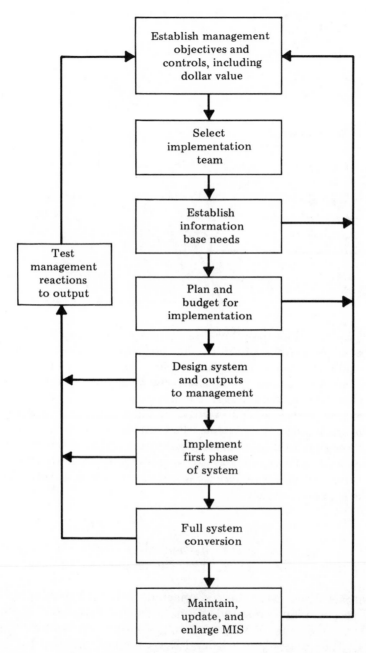

Figure 2. Getting top management involved in designing and implementing an MIS is a prerequisite for success. Flow diagram of implementation steps illustrates this necessity via the ample use of management reviews and tests of MIS progress and results.

Designing an MIS

After management objectives, information values, and data sources have been established, the company is ready to authorize its systems analysts and computer applications specialists to design the system. This study should include a survey of available software and applications programs. But it should not go to the level of detailed programming or other major cost-incurring commitments.

The project should have previously designated work checkpoints. In this way, exposure is limited to a series of minimum steps until success is assured. At each checkpoint, exact costs are forecast and responsibilities for meeting objectives are firm. This incremental approach becomes most critical at the next developmental stage. That is, after preliminary design has been completed, the system tentatively designed by the technicians must be measured against the initial stipulations of management objectives and values. Among veterans of system design wars, this juncture is frequently referred to as "trade-off time."

This is the moment of truth, when broad management stipulations are measured against the realities of costs and operating requirements. At this point, the future course of an MIS can follow three general paths:

1. *If the specified results can be realized within the stipulated budget, a "go" decision is indicated—as long as no other unforeseen considerations have been injected.*
2. *If the cost estimates exceed reasonable values stipulated by management, it may be possible to bring costs and implementation techniques together through compromise.*
3. *If value estimates hold firm and cost-reducing system modifications prove impractical, the project should be aborted. This should be done firmly and cleanly, terminating unproductive investment at the earliest possible moment.*

If either a "go" or an "abort" decision is reached, management need not be involved further at this stage. If the project is "go," the technicians develop the system, coming back to management only if unforeseen problems arise or when they are ready to show results. If the project is aborted, further discussion should be cut off because it would be costly and wasteful.

If a decision is made to look for compromises, management must be in charge until such time as a positive decision is reached for the next step. Typical trade-offs which can be applied at this stage of system development include:

Changes in Deadlines or Format of Delivery

Most frequently this involves weighing the necessary extent of on-line inquiry capabilities—or a decision on whether on-line service is needed at all. Depending on the scope of the projected MIS, communication facilities, equipment, and implementation can account for well over half the total cost of an MIS—both in terms of developmental expenses and operating overhead. Depending on the urgencies of specific types of information, as established by management, it is frequently decided to start an MIS by delivering printed reports on a scheduled basis. Frequently, these reports can be generated by a high-speed printer already available within the company's data processing installation. A single decision of this type could cut MIS development and operational costs by 50%.

Compromise on Information Received

A common reason for high costs of management information systems is a need to create new information files or data processing functions from scratch to support end-product objectives. Where new files or transaction processing systems have to be created especially to support an MIS, expenses will inevitably be high. One management alternative is to accept less information from the MIS. Another version of the same compromise is to implement only part of the system, restricting activities to areas where necessary supporting information files already exist.

Sharing MIS Costs

MIS costs can be shared with other application development activities. Where requisite data files and/or supporting applications have not yet been implemented, management can look at the possibility of developing them in parallel with the overall MIS activity. In such cases, further study will probably be necessary. This study would be aimed at determining where potential improvements derived from designing and implementing basic supporting applications can pay for themselves.

Where this is the case, it might be feasible to absorb the cost of subsidiary application development separately, eliminating charges against the MIS effort for these activities. If this alternative is explored, management must be prepared to take another look and evaluate projected overall results against comparable costs. In such cases, operating and administrative management people will probably enter the picture to establish values for the portions of the system which affect their operations. The same rules of value/cost tradeoffs should apply across the board in such instances.

Should compromise be contemplated, management should be sure to assess the value of the newly-projected results separately. It is important not to fall into the trap of being stuck with the original value rating while accepting lesser results.

Further, management should be careful to restrict any compromises to quantitative areas. Compromises in quality should be ruled out. For example, management might be willing to accept the same information in periodic printouts as was originally stipulated for delivery through terminals located in executive offices. Should such an alternative be considered, the first step is to re-evaluate the new approach to see what this level of service is worth to management. Then, if the system still measures up, management should avoid compromise which might involve the scope, validity, or applicability of the information itself.

Specifically, it is important to recognize that the real controlling element in the results an MIS is capable of delivering is the data base. The data base is the collection of summarized information which is updated and processed to support the inquiries or reports which are the end products of an MIS. The importance of, attention to, and insistence upon quality of the data base cannot be over-emphasized. In this area, one overriding principle should prevail: the data base should be inclusive. It should encompass, from the outset of an MIS, all of the facts which could possibly have any later bearing on information pertinent to management decisions. Thus, in dealing with system designers, management should consider ultimate, as well as current, information requirements. The way to be sure that an information system has the capacity to grow with a company is to apply a long-range view to the planning and specification of the data base which will be made available to an MIS.

In this respect, the data base is different from other elements of an MIS. While compromise can be tried almost anywhere else, it should not be contemplated here. The reason is that restructuring a data base once a system is operational and the desired information is unavailable in computer-compatible format is generally impractical.

For example, a compromise in the area of on-line communication capabilities would leave you with the same basic information.

The only things sacrificed are timeliness and accessibility. Similarly, a decision to use magnetic tape drives within the computer installation in place of random access disk files affects processing speed and flexibility. But, in either case, the system can be expanded later with relative ease.

With the data base, however, a major change would impact the basic file structure and programs. If historic information is involved, capturing of source data might have to start from scratch. Any record file incorporated within a data base should, wherever feasible, include all information available which might have any foreseeable value in management decision making.

31

Information Flow
and Managers' Decisions

Dr. R. J. Beishon, B Sc, D Phil

Published in *Management Accounting*, official journal of the Institute of
Cost and Works Accountants, London, England, November 1970.

Introduction

This paper approaches the question of management information
from the point of view of the behavioural scientist. The behavioural
sciences cover a range of academic disciplines, including parts of
anthropology, psychology, sociology, physiology and zoology,
ergonomics.

Many concepts and ideas are also drawn from systems engineering and cybernetics. All these subjects are concerned in some way
with the behaviour of organisms or systems in their particular
environment, and the behavioural scientist is essentially involved in
the study and understanding of human organisms in their interaction
with the psychological, social and economic systems.

The past decade has seen a steady expansion in the application
of ideas from behavioural science to the workings of industry and
commerce, particularly in the fields of industrial psychology and
ergonomics. In the 1920s and '30s these kinds of efforts were
primarily directed at increasing production and efficiency, although
there has long been a concern with the health and welfare of the
industrial worker in this country. With the changes in the social and
political climate which have come about since the last war, much
more attention has been paid to the 'human component' of the

industrial system. Much interest has been shown in schemes to improve working conditions, not just for efficiency's sake, but to give more interesting and varied jobs. Jobs are designed more and more with job satisfaction in mind and the concept of job enlargement is being applied. There has slowly emerged a recognition that a job is important in a person's life over and above earning a livelihood. People spend up to a third of their time at work and they look to the working environment to provide satisfactions to many of the basic needs they have.

Welcome as this progress may appear, however, there are dangers. The human being is an exceedingly complex 'machine' and our understanding of its functioning and operation is rudimentary. There are, unfortunately, too many examples of well-meaning attempts to apply our little knowledge to improve matters, which have generated only more problems. The behavioural scientist and industrial psychologist have suffered as a result of some of the over-enthusiastic early experiments, and even today it is all too often that a new gimmick system is taken up by industry only to be rejected when the wider implications of the methods are revealed.

These remarks are relevant because there is a natural tendency for the specialists in the field of management information systems to concentrate on solving the technical aspects of their subject. At this relatively early stage in the development of sophisticated systems, especially computer-based systems, there are a number of absorbing technical problems which require urgent solution. We are already seeing some of the effects of the introduction of new systems which have well-developed technical programmes, but which fail because they have failed to consider the fact that they can work only in conjunction with human beings. I want to emphasise the human aspects of management information systems right at the start to draw attention to the dangers of regarding the system as just another technical innovation which people will, or must, adapt to. Information systems involve people more intimately than perhaps is generally realised. We are, ourselves, basically 'information-processing machines', to use the current jargon of experimental psychology, and in the industrial and commercial field it is the manager more than anyone else who does little other than process information.

The purpose of these introductory remarks then is to point out that the psychological and behavioural aspects of information systems are extremely important, but that we still have relatively little understanding of how the human brain works and how human beings will react to changes. Nevertheless, a certain amount of useful information is available in the behavioural science field. In this paper

I want to deal with one or two areas which seem to me to be most relevant, but I shall have to ignore many other areas which ought to be considered in a longer treatment of the subject.

Management and Managers' Behaviour

In a very real sense, the activities of any company or factory are a combination of the behaviour of machines, on the one hand, and of people on the other. The efforts of machines and operatives are directed by management, who exercise a directing and controlling function. This process of management is conventionally seen as a sequence of steps or actions, where the ideal manager carries out the various aspects of his job in an impartial, dispassionate and rational manner. At certain points in the sequence of actions decisions are called for, and here the manager has available a range of aids, technical and mathematical, to assist him in arriving at an 'optimal' decision. The manager also carries out such activities as planning, budgeting, negotiating and so on. There are books on management which make the whole process seem rather easy, and imply that all one has to do is to learn up the chapter headings and become proficient in the subtask to become a good manager.

Behind these conventional views, and also implicit in the way large numbers of managers are treated in industry and commerce, lies a basic assumption. This is that the 'man' within the 'man-ager' acts solely with regard to the company's interests; he is assumed to be directing his activities towards achieving the company's goals and loyally serving the company at all times. Even where there is a conflict between a man's personal interests and those of the company, the man is expected to sacrifice his own interests. There is still very little recognition of the conflicts which can arise; it is blandly assumed that we are all reasonable men and if we could only have a quiet talk without emotion we could settle all our differences and work harmoniously together. It is rare to find personal conflicts referred to at all and, where they are, it is usually only to suggest ways of avoiding conflict and confrontation and of producing an atmosphere of sweetness and light.

The reality of management is, of course, very different. The manager is *not* a rational, dispassionate being capable always of calm, considered decisions. He is a human being in a human environment; he has his own personal aims and aspirations, which may differ from those of his superiors and the company. He has a complex bundle of prejudices and distorted views of reality. He is almost always in competition with others to achieve 'success'. His relationships with other people matter a great deal, often to the exclusion of technical and commercial considerations.

The day-to-day life of a manager is usually full of stress; he is frequently under pressure to make immediate decisions with inadequate data; he rarely has time to stop and think ahead. He is constantly involved in interactions with other people who may be reluctant to co-operate, or are even actively obstructive, and who do not appear to behave rationally or predictably.

This is, of course, an exaggerated view. The truth lies somewhere between the two extremes. The point is, that in considering the manager and his job, we must come to terms with two rather different aspects of the job. There is the rationally-based decision-making activity where a series of actions is carried through in a logical and ordered way, and there is the *non-rational* human interaction and aspiration aspect. For convenience, I will refer to the first aspect as the *formal* component of management, although I do not wish to imply that the conduct of this managerial activity is necessarily formal in the social sense. By formal, I mean the objective and relatively rationally-based side of the job. It is that aspect which is spelt out in a job specification if there is one. The second aspect I will call the *informal* components, to refer to the less explicit and often unrecognised side of the job; where the manager considers how his actions and decisions will affect him personally, where he makes value judgements about actions, and where both conscious and sub-conscious factors influence him.

The formal aspect of management has received a great deal of attention in recent years, and the setting up of business and management schools is an indication of the growth in this area. There are batteries of impressive techniques available to aid the manager— financial control procedures, PERT, critical path analysis and, of course, numerous sophisticated operational research techniques. There is an impression that management can be taught, at least in part, but that the practical side must still be learnt on-the-job.

The informal aspects have, in contrast, been little studied, although there is now a growing recognition of their importance. Interestingly, it has been the semi-serious or humorous writers who have pioneered in this field, eg Parkinson's Law, the Peter Principle. We can all recognise the existence of some truth in these ideas, and Antony Jay has written[1] a very persuasive account of industry where informal behaviours are analysed in terms of the power structure and battles between emperors and empires, kings and barons.

[1] A. Jay, *Management and Machiavelli*. Penguin Books Ltd.

This leads to an interesting contrast between the components of the manager's job, the knowledge he has of the 'words and grammar' which represent the formal component, and the reality of day-to-day working, the 'structured essay or communication', which results from the application of the basic knowledge. It is, perhaps, surprising that we know very little about the second informal aspect in real life. Relatively few studies have been done on the actual way managers spend their time and how they do their job. There are less than a dozen published reports of how managers actually behave, and the findings from these studies are often rather startling. Rosemary Stewart[2] carried out a major survey of 200 managers, using a diary-keeping technique. From this she was able to see how much time was spent communicating, in meetings, on the telephone, travelling, etc. This study was valuable in contrasting different kinds of job and revealing the part played by the various activities. Hesseling, whose work will be referred to in more detail later, also used a diary-keeping method but he was able to analyse his data in more depth. Unfortunately, useful as this approach is, it relies very much on the subjective judgements of the manager himself, and in my own research I have attempted to obtain objectively-based data by direct observation and recording of managers on the job.

I have used a radio transmission system where the manager under study carries a small microphone and transmitter with him during the whole of the working period. Thus, his verbal interactions with others, and many of his activities, are transmitted back to an observer who can record the material and add coded observations himself. This system has the advantage that the observations can be very unobtrusive and the observers need not even be in the same room as the manager. By using a continuously operating tape recorder, an accurate record of the sequence of events throughout the day is obtained. From time to time, at appropriate moments, the manager is questioned about the reasons for his actions and the thinking behind his behaviour; this, of course, is also directly recorded onto the tape.

My colleagues and I have studied a number of managers using this technique, ranging from a power station superintendent to a personnel manager.[3] We have observed these men for periods of several weeks at a time, so that we have an almost complete picture of what a man says and does in the course of his work.

From this data, a number of interesting analyses can be made.

[2] R. Stewart, *Managers and Their Jobs*. Macmillan 1967.
[3] A report of the personnel manager study has appeared in the April 1970 issue of *Personnel Management*.

For example, we have looked at the progression of events throughout the day to see to what extent a manager is free to decide what his next action will be, and we have compared this with the number of times he is forced to respond to events and to do what the situation demands. We classify a manager's behaviours or actions in terms of whether they are 'self-initiated'; 'other-initiated' (higher status); 'other-initiated' (lower status); 'institutionalised', ie, regular meetings which are part of the normal organisation of business; or simply due to a random or chance event such as a meeting in a corridor or in the lunch queue. Further analyses are carried out on the results or effects of these actions or encounters, and also on the future sequences of events which arise from them.

Clearly, from the data we collected, a large number of different aspects can be studied, such as the roles adopted by a manager in different situations, or the language styles used. However, for the purposes of this paper I will concentrate on the informational aspects of the situations, and these will be dealt with in a later section.

Management Information

I should like here to say how I am interpreting the basic terms involved.

Management is regarded as what managers actually do, rather than as what they should do, or ought to do, or say they do.

Information is interpreted, perhaps, more widely than is usual, to include all the signals and data which a manager receives in the course of the day, whether they are apparently relevant to the work or not. This approach regards such things as facial expressions and gestures as information, as well as the more obvious things such as memos and telephone messages.

Direct observational studies of the kind we have done reveal that the amount of information handling that a manager does is remarkably high. One of the most striking findings from observations of managers at work is the amount of inter-personal contact they have. Typically, managers spend 80-90 per cent of their time with other people, and it is not uncommon to find that over half that time they are talking themselves. All this interacting involves communication, both verbal and non-verbal, of information, although much of it may at first sight appear to be irrelevant to the job in hand. We have observed situations where managers even devote time and energy to playing practical jokes on colleagues, and certainly a greal deal of business time is spent discussing cars, houses or gardening. This kind of information is usually ignored in analyses of information flow, but consideration of these factors over a longer time scale suggests that they do in fact play an important part in the managerial situation. The seemingly irrelevant conversations contain data about other people's interests and attitudes. They also are part of the affectional or friendship bonds which grow between colleagues.

The reason these many different interactions, exchanging information at different levels, are important, is quite likely due to the fact that the process of decision-making and acting is more complex than it appears. There are a number of basic steps involved in the making of a decision:

1. *The prospect or possibility of a choice or decision situation arising has first to be recognised.*
2. *Possible courses of action must be enumerated, or action taken to discover what the alternative actions available are.*
3. *The outcomes of the various courses of possible action and the implications of these outcomes for the company, the man, his colleagues, must be postulated. The probabilities of the actual predicted outcomes occurring must be assessed. These outcomes may also involve estimates of the likely reactions of other people to the outcomes, and this can lead to an examination of a complete decision tree as in examining an opponent's likely reply to a chess move.*
4. *Reference has to be made to the value system against which the outcomes are to be judged.*
5. *When the above steps have yielded information the actual decision can be taken.*

There are many more detailed ways of breaking down the decision-making process but the point is, that at several stages in the process, the decision-maker or manager is required to make estimates or judgements about probabilities of events occurring or of the ways in which other human beings will react. It is here that managers will call on their 'experience' and utilise the many different snippets of information they have collected about the situation. They will also relate their feelings about people and their personal value system to the possible outcomes of the actions proposed, and adjust their decision accordingly. In dealing with any specific situation, a manager is going to relate the actions to his longer term goals as well, and there are usually many precedent and bargaining factors to be taken into account. He will say, 'If I take this line which helps X, he is likely to look favourably on a proposal of mine in the future and give me his support', or, 'if I give way this time they will probably ask for more next time'.

The process by which a manager collects information is often rather obscure and devious. He will manufacture excuses to visit other parties to the decision and watch for clues as to their attitudes. He will trade on friendships and the 'old boy net' to obtain additional facts or impressions. He will deliberately place himself in certain locations where he can observe comings and goings which provide yet further clues as to what other people are doing about the matter. People have even been known to read other people's letters upsidedown on their desks. The other side of the coin is that attempts will be made deliberately to suppress information or to distort it in certain directions to influence the decision. We have observed these and many other techniques in operation.

It is of interest at this point to compare these observations with those from a pioneering series of studies by Pyotr Hesseling of Philips Industries, Eindhoven. Hesseling has developed a method for studying the behaviour of a group of managers by arranging for each individual in an interacting group, or set of groups, to keep a detailed diary where he puts down what he is doing every 10 or 15 minutes throughout the day. The diary is kept by anything up to 70 people within a particular structure for a period of a fortnight (10 working days). The participants record on a fairly complex code sheet such things as: type of activity, eg writing a letter to X, telephone call from Y; nature of content, eg technical, personal, etc; status of interactant; and so on. Of particular interest is the coding of the interactions in terms of whether the recorder thought he received or gave an order, or advice, or information. The person he was dealing with would, of course, be completing his diary in the same way, although neither man would see the other's entries. Coded sheets are collected twice a day by the investigators and the material punched up for computer analysis.

A large number of things can be done with the data and comparisons can be made across departments, within departments, and for individuals. For our purpose, the most interesting aspect concerns the information flow from person to person. Firstly, there are many surprisingly large discrepancies between the contacts reported by the two sides of the interactions: typically, department A reports 30 contacts with B, but department B says that they had over 100 contacts with A. The nature, scale and direction of the discrepancies appear to be a function of the relationship which exists between the departments. Harmonious relationships are likely to lead to accurate reports; wide discrepancies suggest that suspicion and distrust exist.

Within departments and structure, Hesseling has found that there is a tendency for subordinates to report that they have spent more time with, and had more contacts with, their superiors than the superiors report from their experience of the same encounters.

Even more striking is the interpretation placed on the contacts by the different parties. Frequently, a superior records that he has issued, say, 20 orders, five pieces of advice and two pieces of information. The recipient, however, records the receipt of, say, one order, 13 advices, and 10 pieces of information. The information flow has not only been distorted from its intended interpretation, but some of it has been lost as well. Clearly, some of these discrepancies can be accounted for by mistakes and misunderstandings, but Hesseling takes particular trouble over briefing sessions and creating an atmosptere of co-operation, and there can be little doubt that the effects are real ones which reflect the widespread nature of information loss and distortion in these situations.

The implications of Hesseling's work are important. He has shown that even in straightforward situations people can seriously misinterpret the information they are given, even when it is in written form and apparently unequivocal. Furthermore, people think that they are issuing clear and specific instructions when, in fact, the truth is very different. There is even greater scope for distortions and misunderstandings in face-to-face interactions where facial expressions and gestures must be judged and correctly interpreted. Social-psychological studies have shown that some people are seriously deficient in their ability to recognise emotion and expression from other people's behaviour, and since we rarely get direct feedback that our impressions are either correct or wrong, these deficiencies can continue indefinitely without rectification.

The Design of Management Information Systems

In approaching the problem of designing an information system we are immediately faced with three questions:

1. *What information should we provide?*
2. *In what form should it be provided?*
3. *To whom should it be given or made available?*

I have not been able to deal with the third question in this paper, although there is a considerable body of knowledge now in the areas of organisational behaviour, organisation psychology, and so on, which is very relevant. But, for the first two questions, some of the findings from behavioural studies, such as those I have briefly referred to earlier, are particularly important. These observation-based studies suggest that managers use informal and semi- or unofficial information sources to a very considerable extent in carrying out their work. There is also evidence that the existing formal services of information frequently provide material which is of little or no use to the man actually making decisions. An example of the kind of thing I mean occurs when one is planning a road journey. A map tells you the distances and the routes to follow, but usually one wants to know how long the journey will take. A map which gave average speeds for the different stretches of road would be very helpful. To some extent we can guess at this information—a stretch of dual carriageway is often marked, and we assume that with reasonable luck this means higher overall speeds on that stretch. But we could easily draw a map which puts towns in positions relative to each other, not on the basis of distance, but time. The introduction of fast inter-city train services alters the map of England consider-ably, because in a practical sense some towns, such as Birmingham, are nearer to London than, say, Bletchley. When I wanted to decide the possible areas in which I could look for a house around London, I drew a time-based map rather than a distance-based map, which produced some rather surprising possible locations I might not otherwise have considered.

There is a further point which seems important here. In a situation where our understanding of how a man does his job is very limited, it is surely rather dangerous to make *a priori* judgements about the information he is going to need. Perhaps more important still, there is a more serious danger in deciding arbitrarily about the information we think he will not need and which, in consequence, we keep from him. Management is still rightly regarded as a peculiarly human skill precisely because, although we can aid the manager, we cannot replace him by explicit sets of rules for action, or even by mathematical equations. Since we, and to a large extent managers themselves, do not consciously know how they reach their decisions or why they make a good rather than a bad one, we must be especially careful in limiting or formalising their information sources. In the absence of specific research findings in the area it would, on the face of it, seem more sensible to allow the manager more freedom to build up his own information system on a trial and error basis and to study these systems in the light of their effectiveness.

An interesting example of our innocence in some of these aspects can be seen from studies of computer control systems for industrial processes. It has been observed that shift operators use input codes to the computer system which were intended purely for engineers' or programmers' use as diagnostic or technical information sources. Somehow, the operators have discovered these codes and experimented with the information obtained, and then found that they could use the material for control purposes. Needless to say, this kind of behaviour is observed more frequently on the night shift. After all, the operators were not supposed to have access to this information.

Quite apart from the difficulties of finding out about the answers to the three questions posed above, there seems to me to be a fourth important question:

   4. *What effects will formalising or changing the information system have on the existing set-up?*

By 'existing set-up', I mean the attitudes and behaviour of people as well as the purely technical or hardware aspects. The implications of this question are worth looking at in more detail, and I have listed below five points which seem particularly relevant. They are not in any order of importance.

(a) Possession of information is, both traditionally and in practice, a source of prestige and power to an individual. Prior information about likely events, exclusive possession of certain facts—these can be very useful and rewarding. At the least, they can give one a feeling of being 'in-the-know', and one can appear knowledgeable to others by revealing undisclosed information and hence increase one's status. Dropping the 'bombshell' in a meeting, so that others must grapple with new and surprising facts which you have had time to assimilate, is a well-known 'ploy' to all of us. In this sense, possession of exclusive information may bring with it very real benefits, and an individual can take steps to protect his interests or even exploit his advantage by beating others in the race. In this connection, it is not surprising to find that people will occasionally restrict the dissemination of information for no other reason but the off-chance that it may pay off eventually.

(b) The traditional status structure of industry and commerce implies certain access routes to information for the more senior people. Objective task analysis may well reveal that, in fact, much more junior people should have information confined to seniors. The number of telephones on an executive's desk is usually a sure indicator of his status, yet it is likely that it is his subordinate who needs the dozen telephones, not the boss. Changes in information flow can, therefore, have effects on status and hierarchy positions which might be totally unexpected.

(c) The chance to make modifications in the information which circulates around an organisation can be important to people. The recent introduction of a computer-based information system was welcomed by a senior man because he now has direct access to raw data from the departments below him. His subordinates were less pleased by the system. However, his reaction to the suggestion that his own boss should also have a terminal and read-out device was one of consternation. "But he would not know how to interpret the raw data I deal with; he could easily get the wrong idea from the figures; they must be presented in the right way", was his comment.

(d) The introduction of data links and transmission systems for information often removes the need for human-to-human contacts. The lack of a chance to maintain the social and psychological bonds between members of a working group or organisation can have serious effects on their morale and satisfaction from the job. Although the human contacts are not essential to the rational decision-making side, they are to the human beings who work there. We have observed people taking confirmatory and unnecessary paper messages by hand, simply so that they can pass the time of day with people they used to come into frequent face-to-face contact with.

(e) The provision of sophisticated information systems often removes the need for the older information-giving type of meeting. So, meetings, which we all know are very time consuming and unnecessary, are done away with or reduced to a minimum. But out with the bath water goes a valuable baby; much is learned in face-to-face meetings, as I have already indicated, and meetings do provide a means for argument and discussion which act to check and recheck on decisions and to generate new ideas.

These, then, are some of the problems which I foresee arising and which, in many cases, have already arisen, after the introduction of new information systems. I am sure that there are many other points which could be added to the list. Studies by sociologists have drawn attention to yet another problem area: how do you get people to accept a new system and to use it? There is evidence that even well-thought-out schemes have failed because people have been suspicious of the motives of the innovators and fearful of the consequences to their personal interests, even when these have been safeguarded.

Conclusion

I have tried in rather a discursive way to draw attention to some of the social and psychological implications associated with the provision of management information. This area is still a very new one and I hope that I have made out a case for involving the behavioural scientist in both the design and implementation stages of management information systems. Although the behavioural scientist cannot provide hard and fast design principles for the human implications he can, at least, make useful suggestions and sound warnings which, if heeded, could raise the probability of getting a successful system working.

32

Managing Management Information

George F. Weinwurm
Reprinted by permission of
Management International Review, January 1970.

I

One of the most portentous conjunctions of computers and management has, in recent years, been widely publicized under the name of "management information systems". Certainly, the proponents of such systems are right in principle in pointing out that decisions that are in some sense effective are largely dependent on the accessibility of relevant information. Hence, the way in which computers can serve to make relevant information more readily accessible to management must, one supposes, be a problem of disproportionate importance.

Unfortunately, most formal information systems are looked upon in retrospect by the managements whose decision-making they are intended to support and facilitate as having failed. It is ironic, and tragic, that, despite the enormous effort and attention that has been lavished upon the development of computer-centered management information systems in recent years, it is indeed rare that a management substantively uses—still less primarily relies upon—the output of a formal information system in making policy decisions of any consequence. Far more typical is the case where, in a crisis, managements' final judgements are based on every conceivable source of information *except* management information systems.

We could, of course, conclude that the common misfortunes in this area have all been isolated events, due entirely to local peculiarities and perturbations. While there is bound to be some truth to this viewpoint, a far more realistic assessment of the situation would be that the "conventional wisdom" regarding computer-centered management information systems is likely to be seriously at fault, i. e., that the process by which such systems are developed and applied is not understood sufficiently well to enable that process to be managed effectively and reliably.

To some extent, the difficulties that so many organizations have been having with computer-centered management information systems can be attributed to gaps in our understanding of the decision-making process itself. Most managers do not know nearly as well as they think they do the way in which they actually make decisions, rather than the way in which they like to think they are making them. Unfortunately, management scientists have not been all that much help either. Especially at the top-management level, most formal decision-making models—whatever may be their conceptual usefulness—are about as far removed from managers' actual thinking processes as are managers' intuitive perceptions of themselves.

Some further part of the disparity between the conceptual potential of computer-centered management information systems and their actual contribution to effective decision-making can be related to shortcomings in the technical state of computerized data management. While every advance in that "state" would certainly be helpful, however, there is no doubt that broad categories of information and aggregating procedures, which have been defined in practice over the years, are able to satisfy most of managements' traditional requirements for status and performance information. I have in mind, for instance, the assortment of financial summaries (e. g., balance sheets, income statements, cash flow projections, capital budgets, and the like) which most managers use although their inherent deficiencies and distortions are widely known. In most cases this sort of information can be refined and expedited and, in a general way, managements' decision-making capabilities will be augmented to some extent as a result.

It is my personal conviction, however, that the major part of managements' disappointments and frustrations regarding computer-centered management information systems stem from the way in which these systems are being perceived—most especially in that they are widely thought of as being analogous to and logical extensions of the traditional accounting and financial reporting procedures with which managements have long been familiar. Now, it is a historical fact that traditional accounting and financial reporting systems have for a very long time served as managements' primary source of formal information; and that most of what we know about "management information" derives from experience with these traditional systems. But it is a different thing entirely to state (or assume) that the two types of systems are necessarily equivalent in concept and in practice, i. e., that computer-centered management information systems ought forever more be nothing but (perhaps) more highly automated extensions of their traditional forbearers. This view, which, unfortunately, has considerable currency among practitioners, has, in my opinion, brought no end of difficulties upon those who have been charged with the responsibility of bringing the fascinating promise inherent in the concept of computer-centered management information into actuality on some reasonable basis.

John Gardner has provided a classic description of this malaise.

> As organizations (and societies) become larger and more complex, the men at the top (whether managers or analysts) depend less and less on firsthand experience, more and more on heavily 'processed' data. Before reaching them, the raw data—what actually goes on 'out there'—have been sampled, screened, condensed, compiled, coded, expressed in statistical form, spun into generalizations and crystallized into recommendations.

> It is a characteristic of the information processing system that it systematically filters out certain kinds of data so that these never reach the men who depend on the system. The information that is omitted (or seriously distorted) is information that is not readily expressed in words or numbers, or cannot be rationally condensed into lists, categories, formulas or compact generalizations by procedures now available to us.

> No one can run a modern organization who is not extraordinarily gifted in handling the end products of a modern information processing system. So we find at the top of our large organizations (and at the top of our government) more and more men who are exceedingly gifted in manipulating verbal and mathematical symbols. And they all understand one another. It is not that they see reality in the same way. It is that through long training they have come to see reality through the same distorting

glasses. There is nothing more heartwarming than the intellectual harmony of two analysts whose training has accustomed them to accept as reality the same systematic distortions thereof.

But what does the information processing system filter out? It filters out all sensory impressions not readily expressed in words and numbers. It filters out emotion, feeling, sentiment, mood and almost all of the irrational nuances of human situations. It filters out those intuitive judgments that are just below the level of consciousness.

So the picture of reality that sifts to the top of our great organizations and our society is sometimes a dangerous mismatch with the real world. We suffer the consequences when we run head on into situations that cannot be understood *except* in terms of those elements that have been filtered out. The planners base their plans on the prediction that the people will react in one way, and they react violently in quite another way.[1]

Managers to whom the above does not seem sadly, and painfully, familiar, need read no further.

II

I contend that the promise of computer-centered management information systems implies in several crucial respects *departures* from the assumptions upon which traditional accounting and financial reporting systems are based. I shall briefly cite several of these departures.

> *First, most practitioners tend to conceive of computer-centered management information systems as being (at least ideally) the* objective *and* neutral *mechanisms for gathering and relating data that traditional accounting and financial reporting systems are purported to be. Management information systems, in fact, are not, and cannot be, objective and neutral for the simple reason that the managers who put information into them are as much a*

[1] *Self Renewal: The Individual and the Innovative Society*, Colophon Edition, Harper & Row, Publishers, Incorporated, New York, 1965. pp. 78, 79.

part of the system as the managers who take information out of them—and they *certainly are not objective or neutral. Indeed, management information systems encompass the people who use them and are used by them: their optimisms, their fears, their biases, their frustrations, and their antagonisms. Depending on the way they are designed and managed, information systems can cause these distortions to resonate or they can tend to mitigate them, but they cannot eliminate them entirely. Moreover, as quickly becomes apparent to anyone who has lived interactively with information systems, the people and not the formal systems dominate the relationship. That is, people almost always succeed in using information systems to achieve* their *ends, however much the systems' designers may have intended otherwise. There is no reason to suspect that the introduction of the computer into the system will substantially alter these dynamic relationships.*

Second, the design of traditional accounting and financial reporting systems continues to be dominated by the fact that, throughout most of history, the cost of acquiring, retaining, manipulating, and disgorging information has been exceedingly high; and, consequently, that the most efficient course has been found to be a reliance on the smallest subset of measures *that can be arbitrarily defined to be meaningful in that context. Within the last decade, however, computers have rendered the historic relationship invalid by decreasing the unit cost of information-handling so drastically that—within rather wide limits—it has become economical to process great quantities of it in the hope that some small portion will eventually become useful to managements' decision-making. Moreover, if such costs continue to decrease exponentially—as is generally expected during the foreseeable future—the residual value of dealing with marginally useful information will continue to exceed its unit cost, most likely by even more than at present. Unfortunately, most practitioners—perhaps in unthinking deference to the tradition—continue to design computer-centered management information systems as though the unit cost of data is far dearer than it is, which has the effect of artificially and unnecessarily filtering the sorts of information that are permitted to enter the system and the sorts of interactions that managers are permitted to have with it. Hence, in the end, computer-centered management information systems are constrained even further away from their true nature and toward resembling the accounting and financial reporting systems that are their forbearers.*

Third, when making a commitment to some sort of computer-centered management information undertaking, most managements seem to have in mind a product *that must be developed and installed rather than a process that must itself be explicitly managed. It is precisely because they have been looked upon as involving mainly problems in technical implementation, and have been staffed largely with specialists in finance and data processing, that so many computer-centered management information projects have failed so catastrophically to satisfy the expectations of their proponents. To realize the purposes for which they are intended, computer-centered management information systems—as distinct from accounting and financial reporting systems—must be predominantly people-oriented, i. e., they should take account of the psychological, political and, above all, motivational dimensions that are the locus of effective managerial decision-making and action. Seen in their true perspective, computer-centered management information systems are, I believe, potentially most powerful as motivational instruments whereby, in a participative sense, managers can seek to achieve and maintain a humanly fulfilling congruity of operative goals throughout an organization. By forcing computer-centered management information systems into a different mold—most often by the simple expedient of assigning developmental and maintenance responsibility to the accounting and/or the financial arm of the organization—managements often unwittingly preclude the very outcomes toward which they ostensibly aspire.*

III

We certainly ought to conclude from the foregoing, I suggest, that the application of computers to the supplying of management information is a *developmental*, and not a production, task, and ought to be managed accordingly.

Let me conclude by mentioning three management imperatives that follow from the aforementioned facts of life; that, in the jargon of our day, tell it like it is.

First, we must manage the system's requirements. Most substantial applications of computers to management information represent a "quantum jump" in informational capability to the user. Consequently, it is simply not possible to define in advance all the eventual purposes of the system. Moreover, even if it were possible, analyzing the requirements of a major user in the necessary depth is a very laborious and time-consuming process, which will usually take longer than the average user is willing to wait. From both the manager's and the technologicist's point of view, evolving a really useful and meaningful (and profitable) computer-centered information system is a long- and not a short-term process; an educational process in the most fundamental sense. The evolution of the system's requirements will not, in Bagehot's phrase, manage itself; it must be managed.

Second, we must manage the system's configuration to insure that modifications to the system are made in accordance with managements' actual desires and users are promptly apprised of them. This process should include at least the following:

Standard approval procedures for modifying existing computer programs and/or data bases.

Standard approval procedures for creating new computer programs and/or data bases, including definition of purpose, size, function flow, interaction with other system programs and/or data bases, descriptors, structure, language, etc.

Standard procedures for documenting and disseminating information about the existing system, and all additions and/or deletions, including formats, minimal contents, etc.

The evolution of the system's configuration will not manage itself; it too must be explicitly and carefully managed.

Thirdly, we must manage the collection of system experience. *There can be little doubt that the installation and evolution of a major, computer-centered management information system at the present state of knowledge will prove to be an arduous and often traumatic process, no matter who is involved, no matter how it is done. It is therefore of paramount importance that some codified experience is gained from the obstacles that must be surmounted during subsequent years. I do not have in mind experience in the general sense, although all who are involved will certainly gain in that respect. The real need is for a comprehensive mechanism for collecting and recording costs and related data in a way that is comparable and amenable to analysis after the fact. A major dividend of the system experience, in retrospect, may lie in the ex post facto knowledge that an organization can gain about itself, its operations, its users, their needs, and what is required to meet those needs in an informational sense. Unfortunately, however, this sort of data will* not *be forthcoming from the usual accounting or administratively-oriented reporting system. It would be well to look upon a commitment to computer-centered management information as a major watershed in a management's experience, one which justified special accounting and reporting procedures. The long-term potential of computer-centered management information warrants more than a bubble of analysis on a whirlpool of processing, to corrupt Keynes' phrase. The collection of experience will not manage itself; it, too, needs the considered attention of management.*

IV

All told, we have exposed more problems than we have illuminated immediate remedies. That, however, is the real state-of-the-art, and therein, I suggest, lies the beginning of the wisdom we need to bring to fruition the impressive potential that waits largely untapped at the confluence of information processing and management.

33

The MIS Mystique:
How to Control It

Ivars Avots

Reprinted by permission of the publisher from *Management Review*.
© October 1970 by the American Management Association, Inc.

"We are five months late with implementation of the management information system."

Earlier it was three months behind, and soon the project may be six months late. Little more can be so disturbing to the company president than a report that the much-awaited computer system is behind schedule. No doubt, another appropriation will be required before it is finished. To add to the problem, the data processing manager does not have a clear explanation of what has gone wrong, and, even worse, he cannot guarantee that his recovery schedule will stick. Management is lucky indeed if the technical approach is still valid and the feasibility of the project is not being questioned.

Disappointment with major systems work is not unusual. Missed schedules and lost budgets seem to go hand in hand with the implementation of major computer-oriented systems. A Midwest company had to add two years of intensive efforts to complete a manufacturing information system. Another major company found itself two years late in implementation of a multi-plant management information system. The story repeats itself in other well organized companies under seasoned data processing managers and controllers.

Reasons for Failure

There are three principal reasons why the development of major computer systems often runs out of control. One reason is that a large-scale systems project is begun without full appreciation of what is to be accomplished. Another is the inability to estimate with any certainty what it takes to develop the programs with a given pool of analysts and programmers. The third reason is the inability to control the programs even after reasonable goals have been set.

This article reviews those characteristics of computer-implementation projects that make them difficult for management to handle and discusses an approach that should help management to raise the odds in favor of success.

In theory, the management of a major systems project should have much in common with the construction of a new plant or launching of a new product. All of these are complex efforts requiring integration of parallel tasks on a tight schedule. In real life, however, systems projects have unique characteristics, both in terms of work content and management, that place them in a separate risk category.

Shortage of Qualified Managers

The field of computer systems has developed at a fast rate over the past decade. This has brought with it a shortage of technically qualified management personnel. Other areas of technical endeavor have pools of managers who are capable of setting objectives, evaluating alternatives, and providing direction in the project management process. This is not true in computer sciences. Few managers are capable of assessing the state-of-the-art implications of any given major computer system and determining what can and cannot be accomplished.

Most large computer system implementation projects are headed by men whose backgrounds are not in software development, but in some more general area of data processing. This affects their management style and technical judgment, which may be influenced by their earlier experience despite the advice they may get from programming experts or consultants. Obviously, there will be no short-term solution to this problem. In the meantime, management will be wise to look at the general qualities of the prospective project manager, rather than concentrate on his experience in any particular part of the computer field. Even if there is not much that can be done about technical qualifications, management can assure that the project manager has proved ability to make commitments and meet them, and the imagination to use all applicable management tools and the ability to conceive and adapt new ones.

Because data processing background as such will not substitute for systems analysis and programming experience, in the final analysis of all pertinent qualifications, an engineering manager, for example, may win out over the computer man. In the crises that are bound to occur, the best chances for survival will go to the project manager who knows the company well, who appreciates his unique role, and who can use staff assistance effectively.

Complexity of Programming

Although the sheer size of major computer systems adds to the difficulties of managing the programming effort, it is the complexity of such systems that presents the real problem. The principal interaction that affects the time and cost of programming is between (1) module complexity and (2) programmer ability.

For every intersection of the module/programmer matrix, the manager has to be concerned with two further issues that contribute to the eventual cost of operating the system. These are computer efficiency and technical impact of the application. Some able programmers can demonstrate great output and write effective programs; however, their documentation is poor or the algorithms are generally such that subsequent revisions become very difficult. On the other hand, some programmers turn out work that is very inefficient from the computer's standpoint. The effectiveness of such programmers depends on the frequency of use of such programs. Obviously, any program that is going to be in day-to-day use requires talent that will maximize the computer efficiency.

Aside from the capabilities of the individual programmer, changes in the state-of-the-art of software and the increasing availability of programs that perform internal management functions make a significant impact on the development of computer systems. Developments in computer technology itself can be significant. These factors, which contribute to complexity in still another dimension, require effective forecasting and interpretation of the state-of-the-art in both software and hardware.

In view of the complexity of the programming tasks, it is not surprising that management finds it difficult to monitor and evaluate progress of the project in any concrete terms. Even if management ignores the multi-dimensional interactions, there are few points at which it is obvious that something has been completed or that a specific goal has been achieved. Fortunately, some of the techniques that have been refined for project management generally are useful in separating program development into components necessary for effective control.

Baseline Definition

Experience has shown that as far as computer systems are concerned, inadequate definition of objectives and coordination of systems development at top management levels, more than any other factor, are responsible for subsequent modification and consequent overruns of schedules and budgets.

In one major company, a new employee benefit program was introduced at about the same time that a new management information system was going through the final testing stage. The change in employee deductions, which had not been communicated to the project manager, required substantial modification of the program, and much of the analysis and design work had to be redone.

In addition to such major communication failures, projects run into difficulties because of poor specifications and inadequate involvement of future users of the system.

Very often, too much is expected of the new system or, at least, the system is too ambitious in view of the expertise of the personnel available. But even where the objectives are realistic and have been adequately coordinated, they must be translated into a set of blueprints that specify what is to be implemented. This can be achieved through development of functional specifications and a work breakdown structure.

The functional specification describes what the program should do, but not how it is to do it. This specification is based on the objectives approved by top management and is usually prepared by the eventual users of the system. Because the programmers should have the final say as to technical feasibility and clarity, it is useful for them to review the specification before it is presented to management. After approval, the functional specification becomes the basis for understanding between the users and the programming project. Any changes to this specification must be approved by both parties.

On the basis of the functional specifications, the project

manager should develop a work breakdown structure that shows in hierarchical fashion all the elements involved in developing and installing the system. It successively breaks down the work to be done beginning with general categories and proceeding to detailed work packages.

It should be noted that the work breakdown structure emphasizes end items rather than functions. It shows all hardware, software, services, and facilities that are necessary to implement the project. As such, it becomes the point of departure for planning, direction, and assignment of responsibilities. If necessary, the accounting and reporting systems can also be broken down along the lines of this structure. Although during the initial stages a work breakdown structure may stay at a relatively high level, eventually, each element needs to be developed further to the detail of work package that can be easily controlled in terms of a schedule and budget.

Company management should be particularly interested in the work breakdown structure because it effectively portrays the composition of a systems development plan. It achieves visual integration of the various aspects of the computer system project, at the same time permitting detail analysis of any single element. In practice, the elements of the second and third levels of the work breakdown structure are usually assigned to individual managers. Thus, in case of any problems, it can be easily determined who has the responsibility for the particular work package.

Planning the Project

In the development of computer systems, the steps from program design to detail design involve a number of unpredictable human events. To make matters worse, the programmers are likely to build without a plan, redefining the program in their own individual ways. For this reason, a carefully designed project plan is necessary to help define the responsibilities and checkpoints that lead to management visibility and control over the project.

A sound starting point for any project manager is the development of a logic diagram to define the relationships between principal program elements and identify the approximate sequence in which they should be tackled. The logic diagram can reveal important facts that can greatly facilitate subsequent detail planning. In addition, the logic diagram is an excellent starting point for a planning network.

Attempts have been made to apply formal PERT techniques to programming, but because of unreliable estimating techniques, results have been unpredictable and much time has been wasted trying to keep PERT in operation. Network planning, however, has distinct and separate uses for planning and for control. There is no question that from the planning standpoint, a network will help management understand the internal relationships of the project and set the initial schedules more intelligently than any other technique.

After a network plan has been drawn up, the next step is to develop detailed manpower assignments. Laying out the network on a date scale and applying the available and planned resources will readily show whether the expected completion time for system implementation is realistic and will permit a more efficient assignment of personnel.

While programmers are often assigned to specific work packages on the basis of their experience with a particular kind of program or programming language, management should also give consideration to the abilities of programmers compared with the characteristics of the modules. For example, high complexity modules should be assigned to high-ability programmers, while modules where extensive systems analysis has been performed can be assigned to less experienced programmers. When the programming of individual modules is laid out in some sort of a critical path network, trade-offs may be possible between module complexities and programmer abilities to achieve a steady and logical programming flow.

In many cases, however, the project manager will never have a chance for such a sophisticated analysis. The first thing that manpower assignment to the network often shows is that programming needs are hopelessly bunched up and that testing soon becomes a bottleneck. These problems should be referred to top management, because their solution usually involves adding personnel, working overtime, compromising on the extent of tests, and taking other similar actions.

Budgeting

By now, it should be obvious that budgeting for a large computer system development is an extremely difficult, although necessary, job. While the project manager should obtain inputs from his first-line supervisors, he should be personally responsible for development of the budget. In doing so, he will have to keep in mind a number of factors at the programming level that can have a pronounced effect on the validity of the budget. Some of the questions the manager should raise are:

Is the program new or a modification of an existing system? If new, is it similar to any previous work?

What degree of complexity is involved with the input-output files, as well as calculations in programming?

What is the size of the program and the expected storage problems?

What is the level of programming language to be used? Are one or more languages required to complete the program?

If more than one person will contribute to a program, how will their efforts be coordinated?

If the program has decision-making capabilities, how will ambiguities be resolved?

Is the problem clearly defined, or will alternations be necessary on the basis of simulation or some interactive process?

If the system to be mechanized exists, is it well documented?

If the system is to be converted from existing computer programs, how much redesign is to be done?

What is the quality of the software that the manufacturer is supplying?

How clean are the input data?

Will adequate machine time be available?

The programming effort and time required for implementation will depend on the answers to these questions. What is more, major computer system efforts extend over a number of years, and it is only natural that in its desire to capitalize on interim advances in the state-of-the-art, management often makes assumptions that would be considered too bold in other fields. While the project manager may be aware of the implications, top management will not have enough technical understanding to evaluate the impact of the answers he gives. Indeed, managers may be so frustrated by the complexity that they may pressure the programming manager for some sort of quantification of programming work.

There have been a number of attempts to develop quantitative guidelines for use in programming assignments, but, except for a certain amount of standardization, these efforts have not been worthwhile.

A budgeting approach that has met with some success involves direct involvement of the programmers. After the program design specification has been developed to tell how the program is expected to work and what must be coded, estimates to complete each module can be requested from the programmers. Programmers are usually optimistic and tend to underestimate, so, in the end, the programming manager must make his own estimate on the basis of the amount of coding, degree of complexity, programmers' experience, and the available computer time. Naturally, each project manager develops his own guidelines for budgeting, and this is one case where experience on similar projects will be useful.

Controlling the Project

The most important ingredient of the project control process is communication. There are two aspects to this. First, the project manager must keep in close touch with the group leaders as well as with individual programmers to evaluate progress and spot any problems that may be developing. To do this, he must speak the programmers language, not only in technical terms, but often in social terms as well.

Second, the project manager must also act as an information filter to protect the programmers from ideas that may interfere with their productivity, for example, program refinements that are suggested at higher levels of management. If these ideas reach the programmers, they may spend considerable effort on features that have not been appropriately evaluated or authorized. It is important, therefore, that strict lines of technical communication be maintained and that the project manager be in control of this information at all times.

Another important aspect of project control relates to trouble-shooting and testing. As the coding process gets under way, it usually becomes obvious that no single person in the entire project understands the full system and its components well enough to diagnose the troubles that develop. This leads to costly delays unless adequate preplanning has been done and methods for handling the situations in a logical manner have been established. Troubleshooting during systems development is usually done on a cause-and-effect basis. On long projects, programmers sometimes repeat errors, but forget the solutions that they found earlier. Careful maintenance of run books in which the complete history of program development is recorded can be of great assistance.

Testing is the point at which the validity of programming efforts is proved. It is also the first point at which most of the serious problems are brought to the surface. A carefully considered test plan can be of importance in keeping such unpleasant surprises to a minimum. Management must realize, however, that tests may take nearly as long to write, debug, and execute as the program itself and, therefore, they cannot be specified in too much detail. So the project manager must not seek a test procedure for each condition, but rather must provide for a definitive philosophy of testing and enforcement of the disciplines required for successful testing. For example, he must assure that programmers adequately test their subroutines to prevent failures further down the line.

When the signal flags are raised, either because some elements of the project require more effort than was budgeted or the results are unsatisfactory, replanning becomes an important part of the project control process.

Using the phased network as a reference point, the project manager can discuss available alternatives with the first-line supervisors responsible for the individual work packages and effect changes in staffing or overtime application to improve the overall health of the project. In many cases, changes in the technical approach or modular structure may be advisable. When this happens, the phased network and related manpower assignments must be revised.

Milestone Reporting

Even in those projects that do not use work breakdown structures and network plans, systems development efforts are usually broken down into phases and identified with milestones for progress reporting. Often the individual programmers are asked to estimate the percentage of completion for the particular units. Because of the many unforeseen difficulties that develop in writing a program, however, it is nearly impossible to estimate that a given programmer's work is 70 or 80 percent complete. Quite often, a program that is 90 percent complete will involve some new condition that necessitates a complete rewriting. Or it may become evident to the programmer that a completely different approach would be better and he begins again.

Despite these problems, formal status monitoring against milestones can be valuable if it is not used as an end in itself, but rather as a signal for more extensive technical progress reviews. From this standpoint, milestone reporting is of particular interest to top management, which may well insist that status be measured at least against the following milestones:

1. *Complete flow-charting of the program.*
2. *First assembly or compilation.*
3. *First execution to end of job with test data.*
4. *Completion of testing using the programmer's test data.*
5. *Completion of testing using independently developed test data.*
6. *First execution with other programs in the system.*
7. *Repeat testing with other programs in the system.*
8. *Testing with actual data or parallel runs.*
9. *Conversion.*

In addition to these milestones, however, a number of specific review points should also be incorporated in the program plan. These should be conducted at the completion of program specifications and prior to commencement of conversion. The purpose of the first review is to assure management that the program to be designed indeed will meet the objectives for which it was intended. The second review gives management a chance to assure itself that all subsystems have been adequately tested and supporting activities have been implemented before the crucial conversion step is carried out. Other points of review should be introduced to suit any particular project.

Section 2

Need for Control

34

Economic Evaluation of Management Information Systems: An Analytical Framework

Norman L. Chervany
and Gary W. Dickson
Reprinted by permission of
Decision Sciences, July–October 1970.

In the years from 1960–1968, the capital outlay for computer hardware in the United States has increased tenfold [see Diebold 9, p. 14]. Added to these equipment components, have been the expenditures in personnel and supplies which are necessary to utilize the hardware. Outlays in the systems and operations sectors are growing even faster than those for hardware [6, p. 142][9, p. 16]. Yet, associated with the increased dollar outlays has been a decrease in managerial satisfaction with the results of this large investment and many writers are suggesting that increasing economic costs have not been matched by increasing economic returns [1, p. 147][9, pp. 14–15][10, pp. 1–3].

A great majority of these increased computer based expenditures have been undertaken for the purpose of providing management information systems (MIS) [8, pp. 18–22]. In the opinion of the writers, the time has come for some reflective consideration of the decision-making processes involved in developing alternative MIS configurations and selecting the best configuration from among these alternatives. The need to analyze the cost/effectiveness of information system investments is of paramount importance. The current state of understanding of cost and benefit functions in MIS development, however, is limited at best [9, p. 15]. A logical framework for systematically identifying and analyzing the decisions encountered in the development of an MIS does not exist. Such a framework is needed to synthesize existing knowledge and coordinate future research. This paper attempts to provide the required framework by: (1) emphasizing the economic decision-making aspects of MIS development, (2) identifying the decision activities required in MIS development, (3) relating the costs and benefits that accrue from these decision activities, and (4) suggesting the research activities necessary to develop workable economic measures of MIS benefits.

MIS Development: A Problem in Decision-making

Various approaches have been suggested for viewing the problem of MIS development and evaluation. With respect to the development of alternative MIS configurations, two types of guidelines have been proposed. The first guideline emphasizes the value, in fact the necessity, of starting with the decision system within an organization as a base for enumerating MIS requirements [1, pp. 153–5][2, pp. 656–8][14, pp. 134–6][15, pp. 654–6]. The second guideline proposes a theoretical approach that focuses upon what the total system should be rather than using the existing system as a basis [4]. Although ideas presented in these two approaches are valuable as guiding premises in MIS development, they are not specific enough to be operational. This operational requirement must be met before the real value of these approaches can be realized.

In the area of economic evaluation of MIS configurations very little concrete work has been done. The major types of costs and benefits have been defined, [9, p. 27][16, p. 3] but attempts to measure these MIS payoffs are sketchy. A simulation approach has been suggested for evaluating MIS by Boyd and Krasnow [5]. Beyond emphasizing some meaningful payoffs that can result from an MIS, e.g., improved control and improved responses to a dynamic environment, this approach is too general to be useful to MIS development specialists. Similarly, attempts to relate the mathematical theory of communication to measuring the value of information [3], while useful in ideas suggested, are several stages from being operationally useful. The Bayesian school of statistical decision theory, e.g., Pratt, Raiffa, and Schlaiffer [13], has done extensive work in developing methods for evaluating sample information in decision situations, but these efforts have not been integrated into the problem of evaluating MIS.

There may be many reasons why the existing research into the problem of evaluation of MIS has not been completely successful. The authors contend, however, that a major source of difficulty is the failure to view MIS development and evaluation as a problem in decision-making. It contains, like any other decision problem, four basic ingredients: (1) controllable variables, (2) constraints, (3) uncontrollable variables, and (4) payoffs [7]. The hardware system utilized, the data collected, the summary statistics calculated, and the reports distributed are examples of variables that can be manipulated by the MIS specialist. His freedom of choice with respect to these variables, however, is often constrained. Constraints may exist in the form and availability of raw data or in legal requirements for the preparation of a specific report. In contrast to the controllable variables, the MIS designer must predict hardware capabilities, future demands on the MIS system, and other factors beyond his immediate control.

It is the prime responsibility of the MIS specialist to synthesize these three elements—controllable variables, constraints, and uncontrollable variables—and project payoff functions (costs *and* benefits) for the alternative MIS configurations under consideration. The development of a successful MIS depends upon the skill by which these payoff functions have been analyzed. The basis for such an analysis must be the various decision problems that arise in the development of an MIS.

Decision Activities in MIS Development

There are many complex decisions that must be resolved in the development of an MIS. Decisions must be made on hardware, personnel, and software. Payoffs vary from clerical cost displacement, which can be determined with relative accuracy, to improved decision-making capability, a nebulous concept at best [9, p. 27].

In order to successfully confront this complexity, a framework must be developed that can be used to isolate, in a meaningful fashion, the decision activities that exist in the MIS development problem. This framework should possess two major characteristics. First, it should increase the probability that all of the relevant dimensions of the problem are considered. Second, it should aid in the analysis of the relevant payoff functions. The framework that the authors suggest is based upon operationally defining two terms—

analysis and design—that are frequently encountered in discussions of MIS development.

Analysis Decisions in MIS Development

Analysis refers to the decision activities involved in determining the requirements of an MIS. The major input into this phase of MIS development is the recognition that an MIS may be useful in assisting management to operate and control the organization. This recognition may come in the form of a managerial directive to automate the accounts receivable/billing procedure. It may also arise in the belief that the development of an MIS may lead to increased effectiveness in the R & D effort within the organization. Based upon problem recognition, analysis concentrates upon the specification of the requirements (or demands) that the MIS must meet.

Stage 1: Specification of the System Scope   A key activity that often determines the success or failure of an MIS is the detail to which the scope of the system has been analyzed. Several authors [1][14][4] have cited the problems that can arise from the failure to specify the purpose of the system under consideration, and the relationships that the system has to other information-decision systems in the organization. It is necessary, therefore, that precise answers must be obtained to several questions: (1) What is the managerial purpose of this system? (2) How does this system interface with other existing systems? and (3) How will this system interact with future MIS developments in the organization?

Stage 2: Specification of the Information Requirements Based upon an analysis of the relationships between the MIS under development and the overall objectives of the organization, the next step is to ascertain what information the system should provide.[1] In this stage decisions must be made concerning the determination of what information is *and* is not required, and the selection of the format (form and timing) for the information that will be supplied.

Stage 3: Specification of the Data Requirements   The final stage in the analysis phase of MIS development is the determination of the data that must be collected. The decisions that specify the information outputs of the MIS must be transplanted into a precise statement of the data that are required to generate this information, and where these data can be found.

A perspective from which to view this set of decisions is to consider the MIS as a production function that converts data

[1] Information is used to denote data that has been summarized and synthesized into a form that can be used for managerial decision-making.

elements into information. The types of value that are associated with the outputs of a production process have been trichotomized into place, form, and time utility [17, pp. 3-4]. The first output from this stage, i.e., the determination of the information to be provided, is the analysis of the place utility aspects of the MIS function. In other words, what value occurs by having certain information delivered to a specific point in the organization? The specification of the format of the information provided, e.g., summary statistics calculated, supporting detail supplied, and the frequency of the reports, focuses upon the form and time utilities of an MIS. In essence, what values occur by delivering the information specified in a specific report form and/or with a specific frequency?

Perhaps the best way to clarify the nature of the analysis decisions in MIS development is to consider briefly two examples with which the authors have had recent experience. One example is the development of a clerical system to process the accounts receivable/billing procedures for a medical clinic. The first requirement was the specification of the manner in which this proposed system was to fit into: (1) the existing accounting system, (2) the administrative functions of recording, processing, and maintaining patients records, and, (3) future plans for automating other information systems in the clinic (Stage 1). Based upon this analysis, the determination was made of the accounting reports required, the statements to be mailed, the form of these documents, and the time pattern to be followed (Stage 2). Finally, the data sources, e.g., requirements for the patients records, were specified (Stage 3).

A second example is the development of an information system to assist the sales manager of a brokerage firm control and evaluate his security salesmen. The first activity undertaken was the identification of the decision and control structure involved in this managerial function (Stage 1). Care was exercised to identify the interfaces this system would have with the remainder of the organization. Based upon this analysis, specification of the information required to manage the salesman, e.g., a report comparing the securities sold to the securities recommended by the firm's research department, and the data sources required, e.g., summary statistics on daily security sales, were determined (Stages 2 and 3).

Design Decisions in MIS Development

The output of the analysis phase of MIS development is a list of system requirements that indicates: (1) the relationships between proposed system and the organization, (2) the information that must be provided, and (3) the data needed to support this information. The design decisions in MIS development center on the resolution of the technical questions concerning: (1) the processing system, (2) the installation methods, and (3) the on-going characteristics of operating the system. If analysis is viewed as specifying the required outputs of the MIS production function, design can be viewed as specifying the production technology necessary to generate the required outputs.

Stage 1: Processing System Requirements   The major technological decision that must be resolved is the determination of the processing system that will be required. Simultaneous consideration must be given to the software that will be employed and the necessary hardware configuration. Several crucial questions should be studied in this stage. First, the interaction between software requirements and hardware capabilities must be considered. Second, the amount and quality of the equipment and support from different manufacturers must be evaluated. Finally, the relationships between current processing capability and future demands should be projected. In this stage, a short-run planning horizon can adversely affect both current and future applications.

Stage 2: Installation Requirements   Implementation decisions concern the procedures to be used to implant the system into the on-going operations of the organization. Many systems have been either failures or only partially successful because careful consideration was not given to alternative tactics for integrating an MIS into useful operation; e.g., parallel operations, management involvement and personnel retraining [11].

Stage 3: Operations Requirements   The final set of technical decisions that must be resolved focus upon providing the requirements for operating and maintaining the system throughout time. The operating personnel must be specified, the frequency the system is to be run determined, and the requirements for system maintenance procedures and personnel identified.

Economic Impact of MIS Development Decisions

This paper is directed toward the development of a framework that can be used in the economic evaluation of an MIS. Aside from a few introductory remarks, however, the topic of evaluation has not been mentioned. This has been intentional and stems from the belief that evaluating existing or proposed MIS configurations cannot be separated from the decision activities of analysis and design.

The question of economic evaluation of MIS's reduces (or explodes) into measuring the economic implications of the six decision stages identified in the previous section. The first step in this measurement problem is the identification of the different types of costs and benefits that can arise from MIS development decisions. These payoff classes are presented in [Table] 1.

Table 1. Economic Impact of MIS's

Costs	Benefits
1. Hardware costs: Purchases Leasing arrangements Physical installation 2. Personnel costs: Management time during analysis Systems analysts Systems programmers Systems operators Clerical positions 3. Supply costs: Cards, tapes, disk packs	1. Cost displacement: Reduced personnel 2. Improved decision-making: Lower costs from improved internal operations, e.g., reduced inventory levels Increased revenues from improved capability to satisfy environmental demands, e.g., a reduction in the time required to process a customer's order Expanded decision-making capability, e.g., computer assisted long range planning

The only comment that needs to be made about the payoffs in [Table] 1 concerns the ability to which these different payoffs can be quantified. The costs, on one hand, can be estimated with reasonable accuracy. Most problems of mis-estimation of costs are a result of over-optimistic (or naive) expectations. The measurement problems on the benefit side, on the other hand, are very complex. Although cost displacement savings are not too difficult to estimate, the values of improved decision-making are hard to enumerate and even harder to evaluate. This is especially true as one moves from improved internal operations to expanded decision capacity.

One frequently presented approach to evaluating MIS payoffs is to consider their time patterns of occurrence [11, p. 357]. This results in a chart similar to [Table] 2. This time oriented perspective for viewing costs and benefits points out the sequence of cost and benefit streams. This orientation emphasizes the time imbalance between the occurrence of costs and benefits. An organization must be willing to incur initial loss years before net benefits are achieved.

Table 2. MIS Development Decision-making

Time Sequence of MIS Payoffs			
Analysis Activities	Design Activities	Implementation Phase	Production Operations
t = 0			t = N
Costs:			
Heavy personnel expenses Light hardware and supplies expenses	Heavy expenditures in all areas	Light to moderate expenses in all areas	Heavy expenses in all areas
Benefits:			
None	None	None	Cost savings
			Improved decision-making

Does the time-oriented analysis presented in [Table] 2 aid in evaluating the net economic benefit of various MIS configurations? The authors contend that it does not! Costs and benefits are the results of decisions, not time; therefore, techniques of economic evaluation of MIS's must be decision-activity oriented. Such an orientation is presented in [Table] 3.

Viewing the MIS payoffs vis-a-vis the decision activities that produce them yields several important insights. First, the only benefits defined are variable benefits, i.e., the benefits only occur as the system operates throughout time. This overlooks benefits related to a more thorough understanding of the firm's operation that is often a result of developing a computer system [11, p. 377]. These benefits, however, could be achieved independently of MIS development. It seems somewhat inappropriate, therefore, to assign them to an MIS. Second, if the premise is accepted that the major benefits of an MIS are the result of improved decision-making [9], the analysis decisions predetermine the bulk of the benefit streams. Third, the fixed costs are incurred because analysis and design decisions must be made. They are a result of the decision-making process rather than the decisions themselves. Finally, the major source of variable MIS costs are the decision alternatives selected in the design activity.

Examination of the payoff/decision classifications reveals the similarities and differences between MIS evaluation in project selection and MIS evaluation in project development. On one hand, project development assumes a commitment from the project selection activity to undertake a given project. This commitment establishes (within a given range) the fixed costs defined in [Table] 3. Evaluation in project development, therefore, becomes a problem of identifying, through the consideration of the analysis and design decision problem, the variable cost and benefit streams associated with alternative MIS configurations.

Table 3. The Relationships between MIS Decision Activities and Payoff Functions

Analysis Decisions	Design Decisions

Benefits:
 (variable)
  Improved decision making
   1. Improved internal
     operations
   2. Improved environmental
     performance
   3. Expanded decision-
     making capability
	Cost savings

Costs:
 (fixed)
  Personnel involved in the analysis
  decision-making process
 (variable)
  Management personnel required to
  maintain or use the system
	Hardware, personnel, and supplies utilized in the design decision-making process:
	  1. Hardware, personnel, and supplies
	    used in production operations
	  2. Reduced benefits due to faulty
	    decisions on the implementation
	    methods

Project selection involves an evaluation problem that takes place, temporally one step before project development. It requires estimating *both* the net benefits (variable benefits minus variable costs) arising from an MIS *and* the fixed costs, i.e., the costs of instituting the analysis and design decision processes, that must be incurred to realize these net benefits. Evaluation in project selection, therefore, is more difficult than in project development because the variable payoffs must be estimated without the knowledge generated in the analysis and design activities.

Implications of the Evaluation Framework

The MIS developmental decisions and the costs and benefits associated with these decisions are the central issue in the economic evaluation of information systems. In order to evaluate the net benefits of alternative MIS configurations, the system developer needs to be able to relate changes in his controllable variables, e.g., different amounts of information supplied, to changes in the dollar values of the relevant costs and benefits. Ideally, this information should be available in a set of mathematical relationships that can be utilized in a specific situation by modifying the parameters that define them. This level of knowledge, especially on the benefit side of MIS evaluation, does not exist.

What are the implications of this lack of cost and benefit functions? For the MIS practitioner, it means that the evaluation of computer applications is going to remain an art form until this type of knowledge is obtained. The classifications of costs and benefits (see [Table] 1) and manner in which they relate to MIS development decisions (see [Table] 3) can provide the MIS developer a logical guideline to use in evaluation. The dollar amounts to costs and benefits will still have to be "guesstimated." The authors feel, however, that a comprehensive emphasis on the decision/payoff relationships significantly improve these "guesstimates."

The absence of economic evaluation functions has some serious implications for the MIS researcher. Research into economic cause-and-effect in MIS's must be undertaken. For given types of MIS's, e.g., MIS's for operation's control or MIS's for financial planning, two basic research activities are needed. First, detailed analysis is needed to find the points at which an information system impacts the organization. Determination of where and how information affects the operating and control decision system is a prerequisite for identifying and measuring costs and benefits. A second research activity concerns the analysis of how a decision-maker converts information into decisions. Do the risk-taking characteristics or does the quantitative aptitude of the decision-makers, for example, influence the impact information has upon the quality of the decision? Research into this particular problem will not be easy. Conversations with MIS practitioners, however, have convinced the authors that this human factor is a prime determinant of MIS value.

Controlled experimentation appears to be the means of undertaking these research areas. The problems in maintaining experimental control and changing experimental variables in real-world systems are well documented [12]. For these reasons, the authors feel that simulation utilizing human decision-makers interacting with a decision environment under the control of the researcher is the most promising avenue of attack.

The decision-oriented framework presented in this paper represents an attempt to synthesize what is involved in MIS evaluation. It is not a finished product that the authors want to set above the research debate. It is, contingent upon improvements and modifications, intended to serve as a vehicle for (1) framing the question of MIS evaluation, and (2) relating various research efforts that must be undertaken into the economic impact of management information systems.

References

1. Ackoff, R., "Management Misinformation Systems," *Management Science*, vol. 14, no. 4, December, 1967.

2. _____, Letter to the Editor, *Management Science*, vol. 14, no. 12, August, 1968.

3. Bedford, N., and M. Onsi, "Measuring the Value of Information—An Information Theory Approach," *Management Services*, vol. 3, no. 1, January–February, 1966.

4. Beged Dov, A., "An Overview of Management Science and Information Systems," *Management Science*, vol. 13, no. 4, August, 1967.

5. Boyd, D. F., and H. S. Krasnow, "Economic Evaluation of Management Information Systems," *IBM Systems Journal*, vol. 2, March, 1963.

6. Burck, G., "The Computer Industry's Great Expectations," *Fortune*, vol. 78, no. 2, August, 1968.

7. Chervany, N. L., "The Ingredients of Economic Decision Making," a paper presented to the Thirteenth Annual Mining Symposium in Duluth, Minnesota, January 15, 1969.

8. Dickson, G. W., "Management Information Decision Systems," *Business Horizons,* vol. 11, no. 6, December, 1968.

9. Diebold, John, "Bad Decisions on Computer Use," *Harvard Business Review*, vol. 47, no. 1, January–February, 1969.

10. Hertz, D. B., "Unlocking the Computer's Profit Potential," A Research Report to Management, McKinsey and Company, 1968.

11. Martin, E. W., Jr., *Electronic Data Processing: An Introduction*, Richard D. Irwin, Inc., Homewood, Illinois, 1961.

12. Naylor, T. H., J. L. Balintfy, D. S. Burdick, and K. Chu, *Computer Simulation Techniques*, John Wiley & Sons, New York, 1966.

13. Pratt, J. W., H. Raiffa, and R. Schlaifer, *Introduction to Statistical Decision Theory*, McGraw-Hill Book Company, New York, 1965.

14. Rappaport, A., "Management Misinformation Systems—Another Perspective," Letter to the Editor, *Management Science*, vol. 15, no. 4, December, 1968.

15. Schrieber, R. J., Letter to the Editor, *Management Science*, vol. 14, no. 12, August, 1968.

16. Swartz, M. H., "Computer Project Selection in Business Enterprise," *Journal of Accountancy*, vol. 127, no. 4, April, 1969.

17. Timms, H. L., *The Production Function in Business*, Richard D. Irwin, Inc., Homewood, Illinois, 1966.

35

Toward a Multi-level, Multi-goal Information System

John E. Field

Reprinted by permission of
The Accounting Review, July 1969.

Organization Structure

Work in industrial operations research has been proceeding now for twenty years. A major by-product of this work is the concept of the firm as a complex total system, resembling a living organism rather than a machine. The relationship between firms and biological systems can, of course, be pushed too far. Transfer of theory from one discipline to another may provide nothing more than superficial analogies. The total system concept, however, is at least a picturesque way of saying that a firm is a set of activities that must be coordinated. A firm certainly is not alive, but it has to behave like a living organism.[1] This desirable result will not be achieved without a great deal of work, unlike the situation in a living organism with its ready-made organization structure. Embedded in the organization structure of a living organism is its information system: this too must be designed for the man-made firm.

A firm should be looked on as an open system, emphasizing its relationship with the supporting environment.[2] It is not surprising that so much effort goes into sales promotion, research, mergers and

[1] S. Beer, *Cybernetics and Management*, (Wiley 1959), p. 17.
[2] D. Katz and R. L. Kahn, *The Social Psychology of Organizations*, (Wiley 1966), p. 9.

other attempts to bring more of the environment under control. Investigation into productivity in British firms concluded that "the most important determinant of a firm's potential for growth and improved efficiency is the ability of its management to learn about its environment. . . ."[3]

The traditional management viewpoint was that division of a firm into parts was desirable, unambiguous and final. This has been challenged as incompatible with technological change.[4] It is considered now that effective organization structure is determined by the work to be done and the resources available to do it.[5]

An organization structure is designed most usefully "from the bottom up," using the production-distribution system as a base.[6] A firm must be run efficiently and this is achieved by division of labor and responsibility for a given work center or basic element in the production-distribution system. On the other hand, the operations of the set of work centers must be coordinated. The point brought out by the system concept is that it is destructive to carry functional specialization right up to the top of the organization structure.

System Theory

To describe the behavior of a system, or to design a man-made system, it is necessary to have an appropriate theory of the structure of systems. A classical example of such a structure is available in feedback system theory as adopted by Forrester.[7] Recently it has been suggested that feedback theory can be extended into a theory of multi-level, multi-goal systems.[8]

[3] "Attitudes in British Management," A P.E.P. Report, Pelican Books 1966, p. 325; originally published as *Thrusters and Sleepers*, (Allen and Unwin, 1965).
[4] S. Beer, "Below the Twilight Arch—A Mythology of Systems," published in D. P. Eckman (Ed), *Systems: Research and Design*, (Wiley, 1961).
[5] W. Brown, *Exploration in Management*, (Heinemann, 1960), p. 19. A similar position has been taken by General Electric Company: see R. N. Anthony, J. Dearden and R. F. Vancil, *Management Control Systems*, (Irwin, 1965), Ch. 2, especially p. 34.
[6] E. D. Chapple and L. R. Sayles, *The Measure of Management*, (Macmillan, 1961), Ch. 2.
[7] Jay W. Forrester, *Industrial Dynamics*, (M.I.T. Press, 1961), p. 13. See also Jay W. Forrester, "A Response to Ansoff and Slevin," *Management Science* (May 1968), p. 604.
[8] D. G. Fleming, M.D. Mesarovic and L. Goodman, "Multi-Level Multi-Goal Approach to Living Organisms," published in K. Steinbuch and S. W. Wagner (Ed), *Neuere Ergebnisse Der Kybernetik*, (Oldenbourg, 1964), pp. 269–282.

Multi-level, multi-goal system theory distinguished first-level goal-seeking units controlling the physical system, from higher-level goal-seeking units that coordinate the first-level control units. This scheme may be generalized into a hierarchy of goal-seeking control units or systems of higher order.[9] Similarly, Forrester points out, "as the basic functions of the business become integrated into a dynamic model, we face more and more the necessity of completing the picture by adding the decision-making characteristics of the higher management levels."[10]

The coordination problem in a complex system is to influence behavior of control units so as to achieve the overall goal. Coordination may be implemented by changing first-level goals, changing decisions delegated to control units, and modifying information supplied to control units. It is through modifying information transfer that accounting is useful in influencing the behavior of the system. Forrester himself points toward this when he writes "as models become more subtle and begin to deal with the very important aspect of top management decision-making, the accounting system becomes an essential part of internal information loops affecting attitudes and decisions."[11]

Survival of the System

For many years it has been considered that the objective of a firm is to earn maximum long-run profit. From a stockholder's viewpoint this continues to be true. One must not lose sight of the primary importance of profit to investors who provide capital for expansion. It has been pointed out that a firm's performance ultimately must be measured in financial terms.[12] Evaluation in terms of other factors is made necessary by inability to measure present value of future benefits, and the belief that satisfactory performance in those factors will contribute to profit in the long run.

Although investors are concerned primarily with profit, managers themselves may not be. The divergence of managers' goals from the stockholders' profit objective has become of greater significance

[9] O. Lange, *Wholes and Parts; A General Theory of System Behavior*, (Pergamon Press, 1965), p. 22.
[10] Forrester, op. cit., p. 329.
[11] Ibid., p. 336.
[12] G. Shillinglaw, chapter in C. P. Bonini, R. K. Jaedicke and H. M. Wagner (Eds) *Management Controls; New Directions in Basic Research*, (McGraw-Hill, 1964), p. 156.

with the continuing increase in size and complexity of business activities. The investors' profit objective is a constraint to be met for the purpose of maintaining share prices. Another constraint of equal importance is managers' own prestige which they may try to satisfy in terms of sales turnover, growth rates and visual expression of social responsibility. Emphasis has shifted toward viewing survival as the ultimate objective.[13] This is consistent with the view of the firm as an open system trying to exist in a more or less hostile environment.

The objective of survival, although descriptive in a general way, is no more operational than the former emphasis on long-run profit maximization. Even if managers did wish to maximize profits, there is no clear way of defining this concept.[14] Similarly, to say that a firm wishes to survive gives no indication of what it must do in order to satisfy this objective.

Multiple Goals

Survival, or alternatively long-run profit maximization, must be broken down into a set of multiple goals.[15] Each goal relates to an area of performance in which the firm wishes to achieve a satisfactory outcome. One of the firm's multiple goals is short-run profit performance. Continual success in terms of profit performance is essential for survival for this provides the means for continued inputs of materials, labor, services and information. Managers are concerned with a variety of factors which they feel are important. In principle, all management actions affect goodwill, and achievement in each area of action is part of short-run changes in the value of the firm. Measurement of the various effects on short-run profit is clearly impossible. Therefore, short-run profit is supplemented by indicators of achievement in relation to markets, employees and so on.

Accountants emphasize profit as an objective because this is part of financial management which historically has been their main

---

[13] H. A. Simon, *Models of Man; Social and Rational*, (Wiley, 1957), Ch. 10. See also S. Beer, op. cit., p. 142.

[14] C. W. Churchman, *Prediction and Optimal Decision*, (Prentice-Hall 1961), pp. 51–56.

[15] J. G. March and H. A. Simon, *Organizations*, (Wiley, 1958), pp. 140–141 and p. 155.

concern. Other specialists emphasize other objectives. Marketing personnel are vitally concerned with market share because a dwindling share means eventual death to the firm. Production managers are concerned with employee relations because they have to keep the plant operating. Many of these objectives from time to time will run counter to rapid increase in short-run profit performance.

Short-run profit position can be improved by cutting down on research, advertizing and other managed costs having long-run consequences. Profit, moreover, can be changed by a change in the accounting treatment of those items. Profit, in fact, has been described as "among the operationally least-defined goals. . . ."[16] It is not surprising that managers look to other performance indicators in the short-run.

Operational Sub-goals

Top management specifies a set of multiple short-run goals describing performance of the total system. Top-level goals must be translated into specific tasks to be performed by subsystems in the firm. Performance in a subsystem can then be measured in terms of degree of success in meeting a prescribed task, quota, standard, budget or plan. A system of subgoals must be designed so that action to improve individual performance will implement total performance.

Assignment of subgoals has been described as a process of decomposing management goals into operational subgoals.[17] The intention is to assign subgoals which are more easily measured, and which consequently are more easily controllable, than top management goals. The process of decomposing goals into subgoals parallels the process of delegating responsibility for decisions. We can go on splitting goals into subgoals, layer by layer, down through the hierarchy of control units in the organization structure. At the physical production-distribution level, the task prescribed for a single operator is intended to contribute toward the firm's ultimate objective.

[16] R. L. Ackoff and M. W. Sasieni, *Fundamentals of Operations Research*, (Wiley, 1968), p. 430.
[17] Y. Ijiri, *Management Goals and Accounting for Control*, (North-Holland Publishing Co., 1965), p. 12.

Management Accounting

The language of the day makes a more or less arbitrary distinction between management accounting and financial accounting. The term management accounting is understood here to be concerned with providing economic information to managers, in contrast with financial accounting which is concerned with economic information for those outside the firm. Management accounting is an economic-behavioral function: financial accounting is concerned largely with legal requirements. Management accounting, in fact, has been described as a branch of organization theory[18] and it is this connotation intended in the present discussion.

If we accept the analogy with a living organism, our attention is directed toward activities essential to survival of the firm. With this perspective we obtain a clearer view of the function of management accounting in the organization, vis-a-vis other information subsystems.

The organization we are concerned with is, at base, a physical production-distribution system. On this base is built a first-level control system structured, so far as possible, like the reflex controls in physiological functions such as digestion and breathing. A first-level, operational control system is not, of course, a set of reflexes controlled by the pons, a part of the nervous system uniting the body with the brain. An operational control system must be designed and implemented in the firm. It is a mixture of programmed controls and rules of thumb arrived at by tradition, trial and error or the implementation of the results of operations research.

Some of the first-level controls are accounting functions. One thinks here of the familiar internal controls over receivables, cash, bank accounts, inventories, payroll and so on. Other operational controls are engineering functions such as production scheduling, inspection, statistical quality control, acceptance sampling and automatic process control.

The intimate interrelationship between information subsystems is shown vividly at the operational level where much of the documentation flows are utilized by both engineering and accounting functions. Production records, for example, originate with inspection routines and flow to the pay office for bonus purposes and to warehouse inventory records. The relationship is shown also in the questions of where to locate the costing office in a manufacturing

---

[18] Churchman, op. cit., p. 64.

firm, in the factory, or in the general office, and who should control the inventory records.

The somewhat arbitrary barrier between information sub-systems is shown by the development of standard costing systems. Originally used by engineers, standard cost routines have been adopted by accountants and integrated with the financial accounts. As the nature of technology changes toward large-scale automation, standard cost systems become less and less relevant in some industries. In view of the history of standard costing, who would be bold enough to say that other processes and statistical controls will not, in time, be accepted as part of the accounting function?

The Top Management Group

In an emergency, the programmed activities of first-level control systems may be over-ridden by top management decision, as if from the motor areas of the cerebral cortex. The cerebrum is the major part of the brain, one set of areas receiving sensory impressions and another set issuing orders to physical activities. A third set, the association areas, is concerned with the highest integrative work of the brain. It is here that sensory information is forged into concepts and motor responses made meaningful instead of remaining a set of reflex actions. The lines of demarcation between areas in the brain appear to be inexact and overlapping,[19] like the changing member-ship of top management committees.

The top management group is concerned with strategic planning,[20] through activities such as long-range planning, operations research and system design. To the extent that accounting has a contribution to make in these activities, specifically in connection with financial appraisal and cost analysis, accounting is a top management function.

Information Systems

In terms of brain structure, the thalamus is a receiving and sorting station for information about the environment and about the state of the physical system. Although dominated by the cerebrum, the

[19] Sidney Ochs, *Elements of Neurophysiology*, (Wiley, 1965), p. 498.
[20] R. N. Anthony, *Planning and Control Systems: A Framework for Analysis*, (Harvard, 1965), p. 24.

thalamus in a very real sense controls the cerebrum through the data it processes and transmits to the sensory areas of the cerebral cortex. In the same way, the top management group in a firm is dependent on information supplied to it.

A wide range of functions is found in a firm's information system. These functions include technological and market research systems scanning the environment, and personnel and buying systems which are concerned with two of the most important inputs required by the firm. Changes in labor markets and supply sources are equal in importance with developments in product markets and technology. Firms grow by expanding their product markets; they also grow by mergers with the complex problem of digesting what has been swallowed.[21]

The accounting function is concerned with some of the information about the state of the system and with some of the information from the environment. Internally, the accounting function must be integrated with the buying, personnel and engineering functions since all subsystems overlap. Externally, accounting is concerned with interfirm comparison and with stock market analysis for capital budgeting and financial management. Accounting information from the environment is integrated with technological and market information in project and new product evaluation.

Middle Management Coordination

Controlling and coordinating the first-level control systems is a group of middle-level managers, supervisors and foremen. This group corresponds to the cerebellum which is a correlation or integration center in the brain.[22] Action specified by the cerebrum is integrated with other information inputs so that physical response is smooth. Removal of the cerebellum does not eliminate motor capabilities but it does interfere with performance. The cerebellum, in other words, is a servo-mechanism which regulates performance of work planned elsewhere.

Design of information systems for middle managers is one of the most important and difficult functions in management account-

---

[21] A. Jay, *Management and Machiavelli*, (Hodder and Stoughton, 1967), p. 31.
[22] Rudolf Nieuwenhuys, "Comparative Anatomy of the Cerebellum," published in C. A. Fox and R. S. Snider (Eds), *The Cerebellum* (Progress in Brain Research, vol. 25); (Elsevier Publishing Co., 1967), pp. 1–93.

ing. Managers need to have a clear understanding of the subgoals assigned to them and to receive a flow of relevant information. This requires a careful screening of the available data from the environment and from the production-distribution level in terms of controllable activities. To a large extent, the first-level control systems can be left alone. Middle managers are coordinators who need information about only those events which appear to be out of control and which they can, and should, correct. As Ackoff has said, although managers lack a good deal of information that they should have, they suffer more from an over abundance of irrelevant information.[23]

The Meaning of Control

Control information is needed so that deviations can be corrected before they become serious, or to show how performance is shaping in relation to goals. Information supplied to a first- or higher-level manager must be relevant to his goals and decisions delegated to him. The information system must be designed so that it is an intrinsic part of the control process as it is in a living organism.

The essential elements of a control system consist of a data processing system, communication channels to distribute information and the control action taken by managers and operators. A control system, in general, consists of a detector, which senses variations in output, a message transmitted by the detector, and a reactor which corrects the input.[24] There may be a "counter feedback" from managers and operators to accounting and data processing, generally enabling information processors to know what reaction is taking place.[25] This may lead to changes in the structure of the information system to achieve the result desired by top management. That is to say, information may be modified to influence the behavior of the system.

There are two distinct ideas in the concept of control. Disagreement about the right way to implement control results frequently from failure to distinguish the two aspects. On the one

[23] Russell L. Ackoff, "Management Misinformation Systems," *Management Science* (December 1967), p. B-150.
[24] P. de Latil, *Thinking by Machine: A Study of Cybernetics*, (Sedgwick and Jackson, 1956), p. 50.
[25] Ibid., p. 64. See also R. J. Chambers, *Accounting, Evaluation and Economic Behavior*, (Prentice-Hall, 1966), p. 161.

hand, "control" means control of the system or what may be termed "operational control." On the other hand, it may mean control of individuals or what may be termed "performance review." This distinction corresponds to control of the physical production-distribution system by first-level control units, as opposed to coordination of those first-level units by higher levels in the hierarchy.

Operational control of the physical production-distribution system depends on planning and a flow of information about what is happening to the system. The term "operational control" is meant to convey the idea of implementation of policies resulting from operations research. Examples are found in production scheduling rules, statistical quality control and inventory replenishment routines. Chapple and Sayles explain control in this sense by the question "how can we predict from our records . . . that a deviation is about to take place in the near or distant future. . . ."[26]

Performance review, in contrast with operational control, is a matter of motivation. There is no attempt to correct current operations in the physical production-distribution system. Budgetary control, responsibility accounting and other forms of performance review are intended as checks on what has happened in respect of previous decisions in lower-level control units. Review of performance is expected to improve control action in the future. This may be achieved by greater experience in the control unit, or by changing subgoals assigned to it, decisions delegated to it or information supplied to it.

The distinction made here between operation control and performance review is the distinction between "current control" and "post control" made by Litterer.[27] Both concepts of control are aspects of management control in general, and both are included in the accounting term "internal control."[28] Internal control, as distinct from external control by stockholders, is the set of procedures designed to control total operations. This includes physical, financial and data processing operations. The accounting concept of internal control includes the area from organization design, through operational control and performance review, to asset protection.

[26] Chapple and Sayles, op. cit., p. 72.

[27] J. A. Litterer, *The Analysis of Organizations*, (Wiley, 1965), p. 234.

[28] C. R. Niswonger and P. E. Fess, *Accounting Principles*, (South-Western, 1965), p. 276.

Conclusions

A committee of the American Accounting Association has stated that the objectives of accounting are, *inter alia*, to provide information for decisions concerning goals and the use of limited resources.[29] Like the operation of the thalamus, the accounting function both assists and controls the management group through the information it selects and transmits to it. The accountant, therefore, must be intimately associated with goal determination and assignment to lower levels, since the goal structure will be the base on which the information system is designed. Success in accounting performance along with that of other information subsystems, is shown by absence of stress or conflict in the organization and by the extent to which top management is able to achieve its goals. Efficient accounting is a necessary (although not sufficient) prerequisite for organizational survival.

The total system concept emphasizes that information handling should be coordinated in the same way as physical operations. An information system is dependent on the structure of control units in the organization, the subgoals assigned to them and the decision-making powers delegated to them. The information system must change as the organization changes in response to its environment. Accounting, like other information subsystems, must be designed to facilitate control of a multi-level, multi-goal organization structure.

[29] American Accounting Association, *A Statement of Basic Accounting Theory*, (American Accounting Association 1966), p. 4 and pp. 39–40.

Section **3**

Need for Management Training

36

Management Information Systems: Training for Businessmen

Robert G. Murdick
and Joel E. Ross

Reprinted by permission of
Journal of Systems Management, October 1969.

The training programs that businessmen need obviously do not meet the educational goals of university students. A business must look for shorter range—now—returns for its large investment in training; it cannot afford to provide long periods of education whose payoff may be both intangible and remote in time. Therefore, companies are concerned mainly with bringing their men abreast of new technologies so that the individuals may then attempt to continue to remain abreast on their own initiative. This applies to training programs for management information systems as well as any other programs.

The program outlined in the following paragraphs is based upon results from two investigations. One study consisted of a government-sponsored workshop in which more than 40 national leaders from industry, education and government assembled to determine the need for systems designers and content of training programs. The other study consisted of a series of field trips and extensive interviews with about ten corporate or division managers with responsibility for management information systems. A number of these held titles such as manager—management information systems, manager—corporate systems and data processing, and manager—business systems and information processing.

Results of both investigations indicate that the leaders in industry and government are groping for ways to organize for and utilize the tremendous payoffs possible with computer-based information systems. The leap from straight data processing to computer-based systems problem solving has been sudden. Understanding and assimilation of the potentialities for decision making have energized leaders in all forms of endeavor. Their first question is, "What do we do to keep from falling behind, to catch up, to forge ahead in this new management approach?" This article, last in a series of three, may provide some answers to this question.

Who Needs It

The impact of management information systems on business has been brought out in the first article of this series. The questions that a company must face are:

1. *Who should we train in MIS?*
2. *What should our objectives be in each case?*
3. *What content and educational level should we strive for in our training courses?*

The investigations indicated that the most pressing needs for training in MIS are for the following groups:

1. *Top managers*
2. *All levels of managers*
3. *Managers of business systems and information systems groups*
4. *Systems analysts and designers*
5. *Computer programmers for systems applications*

Wide variations in type of training and learning objectives appear appropriate for these groups, even though some groups are obviously not mutually exclusive. The content and general objectives for each are first discussed.

General Objectives

For top management, the consensus regarding objectives emerges as:

1. *Orient and familiarize the manager to the end that his information processing system will be more productive*

by: (a) establishing the role of automatic data process-ing (ADP) in the organization; (b) providing tighter control over production of paperwork; (c) getting the manager involved in problem solving ("ADP doesn't solve problems; people do"); and (d) utilizing talents already in the organization.

2. *Close the understanding and appreciation "gap" be-tween management and ADP operations.*

3. *Familiarize the manager with the capability of the computer for improving management effectiveness and productivity through information.*

For operating managers, the objective is more practical. The manager should learn how he could use information systems and the computer in his operations. He must understand how to organize for systems design and implementation. Finally, and very importantly, he must learn how to evaluate MIS in his own operation.

Managers of business systems, the third group, are those responsible for the technical implementation of systems design. They must be able to understand the complexities of top management's problems and translate these into programs for the design of information systems that will aid in their solution. Thus they must be able to speak both language of management and the language of the technician.

The tasks of systems analysts differ considerably among companies, among government agencies, and among other institu-tions. The position description recently developed by the U. S. Civil Service Commission provides a good summary of the systems analyst's duties:

Computer systems analysts develop basic plans of "computer applications" by which subject-matter processes can be organized and accomplished by computer methods. They require a compre-hensive understanding and analysis of subject-matter work processes, actions, criteria, as well as supporting controls, reports, documenta-tion, etc., involved in the function to be automated. Also essential is the ability to devise procedures, to develop methods for generating and processing data, and to integrate these data into processing systems and plans. Typically, specific assignments may include: feasibility or "profitability" studies; the development of detailed systems logic charts and diagrams; the development of data reduction and coding instructions, dictionaries, data banks, and the like. In addition, these positions require a substantial knowledge of com-puter capabilities and processes, and a basic understanding of programming principles and methods. They analyze and organize subject-matter work processes and functions so that they can be converted into workable computer programs and routines. Furthermore, systems analysts must be able to foresee some of the specific problems posed in the subsequent programming processes required, as well as some of the possible solutions to such problems.

The systems analyst for management information systems has developed beyond the old flowchart-operations analysis technician; he is regarded by executives as a logical problem solver with a whole new kit of quantitative and computer tools at his command.

Training Program for Top Management

Top management has very limited time for training "programs," with the result that several one- or two-day seminars over a period of a year may be all that is possible. In this brief time, training must be devoted to the nature of operational systems and closing the gap between the manager and the specialists in management information systems design. The subject areas and level of learning for top management are shown in Table 1. Some "hands on" experience with the computer is highly desirable. BASIC and other time-sharing terminal languages may be explained in a few minutes so that experience at such a terminal is possible.

Training Program for Operational Managers

The training program for operational managers and the level of learning is outlined in Table 1. There are four major subject areas to be covered:

1. Management information systems
   Problem solving and decision making
   Nature of management science
   Nature of management systems
   Organizational problems of system implementation
   Systems evaluation
2. Hardware and how it operates
   The workings of a computer
   Capabilities, limitations and potential
   Input-output devices
   Software considerations

File organization and maintenance
Input-output documentation and display
New technology
3. Computer applications
   Basic existing applications
   Advanced applications
4. "Hands on" experience
   Some experience with time-sharing terminals and language is desirable. The managers should be given an opportunity to ask "what if" questions at the terminal for some model that has been stored in the computer. It is difficult to bring to the manager the potentialities of the computer and time-sharing by just talking about it.

Training for Managers of Systems Groups

Companies have begun to establish positions designated as manager-information systems or manager-business systems. Because in the past the accounting or finance department has had the responsibility for gathering key business information, and because the computer is usually first introduced in a company by this department, it is only natural that top management looks to the accounting or finance department for an expanded role. Figure 1 shows the organizational

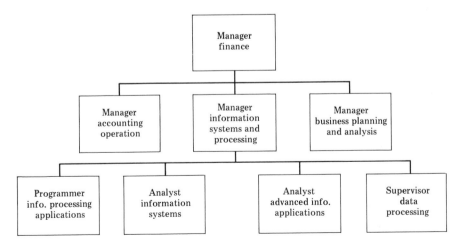

Figure 1.   The MIS organization.

	1: Knowledge 2: Understanding 3: Skill in application 4: Analysis and evaluation 5: Synthesis Analysis, Synthesis, and Design Concepts	Top managers	Operating managers	MIS managers	Systems designers	System computer programmers
I—Problem solving—the theory and practice of logic, decision making and creative thinking. The use of these and other problem-solving principles in the analysis and design of systems.		5	5	5	5	3
II—Organization principles—classical and contemporary principles of organization design and analysis. An understanding of the structure, decision centers, information flow and other organizational considerations in systems design.			2	2	2	
III—Management—the basic functions of management, with special emphasis on planning and controlling through information systems. Consideration and understanding of facilitating the management process with systems.			2	2	2	
IV—Systems planning—determining systems objectives and planning time, cost and resource allocations. Design proposals. PERT/CPM input/output considerations.		2	4	5	5	1
V—Systems theory—theory of information systems operation and design. Control theory. Integrated and total systems concepts. Planning and control through information feedback systems.				5	5	1
VI—Systems evaluation—measuring efficiency against goals. Input/output review and review of objectives.		2	4	4	4	
VII—Human interaction in systems—gaining acceptance and "selling" ADP. The impact of automation on personnel. Getting cooperation. Interpersonal relationships. Applied psychology.		2	2	3	2	
VIII—Quantitative techniques in systems design—application of operations research and other management science techniques. Formulation of decision rules. Simulation and modeling.			1	2	3	3
Analysis and Design Techniques						
IX—Systems planning—network analysis technique for logical structuring of planning. Preliminary systems survey. The feasibility study. The cost evaluation and analysis. Analysis of time requirements. Planning quality elements of the system.			2	3	5	2

Table 1.   Training Programs Summary

1: Knowledge 2: Understanding 3: Skill in application 4: Analysis and evaluation 5: Synthesis	Top managers	Operating managers	MIS managers	Systems designers	System computer programmers
Analysis and Design Techniques (continued)					
X—Systems analysis and design—analytical techniques and documentation (work measurement, flow charting, forms design, source data automation, etc.) Input-output alternatives. Communications, interviewing, and selling. Principles of systems design.	2	4	5	1	
XI—Implementation and follow-up—planning site preparation, personnel, organization, other considerations. Training the user. Evaluation and audit.	5	5	2	1	
Computer Concepts and Capabilities					
XII—Hardware characteristics—mainframe capability, peripheral equipment remotes and linkage input-output devices, time-sharing, on-line systems, etc.	1	1	2	2	5
XIII—Software—languages and compiler options (FORTRAN, COBOL, ALGOL, BASIC, TELCOMP, QUIKTRAN, CAL) Standard programs and models. Systems applications.	1	2	4	4	5
Additional Skill Requirements					
XIV—Programming			1	2	5
XV—Quantitative techniques—management science techniques in systems design.			2	3	4
XVI—Communications—graphics and visual presentations. The oral and written staff report.		5	5	3	3

Table 1. Training Programs Summary (continued)

pattern adopted by many departments (complete businesses) of a large multigroup company.

Very often, the individual put in charge of the information systems group has been trained as an accountant and has picked up some knowledge of computers on the job. He has little knowledge, and often little perspective, of the nature of information systems and management science. In spite of this somewhat narrow background, this individual influences vital decisions. This manager should therefore be trained as soon as he is placed, and preferably before he has been placed in this position.

The MIS manager's training must broaden his understanding of company operations and top management's problems; it must also provide him depth of understanding of the technical areas of management science, systems design and analysis, and computer applications. Proper training is required so that he can staff his organization, guide the training of his people and provide direction for them. His own training must enable him to look ahead beyond the current demands upon his organization; otherwise he becomes simply another technician who fails to fulfill the true needs of his company.

The breadth and depth of his training is suggested in Table 1.

Training Program for the Systems Analyst

The systems analyst must have an understanding of the firm's objectives and management's problems. In this sense, his training must be continuous. His basic contribution is the application of special knowledge to the solution of systems problems. His training should primarily give him greater technical skills. He must gain depth of knowledge of business problems, MIS systems, management science, and computer applications. He must also gain skill in application of analysis and design techniques.

The ideal systems analyst will have a college degree based on either operations research, mathematics or management science. Those without such a background should have the ability to be trained in quantitative methods, and many have been so trained in company programs. Table 1 indicates the subject matter and learning goals for training programs for systems analysts. Programs must, of course, be tailored for the particular individuals employed.

Training of Computer Programmers

In the companies that were visited by the authors, the belief was expressed that some computer programmers should be assigned to the MIS organization. Such programmers actually form a team with systems analysts to perform system design and evaluation. The programmer represents the hardware viewpoint on the team. He takes the position, "Where can the computer be utilized more effectively, in what new applications and for what new systems?" This contrasts with the outlook of the systems analyst who seeks the best system and then looks for hardware to implement it.

Table 1 indicates the kind of in-company training helpful to computer programmers assigned to the systems team.

Conclusion

All managers and many specialists have a direct interest in MIS development. Varied company training programs are required to bring and keep these people abreast of rapidly changing developments in management systems and decision processes. The variations in the training programs are primarily those of depth with respect to a group of central topics.

Each company should examine its current stage of sophistication, the level of sophistication of its MIS people and managers, and the urgency of its need for advanced systems in order to develop feasible and profitable training programs.

37

Educating Potential Managers about the Computer

Daniel Couger

© 1968 by The Regents of the University of California.
Reprinted from *California Management Review*,
Fall 1968, pp. 47–58, by permission of The Regents.

One of five men in college today is majoring in business.[1] Total enrollment in collegiate schools of business is expected to reach 600,000 by 1970.[2] Despite these large numbers, industry recruiters are experiencing considerable difficulty in meeting the needs for management trainees in their firms.

> The problem is especially acute among companies seeking to hire new employees with Master of Business Administration degrees. . . . A man with a M.B.A. can demand as much as $10,000."[3]

Some firms attempt to meet this problem by selecting high potential employees and underwriting the costs for their M.B.A. In either case, the firms expect these costly people to be educated in the techniques and concepts which will enable them to best perform the management function in today's increasingly complex business environment. Unfortunately, most schools of business are neglecting education in one of the most important managerial aids—the

---

[1] "Summary Report on Bachelors and Higher Degrees Conferred," U.S. Department of Health, Education and Welfare (Washington, D.C.: Government Printing Office, 1966).

[2] "New Report Card on the Business School," *Fortune*, Dec. 1965, p. 148.

[3] "The Great Young Man Hunt," *Forbes*, March 1, 1967, pp. 46–47.

computer. A recent survey indicates that the majority of the recipients of diplomas from schools of business this June, both undergraduate and graduate, will have received little education in the use of this valuable managerial tool. This situation is enigmatic in light of the actual business environment, where the computer is an integral part of the managerial process in many firms.

The lack of required computer courses in both graduate and undergraduate programs was revealed in a 1966 survey that I conducted among members of the American Association of Collegiate Schools of Business. Since the AACSB is comprised of the leading 113 schools of business, it is unlikely that many of the other 500 American schools of business have introduced the computer into their curricula to any greater extent. Nor is the problem a result of a disagreement on the appropriateness of computer content in the curriculum. Of the survey respondents, 97 per cent reported that such education should be an objective of the school.

The problem of what to teach and the approach to teaching it are major deterrents to the development of computer curricula in most of these schools. On the other hand, a few progressive schools have been at work on this problem for a number of years and have developed a strong computer curriculum, designed to educate the potential manager concerning ways to use the computer to the best advantage. In addition, these schools have developed some highly sophisticated computer programs for use both in educational and business applications. To make such developments available to all schools and to provide guidelines for incorporation of computer technology into the curriculum, I conducted on-site research in eleven of the most progressive schools of business.[4] Selected from among the ninety respondents to the AACSB survey, these eleven schools include both large-endowment private schools and state-supported schools with relatively moderate budgets.[5]

Accomplishments in these schools are the result of a slow and painstaking evolutionary process. It is anticipated, however, that a report of their successes and problems will help other schools to leap-frog from the usual evolutionary pattern. The gap between curriculum objectives and accomplishments in the majority of business schools needs to be closed as quickly as possible—to permit

---

[4] The research project was made possible through a grant from the International Business Machines Corporation.

[5] The eleven schools were Carnegie Institute of Technology, Dartmouth, Florida, Florida State, Harvard, Pennsylvania, Stanford, Texas, Tulane, U.C.L.A., and Wisconsin.

graduates to utilize effectively a tool capable of handling complex business problems. The results of the research, summarized in this article, will be published in a report to all 613 schools of business during the current year.

How Much Detail

Objectives in Computer Curriculum

The responses in the initial survey indicated that a major problem in developing computer curriculum is determination of the level of detail to provide. More than 90 per cent of the respondents agreed that the minimal goal should be a level of detail to permit the student to recognize the applicability of computers to business.

Considerable disagreement existed on the methods necessary to implement this objective, however. Should the curriculum level be geared to the student about to enter business, or the student already in the first level of supervision, or middle management, or staff positions? Determination of objectives is not a new business school problem. One dean wrote a tongue-in-cheek memorandum to his colleagues on the problem of varying business school objectives, stating,

> . . . a composite of catalog statements suggests that our programs are designed to prepare the candidate for any of the following kinds of careers, in which he is to be both professionally competent and socially responsible:
>
> 1. Both in management and related professions.
> 2. Whether in business, in government, in the armed forces, or in nonprofit organizations.
> 3. Both in integrative and functional management.
> 4. At all levels.
> 5. In all fields without regard to the nature of either the product or service or of the technology involved.
> 6. Anywhere in or out of the United States.
> 7. At all stages of his career.
> 8. Now and in the future.
>
> [The dean concluded] Only the statement of objectives in the corporate charter for U.S. Steel is as comprehensive.

In this context, a disparity in theories on implementation

among the survey respondents was not unexpected. Conversely, the unanimity of approach among the eleven most progressive schools was quite surprising. The statement of objectives in computer curriculum as recorded in the Tulane University catalog is typical of the schools in which the research took place:

> Perhaps the most certain fact of life facing the future manager is the tremendous role that high speed and large capacity computers will have in the management of his enterprise. Thus, an academic program designed to prepare future managers must devote considerable attention to what is now known as the computer sciences.

> Tulane's program requires every student to become operational with a large high-speed computer, currently an IBM 7044 with related equipment. The student must be able to program his own problems, understand computer methodology, and know how to utilize computer information processing and analytical capabilities in management decision-making situations.

> The objective is not to make computer specialists of students. Rather, every graduate is expected to be comfortable in a business environment in which computers are a daily part of managerial activity. He must be able to recognize opportunities to use the computer in his managerial activities, to know what to expect from it, and to know how to communicate effectively with computer specialists so that computerized projects will be properly handled from a technical, as well as managerial, point of view.

Not only were the eleven schools in agreement on the objectives for computer curriculum, their approaches to establishing courses to meet these objectives were quite similar.

What the Manager Needs to Know about Computers

The computer curriculum is highly coordinated with the regular curriculum in these schools. The educational approach consists of four phases:

> *Coverage of computer fundamentals, systems analysis, and design and programming through a course required of all students early in their academic program.*

Coverage of the applications of computers through incorporation of this material into the functional area courses, e.g., computer applications in finance in the finance courses, computer applications in marketing in the marketing courses, etc.

Coverage of computer capabilities for abetting decision making in a dynamic business environment through computer-oriented business games.

Coverage of integration and optimization of computer applications through a course on design and implementation of a sophisticated, computer-based management information system.

Figure 1 illustrates the manner in which material on computer technology is integrated into the regular curriculum.

Teaching Programming

Computer Fundamentals and Programming

All but one of these schools require a course in computer fundamentals or plan to implement such a requirement within the next year. In most schools the requirement is satisfied through a credit course covering fundamentals, systems analysis, and design and programming. In a few schools the programming requirement is satisfied through a noncredit, condensed course, with systems analysis and design covered in one of the functional area courses.

The requirement for computer programming is based on the premise that knowing how to program a computer is the best way to understand its uses and limitations. Knowledge of computer programming techniques provides some important auxiliary benefits, as well:

1. *The logic required in developing effective computer programs helps prepare the student for the decision-making process.*
2. *Such knowledge permits the student to better understand the use of previously developed programs by which he can generate and process data for decision making.*
3. *The student writes programs to handle much more*

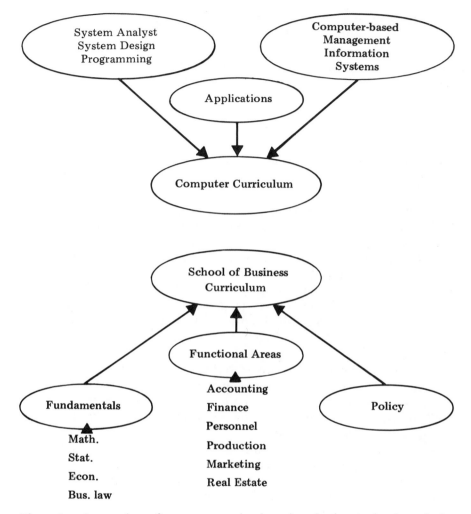

Figure 1.   Integration of computer technology into business school curricula.

> *significant problems than he could solve through manual manipulation.*

Emphasizing the importance of the last benefit, Harvard's Dr. Stanley Buchin commented, "The mass of data to be analyzed and the complexity of the analysis required in accomplishing really significant research projects are rarely possible without the use of computers."

An important change in the approach to course research

projects is evidenced in these schools. In the past, "research" often meant library study, where a student spent many hours rewriting the literature on a specific subject. Now the student is assigned an actual research project, where he utilizes the capabilities of the computer to tackle some significant problems, or variations on problems, which have not been solved previously.

A similar advantage exists in the handling of daily course assignments. Many quantitative techniques are so complex and time-consuming that only trivial problems can be assigned to students for manually derived solutions. The availability of computer programs for use of these techniques permits the student to work on nontrivial problems. Once the student understands the concept, he can better comprehend the advantages and limitations of the technique by gathering data, processing it on the computer, then evaluating the output.

Since the objective is to be able to program, not to become a programmer, all but one of the eleven schools provide instruction in the simplest and most universal programming language, FORTRAN. Not only is FORTRAN an easy language to master, it is a powerful computational language which emphasizes logical thought processes.

The ease in understanding this language is best demonstrated by the way in which it is covered in most of these schools. The usual approach is to require the student to learn the language outside class, through the use of a programmed-instruction manual. The classroom activities consist of review of the computer manufacturer's manual for the specific computer being programmed and discussion of programs written by students.

Despite the limited amount of programming instruction, practice on significant problems produces some surprisingly proficient programmers. In one school 85 per cent of the systems software for a newly released computer was written by undergraduate students, when the computer manufacturer reported it would have to slip the systems software schedule by nine months. In another school a team comprised of student programmers and computer manufacturer programmers is writing the systems software for a third-generation computer to be installed this spring. Many students use programming to pay their way through school, serving as freelance programmers. The rates published on the bulletin boards at Pennsylvania are typical—from $2 to $10 per hour. A professor reported that one of his students is proficient enough to command a fee of $100 per day.

The situation has its disadvantages, however. Despite the many values of programming knowledge, few of the academicians interviewed consider programming an appropriate career for a business school graduate. Many consider the microanalysis aspect of most programming jobs antithetical to the macroanalysis demanded of a manager. Nevertheless, the shortage of programmers enables a business school graduate to start at a salary of $100 to $200 per month higher than salaries paid to management trainees. Some professors counsel their students to consider only those jobs where systems analysis and programming are combined. As a "systegrammer," the student designs and programs the over-all system and is provided valuable experience compatible with that required of a management trainee.

Specialized Courses

Instruction on Computer Applications

Computer fundamentals, system analysis, and design and programming techniques are most effectively covered in specialized courses, prerequisite to course work in the functional fields. Education on computer applications is best provided through the functional areas of the curriculum. Again, strong unanimity in this approach exists among the eleven schools, perhaps best expressed by Dean George Baker of Harvard, "The computer is affecting every aspect of the business enterprise—we need to include in the course content in each curriculum area material on present uses of the computer and the research being conducted on new uses."

While computer simulations of firms operating in a competitive environment have been in use for some time, computer simulations of the operation of major activities within a firm are relatively new. The progressive schools have developed some highly sophisticated computer simulation and applications programs for the functional areas. The purpose is twofold:

To better educate students in the interactive elements of the function.

To educate students in the nature and use of computer simulators.

A few of the simulators and applications programs used in the functional areas are summarized below:

Harvard M.B.A. students in the production core course

write a computer program for digital simulation of a hypothetical two-stage manufacturing process. In describing his course, Dr. James McKenney explained "that the minimal goal was for each student to create a computer program which effectively simulates the material flow and control system for the firm." Part of the task of preparing the program is the definition of decision rules for each of the decisions specified.

U.C.L.A.'s Dr. David Eiteman developed a program for his classes to perform a matrix evaluation on the value of stock, based on current projections. The program provides the values of the alternatives. Professor John Shelton of U.C.L.A. developed a program for financial simulation of the future financial needs of a firm, given various assumptions and historical data. He divides his classes into teams of two or three members and sends them out to study local firms. They gather pertinent data, run complete financial analyses using the computer program, then prepare a written evaluation, which is made available to the firm.

At Stanford, Dr. Peter Winters developed a production simulation program which accepts and utilizes decision procedures programmed by students. Students write a subroutine, called DECIDE, which specifies forty-eight parameters in the planning and scheduling of a simulated factory. The objective of the simulator is to find the decision processes which minimize production costs. Dr. Henry Claycamp of Stanford assigns students of his marketing classes a research project of writing a computer program to utilize the Chicago Tribune Data Bank, for panel analysis of two million records of consumer purchases.

Professor Roy Harris of Texas teaches simulation languages such as G.P.S.S. and SIMSCRIPT to enable his students to write simulators for assembly line balancing and inventory control.

A program designed to prepare production costs reports for process cost accounting has been developed by

Wisconsin's Dr. Werner Frank. His students utilize this program to process cost data for various production departments, with a choice of several cost accounting methods. In another course, Dr. Frank teaches his students a simplified programming language, SIMPAL, to enable them to use an information retrieval program for cost accounting data. Students write programs to retrieve and process the data according to specific accounting techniques.

Dartmouth has been particularly effective in adoption of computer applications materials into the functional areas. Student work on the computer covers a wide and highly challenging range of activities, shown in the boxed list.

Decision-making Practice

Computer-oriented Business Games

The suboptimal and restrictive business games of the 1950's have been greatly sophisticated. All eleven schools are utilizing computer-oriented business games, usually in conjunction with the business policy courses. Although the primary objective of the business game is not the education of the students concerning the use of the computer in a dynamic decision-making environment, computer-oriented games fulfill such a purpose and, as a consequence, are considered as part of the computer curriculum.

The most sophisticated and realistic approach is the Carnegie Management Game. This comprehensive game includes segments in economics, organization theory, finance, marketing, and production. Teams are required to set prices and determine output level. The environment contains the various functions such as the demand curve, which determines the outcome of the decisions made for each firm. The firms receive income statements and balance sheets, and the outcome of their decisions can be traced on the financial statements.

Carnegie introduced and pioneered in the development of this extremely complex management simulation exercise as an integral part of its curriculum. It has become a model on which similar exercises at other schools are based. Currently, twelve business leaders sit on boards of directors for the participating firms (or teams). Their function in the exercise is exactly as it is in actual

Student Work on the Dartmouth
Time-sharing Computer System

1. Probabilistic forecasting of income statements, balance sheets, and cash flow statements
2. Forecasting the ability of a company to meet fixed charges
3. Analyzing a lease proposal
4. Deducing and applying the logic behind bond tables
5. Solving realistic bond problems
6. Developing an understanding of discounting and compounding with computer exercises
7. Manipulating different depreciation methods to establish which is "best" under a given set of assumptions
8. Sensitivity analysis
9. Testing and modifying theories of measuring and evaluating performance of mutual funds, pension funds, and other portfolios
10. Testing, using, and modifying portfolio selection techniques, e.g., Markovitz and Sharpe
11. Devising and testing models for selecting stocks
12. Constructing yield curves, devising switching strategies, and generally solving problems involving bonds
13. Linear programming with library routine
14. Production planning simulation
15. Simulation of bank teller waiting lines
16. Regression analysis
17. Mutually exclusive investment decision involving securities and real property
18. Cost functions
19. Input-output model
20. Decision on factor proportions given production and factor unit cost information
21. Capital budgeting
22. Forecasting models, exponential smoothing
23. Short-term budget forecast for business game
24. Bayesian analysis of marketing research information
25. Queueing simulation
26. Plant layout
27. Simulation of stratified samples
28. Markov chain and simulation model of monopoly

business situations. They suggest policies and review all major decisions made by the firms playing the game and thus have been able to give great educational assistance by providing another dimension of realism to the game experience.

Dr. Kalman Cohen, one of the originators of the game, described the objectives thus:

> The purpose is to provide guided experience in managerial decision making under conditions of competition and uncertainty and to advance students' skills of analysis, advocacy, and negotiations in contacts with outside groups like boards of directors, auditors, and union representatives.

Even functional areas considered by some as inviolate, as far as computer technology is concerned, are heavily involved in the game. The game actually serves as a human relations laboratory where students in this field observe the actions and reactions of participants of the game.

Data Systems Approach

Computer-based Management Information Systems

Courses in the design and use of computer-based management information systems have been added to the required curriculum in eight of the eleven schools. The emphasis in these courses is to identify information needs for each level of management and to develop a conceptual model to integrate all the modules of a computer-based management information system.

Such a course requires a firm foundation in the management sciences, for use of these techniques is required to optimize the M.I.S. In prior years, business school students did not have the quantitative background for such analysis. Now at least twelve hours of undergraduate mathematics, including calculus, are required in most schools. Graduate programs include a minimum of one management science course, in addition to the coverage of many of these techniques in the functional courses.

Students in the M.I.S. course work cooperatively to design a computer-based management information system with the following objectives:

> *To capture or generate all data pertinent to the firm's operations.*

> *To process the data in the most efficient and economical manner, requiring use of the techniques of the management sciences.*

To produce concise and timely information, as required by each level of management for optimum execution of its functional objectives.

Since most managers are heavily involved in the development and continual evolution of a M.I.S., a course of this type is an important curriculum concern.

The Problems

Factors Inhibiting Implementation of Computer Curriculum

Contrary to a pre-research hypothesis, the greatest deterrent to incorporation of computer technology into the curriculum is not the cost associated with use of the computer. The greatest inhibiting factor is the shortage of faculty members capable of teaching this material.

Shortage of Computer Faculty

The rapid expansion in use of computers in the United States (30,785 installed as of January 1, 1967, with more than 11,000 expected to be installed this year[6]) has created an enormous shortage of trained computer personnel. The academic field is no exception. The academic problem is more serious than might appear at first glance. Not only is there a shortage of instructors for the specialized computer courses, there is an even greater shortage of faculty members able to provide proper instruction on the applications of computers in the functional areas of the curriculum. Nor can the shortage be met through recruitment of recent doctoral graduates from institutions with strong computer curricula. The demand far exceeds the supply. The demand for these persons is such that they command a starting salary 10 to 15 per cent higher than their noncomputer-oriented colleagues. The problem is so acute this spring that some schools are including in the recruitment package the rank of associate professor, instead of the normal starting rank of assistant professor.

The only way to meet the critical need is for the existing faculty to acquire a proficiency in this field. However, it's not just a matter of the dean saying "Go to it, men!"

Faculty members are continually retooling, just as the factory

[6] "The Big Prize is Second Place," *Business Automation*, Feb. 1967, p. 40.

laborer confronted with automation must retool. Keeping abreast of new developments in his field of specialization is difficult enough, without adding to the academician the burden of becoming proficient in computer technology. He must be convinced of the importance of such knowledge to give it high priority among retooling needs. In keeping with the tradition of academic freedom, deans are reluctant to require such priority. Instead, they try to establish ways to facilitate the acquisition of computer proficiency. A variety of approaches to faculty education have been used in the eleven progressive schools: special faculty seminars, computer manufacturers' courses, leaves of absence for study at other universities, and grants for developing programs for educational uses.

The most successful approach to the faculty seminar in the eleven schools visited was Florida State's program. Dean Charles Rovetta initiated the seminars three years ago. He relieved the instructor, Dr. Charles Hubbard, of part of his teaching load to permit him to prepare a special program for the faculty. The weekly seminar, of approximately one and one-half hours duration, provides considerable detail concerning computers and the management sciences. A series of excellent handouts has been prepared, including problems for solution outside class. Although the other schools have used the faculty seminar approach, none has achieved the sustained success of Florida State. Dean Rovetta strongly encouraged faculty participation, but did not require it. Deans in the other schools indicated that two principal problems in the faculty seminar approach were:

The difficulty in scheduling seminars at a time which did not conflict with other academic activities.

The widely varying level of knowledge on the subject, making it difficult to teach such a seminar.

Off-campus courses, removing the faculty member from usual pressures, were more effective for some schools. A number of courses are available, such as those provided by computer manufacturers, universities, and professional societies. The cost of travel and tuition, plus the problems arising from a faculty member's absence from the campus for an extended period, limit this educational avenue to the large budget schools or to a select few persons from schools with less financial and reserve faculty resources.

One approach, which is quite effective, is relief from teaching duties for a semester. During the first part of the semester the professor acquires a knowledge of computer fundamentals; in the remaining time he gains proficiency through developing programs to be used in his courses. Although this approach is expensive, it is particularly beneficial for departments where little computer knowledge exists and where an energetic, respected faculty member is selected for the project. As a result of this project, the faculty member generates interest and provides an incentive for his colleagues to acquire such a proficiency—with his help. Such an effect was observed in four of the schools. For example, in a U.C.L.A. department little computer knowledge existed until one faculty member was given a semester for such a project. His success in developing programs for his courses, coupled with his assistance to other faculty members, resulted in four faculty members becoming active in computer projects.

Some schools provide research assistants to write computer programs for classroom or educational use, based on specifications provided by a professor. Few schools can afford enough research assistants for the entire faculty to use this approach, although some have produced improvement in several areas by alternating assistantships between departments.

Although any one of these approaches, or a combination of approaches, might appear to reach a minority of the faculty, the multiplier principle quickly expands the educational effect in several ways:

> In addition to the direct incentive described above, the computer-oriented faculty member also provides an indirect incentive. Through observation of the more frequent and lucrative consulting opportunities for computer-oriented professors, faculty members are induced to acquire computer proficienty.

> The influence of the computer-oriented faculty member on his students has widespread effect also. For example, in three of the eleven schools, leading computer academicians were proteges of Professor Elwood Buffa of U.C.L.A.—a strong advocate of the use of the computer in his field.

> Faculty members are provided the incentive to acquire computer proficiency by computer-oriented students. One of the faculty members at Pennsylvania resisted computer involvement in his courses, explaining to his colleagues, "This is a vocational technique, which should be acquired

on the job." Despite his colleagues' inability to dissuade him, a student who had completed a programming course was able to change his perspective. The student was a member of a class assigned a particularly difficult problem. Previous classes had required 20 to 30 hours to derive a solution, so this class was given a two-week deadline. When the student asked if he could write a computer program and use the computer for the solution of the problem, the professor condescendingly agreed, warning that the two-week deadline still had to be met. When the student arrived at class the next day with the correct solution, the computer field gained a convert.

Computer Costs

Although computer cost is not the major restriction in development of computer curriculum, it is a significant factor. Deans have considerable difficulty in convincing university administration of the need to increase the school's budget for computer use. The administration has reason to question computer budgets in some cases, however. Computer costs have been higher than necessary in some schools, because the dean or influential faculty members insisted that the school have its own computer. The three reasons most often cited in support of a business school computer, instead of using a central campus computer or another department's computer, are:

The ability to acquire the computer best suited for business problems.

Easier access to the computer for students and faculty.

Less turnaround time for processing computer runs.

The first argument is invalidated by actual practice among the respondents to the original survey. Many are using computers which are scientifically rather than business oriented, such as the I.B.M. 1620. The type of problems and research being done in business schools today is such that a minimal gain in efficiency would result from use of a business computer.

It is true that business faculty and students have easier access to a business school computer. On the other hand, less control in use of the computer exists in business school facilities, in terms of machine and operator standards, formal procedures, and job accounting. The result is a higher cost of processing than through use of the central campus facility. In addition, the school can seldom afford a computer with as great a capacity and efficiency as the central computer. Consequently, the types of problems which can be run on the business school computers are often limited.

Turnaround time is not noticeably different for the business school computer, in the schools where the research took place. It is more a function of the extent to which the computer is loaded. In some universities where the business school computer was near saturation, turnaround time was much better at the central computer, and vice versa.

Although these three factors are important, a fourth factor is just as significant. It demonstrates the problems which arise for the school of business when it acquires its own computer. There is a huge investment in faculty to acquire, install, and maintain a computer. The research showed that schools often delude themselves that acquisition of the computer and its operating budget will permit them to obtain sufficient personnel to operate the facility. In actuality, due to the shortage in the field and due to frequent underestimation of operating budget requirements, enough computer people are rarely available. The burden falls on the existing faculty. Although such a situation might result in more faculty involvement in the computer operation, it occurs at a premium cost. The shortage of computer professionals in the business school computer operation results in computer utilization which is rarely as good as that of the central campus facility.

For schools of business which have the financial resources to cover the total investment in personnel as well as computing equipment, a business school computer facility is desirable. Although seven of the eleven schools visited had their own computer facility, in three of these schools the majority of the business school computer work was run on the central campus computer.

Computer Cost per Student

For schools without the financial resources for their own computer, an effective computer curriculum is still possible. The research showed that students can be taught fundamentals and programming with computer costs as low as $15 to $20 per student, by computer processing only half of the programs each student writes. Business games can be run on the computer for costs of $3 to $5 per student. The courses in computer-based management information systems can be taught without incurring any computer costs.

Likewise, computer applications can be taught in the functional areas without use of a computer, although none of the sophisticated simulations described previously could be utilized. Sophistication in any of these areas necessitates a higher computer budget and, without question, provides much greater educational benefit.

Therefore, the four areas of computer technology can be incorporated into the required curriculum for a computer processing cost of $18 to $24 per student. However, in the leading schools where these four areas of computer technology are covered in the required curriculum, computer processing costs ranged from $70 to $515 per student. Figure 2 provides a comparison of computer costs for the minimal level of computer curriculum to that in the schools where the research took place. The comparison is made according to the degree of sophistication in computer curriculum. Carnegie, Stanford, and U.C.L.A. have developed "highly sophisticated" computer curriculum, while the "sophisticated" category consists of Dartmouth, Harvard, and Tulane.

The significant difference in computer costs per student among the eleven schools is consistent with the significant difference in total business school budgets, which range from $435 to $7,000 per student per year. Despite this variation, the low budget schools are doing a creditable job in educating students concerning the computer.

Justifying the Computer Budget

Even with minimal computer use, deans have difficulty in obtaining sufficient computer budget. Although computer costs of $18 to $24 per student may raise the budget by a small percentage, the absolute dollar figure may be significant. For example, the University of Florida will implement a programming requirement this year for its 1,000 students. The additional budget requirements may be anywhere between $15,000 and $45,000, depending upon the number of programs processed per student. Of course, Florida will also need additional budget to staff these courses.

Industry and government leaders can assist in convincing university administration of the need for computer education. Also, the school of business could provide justification through some pragmatic use of systems analysis, design, and programming techniques being taught its students. One way to convince the administration of the value of computer education is to undertake computerization of some university administrative activities as class projects. University administrative practices are notoriously inefficient and could benefit greatly by such effort. Dr. Thomas Williams, of Texas, has undertaken projects of this type, using students in his accounting classes. Another approach would be for the students in the computer-based management information systems course to design a university M.I.S.

Sharing Computer Experience

Costs can be reduced through an increased effort toward sharing computer programs and experience. Overlap in costly and scarce programming effort is occurring among the eleven schools. Several schools were in the process of developing simulation programs in similar areas. Sharing has occurred to a considerable extent on business game computer programs; Carnegie-Mellon, e.g., has shared its game with a number of organizations and sends out updated programs and documentation of all revisions.

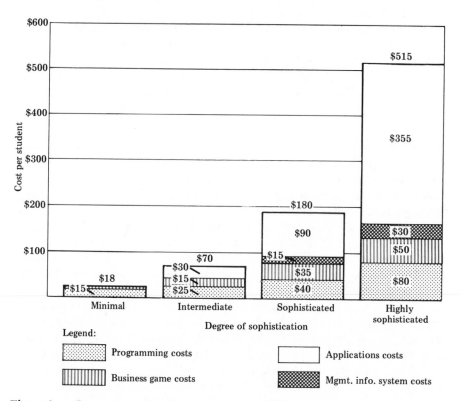

Figure 2.   Computer processing costs for computer curriculum by degree of sophistication.

A limited amount of programs have been made available by other schools, such as U.C.L.A.'s biomedical computer programs for a variety of statistical procedures. Computer manufacturers have provided software packages for some of the management science techniques. Nevertheless, overlap in design and programming investment is occurring in some areas, such as the factory simulator being developed in several schools. Due to the many computer configurations in the schools, existing sharing organizations, such as IBM's SHARE or CDC's CO-OP, are not the solution to this problem. A formal sharing system among the schools of business would require considerable developmental effort, but would benefit both large and small schools.

The Future

The Next Three Years

What is in store for schools of business during the next three years? A visit to Dartmouth provides insight in answering this question. Time-sharing has been a way of life at Dartmouth for two years. Students are frequently at consoles, performing daily homework assignments or working on term research projects. In evidence there is a tremendous motivational effect for students in the process of developing logical solutions to problems and receiving immediate computer evaluation of their solutions.

Time-sharing will be in operation at Stanford, Harvard, Wisconsin, Pennsylvania, Florida, Texas, and U.C.L.A. within the next two years. Dartmouth began using consoles for its business game in March, vividly demonstrating to students how an executive operates in a real-time environment. Carnegie-Mellon is in the process of negotiations for visual display devices to be used to display computer outputs during operation of its management game.

The manner in which computer programming languages will be greatly simplified can be seen in Dartmouth's BASIC time-sharing language, developed under the direction of Professor John Kemeny. The simple instruction "MAT C = A * B" directs the computer to multiply matrix A by matrix B, which together, may comprise a maximum of 8,000 components. Most students become fluent in BASIC, talking freely with the computer after four or five hours of practice. Figure 3 depicts the Dartmouth time-sharing system.

Computer-assisted instruction (C.A.I.) in the classroom will be a regular practice in the near future, greatly improving student

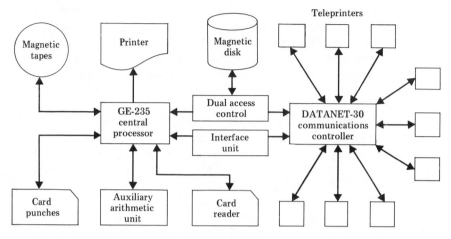

Figure 3.   Dartmouth's GE-235 time-sharing computer system. Serves as many as 40 students and faculty simultaneously from teleprinters in classrooms and dormitories—expanded system using GE-625 processor was operational in June, serving 200 users simultaneously.

motivation and the quality of instruction. Some of the classroom uses of the computer, as projected by Professors George Brown and Arthur Geoffrion of U.C.L.A. are:

> Linear programming. *With a simplex tableau displayed on a Cathode Ray Table (C.R.T.), the manipulations according to the simplex method could be "stepped through" by the student. Various levels of student participation would be possible, from a single instruction, which initiates an entire iteration (sequentially displayed to reveal the various substeps), to detailed instructions such as "Multiply row 5 × 2," which would enable the student to practice the logical aspects of the algorithm without the drudgery of numerical computations.*

> Game theory. *The student could play a matrix game with a computer as his opponent, before he is introduced to the concept of minimax strategy. The computer would be programmed to use the minimax strategy during the play, displaying a running score on the C.R.T. Then the minimax concept would be explained. The improvement in performance during the next play with the computer would greatly enhance the learning experience.*

Inventory theory. *The student could operate (through an IBM 1050 terminal, or similar device) a simple inventory system, with the computer generating stochastic demands and costs. Then the system could be modeled on paper to derive an optimal decision rule. The student would repeat the play, using the decision rule to see the improvement over his previous heuristic method. This approach would greatly facilitate the education of the student on the usefulness of a tractable mathematical model.*

Queueing theory. *The student could watch (via C.R.T.) a simple queueing system start up and approach steady state several times. He would then model the system on paper to derive some of its operating characteristics. The student would observe how closely the theoretical operating characteristics are realized—giving him a feeling for what can be expected of a statistical description of a system. After the analytical topics were covered, some of the key ideas of simulation could be explained.*

Discrete parameter Markov chains. *By displaying a Markov graph on a C.R.T. with transition probabilities labelled on the arcs, the student could observe its sequential operation with the current state of the process being indicated by the position of a bright spot. Numerous concepts relating to Markov chains and their applications could be vividly demonstrated in this way.*

A Need for Action

Conclusion

Although recent surveys indicate that the majority of business schools are graduating students with little education on the use of computers, a number of schools have adopted a strong computer curriculum.

The two major constraints on development of computer curriculum are:

A faculty capable of teaching computer technology.

Adequate budget for computer use.

It is necessary for the faculty member to be provided a proper incentive to rank acquisition of computer proficiency high among his retooling needs. A number of educational avenues are available, although somewhat expensive for the average school. The faculty education process can be expedited through establishment of educational grants from government, industry, and foundations. The cost of computer curriculum is not prohibitive for small budget schools. Use of the central campus computer, a business firm's computer, or a service bureau computer permits a reasonable cost per student. Costs can be kept at a minimum by sharing of programs and experience among schools. Classroom assignments on university administrative applications will aid in justification of computer budgets.

Modern management is often heavily involved in the use of computers. If the universities are to be at the forefront in management education, immediate action is necessary. The experience of the progressive schools should serve as a means for other schools to leapfrog the slow, evolutionary process in developing a proper computer curriculum.

38

Human Relations
and Information Systems

Harry Stern

Reprinted by permission of *Interfaces*,
vol. 1, no. 2, February 1971, pp. 39–43.

Because I believe that the installation of a new computer program or new systems is not a meaningful event unless it causes a change, I was excited by an outline titled "Change Agent Skills" that appeared in the *Reading Book for Laboratories in Human Relations Training*, circulated by the NTL Institute for Applied Behavioral Science (which is associated with the National Education Association). The outline was one of the papers originally prepared for theory sessions at the Institute's laboratories.

Although the material is intended to be "human relations" oriented rather than "information systems" oriented, its application in the area of information systems seems straightforward. An information systems group, setting out to write a system, can consider itself a "Change Agent." Under that description, the user is the "changee," and the skills defined in the outline become directly applicable.

Often the change caused by the introduction of a new system is self evident. Where there is a direct savings in labor, or where an optimum solution to a mix problem results in a change in formulation, then there is only a passing need for a skilled Change Agent. However, where the system is designed to present information that had never before been available, the success of the system is dependent upon the Change Agent's skill. Generally, in a system of this latter type, the value of the system comes from the use of the information in making decisions. If better decisions are not made because of the additional information, then the system is valueless, no matter how cleverly the information is obtained or displayed.

Motivations for Change

In Change Agent Skill Area 1 the outline discusses the skills involved in (1) understanding the motivation of Change Agent himself, (2) determining the need for the changee, and (3) assessing the possibility that change might actually occur.

Skill Area 1

Assessment by the Change Agent of his (or its) personal motivations, and his (or its) relationship to the "changee" ("Change Agent" here may be an individual, a group, or an organization). Some skills and understandings needed for this aspect of change:

1. *Understanding his own motivation in seeing a need for this change and wanting to bring about a change*
2. *Understanding and working in terms of a philosophy and ethics of change*
3. *Predicting the relation of one possible change to other possible changes, or to those that come later*
4. *Determining the possible units of change:*
   (a) What seems to be needed
   (b) What is possible to him (or them)
5. *Determining the size, character, structural make-up of group of changees*
6. *Determining the barriers, the resistance, the degree of readiness to change*
7. *Determining the resources available for overcoming barriers and resistance*
8. *Knowing how to determine his own strategic role in the light of the situation and abilities*

All too often, the information systems designer does not understand his own motivations in wanting to develop a system, or the motivation of a user who asks for a specific report. A basic question is, "What is the need?" Often reports are written because the data exists, and printing it relieves the systems designer of any responsibility for having kept important data from the user.

However, this satisfaction of the Change Agent's need for absolution often leaves the changee unchanged, with only a pile of useless paper. If the systems designer works with the user to uncover a need for information, rather than giving the user that which is easy or convenient, real changes could result from the systems work.

Some organizations are difficult for a particular Change Agent to change. It is usually worthwhile to go to great lengths to create an environment where the changees are actively pushing for the change and are totally involved in the program.

Making the User Aware of the Need for Change

The Change Agent need not be the systems designer. Often problems can be solved by including the systems designer in a team, where the team acts as the Change Agent. This is particularly effective if the team is formed under the auspices of the management of the changee group rather than by the information services group.

Change Agent Skill Area 2 deals with the skills of the Change Agent in preparing the changee for change.

Skill Area 2

Helping changees become aware of the need for change and for the diagnostic process. Some skills and understandings needed for this aspect of change:

1. *Determining the level of sensitivity the changees have to the need for change*
2. *Determining the methods which changees believe should be used in change*
3. *Creating awareness of the need for considering change and diagnosis through: shock, permissiveness, demonstration, research, guilt, "bandwagon," etc.*
4. *Raising the level of aspiration of the changee and making aspirations realistic*
5. *Creating a perception of the potentialities for change expectations*
6. *Creating expectations to use a step-wise plan and to have patience in its use*
7. *Creating perception of possible sources of help in this change*
8. *Creating a feeling of responsibility to engage in this change by active participation*

Note: Each of these steps and the skills categorized under them may be pertinent to changing a person himself, his relations with others, the relations between several others, a total group, a community, or a widely held opinion. Actually, each changee becomes a changer some place in the normal development of the change process.

Understandably, the changee who sees no need for change, and further feels that a change is being imposed upon him arbitrarily, resists. This resistance can range from not using the output to destroying the system by overloading it or by feeding it misinformation. If the user wants to destroy a system, he can usually find a way. The Change Agent who ignores the feelings and needs of the changee reaps what he has sown. The systems designer must remember that the needs of an organization go far beyond needs for data. Prestige, esprit de corps, control, fear, etc., are all motivations which form the basis of needs, and many needs must be taken into consideration if a system is to be successfully designed and installed.

The Place of the Professional Human Relations Consultant

The skills needed to be a systems designer and the skills needed to be a human relations consultant are different. The systems designer must have the technical skills that will allow him to know what is reasonable within the context of existing data, software and hardware systems, and available personnel and funding. But there are human relations, "Change Agent" skills which the systems designer should not be expected to have.

The last five Change Agent Skill Areas deal with skills needed in handling groups and methods for intervening in human systems to cause change. These skills are needed where the change is massive, the group either resistive or large, or where there are human relations problems in the group.

Skill Area 3

Diagnosis by changer and changee in collaboration concerning the situation, behavior, understanding, feeling, or performance to be modified. Some skills and understandings needed for this aspect of change:

1. Making catharsis possible and acceptable when indicated as a starting point

2. *Skill in use of diagnostic instruments appropriate to the problem: surveys, maps, score cards, observation, etc.*
3. *Diagnosis in terms of causes rather than "goods" or "bads"*
4. *Skill in helping changees to examine own motivations*
5. *Examination of the relation of one change to other changes possible in that situation and helping changees understand*
6. *Clarifying interrelationship or roles between changer and changee*
7. *Skill in dealing wisely with changee's ideology, myths, traditions, values*

Skill Area 4

Deciding upon the problem; involving others in this decision; planning action, and practicing these plans. Some skills and understandings needed for this aspect of change:

1. *Techniques in arriving at a group decision*
2. *Examining the consequences of certain possible decisions*
3. *Making a step-wise plan*
4. *Doing anticipatory practice in carrying-out of a plan*
5. *Providing for replanning and assessment at later stages*
6. *Providing administrative organization*
7. *Eliciting and eliminating alternatives*

Skill Area 5

Carrying-out the plan successfully and productively. Some skills and understandings needed for this aspect of change:

1. *Building and maintaining the morale of the changees as they try the change*
2. *Deciding upon the amount of action to be made before pausing for an assessment of process and progress being used*
3. *Understanding the effects of stress on changee's beliefs and behavior*
4. *Defining objectives in a manner that leads to easy definition of methods*
5. *Creating a perception of the need for relating methods to the goal in mind*

Skill Area 6

Evaluation and assessment of changee's progress, methods of working, and human relations. Some skills and understandings needed for this aspect of change:

1. *Skill in the diagnosis of causes when group action becomes inefficient through the use of measuring instruments, interviews, interaction awareness panel*
2. *Skill in use of score cards, rating scales, etc.*

Skill Area 7

Insuring continuity, spread, maintenance and transfer. Some skills and understandings needed for this aspect of change:

1. *Creating perception of responsibility for participation in many persons*
2. *Developing indicated degree of general support for change*
3. *Developing appreciation by others of work of participants who need support*

It is important that the systems designer know that these skills are available from professional human relations consultants. When designing a system whose implementation depends upon the change of a large and diverse group of people, such a consultant should be part of the team.

Conclusion

The successful implementation of a system is often dependent upon the ability of the groups most affected to adapt to a newly imposed environment. It is utter folly to expect adaptation to occur without careful work, planning and involvement of the user group. For that reason, the basic human relations skills are needed, to a greater or lesser extent, in all phases of design and implementation. In many cases, it is sufficient to have a sensitive systems designer, who can handle group problems that arise, whereas in other cases it is necessary to have a human relations professional available. In any case, it is of paramount importance to understand the human relations portion of the design problem.

PART VI

Case Studies
in MIS Applications

It is becoming more and more apparent that if students are to gain further insights into the increasingly complex and diverse nature of systems they must have a chance to observe theory in practice. Therefore the purpose of this section is to provide, through descriptions of applications, a basic framework for stimulating and encouraging conceptualization of systems in process.

It is naive to typify systems solely as a series of parts in interaction without considering the phenomena of the organizational environment in which systems must produce because the real world is one of cooperative endeavor; yet the efforts needed to achieve intensified functional integration in a business firm are often ignored. The success of any subsystem, including an MIS, is largely determined by the effectiveness with which resources can be mobilized to complement the subsystem and the entire organization. Thus, the narrower the boundaries within which one seeks to achieve efficiency the greater the danger that results systematically inconsistent with the operation of the larger whole will be produced. Etzioni phrased it this way: "A study of effectiveness has to include the environmental conditions and the organization's orientation to them" (1).

These readings are intended to: introduce the reader to the nature, scope, and potential of existing systems; focus attention on the managerial dimensions at work in systems; illuminate the unique features of systems; provide a framework for investigating what is necessary to make a system successful; and expose the possible sources of conflict within the system and the residual organizational structure. A persistent need is to synthesize the behavioral dimensions at work in the system; then it is possible to see how they lead to improved relations, system failure, or suboptimization. Not all concepts covered in this book are incorporated in case studies, but they should illustrate formulated, logical relationships from the concepts.

Obviously, the readings in this section were not selected to provide a foolproof prescription for designing and implementing an MIS. That could not be done because each system is necessarily unique in nature and purpose. But the articles should provide the reader an opportunity to study the "hows," "whys," and "why nots" of MIS design and implementation. Specifically they should raise questions about how systems are designed (how conceptualized and built), how they can be improved (or modified), and what is the nature and direction of their growth (which can explain why they are accepted or not accepted).

To prepare himself for positions of responsibility, a student needs to develop, in our way of thinking, his ability to think and act responsibly, to work cooperatively with others, and to develop an appreciation for the efforts, ideals, and applications of others. He can do that through a multidimensional process of learning, one facet of which is to see what others have done. Through the case-application approach the student learns to think for himself, to project himself into the efforts of others, and then to relate the responsibilities in a given situation to circumstances in the application. The real challenge in examining a case, then, is to understand a given situation in all its complexity by pulling the case apart and pushing it back together again, all the while looking for the hows and the whys.

Reference

1. Amitai Etzioni, "Two Approaches to Organizational Analysis: A Critique and a Suggestion," *Administrative Science Quarterly*, p. 262, September 1960.

39

Management Information System for Planning, Forecasting, and Budgeting

John J. Omlor

Reprinted by permission of
Management Accounting, March 1970.

The Columbia-Hallowell Division of Standard Pressed Steel has a completely integrated management information system which provides management with timely, accurate decision making information. The system is used for business planning and profit forecasting through daily, weekly and monthly measurements. A technique has been developed whereby dollar sales forecasts plus firm orders in house are converted into a shipping forecast of specific items. The data, which includes planned increases or decreases in the inventory level, is then converted through existing computer programs to a manpower and facilities projection in terms of standard hours by product line and department. Follow-up reports indicate current accomplishments throughout the period in relation to the target.

Inputs and Outputs

Basically, we can divide the system into two major categories—inputs into the computer and output reports.

Input Reports

1. *Parts list: A parts list is an engineering bill of material adapted for the manufacturing stocking level. The parts list contains each item that must be manufactured, as well as the parts which are to be requisitioned in order to manufacture this part.*
2. *Manufacturing method sheets: These method sheets call out every operation that is to be performed to complete the part, the standard hours required and the facilities needed.*
3. *Fixed and variable budget rate file for each department: Our fixed budget rate is based on cost per day. Each department has its own rate file subdivided for each major category or expense per earned hour, and/or each major category of expense per day. The variable budget rates, on the other hand are based only on a rate per earned direct labor hour. An earned hour is a completed standard hour of labor.*
4. *Customer or manufacturing orders: These are daily routine functions.*
5. *Inventory transactions*
6. *Labor reporting*

Output Reports

1. *Open order registers*
2. *Scheduling documents*
3. *Inventory exceptions and requirement reports*
4. *Business status reports*
5. *Method sheets and standards to manufacture*
6. *Load hours for machine and departments*
7. *Daily, weekly, and monthly variable and fixed budgets*
8. *Normal accounting reports*

Business Planning with MIS

The current backlog is detailed into the system by customer and by part number both in terms of sales dollars and of standard costs. The backlog data will also contain information reflecting standard hours by part, by department, and by facility to manufacture each item. All of this then becomes the basis for determining our next month's shipment forecast.

If we are going to go further out in our forecasting, either to a quarterly or to an annual plan, we will use an incoming forecast in addition to the backlog as the basis for determining the shipments for the planned period. The incoming forecast is taken from an exponentially smoothed history of incoming orders by part number, adjusted to reflect the marketing estimates of business changes. This forecast is converted into "dummy customer orders" and entered into the system exactly as though it were a customer order. These dummy orders together with the real orders we have in-house are then the basis for determining the quarterly or annual shipments forecast. For the purpose of business planning, the dummy orders and backlog are considered to be completely manufactured from beginning to end. That is, we assume no inventory changes since inventory fluctuations from month to month are not significant.

Once the forecast has been incorporated into the management information system, we can produce our shipment dollars and standard cost of goods sold, or the business status report. This report permits us to segregate our sales and standard costs by product line, and it is the basis for determining the product mix effect on the plan.

Each item forecast is exploded into the necessary manufacturing hours by department and facility. The load hours for each department are extended by the budget rate to determine the variable budget cost. This cost plus the fixed budget cost per day times the number of days equals the allowable budget dollars.

The explosion to the load hours helps us to identify machine or manpower bottlenecks. On machine bottlenecks, we can either reschedule, if possible, or use the information as a basis for our Capital Requirements Plan.

Manpower requirements are based upon the load hours by department, factored for projected performance. The performance is determined in two ways:

1. By direct labor performance
2. By the utilization of total available labor, or the direct labor to total labor available ratio

All manpower requirements are computed as equivalent whole people. That is, the required hours divided by eight hours per day times the number of days in the period. For example, Table 1 shows that the press shop's direct labor performance for last month was 114 percent of standard. It also shows that at the end of the month there were 81 people on the payroll although during the month only 74 equivalent whole people worked. These break down into 38 direct

Table 1. Manpower Projection

Department	D. L. Perf %	No. of emp.	Emp. fm WDCS 1 DL	Emp. fm WDCS 1 Ind	% Direct to total labor	Std. hours months	Std. emp.	Perf emp.	Total man power	Std. hours month	Std. emp.	Perf emp.	Total man power
						November—20 days				December—24 days			
Press Shop	114	81	38	36	51.4	8371	53	46	83	10336	54	48	87
Weld	92	28	15	10	60.0	3262	20	22	37	4017	21	23	38
Paint	115	19	9	9	50.0	2419	15	13	25	3058	16	14	26
Assemble	104	38	30	10	75.0	5003	31	30	40	6370	33	32	43
Pack	101	3	2	1	66.7	207	1	1	1	351	2	2	2
Total	107	169	94	66	59.1	19262	120	112	186	24132	126	119	196

labor, and 36 indirect labor. The ratio of direct labor hours to total labor hours for that department was then 51.4 percent.

For November we show 8,371 standard hours required which is equivalent to 53 standard direct labor men. Factored for the 114 percent performance this is equal to 46 direct labor men. Multiplying the 46 direct labor men by the 51.4 percent direct labor to total labor ratio, we find that the department required 83 people to produce the forecast.

This report thus allows us to recognize manpower problems.

If a problem does exist, we have three alternatives:

1. *Change the schedule load hours*
2. *Add or delete men*
3. *Change the performance forecast*

The load hours above are based on current methods of manufacture. Since performance against current methods can be distorted by changes in the standards we shoot for performance of 100 percent against this standard. Therefore, in order not to distort performance levels, we use a measurement against a fixed cost book standard. This is a trend type measurement and the standard always remains the same. Any performance change is indicated by a change in the performance percentage. These two measurements allow us to completely analyze the changes in performance.

Through the use of our Management Information System we have the ability to put together a reliable business plan, and the beauty of it is, if management rejects the results we have the ability to go back, re-do or adjust with a minimum amount of time and effort. Dummy orders, rate files, performance levels, or product mix can all be changed and in a short time we would have a completely new look at the forecast.

Performance to Forecast

Let us assume that management has accepted the forecast. The next step is the measurement of performance compared to the plan. In the management information system we have the ability to measure performance to any forecast on a daily, weekly, and monthly basis.

Daily Measurement

Information necessary to check the performance against plan originates with shipment and labor reporting transactions. Shipment transactions provide data on our actual shipments and standard cost of shipments through one of our existing reports—the Business Status Report. Using this computerized report helps us to prepare a shipment performance graph, [Figure] 1, by product. It is a projection of the to-date shipments in comparison to the forecast shipments. The contribution effect is the volume difference multiplied by the product variable margin rate.

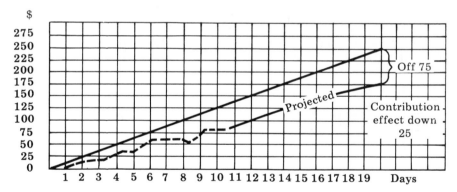

Figure 1.   Shipments.

The labor reporting transaction provides the part manufactured, the time used, the man and department where worked. This information, compared with the standard to manufacture, allows the computation of the daily performance report by department, we summarize the standard direct labor man hours earned and the direct to indirect relationship of the particular department. With this information on a daily basis, and computerized, we have the time and ability to put together reports such as Table 2 which are designed primarily to interpret data presented on the computer reports.

Table 2. Performance to Plan Manpower Requirements

| Department | Today | | | | Balance of Month | | | |
	Planned standard hours by department	Standard hours earned	Plan	Performance daily percent	Percent D/L used to total available	Standard D/L hrs. per day to meet plan	Actual D/L hrs. per day at current performance to meet plan	Equivalent whole men required
Press shop	8371	529	533	108	50	360	345	86
Weld	3262	222	103	121	79	378	356	46
Paint	2419	110	121	96	68	394	306	38
Assemble	5003	220	250	78	82	775	909	114
Pack	207	26	10	98	65	0	0	0
Total	19262	1107	1017	101	67	0	0	284

This is an exception type report issued to the plant manager. Detail of this performance by man in total and by job by man is issued to the foreman. In addition, each department has a graph ([Figure] 2) presenting its performance to plan. The graph also portrays the amount of hours required on a monthly basis. Through a thermometer approach, we measure the department's status at a particular time.

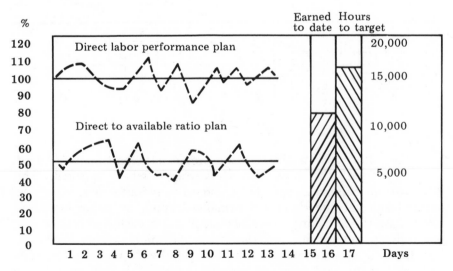

Figure 2.   Daily performance.

All information is personally delivered and interpreted by our plant accountant. At any given day, all concerned know exactly how they stand in relationship to the plan for both earned hours and shipments.

Weekly Measurement

Weekly measurement techniques are very similar to those used daily. However, in measuring weekly performance, one more tool is used—the departmental budget report.

Each report shows the budget dollars or equal to the earned hours multiplied by the variable earned hour budget rate plus the fixed cost budget per day, times the number of days in the period. The variances are segregated according to direct labor and indirect labor, and the direct labor variance is identified as to wage rate and manufacturing performance variance. All this is done mechanically, allowing us time to graphically portray the information to the foremen and plant manager. Using the system to do the brute work allows time for analysis and communications.

Also on a weekly basis, the division runs what we call a "mock closing." In this procedure, we run our regular sales, cost of sales and normal accounting reports. Without going through the formal journal entries, these reports allow us to analyze total performance to plan. We do this two ways. First, we take the month-to-date and project it, assuming performance and/or shipments at the same rate as incurred in the past. Second, we contact the people responsible for the shipments and performance to determine their best estimate for the remainder of the month and prepare an outlook on this basis. Reasons for deviations are categorized as to volume, mix, manufacturing performance, and period cost. Then on each Tuesday afternoon, with this information, we have a financial review with the activity managers of the division.

Monthly Measurement

The monthly performance technique is exactly the same as the weekly performance technique. However, instead of running the mock closing, we run the actual closing; and instead of running the departmental reports on the payroll basis only, the report is complete with actual supplies. The review is the same, perhaps more detailed, but the concept is exactly the same.

Conclusion

Generally, this covers the Columbia-Hallowell Division's use of their management information system for business planning. This technique is used in the annual business plan as well and is no different from that used in any quarterly forecast.

In summary, the major benefits in using this system for business planning, forecasting, and budget measurement are:

1. *The ease in making changes after reviewing the forecast*
2. *The timeliness of the daily, weekly, and monthly measurement technique*
3. *The mechanization of the brute work, allowing accountants to be analysts and communicators of information.*

40

Management Information System

LaVerne G. Milunovich

Reprinted by permission of
Management Services, March–April 1970.

Management information systems have been alternately criticized and praised in recent years, with much of the praise coming from academicians and much of the condemnation from business people who had experimented with them and found them far short of their expectations.

We think this is largely true because of confusion on the part of both groups as to what a management information system actually is, what is involved in developing it, and what its true benefits are.

In the first place, let's define our terms. There is a broad hierarchy of information systems that can exist in any organization. They range from detailed, highly structured production systems to broad, poorly defined environmental study systems.

It is not easy to classify such a spectrum of information systems. One approach to such classification, beginning with the highest level and working down to the lowest, is as follows:

1. *Long-range, future, external, environmental analysis "systems." This could involve a study of fundamental forces—technological, sociological, demographic, political, economic, and philosophical—out, for example, to the year 2000.*

2. *Long-range, strategic, directional study "systems." Based on analyses of the fundamental direction of environmental forces, a pattern of strategic maneuvers can be developed so that the enterprise can capitalize*

on the trend of those forces. This system—if, in fact, it can truly be termed a system—is very broad and ill-structured in nature, as is the first system.

3. *Intermediate-range cyclical planning systems. This is a rhythmic process, such as the five-year plan so frequently employed, whereby areas of an enterprise plan their growth into the future in a fairly coarse manner.*

4. *Short-term, external, environmental forecasting and monitoring systems. This involves a study of economic factors and trends in considerable detail and projections about one year into the future. The one-year economic forecast that precedes sales forecasting and budgeting in manufacturing is an example of this. In addition, it can involve competitor surveillance.*

5. *Program systems. These are special development programs, such as construction of a new building or development of a comprehensive Management Information System. This basically refers to capital expenditure and research and development programs. Such programs can require as much as five years, or so, for completion.*

6. *One-year cyclical or rhythmic planning and control systems. Income, expense, and various resources are budgeted, on a month-by-month basis, by all areas of the business for the coming calendar or fiscal year.*

7. *Day-to-day tactical decision systems, such as bond trade analysis or investment selection programs.*

8. *Historical, corporate-level, custodial reporting systems. This involves reporting of the corporate income statement and balance sheet.*

9. *Special subsidiary systems, such as personnel and customer information systems. These systems provide detail by individual employee and customer. Considerable descriptive, as well as quantitative, data are included in these systems.*

10. *Daily production, posting, and proof systems, such as demand deposit accounting, transit, and installment loan processing systems. Many of these are basically general ledger subsidiary systems.*

Now in several of these systems simulation and optimization models and many of the newer quantitative techniques can be employed profitably. This does not give them the characteristics of a management information system; these are simply tools that can be utilized successfully at any level of planning.

What is an MIS system? An MIS system, fundamentally, is a financial control system, which is the principal basis of a good planning system. The key concepts toward which any good management information system must be geared, then, are planning and control over the enterprise as a whole, not just one aspect of it. This is certainly not a new idea; many of the key concepts were formulated by DuPont and refined at General Motors many years ago. It is an idea that is not completely understood or implemented by too many businesses, however.

The planning and control system must be based on the principles of responsibility accounting.

This relates primarily to point six in the list of information systems, although it generally includes several of the other categories, too, such as points four, five and eight. The resources: people, machines, earning assets, deposits, etc., under the control of each manager are planned, on a month-by-month basis, one year into the future. Actual performance, periodically, is measured against goals, and accountability, or control, is provided by monthly variance reporting. It is a system for measuring the performance of management at all levels of an organization. It basically measures administrative effectiveness. This is why it logically can be called a Management Information System.

To provide a better idea of what MIS is, I would like to outline what we have been doing at the First Wisconsin National Bank of Milwaukee to achieve an MIS Program. The principal reason why the First Wisconsin embarked on a large-scale MIS development program was to improve its earning power by providing rather complete information to managers about many segments of the business. In particular, it was considered desirable to be able to measure profit contribution of different aspects or elements of the enterprise. The program is very comprehensive and will take four years, overall, to complete. A listing of the major concepts being employed is as follows:

   1. *The entire system begins with the corporate-level income statement and balance sheet—the general ledger—and is exploded down from that point. Everything must relate properly to, and integrate well with, the fundamental statements of the business.*

2. *The principal categories of coding are:*
   (a) Responsibility area
   (b) Chart of accounts
   (c) Service line
   (d) Program and project.
   Considerable effort was expended in developing sound, imaginative, and basic coding systems.
3. *The organization structure was precisely defined, since the reporting system is to follow, or roll up, the "chain of command." This is a basic feature of the system. There must be sound control by responsibility, which means by manager.*
4. *Cost is to be measured in three fundamental, mutually exclusive segments:*
   (a) Standards will be developed for production costs, employing work measurement techniques, and flexible budgeting will be used for controlling these costs.
   (b) Program and project costs will be controlled as an integral segment of the reporting system. These costs will be controlled directly on an incurrence or responsibility basis as well as be summarized for evaluation on a program management basis.
   (c) Administrative costs encompass those expenses not included in the other two major categories. These costs tend to have an overhead orientation. We are treating each of the various broad categories of cost in a different manner, based on significant differences in their behavioral characteristics.
5. *Profit will be measured in several ways:*
   (a) By responsibility, or profit center (sales manager)
   (b) By service line (product line manager)
   (c) Eventually, by individual customer.

Profit centers will be stated on a contribution basis; that is, no higher-level overheads will be allocated to profit centers. There will be two profit levels reported in profit centers—marginal profit contribution and contribution to profit and higher-level overhead. We are making provision for incremental analysis. Service line income statements will have two levels of profit—marginal profit contribution and full absorption net profit (principally for major pricing decisions). In general, we will allocate costs only where absolutely necessary.

6. *Standard costs, which are controlled for efficiency purposes by flexible budgeting in production areas, will be charged out at standard, on a service line basis, to profit centers and service lines to provide a better measure of profit contribution.*
7. *Transfer rates will be developed to apply to excesses and deficiencies of investable funds of all fund-oriented areas.*
8. *An automated variance reporting system will be developed which will highlight material variances requiring explanation. By this means, the management by exception principle will be incorporated into the system.*
9. *Balance sheet and a variety of statistical elements will be reported by responsibility, as well as income, cost and profit.*
10. *The general ledger will be fully automated.*
11. *A bill of materials processor will be employed to assemble cost components by service line.*
12. *Not only will after-the-fact reporting of actual against plan data be fully automated, but also the assembly of the plan itself. This is a major task that is frequently overlooked.*
13. *The entire system will be fully integrated. All segments of the system will work from the same data base, and there will be no inconsistencies in the data.*
14. *Very attractive reports will be developed. Esthetics will be given considerable attention.*

The program will be completed near the end of 1970 and is progressing quite well. This represents one of the largest and most comprehensive undertakings of this type being attempted by a bank in this country. A sizable staff has been committed to the effort.

Risks to Watch

There are many risks involved in embarking on a large-scale information system of any kind. The major pitfall is that of suboptimization—development of a segment without possessing a good appreciation of the overall whole and of how the segment should relate to the whole.

This has been one of the principal mistakes made by many companies. Few organizations have devised a broad, high-level concept of the hierarchy of information needs, similar to that previously discussed, and the related systems required for an imaginative organization. It is very important to try to do so, difficult though it be. The whole must be well conceived before developing any of the components. The design of every segment must fit properly into a high-grade master plan. Many banks have failed to take a broad approach to the design of information systems. Random systems development sometimes has resulted from inadequate planning. Some of the major problems that have impeded banks seriously in their efforts are the following:

1. *Top management may not have participated actively in the formulation, design, and control of implementation of information systems. There may be a lack of understanding in regard to the value and use of such systems and a lack of appreciation for employing computers in the process. In many cases, information development programs are sold from levels well down in the organization. Top management approval for initiation may be obtained, but utilization of the system after implementation may be somewhat ineffective.*

2. *Very few banks can muster a development group of sufficient breadth and conceptual power to do a truly effective job. Generally, systems are designed by computer specialists or systems analysts who know computer capabilities rather well. However, they may not have a broad knowledge of the business, may have not served in a line management or staff analytical role, and they may not have used information actively for making decisions. They often may have highly specialized backgrounds and little corporate exposure. They have tended to view computers as production machines, rather than as engines of information analysis. Designing or creating a new decision making system is a much more difficult task than automating an existing processing system. The approach, many times, has been one of achieving cost savings in processing systems, rather than entrepreneurial in formulating analytical and decision systems. A demand deposit accounting system is a very low order of information system. Reports designed by computer staffs sometimes are cluttered and unreadable. Readability is as important as content. There may*

*be a serious lack of appreciation for a sales or public
relations attitude toward users and for display esthetics
or good "packaging" in exhibiting information.*

Many accountants have suffered from the same sort of myopia.
They have been too concerned with handling of transactions and
bookkeeping entries, rather than with analyzing and interpreting
decision information. There has prevailed a processing orientation,
rather than a user orientation.

Finally, line people—the basic users of information—frequently
have not provided a strong contribution, partially due to lack of
interest and dedicated participation, but mostly because they have
not taken the time to really *think deeply* about their aspects of the
business in fundamental and conceptual terms. They, of necessity,
perhaps, have a pronounced, day-to-day, current problem-solving
orientation. Some may view information systems as an impediment
to their work, rather than as a favorable aid.

Thus, there is a great void in requisite capability to perform an
exceedingly difficult task. The necessary attributes are a strong
entrepreneurial posture, user attitude, and a high-level, deep,
conceptual understanding of the business. Technical knowledge and
computer comprehension are secondary in importance. The "make
or break" aspect does not lie mainly in the technical area. The
information design group should be placed at a high level in the
organization and be staffed with the best conceptual brains available.
The members should have had broad and diverse experience in the
business. Then they should read heavily in the literature to educate
themselves in the new disciplines of managerial accounting, managerial economics, information theory, and information systems. There
is little formal education or work experience that provides a
respectable background in this field today.

Establishing a competent group of this sort is the most difficult
aspect of the entire program. This design group should be fully
segregated from the computer operations area, which represents a
production function.

> 3. *Many enterprises have the function of systems develop-
> ment fragmented throughout the organization in an
> array of staff groups, having ill defined and conflicting
> responsibilities. Conflict, lack of progress, and produc-
> tion of unrelated systems components can be the result.*
> 4. *The control of the entire staff and all the other
> resources required to develop the system should be*

*fully centralized in one individual if effective per-
formance is sought. Organizationally, this individual
should report directly to executive management. The
approach involving participation of members, from
various areas, reporting to different superiors, and
under the guidance of a "coordinator," can all too
often be quite inefficient and costly and may result in
poor-quality systems.*

5. *The successful development and implementation of
information systems represents a gigantic, complex, and
costly effort and is not to be undertaken lightly. Yet,
dealing with lesser subsystems will not provide the real
payoff to an organization. Many banks may not have
the caliber of talent to do the job. Competent
individuals may have to be recruited from other more
experienced industries, or a consulting firm may have
to be retained. In dealing with a consulting firm,
choosing the lead representative to be assigned to the
job is at least as significant as selecting the firm itself.*

The First Wisconsin National Bank of Milwaukee retained a
prominent national public accounting firm to work with the bank
staff on the MIS Program. The accounting background was considered to be quite important, since an MIS system is steeped in
managerial accounting theory and is heavily founded on accounting
systems. Banks, essentially, are large accounting machines.

Most banks are engaged in thinking about information systems,
in one manner or another. Many, however, may be having difficulty
in precisely defining problems and, specifically, what they want to
do.

Perhaps a highly competent consulting firm could provide
direction to general problem definition and planning, as well as
guidance in systems design and implementation.

Possible Future Developments

Some of the developments which may occur in the near-term to
intermediate-term future in the general field of information systems
should be mentioned:

1. *Control of information—basic coding, reporting, or
other display methods, systems design, and very
possibly analysis and interpretation of information—*

probably will be centralized in a highly placed staff group in organizations. The totally integrated systems of the future can be produced effectively only on a centralized basis. One cannot obtain integrated systems from fragmented systems groups. Each group will tend to go its own way. Information management, not equipment management, is the key to success.

2. *Information systems will become more sophisticated as business becomes more complex and the competitive pace quickens. There will be no return to simplicity, for the world inexorably is becoming more complex.*

3. *Banks will employ computers as an extension of the thinking process, rather than primarily as arithmetic posting and trial balance printing machines. In the past, banks have tended to concentrate their efforts on the more mundane applications and may not have recognized, adequately and imaginatively, the potential of high-order applications. The information retrieval capability of computers will become fully as important as their computational features.*

4. *A data librarian will be placed in charge of a single, centralized, corporate data bank, containing all internal and external data. Duplication and inconsistencies of data will be avoided. All data will be well classified, coded, and readily addressable. Today, each systems analyst, working with users, establishes his own data requirements and reports, but there may be insufficient control over achieving consistency, uniformity, and full integration among systems. Fragmented systems, inconsistent data, and nonuniform report format and content can be the result of this uncoordinated process.*

5. *Mass, on-line, storage capability soon will become quite economical and will tend to displace sequential storage. Transactions will be posted automatically as they occur, not only within an organization, but among organizations on a global basis. Computers will be interconnected completely among enterprises, as the telephone system is today. Paper will become less important as a medium for storing and transporting of information. Electronic transmission will tend to displace paper flow.*

6. *One person in an organization will be responsible for the format and structuring of all formal reporting and display of information. Centralized control provides full integration and a high level of consistency. The importance of esthetics and appearance in the display and comprehension of information will be recognized more fully. Total integration of all systems will be achieved.*

7. *Centralized, large-screen display and decentralized, tube, or other types of display units will be more heavily employed to access data and charts, in many areas of companies and for a great variety of purposes. The First Wisconsin National Bank has had an operational Management Information Center since the autumn of 1966.*

8. *Interaction of user—salesman, analyst, or anyone else—and the computer will become commonplace. Employing terminals, users can access an index of the complete data library, unrestricted data, and a great array of statistical and analytical programs. Information will be available precisely when it is needed. Alternative solutions to a variety of problems easily can be explored. Mathematical models will be used extensively. Users and computers will come closer together. More flexible machines and systems technology will tend to reduce the relative number of technical people required to develop information systems, in time. We must remember that computers are still in a relatively early, crude state of development.*

9. *Banks are basically giant information processing machines and will become very heavily automated. Few people recognize that the computer is easily the most important invention of mankind. The potential is unbelievable, and all projections in this field will represent vast underestimates. Fifty-year projections are virtually impossible to make and are incomprehensible, if made. Yet, we must attempt to make such projections. The computer will expand the use and efficiency of the mind, rather than serve merely as another piece of production equipment, as has been too frequently the situation in the past.*

10. *Organization structures will change significantly in many ways. For example, analytical staff—"think groups"—will become increasingly centralized. Much staff work is too fragmented and of relatively low quality today. It is easier to waste money in splintered, ineffective staff work than in nearly any other manner. The difficulty of fairly accurate measurement complicates the problem.*

11. *Knowledge will become our most important resource. We will sell an increasingly broad range of advice to customers, rather than mainly process their transactions. The word "bank" may become obsolete in two decades, as we become more deeply involved in consultative activities.*

12. *Enterprise and individual obsolescence rates may increase substantially, because competition will move increasingly into the arena of competing ideas and philosophies. Ideas can become obsolete quickly. The pace will be intense, and the rich innovational rewards will go to the swift and highly competent. The day of comfortable and complacent banking decidedly is over. The competition for high talent will become fierce, for such talent is quite rare in the population. But there will be considerable challenge available for those who actively seek it and have the courage to promote their beliefs and concepts.*

41

Automation: Guidelines for Designing an Automated Commercial Loan Information System and the Use of Computers in Loan Decision Making

Robert H. Long,
Spencer M. Overton,
and James R. Holt

Reprinted by permission of *Journal of Commercial Bank Lending*, January 1969.

Why is research needed? One definition of what research accomplishes is that it determines what you should be doing when you can no longer keep on doing what you are doing now. This leads to the question: Why would we need to change what we're doing in lending?

Perhaps the reason is that growth, complexity, statistical analysis, quantitative measurements, projections, and information systems are fast becoming characteristics of the commercial lending environment. Or, as Marshall McLuhan has said:

> With electric speeds governing industry and social life, explosion in the sense of crash development becomes normal . . . , the old-fashioned kind of "war" becomes as

impractical as playing hopscotch with bulldozers .... Every industry has had to "rethink through" function by function its place in the economy ... the manipulation of information as a means of creating wealth is no longer a monopoly .... Men are suddenly nomadic gatherers of knowledge, nomadic as never before, informed as never before, free from fragmentary specialism as never before, but involved in the total social process as never before since with electricity we extend our central nervous system globally ....

In short, what I think these words mean is that commercial loan systems research is needed because the entire business and social complex of our civilization is undergoing a revolution. This means that if banking's commercial lending activities are to prosper, it must plug in, turn on, and tune in to this change. To do this it helps to know where we are, where we are going, and how we are going to get there. In a sense that's the purpose of the RMA/BAI commercial loan research project.

The RMA/BAI joint research project on automated commercial loan systems has a number of objectives. The primary objectives are to study currently operating commercial loan systems to find out what data they collect, what they do with it, and what they give the loan officers to work with.

In addition, we are studying the information needs of loan officers, attempting to develop commercial loan systems, design guidelines and identify research that could result in substantial improvements in banking's ability to serve its customers or process its loan records.

To learn something about today's automated commercial loan systems we undertook a number of different kinds of activities. The research team of Spencer Overton, vice president, Wachovia Bank & Trust Company, Dave Klipsch, assistant vice president, American Fletcher Bank & Trust Company, and I interviewed bankers, reviewed existing systems, held a workshop in which we discussed commercial loan systems with 35 loan officers and systems designers, and surveyed existing commercial loan systems, characteristics and goals.

Based on these research activities, and a lot of hard thinking and heated discussion, I believe we have begun to develop a reasonable set of design criteria for an automated commercial loan information system.

Basic Findings

To begin our study we examined the entire group of commercial loan activities and decided that from a systems' point of view, commercial lending systems consist of three basic operational elements: the maintenance of data files on customers, loans, and collateral and three basic decision points concerned with new business development, loan plan design, and loan policy development.

Almost all automated commercial loan systems examined emphasized the automation of only one of these elements—the maintenance of loan data files. Since the operations related to the maintenance of loan data files are to a large extent dictated by the requirements of accounting, it is not surprising that we found this to be the state-of-the-art. Accounting has a set of rather well defined requirements, and most information systems must fulfill these requirements before getting on with the task of attempting to improve the information available for officers who make profit making decisions.

Some banks, it is true, were beginning to automate the maintenance and accessibility of customer data and to use the computer to maintain portions of their collateral file. However, no bank, to my knowledge, has even begun to use the computer as a major aid in developing improved administrative loan policies, business development, or loan plan specifications.

While these are admittedly difficult areas to analyze, they also are about the only decision areas that can directly affect the profits of commercial lending.

However, before discussing what banks do not have, let me describe a little more completely what we believe the typical automated commercial loan system of today includes, what appears to be some of its problems, and where most of the development attention is directed.

A Typical Automated Commercial Loan System

According to our survey more than half of the banks with some elements of commercial loan automation has at least these computer prepared reports:

Transaction journal and trial balance

Loan and deposit status

Loan payment and deposit history

New loans

Past due notes

Past due loans

Maturing notes

Delinquent loans

Total direct, indirect, secured, and unsecured liabilities

Portfolio earnings

Customer direct and indirect liability status

Loans by industry and customer classifications and interest rates

Billing and other customer notices

Annual statement of interest paid

In addition, about one-fifth of these banks are producing some information about:

Loans which deviate from the banks' interest rate policy

Loan officer and division performance

Current value of collateral pledged, by loan and by customer

Portfolio cash flow

Participation activity

Status of other accounts and services which the customer has with bank

Problems and Developments

In addition to the general development problems of how to construct and maintain good customer collateral and loan files, the problems of the typical system seem to center around:

Too much paper being generated

Inaccurate or late reports

Difficulty in dealing with special loan agreements

Definition of special status reports and the development of the capability to produce them on demand

The major advance thinking and development efforts in banks seem to be concerned with:

Coding systems linking customer loan accounts, liabilities, and other customer bank services

On-line video information display systems for faster, more selective information retrieval

The development of accounting methods to calculate customer profitability or to help a customer plan his cash flow in order to better assess his financial needs and repayment capabilities

We have not concluded our study so these comments should not be considered as a final judgment or recommendation. They might be called a view from the bridge. From the bridge, through the early morning smog, a number of images are seen with some clarity:

Present commercial loan systems are well on the way to developing automated customer loan and collateral files.

The problems which exist are the standard "period of adjustment" problems of how to impose the standardization and discipline required for good machine systems upon activities which have traditionally been carried out by creative, but rather undisciplined men.

The concerns and "hot" arguments about future commercial loan systems seem to be based on differences of opinion on the boundary line between the decisions that are permanently the province of man and those that can be the province of the programmed machine.

This constitutes the state-of-the-art in today's automated commercial loan systems. It leaves us with the very interesting problem of the future and the questions of:

Are present commercial loan systems developing an adequate data base for future system improvements?

How much automation will it be possible or practical to apply to commercial lending decisions?

What technological breakthroughs will significantly affect commercial loan systems' design and what important contributions might management science produce to aid commercial lending activities?

(At this point Mr. Long introduced Mr. Overton.)

The challenge put to you this afternoon calls for a creative use of the lively human decision making intellect leading to a more effective use of that inanimate, non-decision making, electro-mechanical device, the computer. To the extent you are able to harness the computer to bring into existence true management decision support systems and utilize new analytical methods, including operations research techniques, you will have greater freedom to do the things you do best—decide, plan, negotiate, persuade—in short, manage.

Essential Information Requirements for Commercial Lending/ Commercial Loan Administration

At one point in the BAI/RMA research project, as described by Bob Long, it was thought the project might lead to the development of an ideal commercial loan accounting and management information system. However, after surveying a number of automated commercial loan systems and after many discussions with bank officers about their information needs, it became apparent that due to significant differences in organizational structure, markets served, competition encountered, substantial variations in loan policies, and similar matters, that no one ideal system was feasible. Despite significant differences among commercial banks, the research project did identify a number of essential information needs common to all commercial banks in their commercial lending effort. These essential information needs can be classified as those needed to facilitate operations, control operations, assist in planning, and to assist in evaluating results. The essential information needs were tentatively identified in the research team's field work, and more definitively identified as a result of the response of 42 banks with relatively advanced automated systems to the confidential survey previously mentioned. The needs identified include:

Report on past due loans

Report on loans not handled in accordance with commitments or repayment agreements

Report on loans that deviate from bank's interest rate objectives

Report reflecting past loan and deposit history of borrower or related group of borrowers

Present direct and indirect liability of borrower to bank

Ledger sheet or loan history and status report

Report on portfolio earnings

Measurement of portfolio cash flow or liquidity

Customer profitability evaluation based upon deposit balances, interest income, servicing costs, and other related items of income and expense

In addition to these identified management information needs, responses to the survey concerning projects for research and development gave high priority to the development of a method for measuring loan risk, and the development of a general purpose cash flow model to assist the borrower in planning his cash requirements and borrowing needs.

Limitations of Existent Automated Commercial Loan Systems

At this point, let's examine the ability of existing automated systems to meet identified management information needs to determine where we are so we can chart a course to where we would like to be.

The failure of existent automated commercial loan systems to meet essential management information needs is demonstrated by a consideration of the inability of existing systems to provide a report on loans not handled in accordance with commitments or repayment agreements. While 40 of the 42 respondents to the confidential survey indicated that this report was an essential element of an automated commercial loan system, only 7, or 17%, indicated that such a report was presently available through their automated commercial loan system. This report is needed to enable the loan officer to determine that commitments are met and repayment agreements are properly discharged. This report can be produced as a daily or weekly exception report to the responsible loan officer on loans that exceed commitments, expired commitments, and borrowers who have failed to perform in accordance with agreed upon repayment programs, thus signaling the need for review of the account, discussion with the borrower, and such other appropriate action. The construction of such a report requires that the automated commercial loan system data base contains data on amount and expiration of commitments and agreed upon repayment programs which can be compared with actual performance for the purpose of generating the exception report.

Commercial loan administration, for control purposes, needs this report at less frequent intervals to determine that appropriate action is taken on lines exceeding commitments, expired commitments, and borrowers not meeting repayment agreements. The production of such reports requires that the bank has well defined policies on loan repayment and that clear-cut and realistic understandings on repayment are reached with borrowers. Further, any meaningful forecast of portfolio cash flow or liquidity must be undergirded with a definite and effective policy on loan repayment.

None of the respondents to the survey appears to have a present capability of generating a report on loans not handled in accordance with commitments or repayment agreements which possess any real degree of sophistication. Several banks have a present capability of producing reports on loans of certain types which have not been paid out for some stated period of time, say 30 days or more during the prior 12 months. Others have a capability of reporting certain out-of-bounds conditions—for example, installment loans with a payment 15 days or more past due—but no bank at the time of the survey appeared to have a program that would report loans not handled in accordance with commitments or repayment agreements in a detailed and comprehensive manner.

Forty of the banks surveyed stated that a report on loans that deviate from the bank's interest rate objectives was an essential element of an automated commercial loan system. The purpose of this report is to highlight those borrowing accounts where adjustment in the rate of interest is needed as a result of changes in the prime rate and other money market rates and to assure that loans deviating from the bank's interest rate objectives are properly controlled. To generate such reports for operating and control purposes, it is necessary that the automated system data base contains data on the rate of interest or the rate pattern applicable to the account—for example, prime, prime plus a half, prime plus three quarters with a floor of six and a ceiling of seven, six per cent fixed, and so on. Hence, the actual rate charge can be compared with the rate or rate pattern established for the account to determine whether or not the interest rate objective is being met.

Several banks responding to the survey can produce a print-out of loans categorized by interest rates but a visual review is required to determine those accounts that are out-of-bounds in terms of interest rate objectives. Only one of the participating banks in the survey reported a present capability of generating such an exception report through the inclusion in its data base of the rate objective or rate pattern applicable to the account. All respondents to the survey indicated that a report on past loan and deposit history was essential.

A report on individual commercial borrowers covering amount of commitment, average borrowings, rate of interest, average collected balances and analysis by profit or loss, was generally regarded as a minimum of essential information needed to measure compliance with the bank's policies on compensating balances relative to loans and commitments. While by no stretch of the imagination is such a report an adequate substitute for a comprehensive measurement of customer profitability, it does determine what accounts do and what accounts do not meet the bank's minimum standards on compensation, and it highlights those accounts where someone has some work to do. A report of this type should cover a meaningful time span, say a twelve-month period this year versus last.

To generate such a report through the automated commercial loan system, effective means must be found for pulling together information on commitments, average borrowings, and average collected balances. Means must also be found to pull together all related accounts in a single consolidated grouping—for example, a correspondent bank and the overlines handled for that bank. Many systems provide this essential information, but only a few in a single reporting format. Thus, it becomes necessary to insert clerical personnel at the end of the automated system to pull together computer generated data in a manually prepared report. The survey did uncover two commercial banks with automated systems with a present capability of interfacing vital related data, that is pulling together information on commercial loans and demand deposits for individual accounts and related groups of accounts in a single reporting format. The potential is there but most banks have not achieved the potential.

While some systems analysts question its utility, many loan officers regard the traditional ledger sheet, or if you prefer the loan history and status report, as a necessity in reaching decisions on the extension of credit and in reviewing loans on the bank's books. The survey indicated that all of the respondents wanted certain loan history and status information, including original date and amount of loan, interest rate, date and period of last clean up, type of security, high/low loan balance for the current and previous year, date relationship established, plus certain code information. All respondents indicated this information or portions of it were essential for an automated commercial loan system.

All but two survey respondents indicated that a report measuring the portfolio cash flow or liquidity was an essential element of an automated commercial loan system. Nine indicated that such was available through their systems, but further investigation disclosed that no participating bank had such a report in any really sophisticated form to measure portfolio cash flow. The portfolio cash flow from money market instruments, commercial paper, bankers' acceptances, and the like, can be predictably measured. Portfolio cash flow from repayment of commercial loans extended to the bank's customers can only be approximated at best, and only then if the bank in question has a well defined and effective policy on loan repayment.

A report which seeks to forecast portfolio cash flow by simply spreading the portfolio by types of loans and maturity, loans repayable on demand or 30, 60, and 90 days has no measure of portfolio cash flow. For example, the inclusion of construction loans as loans repayable on demand in the schedule of cash availability is grossly misleading since these loans can only be repaid upon the completion of the project and the permanent financing of the project. Many seasonal commitments are handled on a 90-day note basis with a full expectation that the loan will go through two or three renewals before completion of the seasonal cycle, at which time the borrower hopefully generates the necessary liquidity to retire the indebtedness. In short, it is the achievement of the repayment program agreed upon at the inception of the loan that gives rise to portfolio cash flow, not the theoretic ability of the bank to force the borrower to repay at some future maturity date when in all likelihood he will not have the necessary funds to repay the loan. Further, the ebb and flow of economic activity and the shifts in fiscal and monetary policy have a material impact on loan demand, hence portfolio cash flow.

On some distant day it may be feasible to forecast portfolio cash flow through the application of analytical methods to an expanded data base containing much historical data on the behavior of the loan portfolio under a variety of happenings, but such an application is far in advance of the state of the art today. Before someone takes issue with me on this, let me acknowledge that portfolio cash flow is, at best, a marginal concept. In the long run, the portfolio in a growing bank is not a generator of funds but a consumer of funds. Only in an internal sense does portfolio cash flow produce the liquidity necessary to enable a bank to fund new commitments as borrowers retire existing loans under repayment programs previously agreed upon.

Forty-two of the forty-two respondents indicated that customer profitability analysis was an essential element of an automated commercial loan system. This was also a top priority item for research and development. The achievement of such a reporting capability calls for great sophistication. It necessitates the pulling together of information on the customer's total relationship—at least his total relationship in the commercial banking area. It requires an effective cost system. Several banks have sophisticated indexes of customer profitability, but no bank responding to the survey has a present capability of measuring customer profitability when taking into account all significant items of income and expense associated with the relationship precisely determined. A handful of banks do appear pointed toward the development of systems that will measure customer profitability taking into account all of the factors mentioned.

Now, when you first contemplate the development of a system capable of measuring customer profitability, the task appears overwhelming, but reflect that perhaps ten or fifteen percent of your commercial borrowing customers generate eighty-five to ninety percent of your commercial loan dollars outstanding. Ultimately we may find the answer in terms of an individual determination of profitability for this ten or fifteen percent. The remainder, the eighty-five or ninety percent which produce ten to fifteen percent of our commercial loan dollars, may then be treated in the aggregate to determine that this latter group is at least paying its own way.

On the basis of this examination of existing automated commercial loan systems, I think we can say that today's automated commercial loan systems are essentially accounting systems; provide limited management control and exception reporting; do not, with minor exceptions, interface vital related data; do not, with minor exceptions, provide management information on performance versus objectives; and, finally, are largely lacking in sophisticated measures of profitability. In summary, today's systems provide limited assistance to management in carrying out its responsibilities in planning, in controlling, and in evaluating results.

Now let me repeat that in setting out the limitations of existing automated commercial loan systems, it is not my intention to reflect critically on those involved in system design. My sole purpose is to point out where we are so we may begin to chart a course to where we would like to be.

The Role of the Loan Officer in Systems Design and Development

Why are commercial banks so backward in the development of advanced systems while many industrial companies have made notable progress? One answer is that first priority for automation in commercial banks was given, and properly so, to high volume activities such as demand deposit accounting where needs are critical. Second, since commercial loan accounting represents a low volume complex activity, the limited potential economies arising from automation of commercial loan accounting have given it a low priority. It can be argued that the payoff from the development of automated commercial loan systems lies not in the automation of accounting but in the potential the system offers in terms of freeing management to manage more creatively and effectively, particularly through the development of true management decision support systems and the utilization of advanced analytical methods.

Don't despair that the state of the art is at a low level. This fact enables you to get in on the ground floor and play a significant role in automated commercial loan systems development.

Now, precisely where do you fit in? What is your role in systems development? It should be apparent at this point that one of the important functions of an automated system is to highlight through exception reporting those accounts that are out-of-bounds, those accounts that do not conform to certain policies and objectives. Thus, an essential preliminary step for you in automated system design is a review of your loan policies. What are the bank's policies or objectives on loan repayment, rates of interest for various types of accounts, compensating balances in other fundamental matters? Without clearly defined policies and objectives the data output of the automated system may be interesting but will probably possess little utility for you. Therefore, the first task for you as commercial loan management is to clearly define and clearly state your bank's loan policies and objectives to the fullest extent practical.

The next step involves a review of existing systems of management information and control. Perhaps you have a highly formalized, perhaps also a highly informal, system of management information and control. These systems need to be reviewed carefully and evaluated and reduced to essential elements as part of the process leading to the development of the automated commercial loan system. To accomplish this you're going to have to work very closely with the systems analyst who serves as the link between you, the programmer, and the hardware.

It may clear up some confusion about automated commercial loan systems if we distinguish between computer applications that are logically part of the automated commercial loan system and computer applications that are of interest and potential value but not, by their very nature, part of the automated system. For example, the use of the computer to assist customers in preparing cash forecasts is a sound application of the computer, but it is not an integral part of the automated commercial loan system.

In summary, then, what is your role? It is essentially one of examining and defining commercial loan policies and objectives, reviewing and refining existent systems of management information and control, and conveying needs and preferences to the systems analyst. The systems analyst cannot do this alone. He does not know what you need, when you need it, and in what reporting format. And, if he did know these things, I think the serious question is whether or not he shouldn't have your job.

Having done these things, it is necessary that you maintain a relatively strong, aggressive, insistent posture to see that you get what you want, when you want it, in the format in which you want it, and on a timely basis.

There are several books that may help you in your approach to the computer. *Clarifying the Computer*, by Kevin McLaughlin, Fairchild Publications, New York, is a very readable non-technical work. While it is not necessary at all that you know anything about computer hardware, if you feel you must know what goes on in the guts of these machines, then *Computers and How They Work*, among several other similar works, by James D. Fahnestock, Ziff Davis Publishing Company, New York, will help you there. Finally, if you want some exposure to analytical methods, there is the very excellent *Analytical Methods in Banking*, Cohen and Hammer, Richard D. Irwin, Inc., Homewood, Ill.

Profit Center P & L Accounting and the Measurement of Profit Performance versus Objectives

Despite the potential it possesses, the automated commercial loan system is not a be-all, end-all. It is but one of several automated systems needed to support management decision making. To emphasize this point, let's look at another management decision support system only partially related to the automated commercial loan system—the automated profit center P & L accounting system which measures profit performance against budget objectives.

This automated system derives only a portion of its data from the automated commercial loan system, i.e., data on interest income. Other inputs to the system include other income and expense items relative to the several profit centers, together with detailed budget objectives for income and expense. While relatively few banks have made meaningful progress in the development of automated commercial loan systems, there is good reason to believe that no greater number has developed fully automated profit center P & L accounting systems. "Have you automated your controller?" is still a lively current question.

The Computer and Risk Evaluation

While there is great current interest in the use of the computer to measure loan risk, today's computer's problem solving ability is limited to problems involving binary arithmetic and binary logic which it is programmed to solve. I do not rule out some meaningful role for tomorrow's computer in the measurement of loan risk, but it appears that today's computer has, at best, a very limited contribution to make in this area.

First an evaluation of risk involves a consideration of qualitative and quantitative factors. Today's computer does not have a capability of dealing with judgmental qualitative factors such as the evaluation of the character and capacity of the management of a corporate borrower. Further, risk in large measure depends upon the interplay of human elements as represented by the management of the borrowing corporation and the management of the lending bank. The element of risk present in a loan at any given point in time is in part determined by the skill and effectiveness of the loan officer in negotiating the loan, the quality of the servicing given during the life of the loan, the effectiveness of loan review in detecting deterioration, and effectiveness and intestinal fortitude of bank management in bringing about needed correction in a deteriorating situation.

The Evolving Commercial Loan System

It was a considerable trip from the Ford Trimotor to the Boeing 707, and I suspect it is going to be a considerable, though potentially rewarding, trip from where we stand today to tomorrow's automated commercial loan decision support system. I suspect we will go through at least three stages to get there. For most banks, the first step will involve a conversion of manual accounting systems to automated commercial loan accounting systems. Those banks that have already reached this point will probably be involved for some considerable period of time in the development of a fully effective second generation system that will not only handle accounting but provide, in sophisticated form, the essential information requirements identified earlier. This system may provide a comprehensive measurement of customer profitability on an individual account basis. In a more distant tommorrow, we may see a third generation system with a true management decision support capability, a system with the capabilities of second generation systems plus the capability of liquidity measurement and forecasting, together with other applications arising through the use of advanced analytical methods.

To be or not to be is no longer a valid question relative to automated commercial loan systems. They are here today and will be playing an increasingly significant role as their capabilities are extended. But, make no mistake about this—management decision support systems are not now nor will they ever be a substitute for management.

Recently I heard a banker question the effectiveness of his automated commercial loan system pointing out that while the system produced a past-due report, his bank's past-due loans continued to remain at a high level. I suspect the problem is not in his system but in the deficiencies of commercial loan management. And finally, automation is never going to take the place of that unautomated management information system that goes on-line with the verbal signal, "Come in John, close the door, there's something I want to talk to you about."

(At this point, Mr. Long continued with his remarks.)

Mr. Long: Future Systems

There are two parts to an information processing system: the data base and the processing unit. To understand the problems of what data base will be needed in the future, we must first solve the problem of what the computer will be doing in the future, and this leads to the problem of what men will be doing in the future. In a sense the whole problem is inextricably bound up in the interrelations of its parts.

The entire maze of present and possible future systems can be simplified if we look at information and decision systems as being made up of two parts: man systems, and machine systems. As technology improves and as we become more skillful in its use, it becomes possible to transfer more and more from the "man" subsystem to the machine subsystem in order that the more flexible man subsystem can concentrate more time on those activities in which he excels.

To understand a little more clearly those areas in which men excel and those which machines can perform, let us examine the elements that make up the two information processing systems. Both have memory and input and output mechanisms. Men, however, have a greater variety of input/output mechanisms; eyes, ears, vocal cords, touch, digital manipulative skills, etc.; whereas, computers are much more limited. Men have about 10 billion memory cells—all random access. Computers generally have, at the very most, a few hundred million. Men, however, not only have large random memories, but they seem to have random filing methods and random search methods; whereas the computers of today must have precisely defined data files and orderly retrieval methods. Computers compared to a man, therefore, are terrifically fast, orderly, and expensive. Or, compared to a computer, man is slow, disorderly and inexpensive.

There are, however, a few more important characteristics to be compared. Men conceive dreams, goals, and objectives. Men imagine, evaluate, and combine unrelated ideas to form new concepts or products. Computers do only what they are told to do. This means that whenever we thoroughly understand what data should be used and how it should be analyzed to accomplish a task—we can get a computer to do it. When we do not understand how we do a task or cannot define the information needed, a man must do it.

Armed with this comparison of the strengths and weaknesses of men and computers we can proceed to analyze a little more completely how men and computers may be working together in the future.

In considering the application of computers to decision making problems, two important judgments must be made:

1. *Are significant benefits likely to accrue? While this is usually hard to judge, this estimate is the basis of all R & D activity.*
2. *Do we understand, or can we learn enough, and can we obtain the proper data so that we can instruct the computer to proceed through a complex of logic and arrive at an effective solution?*

Both of these are difficult judgments to make.

If either of them is negative, the decision area will remain in the province of man-systems. If they are both positive and the judgments prove correct, this decision problem will move into the province of machine systems.

Because more and more commercial lending decisions are moving into the computer or machine system area, it is likely that banks will develop two kinds of data files. One data file will be accounting oriented; the other will contain massive amounts of unaggregated data that can be used in the continuous development of improved machine decision making procedures and in the production of specialized management information.

The overall objective in switching as much as possible to the computer is that by allocating certain tasks to a machine we are in effect saying "We do know enough about this aspect of our work to be able to reduce it to rules and patterns that can be taught." By doing this, we hopefully free ourselves to concentrate on those important aspects of our professions which still are on the frontiers of knowledge and require creative insight and a full set of sensory impressions.

I believe the foundation for this kind of system is now being structured. For example, suggestions for future research and development activities collected during our study show these interests:

Loan portfolio liquidity planning models

Method of measuring customers' profitability

Measurement of loan risk

Development of models to help loan officers aid customers in planning cash requirements and to develop better loan plans

If this is the way loan officers are thinking, this is the direction development efforts will take, and these are the milestones that will make a new era of commercial lending feasible.

Perhaps because I am too ignorant of many of the details of commercial lending and too close to the possibilities of the computer, I can see a very different kind of future computer loan system. It might operate as follows: The computer analyzes data from the bank's historical files, economic forecasts, and demographic data and outputs information about blue ribbon loan prospects. The loan officer reviews these prospects, and if he wants to establish a banking connection, makes arrangements to set up a complete customer data file. When the prospect wants a loan the loan officer and the prospect define loan design limits of amount, collateral, term, interest, fees. These are then entered into the computer either from the customer's office over the phone or from the loan officer's desk console.

The computer, using rules and policies set forth by senior loan officers examines the customer's credit worthiness and the bank's policies and economic forecasts and then, if possible, designs a loan plan that fulfills the bank's lending objectives and the customer's borrowing desires. If the first loan plan does not meet the customer's objectives, then the design limitations can be changed and a new loan plan quickly developed. This can be done over and over again until either a loan plan that suits the customer is devised or it becomes obvious that only a loan that violates the bank's present lending policies will satisfy the customer.

If this system ever comes into being, it will allow loan specifications to be sensitive to risk, to the customer's total bank connection, and to current bank loan policies. Lending policies, naturally, will be constructed differently and will change more often than the policies of today. They will be more responsive to general economic conditions, to bank objectives, and to industry forecasts. Such policies will constitute loan design guidelines that will aid the loan officer in negotiating renewals and new loans that are in line with both the bank and the customer's objectives.

In such a system we have two basic kinds of tasks: (1) The machine system tasks of data gathering and program maintenance required to support the mechanized data processing and analysis system and (2) the human system tasks of monitoring the programmed system and evaluating those factors we have not yet been able to completely understand or quantify—such as interpersonal skills judgment, timing, ethics, and the overall evaluation of practicality of business plans.

There are a number of factors that make this kind of a future system seem to be possible. Some of these are:

1. *The growing availability of inexpensive massive data files that permit either loan officers or the computer to quickly retrieve almost any customer or loan data that has ever been recorded. We see these developments in the fields of magnetic storage and in the latest announcements of two way computer/microfilm data transfer equipment.*

2. *Emerging techniques in heuristic and statistical decision models that might enable a computer to literally be "trained" over the years to analyze a statement, within certain limitations judge credit worthiness, and to make predictions of the probability of the success or failure of certain courses of action.*

3. *An increasing willingness of people to conform to a certain extent to the standardization and discipline required to gain the potential benefits of computerization.*

4. *A continued acceleration of growth and complexity in business operations increasing the number and variety of the facts that should be considered in making important business decisions.*

5. *The forecast shortages of highly trained people that will make it more imperative than ever before to use machines wherever we can.*

While commercial loan systems are changing, we must remember that the entire business environment will also be in the process of change. Commercial business will be making more and sophisticated uses of computers, distances will, in effect, shrink, customers will probably shop around for more bank services, financial services may become more customized and even stronger communication and data exchange between banks and their customers may develop, business will become even more international and specialized, and fast moving—all of these and more are occurring now!

The commercial loan information system of the future is already under construction. It began with the development of the bank's first commercial loan processing system. It continues with the integration of this system with other bank data files, the provision for flexible data retrieval, the standardization of loan plan descriptions, the education of your customers on supplying reliable data, and with the transferring your knowledge of commercial lending to a systems designer.

How well your bank competes in the future will depend, more than ever before, upon how well its man system and the machine system work together, how well tasks have been allocated to the unit that can do the best job.

In summary, the commercial loan environment is a complex one. Systems design is complicated by the facts that:

We do not yet explicitly understand how we should judge a commercial customer's credit worthiness.

We do not yet have good yardsticks for measuring liquidity, profitability, or risk.

We do not have techniques for recording all of the loan agreement, so that the computer can have on file a loan officer's expectations, verbal agreements, and estimates of what will happen.

We do not have explicit loan policies which can serve as guidelines for loan plan designs.

However, these problems can be surmounted. I am certain that just as in the near future medical diagnosis, legal research, and investment decisions will be based on results from computers working with extensive data libraries, so will a bank be able to serve its commercial customers in a more personalized way because its commercial lending information system has been kept up-to-date.

Before closing I would like to add one word of caution. I fully believe that advanced systems of computerized decision making will come into being, but success in achieving them will, as always, consist of a proper blend of advance thinking and practicality.

Legend has it that the Greek philosopher Thales fell into a well while strolling along gazing at the stars. It was his penchant for gazing at the heavens that made him great. But failure to keep his eyes on the ground killed him.

(At this point Mr. Long introduced Mr. Holt.)

In Conclusion

Hopefully, Bob and Spence have broadened your horizons about the potential uses of the computer in the lending function. As you have heard, some banks are already starting. Others are investigating approaches that a few years ago would have been considered ridiculous.

But the world of automation is changing very rapidly. In the field of hardware, we now talk about nano-second computers. What is a nano-second? A nano-second is a billionth of a second—this is almost meaningless until we recognize there are almost as many nano-seconds in one second as there are seconds in 33 years.

Great strides are being made in software. We may think that our problems are complex, but there are three locations in the United States where space flights can be simulated on a computer. When we think of what is being done at NASA, our own problems seem to shrink in magnitude. But we can't ignore the fact that, in developing the kind of information system that Bob Long was talking about, there will be many problems to which there are no easy answers. Some of these problems are probably unique in that there may be a different "best" solution for each bank. Other problems lend themselves to industry-wide research, and I think that there may be a fertile field here for additional joint efforts by RMA and BAI. In any event, progress will probably depend on the combined efforts of lending officers and systems analysts, which brings us to one of the problem areas, one which I would like to speak of for a few moments.

There exists a very real and serious communications problem between the systems analyst and the lending officer. Each has his own language. Each language includes words that do not exist in the other's as well as words which have an entirely different meaning to each profession. And the problem goes deeper than just the language. I am convinced that there are real differences in the way these two groups think. The lending officer tends to deal in broad concepts on a rather general basis while the systems analyst tends to be extremely precise, exact, and specific.

How to solve this communication problem? I don't know. At our bank, we've made the assumption that the banking officer is probably more flexible than the systems expert, so we've taken the approach of trying to teach key banking officers how to communicate with systems types, rather than vice versa. After all, the systems man's strength is his knowledge of the art of the possible, he is not competent to define what needs to be done.

Several years ago, we put on a course in computer concepts for our commercial people. It was an eight-hour course spread over four weeks. For Senior Officers, we have a luncheon program in which they are exposed to some of our most far-out research people. These are small groups which lend themselves to informal discussion. We also insist that banking officers participate in automation studies. For example, Lou Gabriel had a guiding influence in developing our commercial loan system. Another of our lending officers played an active role in the development of our Cash Flow Model. Still another possibility is cross training. I'm an example of this. Finally, there are a great many automation schools offered by computer manufacturers and others. For instance, Frank Dyer, one of our Senior Lending Officers, will be attending a manufacturer's automation school in the near future.

I'm sure other banks have been more successful in dealing with this problem than we have. We've found the process to be expensive, time-consuming, and only partially effective. But the brave new world isn't going to happen by itself. It's going to take the combined efforts of the best of both professions to make it happen. Communications is just one of the problems, but I think an important one, which must be solved.

I'm afraid that this panel hasn't given you very many answers. We all have a long way to go. But if it has made you aware of what some of your associates are doing, or trying to do, and has started you thinking about what *you* might be doing, I think it will have served its purpose.

42

Management Information Systems: A New Computer Tool for Life Companies

Thorn Bacon

Reprinted by permission of
Best's Review, Life edition, 71, July 1970, pp. 74–78.

In Dallas recently, Clarence Skelton, the president of Republic National Life, bluntly remarked on a growing dilemma in the life insurance industry—the rising costs of electronic data processing requirements and applications:

"The fact is," he said, "that even the latest computers are by no means omniscient. Nor for that matter are they in any sense self-sufficient, or simple, as we were told. All of them require elaborate and costly preparation of the material to be put into them. We were oversold—oversold in hardware and oversold on the simplicity of programming, and we are constantly overhauling all of the time. I certainly don't think we can place a dollar savings on our data processing installation to date."

Mr. Skelton's accusation places in focus the little publicized truth about the electronic data processing quandary in the life insurance industry which was summed up by one EDP insider, Paul Wrotenbery, senior vice president of Tracor Computing Corp., when he reflected that it reminds him of a classic statement in A. A. Milne's *The House at Pooh Corner:*

"I don't see much sense in that," said Rabbit. "No," said Pooh, humbly, "there isn't. But there was going to be when I began it. It is just that something happened to it on the way."

To learn what that "something" is that has happened to EDP programs in the life insurance industry and what steps are being taken to correct it, involves taking a look at effects to arrive at causes.

It is not generally realized how far the EDP industry in the United States has progressed since the early days of vacuum tube first generation computers in the 1950s.

In 1956, only 570 computers were installed in the U.S. compared to some 63,000 by the end of 1969. Predictions are that by the mid-1970s there will be about 100,000 installations in the U.S. alone whose gross value will reach $40 billion. Even more impressive is the history of "software" sales.

From 1962 through 1966 the total investment in software increased from $10.5 billion to more than $73 billion! By 1973 the total investment in hardware and software is expected to reach a dizzying 12 digits—$100 billion!

One yardstick by which to gauge the impact of the computer on the life insurance industry was revealed in a recent survey on business showing that almost 10% of all plant and equipment expenditures by life companies in 1967 was for data processing equipment. And the survey estimated that these companies would increase the proportion of these expenditures to 29% by 1975.

Outstripping Expectations

The obvious deduction from these figures is that in terms of sales and technical achievement, the computer revolution in the U.S. is outstripping the most optimistic expectations; but in terms of economic payoff on new applications, it is rapidly losing momentum. Many insurance executives familiar with Marshall McLuhan's classic definition of the computer as "The LSD of the business world, transforming its outlook and objectives," bitterly insist they've been taken on a "bad trip" and they are clamoring to get off.

In fairness to the electronic data processing industry, the reasons for this cannot be laid solely at the door of EDP manufacturers. This was put in perspective by McKinsey & Company in a 1968 research report involving 36 companies, three of which were in the life insurance business.

"From a profit standpoint," they said, "our findings indicate computer efforts in all but a few exceptional companies are in real, if often unacknowledged trouble. Faster, costlier, more sophisticated hardware; larger and increasingly complex and ingenious applications: these are in evidence everywhere. Less and less in evidence, as these new applications proliferate, are profitable results. This is the familiar phenomenon of diminishing returns."

Answers Own Question

The McKinsey report went on to answer the question it had raised: What had gone wrong? The rules of the EDP game have changed, but management strategies have not, the report stated. The failure, it pointed out, lay in the fact that, "less than a decade ago management could afford to leave the direction of the corporate effort largely in the hands of technical people. That time is past. Yet the identification and selection of new computer applications are still predominately in the hands of computer specialists, who—despite their professional expertise—are poorly qualified to set the course of the corporate computer effort."

It is not difficult to understand how this situation has come about. Historically, starting about the early 60s, profit-oriented insurance executives guided their companies into computer development work for the singular purpose of improving financial results. The first step was to install a computer system which would function as a sort of superclerk to reduce general and administrative expenses. There is no doubt that computerization has transformed administrative and accounting operations, but the savings have been insignificant compared to the real opportunities inherent in computer technology of solving key operating and management problems—and this, as many life insurance executives have belatedly discovered—is where the greatest computer-oriented profit potential lies.

But a yawning gap exists in this area—between capabilities and practical achievements—for until the life insurance industry puts the computer to work where the leverage on profits is high, the tantalizing prospect of more profits and greater opportunities will continue to be pie in the sky.

Any dispassionate appraisal of present computer development projects would show that, with few exceptions, the main objective in life insurance computer departments is still the refinement of general and administrative procedures and reduction of expenses. And this is the very area where EDP manufacturers have done such a remarkably successful job of selling hardware. Moreover, because the software needed to implement omniverous computer monsters is growing more expensive, a trend has developed to overspend on hardware rather than create software that will maximize machine efficiency [see Figure 1].

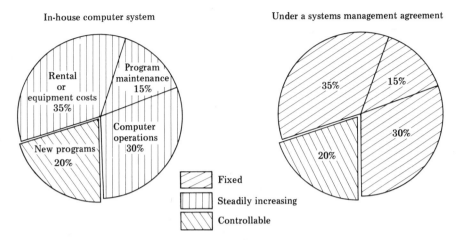

In-house computer system

Under a systems management agreement

For every $100 spent on hardware, companies spend about
$200 on computer staffing, operations, and new applications

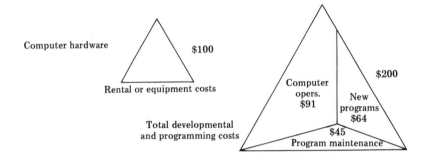

Figure 1.   How TCC figures the distribution of computing costs in the life
insurance industry. According to TCC research, the breakdown for
every $100,000 of total computer expenditures in the life insurance
industry is as follows: $35,000 payroll for computer staff; $15,000
devoted to keeping present systems updated; $20,000 developmental
programming and staff time to new applications which may or may
not pay off. But these can be controlled. TCC's summary: The developmental and operational dollars, as shown above, are typically a
greater fraction of the total than a company's annual bill for hardware rentals—a ratio of about $2 to $1, but in some companies it
goes as high as $3 for each $1 expended on hardware. Thus, this dollar leverage on future costs and benefits is enormous. For a certainty,
they hold the key to the success or failure of a company's computer
effort. TCC maintains that unless the management of a company seg-
regates total EDP costs and fully comprehends the nature of the resources it purchases, the whole direction of future computer development may become bogged down, subject to doubt and eventually
emotional review.

Bad Experience at Pierce National

Ralph Head, president of Pierce National Life of Los Angeles, tells of his company's traumatic experience when it decided in 1966 to develop an integrated computer system. This, unhappily for Pierce National, was before it sought outside help from a firm specializing in computer management information services.

"We figured," says Mr. Head, "on an investment of $300,000 to get an information flow system established and fully functioning. But about a year later, when we discovered we had spent $600,000, we became alarmed. We suddenly found ourselves so deeply involved in the computer business that we increased our investment and started selling time on our machines to recover our outlay which ultimately reached $2.5 million.

"If I were to sound a warning to life insurance company executives, and I think one is certainly timely, it would be this: Like many other life companies we were motivated to reduce administrative costs. But we had no one but the manufacturer to turn to for advice, and hardware manufacturers are in the business to sell equipment. If originally we had done what we did later—pay for expert outside help—we would have saved a lot of money and avoided some terrible headaches.

"Management generally is reluctant to pay the piper for the best advice available before embarking on a course that can cost a whole lot of money.

"I learned this when I attended a computer seminar for management in 1968. There I discovered some of the pitfalls we had already stumbled into, some of the mistakes that can run automation costs up sky-high. In our case it was like shutting the barn door after the horse is out. But at least it put us on the right track. I can't over emphasize that it's far less expensive in the long run to hire competent advice before embarking on a major capital expenditure in computerization than to plunge ahead willy-nilly, then end up paying anyway for somebody to bail you out of your troubles."

Others Skimming Cream

EDP manufacturers are not the only ones who are skimming the cream and some of the milk, too, from life insurance company treasury allotments earmarked for automating information systems including everything from updating policies with renewable term premiums to figuring statutory reserves on a monthly review basis.

Just in the last three years dozens of computer service companies have sprung up across the country offering a range of computing services, including "facilities management" for a fee. Primarily, what they sell are one or more of the following basic services:

Time sharing for a client on machines owned by the supplier.

Application programs which process a client's data— inventory, payroll, etc.

Operations programs that monitor the computer as it processes data from application programs.

Translation programs which convert a common language (English) into a language machines can handle.

One of the major reasons for the success of computer service companies is that their clients, even those who have managed to sidestep some of the perils of computerization that Pierce National fell heir to before it called in help, have found that with computer technology advancing at a record speed and qualified computer personnel scarce and getting scarcer, it is less costly and more effective to contract for a facilities management package. What this boils down to is that a service company shoulders the responsibility for meeting a customer's total data processing requirements.

Short Supply of Programmers

The dearth of qualified computer programmers is so acute that Jerome L. Dryer, executive vice president of the Association of Data Processing Service Organizations, predicts that by 1972, "at least 250,000 systems and programming personnel will be needed. Even now, with a need for less than half that number, we are in short supply." And by the mid-1970s EDP industry experts say requirements will call for a total labor force in electronic data processing of 2.5 million people, certainly a significant percentage of a national labor force of an estimated 80 million.

The manpower problem was a major factor in the decision of Southwestern Life to develop a facilities management contract with Electronic Data Systems Corp., despite the fact that Southwestern had been operating a notably successful data center itself for years.

President William Seay explained his company's reasoning: "We simply felt that EDS, with its highly skilled cadre of professionals, could develop an integrated third generation computer system faster than we could. Hopefully, within 18 months we will have problem-solving applications on stream that will provide an excellent management tool for decision making.

"Of course we are interested in current effectiveness, but the key question is not 'How are we doing?' but 'Where are we heading and why?' "

While giant service companies like EDS are doing a complete job of customer data processing, there is a different sort of EDP company emerging whose philosophy of service goes beyond the nuts and bolts of computerization; it reaches into the heady atmosphere of the board of directors level. These companies, operated by management teams which represent the full spectrum of business science and the arcane art of programming, see a booming market ahead in the life insurance industry by adding a new dimension to sales of their computing-programming packages: This is a vigorous management consulting role to support and help define the client's corporate objectives.

A Concept Called Efficiency

If one word can be used to describe the concept by which these EDP newcomers operate, it is efficiency, the quality Neal J. Dean of Booz, Allen & Hamilton, management consultants, discovered when he reported in the *Harvard Business Review* on 108 large manufacturing companies that were highly successful in utilizing the full capabilities of computers.

Remarked Mr. Dean: ". . . these companies—all of which had superior records of growth in sales and earnings—had discovered ways to apply computers to all major areas of their activities. The main reason for their success was that top management had taken charge. Nearly all had appointed top computer executives who participated in the companies' highest councils."

But there are literally thousands of companies in the United States (including many life companies) that for one reason or another cannot fully utilize or justify a highly paid computer executive. For this reason, management service specialty companies are moving in to provide this expertise contractually. Nearly all of them, like the UNIVAC Division of Sperry Rand, offer most all basic computer services, but a few, like Tracor Computing Corp. (TCC) of Austin, Texas, have taken big strides in the EDP industry by emphasizing the critical role of management consulting in their marketing approach.

TCC's sales effort is headed by Paul Wrotenbery, who preaches a company marketing philosophy with a relish that amounts to a crusading zeal. Mr. Wrotenbery recognizes that some insurance companies do extremely well in utilizing computer potentialities, but is ready with some convincing arguments [see Figure 1] to prove that for great many, "the astonishingly rapid growth of the computer industry has simply not given enough time for the development of true competence on the part of thousands of people engaged in driving their computers, and consequently, fail to astutely relate this effort to the business needs of their employer.

Main Problem Is Future Direction

"The computer management problem confronting corporate insurance executives today is a matter of future direction. The question 'What happened yesterday?' is hardly relevant. What is going to happen a year, five years from now is the most urgent information insurance management needs. And this is the concept behind MIS, the abbreviation in the EDP industry for management information systems."

Mr. Wrotenbery defines the workings of current life insurance management information systems in this fashion:

"Presently, most MIS plans are simply perpetuated daily cycles of administrative and accounting details; necessary, but only a rudimentary task for an integrated computer operation.

"We feel what is critically required is information to cover three vital areas of managerial responsibility: information for long range planning, for control in monitoring performance, and simulation of the total operation of the company."

TCC's concept has produced some surprising results at Pierce National Life.

So far as president Ralph Head is concerned, the program has been immensely successful. Pierce National is presently paying $45,000 monthly (including its hardware) for its total computing requirements—a reduction of $80,000 monthly from the $125,000 it was spending!

TCC's Consulting Service

At the heart of TCC's systems management technique is a data processing and management consulting service. Mr. Wrotenbery explains it this way. "When top management, reviewing a proposal, looks in vain for the promise of profit, in a new data processing application, it has a right to hesitate. I can best put this in focus by relating a proposal we advised one of our clients to reject, for had it been approved, it would have consumed 20% of the computer staff time available for development.

"The project was the design of a revised system of sales call reporting. As envisioned, the computer would analyze salesmen's calls, the type of prospect and customer profitability. Then it would print out detailed instructions to salesmen each week, specifying customers to be called on, sequence of calls, weekly sales quotas, and target sales by product. On the surface, the project looked promising, but it had not been evaluated by the very sales people for whom it was intended. And its performance was to have been based on the company's present account volume, not its future potential."

43

On-line Production Tracking Aids Integrated Management System

R. A. P. Peters
and F. Thumser

Reprinted from the January 1970 issue of *Control Engineering*
by permission of The Reuben H. Donnelley Corporation.
© 1970 by The Reuben H. Donnelley Corporation.

In 1966 Grumman Aerospace Corp. started a comprehensive program to apply advanced electronic data processing to the management of its manufacturing operations. There was a full-scale reorganization of computer personnel and equipment, with all corporate resources placed under the direction of a top executive reporting to the company president. A coordinated total approach has permitted Grumman to design and install a full-range computer-based system for the control of the inherently complex aerospace production cycle. In addition, the technology thus developed formed the basis for creating Grumman Data Systems Corp., a subsidiary company.

The Grumman Management Information System (MIS), viewed functionally, consists of five information systems: Engineering, Material, Manufacturing, Quality Control, and Product Support—running on a complement of large-scale IBM System 360 computers. These systems are integrated throughout the design-procurement-manufacturing cycle of the product, operating on a corporate level but also accommodating individual program requirements:

The Engineering Information System schedules and monitors the release of engineering data and coordinates the activities of all departments participating in the release of engineering data and drawings. These releases plus the manufacturing schedules are used to generate Product Master Files (Figure 1).

The Material Information System generates materials orders based on the master files and monitors delivery and storage of purchased materials and parts.

The Manufacturing Information System automatically generates work orders based on the master files and schedules and loads the production shops. The system tracks detail parts and assemblies through the shops, and labor and payroll data can be collected from production areas by means of remote terminals.

The Quality Control Information System, operating as an integral part of the Material and Manufacturing Information Systems, gathers and processes product quality data.

The Product Support Information System monitors and controls the ordering of spare parts and special support equipment, identifies and lists support equipment, and produces control charts, delivery schedules, and status reports.

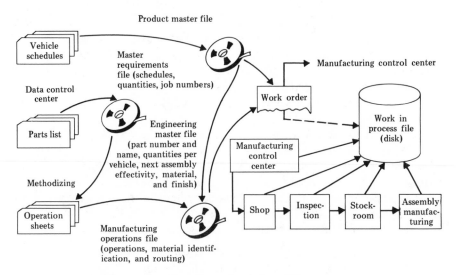

Figure 1.   Manufacturing information system.

The approach of the MIS is suited to research and development, to limited specialized production, and particularly to the highly accelerated production required for such products as the Navy/ Grumman F-14 Air Superiority fighter.

Shop Tracking

The Shop Tracking System provides the source data used by the MIS in the real-time control of Grumman-made aluminum detail parts. (A separate, comparable tracking system is in preparation for Grumman assembly operations.) This system monitors sheet metal parts as they progress through detail shops to the production stockroom.

Information from computer-generated work orders is used to create the Work in Process (WIP) file, a comprehensive disk-stored data bank on all detail work in process. Status information is gathered through 140 data-collection terminals located at dispatching points throughout shops in several plant buildings.

This status information is stored in the WIP file along with the work schedule, and actual progress can be compared with the schedule by querying the computer. The system generates several types of reports on demand or when triggered by specific conditions, enabling close management control of production and flagging delay conditions immediately.

The system embodies a "bus stop" concept of production monitoring, under which a part is reported on to the Management Information System each time it moves from one manufacturing process to the next. The failure of any work to reach its next scheduled bus stop within a specified time is noted by the system, which then generates a Job Behind Schedule report. Printouts in management and production areas aid rapid resolution of problems in production control (missing tools or materials), planning errors (missing or incorrect operations), and maintenance difficulties (machine breakdown).

As the detail part proceeds through its production cycle, the Shop Tracking System monitors part status and collects labor and shop activity data on a real-time basis. When the part reaches the stockroom, this information is used to update vehicle coverage records.

In addition to the management reports the Tracking System provides, real-time action messages are transmitted to the Manufacturing Control Center (Figure 1) for the correction of production control problems, and the tracking system can provide labor data collection for reporting, charging, and payroll.

System Hardware

Figure 2 indicates the hardware configuration of the Shop Tracking System. Data is collected from the shop floor in various plants by means of 140 data-collection terminals made by Data Pathing Inc.

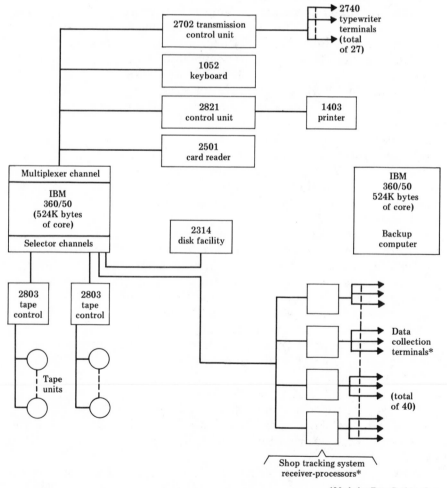

Figure 2.   Shop tracking system hardware.

Messages from these terminals, carrying such data as number, part quantity, part location, quality status, and exception reports, are transmitted via voice-grade telephone lines to four DPI Receiver/Processors located in the computer room. These units store the preprocessing programs and provide code conversion and format sequencing, output-device control, error detection, and message accumulation and control. Edited messages are sent directly to the IBM System 360/50. In addition, each receiver/processor uses two on-line tape drives, independently of the System 360/50, to back up the computer interface.

The System 360/50, operating under OS/MVT, has 524K bytes of core, of which the Shop Tracking System uses a 150K-byte region. Batch jobs, in COBOL, can be executed while the tracking system is operating. Thirteen tape drives support the computer in all its functions; the drives are allocated and released dynamically between tracking and other jobs. Twenty-seven IBM 2740 Inquiry/Response Terminals, located in strategic operating areas and interfaced through an IBM 2702 Transmission Control Unit, operate on-line with the tracking system.

On-line mass storage consists of an IBM 2314 Direct Access Storage Facility. This disk system contains the message queues, checkpoint records, and the heart of the tracking system: the Work in Process (WIP) File. The associated WIP indices are also stored in the disk facility. An IBM 1403 printer, 1052 console, and a "home" 2740 terminal are used to provide system control and monitor the system in the computer room. A second System 360/50, also with 524K bytes of core, can be switched in, in place of the primary Model 50, providing complete computer backup.

File Organization

The WIP file is organized in BDAM (Basic Direct Access Message). It contains 100,000 work-order records of 450 alphanumeric characters each. There are two index files for the WIP, one for part number and one for work-order indexing (each lot of parts for a particular job order has a unique work order number). These index files are organized in ISAM (Indexed Sequential Access Method) and use cylinder and independent overflow.

Additions to the WIP are made to the next available BDAM record. Major additions to the index files are executed daily as new work orders are released into the shops. The new index records are merged with existing indices to write a new file in QISAM (Queued

Indexed Sequential Access Method). Then reorganization to ISAM is accomplished on-line using two copies of each index. At load completion, the new index becomes the active one.

Software

Grumman developed its own approach to systems programming to accommodate the unique requirements and tight implementation schedules of the Shop Tracking System. Message processing is accomplished through QTAM (Queued Telecommunication Access Method). The QTAM message control program attaches the message processing program, which then becomes the control program for the tracking function. The message control and processing programs operate in one MVT region of the 150K bytes. The QTAM message control program acts as the mother task.

The control program for tracking handles all I-O's, attaches all processing routines, and allocates core as work areas and control blocks for each task. The control program also contains standard routines, which are available to all subtasks. All processing programs and routines are coded in reentrant form, so that several tasks can use the same code while it is in core. As many as ten subtasks may be attached for concurrent processing.

All programs are written in IBM 360 assembly language. Subtask testing may be accomplished and "abends" (abnormal endings) encountered without hindering the operating tasks of the tracking system. System-control software is sized to accommodate increased requirements through additional application programming and additional file storage capacity.

Benefits and Economies

It is too early to place quantitative values on the operating benefits Grumman has derived from the MIS system, but a number of gains have been immediately obvious. The primary impact, as might be expected, has been on work-in-process inventory and on production efficiency.

The greatly improved control of the manufacturing process offered by the Shop Tracking System has enabled Grumman to schedule much more closely to its actual needs and to operate with far lower general levels of inventory. By the same token, the rapid computer indication of work delays and out-of-service equipment has significantly improved manufacturing efficiency.

Other direct and indirect improvements have also been noted:

Expediting is more effective, since part location and status is immediately available through real-time inquiry at the Manufacturing Control Center to the WIP data bank.

Clerical efforts will be greatly reduced and accuracy increased when labor data collection is fully operational. Time cards will be virtually eliminated.

"Can't start" problems, such as material shortages or machine outages, are immediately called to the attention of functional experts in the Manufacturing Control Center.

Facility and manpower planning are more effective since the Shop Tracking System creates a comprehensive, consistent data base on production activity.

The volume of routine status reports is vastly reduced, since specific questions on status can be posed to the system.

Comprehensive inspection quality records can be created using the WIP file.

Rework and reinspection activities can be identified by work order, part number, or work center through use of the WIP file.

Work instruction and methodizing errors can be identified rapidly.

"Evaporation" and rejects are identified immediately, so remedial action can be taken to meet assembly schedules.

44

MIS in Higher Education

Roger W. Comstock
Reprinted by permission of *Management Controls*,
Peat, Marwick, Mitchell & Co., September 1970, pp. 190–195.

The use of public funds imposes a fundamental accountability upon educational institutions including higher education. But as higher education's needs enlarge, so do the funding requirements of other worthy social programs. Since all such programs are financed essentially from the same sources, the competition among different programs for the same dollar is likely to increase markedly. In such an environment of constrained resources, choices will have to be made on some rational basis. If higher education is to command the support it needs in these circumstances, it will have to demonstrate its case clearly and objectively. Justification of budget requests, therefore, will have to focus not only on the growing numbers of students being served but, more importantly, on the increased quality and effectiveness of educational programs.

University administrators already are faced with a complex array of informational reporting requirements imposed by state, Federal and other funding sources. While this process may be unnecessarily complicated by conflicting standards and definitions, response to these requests still is mandatory. The development of a uniform set of data classifications and standards on a system-wide basis may help to encourage external funding sources to accept relevant data as they are developed normally within the institutions, thereby eliminating some of the duplication and cost of multiple reporting requirements. This is true whether the "system" be a single university, state-wide, or nation-wide.

The need for a management information system (MIS) for institutions of higher learning is receiving greater recognition—for budget justification, resource management, and planning for expansion. It is needed not only at the level of individual universities and campuses, but by state coordinating boards and legislatures as well, for analysis of current status and past performance and for the forecasting of future requirements.

In MIS design, it is necessary to understand what functions management performs, and how it performs them. One of the key management functions is planning and budgeting. The current add-on, line-item form of budgeting used in most institutions today is not well suited to the demands that will be placed on it in the coming years. The system needed has several characteristics that are often lacking in current practice:

Responsibility for performing the functions of planning and budgeting should be placed directly with the administrators who will carry out the plans—that is, the department heads.

Planning must be performed at the department level and then coordinated for the institution as a whole well in advance of the budgeting process, and certainly before funding requirements are forwarded to the legislature or other funding agency.

In the process of planning and budgeting, some form of recognition must be given to the cross-organizational impact of planning decisions. For example, the establishment of a new program in the School of Engineering would probably require support from Arts and Sciences. This requirement should be defined and entered into the Arts and Sciences planning cycle.

Budgets, once established, should be delegated to the department level for administration.

Some Basics

An MIS can be defined as that combination of men, machines, and methods which supports management in the collection, classification, storage, and retrieval of data needed for managing. It serves as the link between the planning and controlling functions of management and the day-to-day operating procedures.

A distinction should be drawn between operating systems and the management information system itself. Operating systems are those which use detailed data (manual or automated) to support the on-going operation of the university. It is characteristic of operating systems that they:

Deal with transactions concerning single individuals or events, maintaining records on that basis.

Are utilized on a day-to-day or week-to-week basis.

Supply outputs, such as payrolls, that are operational in nature rather than purely informative.

Operate independently of other systems.

Registration, student housing, space allocation, trust fund accounting, and non-academic personnel systems might be some of the operating systems at a particular institution.

In MIS, data tends to be aggregative in nature and is updated and used less frequently than operating data. The balance sheet, a space utilization summary, and a forecast of faculty requirements are typical MIS reports. The tie between the operating systems and the MIS is the former's master files. These must be created and maintained at the detail level before the management information system can be made operational.

The diagram shown as [Figure]1 locates the MIS in relation to institutional operating systems on the one hand and the various aspects of the planning process on the other.

Objectives for Design

Currently, efforts are underway to develop management information systems in a wide spectrum of colleges and universities, both public and private, as well as within groups of institutions at local and state levels. Obviously, objectives for system design will vary from one organization to another, as do the objectives of the organizations themselves. Nevertheless, there is sufficient commonality to warrant discussing the objectives of a particular state-wide public system that will be used for purposes of illustration. In that state, careful

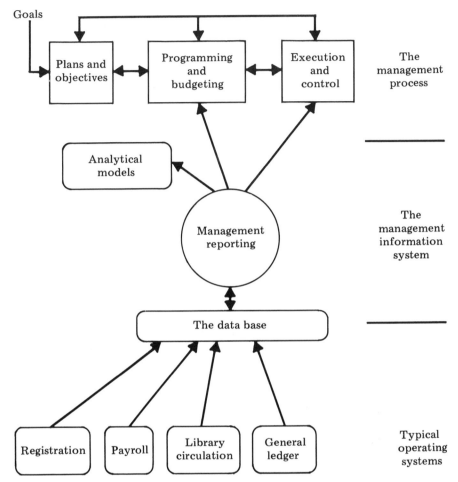

Figure 1. Management process, MIS, and operations.

consideration was given to what should be set as the definitive objectives of the project to develop the higher education management information system. The objectives finally selected included:

The system must provide meaningful management information to the board of regents and to university administrators. This probably will necessitate the development of common but somewhat different systems at individual institutions to meet common but somewhat different needs.

Common definitions must be developed and applied at all universities in order that data supplied by the system may be comparable.

The system taken as a whole must not be oriented to any particular institution or application area.

The plan and resulting systems must be as flexible as possible to permit modification to meet changing objectives and to accommodate new educational methods and procedures. The plan must be devised to provide a firm foundation on which to base new systems development over the next several years. This will not decrease the need to identify as many of the future needs as possible early in the project.

The program for development must be structured so that it can be accomplished in distinct steps. Milestones must be charted at which project progress may be reviewed and new directions taken, if warranted. Provision must be made to review and fund discrete tasks associated with the project, and to pass on their applicability and urgency in the future. The project must also be planned so that some results are achieved at an early date. Confidence and interest tend to lag in direct proportion to the length and cost of the project.

The results of a project of this nature are only as good as the depth of commitment of key administrators and the amount of effort each is willing to devote to its development. The system incorporates many of the tools administrators will use in seeking to satisfy institutional objectives. Hence, the reports to be provided must be fitted closely to the characteristics and requirements of the offices that will use them. For example, the methods by which faculty time utilization is classified can be critical in making decisions with regard to staffing levels, academic personnel policy, and individual advancement.

Unless serious attention is paid to the project plan by key administrators, the resulting systems will fall short of the utility expected. University officials must recognize this and be ready to commit a considerable portion of their time and energy to this project, despite other pressing demands on their time. A broad policy framework within which development of the system can proceed should be established. Procedures as to how information will be controlled and disseminated must be developed. Checks and balances must be built into the administrative structure to ensure against improper issuance or use of data. The integrity and the identity of the individual and of the institution must be preserved.

Conceptual Design

The first step in the actual development of MIS should be the creation of a conceptual design. While many managers do not like to bear the cost of developing such a plan (which has no immediate operational results), it is absolutely essential to develop an overall understanding of the interrelationships of such operating functions as registration, financial aids, space allocation, staffing and course scheduling, and unit costs.

The primary elements of the conceptual plan are definitions of the management-level system outputs, the information flow, the system software and programming languages to be used, the key data elements needed, a data classification scheme, a list of required operating systems, constraints of a planning model, and a plan for implementation. These will now be described in greater detail.

System Outputs; Key Data Elements

The system output generally consists of a set of reports designed to serve management needs at various points in the management process. These may be oriented to such diverse elements of university administration as program planning and budgeting, faculty evaluation, and control of the auxiliary enterprises. Where these are to be provided by MIS, they should be clearly and specifically designed. Such designs should include a definition of each of the fields contained in the report and statements of the purpose of the report, how it will be used, and frequency and manner of distribution.

If MIS is to provide for inquiry via console or specifically written program for such jobs as student accounts and registration, the nature of inquiries that can be allowed and the constraints to be applied to this method of using the system must be defined.

Once the required reporting structure is defined, data elements needed to produce those reports must be identified. These can then be grouped into logical file structures that may assist in the definition of operating system master files.

Information Flow

The information flow description will consist of a system flow chart and a brief narrative. The flow chart should depict the manner in which the key data elements will be handled from the time that they are originated in machine form to the point where they are incorporated into the various system outputs. To do this, it is necessary to define the major operating system file update runs and the major operating system master file structures. Once these have been defined, it is possible to display: the manner in which data is captured by the operating system and in which it flows from one operating system to the next; the basic master file structure; and the techniques by which the management reporting system can extract the data it needs most efficiently. The information flow chart, or "roadmap" as it is sometimes called, should contain all of these elements. A sample of a typical roadmap, depicting the student records subsystem, is shown as [Figure] 2.

Other factors which should be readily apparent from the roadmap are the basic structure of system controls to be used, and the points where interfaces with existing operating systems may be required.

System Software

When system outputs and the information flow chart have been designed, it should be possible for the system designer to prepare gross specifications for the operating software required by MIS. This includes the executive system, the type of file management software to be used, the requirements for inquiry, and the basic programming language for new work. It is logical to include these specifications in the conceptual design.

Data Classification Scheme

A data classification scheme is needed to permit input transactions to be coded so that individual data elements can follow the information flow path to be summarized properly in the management reports. This scheme might include the chart of accounts, the space classification system, course designations, time utilization codes, departmental numbers, etc. While it is impractical for this to be completely defined during the conceptual stage, a basic structure for classification should be provided.

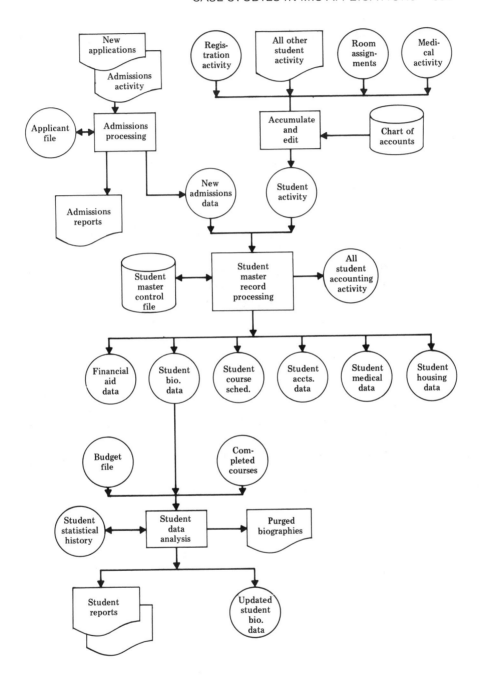

Figure 2.   Student records subsystem.

Operating Systems

The conceptual plan should provide a list of the operating systems which must be functioning to support the management reporting system. This list should identify the following for each operating system:

Name and basic functions.

Frequency of operation.

Gross estimate of time and effort required to make it operational, if applicable.

Priority for implementation in the light of institutional needs and available resources.

If the operating systems are not in operation currently, many of these factors necessarily will be rough. However, such estimates are essential to an informed evaluation of the time and resources required to implement MIS.

Planning Model

An additional element to be considered in the conceptual plan is the university planning model. It provides an analytical description of meaningful relationships among program activity levels and resources under varying circumstances. With the aid of computers, demands on each resource can be computed rapidly for a specified program of activities and policy constraints. The model functions with initial planning data to provide the administration of a college or university with projections of future enrollments, staffing and faculty requirements, facility requirements, and the like.

A general description of the basic modules or computational steps that would constitute a planning model is provided in [Figure] 3 for a structure perhaps applicable to a small college or group of small colleges. Such a model would be developed in stages to be consistent with the available data.

Following are some of the basic estimating relationships to be developed from the initial planning data for use in a planning model:

Fixed and variable costs as a function of grade levels and programs.

Student and staff attrition.

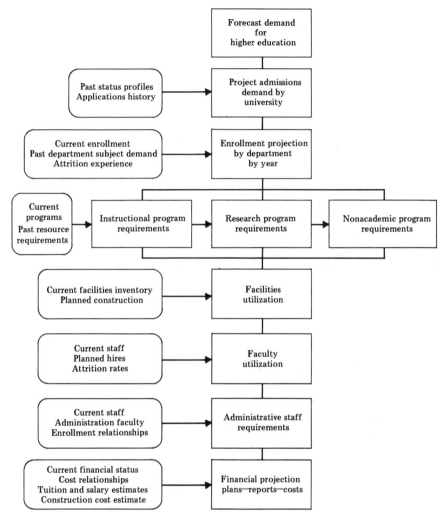

Figure 3.   Planning model.

Instructional hour demand by grade level and major program.

Student/course/classroom-lab space utilization.

Construction cost estimating.

The development of a planning model will be an evolutionary process that improves continually as the data base is expanded.

Implementation Plan

Finally, using the data set forth above, together with similar estimates for the management reporting system(s) and the software required, an implementation plan should be prepared for management approval. The plan should indicate:

Overall time frame for implementation of the MIS, as well as completion dates for subsidiary elements.

Checkpoints for management review and approval. These should be designed in such a way that the project can be redirected or even temporarily halted without undue disruption at each checkpoint, depending upon overall conditions at that time.

Priority schedule for implementation of individual operating subsystems. Is it more important, for example, to start work now on payroll or on a library system?

Estimates of resources required for completion by all parties to the project. These resources include manpower, management participation, vendor assistance, and computer time for program testing.

Once the conceptual plan has been established, it is possible to proceed with the design and implementation of individual operating systems with reasonable confidence that they will fit into the eventual MIS framework.

Some Caveats

While it obviously can produce tangible and exciting benefits, the development of a management information system is a large undertaking calling for the investment of substantial amounts of manpower, money, and time. Problems, pitfalls and untoward consequences should therefore be anticipated if possible. Here are some areas that call for such special inquiry:

User motivation. *This is perhaps the single greatest potential pitfall for an information system. If the user of the system and the individuals responsible for supplying raw data are not disposed to work for the success of the system, it will fail, no matter how well designed. It is a simple matter for a disgruntled employee to "permit" erroneous data to enter the system, or simply not to submit it at all. It is equally easy for an unhappy administrator to not make use of the information the system provides. Every employee involved with the system must be motivated to use it properly; and, conversely, the system must be designed to aid in that motivation.*

Early results. *When senior managements and funding agencies are asked to support multi-year projects with thousands or millions of dollars, they become anxious to see results. The system development should be organized in such a way that tangible system outputs are produced early in the game, preferably within the first year.*

The simple approach. *An information system is a complex undertaking. The expectations of the intended user tend to reinforce the inventiveness and enthusiasm of the system designer, leading to a sophistication of design that is neither desirable nor, in all probability, attainable the first time around. As the system is being developed, managers should opt consistently for the simple approach. To the extent that simplicity can be achieved, the chances of realizing a successful system will increase.*

Maximum system flexibility. *It is in the nature of management to change; else, it would not be management. As management needs change, so do management's requirements of the information system. For this reason, a flexible design is imperative. As a corollary, we should not expect to achieve the optimum system on the first go-around. The system design should be an iterative process, in which the results of earlier experience are built upon to improve the capabilities and responsiveness of the system.*

Data purification. *Early in the project, it will be necessary to develop standard data definitions and promulgate them to all potential sources of data for the information system. Also vital is the review of historical data to determine how it may be incorporated into the information system data base without distortion. An information system that provides reports based on nonstandard data is not only less than useful; it can have a negative impact on the functioning of an institution.*

Conclusion

An information system necessarily must deal with quantified data. Because of this, many administrators, particularly those dealing with academic programs, have become concerned that the information system will eliminate the quality factor from consideration. Their argument is that decisions more often will be made on the basis of quantitative data selected by the system designer for presentation to the administration. In this way, they hold, quality of education will be eclipsed as a factor in educational decisions. Several potential solutions exist.

The information system designer should be aware of this danger and attempt to avoid it. Management, too, must learn to utilize information system outputs interpretively. Rather than expecting the system to provide answers, management must recognize that certain constraints exist with regard to the aggregated data they are supplied. For example, a summary of laboratory hours may include hours spent in chem labs, music practice sessions, and physical education courses. Each of these, in fact, may require separate treatment.

Finally, management must also learn—among other means, perhaps even through well designed management development programs—to question the "facts" neatly presented on a computer print-out; to evaluate them for reasonableness in relation to other known information; and to consider both quantitative and qualitative aspects of a question before reaching a decision.

Bibliography

Periodicals

Ackoff, Russell L.: "Management Misinformation Systems," *Management Science*, December 1967.

_____: "The Evolution of Management Systems," *Journal of the Canadian Operational Research Society*, March 1971.

Albaum, Gerald: "Information Flow and Decentralized Decision Making in Marketing," *California Management Review*, Summer 1967.

Alexander, Tom: "Computers Can't Solve Everything," *Fortune*, October 1969.

Allderige, J. M.: "Off-Line Management," *Datamation*, June 1968.

Allyn, R. G.: "Fine Art of Accounting—the Hot Medium," *Management Accounting*, April 1968.

Ameiss, Albert P., Richard J. Brewer, Harry E. Wood, and Warren A. Thompson: "How to Organize for Shared Systems," *Journal of Systems Management*, December 1970.

Andrus, Roman R.: "Approaches to Information Evaluation," *MSU Business Topics*, Summer 1971.

"Are You Set for Total Data Systems," *International Management,* April 1969.

Argyris, Chris: "Management Information System: The Challenge to Rationality and Emotionality," *Management Science*, February 1971.

Arnoff, E. Leonard: "Operations Research and Decision-Oriented Management Information Systems," *Management Accounting*, June 1970.

Aronson, R. L.: "Computerized Information Control in a Manufacturing Plant," *Management Review*, November 1970.

Atkinson, J.: "Making Computers Pay Their Way," *Managerial Accounting* (Journal of the Institute of Cost and Works Accountants, London), September 1970.

"Auditing EDP — By Computer," *Administrative Management,* December 1970.

Avots, Ivars: "The MIS Mystique: How to Control It," *Management Review*, October 1970.

Axelrod, J. H.: "14 Rules for Building an MIS," *Journal of Advertising Research,* June 1970.

Bacon, T.: "Management Information System: A New Computer Tool for Life Companies," *Best's Review* (*Life* edition), July 1970.

Bagby, Wesley S.: "How We Are Building Our MIS," *Office*, January 1971.

Balk, Walter L.: "The Human Dilemmas of MIS," *Journal of Systems Management*, August 1971.

Barkman, A. I.: "Management Information in an Oil Refinery," *Office*, March 1970.

Barnett, Arnold: "MIS," *AMS Professional Management Bulletins*, February 1971.

Barnett, John H.: "Information Systems: Breaking the Barrier," *Journal of Systems Management*, May 1969.

_____ : "Information System Danger Signals," *Management Services*, January–February 1971.

Barnett, Joseph I.: "How to Install a Management Information and Control System," *Systems and Procedures Journal*, September–October 1966.

Bate, C. F.: "Business Information Systems," *Data Processing*, May 1969.

Baum, B. and E. Burack: "Information Technology, Manpower Development and Organizational Performance," *Academy of Management Journal*, September 1969.

Becker, Richard T.: "Executives Use Computer to Develop EDP Skills," *Administrative Management*, February 1971.

_____ : "Training to Use the Computer as an Executive Tool," *Personnel*, November–December 1970.

Beishon, R. J.: "Intormation Flow and Managers' Decisions," *Managerial Accounting* (Journal of the Institute of Cost and Works Accountants, London), November 1970.

Bell, Jay W.: "Financial Data in a Management Information System," *Management Accounting*, June 1968.

Bellotto, Sam: "Documentation: EDP's Neglected Necessity," *Administrative Management*, January 1971.

Berenson, Conrad: "Marketing Information Systems," *Journal of Marketing*, October 1969.

_____ : "Marketing Information Systems," *Chemical Engineering Progress*, December 1969.

Berkwitt, George J.: "Information Systems: Feedback at the Top," *Management Review*, February 1969.

_____ : "Input-Output: Management's Newest Tool," *Dun's Review*, March 1971.

_____ : "Systems: Too Much Too Soon," *Dun's Review*, June 1968.

Berry, William E.: "What a Personnel EDP System Should Do," *Personnel*, January–February 1969.

Berson, Thomas A.: "Sleuthing Your Data Center," *Computer Decisions*, June 1971.

Beyer, R.: "Positive Look at Management Information Systems," *Financial Executive*, June 1968.

_____ : "Modern Management Approach to a Program of Social Improvement," *Journal of Accounting*, March 1969.

Birch, A.: "Institutional Research is Feedback Link between Administration and Management," *College and University Business*, November 1970.

Bishop, E. B.: "Information For Corporate Planning," *Managerial Accounting* (Journal of the Institute of Cost and Works Accounts, London), August 1970.

Black, C.: "AT and T Pushes Automation Plan," *Electronic News*, May 19, 1969.

Black, Frederick H., Jr.: "The Computer in the Personnel Department," *Personnel*, September–October 1969.

Block, A. C., M. A. Broner, and E. L. Peterson: "What's Going on Here? The Manager's Guide to Systems Analysis," *Management Review*, December 1967.

Bodenstab, C. J.: "Exception Reports for Management Action," *Financial Executive*, November 1969.

Bodington, C. E.: "New California Maintenance-Information Systems Cut Costs," *Oil and Gas Journal*, December 16, 1968.

Boettinger, Henry M.: "What Planning Can Do For You," *Financial Executive*, May 1971.

Bonney, M. C.: "Some Considerations of the Cost and Value of Information," *Computer Journal*, May 1969.

Boulden, James B. and Elwood S. Buffa: "Corporate Models: On-Line, Real-Time Systems," *Harvard Business Review*, July–August 1970.

Brady, Rodney H.: "Computers in Top-Level Decision Making," *Harvard Business Review*, July–August 1967.

Braun, R. J.: "Computers in Management: An Outlook into the Future," *Data Management*, August 1971.

Brien, Richard H. and James E. Stafford: "Marketing Information Systems: A New Dimension for Marketing Research," *Journal of Marketing*, July 1968.

Brink, Victor Z.: "Top Management Looks at the Computer," *Columbia Journal of World Business*, January–February 1969.

Brookfield, Kenneth L.: "Total Systems for Systems Studies," *Journal of Systems Management*, March 1970.

Brown, Robert Goodell: "Towards a Corporate Information System," *Data Processor*, December 1971.

Brown, Warren B.: "Systems, Boundaries, and Information Flow," *Academy of Management Journal*, December 1966.

Browne, D. C.: "What Management Needs to Know," *Inland Printer/American Lithographer*, June 1968.

———: "What Reports Should Your Accountant Provide," *Inland Printer/ American Lithographer*, July 1968.

Bruns, W. J., Jr., and R. J. Snyder: "Management Information for Community Action Programs," *Management Services*, July 1969.

Bull, R. G.: "MIS Planning and Control through PERT," *Best's Insurance News* (*Life* edition), April 1968.

"Business Takes a Second Look at Computers—Special Report," *Business Week*, June 5, 1971.

Butler, D.: "Who's Boss—You or the Computer," *Business Management* (London), March 1968.

Cahill, John J.: "Dictionary/Directory Method for Building a Common MIS Data Base," *Journal of System Management*, November 1970.

Carding, A. D. K.: "Fourth EDP Generation is Here," *Administrative Management*, April 1970.

Carlson, Walter M.: "A Management Information System Designed by Managers," *Datamation*, May 1967.

Caruth, Donald L.: "How Will Total Systems Affect the Corporation," *Journal of Systems Management*, February 1969.

Cathey, P. J.: "Decide Answers You Need, and Leave the System to Us," *Iron Age*, May 15, 1969.

_____ : "How Computer Rates As Manager," *Iron Age*, April 11, 1968.

"Central File and Management Science for a Small Bank," *Bankers Monthly*, December 1968.

Chaplin, Joseph E.: "Integrating Systems, Programming, and Operations," *Journal of Systems Management*, December 1969.

"Charge EDP Field Lags in Management Relations," *Electronic News*, January 13, 1969.

Chervany, Norman L. and Gary W. Dickson: "Economic Evaluation of Management Information Systems: An Analytical Framework," *Decision Sciences* (The Journal for the American Institute for Decision Sciences), July—October 1970.

"CIF Aids Management Decisions and Planning," *Bankers Monthly*, June 1970.

Cleff, Samuel H. and Robert M. Hecht: "Computer Job/Man Matching at Blue-Collar Levels," *Personnel*, January—February 1971.

"Closing a Gap at the Top," *Business Week*, September 20, 1969.

Colantoni, Claude S., Rene P. Manes, and Andrew Whinston: "A Unified Approach to the Theory of Accounting and Information Systems," *The Accounting Review*, January 1971.

Colt, D. G.: "Management Information Systems for Cash Management and Accounts Receivable Application," *Management Accounting*, June 1969.

"Computer-Based Management System," *Data Systems News,* March 11, 1968.

"Computers, Danger or Opportunity," *Administrative Management*, January 1970.

Comstock, Roger W.: "MIS in Higher Education," *Management Controls*, September 1970.

Congdon, Frank P., Jr.: "Advance Planning for the Systems Function," *Journal of Systems Management*, August 1970.

"Container Industry Management Information System," *Paperboard Packaging*, January 1969.

Conway, B.: "Information System Audit: a Control Technique for Managers," *Management Review*, March 1968.

Cook, A. D.: "Top Management Turning on to EDP," *Electronic News*, January 5, 1970.

Cooke, M. J.: "Data Base Revolution," *Systems and Procedures Journal*, March 1968.

Cooke, W. F., Jr., and W. J. Rost: "Standard Cost System: A Module of a Management Information System (Ford)," *Journal of Systems Management*, March 1969.

Cornish, Frederick B.: "Management Information Systems—Cause and Effect," *Managerial Planning*, January/February 1971.

Couger, J. Daniel: "Computer-based Management Information System for Medium-sized Firms," *Journal of Data Management*, August 1967.

_____ : "Educating Potential Managers about Computers," *California Management Review*, Fall 1968.

_____ : "Seven Inhibitors to a Successful Management Information System," *Systems and Procedures Journal*, January 1968.

Cox, Donald F.: "How to Build a Marketing Information System," *Harvard Business Review*, May—June 1967.

Crane, Roger R. and Richard E. Sprague: "A Look at Fourth-Generation Computers," *Management Review*, August 1970.

Cravens, David W.: "An Exploratory Analysis of Individual Information Processing," *Management Science*, June 1970.

Crawford, C. J. and R. A. Grancher: "Dragon's Management Information System," *Pit and Quarry*, July 1969.

Damiani, A. S.: "Plant Engineering an Audio-Visual/Information Center," *Plant Engineering*, April 2, 1970.

Danner, Jack: "MIS: A Tool for Personnel Planning," *Personnel Journal*, July 1971.

"Data Flow: Smooth Currents or Stormy Seas," *Iron Age*, October 9, 1969.

Dawson, Robert I. and Dorothy P. Carew: "Why do Control Systems Fall Apart," *Personnel*, May—June 1969.

Dean, Neal J.: "The Computer Comes of Age," *Harvard Business Review*, January—February 1968.

Dear, Edward P.: "Computer Job Matching Now and Tomorrow," *Personnel*, May—June 1970.

Dearden, John: "Can Management Information be Automated," *Harvard Business Review*, March–April 1964.

___ : "How to Organize Information Systems," *Harvard Business Review*, March–April 1965.

___ : "Time-Span in Management Control," *Financial Executive*, August 1968.

___ : "MIS is a Mirage," *Harvard Business Review*, January–February 1972.

Deckard, Noble S.: "Capturing the Development Costs of an Integrated MIS," *Journal of Systems Management*, January 1970.

De Vos, H. and N. F. O'Connell: "Management Services: Financial Management and Controls," *Journal of Accountancy*, September 1968.

De Witt, Frank: "A Technique for Measuring Management Productivity," *Management Review*, June 1970.

Dickhaut, J. W.: "Accounting Information in Decision Making," *Management Services*, January 1969.

Dickie, P. M. and N. S. Arya: "MIS and International Business," *Journal of Systems Management*, June 1970.

Dickson, G. W.: "Management Information-Decision Systems," *Business Horizons*, December 1968.

Didis, Stephen K.: "Value Analysis of Information Systems," *Journal of Systems Management*, November 1969.

Diebold, John: "Bad Decisions on Computer Use," *Harvard Business Review*, January–February 1969.

Donald, A. G.: "Explaining Systems Concepts," *Managerial Accounting* (Journal of the Institute of Cost and Works Accountants, London), March 1970.

___ : "Understanding Systems," *Managerial Accounting* (Journal of the Institute of Cost and Works Accountants, London), February 1970.

___ : "Systems Theory and MIS," *Management Accounting* (Journal of the Institute of Cost and Works Accountants, London), November 1970.

Donkin, Robert G.: "Management Information Systems: What's Behind the Buzzwords," *The Arthur Young Journal*, Autumn 1968.

___ : "Will the Real MIS Stand Up," *Business Automation*, May 1969.

Dratler, Louise H.: "Facilities Management—Boon or Bane," *Management Services*, September–October 1970.

Dyment, Robert: "Data Center Assists Police in Crime Prevention," *Journal of Systems Management*, January 1970.

Edds, J. A.: "Who Will Manage the Computer," *Canadian Chartered Accountant*, November 1970.

"EDP Controls Personnel Data," *Administrative Management,* October, 1969.

"EDP Hustles the Huffies out of Huffman," *Business Automation,* May 1970.

"EDP to be Controlled by Managers and Not Technicians," *Administrative Management,* March 1970.

Eilon, Samuel: "Some Notes on Information Processing," *Journal of Management Studies*, May 1968.

Elliott, Roger W.: "A Preventive Maintenance Scheduling Information System," *Journal of Systems Management*, June 1970.

Emanuel, F. V.: "Displays in Control: Multiscreen Display Briefs Project Management," *Control Engineering*, June 1968.

"Emerging Management Science," *Bankers Monthly,* November 1969.

Epley, D. R.: "Community Effort Founds Data Bank," *Journal of Systems Management*, May 1970.

Ericson, R. F.: "Impact of Cybernetic Information Technology on Management Value Systems," *Management Science*, October 1969.

Ernst, Martin L.: "Computers, Business, & Society," *Management Review*, November 1970.

Evans, Marshall K. and Lou R. Hague: "Master Plan for Information Systems," *Harvard Business Review*, January–February 1962.

"Every Manager's Dream: His Own Computer," *Iron Age,* January 8, 1970.

Exton, William, Jr.: "The Information Systems Staff: Major Obstacles to Its Effectiveness, and a Solution," *Journal of Systems Management*, July 1970.

Feigenbaum, Donald S.: "The Engineering and Management of an Effective System," *Management Science*, August 1968.

Feltham, G. A.: "Value of Information," *Accounting Review*, October 1968.

Feltz, E. J.: "Corporate Management's Tools of Control," *Personnel Journal*, June 1969.

Fenstermaker, Roy: "Management Systems Engineering—A New Discipline," *Management Review*, October 1969.

Ference, Thomas P.: "Can Personnel Selection be Computerized," *Personnel*, November–December 1968.

Ferguson, R. L. and C. H. Jones: "Computer Aided Decision System," *Management Science*, June 1969.

Field, J. E.: "Toward a Multi-level, Multi-goal Information System," *Accounting Review*, July 1969.

Finney, F. D.: "Contributions of a Management Information System," *Management Accounting*, June 1969.

Firmin, P. A. and J. J. Linn: "Information Systems and Managerial Accounting," *The Accounting Review*, January 1968.

Fisch, Gerald G.: "The Integrated Management Organization," *Management Controls*, May 1969.

Fisher, D. L.: "Management Controlled Information Systems," *Datamation*, June 1969.

"Fourth EDP Generation is Here," *Administrative Management,* April 1970.

Frazier, Dwight M. Jr.: "Systems Test," *Computers and Automation*, September 1970.

Fredericks, Ward A.: "A Manager's Perspective of MIS," *MSU Business Topics*, Spring 1971.

Freed, Roy N.: "Computer Frauds—A Management Trap," *Business Horizons*, June 1969.

_____ : "Negotiating for a Computer without Negotiating Trouble," *Innovation*, August 1969.

_____ : "The Role of Computer Specialists in Contracting for Computers—An Interdisciplinary Effort," *Law and Computer Technology*, January–February 1971.

_____ : "Frisco's Managers Master their Machines," *Railway Age*, May 25, 1970.

Gale, J. R.: "Why Management Information Systems Fail," *Financial Executive*, August 1968.

Galley, T. A.: "Approach to Data Base Design," *Journal of Systems Management*, February 1969.

"Gallion: Blueprint for a Total Management System," *Modern Office Procedures,* February 1970.

Gamer, W. F.: "Fitting Operations Control Reports to Management's Needs," *Management Services*, March 1969.

Gargiulo, Granville R.: "Decision Makers and the Large-Scale System," *Journal of Systems Management*, August 1969.

Garner, B. J.: "Operation of a Management Information Service for Research Planning and Progressing," *Chemistry and Industry*, July 19, 1969.

Garrity, John T.: "The Management Information Dream—The End or a New Beginning," *Financial Executive,* September 1964.

Gellman, H. S.: "Improving Management Information Systems," *Cost and Management*, September and October 1968.

Gerdel, J. K.: "Integrated Data System for Project Management," *Office*, March 1968.

Gerfert, A. H.: "Business Logistics for Better Profit Performance," *Harvard Business Review*, November 1968.

Gershefski, G. W.: "Computer Spotlights Middle Managers," *Petroleum Engineering International*, February 1970.

Gilbreath, U. R.: "Information Processor: Friend or Foe," *Administrative Management*, June 1968.

Giles, P.: "Value of Information for Decision-Making in Insurance," *Operational Research Quarterly*, September 20, 1969.

Godfrey, James T. and Thomas R. Prince: "The Accounting Model from an Information System Perspective," *The Accounting Review*, January 1971.

Goodman, Richard A.: "A System Diagram of the Functions of a Manager," *California Management Review*, Summer 1968.

Gorry, G. Anthony and M. S. S. Morton: "A Framework for MIS," *Sloan Management Review*, Fall 1971.

Greco, Richard J.: "MIS Planning—An Approach," *Data Management*, October 1971.

Green, John F.: "MIS and Corporate Planning," *Long Range Planning*, June 1970.

Green, Paul E.: "Measurement and Data Analysis," *Journal of Marketing*, January 1970.

Greiner, L. E.: "Putting Judgment Back into Decisions," *Harvard Business Review*, March 1970.

Gruber, William H.: "Behavioral Science, Systems Analysis and the Failure of Top Management," *The Industrial Management Review*, Fall 1967.

Guber, William H. and John S. Niles: "Changing Structures for Changing Times," *Financial Executive*, April 1971.

Guerrieri, John A., Jr.: "A Suggested University-Level Curriculum for Business Computer Systems," *Computers and Automation*, September 1969.

Guthrie, G. L. and T. R. Kennedy: "Informing the Nation's President," *SAM Advanced Management Journal*, January 1969.

Hall, A. Lee: "The Executive Faces Computer Programming," part I, *AMS Professional Management Bulletins*, September 1970.

Hamer, Robert W. and Ralph C. Bledsoe: "Information Systems in Management," *SDC Magazine*, January 1970.

Hanold, T.: "President's Views of MIS," *Datamation*, November 1968.

Hartman, H. C.: "Management Control in Real Time is the Objective," *Systems*, September 1965.

Harvey, A.: "Are Total Systems Practical," *Business Automation*, June 1969.

Hawkins, Arthur: "A Predictive Reporting System for Management," *Journal of Management Studies*, October 1968.

Hay, Leon E.: "What is an Information System," *Business Horizons*, February 1971.

Head, Robert V.: "Critical Decisions," *Journal of Systems Management*, November 1970.

____ : "The Final Analysis," *Journal of Systems Management*, December 1970.

____ : "New Breed," *Journal of Systems Management*, May 1969.

____ : "Need for a MIS Organization," *Office*, January 1970.

____ : "Management Information Systems: A Critical Appraisal," *Datamation*, May 1967.

____ : "Management Information Systems: 1970," *Journal of Systems Management*, August 1970.

____ : "Information Systems: the Changing Scene," *Journal of Systems Management*, April 1969.

____ : "MIS Structure," *Data Management*, September 1971.

____ : "Structuring the Data Base for Management Information Systems," *Journal of Systems Management*, January 1969.

———: "MIS: Structuring the Data Base," *Journal of Systems Management*, September 1970.

Hearn, C. P.: "Responsive Management System," *Business Automation*, April 1968.

Hecht, G.: "New Management Information System: Should Auld Accounting Be Forgot," *Management Accounting*, May 1969.

Hein, L. W.: "Management Accountant and the Integrated Information System," *Management Accounting*, June 1968.

Hereford, K.: "New Management Information Systems Due by End of 1972," *Nation's Schools*, May 1970.

Hershman, Arlene: "A Mess in MIS," *Dun's Review*, January 1968.

Heuser, F. L.: "Control vs. Cost of Control," *Management Accounting*, February 1970.

Hirsch, Phil: "WIMMIX: It's the Biggest, but Will It Be the Best," *Datamation*, October 1969.

Hirsch, R. E.: "Value of Information," *Journal of Accountancy*, June 1968.

Hodgson, R. N.: "Design Considerations in Planning and Control Systems," *Managerial Planning*, November–December 1970.

Hofer, Charles W.: "Emerging EDP Pattern," *Harvard Business Review*, March–April 1970.

"Holding EDP Accountable," *Administrative Management,* July 1970.

Holmes, R. W.: "Executive Views Responsibility Reporting," *Financial Executive*, August 1968.

———: "Twelve Areas to Investigate for Better MIS," *Financial Executive*, July 1970.

"Honeywell Targets New Computer at Management Information Usage," *Insurance,* April 19, 1969.

Hook, H. S.: "Bridging the Systems-Management Gap," *Systems and Procedures Journal*, March 1968.

Hoos, Ida R.: "Information Systems and Public Planning," *Management Science*, June 1971.

Hopkins, R. C.: "A Systematic Procedure for Systems Development," *IRE Trans. on Engineering Management*, June 1961.

Hornsell, R.: "Computer as a Management Aid," *Aircraft Engineering*, May 1969.

"How to Get Worldwide Mileage out of Your Management Data," *Business Abroad,* July 1970.

Hudson, Miles H.: "A Technique for Systems Analysis and Design," *Journal of Systems Management,* May 1971.

Humphrey, A. L. and W. G. Munro: "Management Information Retrieval," *Computer Journal,* May 1970.

Hunt, J. G. and P. F. Newell: "Management in the 1980's Revisited," *Personnel Journal,* January 1971.

Hurtado, Corydon D.: "Establishing a Government IMS," *Journal of Systems Management,* June 1971.

"Information for Decision-Making," *Opinion Research Quarterly,* Special Conference Issue, April 1968.

"Information Systems," *Control Engineering,* July 1968.

"Information Systems Need More Trained Specialists," *Steel,* May 5, 1969.

"Ins and Outs of Information: Storage & Retrieval," *Data Systems News,* October 1970.

"Integrated Control of a Factory," *Data Processing,* November 1969.

"Integrated Management Information," *Data Systems News,* June 10–24, 1968.

"International MIS Programs Still Rare, Diebold Group Reports," *Management Services,* July 1970.

International Systems Division, "Getting Involved with Your Systems," and "Closing the Understanding Gap," *AMS Professional Management Bulletins,* February 1971.

Issacs, S. M.: "Total Information System Devised by State Street Bank," *Bankers Monthly,* June 15, 1969.

Jackson, Robert S.: "Computers and Middle Management," *Journal of Systems Management,* April 1970.

Johnson, A. R.: "Organization, Perception and Control in Living Systems," *Industrial Management Review,* Winter 1969.

Johnson, R. L. and I. H. Derman: "How Intelligent is Your MIS," *Business Horizons,* February 1970.

Jones, Curtis H.: "At Last: Real Computer Power for Decision Makers," *Harvard Business Review,* September–October 1970.

Jones, J. Bush: "Centralizing Computer Facilities," *Journal of Systems Management*, June 1971.

Jones, James W.: "Pitfalls of Misinformation: A Case Study," *Management Accounting*, June 1970.

Jones, R.: "Management Chided: Don't Understand the System," *Electronic News*, April 14, 1969.

Joplin, B.: "What Business Are We In? Information!", *Management Accounting*, April 1970.

Joseph, E. C.: "Coming Age of Management Information Systems," *Financial Executive*, August 1969.

_____: "Management Systems in the 70's," *Mechanical Engineering*, November 1969.

Joss, Ernest J. and Jack I. Dahl: "A Management Information System for Cost Control in Government Contracting," *Management Controls*, April 1969.

Judd, J. W.: "When Will We Ever Learn," *Data Processing*, January 1970.

Judge, J. F.: "MASSOP: A New Cost Weapon for Management," *Airline Management and Marketing*, October 1970.

Kahn, G.: "Study of Systems and Procedures," *Business Education World*, April 1969.

Kalb, W. J.: "Time Tools: Small Shops Count, Too," *Iron Age*, November 14, 1968.

Kallab, J.: "Linear Geographical Code for Management Information Systems," *Computers and Automation*, April 1968.

Karp, William: "Management in the Computer Age," *Data Management*, December 1970.

Kast, Fremont E.: "A Dynamic Planning Model," *Business Horizons*, June 1968.

Keegan, W. J.: "Acquisition of Global Business Information," *Columbia Journal of World Business*, March 1968.

"Keeping in Touch: Dynascan 1200 Data Collecting System," *Engineering*, March 20, 1970.

Kennevan, Walter J.: "Management Information Systems," *Data Management*, September 1970.

Kerrigan, William M.: "Organization for a Computer," *Canadian Chartered Accountant*, August 1971.

Kessler, L. M.: "Better Managerial Information," *Office*, January 1970.

Kidd, J. B. and J. R. Morgan: "Predictive Information System for Management," *Opinion Research Quarterly*, June 1969.

Kircher, P.: "Breakthrough in Management Information Systems," *Journal of Data Management*, February 1969.

Kirsch, Carol: "Information Management Part One," *Executive*, August 1970.

Kish, J. L.: "Need for an Efficient Management Reporting System," *Data Systems News*, April 15, 1968.

Kistruck, J. R. S. and W. L. Norman: "Management Information System Survey in Rolls-Royce—A Case History," *Opinion Research Quarterly*, Special Conference Issue, April 1968.

Kohl, M.: "Management Systems Vary According to Builder or User," *Electronic News*, January 1969.

Koprowski, Eugene J.: "Systems Management as a Creative Process," *Journal of Systems Management*, January 1971.

Kosek, M. F.: "Management Information Systems from a Claimsman's Point of View," *Best's Review*, March 1969.

Kotler, Philip: "Corporate Models: Better Marketing Plans," *Harvard Business Review*, July—August 1970.

———: "The Future of the Computer in Marketing," *Journal of Marketing*, January 1970.

Kraemer, Kenneth L.: "The Evolution of Information Systems for Urban Administration," *Public Administration Review*, July—August 1969.

Kramer, R. L. and M. Maertens: "Mini-MIS: The Mod Approach to Information Systems," *Bankers Monthly*, June 1968.

Kriebel, Charles H.: "Information Processing and Programmed Decision Systems," *Management Science*, November 1969.

Kunkel, C. C.: "Management Information System Cuts Job Costs, Raises Efficiency," *Data Processing Magazine*, October 1970.

Lanham, Elizabeth: "EDP in the Personnel Department," *Personnel*, March—April 1967.

Lardas, N. P.: "War Rooms for More Accurate Decision-Making," *Administrative Management*, February 1968.

Laver, Murray: "What Users Should Demand of Computer Designers," *Management Review*, January 1970.

682   BIBLIOGRAPHY

Lewis, A. S.: "Some Techniques for Database Management," *Data Processing,* January 1970.

Liebtag, Wesley R.: "How an EDP Personnel Data System Works for Corporate Growth," *Personnel,* July–August 1970.

Lindgren, LeRoy H.: "Auditing Management Information Systems," *Journal of Systems Management,* June 1969.

"Litton's Electronic Information Machine," *Business Week,* March 28, 1970.

Logue, James A.: "17 Ways Companies Reduce EDP Costs," *Management Review,* February 1971.

Lohara, Charanjit S.: "A New Approach to MIS," parts I and II, *Journal of Systems Management,* July and August 1971.

Long, R. H.: "Automation: Guidelines for Designing an Automated Commercial Loan Information System and the Use of Computers in Loan Decision Making," *Journal of Commercial Bank Lending,* January 1969.

Losty, P. A.: "Designing a Management Information System (MIS)," *The Computer Bulletin,* May 1969.

Lutter, Frederick H.: "EDP Perspective: Danger or Opportunity," *Administrative Management,* January 1970.

_____: "Systems are Underused," *Administrative Management,* January 1971.

_____: "Systems Objectives," *Administrative Management,* May 1970.

_____: "Why MIS Is No Hit," *Administrative Management,* December 1970.

"MACE for Manufacturing Management," *Manufacturing Engineering and Management,* February 1970.

MacVeagh, Charles: "Evaluating an Information System," *AMS Professional Management Bulletins,* July 1970.

Maher, T. P.: "Total Information Systems Could Link Insurance Management Factors," *Insurance,* September 7, 1968.

Malloy, John P.: "Computerized Cost System in a Small Plant," *Harvard Business Review,* May–June 1968.

"Management and the Information Revolution," *Administrative Management,* January 1970.

"Management Information Systems: Fast Facts for Savvy Selling," *Sales Management,* November 15, 1969.

"Management Reporting for Every Man," *Data Systems News,* March 1969.

Mandel, B. J.: "Quality Control of Basic Data," *Quality Progress*, June 1970.

Mapp, George A.: "Planning a Personnel Information System Feasibility and Design Study," *Personnel Journal*, January 1971.

Martenson, H. E.: "New Techniques Permit Old Solutions," *Journal of Systems Management*, February 1970.

Mastromano, F. M.: "Data Base Concept," *Management Accounting*, October 1970.

_____: "Information Technology Applied to Profit Planning," *Management Accounting*, October 1968.

Mathieu, D.: "Management Information System at TI," *Data Systems*, March 1969.

Mayer, S. R.: "Trends in Human Factors Research for Military Information Systems," *Human Factors*, April 1970.

McDonough, A. M.: "Keys to a Management Information System," *Journal of Industrial Engineering*, March 1968.

McFarlan, F. Warren: "Problems in Planning the Information System," *Harvard Business Review*, March–April 1971.

McKechnie, A. K.: "Why It Takes More than Hardware to Make an MIS," *Systems and Procedures Journal*, July 1968.

McKeever, James M.: "Building a Computer-Based MIS," *Journal of Systems Management*, September 1969.

McKnight, R. W.: "Microwave: for NP, a New High in Communications," *Railway Age*, December 16, 1968.

McNamara, James F.: "A State System of Labor Market Information," *American Vocational Journal*, February 1971.

McNiven, M. and B. D. Hilton: "Reassessing Marketing Information Systems," *Journal of Advertising Research*, February 1970.

Mealey, M.: "How Mitsui is Keeping in Touch," *International Management*, March 1970.

Menkhaus, E. J.: "Management's Role in Microfilm," *Management Review*, January 1968.

Menkus, Belden: "Defining Adequate Systems Documentation," *Journal of Systems Management*, December 1970.

Meredith, J. E., Jr.: "Accounting's Contribution to the Selection of Business Investments," *Management Accounting*, April 1968.

Meyers, G. N.: "Obsolescence of Inefficiency," *Office*, January 1970.

Milano, James V.: "Modular Method of Structuring MIS," *Data Management*, February 1970.

Miller-Bakewell, J. B. C.: "Management Information and the Computer," *Management Accounting*, November 1970.

Milunovich, LaVerne G.: "Management Information Systems," *Management Services*, March–April 1970.

_____: "First Wisconsin Installs Management Information System," *Bankers Monthly*, May 1969.

"MIS: Proving Ground for Businessman-Technologist," *Steel,* June 10, 1958.

"MIS—A Status Report on the Concept and its Implementation," *Journal of Accountancy,* June 1970.

"MIS Trips in Vogue," *Sales Management,* April 14, 1969.

Mockler, R. J.: "Developing A New Information and Control System," *Michigan Business Review*, March 1968.

Montgomery, D. B. and G. L. Urban: "Marketing Decision-Information Systems: An Emerging View," *Journal of Marketing Research*, May 1970.

Moore, Michael R.: "Achieving Full Value From Your EDP Operations," *Journal of Systems Management*, February 1970.

Morstein, C. B.: "Information Systems: a Basic Design Consideration," *Journal of Data Management*, January 1968.

Mundhenke, Ehrhard and Harry M. Sneed: "University Information Systems in the Federal Republic of Germany," *Journal of Systems Management*, March 1971.

Murdick, Robert G.: "MIS Development Procedures," *Journal of Systems Management*, December 1970.

_____ and Joel E. Ross: "Management Information Systems: Training for Businessmen," *Journal of Systems Management*, October 1969.

Murphy, D. J.: "Defining Management's Needs Is Key to Designing Successful Information Systems," *Automation*, May 1969.

Murphy, E.: "Guide to an Economically Successful Communications-Based MIS," *Journal of Data Management*, February 1968.

"Must Computer Go on a Data Diet," *Iron Age,* June 5, 1969.

Myers, M. Scott: "The Human Factor in Management Systems," *Journal of Systems Management,* November 1971.

Needles, B., Jr.: "Single Information Flow System for Hospital Data Processing," *Management Services,* September 1969.

Nelson, H. A.: "Teamwork Needed for MIS," *Office,* January 1969.

"New Applications for the Computer in Manufacturing," *Machinery,* September 1969.

"New Computer-Control System Ready," *Oil and Gas Journal,* June 9, 1969.

"New Training Method for System Analysis," *Industrial Electronics,* June 1968.

Nicholson, C. H.: "Management Information Systems in Perspective," *Chemical Engineering Progress,* January 1970.

Nichols, G. E.: "On the Nature of Management Information," *Management Accounting,* April 1969.

"Nixon Likes Litton's System," *Business Week,* March 28, 1970.

Norcross, H. H. and J. R. Poyser: "Sales/Operations Planning and Control," *Director,* May 1970.

Norton, John H.: "Information Systems: Some Basic Considerations," *Management Review,* September 1969.

Norwood, Steven: "Wanted: Human Skills for the Computer," *Management Review,* February 1969.

O'Black, Mary Jane: "Building a Successful MIS," *Journal of Systems Management,* April 1971.

Offord, J.: "Project Evaluation and Profitability," *Data Processing,* November 1969.

O'Haren, Patrick J.: "Total Systems: Operating Objective or Planning Structure," *Journal of Systems Management,* November 1970.

Omlor, John J.: "Management Information System for Planning, Forecasting and Budgeting," *Management Accounting,* March 1970.

Packer, David W.: "Effective Program Design," *Computers and Automation,* July 1970.

Pan, George S.: "The Characteristics of Data Management Systems," *Data Management*, July 1971.

Parnell, Douglass M., Jr.: "A New Concept: EDP Facilities Management," *Administrative Management*, September 1970.

Pedler, C. S.: "New Variables in the Data Processing Equation," *Computer and Automation*, May 1969.

Peirce, R. F.: "Managing an Information Systems Activity," *Management Accounting*, September 1968.

Pelham, R. O.: "Putting Information Systems into the Company Control Structure," *Data Processing Magazine*, July 1970.

Peters, Richard: "Anatomy of a Management Information System," *Business Automation,* November 1969.

Peters, R. A. P. and F. Thumser: "On-Line Production Tracking Aids Integrated Management System," *Control Engineering*, January 1970.

Pirasteh, R.: "Prevent Blunders in Supply and Distribution," *Harvard Business Review*, March 1969.

Pogodzinski, M.: "Management Information System by Honeywell," *Electronic News*, April 14, 1969.

Poindexter, Joseph: "The Information Specialist: From Data to Dollars," *Dun's Review*, June 1969.

Poter, Gordon A.: "Using the Computer to Forecast Factory Indirect Labor," *Managerial Planning*, March/April 1971.

"Production, Inventory and Information Management System Pays Off," *Machinery,* October 1969.

"Programmed Reporting and Information System," *Data Processing,* May 1970.

"Purchasing, Information Processing and Profits," *Purchasing,* October 15, 1970.

"Purdue University's MIS Graduate Program," *Journal of Data Management,* April 1969.

Putnam, A. O.: "Human Side of Management Systems," *Business Automation*, November 1968.

Ramsgard, William C.: "Evaluate Your Computer Installation," *Management Services*, January–February 1971.

Ravitz, L.: "How to Approach a Quality Information System," *Quality Progress*, June 1969.

"Records You Need to Study Feasibility," *Modern Materials Handling*, November 1969.

Research Institute of America: "The Executive Faces Computer Programming," part II, *AMS Professional Management Bulletins,* September 1970.

Reynolds, Carl H.: "Program Control," *Datamation*, October 15, 1970.

Rhind, R.: "Management Information Systems: Some Dreams have turned to Nightmares," *Business Horizons*, June 1968.

Rich, T.: "Data Management Is Systems' Missing Link," *Office*, January 1968.

Rockwell, W. F.: "MIS: a View from the Top," *Dun's Review*, October 1968.

Rosner, W. Norton: "Organizing for Management Information," *Systems & Procedures Journal*, November–December 1968.

Rothery, B.: "Information Model," *Data Processing Magazine*, January 1968.

____ : "Resolutions, Restraints and Reality," *Data Processing Magazine*, February 1968.

Sage, D. M.: "Information Systems: a Brief Look into History," *Datamation*, November 1968.

Sanders, D. H.: "Computers, Organization and Managers: Some Questions and Speculations," *SAM Advanced Management Journal*, July 1969.

Sautebin, J. N.: "Determining System Efficiency," *Data Management*, September 1970.

Schoeters, Ted: "A Case History: The Management Information System of the Hambros Bank of London," *Computers and Automation*, January 1970.

Schroeder, Walter J.: "How to Choose and Manage a Profitable Computer Project," *Business Management*, January 1971.

____ : "The EDP Manager—and the Computer Profit Drain," *Computers and Automation*, January 1971.

Schwab, Bernhard: "The Economics of Sharing Computers," *Harvard Business Review*, September–October, 1968.

"Second Annual Management Meet Examines the Milieu of MIS," *Datamation*, February 1969.

Seese, Dorothy Ann: "Initiating a Total Information System," *Journal of Systems Management*, April 1970.

Sherman, J. R.: "Management's New Helping Hand," *Business Automation*, September 1968.

Shipman, Frederick W.: "Designing M.I.S. for Manager," *Journal of Systems Management*, July 1969.

Shu, F. T. and B. McFarlane, "Management-Information Systems Yield Better Data for Refining," *Oil and Gas Journal*, January 6, 1969.

Siegel, Paul: "Management Information System Planning for the Executive," *Managerial Planning*, May/June 1971.

Sinclair, J. M.: "Basics of an Information System," *Office*, February 1970.

_____ : "Determining What to Put in Reports to Management," *Office*, October 1968.

Singer, J. Peter: "Computer-Based Hospital Information Systems," *Datamation*, May 1969.

Slater, J. G. and G. M. Dawson: "Management Decision Center," *Bankers Monthly*, July 1969.

Smith, August William: "Toward a Systems Theory of the Firm," *Journal of Systems Management*, February 1971.

Smith, R. D.: "Information Systems for More Effective Use of Executive Resources," *Personnel Journal*, June 1969.

Smith, R. L.: "Complete Information for All," *Office*, January 1969.

Sollenberger, Harold M.: "Management Information Systems in the Real World," *Management Services*, November–December 1969.

Spalding, J. E.: "What Can I Do About the Computer," *American Paper Industry*, December 1969.

"Special Report: the Computer and the Business Manager," *Business Management,* May 1970.

Spiro, Bruce E.: "What's a MIS," *Data Management*, September 1971.

Sprague, R. E.: "Personalized Data Systems," *Business Automation*, October 1969.

Staats, E. B.: "Information Needs in an Era of Change," *Management Accounting*, October 1968.

Stanley, W. J. and D. D. Cranshaw: "Use of a Computer-Based Total Management Information System to Support an Air Resource Management Program," *Journal of the Air Pollution Control Association*, March 1968.

Stern, Harry: "Information Systems in Management Science," *The Bulletin of The Institute of Management Science*, February 1971.

_____ (ed.): "Information Systems in Management Science," *Management Science*, June 1970.

_____ (ed.): "Information Systems in Management Science," *Management Science*, October 1969.

_____ : "Information Systems In Management Science," *Management Science*, October 1970.

Stevens, R. G.: "Management Information Systems—Where to Begin in Banking," *Journal of Data Management*, May 1968.

Stevens, W. B.: "Data Analysis and Control Catalog for Management Information Systems," *Computers and Automation*, April 1968.

Stieglitz, Harold: "The Management Information Systems Unit," *The Conference Board Record*, October 1968.

Stubbs, A. W. G.: "Impact of Computers on the Controllership Function," *Management Accounting*, March 1968.

Stults, Fred C.: "Data, Information and Decision Making," *Journal of Systems Management*, June 1971.

Sutherland, John W.: "Tackle System Selection Systematically," *Computer Decisions*, April 1971.

Swyers, W. E.: "Integrated Information Systems and the Corporate Controllership Function," *Management Accounting*, October 1968.

Tanaka, R. I.: "People and Procedure Problem," *Office*, January 1970.

Taylor, W. W.: "Program Package Eases CIF Implementation," *Bankers Monthly*, May 1970.

Thies, James B.: "Computer Modeling and Simulation: A Management Tool for Systems Definition and Analysis," *Financial Executive*, September 1970.

Thomas, D. T.: "Practical Approach to Corporate-Level Computer-Based MIS," *Journal of Data Management*, October 1968.

Thome, P. G. and R. G. Willard: "The Systems Approach: A Unified Concept of Planning," *Aerospace Management*, Fall—Winter 1966.

Thorne, Jack F.: "Internal Control of Real Time Systems," *Data Management*, January 1971.

Toan, Arthur B., Jr.: "Management Information Systems," *The Price Waterhouse Review*, Spring 1970.

"Today's New Managers are Changemakers," *Management Review,* November 1969.

Toles, G. E.: "Information Explosion at Westinghouse," *Business Management* (London), June 1969.

Tolliver, Edward M.: "Myths of Automated Management Systems," *Journal of Systems Management,* March 1971.

————: "Myths of Data Automation," *Journal of Systems Management,* August 1970.

Toma, Charles J.: "Managing Computer Applications," *Systems and Procedures Journal,* September–October 1968.

"Total Systems Revision Repays Better than Speeding Operations," *Management Services,* March 1969.

"Touch Tone Phones Unclog Data Flow," *Steel,* April 15, 1968.

Trentin, H. G.: "Are You a Full-Time Consultant," *Management Services,* March 1969.

Trotter, W. R.: "Organizing a Management Information System," *SAM Advanced Management Journal,* April 1969.

Tucker, R. I.: "Teaching MIS at a British University," *Datamation,* September 1969.

Tyran, M. R.: "Computerized Financial Data Banks: Transition from Conceptual Design to Reality," *Management Accounting,* September 1968.

"UNIPAR: the Magic Word at Union Tank," *Railway Age,* May 10, 1969.

Urban, G. L.: "Ideas on a Decision-Information System for Family Planning," *Industrial Management Review,* Spring 1969.

Verba, Joseph: "Protecting Your EDP Investment," *Management Services,* September–October 1970.

Viste, G. D.: "Property-Liability Information System Is Described in Detail," *National Underwriter,* July 11, 1969.

Waites, William G.: "MIS or IMS," *Journal of Systems Management,* January 1971.

Walker, W. C.: "A Structure for Managing Systems," *Journal of Systems Management,* March 1970.

Walsh, J. A.: "Television Network's On-Line Management Information System," *Office,* May 1968.

Walz, L.: "What's Available for In-Plant Data Collection," *Control Engineering*, February 1968.

Ward, D. S.: "Practical Data Based Design," *Control Engineering*, May 1968.

Wasserman, Joseph J.: "Plugging the Leaks in Computer Security," *Harvard Business Review*, September—October 1969.

Watson, D. B.: "EDP Policy: Control is the Objective," *Administrative Management*, July 1970.

Weatherbee, Harvard Y.: "Personnel Data Systems and the Computer," *Personnel*, July—August 1968.

Weber, J. R.: "Corporate Command Post," *Business Automation*, December 1968.

Webster, Eric: "Information Systems: The First Steps," *Management Review*, February 1969.

Weinwurm, G. F.: "Managing Management Information," *Management International Review*, October 1970.

Weiser, A. L.: "Assigning Priorities to Management Information Reports," *Data Processing Magazine*, July 1970.

Wells, Edmund J.: "Mechanizing the Small Office," *Management Services*, September—October 1970.

"What's the Status of MIS," *EDP Analyzer,* October 1969.

Wheatley, E.: "Putting Management Technics to Work for Education," *College and University Business*, April 1970.

Wheeler, D. P. and G. Campbell: "System Model—an MIS Insurance Policy," *Journal of Data Management*, June 1969.

Whiteside, J. N.: "Integrated Management Planning by Computer," *Managerial Accounting* (Journal of the Institute of Cost and Works Accountants, London), May 1970.

"Who's Afraid of an MIS," *Steel,* November 10, 1969.

"Wide Use Seen for New Electronic Information System for Management," *National Underwriter* (*Life* edition), August 10, 1968.

Widener, W. R.: "New Management Concepts: Working and Profitable," *Business Automation*, August 1968.

Will, Hartmut J.: "Some Comments on Information Systems," *Management Science*, December 1969.

Williams, D. N.: "Computer Rediscovers Foremen," *Iron Age*, May 29, 1969.

Wilson, A. W.: "No Computer Today, Thank You," *Managerial Accounting* (Journal of the Institute of Cost and Works Accountants, London), September 1970.

Wise, D. N.: "All Data Is not Information," *Office*, January 1969.

Withington, F. G.: "Trends in MIS Technology," *Datamation*, February 1970.

Wynne, J. M.: "Management in a Dynamic Economy," *Best's Insurance News* (*Life* edition), February 1968.

Yaffa, Earle and Paul Hines: "Who Should Control The Computer," *Management Review*, March 1969.

Yeatman, R. P.: "Government-Required Data is Management Tool," *College Management*, September 1970.

Young, Stanley: "Organization as a Total System," *California Management Review*, Spring 1968.

Zack, R. A.: "MIS Based on Dynamic Data; Not Big Computers," *Automation*, May 1969.

Zani, William M.: "Real-Time Information Systems: A Comparative Economic Analysis," *Management Science*, February 1970.

―――: "Blueprint for MIS," *Harvard Business Review*, November–December 1970.

―――: "The Coming of the Computer Utility," *Management Review*, December 1970.

Zannetos, Z. S.: "Toward Intelligent Management Information Systems," *Industrial Management Review*, Spring 1968.

Ziegler, James R.: "Computerized Information Systems," *Automation*, April 1970.

Books and Monographs

Ackoff, Russell L.: *A Concept of Corporate Planning* (New York: John Wiley & Sons, Inc., 1970).

Allied Computer Research: *Quarterly Bibliography of Computers and Data Processing* (Phoenix: Applied Computer Research, 1971).

American Federation of Information Processing Societies, Conference Proceedings, vol. 34 (Montvale, N.J.: AFIPS Press, 1969).

American Institute of Certified Public Accountants: *Management Information Systems for the Smaller Business*, Management Services Technical Study No. 8 (New York: American Institute of Certified Public Accountants, 1969).

Association for Systems Management: *An Annotated Bibliography for the Systems Professional* (Cleveland: Association for Systems Management, 1970).

Association for Systems Management: *Business Systems* (Cleveland: Association for Systems Management, 1969).

Association for Systems Management: *Ideas for Management—Papers and Case Histories Presented at the 1970 International Systems Meeting* (Cleveland: Association for Systems Management, 1970).

Association for Systems Management: *Management Information Systems* (Cleveland: Association for Systems Management, 1970).

Association for Systems Management: *Profile of a Systems Man* (Cleveland: Association for Systems Management, 1969).

Awad, Elias M.: *Business Data Processing*, 2d ed. (Englewood Cliffs, N.J.: Prentice-Hall, Inc., 1968).

_____ and Data Processing Management Association: *Automatic Data Processing: Principles and Procedures* (Englewood Cliffs, N.J.: Prentice-Hall, Inc., 1966).

Bailey, Earl L.: *Computer Support for Marketing—A Progress Report* (New York: National Industrial Conference Board, Inc., 1969).

Ballot, Robert: *Materials Management: A Results Approach* (New York: American Management Association, 1971).

Barton, Richard F.: *A Primer on Simulation and Gaming* (Englewood Cliffs, N.J.: Prentice-Hall, Inc., 1970).

Bassett, Glenn A. and Harvard Y. Weatherbee: *Personnel Systems and Data Management* (New York: American Management Association, 1971).

Beckett, John A.: *Management Dynamics: The New Synthesis* (New York: McGraw-Hill Book Company, 1971).

Benjamin, Robert I.: *Control of the Information System Development Cycle* (New York: Interscience Publishers, a division of John Wiley & Sons, Inc., 1971).

Benton, William K.: *The Use of the Computer in Planning* (Reading, Mass.: Addison-Wesley Publishing Company, Inc., 1971).

Berkowitz, Nathan and Robertson Munro, Jr.: *Automatic Data Processing and Management* (Belmont, Calif.: Dickenson Publishing Company, Inc., 1969).

Birkle, John and Ronald B. Yearsley: *Computer Applications in Management* (Princeton, N.J.: Auerbach Publishers, 1970).

Blackburn, Thomas W. and H. Warren White: *Understanding Computers—A Guide for Management* (New York: Clarkson N. Potter, Inc., 1969).

Blumenthal, Sherman C.: *Management Information Systems: A Framework for Planning and Development* (Englewood Cliffs, N.J.: Prentice-Hall, Inc., 1969).

Boore, William F. and Jerry R. Murphy: *The Computer Sampler: Management Perspectives on the Computer* (New York: McGraw-Hill Book Company, 1968).

Boutel, Wayne S.: *Computer-Oriented Business Systems* (Englewood Cliffs, N.J.: Prentice-Hall, Inc., 1968).

Bower, James B. and William R. Welke: *Financial Information Systems—Selected Readings* (Boston: Houghton Mifflin Company, 1968).

———, Robert E. Schlosser, and Charles T. Zlatkovich: *Financial Information Systems: Theory and Practice* (Boston: Allyn and Bacon, Inc., 1969).

Brandon, Dick H.: *Management Planning for Data Processing* (Princeton, N.J.: Brandon Systems Press, Inc., 1970).

Brightman, Richard W.: *Information Systems for Modern Management* (New York: The Macmillan Company, 1971).

———, and B. J. Luskin: *Data Processing for Decision Making* (New York: The Macmillan Company, 1968).

——— and ———: *Data Processing for Decision-Making*, 2d ed., (New York: The Macmillan Company, 1971).

Brinckloe, William D.: *Managerial Operations Research* (McGraw-Hill Book Company, 1969).

Brink, Victor Z.: *Computers and Management: The Executive Viewpoint* (Englewood Cliffs, N.J.: Prentice-Hall, Inc., 1971).

Cantor, Jerry: *Profit Oriented Manufacturing Systems* (New York: American Management Association, 1969).

Carrithers, Wallace M. and Ernest H. Weinwurm: *Business Information and Accounting Systems* (Columbus, Ohio: Charles E. Merrill Books, Inc., 1967).

Chacko, George K.: *Computer-Aided Decision Making* (New York: American Elsevier Publishing Company, Inc., 1971).

Chorafas, Dimitris N.: *Control Systems Functions and Programming Approaches*, vol. A (New York: Academic Press, Inc., 1966).

Churchill, Neil C., John H. Kempster, and Myron Uretsky: *Computer-Based Information Systems for Management: A Survey*, 1st ed. (New York: National Association of Accountants, 1969).

Churchman, C. West: *The Systems Approach* (New York: Delacorte Press, Dell Publishing Co., Inc., 1968).

Cleland, David I. and William R. King: *Systems, Organizations, Analysis, Management: A Book of Readings* (New York: McGraw-Hill Book Company, 1969).

Clifton, H. D.: *Systems Analysis for Business Data Processing* (Princeton, N.J.: Auerbach Publishers, 1969).

Cohen, Burton J.: *Cost-Effective Information Systems* (New York: American Management Association, 1971).

Computing Bibliography: 4th ed. (Colorado Springs: Computing Newsletter, University of Colorado, 1971).

Cross, Hershner: "A General Management View of Computers," *Computers and Management: The 1967 Leatherbee Lectures* (Boston: Harvard Business School, Division of Research, 1967).

Crowley, Thomas H.: *Understanding Computers* (New York: McGraw-Hill Book Company, 1967).

Dearden, John and F. Warren McFarlan: *Management Information Systems* (Homewood, Ill.: Richard D. Irwin, Inc., 1966).

_____,_____, and William M. Zani: *Management Information Systems: Text and Cases* (Homewood, Ill.: Richard D. Irwin, Inc., 1970).

DeGreene, Kenyon B. (ed.): *Systems Psychology* (New York: McGraw-Hill Book Company, 1970).

Diebold, John: *Man and the Computer* (New York: Frederick A. Praeger, Inc., 1970).

_____: *Business Decisions and Technological Change* (New York: Geyer-McAllister Publications, 1971).

Dippel, Gene and William C. House: *Information Systems—Data Processing and Evaluation* (Glenview, Ill.: Scott, Foresman and Company, 1969).

Dun and Bradstreet: *What the Manager Should Know About the Computer* (New York: Thomas Y. Crowell Company, 1969).

Elliott, C. Orville and Robert S. Wasley: *Business Information Processing Systems* (Homewood, Ill.: Richard D. Irwin, Inc., 1965).

____ and ____: *Business Information Processing Systems*, rev. ed. (Homewood, III.: Richard D. Irwin, Inc., 1968).

Ellis, David O. and Fred J. Ludwig: *Systems Philosophy* (Englewood Cliffs, N.J.: Prentice-Hall, Inc., 1962).

Emerick, Paul L. and Joseph W. Wilkinson: *Computer Programming for Business and Social Science* (Homewood, III.: Richard D. Irwin, Inc. and The Dorsey Press, 1970).

Emery, F. E.: *Systems Thinking* (Baltimore: Penguin Books, Inc., 1969).

Emery, James C.: *Organizational Planning and Control Systems—Theory and Technology* (Toronto: Collier-Macmillan Canada, Ltd., 1969).

Enger, Norman L.: *Putting MIS to Work* (New York: American Management Association, 1969).

Exton, William, Jr.: *People and Systems* (New York: American Management Association, 1971).

Gallagher, James D.: *Management Information Systems and the Computer*, AMA Research Study, no. 51 (New York: American Management Association, 1961).

Garrity, John T.: *Getting the Most Out of Your Computer* (New York: McKinsey & Company, 1964).

General Electric Co., R. E. Breen, H. Chestnut, R. R. Duersch, and R. S. Jones: *Management Information Systems, A Subcommittee Report on Definitions* (Schenectady, N.Y.: General Electric Research and Development Center, January 1969).

____ and H. Chestnut: *A Systems Approach to the Economics of the Use of Computers for Controlling Systems in Industry* (Schenectady, N.Y.: General Electric Research and Development Center, February 1970).

____ and R. R. Duersch: *Business Information System Design* (Schenectady, N.Y.: General Electric Research and Development Center, August 1968).

____ and L. A. Gonzalez: *Development of Statewide Information Systems: Problems and Prospects* (Santa Barbara, Calif.: General Electric Company—Tempo Center for Advanced Studies, 1969).

Gentle, Edgar C., Jr.: *Data Communications In Business: An Introduction* (New York: Publishers Service Co., 1965).

Gilmore, Harold and Herbert C. Schwartz: *Integrated Product Testing and Evaluation: A Systems Approach to Improve Reliability and Quality* (New York: Interscience Publishers, a division of John Wiley & Sons, Inc., 1969).

Glans, Thomas B., Burton Brad, David Holstein, William E. Meyers, and Richard N. Schmidt: *Management Systems* (New York: Holt, Rinehart and Winston, Inc., 1968).

Greenwood, Frank: *Managing the Systems Analysis Function* (New York: American Management Association, 1968).

Greenwood, William T.: *Decision Theory and Information Systems* (Cincinnati: South-Western Publishing Company, Incorporated, 1969).

Gruenberger, Fred: *Computers and Communication—Toward A Computer Utility* (Englewood Cliffs, N.J.: Prentice-Hall, Inc., 1968).

Gupta, Roger: *Electronic Information Processing* (New York: The Macmillan Company, 1971).

Handbook of Data Processing Management, six-volume set (Princeton, N.J.: Auerback Publishers, 1971).

Hartman, W., H. Matthes, and A. Proeme: *Management Information Systems Handbook* (New York: McGraw-Hill Book Company, 1970).

Hattery, Lowell H. and Edward M. McCormick (eds.): *Information Retrieval Management* (Detroit: American Data Processing, Inc., 1962).

Heany, Donald F.: *Development of Information Systems—What Management Needs to Know* (New York: The Ronald Press Company, 1968).

Hertz, David B.: *New Power for Management* (New York: McGraw-Hill Book Company, 1969).

Heyel, Carl and Business Equipment Manufacturers Association: *Computers, Office Machines, and the New Information Technology* (New York: The Macmillan Company, 1969).

Higginson, M. Valliant: *Managing with EDP: A Look at the State of the Art* (N.Y.: American Management Association, 1967).

Hodge, Bartow and Robert N. Hodgson: *Management and the Computer in Information and Control Systems* (New York: McGraw-Hill Book Company, 1969).

Hopeman, Richard J.: *Systems Analysis and Operations Management* (Columbus, Ohio: Charles E. Merrill Books, Inc., 1969).

Johnson, Charles B. and William Katzenmeyer (eds.): *Management Information Systems in Higher Education* (Durham, N.C.: The Duke University Press, 1969).

Jordain, Philip B.: *Condensed Computer Encyclopedia* (New York: McGraw-Hill Book Company, 1969).

Kanter, Jerome: *The Computer and the Executive* (Englewood Cliffs, N.J.: Prentice-Hall, Inc., 1967).

Kast, Fremont E. and James E. Rosenzweig: *Organization and Management—A Systems Approach* (New York: McGraw-Hill Book Company, 1970).

Katzan, Harry, Jr.: *Computer Organization and the System/370* (New York: Van Nostrand Reinhold Company, 1971).

Kelleher, Grace J.: *The Challenge to Systems Analysis* (New York: Interscience Publishers, a division of John Wiley & Sons, Inc., 1970).

Kelly, Joseph F.: *Computerized Management Information Systems* (New York: The Macmillan Company, 1970).

Kelly, William F.: *Management Through Systems and Procedures: The Total Systems Concept* (New York: John Wiley & Sons, Inc., 1969).

Konrad, Evelyn et al.: *Computer Innovations in Marketing* (New York: American Management Association, 1970).

Kraplus, W. J. (ed.): *On-Line Computing: Time Shared Man-Computer Systems* (New York: McGraw-Hill Book Company, 1967).

Krauss, Leonard I.: *Administering and Controlling the Company Data Processing Function* (Englewood Cliffs, N.J.: Prentice-Hall, Inc., 1969).

_____: *Computer-Based Management Information Systems* (New York: American Management Association, 1970).

Lazzaro, Victor: *Systems and Procedures: A Handbook for Business and Industry* (Englewood Cliffs, N.J.: Prentice-Hall, Inc., 1968).

LeBreton, Preston P.: *Administrative Intelligence-Information Systems* (Boston: Houghton Mifflin Company, 1969).

Lecht, Charles Philip: *The Management of Computer Programming Projects* (New York: American Management Association, 1967).

Li, David H.: *Accounting, Computers, Management Information Systems* (New York: McGraw-Hill Book Company, 1969).

Lindley, Dennis V.: *Making Decisions* (New York: Interscience Publishers, a division of John Wiley & Sons, Inc., 1971).

Lipperman, Lawrence L.: *Advanced Business Systems*, AMA Research Study 86 (New York: American Management Association, 1968).

Lott, Richard W.: *Basic Systems Analysis* (New York: Harper & Row, Publishers, Incorporated, 1971).

Lyden, Fremont J. and Ernest G. Miller: *Planning, Programming, Budgeting: A Systems Approach to Management* (Chicago: Markham Publishing Company, 1967).

Management Information Systems Index, 1st ed. (Detroit: American Data Processing, 1962).

____: (Detroit: American Data Processing, 1969).

Management Information Systems for the Smaller Business (New York: American Institute of Certified Public Accountants, 1969).

Martino, R. L.: *Management Information Systems* (New York: McGraw-Hill Book Company, 1970).

____: *MIS—Management Information Systems* (Wayne, Pa.: MDI Publications, Management Development Institute Division of Information Industries, Inc., 1969).

McCarthy, E. Jerome, J. A. McCarthy, and Durward Humes: *Integrated Data Processing Systems* (New York: John Wiley & Sons, Inc., 1966).

McKeever, James M.: *Management Reporting Systems* (New York: Interscience Publishers, a division of John Wiley & Sons, Inc., 1971).

McRay, T. W. (ed.): *Management Information Systems* (Baltimore: Penguin Books, Inc., 1971).

Meadow, Charles T.: *The Analysis of Information Systems* (New York: John Wiley & Sons, Inc., 1967).

Meltzer, Morton F.: *The Information Center: Management's Hidden Asset* (New York: American Management Association, 1967).

____: *The Information Imperative* (New York: American Management Association, 1971).

Miller, David W. and Martin K. Starr: *The Structure of Human Decisions* (Englewood Cliffs, N.J.: Prentice-Hall, Inc., 1967).

Monsma, James E., and Kenneth Powell: *An Executive's Guide to Computer Concepts* (New York: Pitman Publishing Corporation, 1969).

Morrison, Edward J.: *Developing Computer-Based Employee Information Systems* (New York: American Management Association, 1969).

Morton, Michael S. Scott: *Management Decision Systems: Computer-Based Support for Decision Making* (Boston: Harvard Business School, Division of Research, 1971).

Murdick, Robert G. and Joel E. Ross: *Information Systems for Modern Management* (Englewood Cliffs, N.J.: Prentice-Hall, Inc., 1971).

Myers, Charles A.: *Computers in Knowledge-Based Fields* (Cambridge, Mass.: The MIT Press, 1970).

_____: *The Impact of Computers on Management* (Cambridge, Mass.: The MIT Press, 1967).

Narahara, Russell M.: *Computer-Aided Design* (New York: Ziff-Davis Publishing, 1969).

Nelson, Oscar S. and Richard S. Woods: *Accounting Systems and Data Processing* (Cincinnati: South-Western Publishing Company, Incorporated, 1961).

O'Brien, James J.: *Management Information Systems: Concepts, Techniques, and Applications* (New York: Van Nostrand Reinhold Company, 1970).

Optner, Stanford L.: *Systems Analysis for Business Management*, 2d ed. (Englewood Cliffs, N.J.: Prentice-Hall, Inc., 1968).

Orlicky, Joseph: *The Successful Computer System* (New York: McGraw-Hill Book Company, 1969).

Pemberton, LeRoy A. and E. Danna Gibson: *Administrative Systems Management* (Belmont, Calif.: Wadsworth Publishing Company, Inc., 1968).

Prince, Thomas R.: *Information Systems for Management Planning and Control* (Homewood, Ill.: Richard D. Irwin, Inc., 1966).

Rappaport, Alfred (ed.): *Information for Decision Making* (Englewood Cliffs, N.J.: Prentice-Hall, Inc., 1970).

Rauseo, Michael J.: *Management Controls for Computer Processing* (New York: American Management Association, 1970).

Reichenbach, Robert R. and Charles A. Tasso: *Organizing for Data Processing* (New York: American Management Association, 1968).

Richards, Max D. and Paul S. Greenlaw: *Management Decision Making,* rev. ed. (Homewood, Ill.: Richard D. Irwin, Inc., 1972).

Rogers, Derek: *Creative Systems Design* (Wembley, England: Anbar Publications Ltd., 1970).

Rosenberg, Jerry M.: *The Computer Prophets* (New York: The Macmillan Company, 1969).

Rosove, Perry E.: *Developing Computer-Based Information Systems* (New York: John Wiley & Sons, Inc., 1967).

Ross, Joel E. and Robert G. Murdick: *Management Information Systems—An Annotated Bibliography* (Cleveland: Association for Systems Management, 1970).

Ross, H. John: *Technique of Systems and Procedures* (New York: Geyer-McAllister Publications, 1970).

Rubin, Martin L.: *Handbook of Data Processing Management* (Princeton, N.J.: Auerbach Publishers, 1969).

Rudwick, Bernard H.: *Systems Analysis for Effective Planning: Principles and Cases* (New York: Interscience Publishers, a division of John Wiley & Sons, Inc., 1969).

Sackman, Harold: *Computers, Systems Science, and Evolving Society* (New York: John Wiley & Sons, Inc., 1967).

Salzer, J. M.: "Evolutionary Design of Complex Systems," in Donald P. Eckman (ed.), *Systems: Research and Design* (New York: John Wiley & Sons, Inc., 1961).

Samaras, Thomas T.: *Fundamentals of Configuration Management* (New York: Interscience Publishers, a division of John Wiley & Sons, Inc., 1971).

Sanders, Donald H.: *Computers and Management* (New York: McGraw-Hill Book Company, 1968).

_____ : *Computers and Management* (paperback) (New York: McGraw-Hill Book Company, 1970).

Schoderbek, Peter P.: *Management Systems—A Book of Readings* (New York: John Wiley & Sons, Inc., 1967).

Shaw, John C. and William Atkins: *Managing Computer System Projects* (New York: McGraw-Hill Book Company, 1971).

Shriver, Richard H. and Russell C. White: *Distribution Planning and Control: Effective Use of Computer Systems and Models*, AMA Research Study 96 (New York: American Management Association, 1969).

Siders, R. A., D. R. Drane, L. W. Ehrhardt, P. Ghent, R. G. C. Hanna, C. W. Hayward, W. B. Heye, Jr., R. A. Meyer, T. G. Rogers, Jr., and J. B. Sabel: *Computer Graphics—A Revolution in Design* (New York: American Management Association, 1966).

Simon, Herbert A.: *The New Science of Management Decisions* (New York: Harper & Row, Publishers, Incorporated, 1960).

Smith, Paul T.: *Computers, Systems, and Profits* (New York: American Management Association, 1969).

_____: *How to Live with Your Computer* (New York: American Management Association, 1967).

Smith, Samuel V., Richard H. Brien, and James E. Stafford: *Readings in Marketing Information Systems* (Boston: Houghton Mifflin Company, 1968).

Solomon, Irving I. and Laurence O. Weingart: *Management Uses of the Computer* (New York: Harper & Row, Publishers, Incorporated, 1966).

Starr, Martin K.: *Systems Management of Operations* (Englewood Cliffs, N.J.: Prentice-Hall, Inc., 1971).

Stokes, Paul M.: *A Total Systems Approach to Management Control* (New York: American Management Association, 1968).

Symonds, Curtis W.: *A Design for Business Intelligence* (New York: American Management Association, 1971).

Systems Approach to Management: An Annotated Bibliography (Springfield, Va.: Scientific and Technical Information Division, National Aeronautics and Space Administration, Office of Technology Utilization, 1969).

Tatham, Laura: *The Use of Computers for Profit—A Businessman's Guide* (New York: McGraw-Hill Book Company, 1970).

Thornton, J. E.: *Design of A Computer—The Control Data* (Glenview, Ill.: Scott, Foresman and Company, 1970).

Toan, Arthur B., Jr.: *Using Information to Manage* (New York: The Ronald Press Company, 1968).

Tomeski, Edward A.: *The Executive Use of Computers* (New York: Collier Books, The Macmillan Company, 1969).

_____: *The Computer Revolution* (New York: The Macmillan Company, 1970).

Tricker, Robert I.: *Management Information Systems* (London: Institute of Chartered Accountants of England and Wales, 1969).

Weik, Martin H.: *Dictionary of Computers and Information Processing* (New York: Hayden Book Company, Inc., 1969).

Weinwurm, George F.: *On the Management of Computer Programming* (Princeton, N.J.: Auerbach Publishers, 1970).

Westin, Alan F. (ed.): *Information Technology in a Democracy* (Cambridge, Mass.: Harvard University Press, 1971).

Whisler, Thomas L.: *Information Technology and Organizational Change* (Belmont, Calif.: Wadsworth Publishing Company, Inc., 1970).

_____ : *The Impact of Computers on Organizations* (New York: Frederick A. Praeger, Inc., 1970).

Wilson, Ira G. and Marthann Wilson: *Information, Computers, and System Design* (New York: John Wiley & Sons, Inc., 1967).

Withington, Frederic G.: *The Real Computer: Its Influences, Uses, and Effects* (Reading, Mass.: Addison-Wesley Publishing Company, Inc., 1969).

_____ : *The Use of Computers in Business Organizations* (Reading, Mass.: Addison-Wesley Publishing Company, Inc., 1966).

_____ : *The Organization of the Data Processing Function* (New York: Interscience Publishers, a division of John Wiley & Sons, Inc., 1972).

Wofsey, Marvin M.: *Management of Automatic Data Processing* (Washington, D.C.: Thompson Book Co., 1968).

Young, Stanley: *Management: A Systems Analysis* (Glenview, Ill.: Scott, Foresman and Company, 1966).

_____ : *Management—A Systems Analysis* (Glenview, Ill.: Scott, Foresman and Company, 1971).

Yourdon, Edward: *Design of On-line Computer Systems* (Englewood Cliffs, N.J.: Prentice-Hall, Inc., 1972).